THE PENGUIN
POCKET THESAURUS

Editors:
Faye Carney and Maurice Waite

MARKET HOUSE BOOKS LIMITED

To Kevin.

Congratulations

on the selection

Cunningham

PENGUIN BOOKS

Penguin Books Ltd, Harmondsworth, Middlesex, England
Viking Penguin Inc., 40 West 23rd Street, New York, New York 10010, U.S.A.
Penguin Books Australia Ltd, Ringwood, Victoria, Australia
Penguin Books Canada Ltd, 2801 John Street, Markham, Ontario, Canada L3R 1B4
Penguin Books (N.Z.) Ltd, 182–190 Wairau Road, Auckland 10, New Zealand

First published 1985

Made and printed in Great Britain by
Cox & Wyman Ltd, Reading
Set in Times by
Market House Books Ltd

PREFACE

A thesaurus (from the Greek word for treasure) is what its name implies, a treasure-house of words. Unlike a dictionary, in which words are listed alphabetically and their meanings explained, a thesaurus consists of words grouped according to their meanings. The aim is to provide a source of words that express the same idea or closely related ideas.

An 'idea', of course, can be a material object, such as food or a machine; it can be a topic or area of activity, such as politics, the cinema, or language; or it can be abstract, such as willingness, innocence, or destruction.

A thesaurus paragraph dealing with a material object, topic, or activity lists the key words in that semantic area, providing a mini-vocabulary of a subject. A paragraph dealing with an abstract quality, on the other hand, lists related words, associations, figurative uses and idiomatic phrases showing different stylistic equivalents in formal or colloquial language. For example, a paragraph on an idea, such as *talkativeness*, will include formal words (*verbosity*), humorous and colloquial usages (*verbal diarrhoea* and *hot air*), and idiomatic phrases (*talk the hind leg off a donkey*).

Thus each paragraph on a particular topic contains a range of words covering different parts of speech and different levels of formality or informality. Vulgar and colloquial terms have all been appropriately labelled in this thesaurus. Words and phrases current on the other side of the Atlantic are labelled as Americanisms. Where necessary, cross-references to related paragraphs are also given. Since there is technically no such thing as a true synonym or exact equivalent, the thesaurus could be said to concentrate on areas of shared meaning, in which usages overlap and shade off into similar ideas. For example, the paragraph on *obstinacy* has cross-references to the paragraphs on *unwillingness* and *perseverance* – all different words related by a central core of common meaning.

This *Pocket Thesaurus* is based on the original *Thesaurus* compiled by Peter Mark Roget in 1852. Roget's arrangement of ideas reflected the thinking and state of knowledge of his day; this framework was considered so obvious to his contemporaries that no index was provided. Over a century later, we order our language differently; priorities have changed, and new fields of knowledge have emerged. As a result it has been necessary to rearrange Roget's original sequence of ideas, and to provide a detailed index for the user. Entries in the index show both parts of speech and paragraph numbers.

As a thesaurus of this size cannot hope to be as exhaustive as Roget's, we have had to omit some rare and obscure terms. However, we have attempted to cover a comprehensive working vocabulary that takes in all levels of language. The end result, we hope, is sufficiently compact to provide a handy means of jogging a recalcitrant memory, while remaining sufficiently comprehensive to serve both as a vocabulary builder and as a source of many hours of useful browsing.

1 EXISTENCE

See also **3** (reality); **322** (life).

n. *existence*, being, life, essence, coexistence; *actuality*, reality, substance, fact, concreteness; *presence*, duration, entity; *universe*, creation, world, cosmos; *coming into being*, realization, materialization, actualization; *survival*, endurance, persistence, continuance; *metaphysics*, ontology, existentialism.

adj. *existing*, being, existent; *actual*, real, substantial, factual, material, physical, concrete; *present*, ongoing, current, prevalent; *surviving*, extant, enduring, lasting, abiding; *metaphysical*, ontological, existential.

vb. *exist*, be, have being, live, breathe; *coexist*, be found, be situated; *be present*, prevail, obtain; *survive*, subsist, remain, endure, continue, last, abide; *come into being*, come about, evolve, arise, take shape; *just exist*, vegetate, stagnate.

adv. *actually*, in (actual) fact, in point of fact, really, truly; *presently*, currently, at the moment; *in one's lifetime*, in all one's born days, man and boy.

2 NONEXISTENCE

See also **4** (unreality); **323** (death).

n. *nonexistence*, nonentity, absence, unreality; *nothingness*, emptiness, vacuum, void, limbo, blankness; *extinction*, death, oblivion, annihilation, nirvana; *nothing*, nil, love, zero; *nullification*, annulment, cancellation, obliteration; *disintegration*, dilapidation, decay, obsolescence; *nihilism*, negativism.

adj. *nonexistent*, absent, missing, minus; *vacant*, empty, blank, null, void; *unreal*, insubstantial, abstract, ideal; *extinct*, dead, defunct, dead and gone, past, obsolete; *nihilistic*, negative, destructive.

vb. *not exist*, be null and void, be over and done with; *cease to exist*, die, pass away, perish, die out; *disappear*, vanish, evaporate, fade, melt, dematerialize; *extinguish*, annihilate, demolish, wipe out, snuff out, quell; *nullify*, abolish, annul, cancel, obliterate,

invalidate, neutralize, negate, veto; *disintegrate*, decay, decompose, go to rack and ruin.

3 REALITY

See also **1** (existence); **282** (material world).

n. *reality*, existence, the here and now; *objectivity*, corporeality, substance, tangibility, palpability, solidity, concreteness; *real world*, universe, creation, physical world, earth, matter; *actuality*, fact, historicity, validity, authenticity; *realism*, naturalism, verisimilitude, cinema vérité, documentary, kitchen sink drama, slice of life; *plausibility*, feasibility, practicality; *realities*, facts of life, home truths, basics, fundamentals, bottom line (*colloq.*), nitty-gritty (*colloq.*), brass tacks, crunch (*colloq.*); *materialism*, realism, empiricism, pragmatism.

adj. *real*, existing, substantial; *objective*, corporeal, tangible, palpable, solid, concrete, physical, material, natural; *actual*, factual, historical, true, valid, authentic; *realistic*, naturalistic, true-to-life, lifelike; *plausible*, feasible, practicable, likely; *practical*, down-to-earth, matter-of-fact, no-nonsense, realistic; *basic*, fundamental, crucial, primary, cardinal; *materialist*, realist, empirical, pragmatic.

vb. *be real*, weigh, bulk large, loom; *objectify*, embody, incarnate, body forth; *validate*, substantiate, corroborate, authenticate; *actualize*, materialize, realize.

adv. *really*, in reality, in fact; *in practice*, in all likelihood, when it comes to the crunch (*colloq.*), when the chips are down (*colloq.*).

4 UNREALITY

See also **2** (nonexistence); **457** (imagination).

n. *unreality*, nonexistence, insubstantiality, incorporeality, abstractness, intangibility, impalpability; *subjectivity*, fantasy, make-believe, fiction, dream world, maya, vision, hallucination, delusion, castle in Spain, pipe-dream; *illusion*, figment of the imagination, mirage, optical illusion, trompe l'oeil, fata morgana, ignis fatuus, will o' the wisp, jack o' lantern; *simulacrum*, shadow, phantom, chimera, ghost, spectre, ectoplasm; *bubble*, fool's paradise, fairy gold, tinsel, nine days' wonder, gossamer, cobweb; *a nothing*, a nobody, nonperson, unperson, hollow man, man of straw, broken reed, paper tiger, puppet; *vain hope*, empty promise, false dawn, pie in the sky (*colloq.*); *empty talk*, hot air (*colloq.*), cock and bull story, bullshit (*colloq.*).

adj. *unreal*, nonexistent, insubstantial, incorporeal, intangible, impapable; *abstract*, ideal, rarefied, bloodless; *subjective*, imaginary, fantastic, make-believe, fictional, dreamlike, hallucinatory, delusory, illusory, chimerical, ghostly, shadowy; *ephemeral*, fleeting, elusive, evanescent; *vague, hazy*, nebulous, tenuous; *spurious*, specious, phoney, flimsy, hollow, meretricious; *token*, nominal, honorary.

vb. *be unreal*, belie, deceive, delude; *idealize*, rarefy, etiolate; *imagine*, fantasize, hallucinate, daydream, hear/see things; *dissolve*, fade, melt, blur, cloud, mist; *falsify*, fudge, distort; *invent*, dissemble, fib, spin a yarn (*colloq.*), waffle (*colloq.*); *invalidate*, refute, puncture, expose, give the lie to.

adv. *ideally*, in theory; *in name*, superficially, to all appearances.

5 ESSENCE

See also **576** (importance).

n. *essence*, substance, gist, heart, stuff; *essential part*, prime constituent, main ingredient, property, attribute; *core*, kernel, backbone, nub, nucleus, marrow, pith, sap, lifeblood; *quintessence*, embodiment, incarnation, personification, epitome, soul; *character*, makeup, constitution, complexion, temperament, stamp, breed, stripe, humour, hue.

adj. *essential*, intrinsic, immanent, inherent; *innate*, inborn, inbred, deep-seated, deep-rooted, ingrained, bred-in-the-bone; *quintessential*, fundamental, constitutional, structural, organic; *integral*, inseparable, ineradicable, built-in.

vb. *be essential*, inhere, belong, be part and parcel of; *characterize*, stamp, inform, mark; *embody*, incarnate, personify, epitomize.

adv. *in essence*, essentially, intrinsically; *at heart*, at bottom, basically, fundamentally.

6 EXTRANEOUSNESS

See also **10** (unrelatedness); **54** (foreign body).

n. *extraneousness*, exteriority, externality; *exterior*, outside, surface, periphery, circumference; *objectification*, externalization, projection; *foreignness*, alienness, unrelatedness, irrelevance, contingency.

adj. *extraneous*, exterior, external, outer, superficial; *foreign*, alien, unrelated, unconnected; *irrelevant*, peripheral, tangential, contingent, incidental, circumstantial.

vb. *be extraneous*, externalize, realize, body forth, objectify; *be irrelevant*, miss the point, talk off the subject, digress.

adv. *outwardly*, on the outside, superficially, prima facie; *off the point*, beside the point, neither here nor there.

7 STATE

See also **5** (essence); **8** (circumstances).

n. *state*, condition, situation, circumstances, lot, plight, estate; *position*, status, standing, footing, rank; *sphere*, realm, world, orbit, walk of life, department (*colloq.*), line of country (*colloq.*); *mode*, manner, modality, modus operandi, modus vivendi; *state of mind*, frame of mind, mood, temper, disposition, attitude, morale, fettle, spirits; *physical condition*, form, shape (*colloq.*), repair, trim, nick (*colloq.*).

adj. *stative*, situational; *modal*, conditional.

vb. *be situated*, stand, lie, sit, be found; *situate*, contextualize, locate.

adv. *as things stand*, in the present situation, in the circumstances.

8 CIRCUMSTANCES

See also **7** (state).

n. *circumstances*, situation, state of affairs, status quo, set-up (*colloq.*); *position*, state of play, lie of the land, story so far; *conditions*, environment, surroundings, setting, milieu, context, background; *occasion*, occurrence, event, episode, incident, happening, coincidence; *stage*, point, juncture, stepping-stone, milestone, turning point, crisis, crossroads.

adj. *circumstantial*, relative, contingent, conditional, provisional, incidental; *surrounding*, environmental, contextual, situational.

adv. *in the circumstances*, as things stand; *in the event*, as it happened; *provisionally*, conditionally.

9 RELATEDNESS

See also **11** (reciprocity); **12** (family relations); **19** (accord); **24** (degree).

n. *relatedness*, relevance, pertinence, bearing, point, appositeness; *relationship*, affinity, kinship, affiliation, bond, tie, rapport; *connection*, relation, link, tie-up, association; *relativeness*, ratio, proportion, scale; *interrelatedness*, correlation, reciprocity, interdependence, cross-reference, complementarity; *correspondence*, agreement, similarity, parallel, comparison, analogy.

adj. *related*, relevant, pertinent, apposite, appropriate, germane, apropos; *corresponding*, connected, similar, parallel, comparable, analogous; *interrelated*, correlative, reciprocal, interdependent, complementary, mutual, respective; *relative*, proportional, commensurate.

vb. *be related*, belong, pertain; *touch*, concern, regard, involve, interest; *relate*, link, connect, tie up, tie in, bracket together; *correlate*, juxtapose, reconcile, compare, contrast, draw a parallel between, cross-refer; *correspond*, approximate, agree, match, accord, fit, tally; *be relevant*, address the question, stick to the point.

adv. *relatively*, proportionally, in proportion, to scale; *in contrast*; *by/in*

comparison, comparatively; *respectively*, mutually.

prep. *relative to*, with respect to, with regard to, as regards, with reference to, concerning, in relation to, re, vis-a-vis.

10 UNRELATEDNESS

See also **6** (extraneousness); **20** (disparity).

n. *unrelatedness*, irrelevance, inappositeness, inappropriateness, extraneousness, red herring (*colloq.*), non sequitur; *unconnectedness*, separateness, dissociation, independence; *randomness*, arbitrariness, coincidence, long shot, shot in the dark, fluke; *disproportion*, disparity, imbalance, asymmetry, distortion.

adj. *unrelated*, irrelevant, inapposite, inappropriate, extraneous, foreign, alien; *unconnected*, incidental, tangential, peripheral, inessential, unimportant, immaterial; *random*, arbitrary, chance, coincidental; *disproportionate*, unbalanced, distorted, asymmetrical.

vb. *be unrelated*, have no bearing on, have nothing to do with; *digress*, miss the point, avoid the issue, get sidetracked.

adv. *beside the point*, off the point; *by the way*, incidentally, in parenthesis.

11 RECIPROCITY

See also **9** (relatedness); **129** (exchange).

n. *reciprocity*, correspondence, interrelation, interdependence, mutuality, interconnectedness, complementarity; *counterpart*, equivalent, opposite number, alter ego, mirror image; *interaction*, interchange, interplay; *exchange*; *alternation*, exchange, give and take, tit for tat, seesaw, vicissitudes, ups and downs, swings and roundabouts.

adj. *reciprocal*, interrelated, interdependent, mutual, interconnected, complementary; *equivalent*, interchangeable, corresponding; *alternating*, seesaw, ding-dong (*colloq.*), retaliatory.

vb. *reciprocate*, exchange, swap (*col-*

loq.), return in kind, give as good as one gets, retaliate; *interact*, interconnect, interrelate, interchange; *alternate*, seesaw, fluctuate, take turn about; *correspond*, match up, tally.

adv. *in turn*, turn and turn about, Box and Cox; *all things being equal*, on balance; *conversely*, on the other hand; *vice versa*, mutatis mutandis.

12 FAMILY RELATIONS

See also 9 (relatedness); 154 (parent).

n. *family relationships*, kinship. tribalism, nepotism, inbreeding, incest; *ancestry*, blood, lineage, descent, matriarchy, patriarchy, genealogy, distaff side, spear side; *family*, clan, folks (*colloq.*), kith and kin, one's own flesh and blood, next of kin, relatives, inlaws, nuclear family, extended family; *parenthood*, motherhood, fatherhood, parenting, fostering, adoption, artificial insemination; *parent*, mother, father, donor, surrogate mother, godparent, stepparent, grandparent; *offspring*, issue, son, daughter, bastardy, illegitimacy, natural child, love child, testtube baby; *sibling*, brother, sister, halfbrother, half-sister, stepbrother, stepsister, twin; *aunt*, uncle, niece, nephew, great-aunt, great-uncle, greatniece, great-nephew, cousin, second cousin; *heredity*, chromosome, gene, DNA, genetic engineering.

adj. *familial*, kindred, cognate, agnate, consanguineous, incestuous; *ancestral*, tribal, genealogical, matriarchal, patriarchal, matrilineal, patrilineal; *filial*; *sibling*, sisterly, brotherly, fraternal; *avuncular*; *hereditary*, inherited, congenital, genetic, inbred.

vb. *be related to*, be descended from, take after, favour; *father*, sire, beget, adopt, foster; *wed*, intermarry, interbreed; *be inherited*, run in the family, be in the blood.

13 SAMENESS

See also 15 (uniformity); 17 (similarity); 21 (imitation).

n. *sameness*, identity, equivalence, similarity, coincidence, congruence, agreement; *likeness*, double, Doppelganger, alter ego, second self, clone, lookalike, spitting image (*colloq.*), chip off the old block (*colloq.*), dead ringer (*colloq.*); *copy*, duplicate, replica, carbon copy, facsimile, analogue, fellow, mate, match, twin, Tweedledum and Tweedledee; *uniformity*, monotony, same old story, nothing new under the sun.

adj. *same*, identical, selfsame, indistinguishable, interchangeable; *similar*, equivalent, like, analogous, congruent; *uniform*, unvarying, monotonous, samey (*colloq.*).

vb. *be the same*, be identical, come to the same thing, be tantamount to; *merge*, coincide, coalesce; *mirror*, repeat, parrot, echo; *copy*, duplicate, replicate, match, twin, clone; *look alike*, be like two peas in a pod.

adv. *similarly*, by the same token, in the same way, likewise; *ditto*.

14 OPPOSITENESS

See also 18 (dissimilarity); 215 (contraposition); 632 (opposition).

n. *oppositeness*, contrariety, contraposition, polarity, contradiction, incompatibility; *opposite*, converse, opposite pole, other extreme, antipodes, antithesis, antonym, negative, counterpoint, foil, antidote; *opposition*, antagonism, hostility, antipathy, conflict, clash; *reverse*, mirror image, wrong side, other side, verso, countercurrent, contraflow; *diametric opposites*, day and night, chalk and cheese, oil and water, yin and yang.

adj. *opposite*, contrary, contradictory, incompatible, inverse, converse; *diametrically opposite*, antithetical, antipodean, contrapuntal, negative; *opposed*, antagonistic, hostile, antipathetic, adversarial; *reverse*, counter, anticlockwise.

vb. *be opposite*, contradict, contrast; *oppose*, antagonize, clash with, conflict with, challenge; *reverse*, negate, counteract, contravene, run counter to, turn the tables on.

adv. *on the contrary*, in contrast; *conversely*, on the other hand; *back to* *front*, inside out, upside down, topsy turvy.

15 UNIFORMITY

See also **13** (sameness); **17** (similarity); **72** (conformity).

n. *uniformity*, evenness, consistency, homogeneity; *continuity*, regularity, constancy, stability; *identity*, accord, agreement, consensus, unison, unity; *conformity*, regimentation, standardization, normalization, mass-production; *mould*, pattern, stamp, stereotype, production line, conveyor belt; *sameness*, drabness, monotony, routine, daily round, groove, rut.

adj. *uniform*, even, consistent, homogeneous, alike, of a piece; *continuous*, constant, regular, unbroken, uninterrupted, rhythmic, stable, unchanging, unvarying; *identical*, mass-produced, unisex, off-the-peg, standard, stereotyped, typecast; *same*, monotonous, repetitive, dull, drab, monochrome, self-coloured; *undifferentiated*, unrelieved, monolithic.

vb. *make uniform*, level, even off, homogenize, grade, size; *regularize*, stabilize, normalize; *standardize*, stereotype, systematize, typecast, mass-produce; *align*, bring into line, rehabilitate, reeducate, drill, regiment.

adv. *uniformly*, across the board; *in line*, in keeping.

16 DIVERSITY

See also **18** (dissimilarity); **38** (mixture).

n. *diversity*, variety, heterogeneity, dissimilarity, contrast, relief, variegation; *nonuniformity*, inconsistency, irregularity, discontinuity, unevenness; *changeability*, instability, variability, versatility; *assortment*, medley, mixed bag, miscellany, motley crew, ragbag, patchwork, mosaic, kaleidoscope, rainbow, coat of many colours, chequered career, everything but the kitchen sink (*colloq.*).

adj. *diverse*, varied, heterogeneous, variegated, chequered; *nonuniform*, inconsistent, irregular, discontinuous, uneven; *changeable*, unstable, variable, kaleidoscopic; *assorted*, mixed, motley, divers, sundry, various, miscellaneous; *versatile*, all-round, multipurpose, multifaceted.

vb. *make diverse*, vary, contrast, variegate, chequer; *mix*, stir up, shake up, jumble, shuffle; *diversify*, have many strings to one's bow, have many irons in the fire, branch out, spread one's wings, broaden one's horizons.

adv. *all anyhow*, in a muddle, higgledy-piggledy (*colloq.*).

17 SIMILARITY

See also **13** (sameness); **15** (uniformity); **19** (accord); **21** (imitation).

n. *similarity*, sameness, synonymy, symmetry, similitude, resemblance, likeness, affinity; *correspondence*, equation, comparability, analogy, simile, parallel, alliteration, assonance, assimilation; *semblance*, simulation, imitation, dissimulation, disguise, camouflage; *counterpart*, twin, copy, clone, soulmate, kindred spirit, two of a king, birds of a feather; *sameness*, equivalence, approximation, much of a muchness (*colloq.*), six of one and half a dozen of the other.

adj. *similar*, same, synonymous, symmetrical, like; *corresponding*, comparable, analogous, parallel, equivalent, approximate, akin; *simulated*, imitation, artificial, cultured, ersatz, synthetic.

vb. *be similar*, resemble, take after, favour, suggest; *reflect*, mirror, echo, evoke, savour of, smack of, be redolent of; *make similar*, equalize, homogenize, assimilate, camouflage, disguise; *compare*, liken, draw a parallel between; *imitate*, emulate, copy, reproduce, duplicate, clone; *correspond*, accord, tally, match, coincide, agree.

adv. *all the same*, at the same time; *similarly*, by the same token, likewise; *in the style/manner of*, à la; *as it were*, so to speak; *in the same boat*, in a similar situation.

18 DISSIMILARITY

See also **14** (oppositeness); **16**

(diversity); **20** (disparity); **418** (discrimination).

n. *dissimilarity*, difference, disparity, diversity, discrepancy, divergence; *unlikeness*, incongruity, incompatibility, contrast, asymmetry, no comparison, nothing in common, another matter/story, different kettle of fish (*colloq.*); *differentiation*, discrimination, distinction, nuance, nicety, nit-picking (*colloq.*).

adj. *dissimilar*, different, disparate, divergent, diverse; *unlike*, incongruous, incompatible, contrasting, poles apart; *distinctive*, unusual, peculiar, out of the ordinary, singular; *discriminating*, discerning, selective, choosy (*colloq.*).

vb. *be dissimilar*, differ, diverge, deviate, depart from; *be unlike*, contrast, conflict, be at odds, be at variance; *differentiate*, distinguish, discriminate, split hairs, nit-pick (*colloq.*), separate the sheep from the goats, tell the men from the boys.

adv. *at different times*, variously; *in contrast*.

19 ACCORD

See also **15** (uniformity); **17** (similarity); **25** (equality); **436** (assent).

n. *accord*, agreement, concord, concert, chorus, harmony, understanding, reconciliation, arbitration; *consensus*, unanimity, unison, unity, cooperation, solidarity; *consistency*, uniformity, coherence, congruity, conformity; *aptness*, fitness, appropriateness, suitability, compatibility, timeliness, right moment, mot juste; *adaptation*, accommodation, adjustment, alignment, synchronization, fine tuning.

adj. *agreeing*, harmonious, reconciled; *unanimous*, united, concerted, joint, cooperative; *consistent*, uniform, coherent, congruent, of a piece; *apt*, appropriate, suitable, fitting, compatible, consonant, commensurate, timely, opportune; *adaptable*, accommodating, flexible, easygoing, conciliatory; *well-adjusted*, balanced, close-fitting, snug, made-to-measure.

vb. *accord*, agree, concur, consent, chorus, chime in, harmonize, reach an understanding; *cooperate*, get along, pull together, hit it off (*colloq.*), be on the same wavelength (*colloq.*), see eye to eye; *fit*, suit, fit the bill (*colloq.*), tally, square, match, dovetail, marry, coincide; *adapt*, adjust, accommodate, align, true up, synchronize, fine-tune.

adv. *in accord*, in chorus, in concert, in step, in phase, in tune, in unison; *in keeping*, in place, in context; *at home*, at ease, in one's element.

20 DISPARITY

See also **10** (unrelatedness); **18** (dissimilarity); **26** (unequality).

n. *disparity*, inequality, imbalance, difference, dissimilarity, divergence; *discrepancy*, inconsistency, gap, margin, overlap, shortfall, surplus, differential; *maladjustment*, mismatch, mésalliance, crossed line, cross-purposes, discord, dissonance, false note; *misfit*, odd man out, eccentric, freak, sport, square peg in a round hole, fish out of water; *unsuitability*, incompatibility, inappropriateness, untimeliness, irrelevancy.

adj. *disparate*, unequal, disproportionate, dissimilar, different, divergent, inconsistent; *discordant*, dissonant, jarring, grating, out-of-tune; *maladjusted*, unbalanced, deviant, eccentric, freakish, odd, ill-matched, ill-assorted; *unsuitable*, unfitting, unbecoming, inappropriate, untimely, inopportune, incompatible, irrelevant.

vb. *be disparate*, differ, diverge, contradict; *conflict*, clash, jar, grate, stick out like a sore thumb (*colloq.*); *misplace*, mistime, mishit, talk out of turn, drop a brick/clanger (*colloq.*).

adv. *out of step*, out of line, out of phase; *at odds*, at variance, at cross-purposes; *out of one's element*, out of place, out of keeping, out of season.

21 IMITATION

See also **13** (sameness); **17** (similarity); **151** (reproduction).

n. *imitation*, mimesis, onomatopoeia, emulation, plagiarism; *copy*, reproduction, duplicate, facsimile, photocopy, carbon copy, replica, clone; *fake*, forgery, counterfeit, sham, simulation, disguise, camouflage; *mimicry*, mockery, travesty, satire, caricature, burlesque, parody, pastiche, impersonation, spoof (*colloq.*), send-up (*colloq.*), takeoff (*colloq.*); *imitator*, follower, emulator, disciple; *copyist*, plagiarist, impersonator, mime, echo, sheep, ape, parrot, copycat; *forger*, counterfeiter, fake, impostor, poseur, charlatan, mountebank; *mimic*, satirist, caricaturist, parodist.

adj. *imitative*, mimetic, onomatopoeic; *derivative*, second-hand, unoriginal, copycat, follow-my-leader; *fake*, counterfeit, false, sham, phoney, pseudo, artificial, synthetic, mock, ersatz, cultured.

vb. *imitate*, emulate, follow, model oneself on, pattern oneself after, follow in the footsteps of; *copy*, reproduce, duplicate, clone, photocopy, borrow, crib, plagiarize; *fake*, forge, counterfeit, sham, simulate, impersonate; *repeat*, echo, ape, parrot, chorus, follow the herd, jump/climb on the bandwagon (*colloq.*); *mimic*, mock, caricature, satirize, burlesque, parody, travesty, send up (*colloq.*), take off (*colloq.*).

adv. *word for word*, verbatim, parrot-fashion; *ditto*; *to the life*.

22 ORIGINALITY

See also **70** (speciality).

n. *originality*, creativity, imagination, inventiveness, innovation; *novelty*, individuality, uniqueness, freshness; *original*, source, model, pattern, mould, matrix, blueprint, prototype, archetype, paradigm, test case, precedent; *originator*, inventor, creator, innovator, deviser; *authenticity*, genuineness, real thing, genuine article, real McCoy (*colloq.*).

adj. *original*, creative, imaginative, inventive, innovative; *novel*, individual, unique, one-off, unparalleled, unprecedented, unheard-of, off-beat (*colloq.*), sui generis, inimitable, incomparable; *seminal*, prototypal, archetypal, stereotypical, standard, classic; *authentic*, genuine, real, echt, bona fide.

vb. *originate*, create, invent, devise,

imagine, dream up, conceive, generate; *patent*, blueprint, copyright, trademark; *model*, mould, pattern, stereotype; *exemplify*, typify, represent.

adv. *from the beginning*, from scratch, ab ovo.

23 QUANTITY

See also **29** (greatness); **30** (smallness); **168** (size); **177** (measurement).

n. *quantity*, amount, amplitude, magnitude, bulk, mass; *dimensions*, longitude, length, latitude, breadth, width, girth, altitude, height, depth; *area*, extension, volume, capacity, weight, heaviness; *strength*, pressure, potential, tension, torque, stress, strain; *definite quantity*, quantum, measure, dose, ration, portion, helping, share, slice of the cake; *small quantity*, thimbleful, cupful, pinch, teaspoonful, ounce, milligram; *large quantity*, bucketful, sackful, armful, bundle, lorryload, hundredweight, kilo, stack, mountain.

adj. *quantitative*, high, long, wide, deep, broad; *large*, ample, bulky, massive, extensive, capacious, voluminous; *small*, compact, light, shallow, neat, diminutive.

vb. *quantify*, measure, estimate; *apportion*, ration, allot, distribute.

adv. *to the tune of*; *in the region of*, approximately, in the right ballpark (*U.S. colloq.*).

24 DEGREE

See also **9** (relatedness).

n. *degree*, extent, proportion, scale, ratio, rate, frequency; *stage*, level, step, rung, point, remove; *rank*, status, class, standing, footing; *gradation*, calibration, differential, interval, nuance; *hierarchy*, taxonomy, series; *gauge*, grid, graph, sliding scale, ladder.

adj. *gradational*, serial, hierarchical; *proportional*, relative, comparative; *gradual*, staggered.

vb. *graduate*, calibrate, measure off, grade, scale, size; *class*, sort, rank, rate.

adv. *by degrees*, gradually, bit by bit,

step by step, little by little; *in some degree*, to some extent, somewhat.

25 EQUALITY
See also **19** (accord); **28** (compensation).

n. *equality*, equivalence, equal footing, identity, sameness, symmetry; *parity*, par, quits, level pegging, six of one and half a dozen of the other; *equilibrium*, balance, poise, even keel, equation, balance of power, balance of terror, mutually assured destruction; *stability*, status quo, stasis, stalemate, deadlock, hung jury; *draw*, tie, dead heat, photo finish (*colloq.*), cliffhanger (*colloq.*); *equalizer*, makeweight, counterweight, ballast, stopgap; *equal*, peer, match, mate, twin, fellow, counterpart, opposite number, oppo (*colloq.*); *egalitarianism*, democracy, equal rights, equal opportunity, positive discrimination, justice.

adj. *equal*, same, equilateral, equidistant, coextensive, identical; *even*, stable, static, self-righting, self-regulating, homoeostatic; *symmetrical*, half-and-half, fifty-fifty, parallel, one-to-one, ding-dong (*colloq.*); *egalitarian*, democratic, equitable, just, fair, impartial.

vb. *be equal*, tie, draw, even out, tally, balance; *equalize*, synchronize, level up/down, round up/down; *compensate*, make good, offset, rob Peter to pay Paul; *stabilize*, strike a balance, redress the balance.

adv. *equally*, by the same token; *on equal terms*, pari passu; *neck and neck*, abreast.

26 INEQUALITY
See also **20** (disparity).

n. *inequality*, disparity, difference, discrepancy, disproportion; *imbalance*, overload, overkill, top-heaviness, shortage, shortfall, deficiency; *handicap*, disadvantage, loaded dice, advantage, privilege, head start; *unevenness*, asymmetry, tilt, camber, list, lopsidedness, odd number, casting vote; *inequity*, injustice, discrimination, prejudice, bias.

adj. *unequal*, disparate, different, disproportionate; *unbalanced*, overweight, underweight, top-heavy, overshot, undershot; *uneven*, asymmetrical, askew, awry, lopsided, skewwhiff (*colloq.*); *inequitable*, undemocratic, unfair, unjust, discriminatory, biased, prejudiced.

vb. *be unequal*, be above/below par, overcompensate, overshoot, fall short; *outweigh*, outrank, outclass, outstrip, outvote; *unbalance*, upset, capsize, destabilize; *bias*, prejudice, skew, disadvantage, handicap, tip the scales.

adv. *of balance*, on the light/heavy side; *at a disadvantage*, up against it, with the odds stacked against one; *at an advantage*, out in front.

27 AVERAGE
See also **63** (middle); **69** (generality).

n. *average*, mean, median, norm, par; *moderation*, middle course, golden mean, happy medium, best of both worlds; *midpoint*, midway, halfway, halfway house, middle age, middle class, middle distance, mid-life crisis; *averageness*, mediocrity, ordinariness, lowest common denominator, middle of the road, common run, common man, man in the street, Joe Bloggs (*colloq.*); *neutrality*, impartiality, mugwumpery, silent majority, floating vote, don't knows.

adj. *average*, mean, median, normal, standard, par for the course; *moderate*, middling, middle-aged, middlebrow, middle-class, middle-of-the-road; *mediocre*, ordinary, commonplace, run-of-the-mill, passable, adequate, so-so (*colloq.*); *neutral*, impartial, tepid, lukewarm, Laodicean.

vb. *average out*, balance out, even out; *take an average*, go halves, split the difference; *be moderate*, strike a balance between, see both sides of the question, sit on the fence (*colloq.*).

adv. *on average*, in general, as a rule, on the whole; *all in all*, on balance, all things considered, at the end of the day; *up to the mark*, up to scratch (*colloq.*), up to snuff (*colloq.*).

28 COMPENSATION

See also **25** (equality).

n. *compensation*, amends, atonement, reparation, redress, restitution; *exchange*, quid pro quo, swap (*colloq.*), give and take; *allowance*, security, insurance, hedge, cover, collateral, safety net, failsafe; *counterweight*, weighting, ballast, makeweight; *refund*, indemnity, costs, damages, reimbursement, repayment.

adj. *compensatory*, reparatory, expiatory.

vb. *compensate*, offset, counterbalance, make amends, atone, make up for, make good; *repay*, refund, redeem, indemnify, reimburse, square up (*colloq.*); *insure against*, secure oneself, cover oneself, hedge; *allow for*, take into account, set against.

adv. *on the other hand*, nevertheless, having said that; *instead*, in lieu, in exchange.

29 GREATNESS

See also **23** (quantity); **47** (whole); **49** (completeness); **168** (size).

n. *greatness*, size, bulk, mass, amplitude, girth, intensity, magnitude, enormity, immensity, infinity; *superiority*, power, might, grandeur, eminence, majesty, authority, distinction, charisma, fame, renown, celebrity, prestige; *greatest part*, lion's share, majority, macrocosm, magnum opus; *maximum*, optimum, ceiling, high point, zenith, peak; *great quantity*, profusion, abundance, host, wealth, plethora, spate, flood, torrent, rush, stream, lots (*colloq.*), heaps (*colloq.*), loads (*colloq.*), masses (*colloq.*), stacks (*colloq.*), bags (*colloq.*), pots (*colloq.*), lashings (*colloq.*), oodles (*colloq.*), tons (*colloq.*), miles (*colloq.*), reams (*colloq.*).

adj. *great*, big, bulky, massive, huge, vast, outsize, enormous, immense, infinite; *greatest*, main, major, best, maximal, optimal; *substantial*, sizable, considerable, respectable, hefty (*colloq.*); *giant*, gigantic, Brobdingnagian, colossal, monumental, monolithic, hulking, strapping, whopping (*colloq.*), whacking (*colloq.*); *ample*, generous, voluminous, capacious, spacious, roomy; *superior*, powerful, mighty, eminent, grand, majestic, authoritative, distinguished, noble, august, charismatic, famous, renowned, celebrated, prestigious; *extraordinary*, outstanding, remarkable, exceptional, prodigious, overwhelming; *plentiful*, abundant, crawling, teeming, swarming, thick on the ground.

vb. *be great*, bulk (large), loom, soar, tower; *prevail*, predominate, rule, dominate, sway; *maximize*, enhance, increase, improve; *abound*, crawl, swarm, teem, brim, overflow.

adv. *greatly*, widely, extensively, amply; *on a large scale*, in a big way (*colloq.*); *largely*, mainly, for the most part, mostly; *very much*, hugely, vastly, enormously, immensely; *substantially*, considerably, materially; *to the utmost*, maximally.

30 SMALLNESS

See also **23** (quantity); **87** (few); **169** (littleness).

n. *smallness*, littleness, diminutiveness, minuteness; *insufficiency*, scantness, paucity, scarcity, sparseness, drop in the ocean; *pettiness*, paltriness, meanness, insignificance, small beer, small fry; *diminution*, contraction, abridgment, reduction, decrease; *smallest part*, minority, microcosm, atom, particle, mote, grain, granule; *minimum*, pittance, low point, floor, nadir, rock bottom; *small quantity*, modicum, fraction, pinch, handful, spoonful, bite, sip, scrap, morsel, crumb, whit, jot, whisper, ray, flicker, trace, tinge, vestige, dash, splash, drop, dribble, trickle, sprinkling; *trifle*, bagatelle, bauble, mite, bean, dime, cent, sou.

adj. *small*, least, little, tiny, diminutive, minute, microscopic, infinitesimal, Lilliputian; *dwarf*, midget, miniature, toy; *insufficient*, scant, scarce, few, rare, sparse, minimal; *narrow*, cramped, confined; *petty*, paltry, mean, insignificant, derisory, minor, trivial, trifling; *slight*, undersized, puny, feeble, meagre, thin, weedy (*colloq.*); *modest*, lowly, humble, unobtrusive, self-effacing.

vb. *become small*, lessen, decrease, diminish, shrink, contract; *make small*, abridge, abbreviate, shorten, reduce, curtail, minimize.

adv. *slightly*, somewhat; *partially*, nearly, almost, virtually; *scarcely*, hardly, barely, narrowly; *at the very least*, minimally; *merely*, simply, only.

31 SUPERIORITY

See also **576** (importance); **651** (success); **665** (master).

n. *superiority*, precedence, primacy, seniority; *pride of place*, prominence, advantage, privilege, prerogative; *lead*, head start, edge, leverage, upper hand, whip hand, trump card; *domination*, rule, sway, ascendancy, hegemony, leadership, supremacy, sovereignty; *quality*, excellence, perfection, high calibre; *elite*, chosen few, happy few, crème de la crème, top people, upper crust, the brightest and best, the pick of the bunch (*colloq.*); *top*, acme, peak, summit, Everest, top of the heap (*colloq.*), top rung of the ladder, vantage point; *superior*, elder, senior, captain, head boy/girl, leader, chief, commander, premier, prime minister, first lady, prima donna; *champion*, prizewinner, victor, world-beater, record-breaker, cock of the walk; *paragon*, model, star, whiz kid (*colloq.*), high-flier, mastermind, superman; *manager*, boss, foreman, gaffer (*colloq.*), governor (*colloq.*); *big battalions*, big boys (*colloq.*), big guns (*colloq.*), top brass, heavyweight (*colloq.*).

adj. *superior*, elder, senior, principal, foremost, prominent; *excellent*, top-level, top-flight, top-notch (*colloq.*); first-class, first-rate, prestigious, five-star, blue-chip, A-1; *outstanding*, matchless, peerless, unparalleled, unrivalled; *leading*, influential, chief, ruling, supreme, paramount, sovereign, royal; *champion*, victorious, world-beating, winning, triumphant.

vb. *be superior*, prevail, predominate, carry the day, win, triumph; *outdo*, defeat, best, worst, outbid, outplay,

outshine, outwit, surpass, be one up on, lick/beat hollow (*colloq.*), hammer (*colloq.*), trounce, knock into a cocked hat; *overshadow*, eclipse, put in the shade, steal someone's thunder, put someone's nose out of joint (*colloq.*); *lead*, head, front, captain, boss, direct, manage, run, spearhead; *culminate*, peak, climax, go through the roof/ceiling (*colloq.*).

adv. *above par*, above average, out of the top drawer, out of the common run; *to crown/cap it all*; *principally*, chiefly, mainly, above all.

32 INFERIORITY

See also **577** (unimportance); **652** (failure); **666** (servant).

n. *inferiority*, dependence, subordination, supporting role, obscurity; *disadvantage*, handicap, uphill struggle, losing battle; *poor quality*, second best, seconds, rubbish, trash, tat (*colloq.*); *subjection*, subjugation, conquest, servitude, bondage, yoke; *dregs*, scum, riffraff, the lowest of the low; *bottom*, record low, minimum, nadir, trough, rock bottom, bottom of the heap (*colloq.*); *inferior*, junior, subordinate, rank and file, second string, assistant, auxiliary, follower, dependant, servant, retainer, underling, hireling, henchman, myrmidon, pawn, tool, creature; *loser*, runner-up, also-ran, nonstarter (*colloq.*), underdog, no-hoper (*colloq.*), has-been (*colloq.*), poor relation.

adj. *inferior*, junior, lower, minor, dependent, subordinate, subject; *secondary*, subsidiary, auxiliary, ancillary, backup; *second-class*, second-rate, mediocre, substandard, imperfect, shopsoiled, shoddy, defective, tatty (*colloq.*), trashy (*colloq.*), crummy (*colloq.*); *common*, low, vulgar, menial.

vb. *be inferior*, submit, yield, bow, knuckle under (*colloq.*), retire defeated, come off second best, lose face, take a beating/hammering (*colloq.*); *efface oneself*, hang back, take a back seat (*colloq.*), play second fiddle (*colloq.*), keep a low profile; *fall short*, not make the grade, leave something to be desired, not come up to the mark, not come up to scratch (*colloq.*), not be a patch on (*colloq.*), not be in the running; *sink*, slump, bottom out, go through the floor (*colloq.*), hit rock bottom.

adv. *below par*, below average; *under someone's heel*, under someone's thumb.

33 INCREASE

See also **35** (addition).

n. *increase*, addition, increment, augmentation, supplement, accretion, accumulation, appreciation, intensification; *growth*, development, advance, progression, acceleration, crescendo, rise, buildup, inflation; *spread*, expansion, enlargement, proliferation multiplication; *sudden increase*, escalation, explosion, bulge, boom, boost, spiral, climb, rising tide, quantum leap; *extra*, bonus, profit, rake-off (*colloq.*).

adj. *increasing*, growing, escalating; *progressive*, cumulative, incremental; *additional*, supplementary, extra; *spiralling*, inflationary.

vb. *increase*, add, accrue, accumulate, appreciate, augment; *grow*, develop, burgeon, sprout, thrive, prosper, advance, progress, accelerate, rise, inflate, wax; *spread*, expand, enlarge, mushroom, proliferate, multiply; *escalate*, climb, spiral, rocket, take off; *intensify*, redouble, treble, step up, hot up (*colloq.*); *boost*, swell, stoke, reinforce, bolster, pad out, flesh out, beef up (*colloq.*).

adv. *increasingly*, more and more; *on the increase*, on the up and up; *into the bargain*, with interest, with knobs on (*colloq.*).

34 DECREASE

See also **36** (subtraction).

n. *decrease*, diminution, abatement, reduction, deduction, subtraction, loss, depreciation, decline; *contraction*, shrinkage, cutback, rundown, retrenchment, deceleration; *recession*, slump, depression, squeeze, freeze, restraint, deflation; *gradual decrease*, diminuendo, decrescendo, ebb, leakage, evaporation, erosion, attrition; *sudden*

decrease, fall, dip, drop, plunge, slide, tumble, crash.

adj. *decreasing*, diminishing, dwindling; *reductive*, subtractive; *depressive*, deflationary.

vb. *decrease*, diminish, reduce, deduct, subtract, lose, depreciate, decline; *contract*, shrink, cut back, retrench, tighten one's belt, deflate, depress, squeeze, freeze; *lessen*, dwindle, ebb, recede, abate, subside, wane, slacken, decelerate; *fall*, dip, drop, plunge, slide, slump, tumble, crash; *cut*, axe, slash, curtail, decimate.

adv. *decreasingly*, less and less; *in decline*, on the wane.

35 ADDITION

See also **33** (increase).

n. *addition*, increase, increment, appendage; *adjunct*, attachment, annexe, extension, arm, wing; *appendix*, supplement, postscript, coda, codicil, addendum, footnote, rider, pendant; *insertion*, interjection, interpolation, parenthesis, filling, padding; *reinforcement*, auxiliary, supernumerary, reserve, backup; *accretion*, agglomeration, agglutination, concatenation; *additive*, admixture, ingredient, seasoning; *accompaniment*, extras, trappings, accessories, trimmings, frills (*colloq.*); *bonus*, perk (*colloq.*), overtime, profit, gain, interest, percentage, golden handshake, windfall; *sequel*, follow-up, encore, epilogue, afterthought.

adj. *additional*, accessory, supplementary; *extra*, spare, reserve, auxiliary, ancillary, supernumerary.

vb. *add*, affix, annex, attach, append; *supplement*, augment, swell, reinforce, pad out, flesh out, top up, beef up (*colloq.*); *insert*, interject, introduce, interpose, interpolate, throw in, chip in (*colloq.*); *add on*, tack on, join on, slap on (*colloq.*), superimpose, overlay, graft.

adv. *in addition*, moreover, furthermore; *plus*, with interest, over the odds; *into the bargain*, to boot; *to the good*, in profit, in the black.

36 SUBTRACTION

See also **34** (decrease).

n. *subtraction*, deduction, removal, withdrawal, elimination, deletion, expurgation, bowdlerization; *curtailment*, cutback, contraction, retrenchment; *reduction*, discount, rebate, loss, decrement, tare; *abridgment*, abbreviation, condensation, summary, precis; *amputation*, excision, decapitation, castration; *erosion*, abrasion, attrition.

vb. *subtract*, deduct, remove, withdraw, eliminate, delete, censor, bluepencil, expurgate, bowdlerize; *curtail*, decrease, cut, cut back, prune, pare, whittle, trim, slim down, dock, chop, axe, slash; *reduce*, abridge, abbreviate, condense, summarize; *amputate*, excise, decapitate, behead, castrate, geld, spay; *erode*, abrade, wear away, grind down.

adv. *less*, minus, without; *at a discount*, at a loss; *out of pocket*, down, in the red.

37 REMAINDER

See also **60** (sequence).

n. *remainder*, residue, remains, remnant, relic; *surplus*, balance, profit, net; *trace*, track, trail, footprint, spoor, vestige; *ruins*, shell, shadow, wreck, husk, skeleton, fossil, ashes; *debris*, detritus, slough, scurf, refuse, litter, rubbish, sewage, excrement; *sediment*, dregs, lees, grounds, scum, dross; *leavings*, leftovers, scraps, scrapings, offscourings, gleanings, stubble, chaff; *rump*, stump, offcut, tail end, fag end (*colloq.*), odds and ends, odds and sods (*colloq.*); *wake*, aftermath, aftereffect, fallout, hangover, by-product, spin-off; *survivor*, orphan, widow, widower, relict, heir, successor.

adj. *remaining*, leftover, residual, vestigial; *surplus*, spare, odd, net, outstanding, superfluous; *sedimentary*, alluvial; *surviving*, alive, extant.

vb. *remain*, survive, outlast, persist, endure.

adv. *to spare*, in hand, to play with (*colloq.*); *on the shelf* (*colloq.*).

38 MIXTURE

See also **16** (diversity); **45** (combination).

n. *mixture*, combination, compound, concoction, infusion, confection; *amalgam*, alloy, blend, fusion, merger; *assortment*, mixed bag, motley crew, miscellany, melange, medley, kaleidoscope, mosaic, patchwork, pot pourri, cocktail, punch; *mishmash*, hotchpotch, ragbag, farrago, job lot, jumble, gallimaufry, ragout, witches' brew, everything but the kitchen sink (*colloq.*); *mixer*, blender, liquidizer, melting pot, crucible; *hybrid*, cross, mongrel, chimera, half-breed, mulatto, creole, androgyne, hermaphrodite, bisexual, transsexual; *admixture*, tinge, trace, dash, sprinkling, hint, soupçon.

adj. *mixed*, combined, composite; *assorted*, miscellaneous, heterogeneous, catholic, eclectic, syncretic; *variegated*, dappled, mottled, brindled, piebald, skewbald, motley, rainbow, kaleidoscopic, psychedelic, technicolour; *hybrid*, mongrel, half-caste, crossbred, bionic, androgynous, bisexual, transsexual, hermaphroditic.

vb. *mix*, combine, amalgamate, fuse, merge; *blend*, shake, stir, dilute, brew, knead, mash, liquidize, homogenize; *mingle*, intersperse, interlard, interlace, interweave, intertwine; *suffuse*, pervade, imbue, impregnate, infuse, permeate; *tinge*, season, spice, sprinkle, lace, spike, adulterate; *intermarry*, interbreed.

adv. *among*, amidst; *pell-mell*, higgledypiggledy (*colloq.*).

39 PURITY

See also **586** (cleanness).

n. *purity*, homogeneity, integrity, immaculateness; *wholeness*, wholefood, health food, macrobiotics; *essence*, distillate, concentrate, extract; *cleanliness*, antisepsis, hygiene, sanitation, pasteurization, sterilization; *purification*, clarification, filtration, distillation; *purgative*, laxative, cathartic.

adj. *pure*, simple, single, unalloyed, irreducible, homogeneous; *integral*, intact, immaculate, pristine, virgin;

natural, whole, raw, unadulterated, unprocessed, untreated, macrobiotic; *clean*, antiseptic, hygienic, sterile, unpolluted, sanitized; *undiluted*, neat, straight; *purebred*, thoroughbred, pedigree.

vb. *purify*, simplify, refine, distil, clarify, concentrate; *filter*, sieve, sift, winnow, weed; *clean*, wash, sterilize, disinfect, pasteurize, purge, flush out, cleanse the Augean stables.

adv. *purely*, simply, merely; *neat*, straight, on the rocks.

40 UNION

See also **42** (connection); **43** (adhesion); **66** (assembly).

n. *union*, combination, conjunction, confluence, convergence, merger, fusion, synthesis; *alliance*, coalition, association, league, brotherhood, guild, trade union, syndicate, cooperative; *meeting*, reunion, gathering, congress, conference; *joint*, link, bond, connection, tie-in, hookup, linkup, ligature, suture, seal, bracket, seam, splice, weld, coupling, yoke; *junction*, intersection, node, nexus, crossroads, interface, hinge, pivot; *consolidation*, compaction, coagulation, coalescence, conglomeration, concretion; *coordination*, cooperation, communication, teamwork, solidarity, symbiosis; *marriage*, wedlock, matrimony; *sexual union*, coitus, coition, coupling, pairing, mating, copulation, sexual intercourse, carnal knowledge, intimacy, nooky (*colloq.*), fucking (*vulg.*), screwing (*vulg.*).

adj. *united*, combined, composite, conjoined, coordinated, interlinked, online; *allied*, associated, joint, symbiotic, corporate, communal, cooperative; *connective*, conjunctive, adhesive, cohesive, copulative; *compact*, close-set, dense, solid, firm, immovable, inextricable; *married*, wed, matrimonial, marital; *coital*, sexual, venereal, intimate.

vb. *unite*, combine, conjoin, compound, coalesce, blend, fuse, merge, incorporate, amalgamate, converge; *ally*, associate, join forces, team up,

organize; *join*, bond, link, connect, bridge, span, straddle; *couple*, harness, hitch, yoke, pair, bracket, lump together; *cement*, solder, seal, splice, tie, knit, sew, bind, lash, stitch, lock, bolt, clamp, staple; *attach*, secure, fasten, nail, hook, pin, screw, stick, gum, plaster; *hinge*, dovetail, mitre, rabbet; *moor*, tether, hobble, fetter, shackle, manacle, handcuff; *marry*, wed, get hitched (*colloq.*), get spliced (*colloq.*); *copulate*, mate, pair, couple, mount, cover, serve, have sex with, know, enjoy, possess, make love to, sleep with, bed, lay (*vulg.*), screw (*vulg.*), fuck (*vulg.*), have it off with (*colloq.*), make it with (*colloq.*), get one's oats, get one's leg over (*colloq.*).

adv. *arm in arm*, hand in hand; *side by side*, shoulder to shoulder, as one man; *hand in glove*, in league, as thick as thieves.

41 SEPARATION

see also **44** (nonadhesion); **46** (disintegration); **67** (dispersion); **790** (unsociability).

n. *separation*, disintegration, fragmentation, decomposition, dissection, analysis; *division*, partition, demarcation, cleavage, dichotomy, divergence, polarization, parting of the ways; *breach*, break, rupture, fracture, split, fission, severance, divorce; *dissociation*, dissolution, disbandment, demobilization, breakup, dispersion, diaspora; *cleft*, crack, fissure, rent, crevasse, chasm; *separatism*, segregation, apartheid, purdah, secession, ghettoism, isolationism, insularity, nonalignment; *seclusion*, quarantine, ghetto, enclave, oasis, reserve; *schism*, sect, faction, splinter group, breakaway group, offshoot, branch; *exclusion*, embargo, boycott, blacklist, blackballing, ostracism.

adj. *separate*, distinct, discrete, unattached, disengaged, free, free-standing; *solitary*, alone, aloof, detached, insular, self-contained, self-sufficient, independent; *apart*, asunder, cleft, cloven, broken, torn, rent; *separatist*, segregationist, isolatinist, secessionist, sectarian, dissident, breakaway; *divisive*, controversial, contentious, polemical.

vb. *separate*, disintegrate, fragment, decompose, dissolve; *break*, breach, rupture, fracture, splinter, split, crack; *dissociate*, disband, disperse, scatter, diverge, divorce, polarize, go one's separate ways; *divide*, halve, split, sever, partition, hive off; *seclude*, sequester, quarantine, segregate, isolate, insulate, cut off; *exclude*, expel, bar, blacklist, blackball, ostracize, send to Coventry, cold-shoulder (*colloq.*); *part*, rend, cleave, sunder, tear, slash, gash, score, slit, scratch, lacerate, chip, shred; *cut down*, hack, chop, dock, clip, shear, prune, fell, scythe, mow.

adv. *apart*, asunder, in two, in twain; *in pieces*, in bits, to shreds, to tatters, to smithereens (*colloq.*), limb from limb.

42 CONNECTION

See also **40** (union).

n. *connection*, association, relation, link, tie, nexus; *bond*, affinity, sympathy, fellow-feeling, rapport; *bridge*, aqueduct, span, arch, stepping-stone, neck, isthmus, causeway, ladder, companionway; *channel*, route, passage, corridor, tunnel, duct, pipeline; *linkup*, hookup, tie-up, hot line (*colloq.*), switchboard, bleeper, intercom, walkie-talkie; *intermediary*, link-man, go-between, middleman, broker, matchmaker, negotiator, pig-in-the-middle (*colloq.*); *fastener*, buckle, hasp, clasp, brooch, bracket, bolt, padlock, latch, nail, peg, dowel, adhesive, glue; *cable*, rope, ligament, tendon, muscle, leash, halter, harness, rein, chain, fetter, manacle, shackle, yoke; *junction*, knot, ligature, suture, seam, hinge, pivot.

adj., vb., adv. *See* **40** (union).

43 ADHESION

See also **40** (union); **539** (resolution); **540** (perseverance); **633** (cooperation).

n. *adhesion*, accretion, agglomeration, consolidation; *cohesiveness*, stickiness, tackiness, viscosity, density, solidity; *association*, adherence, affiliation,

membership, enrolment, matriculation; *solidarity*, esprit de corps, team spirit, serried ranks, united front, phalanx; *mass*, cluster, clump, clot, clod, cake; *adhesive*, gum, glue, paste, fixative, cement, mortar, solder, seal, sticky tape, flypaper; *grasp*, clutch, grip, hug, foothold, toehold, stranglehold; *limpet*, barnacle, leech, bur, clinging vine; *tenacity*, perseverance, resolution, stamina, staying power; *commitment*, dedication, zeal, militancy.

adj. *adhesive*, sticky, gummy, tacky, gluey, viscous, gooey (*colloq.*); *cohesive*, dense, close, solid, compact; *adhering*, clinging, tight-fitting, skintight; *united*, associated, inseparable, indivisible, inextricable; *tenacious*, firm, unshakable, unwavering, persistent, resolute; *committed*, dedicated, engagé, card-carrying, zealous, militant.

vb. *adhere*, stick, cling, cleave; *cohere*, bunch, mass, congeal, cluster, cake, coagulate, set, solidify; *associate*, affiliate, join, enrol, matriculate, subscribe to, adopt, wed, espouse; *glue*, gum, paste, plaster, cement, solder, weld; *grasp*, grip, clutch, clasp, hug, intertwine, interlace, interlock; *persevere*, hold out, stand firm, stay the course; *commit oneself*, take sides, take the plunge (*colloq.*), nail one's colours to the mast, come down on the side of.

adv. *side by side*, shoulder to shoulder, cheek by jowl.

44 NONADHESION

See also **41** (separation); **541** (vacillation).

n. *nonadhesion*, smoothness, slipperiness, runniness, wateriness, looseness, slackness, separateness, detachedness; *independence*, individualism, aloofness, self-sufficiency, nonalignment, separatism, maverick, free spirit, renegade; *irresolution*, vacillation, fickleness, inconstancy, defection; *apathy*, indifference, floating vote, don't knows.

adj. *nonadhesive*, smooth, slippery, runny, watery; *separate*, loose, free, free-floating, flyaway, floppy, slack, baggy; *independent*, aloof, self-sufficient, individualist, nonaligned, separatist; *irresolute*, vacillating, fickle, volatile, inconstant; *uncommitted*, apathetic, indifferent, lukewarm, wishy-washy (*colloq.*).

vb. *not adhere*, slide, slip, flow, thaw, melt, hang, dangle, flap; *unstick*, free, loosen, slacken, release; *be independent*, go it alone, do one's own thing (*colloq.*), stand on one's own two feet, paddle one's own canoe (*colloq.*); *be irresolute*, waver, vacillate, fluctuate, be in two minds, have second thoughts; *be uncommitted*, sit on the fence (*colloq.*), face both ways, hedge one's bets.

adv. *apart*, asunder.

45 COMBINATION

See also **38** (mixture); **633** (cooperation).

n. *combination*, fusion, blend, alloy, amalgam, mixture, merger, synthesis; *union*, marriage, alliance, association, league, confederation, corporation, combine, cartel, cabal, clique, unholy alliance, conspiracy; *cooperation*, partnership, teamwork, joint effort, job-sharing, collective, cooperative; *compilation*, anthology, compendium, miscellany; *composition*, collage, jigsaw, mosaic, patchwork; *unification*, integration, incorporation, absorption, assimilation.

adj. *combined*, corporate, joint, allied, united; *cooperative*, communal, collaborative, symbiotic.

vb. *combine*, mix, fuse, alloy, blend, amalgamate, merge; *unify*, lump together, incorporate, synthesize, assemble, marry up, integrate, homogenize; *unite*, ally, associate, band together, join forces, pool one's resources, team up, get together, pair off.

adv. *in addition*, plus, moreover, on top of that; *in league*, in tandem, in cahoots (*colloq.*), in partnership, in the same boat (*colloq.*).

46 DISINTEGRATION

See also **41** (separation); **593** (deterioration).

n. *disintegration*, fragmentation, fission, breakup, collapse; *decomposition*,

decay, dilapidation, erosion, corrosion; *dissection*, analysis, breakdown, anatomization; *dispersal*, disbandment, dissolution, atomization, pulverization.

adj. *disintegrated*, fragmented, shattered, broken, brittle, fissile; *soluble*, biodegradable, disposable, recyclable; *decomposed*, decaying, dilapidated, crumbling.

vb. *disintegrate*, fragment, break up, collapse, fall apart, go to pieces (*colloq.*), crack up (*colloq.*); *split*, fracture, crack, splinter, shatter, shiver, smash, explode; *decompose*, decay, erode, corrode, crumble, degenerate; *dissect*, analyse, break down, dismantle, dismember, anatomize, put under the microscope; *disperse*, disband, dissolve, scatter, atomize, pulverize.

adv. *apart*, asunder, into pieces, into smithereens (*colloq.*).

47 WHOLE

See also **29** (greatness); **49** (completeness); **51** (inclusion).

n. *whole*, entity, unit, ensemble, complex, total, sum, aggregate, corpus; *wholeness*, unity, integrity, entirety, completeness, totality, universality, fullness, comprehensiveness; *universe*, world, cosmos, globe, microcosm; *panorama*, survey, overview, bird's eye view, synopsis; *everything*, the lot (*colloq.*), the works (*colloq.*), the whole shooting match (*colloq.*), the whole kit and caboodle (*colloq.*); *everyone*, Tom, Dick, and Harry, all the world and his wife.

adj. *whole*, entire, complete, full, total, aggregate, gross; *integral*, organic, intact, virgin, pristine, flawless, seamless, unadulterated, undiluted, unabridged, unedited; *universal*, all-embracing, cosmic, global, holistic, panoramic, omnibus; *comprehensive*, catch-all, sweeping, blanket, exhaustive, wholesale, outright.

vb. *See* **49** (completeness).

adv. *wholly*, entirely, totally, fully, unreservedly, body and soul, one hundred per cent; *outright*, lock, stock, and barrel, hook, line, and sinker, in one fell swoop, at a stroke; *altogether*, all told, in all, as a whole, en masse.

48 PART

See also **50** (incompleteness); **53** (component); **78** (fraction).

n. *part*, portion, segment, section, sector; *share*, cut, whack (*colloq.*), slice of the cake, lion's share; *subdivision*, category, class, branch, offshoot, tributary, feeder, department, compartment; *component*, element, ingredient, constituent, factor, item, detail; *proportion*, percentage, fraction, minority, majority; *instalment*, issue, number, volume, partwork, part-payment, deposit, down payment; *body part*, member, limb, organ, appendage, trunk, torso; *piece*, wedge, chunk, slab, hunk, wodge (*colloq.*); *passage*, extract, snippet, gobbet, excerpt, clip; *small piece*, scrap, morsel, shred, crumb, drop, bite; *fragment*, sliver, shard, splinter, flake, chip, granule.

adj. *partial*, incomplete, unfinished, fragmentary, piecemeal; *scrappy*, bitty, patchy, uneven; *divided*, segmented, fractional, sectional, departmental, compartmentalized.

vb. *part*, split, divide, bisect, section, segment, partition; *subdivide*, branch, ramify, fork, radiate; *disintegrate*, fragment, disband, dissolve, break up; *dissect*, take apart, dismember, dismantle, anatomize, cannibalize.

adv. *partly*, in part; *partially*, incompletely, in some degree; *bit by bit*, piecemeal, in dribs and drabs (*colloq.*), in fits and starts, in snatches.

49 COMPLETENESS

See also **29** (greatness); **47** (whole); **653** (completion).

n. *completeness*, wholeness, entirety, totality; *fullness*, plenitude, repleteness, satiety, bellyful (*colloq.*), skinful (*colloq.*); *refill*, top-up, finishing/last touch, second helping; *maximum*, upper limit, ceiling, summit, acme, crowning glory, ne plus ultra, culmination, apotheosis, saturation point, last straw, clincher (*colloq.*); *comprehensiveness*, exhaustiveness, thoroughness,

inclusiveness, A to Z, alpha and omega, gamut, everything but the kitchen sink (*colloq.*); *all-rounder*, polymath, Renaissance man, jack of all trades, superman, superwoman.

adj. *whole*, entire, total, full-length, full-time, full-scale, full-blown; *replete*, full, sated, brim-full, bursting at the seams, jam-packed, crammed, stuffed, bulging, chock-a-block (*colloq.*); *comprehensive*, exhaustive, inclusive, all-embracing, in-depth, encyclopedic, all-round, wide-ranging; *absolute*, utter, thoroughgoing, radical, wholesale, unmitigated, unqualified, unstinting, wholehearted, unreserved, downright, out-and-out; *sheer*, pure, arrant, rank, gross, regular, arch, dyed-in-the-wool.

vb. *complete*, finish off, follow up/through, round off, put the finishing touches to, perfect, clinch (*colloq.*), set the seal on, despatch, polish off, mop up; *sate*, satisfy, gorge, stuff, cram, pack, fill; *replenish*, refill, top up; *saturate*, swamp, drown, overrun, overwhelm; *do one's utmost*, go all out, go the whole hog (*colloq.*), go for broke (*colloq.*), pull out all the stops, leave no stone unturned.

adv. *completely*, fully, thoroughly, to the hilt, to the top of one's bent, body and soul, down to the ground; *entirely*, root and branch, hook, line, and sinker, lock, stock, and barrel; *absolutely*, unreservedly, wholeheartedly, head and shoulders; *utterly*, wholly, downright, thoroughly, plain, clean, stark, to the core, through and through; *all over*, high and low, far and wide, from top to toe.

50 INCOMPLETENESS

See also **48** (part); **65** (discontinuity); **585** (imperfection); **655** (non-completion).

n. *incompleteness*, inadequacy, deficiency, defectiveness, scantiness, meagreness; *insufficiency*, deficit, shortage, shortfall, short measure, lack, want, need; *superficiality*, perfunctoriness, cursoriness, half measures; *immaturity*, rawness, callowness, greenness, crudity; *unevenness*, scrappiness, patchiness, bittiness, sketchiness, loose ends, curate's egg; *outline*, rough copy, rough draft, sketch, jottings, notes; *gap*, break, breach, hiatus, hole, flaw, omission, lacuna, missing link.

adj. *incomplete*, insufficient, scanty, meagre, underweight, under strength; *inadequate*, deficient, defective, wanting, lacking, missing; *superficial*, perfunctory, cursory, cosmetic; *immature*, raw, green, callow, ill-digested, half-baked (*colloq.*); *uneven*, patchy, scrappy, bitty, sketchy, fragmentary; *provisional*, temporary, makeshift, crude, rough and ready; *unfinished*, half-finished, unpolished, ragged, rough-hewn, uncut, unrefined, coarse.

vb. *be incomplete*, lack, need, want, miss, fall short, leave something to be desired, not come up to scratch, not make the grade; *not complete*, skimp, scamp, bodge, patch up, paper over the cracks; *interrupt*, leave off, break off, leave hanging; *omit*, skip, jump, miss out, skate over.

adv. *incompletely*, partially, nearly, almost, all but, virtually; *in preparation*, under way, nearing completion, on the stocks.

51 INCLUSION
See also **47** (whole); **69** (generality).

n. *inclusion*, incorporation, integration, assimilation, absorption; *inclusiveness*, comprehensiveness, encyclopedicity, blanket coverage, catch-all, package deal; *universality*, catholicity, eclecticness, ecumenicism, broad church, something for everyone; *admission*, membership, admissibility, eligibility.

adj. *including*, comprising, containing, consisting of; *inclusive*, all-in, all-embracing, comprehensive, overall; *universal*, catholic, eclectic, broad-based.

vb. *include*, comprise, subsume, contain, comprehend; *incorporate*, encapsulate, cover, assimilate, encompass, embrace; *admit*, accommodate, receive, number among, count in.

adv. *inclusive*, across the board, from A to Z.

52 EXCLUSION
See also **790** (unsociability).

n. *exclusion*, expulsion, eviction, rejection, banishment, exile, extradition, deportation, excommunication; *prohibition*, ban, embargo, boycott, blockade; *segregation*, colour bar, apartheid, quarantine, ostracism; *barrier*, barricade, closed door, lockout, partition, Iron Curtain, Bamboo Curtain, Berlin Wall, no-man's-land, demilitarized zone, exclusion zone, no-go area; *exclusiveness*, cliquishness, clannishness, freemasonry; *clique*, coterie, in-group, clan, inner circle, elect; *monopoly*, cartel, closed shop, restrictive practices.

adj. *excluding*, debarring, prohibitive, restrictive, monopolistic, protectionist; *exclusive*, clannish, cliquey, snobbish, up-market; *excluded*, inadmissible, struck off, disallowed, debarred.

vb. *exclude*, evict, expel, deport, reject, banish, exile, extradite, outlaw, excommunicate; *prohibit*, ban, boycott, blockade, black, blacklist, blackball; *segregate*, quarantine, demarcate, cordon off, lock out, ostracize, send to Coventry, cold-shoulder (*colloq.*); *except*, omit, pass over, count out, leave out, rule out of court; *prevent*, preclude, forestall, obviate; *monopolize*, corner, hog (*colloq.*), bag (*colloq.*).

adv. *excluding*, barring, excepting, save; *out of the running*, out of the reckoning.

53 COMPONENT
See also **48** (part).

n. *component*, part, piece, element, ingredient, constituent; *unit*, module, building block, Lego (*tdmk.*), Meccano (*tdmk.*); *attachment*, fixture, accessory, spare part; *member*, associate, colleague, cog in the wheel, organization man, party hack, apparatchik; *machinery*, works, innards, insides, guts.

adj. *component*, constituent, essential, intrinsic, inherent; *integral*, fitted, built-in, modular.

vb. *compose*, comprise, make up, constitute; *belong to*, inhere, reside in, consist in, be part and parcel of; *con-*

struct, assemble, compile, fashion, knock together (*colloq.*).

54 FOREIGN BODY

See also **6** (extraneousness); **331** (nationality).

n. *foreign body*, extraneous element, reject, discard, spanner in the works; *foreignness*, ethnicity, alienness, extraneousness, undesirability, superfluousness, irrelevance; *foreigner*, alien, stranger, barbarian, immigrant, incomer, new face, refugee, expatriate, colonial; *intruder*, interloper, trespasser, squatter, gatecrasher, cuckoo in the nest; *misfit*, outsider, black sheep, fish out of water, pariah, leper; *extraterrestrial*, alien, Martian, little green men; *abroad*, overseas, foreign parts, exotica.

adj. *foreign*, alien, extraneous, superfluous, irrelevant, unwanted, undesirable; *strange*, exotic, outlandish, imported, borrowed, ethnic; *extraterrestrial*, alien, space-age, futuristic.

vb. *be foreign*, be out of one's element, stick out like a sore thumb (*colloq.*); *introduce*, borrow, import, naturalize, assimilate; *intrude*, trespass, squat, gatecrash.

adv. *abroad*, overseas.

55 ORDER

See also **57** (arrangement); **64** (consecutiveness); **68** (class).

n. *order*, arrangement, array, disposition, layout; *orderliness*, tidiness, neatness, apple-pie order, alignment; *system*, method, organization, routine, pattern, coordination, regularity, uniformity, coherence; *harmony*, quiet, peace, calm, law and order, rule of law, discipline, stability; *rank*, series, hierarchy, gradation, ascending/descending order, pecking order.

adj. *orderly*, tidy, neat, all shipshape and Bristol fashion, spruce, trim, groomed, dapper, smart, not a hair out of place; *disciplined*, law-abiding, peaceable, docile, well-behaved, obedient; *harmonious*, quiet, peaceful, calm, stable; *serial*, hierarchical, gradational,

ordinal; *systematic*, methodical, organized.

vb. *order*, arrange, dispose, deploy, align; *organize*, sort, sift, classify, systematize, rationalize; *tidy*, neaten, smarten up, spruce up, groom, put to rights, lick/knock into shape (*colloq.*); *restore order*, pacify, discipline, control, police, tighten up on, take in hand; *be in order*, function, work, go like clockwork.

adv. *in order*, O.K., all present and correct, under control; *methodically*, systematically, step by step.

56 DISORDER

See also **58** (disturbance).

n. *disorder*, disarray, untidiness, unkemptness, scruffiness, neglect; *confusion*, muddle, welter, jumble, mix-up, mess, cock-up (*colloq.*), balls-up (*vulg.*); *litter*, clutter, shambles, pigsty, midden, dump (*colloq.*), tip (*colloq.*); *tangle*, snarl, web, warren, jungle, maze, labyrinth; *commotion*, uproar, to-do, trouble, hubbub, hullabaloo, bedlam, babel, pandemonium; *tumult*, turmoil, turbulence, chaos, upheaval, ferment, free-for-all, fracas, melee, rumpus, roughhouse, brawl, punchup (*colloq.*), dustup (*colloq.*), aggro (*colloq.*), breach of the peace, affray, disturbance, riot, anarchy, mob rule.

adj. *disordered*, untidy, unkempt, scruffy, dishevelled, bedraggled, tousled, windswept; *confused*, muddle-headed, incoherent, featherbrained, scatterbrained, disorganized; *careless*, slipshod, neglectful, messy, sloppy, shambolic (*colloq.*); *intricate*, complex, involved, tangled, convoluted, labyrinthine; *random*, desultory, haphazard, rambling, wandering; *turbulent*, tumultuous, chaotic, hell-raising, riotous, disorderly, wild, unruly, undisciplined, harum-scarum, lawless, anarchic.

vb. *make disordered*, untidy, rumple, ruffle, dishevel, bedraggle, tousle; *disorganize*, upset, disperse, throw into disarray, randomize, shuffle, scatter; *confuse*, muddle, botch, mess up, foul up, cock up (*colloq.*), balls up (*vulg.*); *complicate*, entangle, embroil, ensnare;

be disorderly, riot, rampage, storm, mob, run wild/amuck, get out of hand. **adv.** *in disorder*, in disarray, pell-mell, haywire, higgledy-piggledy (*colloq.*), all anyhow, upside down, topsy turvy, arsy versy (*colloq.*); *confusedly*, at sixes and sevens, at cross-purposes; *out of order*, off the rails, kaput, on the blink (*colloq.*).

57 ARRANGEMENT

See also **55** (order); **76** (list); **559** (preparation).

n. *arrangement*, order, disposition, layout, line-up (*colloq.*), distribution, composition, organization, structure; *classification*, categorization, listing, hierarchy, taxonomy, paradigm, pattern, system; *catalogue*, directory, list, table, index, inventory, checklist, register, file, slot, niche, pigeonhole; *chart*, diagram, schema, programme, agenda, timetable, schedule, graph, flow chart, critical path.

adj. *arranged*, ordered, classified, graded, sorted; *schematic*, diagrammatic, tabular, paradigmatic; *systematic*, methodical, organizational.

vb. *arrange*, order, dispose, array, marshal, group, deploy, distribute, sort, label, rank, range, grade, size, alphabetize; *catalogue*, tabulate, programme, index, timetable, schedule, cross-refer, file, pigeonhole, compartmentalize.

adv. *in place*, in line, in order.

58 DISTURBANCE

See also **56** (disorder); **161** (displacement); **447** (insanity).

n. *disturbance*, displacement, dislocation, dislodgment, derailment, disorientation, dispersion; *upset*, upheaval, convulsion, perturbation, agitation; *interference*, interruption, perversion, subversion, agitprop, sabotage; *derangement*, madness, insanity, a screw loose (*colloq.*).

adj. *disturbed*, displaced, dislocated, disorientated, dispersed; *upset*, perturbed, agitated, confused, disconcerted; *deranged*, mad, unhinged, unbalanced, insane.

vb. *disturb*, displace, dislocate, dis-lodge, derail, unseat, disorientate, throw off course; *upset*, agitate, discompose, disconcert, perturb, ruffle, fluster, put off one's stride/stroke; *disperse*, scatter, shuffle, jumble, randomize; *interfere*, interrupt, pervert, subvert, sabotage, throw out of joint, throw a spanner in the works; *derange*, unhinge, unbalance, drive insane, drive round the bend (*colloq.*).

adv. *on the wrong track*, off the rails, off course; *out of gear*, out of joint, out of place.

59 PRECEDENCE

See also **61** (beginning); **99** (priority).

n. *precedence*, antecedence, ancestry, pedigree, primogeniture; *priority*, pride of place, head start, initiative, first come first served, front of the queue, forefront, avant-garde, vanguard; *forerunner*, eldest, firstborn, ancestor, precursor, senior, predecessor; *guide*, scout, outrider, pilot, beacon, harbinger, messenger, pioneer, trail-blazer, pathfinder, trendsetter; *precedent*, antecedent, example, sample, preview, foretaste, forecast, prognosis, trailer, prequel; *introduction*, initiation, inauguration, baptism of fire, christening; *preliminary*, preface, prologue, foreword, frontispiece, prelude, preamble, overture, curtain-raiser, aperitif, starter, appetizer.

adj. *preceding*, antecedent, anterior, prior, former, previous, foregoing, aforementioned; *leading*, foremost, avant-garde, pioneering, innovative, exploratory; *introductory*, initial, preliminary, prefatory, initiatory, inaugural, baptismal; *elder*, senior, superior.

vb. *precede*, antedate, predate, anticipate, preempt, preclude, forestall; *lead*, go before, front, head, spearhead, pioneer, explore, blaze a trail; *announce*, herald, forecast, presage, foretell, usher in, advertise, trail (*colloq.*); *introduce*, preface, initiate, baptize, christen, inaugurate, blood.

adv. *first*, above all, first and foremost; *ahead*, in front, upfront (*colloq.*); *in advance*, previously, beforehand.

60 SEQUENCE

See also 37 (remainder); 64 (consecutiveness); 100 (succession).

n. *sequence*, series, succession, chain, string, progression; *posterity*, line, lineage, issue, progeny, offspring; *consequence*, effect, end result, outcome, upshot, legacy, by-product, spin-off, aftereffect, aftermath, sequel, hangover (*colloq.*), fallout; *appendage*, follow-up, tailpiece, epilogue, afterword, postscript, coda, afterthought, supplement, post mortem, dessert, afters (*colloq.*); *rear*, posterior, train, trail, wake, tail; *rearguard*, runner-up, straggler, sweeper, tail-end Charlie (*colloq.*), last man in, booby prize, wooden spoon.

adj. *sequential*, successive, consecutive, serial; *succeeding*, following, subsequent, next, later, resulting, ensuing; *rear*, posterior, hindmost.

vb. *succeed*, come after, follow, come in the wake of, tread on the heels of, follow in the footsteps of, step into someone's shoes, supplant, supersede; *pursue*, tail, trail, shadow, dog someone's footsteps; *result*, ensue, turn out, come to pass; *come last*, bring up the rear, lag, dawdle.

adv. *in succession*, in turn, one after the other, back to back (*colloq.*); *in sequence*, in order; *next*, then, afterwards, subsequently; *in consequence*, as a result, therefore; *behind*, in someone's wake/train.

61 BEGINNING

See also 59 (precedence); 132 (cause).

n. *beginning*, start, commencement, onset; *foundation*, inception, inauguration, instigation, institution; *initiation*, christening, baptism, honeymoon, debut, first night, premiere, maiden speech, maiden voyage, launch, housewarming, send-off; *starting-point*, outset, first base, first lap, first round, qualifier, square one, zero, alpha, kick-off (*colloq.*); *introduction*, opening gambit, preliminaries, lead-in, foreword, preface; *preparation*, rudiments, first principles, groundwork, spadework (*colloq.*), trial run, teething troubles, growing pains, birth pangs; *origin*, birth, infancy, dawn, morning, cradle, genesis; *germ*, seed, bud, embryo, nucleus, primordial soup; *beginner*, apprentice, learner, novice, tyro, probationer, new boy, new bug (*colloq.*).

adj. *beginning*, primary, initial, first; *primal*, primordial, primeval, aboriginal; *introductory*, preliminary, prefatory, initiatory, preparatory, inaugural, baptismal; *fundamental*, rudimentary, elementary, basic; *infant*, embryonic, budding, incipient, nascent.

vb. *begin*, start, commence, make a start, set about, get under way, set in motion, tackle, broach; *set out*, kick off (*colloq.*), set the ball rolling, blast off, fire away, take the plunge, break the ice, pull one's finger out (*colloq.*), get weaving/cracking (*colloq.*), clock in; *initiate*, inaugurate, instigate, found, institute, launch, christen, baptize, be in on the ground floor; *originate*, generate, provoke, prompt, sow the seeds of, trigger off, spark off; *pioneer*, explore, embark on, break new ground, blaze a trail; *arise*, appear, emerge, see the light of day, spring up, crop up; *recommence*, resume, make a fresh start, go back to square one, go back to the drawing board.

adv. *from the beginning*, ab ovo, from scratch (*colloq.*), from the word go (*colloq.*); *in the beginning*, at first, at the outset, initially, early on, to begin with; *in the first place*, firstly, for a start, for a kick-off (*colloq.*).

62 END

See also 60 (sequence); 133 (effect); 323 (death).

n. *end*, cessation, termination, completion, conclusion, end result, payoff, expiry; *ending*, final, finale, death, demise, last words, last gasp, swansong; *end point*, terminus, goal, omega, last lap, last round, home stretch, end of the road; *extremity*, boundary, limit, peak, summit; *finality*, final offer, ultimatum, deadline, last orders, time up, closing time, close of play, closedown, adjournment, dissolution; *climax*, resolution, denouement, death blow, coup de grâce, clincher (*colloq.*); *last judgment*, last trump, doomsday, apocalypse, twilight of the gods, holocaust.

adj. *final*, last, terminal, ultimate, concluding; *rear*, back, hindmost, posterior; *finished*, ended, over and done with, played out, kaput (*colloq.*), clapped out (*colloq.*), washed up (*colloq.*); *apocalyptic*, eschatological.

vb. *end*, finish, cease, stop, terminate, conclude, close down, ring down the curtain, shut up shop, sign off, clock off, call it a day; *come to an end*, die, expire, run one's course, run out of time, fade out, peter out, fizzle out (*colloq.*), tail off; *bring to an end*, conclude, terminate, discontinue, dispose of, drop, write off, wash one's hands of, wind up (*colloq.*), wrap up (*colloq.*); *complete*, finish off, round off.

adv. *in the end*, finally, at last, at the end of the day, in the final analysis, in the long run, when the chips are down (*colloq.*); *once and for all*, for good, forever, conclusively, definitively.

63 MIDDLE
See also **27** (average).

n. *middle*, midst, centre, thick, heart, core, kernel, marrow, focus, hub, nucleus, pivot, fulcrum; *midpoint*, midway, midweek, midsummer, midwinter, midstream, middle distance, equator, midriff, middle age, mid-life crisis, halfway house; *average*, mean, median, happy medium; *mediation*, intervention, arbitration, compromise, no-man's-land, middle ground, grey area, borderline case; *intermediary*, middleman, agent, broker, mediator, go-between, buffer, arbitrator, third force, pig-in-the-middle (*colloq.*).

adj. *middle*, central, mid, medial, median, interim, equidistant; *mean*, average, middle-of-the-road; *intermediate*, neutral, halfway, grey, indeterminate.

vb. *straddle*, lie betwixt and between, hold the centre, occupy the middle ground; *compromise*, meet someone halfway, steer a middle course, fall

between two stools, be neither fish nor fowl; *intervene*, mediate, come between; *split down the middle*, halve, divide fifty-fifty, bisect.

adv. *midway*, halfway; *amidst*, among; *in between*, between Scylla and Charybdis, between the devil and the deep blue sea.

64 CONSECUTIVENESS
See also **55** (order); **60** (sequence).

n. *consecutiveness*, sequence, succession, causality, cause and effect, domino theory, knock-on effect, repercussion; *continuity*, stability, routine, flow, trend, run; *series*, string, chain, ladder, suite, scale, arpeggio, spectrum, hierarchy, colonnade, dynasty, line, family tree; *one of a series*, instalment, row, tier, storey, echelon, rank, course; *continuum*, assembly line, conveyor belt, treadmill, endless band, Mobius strip, vicious circle; *procession*, column, cortege, train, caravan, queue, crocodile, tailback.

adj. *consecutive*, successive, following, serial; *continuous*, perpetual, endless, nonstop, unbroken, seamless, running, ongoing; *progressive*, linear, gradual.

vb. *be consecutive*, succeed, run on, follow on, overlap; *continue*, extend, run, flow, persist, endure; *arrange in succession*, range, rank, line up, stagger.

adv. *consecutively*, successively, one after another, back to back (*colloq.*), in succession, in turn; *continuously*, nonstop, day in day out, round the clock, on the trot (*colloq.*); *end to end*, nose to tail, bumper to bumper.

65 DISCONTINUITY
See also **50** (incompleteness).

n. *discontinuity*, disconnectedness, disjointedness, alternation, unevenness, sporadicness, jerkiness; *disruption*, break, gap, breach, interval, caesura, hiatus, pause, stopover, time lag, time-warp, missing link, non sequitur, anacoluthon; *interruption*, digression, parenthesis, interjection, interpolation; *irregularity*, collage, patchwork, crazy paving.

adj. *discontinuous*, discrete, broken,

uneven, distinct; *disconnected*, disjointed, fitful, jerky, spasmodic, sporadic, episodic; *intermittent*, desultory, irregular, alternate, periodic, stop-go, on-off; *digressive*, parenthetical, interjectional.

vb. *discontinue*, suspend, terminate, interrupt; *break off*, leave off, stop off/over, digress, pause, take time out (*colloq.*); *interject*, interpose, intervene, cut in, butt in, chip in, put one's oar in; *omit*, miss out, jump, skip, leapfrog (*colloq.*); *alternate*, oscillate, fluctuate, blow hot and cold (*colloq.*).

adv. *discontinuously*, periodically, now and then, occasionally, off and on, at intervals; *by degrees*, by fits and starts, in dribs and drabs (*colloq.*).

66 ASSEMBLY
See also **40** (union).

n. *assembly*, meeting, rally, convention, conference, company, congregation, caucus, party, rendezvous, tryst, get-together (*colloq.*); *collection*, compilation, compendium, anthology, roundup (*colloq.*); *group*, band, troupe, collective, syndicate, union, guild, team, stable, string, squad, crew, posse, force, regiment; *social group*, circle, family, clan, tribe, peer group, age group, generation, clique, coterie, mafia; *crowd*, throng, mob, press, huddle, scrum, crush, swarm, bevy, gang; *multitude*, host, galaxy, constellation, storm, shower, hail, volley, deluge, spate, flood, slew (*colloq.*), raft (*colloq.*); *bunch*, bouquet, spray, knot, clump, cluster, bundle, parcel, bale, roll, bolt, skein, hank, truss, sheaf, conglomeration, heap, pile, mass; *flock*, herd, shoal, pack, drove, brood, school, clutch, litter, covey (partridges), flight/gaggle/skein (geese), pride (lions), leap (leopards), kindle (kittens), skulk (foxes), charm (goldfinches), exaltation (larks).

adj. *assembled*, gathered, congregated; *crowded*, congested, packed, teeming, milling, seething, crawling (*colloq.*), chock-a-block (*colloq.*); *converging*, centripetal.

vb. *assemble*, collect, forgather, meet,

unite, congregate, get together, rendezvous, fall in, join forces, team up, band together, gang up; *crowd*, flock, mass, mill, seethe, swarm, teem, pack, huddle, throng; *bring together*, summon, convoke, convene, rally, mobilize, herd, muster, shepherd, round up; *bunch*, bundle, parcel, package, clump, knot, cluster, bind, truss; *accumulate*, amass, agglomerate, stack, heap, pile; *compress*, cram, crush, squash, stuff, squeeze.

adv. *collectively*, all together, as one, in a body, en masse.

67 DISPERSION
See also **41** (separation).

n. *dispersion*, diffusion, dissemination, propagation, distribution, spread; *disbandment*, dissolution, breakup, demobilization, decentralization; *divergence*, branching, radiation, ramification; *emigration*, exodus, diaspora, population drift, overspill, new town, suburbia, urban sprawl, ribbon development.

adj. *dispersed*, scattered, far-flung, widespread; *sparse*, strung out, dotted about, sporadic, few and far between, thin on the ground; *loose*, stray, straggling, wandering, sprawling; *divergent*, branching, radiating, centrifugal.

vb. *disperse*, diffuse, spread, disseminate, propagate, broadcast, distribute; *disband*, disintegrate, dissolve, break up, fall out, demobilize, decentralize; *scatter*, strew, sprinkle, litter, spatter; *emigrate*, wander, drift, stray, straggle, sprawl; *diverge*, branch, radiate, ramify, fan out, hive off.

adv. *here and there*, round and about; *in all directions*, to the four winds, to the four corners of the earth.

68 CLASS
See also **55** (order).

n. *class*, category, variety, kind, sort, strain, brand, make, marque; *division*, group, species, genus, order, phylum; *type*, manner, stamp, mould, stripe, breed, race, tribe, ilk, kidney, cast, colour, complexion, hue; *classification*,

rank, order, system, hierarchy, taxonomy.
adj. *classificatory*, hierarchical, taxonomic; *typical*, representative, generic, stereotypical.
vb. *class*, group, divide, sort, grade, range, rank; *classify*, typify, categorize, identify, label, brand, stamp.

69 GENERALITY
See also **27** (average); **51** (inclusion).
n. *generality*, universality, comprehensiveness, inclusiveness, catholicity, ecumenicalism, broad church, eclecticism, cosmopolitanism; *nonspecificness*, broad canvas, broad spectrum, blanket coverage, catch-all, dragnet, grapeshot, panacea, cure-all, open house, open meeting, open letter, circular, something for everyone; *average*, ordinariness, common run, lowest common denominator; *everyman*, man in the street, man on the Clapham omnibus, Joe Bloggs, Tom, Dick, and Harry, every man Jack; *common people*, general public, masses, admass, grassroots, vox populi.
adj. *general*, nonspecific, generic, representative, typical, standard; *universal*, comprehensive, all-inclusive, blanket, across-the-board; *common*, ordinary, popular, middlebrow, vernacular, vulgar, down-market; *prevalent*, widespread, ubiquitous, worldwide, global, endemic; *multipurpose*, versatile, adaptable.
vb. *generalize*, spread, broaden, widen, popularize, vulgarize, broadcast, disseminate; *prevail*, obtain, predominate.
adv. *generally*, in general, as a rule, by and large, in the main, broadly speaking, typically.

70 SPECIALITY
See also **22** (originality); **79** (one).
n. *speciality*, individuality, originality, uniqueness, particularity, singularity, distinctiveness, specificity; *feature*, attribute, trait, peculiarity, characteristic, quirk, idiosyncrasy, hallmark, trademark; *particulars*, specifications, details, minutiae, ins and outs (*col-*

loq.); *exception*, special case, one-off, nonce word, rara avis; *subjectivity*, individualism, egoism, self, number one, ego-trip (*colloq.*), solipsism, me generation.
adj. *special*, particular, peculiar, specific, unique, singular, distinctive, original, individual; *characteristic*, idiomatic, peculiar, typical, personal, idiosyncratic, quirky, eccentric; *exceptional*, one-off, unique, sui generis, inimitable, esoteric, way-out (*colloq.*); *exclusive*, bespoke, made-to-order, made-to-measure, custom-made, personalized, own-brand; *subjective*, individualistic, self-centred, egotistical, solipsistic.
vb. *specify*, enumerate, list, detail, itemize, spell out; *particularize*, cite, mention, quote, name names; *isolate*, distinguish, individuate, pick out, single out, highlight, pinpoint, put one's finger on (*colloq.*); *stand out*, shine, excel, be in a class of one's own, be out of the ordinary, be off the beaten track.
adv. *especially*, in particular, above all; *specifically*, namely, respectively; *personally*, ad hominem.

71 RULE
See also **549** (habit); **657** (authority); **852** (legality).
n. *rule*, regulation, ruling, standing order, injunction, law, degree, edict, statute, bylaw; *code*, canon, rulebook, charter, statute book, constitution; *precept*, guideline, criterion, standard, benchmark, litmus test, principle, tenet, prescription, precedent; *procedure*, system, method, practice, drill, routine, form.
adj. *regulatory*, normative, prescriptive; *legal*, compulsory, obligatory, de rigueur, statutory, mandatory; *standard*, normal, conventional, orthodox, canonical; *procedural*, routine, formulaic, copybook.
vb. *rule*, prescribe, ordain, decree, lay down the law; *regulate*, standardize, normalize, bring into line, regularize; *obey orders*, stick to the rules, keep to the straight and narrow, keep one's

nose clean (*colloq.*), toe the line (*colloq.*), work to rule, mind one's Ps and Qs.

adv. *according to the rules*, by the book.

72 CONFORMITY

See also **15** (uniformity); **549** (habit).

n. *conformity*, agreement, harmony, consistency, compatibility; *usage*, convention, orthodoxy, conservatism, traditionalism, Babbitry, conventional wisdom, done thing, order of the day, received idea, party line; *assimilation*, absorption, levelling, acclimatization, adaptation, indoctrination, reeducation, rehabilitation; *pattern*, mould, stereotype, matrix; *conformist*, traditionalist, silent majority, herd, sheep, copycat, running dog, yes-man, company man, timeserver, party hack, apparatchik.

adj. *conformist*, conventional, orthodox, conservative, law-abiding, traditionalist, bourgeois; *consistent*, compatible, harmonious, consonant; *typical*, stock, standard, identikit, average, common or garden, unexceptional; *adaptable*, flexible, malleable, compliant, pliable.

vb. *conform*, accord, agree, correspond, match, tally, run true to form; *make conform*, standardize, stereotype, process, assimilate, bring into line, adapt, adjust, mould; *indoctrinate*, brainwash, reeducate, rehabilitate; *follow suit*, fall into line, follow the crowd, keep up appearances, keep up with the Joneses, jump on the bandwagon, swim with the tide.

adv. *in place*, in keeping, in line.

73 NONCONFORMITY

See also **20** (disparity).

n. *nonconformity*, disparity, disagreement, inconsistency, incompatibility, incongruity, contrast; *nonconformism*, unorthodoxy, heresy, schism, iconoclasm, revolt, dissent, protest, deviationism; *unconventionality*, eccentricity, oddity, rarity, singularity; *nonconformist*, maverick, renegade, lone wolf, outsider, outlaw, outcast, pariah,

blackleg, scab, marginal, lunatic fringe; *rebel*, Bohemian, hippie, dropout, angry young man, dissident, young Turk, radical, freethinker, iconoclast, heretic; *exception*, anomaly, aberration, abnormality, special case, odd man out; *eccentric*, character, card (*colloq.*), crank, weirdo (*colloq.*), oddball, freak, misfit, deviant; *homosexual*, gay, lesbian, dyke (*colloq.*), queer (*colloq.*), poofter (*colloq*), woofter (*colloq.*), pansy (*colloq.*), fairy (*colloq.*), bisexual, transvestite, crossdresser, transsexual, hermaphrodite.

adj. *nonconformist*, inconsistent, incompatible, incongruous, contrasting; *unorthodox*, independent, freethinking, radical, iconoclastic, heretical; *rebellious*, Bohemian, dissident, deviationist; *eccentric*, unconventional, odd, rare, unusual, exotic, out-of-the-ordinary, fringe, outlandish, offbeat (*colloq.*), way-out (*colloq.*), weird; *exceptional*, anomalous, aberrant, abnormal, deviant; *homosexual*, gay, lesbian, queer (*colloq.*), bent (*colloq.*), bisexual, AC/DC (*colloq.*).

vb. *not conform*, diverge, dissent, protest, rebel, kick over the traces, rock the boat (*colloq.*); *be independent*, deviate, break ranks, step out of line, go one's own way, do one's own thing (*colloq.*), break the mould, drop out (*colloq.*).

adv. *out of step*, out of keeping, out of line, out on a limb; *out of the way*, out of the common run, off the beaten track.

74 NUMBER

See also **75** (calculation).

n. *number*, numeral, digit, figure, integer, character, cipher, decimal; *sum*, total, aggregate, remainder; *factor*, multiple, quotient, product, function, variable, expression, coefficient, formula; *fraction*, numerator, denominator, vulgar fraction, common fraction; *power*, exponent, root, square, logarithm, mantissa.

adj. *numerical*, digital, prime, whole, real, even, odd, cardinal, ordinal, binary, decimal.

vb. *number*, enumerate, count, tell, reckon, tick off (*colloq.*); *amount to*, total, come to, make, notch up (*colloq.*).

75 CALCULATION
See also **74** (number).

n. *calculation*, estimation, computation, numeration, addition, subtraction, multiplication, division; *count*, score, tally, census, poll, head-count, stocktaking, roll call; *mathematics*, arithmetic, calculus, algebra, geometry, trigonometry, statistics; *data processing*, computing, numbercrunching (*colloq.*), information retrieval, cybernetics; *computer*, mainframe, microcomputer, minicomputer, personal/desk computer, microprocessor, chip, circuit, hardware, visual display unit, printout, core, memory, floppy disk, software, program, machine code; *abacus*, ready reckoner, slide rule, calculator; *numerator*, mathematician, accountant, actuary, teller, statistician, programmer, systems analyst, liveware.
adj. *computational*, actuarial, mathematical, arithmetical, statistical, geometric, algebraic.
vb. *calculate*, estimate, compute, add, subtract, multiply, divide, square, cube; *automate*, computerize, process, input, throughput, program.

76 LIST
See also **57** (arrangement).

n. *list*, record, register, table, file, listing; *index*, catalogue, directory, inventory, checklist, bibliography, filmography, discography; *agenda*, programme, timetable, schedule, bill of fare, table of contents, prospectus; *vocabulary*, glossary, lexicon, dictionary, thesaurus, gazetteer, almanac, yearbook; *roll*, roster, rota, short list, waiting list, blacklist, dramatis personae, credits.
vb. *list*, enter, log, register, record, table, file; *catalogue*, index, inventorize, schedule, timetable, minute; *enrol*, inscribe, enlist, matriculate, sign on.

77 ZERO

n. *zero*, nothing, none, naught, nix, nada, zilch (*colloq.*), sweet f.a. (*colloq.*); *nought*, nil, null, love, duck; *nullity*, nothingness, blank, cipher, void.
adj. *zero*, no, nil.

78 FRACTION
See also **30** (smallness); **48** (part).

n. *fraction*, part, piece, portion, section, segment, percentage, proportion; *fragment*, particle, atom, iota, scrap, shred, whit, jot; *less than one*, quarter, half, three quarters.
adj. *fractional*, small, tiny, slight, infinitesimal; *partial*, fragmentary, incomplete.
adv. *fractionally*, slightly, marginally, partially.

79 ONE
See also **40** (union); **70** (speciality).

n. *one*, ace, unit, entity, individual, atom, monad; *item*, detail, bit, isolated instance; *oneness*, unity, wholeness, integrity, indivisibility, indissolubility; *individualism*, separatism, isolationism, unilateralism; *solitariness*, isolation, aloneness, solitude, loneliness; *soloist*, one-man band, one-man show, solo effort, monologue, soliloquy; *single person*, spinster, bachelor, bachelor girl, single parent, widow, widower, celibacy, monogamy; *monopoly*, cartel, multinational.
adj. *one*, solo, single, mono, unified, whole, indivisible, indissoluble; *individual*, separatist, isolationist, unilateralist, insular; *solo*, single-handed, alone, isolated, solitary; *single*, unmarried, celibate, monogamous.
vb. *be one*, stand alone, plough a lonely furrow, stand on one's own two feet, do one's own thing (*colloq.*), paddle one's own canoe (*colloq.*); *become one*, unite, cohere, combine, merge, fuse; *isolate*, single out, specify, prick out.
adv. *one by one*, singly, one at a time; *on one's own*, by oneself, on one's tod (*colloq.*); *solely*, only, merely, simply; *in unison*, as one.

80 PLURALITY

See also **86** (multitude).

n. *plurality*, majority, multiple; *variety*, multiplicity, multifariousness, multilateralism, polygamy, polysemy, pluralism; *all-rounder*, polymath, Renaissance man, pluralist.

adj. *plural*, many, numerous, multiple; *various*, divers, sundry, several; *versatile*, multifarious, multipurpose, pluralist, multilateralist, polygamous, polysemous, polytheist.

81 TWO

n. *two*, deuce, pair, couple, duo, brace, span, twosome, twins; *double*, couplet, doublet, duet, two-hander, diptych, double-decker, tandem, two-seater, two-wheeler, bicycle, biplane; *duality*, dichotomy, polarity, dualism, bilingualism, bisexuality, ambidexterity, ambiguity, ambivalence, duplicity, double-dealing; *duplication*, doubling, repetition, reproduction; *bisection*, bifurcation, fork, branch, swallowtail; *half*, moiety, hemisphere, semicircle, semitone, semibreve.

adj. *dual*, double, binary, duple, duplex, twofold, double-barrelled, biennial, biannual; *both*, amphibious, ambidextrous, bilingual, bisexual, ambiguous, ambivalent, double-edged, duplicitous, double-dealing, two-faced; *two-way*, dual-purpose, reciprocal, bilateral, bipartite, binaural, split, cloven; *duplicate*, second, repeat, twin.

vb. *double*, duplicate, repeat, copy, mirror, echo, second; *pair*, twin, match, mate; *bisect*, halve, bifurcate, split, cleave; *go halves*, go fifty-fifty; *have it both ways*, have the best of both worlds, have one's cake and eat it (*colloq.*).

adv. *twice*, twofold, as much again, doubly.

82 THREE

n. *three*, triad, trio, trinity, triune, threesome, troika, triumvirate; *treble*, triplet, tercet, trilogy, three-decker, three-hander, triangle, triptych, three-wheeler, tricycle, trident, tripod, trimester, hat trick; *third*, tierce, third party, Third World.

adj. *triple*, ternary, triplex, threefold, triplicate, three-ply, three-dimensional; *three-way*, triangular, trilateral, tripartite; *third*, tertiary.

vb. *triple*, treble, cube, triplicate.

adv. *thrice*, trebly, threefold, in triplicate.

83 FOUR

n. *four*, quartet, tetrad, foursome, quaternity, quadriga, four-in-hand, four-poster; *quadruplicate*, quadrangle, square, tetrahedron, quadruped, quadruplet, quad, tetralogy, quatrain, tetrameter, four-letter word; *quarter*, fourth, quarterly, quarto, tetrarch.

adj. *quadruple*, quaternary, fourfold; *square*, foursquare, quadrate, quadrilateral, tetrahedral; *quarterly*, quadraphonic, quadrennial.

vb. *quadruple*, quadruplicate, square, quadrate; *quarter*.

adv. *fourfold*; *squarely*, foursquare.

84 FIVE AND OVER

n. *five*, quintet, quintuplet, quin, fiver (*colloq.*), pentad, pentagon, pentangle, quincunx, pentameter, Pentateuch, pentathlon; *six*, half a dozen, sextet, sextuplet, sixer, hexad, hexagon, hexameter, sestina, Hexateuch; *seven*, heptad, septet, heptagon, Sabbath, sabbatical, Heptateuch; *eight*, octet, octad, octagon, octave, octoroon, octopus, octavo; *nine*, nonet, nonagon, novena; *ten*, tenner (*colloq.*), decade, decalogue, decagon, decathlon, tenth, decimal, tithe; *eleven*, double figures; *twelve*, dozen, dodecahedron, alexandrine; *thirteen*, baker's dozen, long dozen, teens; *twenty and over*, score, fifty, quinquagenarian, sixty, sexagenarian, seventy, septuagenarian, eighty, octogenarian, ninety, nonagenarian; *hundred*, centenarian, century, three figures, gross, bicentenary, tercentenary, quadricentennial, quincentenary; *thousand*, K, millennium, grand (*colloq.*); *million*, billion, trillion.

adj. *fifth*, fivefold etc., quintuple, sixth, sextuple, seventh, septuple, eighth, octuple, ninth, nonary, tenth, decimal, twelfth, duodecimal, centennial, millionth, billionth.

vb. *quintuple etc.*, multiply; *decimate*, decimalize.

adv. *fivefold etc.*, hundredfold.

85 ACCOMPANIMENT
See also **35** (addition); **789** (sociability); **793** (friendship).

n. *accompaniment*, coexistence, symbiosis, conjunction, cohabitation, company, society, fellowship, companionship, friendship, togetherness, mateyness (*colloq.*); *companion*, friend, comrade, mate, buddy (*colloq.*), colleague, partner, cohabitee, consort; *escort*, guide, convoy, outrider, attendant, chaperon, bodyguard, minder (*colloq.*); *follower*, dependant, satellite, hanger-on, camp follower, shadow, tail; *concomitant*, attribute, feature, symptom, accessory, appurtenance, appendage, corollary, sine qua non, prerequisite.

adj. *accompanying*, attendant, associated, concomitant, accessory, incidental; *parallel*, simultaneous, contemporaneous, coexistent; *inseparable*, thick as thieves, symbiotic.

vb. *accompany*, escort, guide, convoy, attend, partner, chaperon, squire, mind (*colloq.*); *attach oneself to*, dance attendance on, tag along, string along, dog the footsteps of, shadow, tail, track; *belong with*, complement, go together, go hand in hand; *associate*, consort, frequent, hobnob (*colloq.*), socialize, club together, team up, gang up.

adv. *together*, in a body; *in convoy*, in tow, in someone's wake, on someone's coat-tails.

86 MULTITUDE
See also **29** (greatness); **80** (plurality).

n. *multitude*, multiplicity, infinity, myriad, zillions (*colloq.*); *host*, army, legion, horde, fleet, swarm, brood, sea, forest, galaxy; *throng*, crowd, masses, mob, press, crush.

adj. *multitudinous*, countless, number-

less, innumerable, myriad; *endless*, infinite, boundless, vast, untold, inexhaustible; *numerous*, many, manifold, ample, abundant, profuse, plenty, bumper, umpteen (*colloq.*), galore (*colloq.*); *crowded*, packed, overcrowded, overmanned, overpopulated, high-density, thick on the ground.

vb. *crowd*, throng, flock, troop, pour, flood, stream; *swarm*, crawl, infest, mill, seethe, teem, pullulate, multiply; *overrun*, outnumber, swamp, snow under.

adv. *in droves*, en masse, thick and fast.

87 FEW
See also **30** (smallness).

n. *few*, handful, trickle, sprinkling, minority, low turnout; *scarcity*, paucity, shortage, scantiness; *sparseness*, rarity, infrequency.

adj. *few*, scant, scarce, straggly, wispy, few and far between; *sparse*, infrequent, intermittent, dotted about, strung out, scattered; *underpopulated*, low-density, thin on the ground, understaffed, undermanned.

vb. *scatter*, sprinkle, dot; *thin*, reduce, rarefy, weed out, eliminate, decimate.

adv. *thinly*, in ones and twos, in dribs and drabs (*colloq.*); *seldom*, rarely, infrequently, occasionally.

88 REPETITION
See also **119** (regularity).

n. *repetition*, recapitulation, reiteration, tautology, reproduction, duplication; *renewal*, resumption, reprise, rehearsal, repeat, rerun, replay, reprint, remake, reissue, rehash; *recurrence*, reappearance, renaissance, rebirth, return, cycle, revival, relapse, reversion; *regularity*, rhythm, beat, pulse, rhyme, alliteration, assonance; *refrain*, chorus, encore, repeat performance, second helping; *repetitiveness*, routine, monotony, familiarity, cliché, chestnut (*colloq.*), same old story, mixture as before.

adj. *repetitive*, reiterative, tautological, repetitious; *recurrent*, regular, rhythmical, periodic, cyclical; *monotonous*, routine, familiar, stale, hackneyed, trite.

vb. *repeat*, recapitulate, reiterate, restate, reemphasize, hammer into, din into, harp, nag; *reproduce*, copy, mirror, duplicate, echo, chorus, parrot; *renew*, resume, revive, reprise, rehearse, rerun, replay, remake, reissue, reprint, rehash, recycle; *recur*, reappear, return, crop up; *relapse*, regress, revert, retrace one's steps, go back over old ground.

adv. *repeatedly*, again and again, time after time, over and over, ad nauseam; *once more*, da capo.

89 INFINITY

See also **95** (eternity).

n. *infinity*, infinitude, immensity, boundlessness, limitlessness, vastness, abyss; *eternity*, perpetuity, immortality, everlastingness.

adj. *infinite*, boundless, limitless, bottomless, immeasurable, vast, unfathomable, ineffable; *countless*, innumerable, incalculable, numberless, untold; *endless*, indefinite, open-ended, neverending, interminable, inexhaustible; *eternal*, immortal, perpetual, everlasting.

vb. *be infinite*, know no bounds, go on and on, last forever.

adv. *infinitely*, immeasurably, incalculably, vastly, ineffably; *ad infinitum*, to the nth degree, forever, eternally, perpetually; *indefinitely*, sine die.

90 TIME

See also **92** (period); **97** (timekeeping).

n. *time*, spacetime, duration, continuity; *age*, epoch, aeon, century, lifetime, time immemorial, time out of mind; *period*, span, course, season, spell, phase; *interim*, meanwhile, meantime, interval, interlude, time lag, timewarp; *hour*, zero hour, moment, point in time, local time, time zone, standard time, summer time, man hour, flexitime, overtime.

adj. *temporal*, periodical, seasonal; *continual*, ongoing, present, current, pending.

vb. *pass*, elapse, continue, run, roll, glide; *pause*, take time out, bide one's time, stand still, tick over, vegetate; *spend,* while away, kill (*colloq.*), waste, idle, fritter, squander.

adv. *meanwhile*, in the meantime, in the interim, for the time being; *at present*, now, currently; *soon*, in time, one fine day; *sometimes*, from time to time, at times; *once*, once upon a time, at one time.

91 TIMELESSNESS

See also **95** (eternity).

n. *timelessness*, eternity, perpetuity, unchangingness, immutability; *immortality*, agelessness, datelessness, everlastingness.

adj. *timeless*, eternal, perpetual, unchanging, immutable; *immortal*, ageless, dateless, classic, evergreen.

adv. *never*, at no time, not in a month of Sundays, over one's dead body; *indefinitely*, sine die, till the cows come home (*colloq.*).

92 PERIOD

See also **90** (time); **120** (irregularity).

n. *period*, season, cycle, span, spell, phase, stint, watch, stretch, bout, round, innings; *term*, quarter, trimester, semester; *hour*, rush hour, lunch hour, witching hour, small hours; *day*, weekday, rest day, red-letter day; *week*, fortnight, month, calendar month, lunar month; *year*, twelvemonth, leap year, light-year, solar year; *decade*, century, millennium; *anniversary*, birthday, saint's day, jubilee, centenary, bicentenary, tercentenary; *age*, epoch, generation, aeon.

adj. *periodic*, seasonal, cyclical; *daily*, quotidian, weekly, hebdomadal, fortnightly, monthly, menstrual, quarterly, biannual, yearly, annual, biennial, centennial, perennial.

vb. *be periodic*, recur, come round, go in phases; *alternate*, take one's turn.

adv. *periodically*, from time to time, sometimes, now and then, at times.

93 DURATION
See also **95** (eternity); **124** (continuity).

n. duration, continuance, permanence; *long time*, lifetime, ages, month of Sundays (*colloq.*), donkey's years (*colloq.*), yonks (*colloq.*), long haul, marathon; *protraction*, prolongation, filibustering, stonewalling; *durability*, toughness, endurance, stamina, staying power, persistence, survival instinct.

adj. *lasting*, abiding, enduring, continuing, ongoing, permanent, surviving; *long-term*, long-haul, long-standing, lifelong; *protracted*, long-drawn-out, time-consuming, longwinded, interminable; *durable*, tough, long-lasting, imperishable, evergreen, perennial.

vb. *last*, abide, endure, continue, remain, persist; *survive*, outlast, outstay, outlive, have nine lives; *protract*, prolong, spin out, linger, dawdle, take forever, play for time, temporize, filibuster, stonewall.

adv. *for a long time*, at length, for ages; *in the long run*, in the end, at the end of the day.

94 TRANSIENCE
See also **130** (changeableness).

n. *transience*, impermanence, evanescence, brevity, instantaneity; *changeability*, volatility, instability, precariousness, fragility, brittleness, perishability; *shooting star*, bubble, spindrift, flare, flicker, shifting sand, nomad, bird of passage, ship that passes in the night, nine days' wonder, flash in the pan (*colloq.*).

adj. *transient*, ephemeral, shortlived, evanescent, passing, fleeting, brief, cursory, momentary, transitory; *temporary*, makeshift, provisional, ad hoc, short-term, impermanent, disposable, throwaway; *changeable*, volatile, mutable, perishable, fragile, brittle; *precarious*, unstable, unsettled, drifting, rootless, nomadic.

vb. *pass*, fade, die, expire, disappear, vanish, melt, evaporate; *flare*, flicker, flash, spurt, explode.

adv. *briefly*, momentarily; *temporarily*, provisionally, for the time being.

95 ETERNITY
See also **89** (infinity); **91** (timelessness); **93** (duration).

n. *eternity*, perpetuity, infinity, forever; *timelessness*, agelessness, immortality, imperishability, indestructibiity, permanence, endurance.

adj. *eternal*, perpetual, sempiternal, everlasting; *immortal*, deathless, undying, imperishable, indestructible, self-perpetuating; *timeless*, ageless, classic, evergreen; *endless*, ceaseless, neverending, unremitting, relentless.

vb. *perpetuate*, immortalize; *preserve*, conserve, freeze, embalm, mummify.

adv. *eternally*, for ever, for ever and a day, for good, for keeps (*colloq.*), till doomsday, for good and all; *endlessly*, incessantly, nonstop, relentlessly, around the clock.

96 IMMEDIACY
See also **94** (transience); **245** (speed).

n. *immediacy*, instantaneousness, simultaneity, suddenness, abruptness; *promptness*, speediness, alacrity, spontaneity, impulsiveness.

adj. *immediate*, instant, instantaneous, simultaneous; *sudden*, abrupt, spontaneous, impulsive, unpremeditated; *prompt*, punctual, speedy, rapid-fire, staccato.

vb. *act on impulse*, improvise, extemporize, ad-lib; *start*, dart, flit, bolt, pelt, flash, dash.

adv. *immediately*, forthwith, pronto (*colloq.*), overnight; *suddenly*, in a flash, on the spur of the moment, at the drop of a hat, off the cuff; *at once*, at a stroke, in one fell swoop; *punctually*, on time, to the second, on the dot (*colloq.*), on the nail.

97 TIMEKEEPING
See also **90** (time).

n. *timekeeping*, horology, chronometry, timing, clockwatching; *dateline*, time zone, meridian, daylight saving, local time, standard time; *chronology*, calendar, almanac, agenda, timetable, schedule, timesheet, journal, diary, logbook, chronicle, annals; *timepiece*, chronometer, sundial, waterclock, hourglass, siren, hooter, time signal, gong, chimes, speaking clock, metronome; *clock*, grandfather clock, alarm, repeater, fobwatch, hunter, turnip, wristwatch, digital watch, stopwatch, dial, face, hand, pendulum, escapement, mainspring.

adj. *timekeeping*, chronometrical, horological; *chronological*, temporal, historical.

vb. *record*, chronicle, log, clock up, time, timetable, schedule.

adv. *clockwise*; *around the clock*, twenty-four-hours a day; *anticlockwise*, against the clock, out of time.

98 WRONG TIME

n. *wrong time*, mistiming, bad timing, untimeliness, wrong moment; *anachronism*, precocity, prematurity, outdatedness, unfashionableness.

adj. *mistimed*, untimely, unseasonable, inopportune; *unpunctual*, late, tardy, dilatory, behindhand, early, previous; *anachronistic*, precocious, premature, overdue, outdated, posthumous, old-fashioned.

vb. *mistime*, bring forward, antedate, jump the gun (*colloq.*); *delay*, retard, postdate, hold up, tarry, be slow off the mark, be behind the times, put the clock back, regress.

adv. *in advance*, prematurely, ahead of time; *belatedly*, tardily, late in the day.

99 PRIORITY

See also **59** (precedence).

n. *priority*, anteriority, preexistence, prehistory; *precedence*, primogeniture, antecedence, right of way, early bird, first come first served; *firstborn*, eldest, antecedent, forbear, precursor; *premonition*, presentiment, forewarning, briefing, prior notice, foresight.

adj. *prior*, previous, preexisting, anterior, antecedent, earlier, first; *former*, onetime, erstwhile, sometime; *preemptive*, preventive, anticipatory.

vb. *precede*, predate, preexist, predecease; *foreshadow*, presage, anticipate, forestall, obviate, prevent; *preempt*,

preclude, steal a march on, jump the queue, present with a fait accompli.

adv. *before*, beforehand, in advance, previously.

100 SUCCESSION

See also **60** (sequence).

n. *succession*, posterity, issue, inheritance, legacy; *aftereffect*, aftermath, fallout, upshot, outcome; *youngest*, junior, benjamin, latecomer; *successor*, heir, descendant, inheritor; *afterthought*, hindsight, second thoughts, post mortem, debriefing.

adj. *successive*, subsequent, following, last, posterior, next, rear; *future*, budding, would-be, elect, designate; *posthumous*.

vb. *succeed*, follow, take over from, inherit the mantle of, step into the shoes of; *defer*, put off, postpone, postdate.

adv. *after*, afterwards, subsequently, thereafter, thereupon.

101 PRESENT TIME

See also **96** (immediacy); **103** (same time); **106** (newness).

n. *present time*, present, simultaneity, contemporaneousness, present day, here and now, modern times; *contemporary*, one's generation, age group, peer group; *topicality*, currency, current affairs, news; *present event*, happening, occurrence, incident, episode, development, affair, matter, concern, transaction; *crisis*, turn of events, emergency, chapter of accidents, vicissitudes, ups and downs (*colloq.*).

adj. *present*, existing, extant, ongoing, actual, current, contemporaneous, simultaneous, live; *present-day*, contemporary, modern, up-to-date, topical, latest, up-to-the-minute, now (*colloq.*); *temporary*, provisional, ad hoc, makeshift, stopgap.

vb. *be present*, be in the air, be in the wind; *exist*, live from hand to mouth, live for the present; *attend*, show up, put in an appearance, turn up; *take place*, happen, occur, come about, coincide, arise, spring up, crop up (*colloq.*), transpire, supervene; *experience*, encounter, undergo, go through.

adv. *at present*, at the moment, today, nowadays, these days, in this day and age; *now*, now or never, immediately, instantly, on the spot; *until now*, hitherto, to date; *for the present*, for the time being, temporarily, provisionally.

102 DIFFERENT TIME
See also **98** (wrong time).

n. *different time*, another time, alternative date; *past*, days gone by, better days; *future*, days to come, distant future.

adj. *out-of-date*, anachronistic, behind the times, overdue, advanced, futuristic.

adv. *not now*, later, some time, one of these days, one fine day, sooner or later; *then*, earlier, previously, at one time; *out of step*, out of phase, out of sync.

103 SAME TIME
See also **101** (present time).

n. *same time*, synchronism, coexistence, coincidence, simultaneity, clash, concurrence, contemporaneusness, unison, chorus; *same age*, vintage, generation, peer group, age group, contemporary, coeval; *synchronization*, sync, meridian, time zone, dead heat, photo finish.

adj. *synchronous*, synchronic, simultaneous, contemporaneous, concurrent, coexistent, coincidental; *contemporary*, coeval, isochronous.

vb. *synchronize*, tune, phase, align; *coincide*, come together, clash, double-book; *chorus*, chime, chant; *keep up*, keep abreast, keep in step.

adv. *at the same time*, simultaneously, concurrently, in the same breath; *in step*, in phase, in sync, in concert, in unison.

104 FUTURE TIME
See also **100** (succession); **450** (expectation).

n. *future time*, futurity, tomorrow, morrow, time to come; *future*, prospect, outlook, expectation, lookout

(*colloq.*); *potential*, promise, raw material; *imminence*, proximity, approach, advent; *fate*, destiny, karma, predestination, inevitability; *horoscope*, stars, forecast, prediction, divination, futurology, crystal-gazing; *afterlife*, hereafter, next world, millennium, doomsday.

adj. *future*, coming, approaching, impending, imminent, due, ahead; *potential*, promising, budding, aspiring, would-be, prospective; *predestined*, fated, doomed, inevitable, inescapable.

vb. *lie ahead*, threaten, loom, draw nigh, be just around the corner; *anticipate*, foresee, foreshadow, predict, divine.

adv. *in future*, henceforth, from now on; *eventually*, in due course, in the fullness of time, in the long run; *at hand*, in view, in the offing, on the horizon, on the cards, on the agenda.

105 PAST TIME
See also **107** (oldness).

n. *past time*, bygone days, yesteryear, days of yore, good old days, auld lang syne; *souvenir*, memento, retrospective, golden oldie (*colloq.*); *blast from the past* (*colloq.*); *recollection*, memory, remembrance, nostalgia, hindsight; *regression*, atavism, reversion, relapse, throw-back; *obsoleteness*, antiquity, time immemorial, prehistory, Dark Ages, Stone Age; *relic*, archaism, antique, fossil, dinosaur, ruin, ancient monument, museum, archive; *archaeology*, palaeology, palaeography, antiquarianism; *thing of the past*, dead letter, ancient history, old news, has-been (*colloq.*), yesterday's man; *revival*, resurrection, resuscitation, exhumation.

adj. *past*, bygone, archaic, antiquated, obsolete, extinct; *retrospective*, nostalgic, retroactive, regressive, atavistic; *ancient*, prehistoric, Stone-Age, antediluvian; *lapsed*, date-expired, finished with, over and done with, irrevocable, irreversible; *former*, late, erstwhile, onetime, sometime, previous.

vb. *be past*, have run its course, have had its day, have seen better days; *pass*, elapse, expire, run out, die out, fade away, blow over (*colloq.*); *recollect*, remember, recall, look back, hark back, put the clock back, go over old ground, regress, revert; *revive*, exhume, resurrect, resuscitate.

adv. *in the past*, formerly, previously, before, at one time, time was; *long ago*, once upon a time, in the dim and distant past.

106 NEWNESS

See also **101** (present time); **111** (youth).

n. *newness*, recentness, freshness, bloom; *novelty*, innovation, neologism, scoop, exclusive; *modernity*, up-to-dateness, topicality, currency, trendiness, latest thing, last word, dernier cri, flavour of the month (*colloq.*); *avant-garde*, modernism, new wave, futurism; *modernization*, revolution, renovation, restoration, facelift, overhaul, update, new edition, new look, revision; *immaturity*, greenness, rawness, callowness, inexperience; *novice*, raw recruit, tyro, fledgling, apprentice, greenhorn (*colloq.*), new boy, new bug (*colloq.*), newcomer, new broom, new blood; *rising generation*, bright young thing (*colloq.*), trendy (*colloq.*), upstart, parvenu, nouveaux riches.

adj. *new*, brand-new, born-again, fresh, virgin, pristine, evergreen; *novel*, innovative, new-minted, hot off the press; *modern*, up-to-date, current, topical, up-to-the-minute, fashionable, trendy (*colloq.*), with-it (*colloq.*); *immature*, green, callow, raw, inexperienced, untried, new to the game, budding.

vb. *make new*, modernize, renew, renovate, refurbish, rejuvenate, freshen up, give a new lease of life, update, revise, overhaul; *innovate*, introduce, invent, patent, coin, mint.

adv. *newly*, recently, lately, of late; *as new*, in mint condition; *anew*, afresh.

107 OLDNESS

See also **105** (past time); **112** (age).

n. *oldness*, age, antiquity, archaism, obsolescence, obsoleteness; *antique*, heirloom, collector's piece, museum piece, relic, fossil; *tradition*, custom, oral history, folklore, mythology; *maturity*, ripeness, experience, seniority, wisdom; *veteran*, old hand, old-timer (*colloq.*), doyen, father figure; *old age*, longevity, senility, senescence; *decay*, decline, dilapidation, erosion, ruin.

adj. *old*, age-old, ancient, olden, bygone, antique, vintage, old-world, archaic, obsolescent, obsolete, antediluvian; *traditional*, time-honoured, long-standing, historical, old as the hills, mythological, primordial; *outdated*, outmoded, antiquated, superannuated, passé, discontinued, old hat (*colloq.*), out of the ark (*colloq.*); *dilapidated*, mouldering, crumbling, motheaten, threadbare, clapped out (*colloq.*), rusty, musty, distressed; *aged*, venerable, hoary, geriatric, past it (*colloq.*), senile, gaga (*colloq.*).

vb. *grow old*, age, wither, fade, crumble, moulder, decay, rust.

adv. *for ages* (*colloq.*), since the year dot, since Adam was a boy.

108 SEASON

n. *season*, high/low season, close season; *spring*, springtime, seedtime, youth, vernal equinox; *summer*, summertime, midsummer, high summer, dog days, summer solstice; *autumn*, fall (*U.S.*), back end, Indian summer, autumn equinox; *winter*, wintertime, Christmas, yuletide, festive season, midwinter, hibernation, decline, decay, winter solstice.

adj. *seasonal*, springlike, vernal, burgeoning, summery, aestival, autumnal, equinoctial, wintry, hibernal, bleak.

109 MORNING

n. *morning*, morn, daybreak, dawn, sunrise, Aurora, cockcrow, sunup; *forenoon*, elevenses, noon, midday, high noon; *dawn chorus*, early bird, early riser, reveille, matins.

adj. *morning*, matutinal, daytime, diurnal.

adv. *a.m.*, ante meridiem; *at first light*, at the crack of dawn, with the lark.

110 EVENING

n. *evening*, eventide, eve, sunset, sundown, twilight, half-light, dusk, gloaming, cockshut; *night*, nightfall, nighttime, darkness, moonrise, dead of night, midnight, witching hour, small hours; *afternoon*, matinée, soiree, cocktail, sundowner, evensong, vespers, lights out, curfew, lighting-up time, last post, bedtime, night hawk, night owl, moonlight flit.

adj. *nightly*, nocturnal, dark, twilight, crepuscular, overnight.

adv. *p.m.*, post meridiem; *by night*, overnight, under cover of darkness.

111 YOUTH

See also **106** (newness).

n. *youth*, springtime, heyday, salad days; *youthfulness*, freshness, immaturity, callowness; *babyhood*, infancy, childhood, tender years, formative years; *adolescence*, teens, puberty, awkward age, pubescence, growing pains; *cradle*, nursery, kindergarten, playschool; *pupillage*, nonage, tutelage, wardship; *youngster*, infant, babe in arms, suckling, toddler, tot, mite; *child*, kid (*colloq.*), brat (*colloq.*), urchin, nipper (*colloq.*), minx, madam, moppet; *adolescent*, juvenile, teenager, delinquent, whippersnapper (*colloq.*), stripling, tearaway, skinhead, yob (*colloq.*), lass, teenybopper, tomboy, nymphet, Lolita; *pupil*, ward, minor.

adj. *young*, youthful, fresh, young-at-heart, ageless; *immature*, green, callow, wet behind the ears (*colloq.*); *newborn*, babyish, infantile, preschool, childish, puerile, adolescent, pubescent, virginal, coltish, junior, teenage.

112 AGE

See also **107** (oldness).

n. *age*, older generation, adulthood, manhood, legal age, majority, seniority; *middle age*, prime, maturity, menopause, climacteric, change of life, mid-life crisis, mutton dressed as lamb, no spring chicken (*colloq.*); *old age*, longevity, ripe old age, declining years, evening of one's life, second childhood, senility, dotage; *old person*, adult, grown-up, matriarch, matron, patriarch, oldster (*colloq.*), old-age pensioner, senior citizen, grandfather, grandad (*colloq.*), old boy (*colloq.*), old fogy, old buffer (*colloq.*), greybeard, grandmother, granny (*colloq.*), old dear (*colloq.*), crone, hag, Darby and Joan; *old hand*, veteran, expert, old-timer, elder, elder statesman, grand old man, doyen, grande dame, doyenne; *gerontocracy*, gerontology, geriatrics, old folks' home, granny flat.

adj. *old*, adult, grown-up, mature; *middle-aged*, menopausal, matronly, of a certain age, ageing, getting on (*colloq.*), long in the tooth (*colloq.*); *aged*, elderly, sprightly, geriatric, doddering, failing, senile, gaga (*colloq.*), white-haired, with one foot in the grave (*colloq.*).

113 EARLINESS

See also **99** (priority).

n. *earliness*, promptness, dispatch, timeliness, immediacy, punctuality; *prematurity*, precocity, forwardness; *immaturity*, unreadiness, unpreparedness, unripeness; *foresight*, anticipation, preparedness, forward planning, prior warning, head start.

adj. *early*, prompt, immediate, punctual, timely; *premature*, precocious, previous, forward, advanced; *immature*, unripe, unready, unprepared; *preliminary*, preparatory, anticipatory.

vb. *be early*, reserve, book, get in first, jump the queue, jump the gun (*colloq.*); *preempt*, take the initiative, forestall, nip in the bud; *dispatch*, expedite, lose no time, take time by the forelock.

adv. *early on*, first thing; *beforehand*, in advance, before one's time, out of turn.

114 LATENESS

See also **100** (succession).

n. *lateness*, late hour, small hours, eleventh hour, last minute, high time, brinksmanship; *tardiness*, slowness, delayed reaction, time lag, afterthought; *dilatoriness*, unpunctuality, delay, holdup, latecomer; *backward-*

ness, retardation, slow starter, late developer; *postponement*, adjournment, deferment, procrastination, suspension, reprieve, moratorium.

adj. *late*, late in the day, last-minute, deathbed, posthumous; *belated*, overdue, behindhand, tardy, dilatory, unpunctual; *backward*, retarded, slow; *postponed*, deferred, suspended.

vb. *be late*, oversleep, keep late hours, burn the midnight oil; *be slow*, linger, dawdle, tarry, loiter, dilly-dally (*colloq.*); *postpone*, put off, defer, adjourn, shelve, mothball, put on ice/in cold storage, procrastinate; *delay*, stall, stonewall, filibuster, play for time, suspend, hang fire, sleep on it, take one's time, cool one's heels, wait and see.

adv. *late*, till all hours; *at last*, ultimately, in the end; *tardily*, belatedly, at the last minute, in the nick of time.

115 TIMELINESS

See also **580** (convenience).

n. *timeliness*, opportuneness, convenience, expediency, right moment; *opportunity*, golden opportunity, chance, break (*colloq.*), piece of luck, opening; *key moment*, psychological moment, moment of truth, pinch (*colloq.*), push (*colloq.*), crunch (*colloq.*); *critical point*, crux, turning point, crisis, emergency, narrow escape, close shave.

adj. *timely*, welcome, seasonable, fortuitous, well-timed, auspicious, opportune, providential, propitious, heavensent; *convenient*, handy, expedient, advantageous.

vb. *seize one's opportunity*, profit by, take advantage of, exploit, turn to good account, capitalize on, strike while the iron is hot, make hay while the sun shines.

adv. *at the right moment*, conveniently, not before time, in the nick of time.

116 UNTIMELINESS

See also **581** (inconvenience).

n. *untimeliness*, inconvenience, inopportuneness, wrong moment, evil hour, off-day, one of those days; *mistiming*, intrusion, interruption, misjudgment, blunder, clanger (*colloq.*).

adj. *untimely*, inopportune, inauspicious, untoward, disadvantageous, unlucky, ill-starred; *mistimed*, intrusive, misjudged, malapropos, awkward, inconvenient.

vb. *mistime*, misjudge, miss one's opportunity, miss the boat (*colloq.*), blow it (*colloq.*); *intrude*, break in on, talk out of turn, put one's foot in it (*colloq.*), drop a brick (*colloq.*).

adv. *at a bad time*, at the wrong moment, inopportunely, inconveniently.

117 FREQUENCY

See also **88** (repetition); **119** (regularity).

n. *frequency*, recurrence, regularity, repetition, rhythm; *predictability*, familiarity, commonness, monotony, banality.

adj. *frequent*, numerous, recurrent, periodic, regular, repeated, rhythmic; *continual*, sustained, constant, monotonous, relentless, remorseless; *predictable*, familiar, common, prevalent, banal, two a penny.

vb. *be frequent*, recur, keep on, continue.

adv. *frequently*, often, many a time; *repeatedly*, constantly, again and again, time and time again, regularly, continually; *commonly*, generally, more often than not.

118 INFREQUENCY

See also **87** (few); **120** (irregularity).

n. *infrequency*, rarity, scarcity, scantness, sparseness; *intermittence*, irregularity, unpredictability.

adj. *infrequent*, rare, few and far between, spaced out, occasional, scarce, sparse; *intermittent*, irregular, unpredictable, uncommon, unusual.

adv. *infrequently*, rarely, seldom; *occasionally*, once in a while, every now and then, once in a blue moon (*colloq.*); *intermittently*, off and on, now and then.

119 REGULARITY
See also **88** (repetition); **92** (period); **117** (frequency).

n. *regularity*, rhythm, recurrence, repetition, periodicity; *reliability*, steadiness, constancy, predictability, uniformity; *beat*, throb, tick, pulse, measure, refrain, chorus; *alternation*, ebb and flow, to and fro, shuttle service, swing, pendulum, piston; *rotation*, rota, roster, revolution, circuit, cycle, menstruation, biorhythms; *routine*, daily round, nine to five, treadmill; *anniversary*, birthday, leap year, immovable feast.

adj. *regular*, rhythmic, repeated, recurring, periodic; *reliable*, predictable, steady, constant, uniform, even, measured; *alternating*, seasonal, cyclical, rotational.

vb. *recur*, come round again, revolve, rotate, alternate, reciprocate, take turn about; *be rhythmic*, beat, throb, tick, chime, swing; *go to and fro*, ply, commute.

adv. *regularly*, at regular intervals, seasonally, cyclically; *periodically*, at intervals, now and again; *alternately*, in rotation, in turn; *to and fro*, back and forwards.

120 IRREGULARITY
See also **118** (infrequency).

n. *irregularity*, variability, unpredictability, randomness, inconstancy, capriciousness; *unevenness*, unsteadiness, fitfulness, jerkiness, sporadicness, spasmodicness, fluctuation; *caprice*, whim, variable, unknown quantity, movable feast.

adj. *irregular*, variable, unpredictable, random, changeable, capricious, erratic; *uneven*, unsteady, fitful, jerky, sporadic, spasmodic, intermittent, arhythmic, stop-go.

vb. *be irregular*, vary, change, waver, flicker, fluctuate, come and go.

adv. *irregularly*, off and on, spasmodically, in fits and starts.

121 CHANGE
See also **125** (conversion); **127** (revolution); **130** (changeableness).

n. *change*, alteration, modification, version, adjustment, modulation, inflection, mutation; *transformation*, transfiguration, transmogrification, metamorphosis, conversion; *adaptation*, variation, permutation, shift; *transition*, changeover, switch, substitution, transposition, transference; *flux*, flow, mobility, impermanence, instability, vicissitudes, ups and downs (*colloq.*); *improvement*, reformation, revision, upturn, change for the better/worse, deterioration, degeneration, downturn; *fluctuation*, seesaw, change of mind, vacillation, change of direction, deviation, diversion, U-turn, volte-face, about-turn; *revolution*, overthrow, upheaval, sea change, wind of change, innovation, reform, reconstruction, reorganization; *adapter*, alterant, transformer, catalyst, metabolism, alchemy, enzyme, leaven, yeast; *reformer*, radical, revolutionary, agitator, new broom.

adj. *changing*, fluid, plastic, mobile, unstable, protean, impermanent, volatile; *transitional*, provisional, temporary, interim, ad hoc; *revolutionary*, radical, progressive, innovative, reformist.

vb. *change*, alter, modify, adjust, temper, modulate, inflect, mutate; *transform*, transfigure, transmogrify, transmute, metamorphose, convert, metabolize; *vary*, diversify, adapt, ring the changes; *improve*, reform, turnover a new leaf, change for the better/worse, deteriorate, degenerate, fall away; *fluctuate*, vacillate, change one's tune, shift, veer, chop and change, blow hot and cold (*colloq.*); *interchange*, swap (*colloq.*), switch, change round, substitute, transpose, transfer; *revolutionize*, revamp, remodel, reconstruct, refurbish, reorganize, revise; *process*, treat, adulterate, denature, doctor, massage.

adv. *mutatis mutandis*, vice versa.

122 PERMANENCE
See also **131** (stability).

n. *permanence*, unchangingness, immutability, fixity, immobility, stasis;

endurance, continuity, persistence, subsistence, survival; *stability*, steadiness, constancy, firmness, bedrock, solidity; *tradition*, custom, habit, routine, status quo, conservatism, laissez-faire; *conservative*, reactionary, hawk, diehard, stick-in-the-mud (*colloq.*); *invariability*, inflexibility, rigidity, immovableness, stubborness, obstinacy.

adj. *permanent*, unchanging, immutable, fixed, stationary, immobile, static; *enduring*, persistent, continuing, lasting, surviving; *stable*, steady, constant, firm, solid, unbudgeable, unwavering, steadfast; *invariable*, inflexible, rigid, immovable, stubborn, obstinate.

vb. *be permanent*, endure, last, abide, subsist, persist, survive; *remain*, stay, tarry, stay put, stand still, dig in one's toes, tread water, mark time; *settle*, establish, fix, entrench, put down roots; *maintain*, sustain, uphold, persevere, conserve.

adv. *permanently*, for good, for ever.

123 CESSATION
See also **235** (motionlessness).

n. *cessation*, discontinuation, termination, closure, shutdown, closedown, collapse, failure, crash; *stop*, halt, standstill, deadlock, stasis, stalemate, checkmate; *hitch*, check, holdup, snag, hiccup, blockage, bottleneck, jam; *stoppage*, walkout, strike, work-to-rule, go-slow, lockout, sit-in; *pause*, lull, break, interruption, letup, rest, breather (*colloq.*), respite, cooling-off period; *suspension*, freeze, abeyance, moratorium, truce, ceasefire, armistice, amnesty; *end*, conclusion, expiry, enddate, terminus, end of the road.

vb. *cease*, stop, desist, refrain, hold off; *halt*, stop short, stop in one's tracks, pull up, baulk, stall, seize up; *discontinue*, pause, break off, leave off, ring off, knock off (*colloq.*); *strike*, walk out, down tools, come out, work to rule, go slow, occupy; *check*, arrest, stem, block, veto, thwart, foil, parry, checkmate; *suspend*, drop, hold over, put on ice, freeze, shelve, mothball; *end*, terminate, finish, conclude, expire, run out, peter out, fizzle out (*colloq.*);

collapse, fail, fold, go into liquidation, wind up, shut up shop, ring down the curtain; *retire*, resign, stand down, pull out, withdraw, scratch.

124 CONTINUITY
See also **93** (duration).

n. *continuity*, continuation, perpetuation, maintenance, prolongation; *flow*, run, course, progress, current; *regularity*, constancy, uniformity, steadiness, smoothness, monotony; *link*, bridge, stopgap, potboiler (*colloq.*), filler, padding.

adj. *continuous*, uninterrupted, unbroken, nonstop, ongoing, flowing, seamless; *perpetual*, unceasing, incessant, neverending, inexhaustible, undying; *continual*, steady, constant, uniform, regular, recurrent, monotonous, unremitting, relentless.

vb. *continue*, proceed, progress, advance, carry on, keep on; *maintain*, uphold, sustain, preserve, conserve, perpetuate; *endure*, persist, persevere, hang on, plod on, peg away (*colloq.*), stick; *prolong*, protract, extend, spin out, drag out.

adv. *continuously*, on and on, to the bitter end; *continually*, repeatedly.

125 CONVERSION
See also **121** (change).

n. *conversion*, mutation, switch, changeover, transformation, metamorphosis; *processing*, treatment, chemistry, alchemy, evaporation, liquefaction, crystallization, solidification; *convertibility*, adaptability, versatility, flexibility; *laboratory*, melting pot, crucible, test tube; *convert*, proselyte, neophyte, apostate, turncoat, deserter.

adj. *convertible*, mutable, adaptable, versatile, flexible, recyclable, biodegradable; *converted*, reborn, bornagain, reformed; *proselytizing*, evangelical, crusading, missionary, revivalist.

vb. *convert*, adapt, change, assimilate, mutate, metamorphose, transform; *process*, treat, liquefy, evaporate, solidify, crystallize, recycle, break down; *proselytize*, evangelize, win over, persuade; *be converted*, change one's mind, defect, go over to the other side, desert.

126 REVERSION
See also 254 (backward motion).

n. *reversion*, return, regression, atavism, throwback; *relapse*, recidivism, backsliding, recurrence, recrudescence; *reaction*, response, feedback, backlash, whiplash, recoil, retaliation, repercussion, reverberation; *reversal*, overthrow, overturn, upset, about-turn, U-turn, volte-face, swing of the pendulum; *restoration*, recovery, retrieval, restitution, reinstatement; *retreat*, withdrawal, retraction, retrogression, retrenchment, recession.

adj. *reverted*, reflexive, retrogressive, retroactive; *retrograde*, reactionary, unreconstructed, backward-looking, retrospective, regressive; *reacting*, responsive, reflex, repercussive, reverberative; *reversible*, convertible, inverted, two-way.

vb. *revert*, return, relapse, regress, retrace one's steps, retreat, recede, withdraw; *undo*, unmake, overthrow, overturn, upset; *react*, respond, retort, counter, recoil, rebound; *restore*, reinstate, redress, recover, retrieve.

adv. *inside out*, back to front, upside down; *as you were*, back to square one, back to the drawing board.

127 REVOLUTION
See also 121 (change); 662 (disobedience).

n. *revolution*, unpheaval, upset, convulsion, shakeup, coup d'état, overthrow; *rotation*, full circle, circuit, lap, turn; *revolt*, uprising, insurrection, rebellion, insurgency, mutiny; *extremism*, militancy, radicalism, agitprop, entryism, subversion, sedition; *complete change*, clean sweep, clean slate, tabula rasa, new dawn; *revolutionary*, militant, radical, extremist, fanatic, rebel, insurgent, guerrilla, freedom fighter, fifth column.

adj. *revolutionary*, radical, extreme, far-reaching, sweeping, thoroughgoing, draconian, root and branch; *rebellious*, mutinous, bolshie (*colloq.*), militant,

extremist, insurgent, underground, seditious, subversive, entryist, anarchistic.

vb. *revolutionize*, shake up, change the face of, remodel, reconstruct; *overturn*, overthrow, subvert, undermine, infiltrate; *revolt*, rebel, rise up, mutiny, kick over the traces.

128 SUBSTITUTION
See also 129 (exchange).

n. *substitution*, exchange, switch, swap (*colloq.*), changeround, shuffle, musical chairs; *substitute*, agent, deputy, proxy, replacement, stand-in, surrogate, understudy, relief, reserve, locum, whipping boy, scapegoat; *equivalent*, approximation, imitation, second best, makeshift, expedient, stopgap.

adj. *substitutable*, surrogate, alternative, equivalent, interchangeable, vicarious; *substitute*, imitation, fake, ersatz, mock.

vb. *substitute*, exchange, switch, swap (*colloq.*), change round, shuffle; *replace*, supplant, oust, supersede, take over from; *deputize*, stand in for, understudy, cover up for, impersonate.

adv. *instead*, in lieu; *in one's place/stead*, in one's shoes, by proxy.

129 EXCHANGE
See also 11 (reciprocity); 128 (substitution).

n. *exchange*, barter, trade, handover, transfer, swap (*colloq.*); *reciprocity*, give and take, mutuality, quid pro quo, retort, rejoinder, riposte, repartee, dialogue; *interaction*, interplay, interchange, cooperation; *substitution*, transposition, transliteration, transcription; *retaliation*, requittal, reprisals, tit for tat (*colloq.*).

adj. *exchanged*, mutual, reciprocal, cooperative, two-way; *interchangeable*, substitutable, equivalent, convertible.

vb. *exchange*, barter, trade, swap (*colloq.*), hand over, transfer; *reciprocate*, retaliate, retort, bandy words; *interchange*, switch, transpose, transcribe, shuffle, substitute.

adv. *in exchange*, instead, in kind, in return.

130 CHANGEABLENESS

See also 94 (transience); 121 (change).

n. *changeableness*, changeability, mutability, variability; *fluidity*, plasticity, malleability, flexibility, versatility, adaptability; *inconstancy*, impermanence, instability, volatility, unreliability, unpredictability, waywardness, fickleness, capriciousness; *fluctuation*, vacillation, hesitation, indecision, irresolution; *mobility*, restlessness, unease, fidgetiness, *changeable thing*, kaleidoscope, prism, chameleon, mercury, quicksilver, shot silk.

adj. *changeable*, mutable, variable, unstable, impermanent; *fluid*, plastic, malleable, flexible, versatile, adaptable, quick-change, protean, mercurial; *inconstant*, volatile, fickle, flighty, unreliable, wayward, capricious, erratic, unpredictable; *vacillating*, hesitant, indecisive, irresolute, uncertain; *mobile*, restless, shifty, fidgety, uneasy; *desultory*, fitful, spasmodic, sporadic.

vb. *vary*, change, shift, fluctuate, waver, vacillate, hesitate, blow hot and cold (*colloq.*); *move*, dart, dance, flit, flicker, twinkle, gutter, shimmer.

adv. *spasmodically*, off and on.

131 STABILITY

See also 122 (permanence).

n. *stability*, steadiness, firmness, fixity, permanence, solidity, immobility; *balance*, equilibrium, homoeostasis, self-regulation, self-control, composure, even-temperedness, even keel; *reliability*, predictability, invariability, constancy, regularity, sureness; *stabilizer*, ballast, counterweight, prop, buttress, foundation, pillar, bedrock, anchor, mooring; *confirmation*, ratification, validation, corroboration.

adj. *stable*, steady, firm, fixed, permanent, immobile; *balanced*, homoeostatic, self-regulating, self-controlled, calm, composed, even-tempered; *immovable*, entrenched, solid, unwavering, inalterable, unshakable, unassailable; *reliable*, predictable, invariable, constant, regular, perennial; *indelible*,

fast, ingrained, deep-rooted, deep-seated, ineradicable.

vb. *be stable*, stand firm/fast, stay put, dig in, settle down, put down roots; *stabilize*, support, buttress, shore up, prop up, anchor, embed, entrench, fix; *confirm*, establish, validate, ratify, corroborate.

132 CAUSE

See also 61 (beginning); 134 (motive).

n. *cause*, motive, reason, casus belli, ground, explanation, rationale, factor, influence, determinant; *causality*, instrumentality, aetiology, necessity, determinism; *motivation*, mainspring, provocation, stimulus, impetus, encouragement, inducement; *creator*, prime mover, author, inventor, originator, founder, architect; *source*, fount, fountainhead, cradle, womb, nursery, seed bed, breeding ground, hotbed; *genesis*, origin, ancestry, roots, derivation, etymology; *instrument*, means, motor, pivot, lever, hinge, dynamo; *germ*, seed, fetus, embryo, raw material.

adj. *causal*, instrumental, determinant, pivotal, influential, formative; *basic*, original, primary, fundamental, elemental, embryonic; *creative*, dynamic, innovative, inventive, productive, generative, fertile, seminal.

vb. *cause*, give rise to, create, generate, produce, originate; *found*, establish, institute, launch, initiate; *bring about*, occasion, unleash, precipitate, trigger; *organize*, set up, engineer, stage-manage; *provoke*, elicit, evoke, release; *stimulate*, kindle, inspire, encourage, foster, promote; *determine*, decide, entail, require, necessitate.

prep. *because of*, owing to, due to, as a result of.

133 EFFECT

See also 62 (end).

n. *effect*, consequence, result, end result, development, outcome, upshot; *aftereffect*, sequel, aftermath, fallout, reaction, backlash, ripple effect, knock-on effect, chain reaction; *prod-*

uct, produce, crop, harvest, fruit, output; *derivative*, by-product, side effect, spin-off, legacy.

adj. *resultant*, consequent, subsequent, secondary, ensuing; *dependent*, contingent, concomitant; *derivative*, inherited, hereditary, genetic.

vb. *result*, develop, arise, unfold, evolve, spring up, issue, emerge; *derive from*, emanate from, go back to, originate in, have one's roots in; *depend on*, hinge, pivot, turn, hang.

adv. *consequently*, hence, as a result, in consequence.

134 MOTIVE
See also **132** (cause); **551** (persuasion).

n. *motive*, reason, hypothesis, theory, inference, assumption, grounds, basis; *explanation*, occasion, pretext, excuse, justification, rationale; *motivation*, impetus, driving force, impulsion, mainspring, trigger, inspiration, inducement, carrot; incentive; *attribution*, imputation, responsibility, accountability, credit, blame.

adj. *motivated*, caused, inspired, occasioned; *attributable*, assignable, ascribable, accountable, responsible, culpable; *inferred*, assumed, hypothetical, putative.

vb. *motivate*, cause, occasion, instigate, inspire; *attribute*, ascribe, assign, put down to, lay at the door of, blame, implicate; *explain*, account for, justify, interpret; *assume*, infer, derive, hypothesize.

adv. *hence*, for this reason; *therefore*, consequently.

prep. *owing to*, on account of, because of.

135 LACK OF MOTIVE
See also **554** (chance).

n. *lack of motive*, fortuitousness, gratuitousness, arbitrariness, randomness; *chance*, luck, fortune, pot luck, hazard, accident, fluke; *unaccountability*, unpredictability, coincidence, haphazardness, indeterminacy.

adj. *motiveless*, groundless, causeless, gratuitous, uncalled-for, arbitrary, random; *unmotivated*, unintentional, accidental, coincidental, fortuitous, lucky; *unpredictable*, unaccountable, inexplicable, unexpected, chance, haphazard.

vb. *chance*, light upon, stumble upon, hit upon.

adv. *by chance*, accidentally, coincidentally; *unpredictably*, unexpectedly, out of the blue.

136 OPERATION
See also **138** (instrumentality); **567** (means).

n. *operation*, action, agency, influence, power, stress, pressure; *execution*, implementation, performance, application, effect, force; *process*, function, working, running, handling, administration.

adj. *operative*, effective, conducive, influential; *operational*, functional, working, active, live, on-stream; *practical*, feasible, applicable, manageable; *executive*, administrative, managerial.

vb. *operate*, work, function, run, tick over, idle; *execute*, perform, carry out, put into effect/practice; *affect*, influence, work on, act on, take effect; *activate*, power, drive, run, switch on, plug in, wind up.

adv. *into action*, into operation, into force, into play.

137 COUNTERACTION
See also **28** (compensation); **632** (opposition).

n. *counteraction*, opposition, retaliation, reprisals, counterattack, counterblast, counterrevolution; *reaction*, response, retort, riposte, repercussion, backlash; *recoil*, resistance, friction, drag; *compensation*, counterbalance, counterweight, foil, corrective, checks and balances, antidote, remedy, cure.

adj. *counteractive*, counter, contrary, counterproductive, opposing, retaliatory; *reactionary*, counterrevolutionary, resistant, recalcitrant; *compensatory*, countervailing, makeweight; *restorative*, corrective, remedial, curative.

vb. *counteract*, counter, oppose, combat, militate against; *react*, retaliate, respond, answer, riposte, retort; *com-*

pensate, offset, make up for, counterbalance, neutralize, defuse, cancel out; *check*, prevent, foil, thwart, cross, obviate; *remedy*, cure, restore, correct.

138 INSTRUMENTALITY
See also **136** (operation); **568** (tool); **631** (help).

n. *instrumentality*, agency, means, services, action, aid, assistance; *intervention*, intercession, mediation, intermediary; *mechanism*, device, contrivance, deus ex machina, means to an end; *utility*, usefulness, helpfulness, serviceability, convenience, handiness.

adj. *instrumental*, effective, influential, conducive; *useful*, serviceable, practicable, convenient, handy; *helpful*, contributory, favourable, supportive.

vb. *be instrumental*, work, act, influence, affect; *serve*, help, encourage, support, promote, foster, advance; *intervene*, intercede, interpose, mediate, have a hand in.

prep. *by means of*, through, via, per; *thanks to*, courtesy of; *on behalf of*, for the sake of.

139 INFLUENCE
See also **551** (persuasion).

n. *influence*, dominance, sway, ascendancy, power, hegemony; *leverage*, pull, weight, clout (*colloq.*), whip hand, upper hand, casting vote; *persuasion*, suggestion, manipulation, string-pulling, lobbying, propaganda, soft sell, brainwashing; *charm*, magnetism, charisma, hypnotism, mesmerism, sorcery, magic, seduction, fascination; *patronage*, nepotism, freemasonry, old-boy network, friend at court, powers that be, Establishment; *moving force*, lobby, pressure group, ginger group, power behind the throne, grey eminence, agent provocateur, mole; *infiltration*, subversion, entryism.

adj. *influential*, important, dominant, prevailing, powerful, pervasive; *persuasive*, suggestive, convincing, manipulative, subversive; *charming*, charismatic, magnetic, hypnotic, mesmeric, bewitching, fascinating.

vb. *influence*, dominate, override, out-

weigh, master, subdue, have under one's thumb. *have influence*, count, tell, weigh, matter, carry weight, wear the trousers, call the tune; *persuade*, convince, manipulate, sway, have the ear of, work on, lean on, prevail on, pressurize, lobby; *charm*, mesmerize, hypnotize, bewitch, fascinate, captivate; *permeate*, infiltrate, penetrate, subvert, undermine.

140 TENDENCY
See also **430** (misjudgment).

n. *tendency*, trend, tenor, course, direction, mainstream, current; *inclination*, leaning, penchant, proclivity, propensity, predilection, soft spot; *predisposition*, cast, bent, bias, prejudice; *proneness*, liability, susceptibility, likelihood, vulnerability; *aptitude*, instinct, flair, gift.

adj. *tending*, conducive, leading, tendentious, biased, partisan, partial; *predisposed*, inclined, prone, apt, liable, susceptible, likely.

vb. *tend*, incline, lean, gravitate, verge; *predispose*, bias, prejudice, influence.

141 POWER
See also **143** (strength); **145** (vigour).

n. *power*, might, omnipotence, rule, authority, dominance, ascendancy, hegemony, influence, sway; *strength*, forcefulness, cogency, impact, effectiveness, teeth, muscle; *vigour*, life, energy, dynamism, drive, overdrive; *ability*, capability, potential, competence, reach, grasp, aptitude; *powerful person*, chief, mandarin, mogul, magnate, tycoon, big battalions, power behind the throne, linchpin, moving spirit, driving force; *energy*, impetus, momentum, propulsion, drive, thrust, pressure, horsepower, locomotion; *energy source*, fuel, gas, electricity, atomic power, wave power, solar energy, fossil fuel, hydroelectricity; *motor*, engine, generator, turbine, dynamo, battery, reactor, power station.

adj. *powerful*, mighty, all-powerful, omnipotent, dominant, influential, authoritative; *strong*, forceful, cogent, telling, hard-hitting, effective; *able*, capable, competent, efficacious, adequate; *powered*, locomotive, automated, self-propelled, souped-up; *active*, live, operative, on-stream, working.

vb. *power*, drive, charge, propel, electrify, automate, mechanize; *activate*, plug in, switch on, wire up; *strengthen*, invigorate, energize, galvanize, boost; *dominate*, rule, govern, hold sway, prevail, pull rank, rule the roost, wear the trousers (*colloq.*).

adv. *in power*, in force, in operation.

142 POWERLESSNESS

See also **144** (weakness); **593** (deterioration).

n. *powerlessness*, impotence, helplessness, defencelessness, vulnerability; *weakness*, frailness, feebleness, debility, disablement, handicap, senility; *inability*, incapacity, incompetence, unfitness, ineffectiveness, inadequacy; *prostration*, exhaustion, paralysis, lifelessness, torpor, inertia, atrophy; *broken reed*, sitting duck, lame duck, paper tiger, man of straw.

adj. *powerless*, impotent, helpless, defenceless, vulnerable; *weak*, frail, feeble, disabled, handicapped, hamstrung, senile, debilitated, incapacitated; *prostrate*, inert, paralysed, lifeless, torpid, comatose, exhausted, all in, laid up, invalid, bedridden; *unable*, incompetent, ineffectual, unfit, inadequate, spineless, toothless.

vb. *make powerless*, disarm, disable, put out of action, neutralize, invalidate; *weaken*, undermine, sap, cripple, handicap, cramp someone's style, put a spoke in someone's wheel; *prostrate*, exhaust, paralyse, atrophy, drain.

adv. *out of commission*, hors de combat, in dock (*colloq.*).

143 STRENGTH

See also **141** (power); **664** (compulsion).

n. *strength*, might, brute force, muscle, brawn, toughness, hardness, steel, iron; *potency*, virility, manliness, ruggedness, fitness, health, soundness;

endurance, resistance, durability, stamina, staying power, grit, backbone, guts, bottle (*colloq.*), pluck; *vigour*, force, energy, assertiveness, strength of character, resolution; *invulnerability*, impregnability, impermeability, indomitability, resilience; *athleticism*, gymnastics, weightlifting, body building, pumping iron (*colloq.*); *weightlifter*, strong man, amazon, Samson, Tarzan, Hercules, muscleman, he-man (*colloq.*), beefcake (*colloq.*); *support*, reinforcement, rampant, buttress, mainstay, pillar, tower of strenth.

adj. *strong*, powerful, mighty, well-armed, tough, hard, steely; *potent*, virile, manly, rugged, robust, fit, healthy, sound; *vigorous*, energetic, dynamic, forceful, assertive, resolute; *invulnerable*, impregnable, impermeable, indestructible, durable; *resilient*, plucky, indomitable, unflagging, staunch, stalwart, doughty; *athletic*, able-bodied, muscular, brawny, burly, hefty, strapping, amazonian.

vb. *strengthen*, reinforce, fortify, buttress, brace, steel, nerve, gird one's loins; *assert*, affirm, stress, underline, emphasize; *invigorate*, energize, hearten, enliven, animate.

adv. *strongly*, with might and main, forcefully.

144 WEAKNESS

See also **142** (powerlessness).

n. *weakness*, feebleness, puniness, slightness, frailty; *flimsiness*, fragility, brittleness, delicacy, fineness; *ineffectiveness*, impotence, powerlessness, helplessness, vulnerability, uselessness; *softness*, tenderness, womanliness, effeminacy, effeteness; *limpness*, flaccidity, flabbiness, slackness, sponginess; *debility*, infirmity, weakliness, decrepitude, sickliness, invalidism, valetudinarianism; *prostration*, fatigue, languor, listlessness, lethargy, lassitude; *insipidness*, tastelessness, wateriness, thinness, pallor, bloodlessness, anaemia; *instability*, insecurity, shakiness, unsteadiness, precariousness, house of cards, matchwood; *weak point*, soft spot, foible, Achilles' heel, inadequacy, defect, flaw, weak link, chink in someone's armour; *weakling*, milksop, sissy, lame duck, invalid, jellyfish, doormat, wet (*colloq.*), wimp (*colloq.*), drip (*colloq.*), weed (*colloq.*).

adj. *weak*, feeble, puny, slight, frail, fragile, brittle, delicate, flimsy; *ineffectual*, impotent, powerless, helpless, unarmed, unaided, vulnerable; *soft*, tender, womanly, effeminate, babyish, effete; *weak-willed*, irresolute, gutless, weak-kneed, spineless, wet (*colloq.*), drippy (*colloq.*), wimpish (*colloq.*); *limp*, flaccid, flabby, slack, spongy; *infirm*, sickly, weakly, decrepit, invalid, disabled, lame, halt; *prostrate*, weary, languid, spent, listless, lethargic, burnt-out; *insipid*, tasteless, watery, thin, pale, anaemic, dilute, wishy-washy (*colloq.*), washed out; *unstable*, insecure, shaky, wobbly, rocky, rickety, precarious, ramshackle, gimcrack.

vb. *weaken*, sap, undermine, disarm; *disable*, maim, lame, cripple, enfeeble, debilitate, enervate; *decline*, dwindle, fade, wither, wilt, languish, flag, sag, slacken; *mitigate*, extenuate, lessen, soften, cushion, muffle, blunt; *dilute*, thin, water down, adulterate, tone down, moderate; *shake*, waver, quaver, tremble, totter, teeter, dodder.

145 VIGOUR

See also **141** (power); **507** (emphasis).

n. *vigour*, energy, life, vitality, dynamism, dash, elan, liveliness, impetus, vim, pep (*colloq.*), zap (*colloq.*), oomph (*colloq.*); *enthusiasm*, fervour, zest, joie de vivre, gusto, relish; *enterprise*, initiative, drive, dynamism, aggressiveness, thrust, punch, attack, verve, get-up-and-go (*colloq.*); *spirit*, mettle, fire, guts (*colloq.*), pluck, spunk (*colloq.*), bottle (*colloq.*); *stimulus*, boost, shot in the arm, fillip, tonic, stimulant, pick-me-up (*colloq.*), upper (*colloq.*), pep talk (*colloq.*); *whiz kid*, livewire (*colloq.*), bright spark (*colloq.*), self-starter, go-getter (*colloq.*).

adj. *vigorous*, energetic, lively, animated, racy, spirited, zappy (*colloq.*); *enthusiastic*, keen, go-ahead, enterprising, high-powered; *forceful*, aggressive, thrusting, punchy (*colloq.*); *stimulating*, invigorating, bracing, tonic, brisk, no-nonsense (*colloq.*).

vb. *invigorate*, enliven, animate, energize, vitalize, galvanize, electrify, ginger up, put a bomb under (*colloq.*); *stimulate*, rouse, encourage, boost, kindle, inflame, intoxicate; *drive*, thrust, push, attack, go at, pull out all the stops; *be vigorous*, thrive, blossom, bloom, flourish, be in fine fettle.

adv. *vigorously*, hard, full steam ahead.

146 INERTNESS

See also **144** (weakness); **608** (inaction); **610** (inactivity).

n. *inertness*, inactivity, languor, sluggishness, lethargy, inertia, torpor, listlessness; *immobility*, stillness, stagnation, hibernation, dormancy; *dullness*, apathy, passivity, sloth, indolence, laziness, stolidity, impassivity, nonchalance.

adj. *inert*, inactive, languid, lethargic, sluggish, torpid; *immobile*, still, stagnant, dormant, fallow; *lifeless*, heavy, sleepy, numb, paralysed; *dull*, apathetic, lazy, idle, slothful, indolent, passive, indifferent, nonchalant, stolid.

vb. *be inert*, stagnate, vegetate, tick over, idle; *sleep*, doze, slumber, hibernate.

147 VIOLENCE

See also **639** (attack).

n. *violence*, vehemence, intensity, force, power; *outbreak*, outburst, spasm, paroxysm, convulsion, eruption, earthquake, upheaval, explosion, cataclysm; *onrush*, torrent, tidal wave, hurricane, storm, tempest; *turbulence*, turmoil, uproar, furore; *ferocity*, savagery, brutality, frenzy, rage, passion; *assault*, hammering (*colloq.*), thrashing, grievous bodily harm, rape, battering, mugging; *fight*, punchup (*colloq.*), dustup (*colloq.*), brawl, melee, aggro (*colloq.*), bovver (*colloq.*), hooliganism, thuggery, riot, mayhem, mob rule; *killing*, murder, homicide, massacre, slaughter, carnage; *brute*, beast, savage, barbarian, thug, hooligan, ruffian, bully, yob (*colloq.*); *killer*, assassin, murderer, butcher, axeman, hatchetman; *fury*, spitfire, termagant, virago, hothead, firebrand.

adj. *violent*, vehement, intense, forceful, powerful; *turbulent*, tumultuous, cataclysmic, explosive, convulsive, volcanic; *wild*, frenzied, frantic, hysterical, unrestrained, unbridled, sweeping, overwhelming; *rampant*, raging, rabid, fuming, tempestuous, stormy; *fierce*, ferocious, vicious, brutal, savage, murderous, bloodthirsty; *aggressive*, belligerent, tough, rowdy, boisterous, riotous.

vb. *be violent*, convulse, erupt, explode, burst, let fly, lash out; *rage*, storm, fume, rant, see red, go berserk; *charge*, stampede, rampage, riot, run amuck; *surge*, gush, flood, inundate, overwhelm; *dash*, hurtle, rush, fling, pelt, hurl; *smash*, crash, break, shatter, demolish, pulverize, crush; *assault*, rape, violate, strike, punch, mug, lay into, beat up, thrash, hammer (*colloq.*), batter, work over, dust up (*colloq.*); *make violent*, rouse, goad, lash, whip up, exasperate, infuriate, enrage, madden.

adv. *violently*, tooth and nail, hammer and tongs; *precipitately*, headlong, headfirst, at full tilt.

148 MODERATION

See also 63 (middle); 733 (impassivity).

n. *moderation*, reasonableness, rationality, sanity, sobriety, common sense; *calmness*, composure, restraint, self-control, cool-headedness, impassivity; *middle way*, golden mean, happy medium, middle of the road; *mildness*, harmlessness, innocuousness, gentleness, blandness; *alleviation*, mitigation, abatement, relief, easing, relaxation; *pacification*, mollification, appeasement; *palliative*, balm, emollient, lubricant, salve, sedative, tranquillizer, opiate, downer (*colloq.*), analgesic; *mediator*, peacemaker, arbitrator, conciliator; *brake*, check, curb, rein, damper, cushion, wet blanket (*colloq.*);

moderate, centrist, reformist, pinko (*colloq.*), woolly liberal (*colloq.*).

adj. *moderate*, reasonable, rational, sensible, sane, sober; *calm*, composed, impassive, restrained, low-key, subdued, tame; *mild*, gentle, soothing, bland, anodyne, insipid; *average*, middlebrow, middle-of-the-road.

vb. *moderate*, temper, mitigate, lessen, tone down, dampen, muffle, blunt, take the edge off; *curb*, check, quell, subdue, tame, bring to heel; *alleviate*, allay, assuage, relieve, deaden, numb, dull; *pacify*, calm, appease, lull, soothe, pour oil on troubled waters.

adv. *in moderation*, within reason, within bounds; *gradually*, softly softly (*colloq.*).

149 PRODUCTION

See also 152 (fertility); 611 (work).

n. *production*, creation, origination, generation, invention; *manufacture*, fabrication, concoction, preparation, formation, construction; *industrialization*, mass production, factory farming, assembly line, automation, new technology; *industry*, trade, craft, skill, cottage industry, homeworking; *product*, end-product, output, throughput, yield, productivity, produce, crop, harvest, by-product, waste, extract; *artefact*, handiwork, ware, goods, merchandise, finished article; *composition*, piece, opus, oeuvre, work of art, chef d'oeuvre, masterpiece, brainchild; *handicrafts*, ceramics, pottery, metalworking, silversmithing, weaving, tapestry, embroidery, patchwork, crochet, knitting, macramé; *producer*, creator, maker, originator, inventor, founder, author, architect, engineer, composer, designer; *manufacturer*, industrialist, workman, labourer, craftsman, artisan; *farmer*, grower, breeder, market gardener.

adj. *productive*, creative, generative, inventive, constructive; *fruitful*, rich, prolific, fertile, profitable; *synthetic*, artificial, man-made, ready-made.

vb. *produce*, create, originate, generate, invent, devise, conceive, design; *make*, fabricate, concoct, frame, fashion, forge, cast, coin, mint, cobble together; *craft*, sew, knit, spin, weave, embroider; *manufacture*, machine, synthesize, process, treat, mass-produce, assemble, turn out; *accomplish*, achieve, contrive, engineer, develop, exploit; *farm*, grow, breed, cultivate, propagate.

150 DESTRUCTION

See also 324 (killing); 593 (deterioration).

n. *destruction*, obliteration, nullification, abolition, deterioration, erosion, eradication, extirpation; *extinction*, annihilation, extermination, liquidation, decimation, assassination, murder, slaughter, massacre, genocide; *demolition*, bombardment, blitz, scorched-earth policy, defoliation; *disaster*, catastrophe, cataclysm, holocaust, earthquake, flood, disaster area; *devastation*, chaos, ruin, wreckage, damage, harm, ravages, shambles; *collapse*, smash-up, crash, collision, wreck; *destructiveness*, vandalism, sabotage, arson, character assassination, smear campaign; *destroyer*, vandal, wrecker, arsonist, saboteur, killer, assassin, butcher, hitman (*colloq.*); *blight*, bane, cancer, canker, poison, toxin, corrosive; *battering ram*, bulldozer, steamroller, juggernaut.

adj. *destructive*, disastrous, catastrophic, cataclysmic, ruinous, fatal, terminal; *harmful*, injurious, pernicious, corrosive; *murderous*, homicidal, suicidal, deadly, lethal, self-destructive; *destroyed*, ruined, undone, washed up, burnt-out, kaput (*colloq.*), done for (*colloq.*).

vb. *destroy*, harm, damage, injure, erode; *obliterate*, nullify, delete, expunge, erase, cancel out, undo, unmake; *abolish*, extinguish, eradicate, extirpate, stamp out, wipe out, annihilate; *exterminate*, liquidate, assassinate, decimate, murder, massacre, slaughter, butcher, do in (*colloq.*); *engulf*, consume, devour, swallow up, swamp, drown; *devastate*, ravage, despoil, ransack, pillage, lay waste; *flatten*, blitz, raze, level, bulldoze, demolish; *ruin*, wreck, vandalize, sabotage, torpedo, sink, scuttle, scupper (*colloq.*), put the mockers/kibosh on (*colloq.*); *dismantle*, scrap, shred, pulp, break up, make mincemeat of (*colloq.*); *crash*, collide, write off, smash up, shatter; *suppress*, quell, quash, smother, stifle, strangle, suffocate, nip in the bud; *be destroyed*, go under/down, go to rack and ruin, go to the wall, succumb, go to the dogs (*colloq.*).

adv. *on the scrapheap*, on the rocks (*colloq.*).

151 REPRODUCTION

See also 21 (imitation); 88 (repetition).

n. *reproduction*, procreation, regeneration, reincarnation; *reduplication*, repetition, multiplication, mass production; *remake*, reprint, reissue, repeat, copy; *renewal*, revitalization, resurgence, renaissance, rebirth, resuscitation, revival.

adj. *reproductive*, regenerative, procreative, prolific; *resurgent*, born-again, rejuvenated.

vb. *reproduce*, procreate, breed, multiply; *repeat*, duplicate, copy, mass-produce, churn out; *remake*, rebuild, reprint, reissue; *renew*, revive, resurrect, resuscitate.

152 FERTILITY

See also 149 (production).

n. *fertility*, fecundity, virility, potency; *procreation*, propagation, proliferation, multiplication, reproduction, facts of life, birds and the bees (*colloq.*); *productiveness*, abundance, richness, glut, cornucopia, horn of plenty, baby boom, population explosion; *motherhood*, maternity, childbearing, midwifery, obstetrics; *fertilization*, insemination, pollination, irrigation, artificial insemination, conception, gestation, pregnancy, test-tube baby; *childbirth*, birthing, parturition, confinement, delivery, happy event, stillbirth, miscarriage; *womb*, uterus, ovary, cervix, loins; *ovum*, seed, sperm, semen, pollen; *genitals*, private parts, vagina, cunt (*vulg.*), twat (*vulg.*), fanny (*colloq.*), pudenda, penis, phallus, pizzle, cock (vulg.), prick (*vulg.*), dick (*colloq.*), testicles, balls (*vulg.*), bollocks (*vulg.*), goolies (*vulg.*).

adj. *fertile*, fecund, procreative, potent, virile, productive, seminal; *pregnant*, gravid, expecting, broody, with child, antenatal, obstetric; *abundant*, copious, rich, plentiful, fruitful.

vb. *fertilize*, impregnate, inseminate, pollinate, irrigate, manure; *procreate*, propagate, breed, spawn, cultivate, rear, multiply, increase; *conceive*, fall, beget, engender, sire; *give birth*, bring forth, drop, lamb, farrow, whelp, pup, litter, hatch; *proliferate*, sprout, mushroom, blossom, burgeon, bloom, flourish.

adv. *with child*, in the family way, up the spout (*colloq.*), in the club (*colloq.*).

153 INFERTILITY
See also 579 (uselessness).

n. *infertility*, sterility, impotence, barrenness, unproductiveness, aridity; *fruitlessness*, futility, unprofitability, zero growth, stagnation; *desolation*, desert, tundra, wasteland, dustbowl, famine, dearth; *contraception*, family planning, birth control, abortion, sterilization, vasectomy, menopause, castration; *eunuch*, castrato, gelding, neuter, freemartin, hermaphrodite.

adj. *infertile*, sterile, impotent, barren, childless, subfertile; *unproductive*, fruitless, arid, unprofitable, fallow, stillborn.

vb. *be unproductive*, lie fallow, stagnate, wither on the vine, abort, miscarry, die aborning; *sterilize*, castrate, emasculate, geld, neuter, spay.

154 PARENT
See also 12 (family relations).

n. *parent*, parenthood, parenting, single parent, one-parent family, donor, godparent, foster parent, guardian; *family*, blood, stock, strain, line, pedigree, extraction, ancestry; *motherhood*, maternity, mother-to-be, earth mother, surrogate mother, mum (*colloq.*), mater, mamma, matron, matriarch; *fatherhood*, paternity, sire, progenitor,

dad (*colloq.*), pater, papa, paterfamilias, patriarch.

adj. *parental*, familial, ancestral; *maternal*, motherly, matronly, matriarchal; *paternal*, fatherly, patriarchal.

vb. *father*, sire, beget.

adv. in loco parentis.

155 OFFSPRING
See also 111 (youth).

n. *offspring*, progeny, issue, young, spawn, litter, brood; *heir*, heiress, successor, descendant, posterity, offshoot, branch, scion, love child, bastard; *descent*, lineage, succession, dynasty, illegitimacy.

adj. *familial*, lineal, filial, hereditary, genetic.

156 SPACE
See also 157 (region).

n. *space*, space-time, extension, outer space; *dimensions*, proportions, size, extent, area, volume, capacity, circumference; *range*, span, compass, coverage, radius, sweep, scope, spread; *region*, expanse, tract, reach, stretch; *room*, latitude, margin, clearance, leeway, legroom, headroom, accommodation.

adj. *spatial*, three-dimensional, spatio-temporal; *extensive*, widespread, far-reaching, global, worldwide; *spacious*, roomy, capacious, voluminous, commodious, expansive.

vb. *extend*, range, spread, stretch, sweep; *span*, straddle, cover, enclose, encompass, contain, accommodate.

adv. *extensively*, far and wide, all over, high and low.

157 REGION
See also 156 (space).

n. *region*, locality, area, zone, belt, heartland, parallel, latitudes, climes, parts, neck of the woods (*colloq.*); *sphere*, field, domain, arena, theatre; *territory*, enclave, ghetto, exclusion zone, precinct; *state*, realm, kingdom, dominion, protectorate, colony, dependency, republic; *district*, county, province, shire, parish, ward, borough, hamlet, village; *city*, town, built-up area, new town, conurbation, inner city, city centre, quarter; *suburb*, dormitory town, green belt, stockbroker belt; *environs*, neighbourhood, vicinity, outskirts, hinterland.

adj. *regional*, zonal, provincial; *local*, municipal, parochial, urban, suburban.

158 LOCATION
See also **165** (habitat).

n. *location*, situation, site, whereabouts, seat; *haunt*, habitat, patch, pitch, beat, territory, stamping ground; *abode*, residence, quarters, address, premises; *place*, spot, corner, nook, niche, hole, slot, groove; *enclosure*, stockade, compound, pen, paddock, field, quadrangle, courtyard; *compartment*, recess, alcove, cubicle, locker, pigeonhole.

vb. *locate*, site, situate, place; *quarter*, billet, station, post; *reside in*, inhabit, frequent, haunt; *pinpoint*, track, home in, zero in.

adv. *locally*, on the spot.

159 SITUATION
See also **160** (placement).

n. *situation*, position, setting, locale, scene, venue; *orientation*, direction, bearings, standpoint, viewpoint; *geography*, topography, orienteering, mapreading.

adj. *situated*, orientated, positioned, located; *geographical*, topographical, directional.

vb. *situate*, site, position, station, post, locate; *orientate*, direct, head.

adv. *in place*, in situ, on site; *on course*, on the right track.

160 PLACEMENT
See also **159** (situation).

n. *placement*, emplacement, installation, settlement, establishment; *post*, position, station, base, depot, camp, encampment, depot; *niche*, resting-place, berth, anchorage, garage, storehouse, repository.

adj. *placed*, lodged, installed, ensconced, entrenched, dug in.

vb. *place*, position, install, station, post; *lodge*, establish, embed, fix, house; *anchor*, moor, tether, berth,

dock, park; *settle*, colonize, encamp, camp, dig in, pitch, squat.

adv. *in position*, in place; *at rest*, at anchor.

161 DISPLACEMENT
See also **58** (disturbance); **266** (expulsion).

n. *displacement*, dislocation, dislodgment, disturbance; *transfer*, transposition, removal, relocation, evacuation; *deposition*, overthrow, coup, takeover, palace revolution; *relegation*, demotion, expulsion, banishment, exile, eviction, homelessness; *dismissal*, sacking, redundancy, lay-off; *displaced person*, refugee, evacuee, waif, stray, guest worker, immigrant.

adj. *displaced*, dislocated, disturbed; *disorientated*, uprooted, rootless, homeless; *misplaced*, mislaid, lost, gone astray.

vb. *displace*, dislocate, dislodge, disturb; *transfer*, transpose, shunt, remove, relocate, evacuate; *depose*, unseat, dethrone, usurp, oust, supersede; *relegate*, demote, dismiss, lay off, sack, fire, kick upstairs (*colloq.*), banish, exile, expel; *misplace*, mislay, lose.

adv. *out of place*, out of joint; *out of the running*, out of the picture, out in the cold (*colloq.*), in limbo.

162 PRESENCE
See also **85** (accompaniment).

n. *presence*, existence, pervasiveness, omnipresence, ubiquitousness; *situation*, location, position, whereabouts; *availability*, readiness, handiness, convenience; *attendance*, appearance, participation, accompaniment; *residence*, occupancy, habitation; *conspicuousness*, obviousness, visibility; *spectator*, onlooker, audience, bystander, eye-witness, participant.

adj. *present*, existent, pervasive, omnipresent, ubiquitous; *available*, ready, handy, convenient; *attendant*, participant, concomitant, accompanying; *resident*, live-in, in-house, residential; *conspicuous*, obvious, visible, eye-catching.

vb. *be present*, pervade, permeate, imbue; *reside*, occupy, inhabit, live in;

participate, take part, watch, witness, assist at, spectate; *attend*, turn up, present oneself, show up, put in an appearance, look in; *be conspicuous*, stand out, stick out like a sore thumb (*colloq.*), make one's presence felt.

adv. *at hand*, on the spot, on the ground; *to hand*, within reach, on call, on tap; *close to*, under one's nose, to one's face, before one's very eyes; *in person*, live; *at home*, in town, on the premises.

163 ABSENCE
See also **2** (nonexistence).

n. *absence*, nonexistence, disappearance, loss; *nonappearance*, nonattendance, absenteeism, truancy, desertion, defection, French leave; *emptiness*, vacuum, blankness, void, vacancy, gap, omission; *lack*, shortage, want, scarcity, deficiency; *absentee*, nonperson, missing person, defector, deserter; *leave of absence*, furlough, holiday, vacation.

adj. *absent*, nonexistent, gone, lost, flown, fled; *away*, out, unavailable, off (*colloq.*); *empty*, vacant, void, blank, vacuous, hollow; *lacking*, missing, minus, devoid, deficient, short; *unoccupied*, deserted, abandoned, depopulated, godforsaken.

vb. *be absent*, stay away, be conspicuous by one's absence, vote with one's feet; *depart*, withdraw, retreat, absent oneself, make oneself scarce (*colloq.*); *abandon*, desert, defect, forsake, walk out on; *miss*, skip, go AWOL, play hooky (*colloq.*).

adv. *in one's absence*, in absentia, behind one's back; *off the premises*, out of house; *on leave*, on vacation, on holiday, out of town.

164 INHABITANT
See also **165** (habitat).

n. *inhabitant*, dweller, citizen, denizen; *occupant*, resident, householder, owner-occupier; *tenant*, lodger, boarder, paying guest, au pair; *inmate*, incumbent, in-patient; *native*, aborigine, local, villager, parishioner, townee, suburbanite, commuter, city slicker (*colloq.*);

cottager, crofter, smallholder, peasant, rustic, yokel, country bumpkin; *incomer*, immigrant, settler, colonist, squatter; *household*, ménage, commune, colony, community, population.

adj. *inhabited*, occupied, rented, leased; *native*, indigenous, aboriginal, ethnic, vernacular; *domestic*, local, household, home.

165 HABITAT
See also **158** (location); **164** (inhabitant); **762** (recreation).

n. *habitat*, abode, dwelling, domicile, residence, haunt, hang-out (*colloq.*); *base*, headquarters, seat, camp, bivouac, pad (*colloq.*); *accommodation*, quarters, billet, lodgings, digs (*colloq.*), squat, hostel, dormitory, dosshouse (*colloq.*); *home*, hearth, fireside, homestead, cradle, home town, birthplace, stamping ground, motherland, fatherland; *lair*, den, burrow, warren, earth, sett, holt, nest, drey, aviary, apiary; *house*, villa, bungalow, chalet, prefab, townhouse, houseboat, caravan, mobile home; *cottage*, cabin, shack, hovel, lean-to, outhouse; *flat*, maisonette, studio, apartment, mews, penthouse, pied-à-terre, bedsitter, granny flat; *mansion*, seat, hall, grange, manor, chateau, stately home; *housing*, conurbation, housing estate/scheme, tower block, slum, shanty town; *stable*, byre, cowshed, sty, kennel, fold, stall, coop, hutch; *hotel*, bed & breakfast, motel, roadhouse, inn, tavern, public house, pub, hostelry, local (*colloq.*), boozer (*colloq.*); *restaurant*, wine bar, bistro, brasserie, trattoria; *cafe*, cafeteria, snack bar, tearoom, canteen, buffet, takeaway, diner; *retreat*, haven, refuge, sanctuary, halfway house, hospice; *park*, gardens, allotment, arbour, pergola, gazebo, folly, conservatory, glasshouse.

adj. *residential*, built-up, metropolitan, urban, surburban; *detached*, semidetached, terraced, purpose-built, multistorey, high/low rise; *rural*, rustic, countrified; *local*, parochial, municipal.

vb. *inhabit*, occupy, people, settle, colonize, populate; *reside*, dwell, sojourn, lodge, put up at, doss down (colloq.), crash (colloq.), camp; frequent, haunt, visit, hang out at (colloq.).

166 CONTENTS

See also **53** (component).

n. contents, ingredients, components, stuffing, filling, centre; insides, guts, entrails, bowels, pith, marrow; containment, load, cargo, shipment, freight.
vb. contain, hold, enclose, conceal; insert, stuff, pack, cram; take in, absorb, assimilate, ingest; containerize, load, freight, ship, transport.

167 CONTAINER

n. container, receptacle, holder, frame; cover, case, envelope, wrapper, packaging, sheath, cocoon; depository, reservoir, store, warehouse, treasury; boxroom, cloakroom, strongroom, cellar, bunker, attic; compartment, locker, cupboard, cabinet, closet; box, chest, casket, coffer, crate, hamper, basket, punnet; suitcase, overnight bag, holdall, grip, trunk, baggage; capsule, pillbox, canister, carton, caddy, tin, can, tub; bag, knapsack, rucksack, haversack, backpack, kitbag, duffel bag; satchel, pannier, creel, saddlebag; purse, wallet, money-belt, briefcase, attaché case, file, portfolio; vessel, barrel, cask, vat, tun, tank, keg, cistern; vase, jug, pitcher, carafe, decanter, vial, phial, flagon, carboy; bucket, pail, bin, hopper, silo; basin, ewer, pan, pot, urn, kettle, cauldron; cup, chalice, goblet, wineglass, schooner, beaker, tumbler, tankard, mug; bottle, demijohn, magnum, jeroboam, rehoboam, methuselah; bowl, porringer, ramekin, tureen; plate, platter, charger, salver.

168 SIZE

See also **23** (quantity); **29** (greatness).

n. size, proportions, dimensions, amplitude, girth, bulk, magnitude; extent, area, volume, mass, weight; largeness, bigness, hugeness, vastness, immensity, enormity; colossus, mountain, skyscraper, pyramid, mausoleum; giant, monster, leviathan, whale, whop-

per (colloq.); fatness, obesity, corpulence, portliness, fleshiness, corporation, beer belly, midriff bulge, spare tyre (colloq.), flab (colloq.); fat person, fattie (colloq.), hulk, Falstaff, Billy Bunter, slimmer, weight watcher.
adj. large, big, sizable, considerable, hefty (colloq.); large-scale, life-size, full-grown, king-size, mammoth, jumbo, outsize, giant; massive, bulky, huge, enormous, hulking, whopping (colloq.); gigantic, colossal, monumental, immense, vast, astronomical, gargantuan, Brobdingnagian; fat, stout, corpulent, obese, overweight, portly, rotund, plump, chubby, podgy, roly-poly, tubby, buxom, pot-bellied, Falstaffian.

169 LITTLENESS

See also **30** (smallness); **179** (shortness).

n. littleness, diminutiveness, minuteness, smallness, scantiness, meagreness, paucity, skimpiness; miniature, mini, baby, microcosm, pinhead, atom, particle, molecule; dwarf, midget, manikin, pygmy, Tom Thumb, homunculus; gnat, flea, sprat, tiddler, minnow, shrimp, runt, small fry; microorganism, microbe, germ, virus, bacterium; microelectronics, microcomputer, microprocessor, integrated circuit; spot, fleck, dot, speck, mote, crumb, grain, granule, drop, shred.
adj. little, small, diminutive, minute, tiny, petite, dainty, dinky (colloq.); small-scale, toy, baby, mini, miniaturized, pint-sized, wee, titchy (colloq.), Lilliputian; dwarfish, puny, runty, stunted, undersized; scanty, meagre, insufficient, skimpy.

170 EXPANSION

See also **33** (increase); **180** (breadth).

n. expansion, increase, enlargement, augmentation, amplification, aggrandizement; development, spread, deployment, sweep, sprawl; inflation, distension, swollenness, inflammation, tumescence, puffiness, turgidity, dilation; extensibility, elasticity, stretchiness, give; *padding*, stuffing, wadding, waffle (*colloq.*), bombast.

adj. *expanded*, inflated, bloated, distended, dilated, taut; *expandable*, stretchy, elastic, extensible; *swollen*, turgid, overblown, tumescent, tumid, bulbous, distended, pot-bellied; *wide*, gaping, flared, bell-bottomed, splayed, spreadeagled, outstretched.

vb. *expand*, broaden, widen, flare, splay; *increase*, augment, enlarge, magnify, wax, amplify; *spread*, develop fan out, deploy, sprawl, mushroom; *inflate*, balloon, belly, dilate, distend, puff up, swell, inflame; *pad*, stuff, bulk up, beef up (*colloq.*).

171 CONTRACTION
See also **34** (decrease); **179** (shortness).

n. *contraction*, shrinkage, reduction, abatement, diminution, decrease, attenuation; *curtailment*, abbreviation, abridgment, constriction, compaction, compression; *decline*, falling-off, slump, recession, squeeze; *compressor*, constrictor, tourniquet, straitjacket, corset.

adj. *contracted*, shrunk, compacted, condensed, abridged, compressed; *constricted*, pinched, drawn, wizened, shrivelled, stunted; *astringent*, tight, constricting, binding.

vb. *contract*, diminish, lessen, decrease, reduce, curtail; *compress*, condense, abridge, abbreviate, boil down; *constrict*, nip, pinch, tighten, clench; *compact*, pack, squeeze, bind, cramp, squash, flatten; *narrow*, taper, attenuate, thin, slim, extrude; *shrivel*, wrinkle, wizen, pucker, crease; *dwarf*, stunt, shorten.

172 DISTANCE
See also **178** (length).

n. *distance*, farness, remoteness, inaccessibility; *extent*, range, reach, span, sweep, coverage; *long distance*, long haul, trek, marathon; *outskirts*, purlieus, periphery, frontier, outback, back of beyond; *horizon*, skyline, background, middle distance; *aloof-*

ness, detachedness, reserve, stand-offishness.

adj. *distant*, far, far-away, far-off, far-flung, farthest; *remote*, outlying, offshore, peripheral, inaccessible, out-of-the-way, godforsaken; *foreign*, antipodean, overseas, exotic; *long-distance*, long-range, long-haul; *aloof*, stand-offish, unapproachable, reserved.

vb. *distance*, outdistance, outstrip, outrun, outdo; *carry*, extend, stretch, reach; *keep one's distance*, keep clear of, give a wide berth to, not touch with a bargepole (*colloq.*).

adv. *afar*, far afield, far off, far and wide, to the ends of the earth; *off the beaten track*, in the middle of nowhere, out in the sticks (*colloq.*); *at a distance*, at arm's length; *out of range*, out of sight, out of earshot.

173 NEARNESS
See also **176** (juxtaposition).

n. *nearness*, proximity, propinquity, juxtaposition, closeness; *locality*, vicinity, neighbourhood, environs; *close range*, close quarters, pointblank range, foreground, ringside seat; *edge*, brink, verge, border; *short distance*, shortcut, beeline, walking distance, hop, step, and jump, stone's throw, spitting distance, hair's breadth; *closeness*, intimacy, understanding, rapport, affection.

adj. *near*, close, approximate, rough; *nearby*, adjoining, local, neighbouring, accessible, handy; *short-distance*, shortrange, short-haul; *close*, affectionate, intimate, inseparable; *crowded*, packed, serried.

vb. *be near*, hug, skirt, brush, graze, skim; *approximate*, approach, be in the right ballpark (*colloq.*); *adjoin*, abut, border, verge, touch; *close up*, close ranks, huddle, press, crowd, jostle, elbow, rub shoulders; *follow*, shadow, tail, dog someone's footsteps, tread on someone's heels.

adv. *nearly*, almost, approximately, circa, thereabouts; *nearby*, close to, face to face, eyeball to eyeball; *within range*, within earshot, in view; *nigh*, at

hand; *practically*, virtually, to all
intents and purposes.

174 INTERVAL
See also 65 (discontinuity).

n. *interval*, space, gap, interstice, hole,
lacuna; *breach*, break, fissure, rupture,
crevice, crack, rift, chasm, gulf; *network*, lattice, mesh, trellis, reticulation;
margin, clearance, leeway, headroom.

adj. *spaced out*, intermittent, sporadic,
periodic; *latticed*, criss-cross, gap-
toothed, crenellated, filigree, lacy.

vb. *space out*, stagger, intersperse;
gape, yawn, split, tear, rend, crack;
lattice, mesh, criss-cross, reticulate,
interweave.

adv. *at intervals*, now and then, off
and on, here and there.

175 LAYER
See also 202 (covering).

n. *layer*, stratum, bed, course, string,
vein, seam, band; *level*, floor, storey,
tier; *thickness*, ply, coat, overlay, topcoat, veneer; *lamina*, sheet, strip, foil,
leaf; *flake*, scale, wafer, slice, lamella,
shavings, peelings, parings; *sandwich*,
double-decker, onion, Chinese boxes,
nest of tables.

adj. *layered*, laminated, lamellate;
flaky, peeling, scaly, squamose; *overlaid*, overlapping, shingled, clinker-
built.

vb. *layer*, laminate, stratify, deck; *overlay*, plate, veneer, coat; *flake*, peel,
pare, shave; *overlap*, tile, flag, shingle.

176 JUXTAPOSITION
see also 173 (nearness); 207 (interface).

n. *juxtaposition*, contiguity, contact,
tangency, proximity; *border*, dividing
line, demarcation, watershed, interface,
meeting, junction.

adj. *juxtaposed*, adjacent, coterminous,
contiguous, adjoining, interconnecting.

vb. *juxtapose*, bring together, butt,
dovetail, overlap; *adjoin*, border, abut,
skirt, fringe, hem.

adv. *side by side*, cheek by jowl, arm
in arm, abreast; *end to end*, bumper to
bumper.

177 MEASUREMENT
See also 23 (quantity).

n. *measurement*, mensuration, triangulation, calculation, computation, quantification; *valuation*, estimation, assessment, appreciation, appraisal;
geometry, trigonometry, surveying,
sounding; *measure*, gauge, scales, balance, ruler, yardstick, footrule, tape
measure; *compass*, callipers, protractor,
sextant, quadrant, theodolite; *meter*,
thermometer, barometer, speedometer,
tacheograph, metronome, Geiger
counter; *reference point*, grid, water
line, tidemark, Plimsoll line, bench
mark.

adj. *metric*, imperial, avoirdupois, troy,
SI.

vb. *measure*, mensurate, compute, calculate, quantify; *estimate*, sound,
reckon, weigh up, pace out, valuate,
assess, gauge; *rule*, graduate, calibrate,
mark off.

178 LENGTH
See also 172 (distance).

n. *length*, extent, expanse, reach,
stretch, span; *lengthening*, elongation,
extension, extrusion; *protraction*, prolongation, slowness, longueur, tedium;
line, queue, file, string, crocodile; *longitude*, parallel, wavelength, waveband,
frequency.

adj. *long*, longitudinal, extended, elongated, extruded; *lengthy*, protracted,
prolonged, long-drawn-out, long-
winded, tedious; *full-length*, uncut,
unabridged.

vb. *lengthen*, elongate, extend, extrude,
stretch, expand; *protract*, prolong,
draw out, spin out, drag out.

adv. *lengthways*, from stem to stern,
from top to toe; *at length*, lengthily,
long.

179 SHORTNESS
See also 169 (littleness); 171 (contraction).

n. *shortness*, scarcity, scantiness,
skimpiness; *abridgment*, condensation,
summary, precis, résumé; *conciseness,*
compression, succintness, terseness,
ellipsis, thumbnail sketch; *brevity*,

transience, fleetingness; *squatness*, dumpiness, stockiness, stubbiness.

adj. *short*, scanty, scarce, insufficient, skimpy; *abridged*, condensed, potted, cut; *concise*, terse, succinct, elliptical, laconic, curt; *brief*, transient, fleeting, short-lived; *curtailed*, foreshortened, truncated, headless, retroussé, blunt; *squat*, dumpy, stocky, petite, stubby, stunted.

vb. *shorten*, cut, curtail, reduce, contract; *abridge*, abbreviate, condense, summarize, precis, telescope, compress; *cut short*, interrupt, truncate, guillotine, behead, foreshorten, dock, prune, lop.

adv. *in short*, briefly, in sum, to cut a long story short, in a nutshell.

180 BREADTH
See also **170** (expansion).

n. *breadth*, width, girth, latitude, span, diameter; *amplitude*, scope, range, extent; *expanse*, panorama, vista, sweep; *broad-mindedness*, tolerance, permissiveness, liberalness.

adj. *broad*, wide, wide-angle, wide-bodied, broad in the beam, broad-shouldered, flared, bell-bottomed; *wide-ranging*, extensive, sweeping, far-reaching; *expansive*, roomy, spacious, ample; *broad-minded*, liberal, tolerant, permissive.

vb. *broaden*, widen, extend, stretch, spread one's wings; *splay*, sprawl, spreadeagle, flare, bell.

adv. *widthways*, across; *broadly*, loosely, roughly.

181 NARROWNESS
See also **171** (contraction); **183** (thinness).

n. *narrowness*, tightness, constriction, compression, contraction; *confinement*, restrictedness, crampedness, overcrowding, tight fit, tight squeeze, no room to swing a cat; *narrow space*, corner, cranny, nook, crack, cleft, chink, crevice; *strait*, gully, gorge, ravine, pass, defile; *neck*, isthmus, chimney, funnel, bottleneck, hourglass; *line*, path, strip, vein, streak, stripe, ribbon, knife-edge, pinhead; *narrow-*

mindedness, intolerance, prejudice, bigotry.

adj. *narrow*, tight, constricted, compressed, pinched; *skin-tight*, figure-hugging, clinging, slinky; *confined*, overcrowded, cramped, restricted, straitened; *narrow-minded*, intolerant, prejudiced, bigoted.

vb. *narrow*, converge, streamline, taper, funnel; *tighten*, contract, pinch, squeeze, constrict; *confine*, cramp, restrict, tether, hobble, fetter; *cling*, hug, cleave, adhere, stick like glue.

182 THICKNESS
See also **168** (size); **317** (semiliquid).

n. *thickness*, solidity, massiveness, bulk, body, density, consistency; *breadth*, ampleness, generosity, fullness, abundance; *viscosity*, tackiness, lumpiness, stodginess, clottedness, pulpiness, soupiness; *sediment*, mud, silt, jelly, curd, soup, pulp; *thickener*, padding, wadding, stuffing, bulk, starch, emulsifier; *thick-headedness*, dullness, stolidness, crassness, stupidity.

adj. *thick*, solid, massive, bulky, dense; *ample*, generous, lavish, full, plentiful, abundant, thick on the ground; *clotted*, lumpy, stodgy, starchy, soupy, pulpy, viscous, tacky; *thick-headed*, dull, stolid, obtuse, crass, stupid, block-headed.

vb. *thicken*, fatten, pad, wad, stuff, bulk up; *solidify*, coagulate, clot, curdle, congeal, gel.

183 THINNESS
See also **171** (contraction); **181** (narrowness).

n. *thinness*, slimness, slenderness, leanness, skinniness, emaciation, anorexia; *thin person*, beanpole, rake, scarecrow, anorexic; *filament*, stalk, tendril, antenna, wire, thread, fibre, capillary; *streak*, strand, splinter, sliver, wafer, shavings; *fineness*, delicacy, transparency, translucency, sheerness; *gauze*, tulle, chiffon, gossamer, cobweb, eggshell; *sparseness*, rarity, infrequency.

adj. *thin*, slim, slender, svelte, willowy,

lissom, lithe, leggy, lean, wiry, sinewy, spare; *underweight*, skinny, skeletal, emaciated, anorexic, spindly, lanky, scraggy, scrawny, gaunt, haggard, raw-boned; *threadlike*, filamentous, fine-spun, stringy, fibrous, streaky; *flimsy*, fragile, delicate, transparent, translucent, sheer, diaphanous; *fluid*, runny, watery, dilute, weak; *sparse*, infrequent, thin on the ground.

vb. *thin*, reduce, slim down, streamline, prune, weed out; *rarefy*, attenuate, dilute, water down, liquefy, melt; *contract*, narrow, taper, shrink.

184 HEIGHT

See also **188** (summit); **190** (verticality); **274** (ascent); **276** (raising).

n. *height*, altitude, elevation, stature, tallness, loftiness, verticality, steepness; *high point*, summit, climax, zenith, ceiling, heavens, sky; *vantage point*, bird's eye view, overview, watchtower, lookout, crow's nest, platform, dais, rostrum; *heights*, highland, upland, mountain, alp, peak, crest, Everest; *cliff*, precipice, bluff, escarpment, slope, gradient, incline; *tower*, spire, steeple, mast, skyscraper, tower block, penthouse, attic, rooftop, Empire State Building; *ascent*, climb, rise, takeoff.

adj. *high*, sky-high, aerial, elevated, lofty; *steep*, vertical, vertiginous, precipitous; *mountainous*, alpine, multi-storey, high-rise, towering, soaring; *tall*, lanky, rangy, gangly.

vb. *heighten*, raise, elevate, uplift; *tower*, soar, hover, overlook, overhang; *ascend*, rise, climb, scale, mount.

adv. *above*, overhead, upstairs, on high, aloft.

185 LOWNESS

See also **189** (base); **275** (descent); **277** (lowering).

n. *lowness*, smallness, squatness, dwarfishness; *flatness*, floor, sea level, plain, foothills, depression, flats, lowland, valley; *low point*, nadir, base, rock bottom, plinth, foot, ground; *underneath*, underside, underbelly,

worm's eye view; *descent*, dip, fall, drop, decline.

adj. *low*, supine, prostrate, laid low, flat out; *bent*, hunched, bowed, stooping, crouched; *small*, squat, petite, stunted, dwarfish; *low-lying*, flat, level, sunken, depressed, subterranean, underground.

vb. *lower*, depress, flatten, level, raze, lay low; *bend*, stoop, hunch, crouch, cower, duck, crawl, kneel, knuckle under, bow; *descend*, fall, tumble, dip, plunge.

adv. *below*, underfoot, underneath, underground, downstairs.

186 DEPTH

See also **277** (lowering).

n. *depth*, deep end, depression, hollow, crater, pit, shaft, well, mine, excavation; *depths*, the deep, abyss, chasm, bowels, underworld; *plunge*, dive, immersion, submersion; *cellar*, basement, vault, crypt, dungeon; *profundity*, deep thought, searching, thoroughness.

adj. *deep*, profound, thorough, probing, in-depth; *cavernous*, yawning, gaping, bottomless, fathomless, unplumbed; *entrenched*, embedded, deep-seated, deep-rooted; *buried*, underground, subterranean, deep-sea, underwater.

vb. *deepen*, darken, worsen, intensify; *excavate*, dig, hollow, gouge out; *sound*, probe, fathom, plumb the depths; *bury*, entrench, embed, entomb; *sink*, submerge, plummet, dive, plunge.

adv. *deeply*, profoundly, intensely; *at bottom*, deep down; *out of one's depth*, over one's head, in deep water.

187 SHALLOWNESS

See also **577** (unimportance).

n. *shallowness*, slightness, cursoriness, superficiality, triviality; *shallows*, shoals, ford, puddle; *surface*, facade, overlay, topcoat, veneer, gloss; *surface wound*, scratch, pinprick, graze, scrape.

adj. *shallow*, slight, perfunctory, cursory, trivial, lightweight; *surface*, skin-deep, cosmetic; *thin*, light, sparse, meagre.

vb. *be shallow*, skim, graze, scrape, brush, tickle; *dabble*, paddle, tinker, scratch the surface, make no impression on; *face*, coat, gloss, veneer, touch up.

188 SUMMIT
See also **184** (height).

n. *summit*, brow, top, peak, crest, pinnacle, tip, crown, apex, vertex; *high point*, zenith, acme, apogee, apotheosis, culmination, climax; *maximum*, highwater mark, ceiling, upper limit; *roof*, coping, capstone, steeple, spire; *head*, pate, poll, noddle (*colloq.*), bonce (*colloq.*), block (*colloq.*), nut (*colloq.*), loaf (*colloq.*). **adj.** *topmost*, top, highest, uppermost, maximal; *crowning*, climactic, supreme. **vb.** *top*, cap, crown, tip, crest; *climax*, peak, go through the roof. **adv.** *at the top of the tree*, on the top rung of the ladder.

189 BASE
See also **185** (lowness); **193** (support).

n. *base*, foot, bottom, root, underneath; *foundation*, basis, infrastructure, underlay, substratum, bedrock; *support*, plinth, pedestal, stand; *ground*, ground floor, basement, mezzanine, entresol; *minimum*, floor, lower limit, rock bottom, nadir; *starting-point*, first base, square one; *foot*, plates of meat (*colloq.*), toe, tootsie (*colloq.*).
adj. *base*, bottom, lowest, underlying, nethermost; *basic*, fundamental, rudimentary, elemental.
vb. *base*, ground, set, establish, found; *support*, underpin, underlie, maintain, uphold; *bottom out*, go through the floor, hit bedrock.
adv. *basically*, at bottom, when you get down to it.

190 VERTICALITY
See also **184** (height).

n. *verticality*, perpendicularity, uprightness, erectness; *steepness*, precipitousness, sheerness, plumbness; *vertical*, upright, pillar, column, ramrod, obelisk, stalagmite, standing-stone, menhir; *wall*, cliff, precipice, bluff, escarpment, sheer drop.

adj. *vertical*, upright, erect, perpendicular, standing, rampant; *steep*, precipitous, sheer, abrupt, plumb, vertiginous.
vb. *be vertical*, rear, stand, be upstanding; *erect*, pitch, raise, upend, cock, stick up, prick up; *plunge*, plummet, drop like a stone.
adv. *vertically*, on end, bolt upright; *from north to south*, from top to toe.

191 HORIZONTALITY
See also **292** (smoothness).

n. *horizontality*, flatness, breadth, levelness, proneness, supineness; *sweep*, vista, panorama, horizon, skyline; *plane*, level, plateau, tableland, steppe, flats, fens; *ledge*, shelf, terrace, tier, balcony; *iron*, bulldozer, steamroller, juggernaut.
adj. *horizontal*, level, plane, even, flush, flat; *prone*, prostrate, reclining, recumbent, supine, couchant.
vb. *be horizontal*, stretch, sweep, sprawl, extend; *recline*, repose, loll, lie back; *flatten*, level, even, roll, iron out, tread, trample, stamp; *raze*, floor, ground, bring down, topple.
adv. *horizontally*, widthways, from side to side, from east to west.

192 SUSPENSION

n. *suspension*, hanging, pendency, fall; *droopiness*, pendulousness, bagginess, looseness; *droop*, sag, hang, swing; *pendulum*, bob, plumbline, pendant, tassel, earring, icicle, stalactite, chandelier, hammock; *curtain*, hanging, drapery, train, skirt; *dewlap*, jowls, lobe, wattle, double chin; *hanger*, suspender, hook, spar, boom, gallows, gibbet, crane, jib.
adj. *suspended*, hanging, pendent; *pendulous*, saggy, droopy, baggy, slack; *loose*, dangling, trailing, weeping; *freehanging*, floating, flyaway, free-floating.
vb. *suspend*, hang, drape, hitch, hook; *fall*, droop, sag, bag; *dangle*, swing, flap, trail, weep, straggle, stream, float.

193 SUPPORT

See also **189** (base).

n. *support*, underpinning, chassis, undercarriage, mounting; *reinforcement*, back-up, encouragement, sponsorship; *foundation*, base, cornerstone, mainstay, bedrock, backbone; *prop*, shore, strut, stay, buttress, pier, beam, joist, rafter, girder; *cane*, staff, walking stick, crutch, shooting stick; *stand*, tripod, trivet, easel, trestle, pedestal, plinth; *bolster*, cushion, mattress, pillow, headrest, footstool; *brace*, truss, corset, foundation garment, splint, surgical collar; *floor*, ground, pavement, terra firma, dry land; *banister*, balustrade, handrail, parapet; *bracket*, shelf, ledge, sill, platform, counter; *pivot*, fulcrum, lever, axle, spine; *supporter*, backer, sponsor, patron, ally, helpmate, tower of strength.

adj. *supporting*, structural, sustaining.

vb. *support*, sustain, maintain, carry, bear, shoulder, uphold; *prop*, shore up, underpin, buttress, brace, bolster, stay; *reinforce*, back, stand by, stick up for, sponsor, buoy up, encourage; *frame*, mount, cradle, pillow, cushion.

194 PARALLELISM

n. *parallelism*, equidistance, coextension; *correspondence*, similarity, analogy, comparison; *parallelogram*, trapezium, rectangle, tramlines, railway lines.

adj. *parallel*, equidistant, coextensive; *similar*, corresponding, analogous, comparable.

vb. *be parallel*, correspond, match, tally; *compare*, liken, equate, draw a parallel.

adv. *in parallel*, side by side, alongside, abreast.

195 OBLIQUENESS

See also **220** (angle).

n. *obliqueness*, indirectness, implicitness, ellipsis; *diagonal*, tangent, zigzag, chevron, herringbone; *deviation*, divergence, bias, slant; *slope*, incline, gradient, ramp, bank; *angle*, batter, bevel, rake, cant, list.

adj. *oblique*, indirect, implicit, ellipti-

cal, circuitous, roundabout; *angled*, squint, aslant, diagonal, transverse, sideways, sidelong.

vb. *be oblique*, lean, list, tilt, pitch, tip; *slope*, incline, shelve, bank, slant, cant, careen; *diverge*, sidestep, jink, dodge, zigzag, edge, sidle; *angle*, bevel, warp, camber, chamfer, mitre.

adv. *obliquely*, at an angle, edgeways, crabwise; *to one side*, out of true, out of plumb.

196 INVERSION

See also **126** (reversion); **129** (exchange).

n. *inversion*, transposition, substitution, swap (*colloq.*), changeover, retroversion, eversion; *anagram*, metathesis, palindrome, spoonerism; *upset*, capsizal, somersault, cartwheel, revolution; *reversal*, about-turn, U-turn, volte-face.

adj. *inverted*, inverse, topsy-turvy, upside-down.

vb. *invert*, transpose, interchange, change round, put the cart before the horse, reverse, turn the tables; *capsize*, overturn, upset, upend, stand on its head; *revolve*, somersault, turn turtle, come full circle; *tip*, tilt, keel over, topple.

adv. *inversely*, vice versa; *back to front*, inside out, upside down, head over heels, topsy turvy.

197 INTERWEAVING

See also **174** (interval); **299** (texture); **569** (materials).

n. *interweaving*, criss-crossing, network, complex, figure of eight, wickerwork, basketry; *grid*, grille, lattice, trellis, reticulation, netting, webbing; *tracery*, fretwork, filigree, honeycomb, mesh, openwork, yarn, fabric, textile; *braid*, wreath, plait, skein, cat's cradle, knot, tangle, snarl; *cross*, intersection, crossroads, crucifix, ankh, saltire, swastika.

adj. *interwoven*, interlocking, pleached, criss-cross, cruciform; *complex*, intricate, involved, tangled, ravelled, matted.

vb. *interweave*, interlace, interlock, intertwine; *plait*, braid, wreathe, pleach, twist, spin, weave, darn; *cross*, intersect, cut across, criss-cross; *enmesh*, entangle, ravel, snarl, embroil, implicate, involve.

198 EXTERIOR
See also **6** (extraneousness); **52** (exclusion).

n. *exterior*, periphery, circumference, perimeter, sidelines; *surface*, appearance, face, facade, shell, mask; *externalization*, extroversion, embodiment, concretization, materialization; *exclusion*, eviction, expulsion, ejection; *outside*, out of doors, open air, great outdoors, outdoor type, fresh-air fiend; *outside world*, parole, day release, day boy, outsider, ex-prisoner.

adj. *exterior*, external, outlying, peripheral, extraneous; *outer*, surface, superficial, prima facie, skin-deep, cosmetic, facial; *extrovert*, outward-looking, outgoing; *outside*, outdoor, out-of-house, extramural, public.

vb. *externalize*, embody, body forth, project, materialize; *expel*, eject, exclude, evict, banish; *cover*, surround, circumscribe, enclose.

adv. *on the outside*, out in the cold, in limbo; *on the face of it*, to all appearances, at first sight; *outside*, in the open, al fresco, out and about.

199 INTERIOR
See also **5** (essence); **166** (contents).

n. *interior*, inside, centre, heartland, core, hub, nub, heart, nerve centre; *pith*, marrow, quick, kernel, heartwood; *insides*, innards, inner man, vitals, viscera, entrails, guts, bowels; *introversion*, introspection, self-absorption, egotism; *insider*, inmate, internee, boarder, stay-at-home, homebody; *insertion*, injection, introduction, intromission; *absorption*, assimilation, incorporation, ingestion.

adj. *interior*, internal, inner, innermost, central; *inside*, private, intimate, domestic, home, indoor, in-house; *endemic*, deep-seated, ingrained, ingrown; *introverted*, inward-looking, introspective.

vb. *internalize*, incorporate, assimilate, absorb, ingest, inhale; *enclose*, enfold,

embrace, encapsulate; *confine*, intern, imprison, shut in.

adv. *inside*, indoors, at home, en famille; *inwardly*, deep down, at heart.

200 CENTRE
See also **63** (middle).

n. *centre*, heart, nucleus, hub, epicentre, bull's eye; *middle*, waistline, midriff, diameter, watershed, parting; *pivot*, fulcrum, hinge, axis; *focus*, centre of attraction, cynosure, centrepiece; *meeting point*, junction, rallying point, node; *centrality*, importance, relevance.

adj. *central*, focal, key, crucial, vital, pivotal; *centripetal*, convergent.

vb. *centralize*, converge, concentrate, focus, home in on, zero in on; *centre on*, hinge on, turn on, pivot on.

adv. *at the heart*, at the core.

201 LINING
See also **202** (covering).

n. *lining*, liner, facing, interlining, inlay; *filling*, wadding, padding, quilting, stuffing; *insulation*, soundproofing, backing, panelling, cladding; *coating*, furring, encrustation, scale.

vb. *line*, face, interline, inlay; *fill*, stuff, wad, pad, quilt, pack; *coat*, fur, encrust.

202 COVERING
See also **175** (layer); **201** (lining); **378** (screen).

n. *covering*, surface, overlay, overlap, superimposition; *cover*, coating, topping, wrapping, packaging, lagging; *lid*, flap, shutter, trapdoor, cap, stopper, plug, bung; *envelope*, sheath, scabbard, ferule, holster; *tarpaulin*, loose cover, dustsheet, pillowcase, tea cosy; *case*, wrapper, dust jacket, boards, record sleeve, folder; *roof*, thatch, canopy, awning, tent, marquee; *hood*, umbrella, sunshade, blind, screen, curtain; *cocoon*, shroud, winding sheet, swaddling clothes, bandage; *skin*, epidermis, integument, bark, peel, rind, husk, pod, jacket; *shell*, armour, carapace, shield, crust, scab; *fur*, pelt, fleece, hair, hide, plumage; *blanket*, sheet, mantle, robe, cloak, veil, pall, mask, disguise; *veneer*, varnish, lacquer, enamel, glaze, paint, whitewash; *flooring*, linoleum, vinyl, matting, paving, cobblestones, screed, asphalt, tarmac.

adj. *covered*, overlaid, surfaced, paved, metalled; *wrapped*, veiled, cloaked, clad, enveloped.

vb. *cover*, overlay, superimpose, layer; *coat*, spread, smear, smother; *envelop*, cloak, blanket, shroud; *wrap*, bandage, swathe, cocoon; *encase*, encapsulate, enclose, sheathe, box, pack; *roof*, thatch, tile, slate, cap, top; *surface*, floor, pave, metal, tarmac; *paint*, render, whitewash, varnish, veneer, lacquer, enamel, glaze; *mask*, hood, conceal, disguise, draw a veil over.

203 UNCOVERING
See also **205** (undress); **469** (disclosure).

n. *uncovering*, stripping, denudation, defoliation, shedding, moulting; *bareness*, undress, nakedness, baldness, alopecia; *disclosure*, unveiling, revelation, exposure; *paint-remover*, stripper, solvent, depilatory, hair-remover, defoliant; *detective*, private eye, sleuth, investigator.

adj. *uncovered*, bare, naked, stripped, denuded, threadbare; *hairless*, bald, leafless, plucked, skinned, cleanshaven, thin on top.

vb. *uncover*, divest, disrobe, strip; *skin*, flay, scalp, pluck, peel, husk, pod, shell; *shed*, cast, moult, slough; *denude*, lay bare, defoliate, devastate; *unpack*, unwrap, unfold, expose; *disclose*, divulge, reveal, unmask, unveil, take the lid off (*colloq.*).

204 DRESS
See also **202** (covering).

n. *dress*, cover, clothing, apparel, attire, garb, costume, raiment; *wardrobe*, outfit, ensemble, rig-out (*colloq.*), wear, gear, togs (*colloq.*), clobber (*colloq.*), duds (*colloq.*); *garment*, coordinates, separates, underwear, lingerie, outerwear, headgear, footwear; *dressing-up*, evening dress, white tie, finery,

toilette, Sunday best, best bib and tucker, glad rags (*colloq.*), fancy dress; *uniform*, regalia, livery, subfusc, weeds, mourning, khaki, fatigues; *old clothes*, rags, hand-me-downs, cast-offs; *clothier*, tailor, costumier, outfitter, designer, couturier; *fashion*, rag trade, haute couture, high fashion.

adj. *dressed*, clad, decent, got up, overdressed, dressed up to the nines (*colloq.*), tarted up (*colloq.*), dolled up (*colloq.*); *well-dressed*, soigné, groomed, fashionable, well turned-out, smart; *tailored*, bespoke, made-to-measure, custom-made, off-the-peg, ready-to-wear.

vb. *dress*, clothe, array, robe, garb, deck out; *wear*, don, sport, try on, slip on, throw on; *dress up*, spruce up, titivate, prink, smarten up.

205 UNDRESS
See also **203** (uncovering).

n. *undress*, casual wear, civvies, plain clothes, mufti, dishabille; *nakedness*, nudity, indecent exposure, naturism, striptease, birthday suit (*colloq.*); *stripper*, ecdysiast, flasher (*colloq.*), streaker (*colloq.*), exhibitionist, nudist, naturist.

adj. *undressed*, bare, half-dressed, underdressed, barelegged, barefooted, naked, nude, starkers (*colloq.*); *décolleté*, plunging, low-necked, revealing, skimpy, mini.

vb. *undress*, strip, peel off (*colloq.*), disrobe, divest oneself; *undo*, untie, unbutton, unzip; *take off*, throw off, slip out of.

adv. *in the nude*, in the altogether (*colloq.*), in the buff (*colloq.*), in the raw (*colloq.*), without a stitch on.

206 SURROUNDINGS
See also **210** (enclosure).

n. *surroundings*, milieu, environment, background, setting, frame; *circumference*, perimeter, periphery, outskirts, boundary, environs, purlieus; *neighbourhood*, vicinity, precincts, region; *ambience*, atmosphere, mood, climate. **adj.** *surrounding*, peripheral, environmental, climatic, ambient, atmospheric.

vb. *surround*, encompass, encircle, envelop, enclose, embrace; *ring*, circumscribe, contain, cordon off, hem, circle.

adv. *on all sides*, all around, to right and to left.

207 INTERFACE

See also **176** (juxtaposition); **269** (insertion).

n. *interface*, meeting point, junction, crossroads, intersection; *boundary*, frontier, divide, watershed, parting; *midpoint*, median, midriff, diaphragm; *partition*, curtain, screen, party wall, buffer, bulkhead; *intervention*, intercession, interception, interference.

adj. *intervening*, interjacent, juxtaposed; *intermediate*, coterminous, contiguous; *interfering*, intrusive, obtrusive.

vb. *put between*, layer, sandwich, wedge, bracket; *interpose*, intercalate, introduce, interleave, interlard; *interfere*, intercede, intercept, intervene; *divide*, come between, separate, demarcate.

208 OUTLINE

See also **223** (circularity).

n. *outline*, profile, silhouette, relief, contour, shape; *frame*, border, surround, rim, edge, periphery, circumference; *sketch*, diagram, figure, delineation; *broad/rough outline*, skeleton, germ, gist, embryo.

vb. *outline*, delineate, trace, frame, silhouette, profile; *sketch*, jot, rough out, map out, block out.

209 EDGE

See also **211** (limit).

n. *edge*, verge, brink, fringe, margin, tip, corner; *lip*, rim, brim, flange, welt; *boundary*, extremity, outer limit, perimeter, confines; *coastline*, seaboard, littoral, shoreline, beach; *roadside*, kerb, verge, gutter, hard shoulder; *threshold*, sill, doorstep, porch; *edging*, frame, mounting, hem, border, frill, trim, piping.

adj. *marginal*, peripheral, borderline, fringe; *riverside*, riparian, wayside, roadside; *scalloped*, bevelled, deckle-edged.

vb. *edge*, trim, hem, fringe, border; *rim*, skirt, verge.

210 ENCLOSURE

See also **206** (surroundings).

n. *enclosure*, fold, pen, compound, paddock, stockade, corral; *arena*, pitch, ring, court, yard, rink, ground, stadium, amphitheatre; *fence*, railing, cordon, paling, barrier, palisade, hedge; *ditch*, trench, moat, ha-ha; *case*, envelope, wrapper, jacket, cover.

vb. *enclose*, pen, cage, hem in, fence in, wall up, immure, confine, corral; *encircle*, encompass, surround, besiege, picket, seal off, cordon off; *encase*, enfold, wrap, envelop.

211 LIMIT

See also **209** (edge).

n. *limit*, threshold, edge, boundary; *upper/lower limit*, ceiling, cut-off point, sticking point, saturation point; *extremity*, end, terminus, finishing line, winning post, destination; *frontier*, border, no-man's land, borderline; *dateline*, horizon, equator, skyline; *deadline*, time limit, ultimatum, final offer; *delimitation*, definition, circumscription, demarcation, restriction.

adj. *limited*, defined, demarcated, set; *bordering*, coterminous, edging.

vb. *limit*, bound, border, edge, mark out, demarcate; *delimit*, define, outline, circumscribe; *curb*, confine, restrict, contain.

212 FRONT

See also **59** (precedence).

n. *front*, fore, forefront, foreground, prominence, high profile; *anteroom*, forecourt, threshold, entrance; *frontage*, facade, fascia, facing, veneer; *vanguard*, spearhead, avant-garde, front line, firing line; *bow*, prow, nose, beak, brow, forehead; *right side*, topside, recto, heads; *face*, countenance, physionomy, kisser (*colloq.*), mush (*colloq.*), dial (*colloq.*), mug (*colloq.*); *front man*, presenter, spokesperson, figurehead, cover, decoy.

213 REAR

adj. *frontal*, forward, anterior, full-frontal; *facing*, opposite, oncoming, head-on; *advance*, leading, head, foremost, prominent, up-front (*colloq.*).
vb. *front*, lead, head up, spearhead; *come to the fore*, step forward, advance, forge ahead, be out in front; *face*, confront, brave, breast.
adv. *in front*, forward, downstage; *ahead*, in advance, in the forefront.

213 REAR
See also **60** (sequence).

n. *rear*, tail, stern, back end, wake, train; *rearguard*, sweeper, back, backstop; *background*, back seat, low profile, back-room boy; *backdrop*, backstage, back door, hinterland; *reverse*, verso, flipside, tails; *hindquarters*, buttocks, backside (*colloq.*), behind (*colloq.*), posterior, bum (*colloq.*), arse (*vulg.*).
adj. *rear*, back, hind, hindmost, rearmost; *reverse*, backward, back-to-front; *dorsal*, vertebral, lumbar.
vb. *back*, reverse, retrace one's steps, double back, turn tail; *bring up the rear*, lag, trail, straggle.
adv. *in the rear*, behind, upstage, aft, astern, backwards.

214 SIDE
See also **252** (deviation).

n. *side*, flank, broadside, wing, profile; *sidelines*, siding, edge, margin, fringe; *diversion*, deflection, sidestep, bypass, digression, tangent; *right*, right hand, off side, starboard; *left*, left hand, near side, on side, port, larboard, southpaw.
adj. *lateral*, side, sidelong; *oblique*, tangential, indirect, roundabout, circuitous; *right*, clockwise, ambidextrous, dextral; *left*, anticlockwise, sinistral.
vb. *flank*, edge, sidle, skirt, border; *divert*, sidetrack, deflect; *deviate*, digress, sidestep, bypass.
adv. *sideways*, crabwise; *side by side*, abreast, alongside.

215 CONTRAPOSITION
See also **14** (oppositeness).

n. *contraposition*, polarity, contrariety;

opposite, antithesis, reverse, inverse; *polarization*, confrontation, opposition.
adj. *opposite*, contrary, counter, antithetical, opposed, adverse; *polar*, antipodean, arctic, antarctic.
vb. *be opposite*, face, confront, oppose, run counter to, challenge.
adv. *against*, contrariwise.

216 FORM
See also **149** (production); **298** (structure).

n. *form*, shape, figure, configuration; *outline*, silhouette, contour, profile; *design*, style, appearance, look, lines, format; *structure*, build, architecture, skeleton, framework, infrastructure; *pattern*, mould, template, die, stamp, prototype; *formation*, production, creation, formulation, expression.
adj. *formative*, architectural, structural; *plastic*, fictile, malleable, pliable, impressionable; *shaped*, defined, solid, three-dimensional.
vb. *form*, make, create, produce, shape, fashion, style; *outline*, sketch, design, draft; *pattern*, mould, die, stamp, coin; *model*, carve, turn, throw, sculpt, chisel, hew, cast, forge; *formulate*, express, devise, work up, lick/knock into shape (*colloq.*); *take shape*, materialize, develop, come into being.

217 SHAPELESSNESS
See also **219** (distortion).

n. *shapelessness*, amorphousness, formlessness, chaos; *indefiniteness*, indistinctness, vagueness, fuzziness, woolliness, blur; *fluidity*, liquidity, volatility, mobility, changeability; *raw material*, rough diamond, embryo, amoeba; *scribble*, scrawl, doodle, squiggle.
adj. *shapeless*, amorphous, formless, featureless, unformed, inchoate; *indefinite*, indeterminate, vague, indistinct, nebulous, blurred, fuzzy, woolly, messy, chaotic; *fluid*, liquid, volatile, mobile, unstable, protean. *raw*, rough, crude, brute, embryonic; *unfinished*, unprocessed, rough-hewn, uncut, unpolished.
vb. *deform*, warp, twist, distort, knock out of shape; *blur*, smudge, confuse,

jumble, mess up; *dissolve*, melt, thaw, liquefy.

218 SYMMETRY
See also **25** (equality).

n. *symmetry*, proportion, balance, equilibrium; *correspondence*, equivalence, analogy, parallelism; *harmony*, regularity, evenness, rhythm.

adj. *symmetrical*, proportional, balanced, equal; *corresponding*, parallel, analogous, similar; *harmonious*, regular, even, classical.

219 DISTORTION
See also **217** (shapelessness).

n. *distortion*, contortion, twistedness, convolution, tortuousness; *asymmetry*, inequality, imbalance, irregularity, disproportion, lopsidedness, squintness; *deformity*, malformation, abnormality, disfigurement, mutilation; *misrepresentation*, bias, skew, exaggeration, perversion.

adj. *distorted*, contorted, convoluted, tortuous, twisted, gnarled; *asymmetrical*, unequal, disproportionate, uneven, irregular; *askew*, awry, crooked, squint, lopsided, skew-whiff (*colloq.*); *bent*, buckled, bowed, bandy, hunch-backed, knock-kneed; *deformed*, misshapen, abnormal, stunted, crippled; *biased*, loaded, skewed, perverted.

vb. *distort*, contort, twist, screw, knot; *bend*, buckle, bow, warp, crumple, give; *grimace*, scowl, pucker, frown, pull a face; *deform*, disfigure, mangle, mutilate, cripple, stunt; *misrepresent*, misconstrue, pervert, fudge, bias, weight, skew.

220 ANGLE
See also **195** (obliqueness).

n. *angle*, crook, bend, hook, elbow, dog-leg, branch, fork, crutch; *corner*, nook, recess, niche, cranny; *triangle*, wedge, arrowhead, chevron, prism, pyramid; *square*, cube, rectangle, oblong, diamond, lozenge, rhombus, parallelogram; *polygon*, pentangle, Star of David, hexagon, octagon.

adj. *angular*, aquiline, hooked, right-angled, L-shaped; *bent*, akimbo,

forked, pointed, jagged, zigzag; *triangular*, cuneiform, pyramidal, wedge-shaped; *square*, cuboid, rectangular, rhomboid; *polygonal*, hexagonal, octagonal.

vb. *angle*, point, corner, hook, bend, crook, fold, zigzag; *fork*, branch, ramify, deviate, go off at a tangent.

221 CURVE
See also **224** (convolution); **226** (convexity).

n. *curve*, flexion, arc, trajectory, parabola, sweep; *curvature*, sinuosity, concavity, convexity; *deflection*, swerve, deviation, detour; *bend*, turn, hairpin, U-turn, horseshoe, oxbow, bay, bight, cove. *loop*, endless belt, Möbius strip, oval, scallop, festoon, swag; *bow*, arch, arcade, vault, ogive, crescent, sickle, half-moon; *hump-back*, wave, undulation, S-bend, figure of eight, switchback, roller coaster.

adj. *curved*, arched, bent, ovoid, rounded, curvilinear; *semicircular*, convex, concave, domed, hemispherical; *curvy*, shapely, curvaceous, voluptuous, pear-shaped; *wavy*, undulating, rolling, sinuous; *heart-shaped*, bow-legged, bandy-legged, swan-necked; *turned-up*, retroussé, tip-tilted.

vb. *curve*, swerve, turn, bend, sweep; *bow*, flex, round, arch, vault, dome; *loop*, coil, scallop, festoon, swag; *roll*, undulate, unfold, unfurl.

222 STRAIGHTNESS
See also **190** (verticality); **191** (horizontality).

n. *straightness*, alignment, linearity, directness, verticality, horizontality, perpendicularity; *rigidity*, stiffness, tautness, inflexibility; *straight line*, bee-line, direct route, short cut; *vertical*, horizontal, upright, poker, plumb, ramrod.

adj. *straight*, linear, rectilinear, true, level, horizontal; *vertical*, perpendicular, upright; *direct*, undeviating, unswerving, unbending, rigid, inflexible, stiff.

vb. *straighten*, align, level, even out, flatten, smooth, iron out; *stretch*, extend, unfold, unroll, uncurl, uncoil, unbend.

adv. *straight*, plumb, in true; *direct*, as the crow flies.

223 CIRCULARITY

See also **208** (outline); **225** (roundness); **251** (circuit); **279** (rotation).

n. *circularity*, roundness, rotundity, curvedness; *circumference*, equator, orbit, circuit, cycle; *circulation*, rotation, revolution, gyration, spin, pirouette; *circle*, ring, torus, round, disc, wheel, loop, saucer; *sphere*, orb, globe, bulb, ball; *dome*, hemisphere, boss, knob, stud; *crown*, circlet, coronet, halo, nimbus, corona, aureole; *collar*, necklace, garland, wreath, bracelet, anklet, belt, girdle.

adj. *circular*, round, discoid, toroid, annular; *spherical*, globular, tubular, cylindrical; *cyclic*, circulatory, rotatory, gyratory.

vb. *circle*, orbit, lap, wheel; *rotate*, revolve, circulate, gyrate, spin, spiral, pirouette; *encircle*, surround, loop, girdle, circumscribe.

224 CONVOLUTION

See also **221** (curve); **279** (rotation).

n. *convolution*, twist, torsion, contortion; *roll*, coil, winding, spring, spiral, screw, helix, worm, corkscrew; *curl*, wave, lock, kink, ringlet, frizz, tendril; *ripple*, swirl, whorl, vortex, whirlpool; *scroll*, flourish, curlicue, squiggle; *maze*, network, labyrinth, warren; *convolutedness*, intricacy, complexity, tortuousness, sinuousness.

adj. *convoluted*, twisted, contorted, knotted; *tortuous*, sinuous, intricate, involved, complex, labyrinthine; *spiral*, helical, loopy, coiled, serpentine, snaky, squiggly; *wavy*, corrugated, rippling, crinkly, curly, kinky, frizzy, crimped.

vb. *twist*, contort, corkscrew, writhe, squirm, wriggle, worm; *roll*, undulate, meander, loop, coil, snake; *entwine*, wreathe, enmesh, embroil; *curl*, wave, perm, crimp, crinkle, corrugate.

225 ROUNDNESS

See also **223** (circularity); **226** (convexity).

n. *roundness*, curvedness, circularity, rotundity, convexity; *sphere*, globe, balloon, bubble, ball, orb, bulb, bullet, pea, globule, bead, drop; *cylinder*, cone, tube, roller, rung, bole, trunk, drum, barrel; *paunch*, pot-belly, corporation, beer gut; *bulge*, swelling, hump, dome, hemisphere.

adj. *round*, curved, circular, beady, convex; *spherical*, globular, globose, bulbous, swollen; *cylindrical*, tubular, columnar, conical; *rotund*, rounded, paunchy, pot-bellied, barrel-chested.

vb. *round*, arch, curve, bend; *bulge*, swell, balloon, distend, inflate; *ball*, roll, coil, furl.

226 CONVEXITY

See also **221** (curve); **225** (roundness); **228** (prominence).

n. *convexity*, curvature, roundedness, tumescence, swollenness; *hemisphere*, dome, cupola, beehive, cup; *bulge*, hump, bow, arch, curve, ridge, hog's back, camber; *swelling*, excrescence, growth, tumour, nodule, lump; *pimple*, blister, boil, carbuncle, bunion; *knob*, boss, bump, nubble, bud, button; *breast*, bosom, pap, udder, dug, nipple, teat, bust, boobs (*colloq.*), bristols (*colloq.*), tits (*colloq.*), knockers (*colloq.*).

adj. *convex*, round, curved, arched, domed, hemispherical, bouffant; *swollen*, puffy, tumescent, tumid, distended, bloated; *raised*, embossed, bumpy, lumpy, nubbly, pimply; *curvaceous*, busty, buxom, bosomy, well-stacked (*colloq.*).

vb. *be convex*, arch, curve, rise, bow; *bulge*, swell, belly, billow.

227 CONCAVITY

See also **221** (curve); **231** (furrow).

n. *concavity*, hollow, depression, dip, indentation, impression; *cavity*, hole, recess, nook, alcove, burrow, cave, grotto, cavern, pothole; *basin*, pan, saucer, bowl, dish, cup; *dent*, dimple, pockmark, perforation; *pit*, crater, well, shaft, borehole, tunnel; *valley*, gorge, gully, ravine, crevasse; *groove*, socket, channel, furrow, trench; *spoon*, scoop, ladle, trowel, bucket.

adj. *concave*, hollow, cavernous, gaping, yawning; *pitted*, dented, dimpled, pockmarked, perforated; *recessed*, indented, sunken, excavated; *grooved*, channelled, furrowed, corrugated.

vb. *make concave*, buckle, dent, stave in, cave in; *hollow*, indent, recess, depress; *gouge*, groove, channel, bore, burrow, excavate; *hole*, pit, pockmark, perforate.

228 PROMINENCE
See also **226** (convexity).

n. *prominence*, eminence, height, conspicuousness, high profile; *projection*, tongue, salient, promontory, headland, spur, point, spit; *overhang*, shelf, ledge, outcrop, crag, ridge, buttress; *protuberance*, excrescence, outgrowth, lump, bump, hump; *beak*, bill, nose, conk (*colloq.*), snout, proboscis, antenna, feeler, horn; *relief*, convexity, embossing, cameo, high relief.

adj. *prominent*, high, conspicuous, noticeable; *projecting*, salient, jutting, overhanging, beetle-browed, craggy, buck-toothed; *protuberant*, raised, convex, bulging, lumpy, humped, popeyed.

vb. *project*, jut, stick out, stand out, protrude, bulge; *rise*, bristle, cock, prick up, erect.

229 NOTCH
See also **296** (sharpness).

n. *notch*, serration, indentation, crenellation, scallop, zigzag, deckle edge; *nick*, V-shape, snick, cut, gash, incision; *tooth*, sprocket, ratchet, comb, saw.

adj. *notched*, serrated, jagged, ragged, saw-toothed; *stepped*, crenellated, indented, scalloped.

vb. *notch*, serrate, tooth, mill; *indent*, crimp, pink, scallop; *nick*, snick, cut, snip, clip.

230 FOLD
See also **231** (furrow).

n. *fold*, pleat, tuck, gather; *frill*, flounce, ruffle, ruche; *lapel*, cuff, turn-up, crease; *ridge*, furrow, groove, corrugation; *wrinkle*, crinkle, pucker, frown, crow's feet.

adj. *folded*, plicate, ridged, gathered, pleated, frilly; *crumpled*, creased, crushed, crinkled, dog-eared, puckered, corrugated, lined.

vb. *fold*, furl, drape, swathe, festoon; *furrow*, groove, corrugate, wrinkle, pucker, crinkle, purse, concertina; *frill*, ruffle, ruche, pleat, gather, tuck.

231 FURROW
See also **227** (concavity); **230** (fold).

n. *furrow*, groove, chase, channel, track, slot, rut; *slit*, chink, cranny, crack, crevice; *hollow*, trough, gutter, gully, ditch, trench, moat; *wave*, ripple, fluting, ribbing, corduroy; *wrinkle*, frown, corrugation, rifling, etching, incision, gash, slash.

adj. *furrowed*, wrinkled, puckered, lined, etched, incised; *grooved*, fluted, ribbed, ridged, rutted, striated.

vb. *furrow*, groove, chase, channel, chamfer, flute, rifle; *plough*, rut, rib, corrugate, wrinkle; *line*, etch, incise, score, gash, slash.

232 OPENING
See also **174** (interval).

n. *opening*, aperture, gap, hole, breach, lacuna, hiatus, break; *space*, crack, chink, interstice, cavity, pocket, orifice; *perforation*, pore, puncture, indentation, bore, pinhole, eyelet; *sieve*, strainer, colander, riddle; *mesh*, netting, fretwork, openwork, lace, filigree, broderie anglaise; *outlet*, nozzle, vent, spout, gullet, nostril, mouth, maw, gob (*colloq.*), trap (*colloq.*), cakehole (*colloq.*); *compartment*, slot, keyhole, pigeonhole, letterbox; *window*, grille, fanlight, skylight, porthole, loophole, peephole; *door*, gate, portal, entrance, hatch, trapdoor, manhole, flap; *tunnel*, shaft, bolthole, burrow, foxhole; *funnel*, chimney, flue, duct, tube; *open space*, clearing, glade, bomb site, waste ground, vista, panorama; *opener*, aperient, purgative, open sesame, password; *tin-opener*, corkscrew, key, handle, knob; *punch*, bodkin, skewer, gimlet, drill, auger, bradawl; *openness*, accessibility, penetrability, permeability, porosity.

adj. *open*, ajar, agape, yawning, open-mouthed; *perforated*, riddled, honey-combed, shot through; *holey*, lacy, leaky, porous, permeable, absorbent; *accessible*, clear, unobstructed, uncluttered.

vb. *open*, unlock, unfasten, uncork, unwrap, unpack, undo; *gape*, yawn, split, rend, part, burst, explode, leak; *pierce*, puncture, perforate, gore, hole, bore, drill, punch, tattoo, riddle, pepper; *stab*, prick, skewer, nail, spear, transfix, impale; *enter*, penetrate, permeate, pervade.

adv. *openly*, out in the open, open to the four winds, al fresco.

233 CLOSURE
See also **202** (covering).

n. *closure*, occlusion, strangulation, obstruction, blockage, stoppage; *impasse*, dead end, cul de sac, road block, barricade; *impermeability*, imperviousness, staunchness, impenetrability; *stopper*, cork, bung, spigot, plug, wad, tampon; *valve*, tap, stopcock, ballcock, choke, damper; *gag*, muzzle, tourniquet, compress; *cover*, top, lid, cap, seal, shutter; *lock*, bolt, bar, latch, deadlock.

adj. *closed*, shut, barred, bolted, shuttered; *impermeable*, impenetrable, impervious, staunch, watertight, airtight, hermetically sealed; *impassable*, inaccessible, blocked, barricaded.

vb. *close*, shut, occlude, strangulate, obstruct, clog; *lock*, bar, bolt, fasten; *stop*, plug, bung, caulk, cork, seal; *block*, dam, choke, throttle, gag, muzzle.

234 MOTION
See also **236** (land travel); **239** (transfer).

n. *motion*, movement, mobility, locomotion, perambulation; *momentum*, impetus, propulsion, impulsion; *advance*, progress, headway, ascent; *retreat*, regression, withdrawal,

descent; *oscillation*, fluctuation, vibration, agitation, tremor; *activity*, unrest, stir, bustle, traffic; *passage*, transit, transfer, shift, transport, conveyance; *flow*, flux, drift, current, course, run; *gait*, walk, carriage, bearing, tread, stride.

adj. *moving*, mobile, motile, locomotive, automotive, self-propelled; *transitional*, passing, shifting, fleeting; *wandering*, ambulant, peripatetic, nomadic, restless, drifting; *kinetic*, dynamic, cinematographic.

vb. *move*, go, walk, proceed, make one's way, advance, progress; *march*, tramp, stride, lope, jog, amble, saunter, stroll, waddle, shuffle; *stalk*, strut, swagger, mince; *run*, race, gallop, hare, fly, dash; *roll*, taxi, trundle, chug, wheel, coast, cruise, freewheel; *travel*, roam, wander, drift, stray; *transfer*, transport, shift, convey, dispatch; *push*, shove, budge, drive, hustle; *draw*, pull, drag, tug, haul.

adv. *in motion*, on the move, on the go, up and about; *under way*, on the road, en route, in transit.

235 MOTIONLESSNESS
See also **123** (cessation).

n. *motionlessness*, stillness, rest, immobility; *stability*, equilibrium, poise, balance, stasis; *suspension*, cessation, stagnation, inertia, deadlock, stalemate; *standstill*, stop, halt, pause, truce, lull; *stoppage*, embargo, freeze, strike; *calm*, still, quiet, hush.

adj. *motionless*, still, immobile, becalmed; *static*, stationary, stagnant, inactive, idle; *immovable*, stuck, rigid, paralysed, unbudgeable; *transfixed*, spellbound, rooted to the spot, stock-still; *sedentary*, stay-at-home, home-loving, housebound, bedridden, disabled.

vb. *be motionless*, stand still, stay put, sit tight, mark time, stagnate; *cease*, stop, come to a halt, settle, subside, die down; *pause*, rest, tarry, take a breather (*colloq.*), rest on one's oars; *immobilize*, lock, jam, stick, lodge, catch; *halt*, stop short, stop in one's tracks, brake, check, pull up.

236 LAND TRAVEL

See also 234 (motion); 242 (vehicle); 762 (recreation).

n. *land travel*, tourism, globe-trotting, sightseeing, exploration, peregrination; *journey*, voyage, odyssey, expedition, trek, safari; *trip*, jaunt, outing, excursion, spin, ride; *walk*, constitutional, stroll, ramble, hike, tramp, march, walkabout, Shank's pony; *run*, jog, race, sprint, cross-country, marathon; *route*, itinerary, stopover, terminus, destination, journey's end; *traveller*, voyager, passenger, commuter, tourist, wayfarer, sightseer, tripper; *walker*, pedestrian, hiker, rambler, jogger, runner, sprinter; *wanderer*, rover, globe-trotter, migrant, drifter, rolling stone, vagabond, vagrant, tramp, gentleman of the road.

adj. *travelling*, itinerant, peripatetic, globe-trotting, ambulant; *wandering*, migratory, nomadic, restless, vagrant, vagabond, errant.

vb. *travel*, journey, voyage, explore, tour, shuttle, commute, knock about (*colloq.*); *walk*, pace, saunter, stroll, amble; *hike*, trek, tramp, march, ramble; *trudge*, plod, slog, stump, hoof it, foot it, leg it; *run*, race, jog, sprint; *wander*, rove, roam, migrate, traipse.

adv. *by road*, overland, on foot; *on the road*, on the trail, on the beat.

237 WATER TRAVEL

See also 243 (ship); 762 (recreation).

n. *water travel*, sailing, navigation, cruising, yachting, boating; *voyage*, circumnavigation, cruise, crossing, sail; *seamanship*, seafaring, sea legs, weather eye; *navy*, fleet, merchant navy, shipping, flotilla; *water sport*, aquatics, surfing, swimming, natation, diving, windsurfing, canoeing, sculling, rowing; *seaman*, mariner, sailor, submariner, seafarer, sea dog, old salt; *captain*, crew, boatswain, master, mate, pilot, navigator; *coastguard*, lifeboatman, boatman, ferryman, Charon.

adj. *seafaring*, maritime, marine, naval, nautical, navigational, aquatic, deep-sea, ocean-going, longshore, seaworthy, waterborne.

vb. *put to sea*, set sail, embark, cast off, launch, weigh anchor; *voyage*, sail, cruise, ply, steam, ferry, run, circumnavigate; *navigate*, steer, pilot, captain; *disembark*, land, dock, berth, tie up, moor, drop anchor; *row*, scull, canoe, punt, paddle; *swim*, float, tread water, bathe, surf, windsurf, wade, paddle.

adv. *at sea*, aboard, afloat, on the high seas.

238 AIR TRAVEL

See also 244 (aircraft).

n. *air travel*, aeronautics, aerospace, aerodynamics; *flying*, aviation, gliding, hang-gliding, ballooning, parachuting, sky-diving, aerobatics; *airline*, airlift, charter, flight, airlane; *airport*, airfield, aerodrome, landing strip, runway, airstrip, terminal; *takeoff*, touchdown, landing, crash-landing, nosedive, prang (*colloq.*); *space travel*, space flight, countdown, liftoff, blastoff, orbit, docking, reentry, splashdown; *pilot*, aeronaut, aviator, aviatrix, airman/woman, flier, balloonist, parachutist, paratrooper; *astronaut*, cosmonaut, spaceman/woman, space traveller.

adj. *flying*, aeronautic, aerodynamic, aerobatic; *aerial*, airborne, in-flight, airworthy.

vb. *fly*, pilot, aviate, glide, balloon, parachute, jet; *take off*, taxi, overfly, hover, fly, drift, cruise; *come down*, touch down, land, crash, nosedive, crashland, ditch, bail out, eject; *lift off*, blast off, orbit, dock, splash down.

adv. *in flight*, in the air, in orbit, on the wing.

239 TRANSFER

See also 234 (motion); 697 (transfer of property).

n. *transfer*, relocation, shift, removal, transferal, transplantation, deportation; *transmission*, conduction, convection, transfusion, contagion; *transportation*, conveyance, dispatch, transshipment, exportation, importation, delivery; *carriage*, transport, haulage, cartage; *freight*, consignment, shipment, cargo, container.

adj. *transferable*, movable, portable; *transmissible*, communicable, contagious, infectious.

vb. *transfer*, shift, move, convey, transmit; *dispatch*, transport, ship, transship, export, import; *send*, consign, post, mail, forward.

adv. *in transit*, on the way, en route, under way.

240 WAY

See also **271** (passage); **315** (channel).

n. *way*, manner, method, procedure, modus operandi, measures, steps; *course*, route, direction, line, tack, short cut, detour; *approach*, access, entrance, passage, right of way; *path*, track, orbit, trajectory, channel; *trail*, footpath, bridlepath, towpath; *walk*, drive, avenue, boulevard, promenade; *road*, highway, thoroughfare, artery, trunk road, ring road, bypass, dual carriageway, motorway; *street*, terrace, crescent, circus; *sidestreet*, lane, alley, close, wynd; *railway*, railroad, main line, branch line, siding, marshalling yard; *underground*, subway, tube, funicular, monorail; *bridge*, footbridge, drawbridge, viaduct, aqueduct, flyover, cloverleaf; *causeway*, gangway, catwalk, aisle, underpass.

241 CARRIER

n. *carrier*, bearer, porter, coolie, messenger, courier, runner, postman; *common carrier*, transporter, shipper, haulier, carter, importer, exporter; *beast of burden*, packhorse, draught horse, mule, donkey; *carrier bag*, tote bag, trolley, stretcher, litter, conveyor belt.

vb. *carry*, bear, shoulder, hump, cart, heave, haul, lug, tote (*colloq.*), shlepp (*colloq.*); *convey*, post, send, forward, transport, ship, ferry.

242 VEHICLE

See also **236** (land travel).

n. *vehicle*, conveyance, transport, wheels (*colloq.*); *wagon*, dray, cart, tumbril; *carriage*, landau, brougham,

hansom, buggy, gig, fly, trap; *bicycle*, tandem, pushbike, tricycle, trike, moped, scooter, motorcycle, motorbike; *car*, motor car, automobile, saloon, hatchback, convertible, coupé, shooting brake, station wagon, runabout, limousine; *van*, camper, pickup, float, pantechnicon, hearse, Black Maria, ambulance, lorry, truck, juggernaut; *bus*, coach, charabanc, double-decker, tram, trolleybus, streetcar (*US*); *stagecoach*, post chaise, hackney carriage, cab, taxi, minicab, rickshaw, trishaw; *train*, express, high-speed train, locomotive, tender, tanker, goods train, underground, subway.

adj. *vehicular*, wheeled, motorized, automotive, locomotive.

243 SHIP

See also **237** (water travel).

n. *ship*, vessel, boat, craft, tub (*colloq.*); *passenger ship*, ferry, packet, steamer, paddleboat, hovercraft, hydrofoil, liner; *freighter*, barge, tramp, tanker, collier, dredger, tug, supertanker; *launch*, lighter, painter, dinghy, wherry, lifeboat; *sailing ship*, galleon, sloop, schooner, ketch, yawl, clipper, merchantman, Indiaman; *fishing boat*, trawler, drifter, smack, whaler, factory ship; *yacht*, skiff, catamaran, junk, sampan, dhow, caique, felucca; *rowing boat*, scull, canoe, punt, coracle, gondola, kayak, pirogue; *warship*, man o' war, battleship, frigate, corvette, cruiser, destroyer, aircraft carrier.

adj. *nautical*, maritime, marine, seagoing, oceangoing, transatlantic.

244 AIRCRAFT

See also **238** (air travel).

n. *aircraft*, aeroplane, plane, flying machine, monoplane, biplane, seaplane, crate (*colloq.*); *airliner*, jet, jumbo jet, airbus, shuttle, Concorde; *helicopter*, whirlybird (*colloq.*), chopper (*colloq.*), fighter, bomber; *airship*, dirigible, balloon, glider, hang-glider; *spaceship*, satellite, rocket, capsule, module.

adj. *aviational*, aeronautical, wide-bodied, heavier-than-air, supersonic.

245 SPEED
See also **96** (immediacy); **615** (haste).

n. *speed*, velocity, rapidity, swiftness; *quickness*, alacrity, promptness, suddenness, instantaneity; *pace*, rate, tempo, momentum, rate of knots (*colloq.*), lick (*colloq.*); *haste*, hurry, rush, dispatch; *acceleration*, flying start, spurt, sprint, full throttle; *run*, race, dash, charge, gallop, stampede; *runner*, racer, speed merchant (*colloq.*), harrier, sprinter; *racehorse*, greyhound, hare, cheetah, gazelle.

adj. *speedy*, fast, swift, rapid, meteoric; *quick*, lively, snappy, quick-fire, brisk, smart; *prompt*, immediate, sudden, double-quick, alacritous, hasty, expeditious; *light-footed*, nimble, agile, fleet-footed, mercurial; *high-speed*, breakneck, headlong, precipitous, runaway.

vb. *speed*, race, flash, streak, shoot, fly; *dart*, flit, whisk, zoom, whiz (*colloq.*), zip, rush, tear, dash; *run*, gallop, hare, sprint, hot-foot it, belt, pelt, hurtle, career, stampede; *dive*, pounce, spring, swoop, lunge; *run away*, bolt, scoot, take to one's heels, scamper, scuttle, scarper (*colloq.*), skedaddle (*colloq.*); *accelerate*, hurry, hasten, quicken, hustle, step on it (*colloq.*), get a move on (*colloq.*), get weaving/cracking (*colloq.*), get one's skates on (*colloq.*), jump to it.

adv. *at full speed*, swiftly, flat out, hell for leather, post haste, helter skelter, apace; *promptly*, pronto (*colloq.*), smartish (*colloq.*), at the double, in a trice, before you can say Jack Robinson.

246 SLOWNESS
See also **616** (lack of haste).

n. *slowness*, sluggishness, lethargy, languor, inertia, slackness; *lack of haste*, patience, methodicalness, deliberation, unhurriedness, leisureliness; *hesitation*, tardiness, reluctance, unwillingness; *delay*, holdup, slowdown, work-to-rule, go-slow; *deceleration*, brake, curb,

restraint, retardation; *slow motion*, snail's pace, amble, stroll, saunter, dawdle; *slow creature*, slowcoach (*colloq.*), sloth, tortoise, snail.

adj. *slow*, sluggish, lethargic, listless, languid, slack; *deliberate*, patient, painstaking, methodical, unhurried, leisurely; *hesitant*, reluctant, unwilling, tardy, dilatory, slow off the mark.

vb. *move slowly*, amble, saunter, dawdle, stroll, linger, loaf; *creep*, crawl, inch, trickle, drip, ooze; *plod*, trudge, limp, hobble, shuffle, shamble, mooch (*colloq.*); *lag*, delay, dilly-dally (*colloq.*), drag one's feet, take one's time, run out of steam, falter; *slow down*, decelerate, slacken, retard, brake, backpedal, ease off, let up.

adv. *slowly*, adagio, largo, little by little, softly softly (*colloq.*).

247 IMPULSION
See also **255** (propulsion).

n. *impulsion*, impetus, momentum, thrust, drive, propulsion, force, charge; *impact*, brunt, shock, jolt, nudge, bump, cannon, collision, crash, smash; *blow*, bang, thud, knock, rap, punch, thwack, thump; *stroke*, hit, smack, cuff, slap, clap, lash, flick, tap; *hammer*, club, cudgel, cosh, truncheon, knocker, ram, bulldozer.

vb. *impel*, thrust, drive, kick, charge; *throw*, fling, propel, launch, hurl, toss; *push*, shove, force, press, ram, bulldoze; *jerk*, jog, jolt, jar, nudge, butt, wrench, tug; *collide*, smash, crash, bang, cannon, bump, careen; *hit*, strike, clout, cuff, spank, smack, slap, rap, tap, knock; *punch*, slug, pummel, pound, bludgeon, hammer; *beat*, bash, thrash, wallop (*colloq.*), clobber (*colloq.*), belt (*colloq.*), slosh (*colloq.*), whack (*colloq.*).

248 RECOIL
See also **137** (counteraction).

n. *recoil*, rebound, bounce, spring, swing of the pendulum; *reflex*, kickback, ricochet, boomerang, cannon; *echo*, reflection, repercussion, reverberation, backlash; *reflector*, mirror, sounding board, echo chamber;

response, reply, retort, riposte, rebuff; *reaction*, double take, wince, start.

adj. *reactive*, responsive, reflexive, knee-jerk (*colloq.*); *echoey*, resonant, reverberative, repercussive; *springy*, bouncy, elastic.

vb. *recoil*, rebound, cannon, boomerang, ricochet; *spring*, bounce back, kick back, backfire; *echo*, reflect, mirror, reverberate; *react*, respond, reply, retort, rebuff.

249 DIRECTION
See also **159** (situation).

n. *direction*, bearings, situation, orientation, location, compass point, cardinal point; *trend*, tendency, drift, thrust, tack, line; *course*, route, short cut, beeline; *destination*, goal, aim, target, objective; *compass*, direction finder, signpost, map, tracking device.

adj. *directed*, headed, bound for, set.

vb. *direct*, indicate, signpost, guide, steer, level, point, aim; *orientate*, situate, take one's bearings, pinpoint, locate, track; *head for*, make for, aim for, make tracks for.

adv. *direct*, straight, point blank; *on course*, on the right track, on the right lines.

250 MIDDLE WAY
See also **63** (middle); **148** (moderation).

n. *middle way*, short cut, beeline, diameter, centre; *middle course*, median, average, happy medium, golden mean; *midpoint*, central reservation, traffic island; *middle of the road*, halfway house, compromise, moderation.

adj. *middle*, central, equidistant, direct, straight; *midway*, halfway, intermediate, medial; *neutral*, moderate, middle-of-the-road, unextreme.

251 CIRCUIT
See also **223** (circularity).

n. *circuit*, detour, bypass, loop, ring road; *digression*, deviation, way round, circumlocution.

adj. *circuitous*, roundabout, out-of-the-

way; *circumlocutious*, long-winded, indirect.

vb. *circuit*, lap, loop, ring; *deviate*, digress, go out of one's way; *bypass*, skirt, avoid, give a wide berth.

252 DEVIATION
See also **214** (side); **260** (divergence).

n. *deviation*, aberration, wrong turning, disorientation; *detour*, side-step, zigzag, swerve, veer; *diversion*, shift, deflection, divergence; *digression*, aside, tangent, parenthesis.

adj. *deviant*, aberrant, off-course, off-beam, stray, wide of the mark; *digressive*, wandering, rambling, off the point, discursive.

vb. *deviate*, wander, stray, lose one's bearings, be on the wrong track; *side-step*, diverge, veer, slew, zigzag; *digress*, go off at a tangent, get sidetracked.

253 FORWARD MOTION
n. *forward motion*, progress, advance, headway; *course*, march, tide, current, flood; *step*, stride, leap, jump, spurt; *advancement*, preferment, promotion, leg-up; *development*, growth, evolution, furtherance; *improvement*, betterment, perfectibility.

adj. *forward*, progressive, advanced, up-to-date, forward-looking; *go-ahead*, enterprising, go-getting (*colloq.*); *ongoing*, continuing, inexorable, irreversible.

vb. *go forward*, proceed, progress, advance, make headway, get the go-ahead (*colloq.*); *keep on*, press on, push on, make strides, gain ground, forge ahead, get somewhere (*colloq.*); *develop*, evolve, further, bring on; *promote*, upgrade, better, improve.

adv. *forward*, onward, ahead; *progressively*, by leaps and bounds.

254 BACKWARD MOTION
See also **126** (reversion).

n. *backward motion*, recession, retraction, retreat, withdrawal, retirement, flight; *retroaction*, retrospection, regression, nostalgia; *reversion*, backward step, relapse, backsliding; *decline*, fall off, slump, ebb; *about-turn*, volte-face, U-turn.

adj. *backward*, retrograde, retrogressive; *receding*, recessive, retreating, retractile; *retroactive*, retrospective, nostalgic.

vb. *recede*, retire, withdraw, back off, fall back; *regress*, return, revert, hark back, relapse, backslide; *reverse*, back, backtrack, backpedal, retrace one's steps, double back; *turn tail*, about-face, wheel, turn on one's heel.

adv. *backwards*, in reverse, anticlockwise, widdershins (*dial.*).

255 PROPULSION
See also 247 (impulsion).

n. *propulsion*, impulsion, drive, momentum, impetus, kick; *throw*, cast, toss, pitch, bowl; *discharge*, volley, salvo, bombardment, cannonade; *archery*, toxophily, ballistics, gunnery, artillery; *missile*, projectile, arrow, dart, bullet, shot, pellet, shell, cannonball, torpedo, rocket; *propellant*, charge, explosive, dynamite; *propeller*, pedal, oar, turbine, booster, thruster; *firearm*, shotgun, rifle, catapult, sling, bow, peashooter; *shooter*, marksman, crack shot, gunner, sniper, archer, bowler, pitcher.

adj. *propulsive*, propellent, expulsive, ballistic.

vb. *propel*, launch, project, impel, drive, thrust, kick; *throw*, cast, toss, pitch, bowl, chuck, fling, hurl, lob, bung; *fire*, catapult, pitchfork, send flying; *shoot*, discharge, loose off, volley, bombard.

256 TRACTION
See also 257 (attraction).

n. *traction*, haulage, draught, pulling, tug of war; *pull*, tug, heave, tow, trawl, haul, drag, friction; *magnetism*, attraction, charisma, drawing power; *tractor*, towrope, tugboat, windlass, dragnet, magnet.

adj. *retractive*, retractable, ductile; *magnetic*, attractive, charismatic.

vb. *draw*, pull, haul, heave, tow; *drag*, trawl, dredge, winch, reel in; *pull at*, tug, jerk, tweak, pluck, yank; *draw in*, withdraw, retract, sheathe; *attract*, magnetize, spellbind.

257 ATTRACTION
See also 256 (traction).

n. *attraction*, pull, draw, influence, gravity, magnetism; *allure*, fascination, seductiveness, charm; *lure*, bait, decoy, snare, siren, temptress; *focal point*, cynosure, centre of attraction, magnet, lodestone.

adj. *attractive*, seductive, charming, irresistible; *magnetic*, gravitational, focal, centripetal, convergent.

vb. *attract*, pull, draw, influence; *lure*, bait, ensnare, seduce; *tempt*, captivate, enthral, magnetize, mesmerize.

258 REPULSION
See also 266 (expulsion).

n. *repulsion*, rejection, rebuff, dismissal, snub, brush-off (*colloq.*); *deflection*, defence, counterstroke, parry, foil, counterattack, resistance.

adj. *repulsive*, repellent, antipathetic, offensive, off-putting; *defensive*, resistant, hostile, dismissive.

vb. *repel*, drive away, chase, dismiss; *deflect*, ward off, fend off, keep at bay, head off, parry; *reject*, rebuff, snub, cold-shoulder; *eject*, throw out, show the door, send packing (*colloq.*).

259 CONVERGENCE
n. *convergence*, confluence, concurrence, concourse, concentration; *approach*, advance, confrontation, collision course; *union*, meeting, congress, assembly, congregation; *focus*, centre, pivot, hub.

adj. *convergent*, centripetal, confluent, advancing, oncoming.

vb. *converge*, close in, approach, draw near; *come together*, assemble, congregate, concentrate, gather, cluster; *focus*, centre, home in, zero in.

260 DIVERGENCE
See also 252 (deviation).

n. *divergence*, difference, deviation, contradiction, contrariety; *radiation*, branching, ramification, bifurcation;

crossroads, fork, intersection, parting of the ways.
adj. *divergent*, radial, centrifugal; *branching*, forked, splayed, spread-eagled.
vb. *diverge*, radiate, fan out, diffuse, go one's separate ways; *branch*, ramify, fork, splay, spreadeagle.

261 ARRIVAL

n. *arrival*, advent, approach, coming, onset, advance; *entrance*, appearance, emergence, debut; *attainment*, accession, achievement, fulfilment; *landing*, disembarkation, landfall, touchdown; *destination*, goal, journey's end, terminus; *reception*, welcome, greeting, handshake, hospitality. **adj.** *arriving*, incoming, immigrant; *approaching*, impending, imminent, oncoming, advancing; *attainable*, approachable, accessible, get-at-able (*colloq.*); *welcoming*, inviting, hospitable. **vb.** *arrive*, reach, approach, draw up, gain, attain, get to, end up in, fetch up in; *land*, dismount, alight, set foot in, touch down, disembark, dock, moor; *appear*, turn up, show up, roll up (*colloq.*), drop in (*colloq.*), blow in (*colloq.*), make an entrance; *receive*, greet, welcome, kill the fatted calf.

262 DEPARTURE

n. *departure*, going, leaving, setting out; *embarkation*, takeoff, liftoff, blast-off; *emigration*, exodus, evacuation, exit, walkout; *flight*, retreat, escape, getaway, decampment, elopement, moonlight flit; *parting*, farewell, leavetaking, separation, send-off; *good-bye*, adieu, parting shot, valediction, obituary; *point of departure*, starting point, outset, springboard, jumping-off point.
adj. *departing*, farewell, valedictory; *outgoing*, outward bound, emigratory.
vb. *depart*, leave, quit, turn one's back on, vote with one's feet; *move out*, emigrate, pull out, evacuate, strike camp; *set out*, embark, set sail, take off, get under way; *escape*, flee, decamp, elope, abscond, bolt; *retire*, withdraw, retreat, bow out, sign off;

separate, bid farewell, part company, take one's leave; *be off*, make tracks, up sticks, clear off (*colloq.*), push off (*colloq.*), slope off (*colloq.*), buzz off (*colloq.*); *rush off*, make oneself scarce (*colloq.*), beetle off (*colloq.*), vamoose (*colloq.*), skedaddle (*colloq.*), scarper (*colloq.*), beat it (*colloq.*), scram (*colloq.*).

263 ENTRY

See also **265** (admittance); **269** (insertion).

n. *entry*, admission, access, ingress; *influx*, incursion, invasion, intrusion; *inroad*, encroachment, penetration, infiltration; *enrolment*, enlistment, initiation, induction; *intake*, immigration, importation, open door, free trade; *entrance*, way in, door, gate, mouth, orifice, inlet; *entrant*, incomer, immigrant, settler, colonist; *intruder*, invader, gatecrasher, housebreaker, burglar.
adj. *incoming*, immigrant, imported; *invasive*, incursive, intrusive.
vb. *enter*, gain admittance, set foot in, cross the threshold, drop in (*colloq.*), pop in (*colloq.*); *enrol*, enlist, inscribe, induct, sign on, initiate, admit; *invade*, irrupt, trespass, encroach, gatecrash, break and enter, burgle; *penetrate*, infiltrate, permeate, percolate; *rush in*, breeze in, barge in, butt in, muscle in (*colloq.*).

264 EXIT

See also **266** (expulsion); **270** (extraction).

n. *exit*, egress, way out, fire escape; *outflow*, effluent, issue, outpouring, discharge, leak; *emanation*, emission, seepage, exudation, secretion; *eruption*, outburst, breakout, sortie, sally; *emigration*, exodus, walkout, departure; *vent*, outlet, outfall, spout, drain, overflow; *escape route*, loophole, back door, let-out.
adj. *outgoing*, emigrant, departing; *leaky*, oozy, weeping, escaping.
vb. *exit*, emerge, issue, debouch; *erupt*, sally forth, break out, escape; *emigrate*, evacuate, clear out, bale out;

emit, discharge, exude, secrete; *ooze*, weep, bleed, leak, seep; *pour*, overflow, gush, jet, spout.

265 ADMITTANCE

See also 263 (entry).

n. *admittance*, access, admission, reception, acceptance; *receptivity*, openness, accessibility, open arms, hospitality; *acceptability*, admissibility, suitability; *introduction*, initiation, rite of passage, baptism, enrolment, registration; *intake*, incorporation, absorption, ingestion.

adj. *admissible*, acceptable, suitable; *receptive*, open, accessible, welcoming, inviting, hospitable; *initiatory*, introductory, baptismal; *absorbent*, assimilative, digestive.

vb. *admit*, receive, take in, shelter; *welcome*, embrace, adopt, accept; *register*, enrol, enlist, inscribe, include; *initiate*, baptize, introduce, show the ropes (*colloq.*); *incorporate*, assimilate, internalize, absorb, digest.

266 EXPULSION

See also 161 (displacement); 258 (repulsion); 264 (exit); 270 (extraction).

n. *expulsion*, ejection, eviction, dislodgment; *dismissal*, discharge, rustication, excommunication, disbarment, the sack, the push (*colloq.*), the boot (*colloq.*), the bum's rush (*colloq.*); *deportation*, extradition, banishment, exile, repatriation, relegation; *removal*, elimination, evacuation, clearance, voidance; *ejector*, bouncer (*colloq.*), chucker-out, heavy (*colloq.*); *nausea*, vomiting, sickness, expectoration.

adj. *expulsive*, expellant, emetic, purgative, cathartic, excretory.

vb. *expel*, eject, evict, dislodge, turn out; *dismiss*, discharge, excommunicate, rusticate, send down, strike off, disbar, sack, fire; *throw out*, turf out, chuck out, drum out, root out, eradicate; *deport*, repatriate, extradite, banish, exile, relegate; *eliminate*, evacuate, void, empty, clear, purge; *emit*, disgorge, spit out, vomit, spew, retch, throw up (*colloq.*), puke (*colloq.*).

267 INGESTION

n. *ingestion*, digestion, consumption, imbibing, mastication, chewing; *nutrition*, sustenance, alimentation, dietetics, domestic science, home economics; *gluttony*, gourmandise, overeating, voraciousness; *gastronomy*, epicureanism, haute cuisine, cookery; *eater*, diner, gourmet, gastronome, connoisseur, epicure, trencherman; *provisions*, provender, foodstuffs, victuals, comestibles, rations; *food*, staff of life, ambrosia, tuck (*colloq.*), grub (*colloq.*), nosh (*colloq.*), chow (*colloq.*); *convenience food*, fast food, junk food, TV dinner, health food, wholefood; *meal*, fare, snack, titbit, morsel, bite, brunch, elevenses, tiffin; *feast*, banquet, junket, beanfeast (*colloq.*), bunfight (*colloq.*), beano (*colloq.*), slap-up meal (*colloq.*), blowout (*colloq.*); *dish*, hors d'oeuvres, starter, appetizer, entree, pudding, sweet, dessert, afters (*colloq.*); *beverage*, infusion, cocktail, brew, tipple, poison (*colloq.*); *alcohol*, spirits, hard stuff (*colloq.*), booze (*colloq.*), hooch (*colloq.*), vino (*colloq.*), plonk (*colloq.*), rotgut (*colloq.*); *drink*, draught, sip, gulp, swig (*colloq.*), dram, snort (*colloq.*), nightcap.

adj. *edible*, digestible, nutritious, drinkable, potable; *appetizing*, wholesome, tasty, palatable, moreish (*colloq.*), scrumptious (*colloq.*); *culinary*, dietary, gastronomic, cordon bleu, underdone, oven-ready, rare; *carnivorous*, herbivorous, vegetarian, omnivorous, gluttonous.

vb. *ingest*, digest, chew, masticate, consume; *eat*, feed, feast, dine, sup, put away (*colloq.*), tuck into (*colloq.*), polish off; *devour*, bolt, wolf, gorge, gobble, guzzle; *taste*, nibble, peck at, sample; *drink*, imbibe, sip, quaff, down, gulp, knock back, tipple, booze (*colloq.*); *cook*, prepare, fix (*US*), boil, simmer, poach, stew, braise, grill, roast, bake, serve up, dish up.

268 EXCRETION

n. *excretion*, secretion, exudation, discharge, expulsion, ejection, expectoration; *defecation*, evacuation, voidance, bowel movement, constipation, dysentery, diarrhoea, runs (*colloq.*), trots (*colloq.*), Delhi belly (*colloq.*); *urination*, micturation, call of nature, incontinence, weak bladder, enuresis; *excreta*, excrement, faeces, stool, turd (*vulg.*), dung, muck, shit (*vulg.*), crap (*vulg.*), manure, droppings, guano; *urine*, water, pee (*colloq.*), piddle (*colloq.*), wee (*colloq.*), piss (*vulg.*); *saliva*, mucus, catarrh, spittle, sweat, perspiration.

adj. *excretory*, diuretic, laxative, purgative, cathartic; *faecal*, urinary, excremental, shitty (*vulg.*), crappy (*vulg.*); *continent*, toilet-trained, housetrained.

vb. *excrete*, evacuate, discharge, expel, eject, pass; *defecate*, foul, soil, be caught short, shit (*vulg.*), crap (*vulg.*); *urinate*, relieve oneself, micturate, spend a penny (*colloq.*), pee (*colloq.*), piddle (*colloq.*), widdle (*colloq.*), piss (*vulg.*); *secrete*, exude, perspire, sweat; *expectorate*, spit, salivate, drool, slobber, hawk.

269 INSERTION
See also **207** (interface); **263** (entry).

n. *insertion*, introduction, interjection, interpolation, intercalation; *injection*, inoculation, vaccination, transfusion, implantation, impregnation; *insert*, inlay, inclusion, filling, stuffing.

adj. *inserted*, included, interjectional, parenthetical, by-the-by (*colloq.*).

vb. *insert*, introduce, interject, interpolate, intercalate, include, drag in (*colloq.*); *infuse*, instil, imbue, impregnate; *inject*, inoculate, vaccinate, transfuse, implant; *inset*, inlay, embed, encapsulate, sheathe, encase; *immerse*, plunge, bury, steep, souse, dunk.

270 EXTRACTION
See also **264** (exit); **266** (expulsion).

n. *extraction*, removal, withdrawal, excision; *displacement*, dislodgment, excavation, extrication, suction, aspiration; *extortion*, squeezing, expression, wringing out; *distillation*, separation, refinement, condensation; *extract*, essence, distillate, sublimate; *extractor*, excavator, dredger, digger, scoop; *for-

ceps*, tweezers, pliers, wrench, syringe, siphon, pump.

vb. *extract*, remove, withdraw, excise; *displace*, dislodge, extricate, winkle out; *extort*, elicit, squeeze, force, express, wring out, get blood out of a stone; *excavate*, mine, quarry, dredge, dig up; *pump*, suck, vacuum, aspirate, siphon off, tap, milk; *distil*, refine, separate, condense, cream off.

271 PASSAGE
See also **240** (way).

n. *passage*, movement, transit, crossing, journey, voyage; *access*, right of way, thoroughfare, traffic, circulation; *entrance*, infiltration, penetration, permeation, percolation, osmosis; *crossing point*, bridge, ford, zebra crossing, frontier post, checkpoint; *passport*, visa, safe-conduct, laissez-passer, ID.

vb. *pass*, proceed, move through, circulate, journey, voyage, patrol, do the rounds (*colloq.*); *cross*, traverse, negotiate, transit, overfly; *enter*, penetrate, permeate, osmose, percolate, infiltrate; *bridge*, ford, straddle, span.

272 OVERSTEPPING
See also **575** (excess); **820** (lack of entitlement).

n. *overstepping*, trespass, entrenchment, encroachment, intrusion, invasion; *transgression*, violation, infringement, infraction, breach; *excessiveness*, exaggeration, overestimation, hyperbole.

adj. *excessive*, undue, unwarranted, uncalled-for; *intrusive*, invasive, encroaching; *exaggerated*, overdone, far-fetched, over the top (*colloq.*).

vb. *overstep*, go too far, overshoot, overrun, overreach; *trespass*, entrench, encroach, impinge, intrude, invade, poach, muscle in on; *transgress*, violate, infringe, usurp, breach; *exceed*, surpass, outdo, excel, transcend; *exaggerate*, overdo, overrate, overestimate.

273 SHORTFALL
See also **574** (insufficiency).

n. *shortfall*, insufficiency, short measure, shortage, deficit; *lack*, want, dearth, scarcity, famine; *shortcoming*, inadequacy, imperfection, defect, deficiency; *incompleteness*, half measures, perfunctoriness, cursoriness.

adj. *short*, deficient, minus, wanting, lacking, missing; *defective*, imperfect, inadequate, substandard; *incomplete*, half-done, perfunctory, cursory.

vb. *fall short*, miss, lack, want, need, require, cry out for; *fail*, fall through, disappoint, leave something to be desired, not come up to scratch (*colloq.*).

274 ASCENT

See also **184** (height); **276** (raising).

n. *ascent*, climb, rise, ascension, levitation, liftoff, takeoff; *upturn*, upsurge, upswing, increase, spiral, quantum jump; *jump*, leap, vault, spring, bound, hop, skip, high jump; *mountaineering*, climbing, alpinism; *gradient*, incline, slope, hill, ramp; *stairway*, ladder, steps, escalator, lift; *climber*, mountaineer, alpinist, steeplejack, high-jumper, hurdler, steeplechaser.

adj. *ascending*, upward, uphill; *rising*, mounting, buoyant, bullish.

vb. *ascend*, climb, rise, mount, soar, spiral; *take off*, lift off, rocket, surge; *jump*, spring, leap, vault, bound, hop, skip; *scale*, top, breast, clear, hurdle, shin up.

adv. *upwards*, in the ascendant, on the up and up (*colloq.*).

275 DESCENT

See also **185** (lowness); **277** (lowering).

n. *descent*, plunge, dive, swoop, slide, dip, landing, touchdown; *decline*, fall, drop, slump, downturn, tumble, spill; *collapse*, failure, comedown, demotion, downfall, débâcle; *avalanche*, subsidence, cascade, waterfall, chute, precipice; *caving*, potholing, mining, speleology; *diver*, submariner, caver, potholer, speleologist.

adj. *descending*, downward, downhill; *falling*, sinking, declining, bearish; *sagging*, droopy, depressed, down in the mouth (*colloq.*).

vb. *descend*, plunge, dive, swoop, settle, subside, dip; *land*, touch down,

alight, dismount, get down; *decline*, fall, drop, plummet, crash, slump, tumble, spill; *cascade*, overflow, pour, shower; *sink*, submerge, drown, go under; *trip*, stumble, lurch, totter, stagger, collapse, nosedive, bite the dust (*colloq.*).

276 RAISING

See also **184** (height); **274** (ascent).

n. *raising*, erection, elevation, uplift, levitation; *boost*, promotion, upgrading, leg-up (*colloq.*); *height*, eminence, loftiness, sublimity; *raising agent*, leaven, yeast, fermentation; *lifter*, crane, derrick, lever, hoist, jack, lift, escalator, dumb waiter, springboard.

adj. *raised*, erect, upstanding, vertical; *elevated*, sky-high, lofty, eminent, high-flown, sublime.

vb. *raise*, erect, build, put up; *lift*, uplift, hoist, lever, jack up, prop up, shoulder; *send up*, lob, loft, flight; *elevate*, enhance, exalt, put on a pedestal; *arise*, rear, jump up, be upstanding, jump to one's feet.

277 LOWERING

See also **185** (lowness); **186** (depth); **275** (descent).

n. *lowering*, depression, deflation, levelling, demolition; *debasement*, demotion, downgrading, humilation; *overthrow*, overturn, upset, toppling; *crouch*, hunch, duck, bend, stoop, bob, curtsy, genuflection.

adj. *lowered*, depressed, deflated, flattened; *lowering*, humiliating, debasing, demeaning.

vb. *lower*, depress, deflate, squash; *flatten*, level, raze, demolish, fell, ground; *bring down*, topple, floor, overthrow, undermine, torpedo, scuttle; *demote*, downgrade, debase, humble, cashier; *crouch*, stoop, bend, hunch, duck, curtsy, bob, kneel, genuflect.

278 ORBITAL MOTION

See also **279** (rotation).

n. *orbital motion*, rotation, revolution, circulation, circumnavigation; *orbit*, lap, circuit, tour, round trip; *circle*, wheel, spiral, gyre; *satellite*, moon, planet, spaceship, sputnik; *ring road,* orbital, bypass.

adj. *orbital,* roundabout, circular, circuitous.

vb. *orbit,* turn, lap, circuit, revolve, rotate, spiral, wheel; *ring,* circle, circumscribe, gird, loop.

279 ROTATION

See also **223** (circularity); **224** (convolution); **278** (orbital motion).

n. *rotation,* revolution, orbit, cycle; *turn,* roll, spiral, gyration, twirl, corkscrew, pirouette, whirl; *swirl,* eddy, whirlpool, vortex, maelstrom, whirlwind, cyclone, tornado; *roundabout,* merry-go-round, carousel, turntable; *rotor,* propeller, screw, turbine, windmill; *spindle,* axle, lathe, shaft, pivot.

adj. *rotary,* gyratory, spinning, revolving, cyclic.

vb. *rotate,* revolve, orbit, circuit; *turn,* spiral, corkscrew, pirouette, twirl, whirl, swirl; *roll,* wind, reel, spin; *pivot,* swivel, hinge.

280 OSCILLATION

See also **119** (regularity); **281** (agitation).

n. *oscillation,* fluctuation, alternation, reciprocation, undulation, ebb and flow; *vibration,* flutter, tremor, agitation, shake, quiver; *palpitation,* pulse, throb, beat; *pendulum,* bob, oscillator, vibrator, metronome; *rocker,* seesaw, cradle, shuttle, swing; *vacillation,* wavering, indecision, hesitation.

adj. *oscillating,* fluctuating, alternating, reciprocating; *vibrating,* pulsating, throbbing, rhythmical; *vacillating,* hesitant, indecisive, irresolute.

vb. *oscillate,* swing, alternate, fluctuate, reciprocate, undulate; *vibrate,* quake, tremble, quiver, flutter, palpitate; *pulsate,* throb, beat, pound, tick; *rock,* sway, seesaw, zigzag, teeter, reel, stagger; *vacillate,* waver, hesitate, falter.

adv. *to and fro,* from side to side, back and forth.

281 AGITATION

See also **280** (oscillation).

n. *agitation,* vibration, jerkiness,

unsteadiness, tremulousness, palpitation; *tumult,* turmoil, commotion, confusion, stir, bustle; *fuss,* bother, song and dance (*colloq.*), fluster, flap (*colloq.*), tizz (*colloq.*); *turbulence,* ferment, effervescence, seethe, swell, squall; *disturbance,* perturbation, nervousness, jumpiness, edginess, butterflies (*colloq.*), jitters (*colloq.*), heebie-jeebies (*colloq.*), collywobbles (*colloq.*); *restlessness,* feverishness, itchiness, fidgetiness, twitchiness; *tremor,* quiver, shiver, shudder, judder, throb; *convulsion,* paroxysm, spasm, fit, throes, seizure; *jolt,* jar, shock, start, jerk, twitch.

adj. *agitated,* troubled, disturbed, confused, shaken, shocked; *restless,* feverish, fidgety, itchy, twitchy; *nervous,* anxious, perturbed, jumpy, edgy, jittery (*colloq.*), nervy, like a cat on hot bricks (*colloq.*); *flustered,* fussing, fluttery, hot and bothered (*colloq.*); *convulsive,* jerky, fitful, spasmodic, paroxysmic; *turbulent,* stormy, tempestuous, seething, effervescent; *tremulous,* shaky, wobbly, quaking, quivering, trembling.

vb. *be agitated,* boil, churn, heave, seethe, ferment, bubble, effervesce; *convulse,* writhe, squirm, thresh, toss and turn; *vibrate,* quake, throb, palpitate, tremble, flutter, quiver, shiver, shake; *shudder,* judder, jolt, jar, jerk, twitch; *disturb,* rumple, ruffle, muddy, stir, whisk, beat; *flicker,* twinkle, sparkle, glimmer, gutter, sputter.

282 MATERIAL WORLD

See also **3** (reality).

n. *material world,* matter, mass, substance, stuff, body, material, fabric; *embodiment,* incarnation, materialization, solid object, flesh and blood; *concreteness,* corporeality, solidity, tangibility, palpability; *thing,* object, article, gadget, thingamajig (*colloq.*); *ingredient,* element, constituent, component, particle, atom, molecule.

adj. *material,* real, physical, actual, objective; *concrete,* solid, palpable, tangible, sensible; *corporeal,* bodily, fleshly, carnal, worldly, materialistic.

vb. *materialize*, embody, body forth, objectify, incarnate.

283 NONMATERIAL WORLD
See also **396** (intellect).

n. *nonmaterial world*, unreality, insubstantiality, incorporeality, intangibility, impalpability; *spirituality*, otherworldliness, idealism, transcendence, unearthliness; *occultism*, spiritualism, mysticism, paranormal, extra-sensory perception; *psyche*, mind, intellect, soul, spirit, subjectivity, self.

adj. *immaterial*, incorporeal, intangible, ideal, abstract, nonphysical, insubstantial; *disembodied*, shadowy, ghostly, ethereal, unreal; *spiritual*, otherworldly, transcendent, unearthly; *occult*, mystical, psychic, spiritualist.

vb. *dematerialize*, disembody, disintegrate; *idealize*, intellectualize, conceptualize, spiritualize.

284 UNIVERSE

n. *universe*, world, creation, cosmos, macrocosm, space, outer space, galaxy; *earth*, globe, sphere, planet earth, spaceship earth; *heavens*, firmament, empyrean, primum mobile, ether, atmosphere; *celestial body*, planet, star, constellation, comet, meteor, asteroid, satellite, quasar, pulsar, black hole, nova, nebula, falling/shooting star, meteorite; *zodiac*, horoscope, house, ascendant, astrological sign; *sun*, solar system, eye of heaven, daystar, midnight sun; *astronomy*, stargazing, astrophysics, cosmology, cosmography; *earth sciences*, geology, geography, orography, hydrography, cartography.

adj. *universal*, cosmic, macrocosmic, galactic, interstellar; *earthly*, global, worldly, terrestrial, earthbound, tellurian; *celestial*, heavenly, extraterrestrial, ethereal, empyreal, alien; *starry*, stellar, astral, sidereal; *solar*, lunar, nebular, planetary, asteroidal; *astronomical*, cosmological, astrophysical; *geological*, geographical, orographic, cartographic.

285 HEAVINESS
See also **287** (density).

n. *heaviness*, gravity, weight, bulk; *mass*, force, pressure, density; *load*, burden, encumbrance, cargo, freight, ballast, counterweight, counterpoise; *heavy object*, paperweight, sandbag, millstone, lead, stone, plumb, sinker, lead balloon, ton of bricks (*colloq.*); *weighing machine*, scales, balance, weighbridge; *weightiness*, ponderousness, gravitas, seriousness.

adj. *heavy*, bulky, massive, solid, dense; *overweight*, top-heavy, laden, charged; *burdensome*, onerous, cumbersome, unwieldy, clumsy, awkward; *leaden*, oppressive, crushing, insupportable; *weighty*, ponderous, grave, serious, heavyweight (*colloq.*).

vb. *weigh*, balance, outweigh, tip the scales; *pressurize*, lean on, weigh on, encumber, oppress; *burden*, saddle, weigh down, load, overload, weight.

286 LIGHTNESS
See also **306** (air).

n. *lightness*, weightlessness, buoyancy, portability; *airiness*, thinness, transparency, translucence, flimsiness, delicacy, fluffiness; *light object*, cork, float, bob, buoy, inflatable; *air*, foam, froth, bubble, fluff, gauze, gossamer, feather, thistledown; *raising agent*, leaven, yeast, aerator, lightener, thinner.

adj. *light*, buoyant, weightless, portable; *lightweight*, underweight, flyweight, bantamweight; *insubstantial*, flimsy, floaty, feathery, fluffy, frothy; *thin*, gauzy, diaphanous, transparent, translucent.

vb. *be light*, levitate, rise, surface, float, hover, waft, soar; *lighten*, leaven, thin, reduce; *unload*, disencumber, throw overboard, jettison, discard.

287 DENSITY
See also **182** (thickness); **285** (heaviness).

n. *density*, solidity, compactness, concreteness; *mass*, bulk, body, thickness, consistency; *consolidation*, concretization, crystallization, solidification, coagulation; *condensation*, concentration, congestion, saturation; *impenetrability*, impermeability, imperviousness, incompressibility; *solid*, block, lump, nugget, clot, cake.

adj. *dense*, solid, compact, concrete, hard, stiff; *bulky*, massive, substantial, thick; *clotted*, curdled, caked, matted; *condensed*, packed, serried, concentrated, thick on the ground; *impenetrable*, impermeable, nonporous, incompressible.

vb. *become dense*, crystallize, harden, stiffen, set, freeze; *solidify*, congeal, coagulate, thicken, clot, curdle, cake; *make dense*, pack, compress, condense, concentrate; *crowd*, mass, throng, accumulate.

288 SPARSENESS
See also **183** (thinness).

n. *sparseness*, thinness, fineness, wispiness; *rarefaction*, dilution, attenuation, adulteration; *rarity*, infrequency, smattering, sprinkling.

adj. *sparse*, thin, fine, wispy, straggly; *rare*, infrequent, intermittent; *scattered*, dotted, strung out, thin on the ground.

vb. *rarefy*, thin, reduce, adulterate, attenuate, dilute; *scatter*, dot, sprinkle, strew.

289 HARDNESS
See also **294** (toughness).

n. *hardness*, toughness, resilience, resistance, firmness, resoluteness; *stiffness*, rigidity, inflexibility, intractability; *petrification*, ossification, fossilization, sclerosis; *hard-heartedness*, unyieldingness, harshness, callousness, insensitivity; *hard substance*, stone, grit, flint, rock, granite, cement, brick, marble, diamond, steel, iron; *hardwood*, oak, teak, board, bone, horn, shell, armour, carapace.

adj. *hard*, tough, resilient, resistant, firm, unyielding; *rock-hard*, unbreakable, shatterproof, adamantine; *stiff*, rigid, inflexible, intractable, unbending; *stony*, gritty, flinty, steely, rocky; *bony*, horny, woody, crystalline, glassy, vitreous; *hardened*, reinforced, tempered, case-hardened, vitrified; *hardhearted*, callous, harsh, insensitive.

vb. *harden*, toughen, reinforce, temper;

stiffen, starch, freeze, solidify; *petrify*, ossify, fossilize, crystallize, vitrify.

290 SOFTNESS
See also **293** (elasticity); **317** (semiliquid).

n. *softness*, suppleness, springiness, elasticity, give; *pliancy*, flexibility, plasticity, malleability, tractability, ductility; *flaccidity*, limpness, flabbiness, floppiness, slackness, sponginess, doughiness; *tenderness*, gentleness, mildness, mellowness; *pulp*, mud, clay, dough, putty, butter, wax; *down*, velvet, cushion, pillow, feather bed, padding, wadding.

adj. *soft*, yielding, springy, supple, elastic; *pliant*, flexible, plastic, malleable, tractable, ductile; *flaccid*, limp, flabby, floppy, slack; *spongy*, doughy, soggy, pulpy, mushy; *downy*, velvety, cushiony, feathery; *tender*, gentle, mellow, mild.

vb. *soften*, tenderize, mash, pulp, squash, dissolve, melt; *yield*, give, bend, flex; *relax*, ease, sag, flop, slacken; *cushion*, pillow, pad, buffer; *mellow*, relent, temper, sweeten.

291 ROUGHNESS
See also **301** (friction).

n. *roughness*, asperity, harshness, coarseness, crudity; *hairiness*, shagginess, scaliness, scratchiness; *ruggedness*, cragginess, unevenness, jaggedness, knobbliness, brokenness; *rough object*, file, sandpaper, emery board; *bristle*, prickle, tweed, sackcloth, scab, scale, encrustation.

adj. *rough*, harsh, grating, coarse, grainy, gravelly; *uneven*, rutted, pitted, ridged, bumpy, knobbly; *crude*, unfinished, roughcast, rough-hewn; *rugged*, gnarled, craggy, jagged, serrated; *hairy*, hirsute, shaggy, unshaven, dishevelled, unkempt, tousled; *bristly*, scratchy, prickly, tweedy, scaly, scabby, encrusted.

vb. *roughen*, coarsen, harshen; *ridge*, corrugate, serrate, notch; *ruffle*, ripple, dishevel, tousle; *bristle*, prickle, chafe, grate, abrade.

292 SMOOTHNESS
See also **191** (horizontality); **302** (lubrication).

n. *smoothness*, evenness, flatness, levelness; *continuity*, unbrokenness, uninterruptedness; *softness*, silkiness, shininess, glassiness; *slipperiness*, slitheriness, oiliness, greasiness; *suavity*, urbanity, polish, sleekness; *finish*, glaze, lustre, sheen, gloss, shine, varnish; *velvet*, satin, glass, marble, mirror, millpond; *roller*, iron, sandpaper, file.

adj. *smooth*, even, flat, level; *continuous*, uninterrupted, unbroken, smooth-running, streamlined; *soft*, silky, satiny, velvety, clean-shaven; *shiny*, glassy, glossy, lustrous; *sleek*, suave, urbane, polished; *slippery*, slithery, greasy, oily.

vb. *smooth*, even, plane, level, flatten, roll, iron out; *shine*, gloss, polish, buff, glaze, finish; *oil*, grease, slick, lubricate; *slide*, slip, glide, skate, coast.

293 ELASTICITY
See also **290** (softness).

n. *elasticity*, pliability, flexibility, ductility; *expandibility*, extensibility, stretch, give; *spring*, bounce, recoil; *rubberiness*, resilience, buoyancy; *elastic band*, indiarubber, spring, coil.

adj. *elastic*, pliable, flexible, ductile, tensile; *expandable*, extensible, stretchy; *springy*, bouncy, rubbery, resilient, buoyant.

vb. *be elastic*, stretch, expand, give, extend, flex; *bounce*, recoil, spring, rebound.

294 TOUGHNESS
See also **289** (hardness).

n. *toughness*, hardness, strength, durability; *resistance*, tenacity, resilience, stamina; *leatheriness*, chewiness, rubberiness, elasticity; *fibre*, sinew, cartilage, gristle.

adj. *tough*, hard, strong, unbreakable; *durable*, hard-wearing, long-lasting, imperishable; *resistant*, tenacious, unflagging, indefatigable; *leathery*, chewy, rubbery, gristly, cartilaginous; *fibrous*, woody, stringy, sinewy.

vb. *be tough*, wear, outlast, survive, stay the course; *toughen*, harden, strengthen, temper.

295 BRITTLENESS
n. *brittleness*, breakability, frangibility, fragility; *frailty*, flimsiness, delicateness, fineness; *sharpness*, crispness, crunchiness, flakiness, crumbliness, friability; *brittle substance*, glass, eggshell, matchwood, thin ice.

adj. *brittle*, breakable, frangible, fragile; *frail*, flimsy, insubstantial, delicate, papery, wafer-thin; *sharp*, crisp, crunchy, crispy, flaky, crumbly, friable, powdery.

vb. *be brittle*, snap, crack, split, chip, break; *fragment*, fracture, splinter, disintegrate, flake, crumble.

296 SHARPNESS
See also **229** (notch).

n. *sharpness*, pointedness, jaggedness, prickliness, serratedness; *incisiveness*, acuteness, keenness, acuity, mordancy, trenchancy; *sting*, bite, prick, cut, stab; *needle*, pin, nail, barb, point, prong, spur, spike, tine; *spine*, prickle, thorn, tooth, fang, tusk, incisor; *cutting edge*, blade, razor, knife, scissors, shears, secateurs, scalpel, cleaver, guillotine; *sharpener*, file, whetstone, grindstone, carborundum, steel.

adj. *sharp*, pointed, jagged, toothed, serrated, notched; *prickly*, spiny, thorny, barbed, spiky; *razor-sharp*, cutting, keen, trenchant, biting, acute, incisive, trenchant, mordant.

vb. *sharpen*, grind, hone, file, whet, edge; *point*, taper, barb, spur; *prick*, sting, bite, pierce, stab, lance.

297 BLUNTNESS
n. *bluntness*, smoothness, roundedness, stubbiness, flatness; *dullness*, obtuseness, insensitivity; *outspokenness*, frankness, directness, straightforwardness.

adj. *blunt*, smooth, rounded, stubby, snub, flat; *dull*, obtuse, insensitive; *outspoken*, frank, direct, straightforward.

vb. *blunt,* dull, bate, take the edge off, flatten, round.

298 STRUCTURE

See also **216** (form).

n. *structure,* organization, arrangement, pattern, plan; *form,* shape, architecture, make-up, composition, constitution; *framework,* fabric, bodywork, skeleton, anatomy, infrastructure; *construction,* building, edifice, erection, superstructure, elevation.

adj. *structural,* organizational, constructional, architectural, tectonic; *organic,* anatomical, formal, skeletal.

vb. *structure,* organize, plan, pattern, arrange; *shape,* form, construct, build, erect, raise, assemble.

299 TEXTURE

See also **197** (interweaving).

n. *texture,* structure, tissue, web, network; *finish,* surface, feel, touch, sensation; *weave,* grain, warp, weft, woof, nap, pile; *fibre,* filament, yarn, thread, string, tow; *textile,* cloth, material, fabric.

adj. *textural,* textile, woven, spun; *rough,* ribbed, hairy, woolly, tweedy, fibrous, coarse-grained, granulated; *smooth,* finespun, delicate, silky, satiny, cottony.

300 POWDERINESS

n. *powderiness,* dustiness, frosting, efflorescence, bloom; *crumbliness,* flakiness, friability, looseness; *pulverization,* grinding, pounding, erosion, abrasion, attrition; *powder,* dust, sand, pollen, flour, grit, talc, ash, chalk; *granule,* grain, speck, mote, particle, flake, crumb; *grinder,* crusher, mill, hammer, pestle.

adj. *powdery,* dusty, sandy, floury, farinaceous, chalky; *crumbly,* flaky, friable, loose; *ground,* granulated, pulverized, gritty, grainy.

vb. *powder,* dust, sand, flour, sprinkle; *pulverize,* pound, grind, bruise, crush, mill; *crumble,* flake, granulate, chip.

301 FRICTION

See also **291** (roughness).

n. *friction,* drag, resistance, roughness; *rubbing,* abrasion, erosion, corrosion, attrition; *rub,* scrape, graze, polish, elbow grease; *irritation,* grating, tension, irascibility, prickliness; *rubber,* eraser, scraper, sander, emery paper, pumice, sandpaper, file, rasp.

adj. *frictional,* abrasive, irritant; *rough,* rasping, grating.

vb. *rub,* smooth, burnish, scour, polish, buff; *abrade,* scrape, scuff, bark, graze, scratch; *erode,* corrode, wear away, fray; *grind,* rasp, file, plane; *irritate,* chafe, grate, fret, rub up the wrong way.

302 LUBRICATION

See also **292** (smoothness); **319** (oiliness).

n. *lubrication,* nonfriction, smoothness, slipperiness; *oiliness,* greasiness, unctuousness, waxiness; *lubricant,* oil, wax, grease, tallow; *ointment,* salve, balm, cream, lotion, emollient.

adj. *lubricated,* oiled, smooth-running; *oily,* greasy, waxy, slippery.

vb. *lubricate,* oil, grease, wax; *smear,* anoint, cream, daub; *ease,* smooth over, oil the wheels, pour oil on troubled waters.

303 FLUID

n. *fluid,* liquid, gas, condensation, water; *juice,* sap, liquor, gravy, stock, whey; *body fluid,* blood, rheum, pus, saliva, lymph, mucus, plasma, serum; *solution,* infusion, suspension, decoction; *fluidity,* liquidity, juiciness, wateriness, runniness; *liquefaction,* liquidization, dissolution, deliquescence, thaw; *flow,* flux, haemorrhage, suppuration, secretion; *solvent,* liquidizer, blender, liquefier.

adj. *fluid,* liquid, gaseous, soluble; *watery,* runny, juicy, sappy, moist; *molten,* liquefied, dissolved, deliquescent; *rheumy,* weeping, bleeding, pussy, suppurating.

vb. *make fluid,* liquefy, dissolve, deliquesce, condense; *liquidize,* melt, thaw, defrost, render, melt down, smelt; *flow,* run, pour, stream, well up.

304 GAS

n. *gas*, air, ether, atmosphere, exhalation; *smoke*, steam, fumes, reek, cloud, miasma; *vaporization*, distillation, evaporation, atomization; *vaporizer*, atomizer, spray, aerosol, condenser; *gaseousness*, volatility, effervescence, fermentation, fizziness.

adj. *gaseous*, vaporous, volatile, airy, atmospheric, ethereal; *smoky*, steamy, cloudy, misty; *gassy*, fizzy, effervescent, carbonated, sparkling, bubbly.

vb. *gasify*, evaporate, vaporize, volatilize, atomize, distil; *aerate*, fumigate, oxygenate, carbonate; *smoke*, steam, fume, reek, exhale, give off.

305 WATER

See also **308** (moisture).

n. *water*, H_2O, fluid, liquid, wet; *moisture*, steam, vapour, condensation; *sweat*, perspiration, exudate, tears, saliva, spittle; *wateriness*, wetness, dampness, runniness; *dilution*, solution, saturation, hydration; *rainwater*, sea water, fresh water, meltwater, ice, salt water, brine; *shower*, douche, bath, dip, wash, hydrotherapy, irrigation; *irrigator*, well, oasis, hydrant, tap, standpipe, sprinkler.

adj. *watery*, fluid, aqueous, liquid, aquatic; *dilute*, hydrated, saturated, watered down; *wet*, soaked, drenched, streaming, dripping, wringing, sopping, waterlogged, awash.

vb. *water*, moisten, sprinkle, irrigate, hydrate; *water down*, dilute, thin, adulterate, dissolve; *wet*, soak, souse, douse, steep, immerse, wash, bathe, rinse, sluice, hose down; *drench*, flood, inundate, saturate, waterlog, deluge, swamp.

306 AIR

See also **286** (lightness); **316** (wind).

n. *air*, gas, ether, atmosphere, oxygen, ozone; *wind*, breeze, blast, gust; *open air*, open, fresh air, great outdoors; *ventilation*, air-conditioning, airing, exposure; *airiness*, lightness, buoyancy, weightlessness; *air bubble*, froth, foam, suds, lather, spray, spindrift, mousse,

soufflé, meringue; *aeration*, fermentation, leavening, yeast, raising agent.

adj. *airy*, gaseous, ethereal, weightless; *aerial*, buoyant, inflated, lighter-than-air, pneumatic; *bubbly*, foamy, frothy, aerated, yeasty, fizzy; *breezy*, windy, blowy, fresh, gusty; *open-air*, outdoor, al fresco.

vb. *aerate*, inflate, oxygenate, air, ventilate, expose; *blow*, blast, gust, puff, huff; *bubble*, froth, foam, sparkle, fizz, gurgle, simmer, ferment.

307 WEATHER

See also **308** (moisture); **316** (wind).

n. *weather*, elements, weather conditions, climate; *high*, anticyclone, blue skies, heatwave, scorcher (*colloq.*), dry spell, drought; *low*, depression, cyclone, precipitation; *rainfall*, rain, drizzle, shower, downpour, cloudburst, deluge, monsoon, rainy season, rains; *fog*, mist, haze, smog, pea-souper (*colloq.*); *snow*, sleet, hail, snowfall, snowstorm, blizzard, black ice, frost, cold snap; *storm*, high wind, squall, gale, hurricane, typhoon, whirlwind, tornado; *cloud*, cloud cover, cumulus, cirrus, nimbus, stratus, mackerel sky; *barometer*, glass, weather vane, weathercock, windsock, weather forecast, weatherman, meteorologist, climatologist.

adj. *meteorological*, climatic, atmospheric, barometric; *windy*, stormy, squally, blustery; *rainy*, showery, drizzly, snowy, freezing, wintry; *cloudy*, overcast, misty, hazy, foggy; *fair*, clear, sunny, bright, hot, baking, scorching, boiling, sweltering.

vb. *rain*, pour, sleet, hail, snow, freeze; *clear up*, change, brighten up, shine, break through; *blow*, gust, blow up, brew.

308 MOISTURE

See also **305** (water); **307** (weather).

n. *moisture*, dampness, humidity, dankness, wetness; *vapour*, steam, condensation, rising damp, seepage; *perspiration*, sweat, dew, drizzle, spray, precipitation, mist; *mud*, wet, slime, mire, ooze, sludge; *marsh*, swamp, bog, quicksand, quagmire, wetlands, fen, floodplain.

adj. *moist,* humid, damp, dank, clammy, muggy, close; *wet,* tear-stained, dewy, sweaty, misty, drizzly; *marshy,* swampy, boggy, oozy, soggy, squelchy, muddy, sodden, sludgy, waterlogged, splashy, slushy.

vb. *moisten,* dampen, humidify; *sprinkle,* spatter, spray, dabble, splash, slosh (*colloq.*); *be moist,* perspire, sweat, ooze, leak, seep, trickle, dribble.

309 DRYNESS

n. *dryness,* aridity, parchedness, thirst, drought; *dehydration,* drainage, evaporation, desiccation; *desert,* sand dune, dustbowl, wasteland, Sahara; *dryer,* absorbent, blotter, sponge, mop, towel, wringer, spin-dryer, tumble-dryer.

adj. *dry,* bone-dry, parched, thirsty; *desert,* arid, rainless, sandy, dusty, barren; *dehydrated,* desiccated, sun-dried, baked; *waterproof,* dampproof, rainproof, showerproof, watertight; *dried-up,* withered, shrivelled, sere.

vb. *dry,* freeze-dry, drain, dehydrate, evaporate, desiccate; *absorb,* blot, mop up, wipe, sponge, towel; *dry up,* parch, wither, shrivel, bake, toast; *drip-dry,* spin-dry, tumble-dry, wring.

310 OCEAN

See also **314** (running water).

n. *ocean,* sea, briny, the deep, the blue, drink (*colloq.*); *high seas,* open sea, seven seas, main, waters; *seaboard,* coastline, littoral, inshore waters; *channel,* sound, strait, fiord, sea loch, inlet; *estuary,* mouth, delta, firth; *gulf,* bay, bight, cove, lagoon, creek; *wave,* billow, breaker, roller, surf, white horses; *oceanography,* hydrography, hydrology.

adj. *oceanic,* pelagic, deep-sea, marine, maritime, underwater, submarine; *coastal,* littoral, inshore, offshore, sea-going, oceangoing.

311 LAND

See also **313** (plain); **321** (mineral).

n. *land,* ground, terrain, dry land, terra firma; *mainland,* continent,

inland, interior, hinterland; *island,* isle, islet, atoll, reef, sandbank, archipelago; *peninsula,* promontory, headland, isthmus, spit; *plain,* desert, steppe, tundra, polder, highland, lowland; *shore,* strand, beach, seaside, riverbank, floodplain; *earth,* soil, topsoil, alluvium, clay, loam, gravel; *rock,* stone, boulder, pebble, scree; *crag,* outcrop, cliff, escarpment; *limestone,* sandstone, granite, shale, schist, chalk.

adj. *terrestrial,* mainland, inland, continental, overland; *coastal,* onshore, riparian, riverine; *rocky,* stony, pebbly, gritty, gravelly, sandy; *clayey,* alluvial, loamy, chalky, flinty, slaty; *insular,* peninsular, sea-girt, marooned, high and dry, cast away.

312 LAKE

n. *lake,* loch, lough, lagoon, inland sea, sea loch, fiord; *creek,* basin, mudflat, wash, fen, marsh; *pool,* pond, tarn, mere, millpond, reservoir, dam; *waterhole,* oasis, puddle, wallow, well.

313 PLAIN

See also **311** (land).

n. *plain,* expanse, open country, downs, wold, champaign, plateau, tableland; *lowland,* flats, valley, basin, delta; *desert,* tundra, heath, moorland; *grassland,* prairie, steppe, savannah, pampas, veld; *pasture,* field, meadow, lea, park, grounds, green belt, greensward, common.

314 RUNNING WATER

See also **310** (ocean); **315** (channel).

n. *running water,* flow, tide, bore, current, undertow; *river,* waterway, watercourse, canal; *stream,* tributary, feeder, rivulet, brook, burn, beck, rill, runnel; *torrent,* freshet, rapids, white water; *waterfall,* cataract, cascade, falls, weir, Niagara; *flood,* spate, flash flood, tidal wave, tsunami; *spring,* fountain, jet, geyser, waterspout; *wash,* backwash, wake, eddy, swirl, millrace, whirlpool.

adj. *running,* flowing, tidal, fluvial; *choppy,* broken, rough, gurgling, babbling; *smooth,* calm, glassy, meandering, sluggish.

vb. *run*, flow, pour, stream, course, race, rush; *tumble*, surge, roll, dash, swirl, eddy; *gush*, spout, squirt, well up, bubble up; *splash*, lap, swash, wash, slosh (*colloq.*), plash; *trickle*, dribble, ooze, leak, seep. *flow gently*, murmur, babble, gurgle, meander, wind, glide, slide; *flood*, cascade, overflow, spill, inundate, deluge.

315 CHANNEL
See also **240** (way); **314** (running water).

n. *channel*, conduit, course, canal, waterway; *ditch*, trench, moat, riverbed, gutter, pipeline, aqueduct; *lock*, sluice, floodgate, watergate, weir, barrier; *drain*, gully, overflow, culvert, outfall, waterspout, sewer, downpipe, drainpipe.

316 WIND
See also **306** (air); **307** (weather).

n. *wind*, air, draught, downdraught, current, thermal; *blast*, headwind, crosswind, airstream, slipstream, jet-stream, tailwind; *trade wind*, sirocco, chinook, föhn, mistral, harmattan; *breeze*, zephyr, whiff, waft, puff, breath; *squall*, flurry, storm, tempest, hurricane, typhoon, whirlwind, tornado; *bellows*, windbag, air pipe, airway, lung, gill, nostril, blowhole; *respiration*, breathing, inhalation, exhalation, expiration, flatulence, belch, burp (*colloq.*), hiccup, fart (*vulg.*); *pant*, gasp, sigh, sniff, wheeze, cough, sneeze, asthma.

adj. *windy*, airy, draughty, exposed, windswept; *breezy*, blowy, gusty, squally, blustery, stormy; *panting*, out of breath, snuffly, wheezy, chesty, asthmatic.

vb. *blow*, waft, sigh, sough, stir; *blast*, gust, buffet, bluster, blow up, freshen, storm, rage; *air*, fan, ventilate, air-condition; *breathe*, inhale, exhale, expire; *pant*, gasp, puff, wheeze, sniff, snuffle, snort; *belch*, burp (*colloq.*), hiccup, break wind, fart (*vulg.*).

317 SEMILIQUID
See also **182** (thickness); **290** (softness).

n. *semiliquid*, semifluid, emulsion, paste, colloid; *soup*, stew, gruel, porridge, slops; *mud*, slush, ooze, slime, silt, sludge, lava; *pulp*, puree, pap, mush, stodge, curd, batter; *pulpiness*, sponginess, squelchiness, sogginess, squashiness, runniness; *juiciness*, succulence, sappiness, overripeness.

adj. *semiliquid*, semifluid, runny, watery; *juicy*, sappy, succulent, overripe; *thick*, clotted, curdled, coagulated; *pulpy*, soupy, mushy, squashy, spongy, squelchy, soggy, sloppy, sludgy.

vb. *pulp*, puree, mash, liquidize, stew; *thicken*, curdle, clot, congeal, emulsify.

318 VISCOSITY
n. *viscosity*, viscidity, stickiness, clamminess, glutinousness, adhesiveness, tackiness; *adhesive*, glue, gum, resin, paste, size, birdlime, tar; *mucus*, phlegm, albumen, pus, matter; *glaze*, gelatine, syrup, honey, treacle, jelly, slime, goo (*colloq.*), gunge (*colloq.*).

adj. *viscous*, viscid, sticky, tacky, clammy; *adhesive*, gluey, gummy, resinous, tarry; *slimy*, mucous, syrupy, treacly, gooey (*colloq.*), gungy (*colloq.*).

319 OILINESS
See also **302** (lubrication).

n. *oiliness*, unctuousness, greasiness, fattiness, soapiness; *oil*, lubricant, petroleum, paraffin, kerosene; *fat*, grease, soap, tallow, lanolin, blubber, suet, lard, dripping, butter, cream; *ointment*, unguent, salve, liniment, embrocation, pomade, brilliantine.

adj. *oily*, unctuous, oleaginous, slippery, lubricated; *fatty*, soapy, greasy, adipose, pinguid, blubbery, waxy, buttery, creamy.

vb. *oil*, lubricate, grease, wax, soap; *smear*, spread, anoint, baste, butter, cream.

320 ORGANISM
See also **322** (life).

n. *organism*, microorganism, bacterium, virus, germ; *cell*, protoplasm, enzyme, protein, gene, chromosome, DNA; *animal*, plant, flora, fauna, creature, being; *life sciences*, biology, biochemistry, ecology, botany, zoology; *evolution*, development, natural selection, Darwinism, genetics, biotechnology, genetic engineering.

adj. *organic*, bacterial, viral, microscopic; *cellular*, single-celled, chromosomal, genetic; *biological*, ecological, zoological, biochemical, botanical.

321 MINERAL
See also **311** (land).

n. *mineral*, rock, ore, gemstone, metal, precious metal, alloy; *petrification*, fossil, fossil fuel, coal, lignite; *deposit*, vein, stratum, layer, coal measures; *quartz*, topaz, beryl, corundum, feldspar, basalt, obsidian; *mineralogy*, geology, metallurgy.

adj. *mineral*, inorganic, inanimate; *fossilized*, crystalline, glassy, hard, metallic; *mineralogical*, geological, metallurgical.

322 LIFE
See also **1** (existence); **152** (fertility); **320** (organism).

n. *life*, living, being, animation, growth, vital force; *creation*, propagation, birth, nativity, procreation; *existence*, lifetime, one's born days, life history, life cycle, longevity; *soul*, spirit, heart, lifeblood, breath, wind; *creature*, being, mortal, individual, human, organism; *mortality*, way of all flesh, human condition, man's estate, life expectancy, quality of life; *resuscitation*, survival, artificial respiration, kiss of life, lifesaver, life-support system; *vitality*, vigour, vivaciousness, liveliness, verve, energy.

adj. *living*, live, alive and kicking, breathing, quick, viable; *vital*, lively, animated, vivacious, spirited, vigorous; *human*, mortal, finite, ephemeral; *existing*, surviving, long-lived.

vb. *live*, exist, breathe, draw breath; *survive*, outlive, be spared, keep body and soul together, have nine lives, be in the land of the living; *be born*, hatch, come into the world, arrive, see the light of day; *revitalize*, revive, resuscitate, breathe new life into, give a new lease of life; *animate*, enliven, liven up, invigorate, energize.

323 DEATH
See also **2** (nonexistence); **62** (end); **324** (killing); **325** (burial).

n. *death*, mortality, fatality, casualty, losses, death toll; *extinction*, decease, departure, exit, demise, release; *natural death*, accidental death, brain death, stillbirth, miscarriage, abortion; *unnatural death*, murder, foul play, suicide, mercy killing, euthanasia; *deathbed*, death knell, dying day, last hour, dying breath, death rattle, death throes, last words, last rites, last will and testament; *afterlife*, eternity, other side, next world, heaven, hell, happy hunting grounds (*colloq.*), underworld, Hades, Valhalla; *the dead*, ancestors, forefathers, spirits, shades; *death notice*, death certificate, obituary, post mortem, autopsy, inquest; *bereavement*, loss, mourning, widowhood, orphanage.

adj. *dying*, moribund, half-dead, not long for this world, done for, slipping away, in extremis; *dead*, deceased, departed, stone dead, dead and gone, dead as a doornail, extinct, defunct, kaput (*colloq.*); *lifeless*, inert, inanimate, stillborn; *deathly*, fatal, mortal, lethal, deadly; *surviving*, bereaved, widowed, orphaned; *late*, lamented, sainted, posthumous.

vb. *die*, perish, expire, pass over/away, fall asleep, give up the ghost, depart this life, croak (*colloq.*), snuff it (*colloq.*), peg out (*colloq.*), pop one's clogs (*colloq.*), kick the bucket (*colloq.*), push up daisies (*colloq.*); *die out*, wither, fade, go west, go the way of all flesh, go for a burton (*colloq.*); *be dying*, have one foot in the grave (*colloq.*), be on one's last legs (*colloq.*), be at death's door, be a goner (*colloq.*); *drop dead*, die in harness, fall, lay down one's life, be slain.

324 KILLING
See also **150** (destruction); **323** (death).

n. *killing*, destruction, bloodshed, bloodletting, bloodsports, cull; *murder*, homicide, manslaughter, suicide, self-slaughter, hara kiri, felo de se; *execution*, capital punishment, decapitation, hanging, the rope, the gallows, electrocution, garrotte, the stake, auto-da-fe; *assassination*, liquidation, extermination, annihilation, genocide; *carnage*, massacre, bloodbath, butchery, slaughter, holocaust, pogrom, night of the long knives; *killer*, murderer, butcher, assassin, hitman (*colloq.*), executioner, hangman, lynch mob, cutthroat, axeman; *corpse*, body, remains, cadaver, stiff (*colloq.*), mummy, carcass.

adj. *deadly*, destructive, lethal, fatal, toxic, malignant; *murderous*, homicidal, bloodthirsty, psychopathic; *suicidal*, self-destructive, kamikaze; *cadaverous*, corpselike, deathly.

vb. *kill*, slaughter, destroy, put down, butcher, massacre, exterminate, liquidate, annihilate, decimate; *murder*, assassinate, do in (*colloq.*), lynch, bump off (*colloq.*), rub out (*colloq.*); *slay*, dispatch, bring down, shoot, stab, run through, string up, strangle, smother, suffocate; *execute*, hang, decapitate, behead, guillotine, electrocute, gas, garrotte; *kill oneself*, take one's life, commit suicide, do oneself in (*colloq.*).

325 BURIAL
See also **323** (death).

n. *burial*, interment, entombment, cremation; *funeral*, obsequies, last rites, lying-in-state, mourning, wake, cortege; *cemetery*, graveyard, crematorium, churchyard, Calvary, golgotha, catacombs; *grave*, tomb, shrine, sepulchre, mausoleum, vault, crypt; *funeral parlour*, mortuary, morgue; *coffin*, sarcophagus, catafalque, bier, pyre, hearse, pall, shroud, winding sheet; *requiem*, dead march, dirge, lament, elegy, epitaph, obituary.

adj. *buried*, interred, dead and buried, six feet under; *funeral*, funerary, mortuary, elegiac, sepulchral.

vb. *bury*, inter, lay to rest, entomb, enshrine, cremate, embalm, mummify; *mourn*, lament, regret, keen, pay one's last respects; *disinter*, exhume, dig up, unearth.

326 ANIMAL
See also **328** (agriculture).

n. *animal*, beast, dumb animal, creature, wildlife, fauna; *quadruped*, biped, invertebrate, vertebrate, omnivore, herbivore, carnivore; *mammal*, amphibian, reptile, marsupial, ruminant, rodent, crustacean, fish; *domestic animal*, livestock, pet, vermin; *wild animal*, game, endangered species; *bird*, fowl, poultry, bird of prey, hen, cock, chick, fledgling; *cow*, cattle, heifer, bull, calf, bullock, ox, milch cow; *horse*, mare, stallion, foal, filly, colt, pony, nag (*colloq.*), hack, hunter, gee-gee (*colloq.*); *sheep*, ewe, ram, lamb, wether; *pig*, swine, sow, boar, piglet, hog; *dog*, bitch, pup, mongrel, cur, hound, tyke (*colloq.*), mutt (*colloq.*), pooch (*colloq.*), bow-wow (*colloq.*), man's best friend; *cat*, tabby, tom, kitten, pussy (*colloq.*), moggy (*colloq.*), big cat, wildcat; *insect*, larva, grub, pupa, imago, creepy-crawly (*colloq.*); *zoo*, menagerie, safari park, game reserve, aviary, apiary, aquarium.

adj. *animal*, bestial, brutish, feral, wild; *domestic*, tame, house-trained, broken in; *mammalian*, reptilian, amphibian, bovine, equine, ovine, porcine, canine, feline; *omnivorous*, herbivorous, carnivorous, insectivorous.

327 PLANT
See also **329** (horticulture).

n. *plant*, flower, vegetable, weed, herb, shrub, bush, tree, sapling; *plant life*, flora, vegetation, biomass, greenery, verdure; *wood*, forest, jungle, greenwood, woodland, heath, scrub, undergrowth; *copse*, thicket, spinney, plantation, orchard, grove; *branch*, bough, twig, shoot, leaf, foliation, stem, stalk, trunk, bole; *root*, tuber, bulb, corm, rhizome, seed; *flowerhead*, bloom, floret, bud, petal, inflorescence, raceme, panicle; *grass*, pasture, sward, lawn, turf, sod, divot.

adj. *vegetal*, floral, botanical, horticultural; *evergreen*, deciduous, coniferous, hardy, annual, biennial, perennial; *verdant*, leafy, grassy, herbaceous, lush, overgrown, rank; *woody*, sylvan, arboreal, bosky, scrubby, shrubby, jungly.

vb. *plant*, afforest, cultivate, garden, botanize; *grow*, germinate, sprout, shoot, take root, strike.

328 AGRICULTURE

See also 326 (animal).

n. *agriculture*, farming, stockbreeding, factory farming, animal husbandry, agronomy, veterinary science; *farm*, ranch, hatchery, stud farm, battery, piggery; *stable*, byre, cowshed, sheepfold, pen, coop, sty, hutch; *farmstead*, collective farm, kolkhoz, kibbutz, estate, smallholding, croft; *farmer*, agronomist, tenant farmer, peasant, yeoman, smallholder, crofter, shepherd, farmhand, serf; *crop*, produce, yield, harvest, glut.

adj. *agricultural*, agronomic, agrarian; *arable*, pastoral, bucolic, rustic, rural; *purebred*, thoroughbred, crossbred, hybrid, domesticated.

vb. *farm*, ranch, raise, rear, breed, grow; *dig*, till, plough, cultivate, rotivate, drain, reclaim; *irrigate*, fertilize, manure, rake, harrow, hoe; *sow*, broadcast, drill, mow, reap, harvest, gather in, thresh, winnow.

329 HORTICULTURE

See also 327 (plant).

n. *horticulture*, arboriculture, viticulture, market gardening, landscape gardening, topiary; *nursery*, garden centre, orchard, plantation, vineyard; *garden*, allotment, kitchen garden, cabbage patch, herbaceous border, shrubbery, rockery; *park*, arboretum, botanical gardens, herbarium; *hothouse*, greenhouse, glasshouse, orangery, conservatory, cold frame, cloche; *gardener*, horticulturalist, nurseryman, seedsman, market gardener, planter.

adj. *horticultural*, floral, herbal, herbaceous, alpine, hardy, exotic.

vb. *cultivate*, garden, grow, propagate, force, graft; *sow*, plant out, harden off, prick out, transplant; *fertilize*, manure, topdress, mulch.

330 HUMANKIND

n. *humankind*, humanity, human race, mankind, womankind; *human being*, creature, homo sapiens, android, humanoid; *hominid*, apeman, Neanderthal man, troglodyte, savage, barbarian; *person*, individual, mortal, soul, body, personage, figure; *fellow*, character (*colloq.*), customer (*colloq.*), card (*colloq.*), cove (*colloq.*); *family*, house, tribe, clan, sept, line, dynasty; *community*, public, society, masses, tribalism, herd instinct; *population*, populace, people, nation, civilization, culture.

adj. *human*, humanoid, anthropoid, hominoid; *anthropological*, sociological, cultural, ethnological; *interpersonal*, familial, tribal, social, communal, collective, public, civic.

331 NATIONALITY

n. *nationality*, ethnicity, nationhood, statehood; *nationalism*, patriotism, chauvinism, jingoism, racism, antisemitism; *nation*, state, commonwealth, republic, people, ethnic minority; *native*, Brit (*colloq.*), Pommie (*colloq.*), Sassenach (*derog.*), Jock (*colloq.*), Paddy (*colloq.*), Mick (*derog.*), Taffy (*colloq.*); *foreigner*, outsider, immigrant, wop (*derog.*), wog (*derog.*), black, coloured, darkie (*derog.*), coon (*derog.*), nigger (*derog.*), Asian, Pakki (*derog.*); *Latin*, Continental, Frog (*derog.*), Kraut (*derog.*), Eyetie (*derog.*), dago (*derog.*), Polack (*derog.*), Yid (*derog.*), Argie (*derog.*), Yank (*colloq.*).

adj. *national*, racial, ethnic; *nationalistic*, patriotic, jingoistic, chauvinist, racist.

332 MALE

n. *male*, he, man, boy, youth, lad, stripling, Adam, spear side; *masculinity*, manliness, virility, manhood, mannishness, patriarchy, machismo; *gen-*

tleman, lord, master, sir, mister; *fellow*, chap (*colloq.*), bloke (*colloq.*), geezer (*colloq.*), codger (*colloq.*), buffer (*colloq.*), guy (*colloq.*), mate (*colloq.*), buddy (*colloq.*), squire (*colloq.*), governor (*colloq.*); *he-man*, beefcake (*colloq.*), stud, male chauvinist, MCP, misogynist; *bachelor*, homosexual, boyfriend, escort, husband, bridegroom, family man, househusband, paterfamilias, widower, patriarch; *male animal*, cock, drake, gander, capon, jack, buck, stag, dog, stallion, bull, ox, colt, boar, ram, billy, tom.

adj. *male*, masculine, manly, virile, mannish, butch (*colloq.*), macho; *unmanly*, womanish, effeminate, androgynous.

333 FEMALE

n. *female*, she, woman, Eve, fair sex, weaker sex, distaff side; *femininity*, womanhood, womanliness, motherliness; *feminism*, sisterhood, Women's Movement, Women's Lib/Liberation, matriarchy, misandry, lesbianism; *girl*, lass, wench, damsel, maiden, colleen, nymphet, dolly bird; *bachelor girl*, career woman, spinster, old maid, girlfriend, bride, wife, homemaker, housewife, widow, dowager; *lady*, madam, ma'am, dame (*colloq.*), chick (*colloq.*), doll (*colloq.*), bird (*colloq.*), skirt (*colloq.*), crumpet (*colloq.*), cheesecake (*colloq.*); *female animal*, hen, goose, duck, bitch, vixen, heifer, mare, ewe, filly, nanny, doe, hind.

adj. *female*, feminine, gynaecological, obstetric; *womanly*, ladylike, matronly, maternal; *feminist*, liberated, sisterly, lesbian.

334 SENSATION

See also **729** (feeling); **730** (sensitivity).

n. *sensation*, feeling, sensitivity, sensibility; *hypersensitivity*, allergy, soreness, tenderness, rawness; *sense*, feel, touch, perception, awareness; *response*, reaction, reflex, impression; *physicality*, sensuality, body language:

adj. *sentient*, sensible, sensory; *sensitive*, responsive, perceptive, aware,

impressionable, susceptible; *sore*, tender, raw, exposed, hypersensitive, allergic; *physical*, bodily, sensuous.

vb. *sense*, feel, see, hear, touch, taste, smell; *respond*, react, register, realize; *awaken*, arouse, sensitize, impress.

335 INSENSIBILITY

See also **731** (insensitivity).

n. *insensibility*, deadness, numbness, dullness, anaesthesia; *insensitivity*, indifference, callousness; *inertness*, paralysis, catalepsy, catatonia, stupor; *unconsciousness*, coma, trance, faint, swoon, blackout; *anaesthetic*, analgesic, painkiller, sedative, tranquillizer, narcotic.

adj. *insensible*, numb, dead, dull, anaesthetized; *inert*, paralysed, catatonic, cataleptic; *unconscious*, comatose, stupefied, punch-drunk; *insensitive*, unfeeling, callous, thick-skinned.

adj. *desensitize*, deaden, numb, dull, anaesthetize; *drug*, dope, put under, knock out, sedate, tranquillize; *lose consciousness*, swoon, faint, pass out, black out.

336 PHYSICAL PLEASURE

See also **734** (joy).

n. *physical pleasure*, enjoyment, satisfaction, gratification; *pleasure-seeking*, sensuality, debauchery, dissipation, hedonism; *excitement*, arousal, kick (*colloq.*), thrill, turn-on (*colloq.*), orgasm, ecstasy; *ease*, comfort, contentment, wellbeing, euphoria, creature comforts, bed of roses, lap of luxury.

adj. *pleasurable*, agreeable, enjoyable, gratifying, titillating; *comfortable*, easy, luxurious, cosseted, pampered, cushy (*colloq.*); *sensual*, voluptuous, rakish, debauched, hedonistic, dissipated.

vb. *enjoy*, relish, savour, revel, wallow, bask, luxuriate; *excite*, titillate, arouse, thrill, turn on (*colloq.*); *thrive*, prosper, be in clover, live the life of Riley (*colloq.*).

337 PHYSICAL PAIN

See also **735** (sorrow).

n. *physical pain*, illness, suffering, distress, discomfort; *hurt*, injury, wound, trauma, shock, anguish, agony; *wound*, cut, gash, abrasion, bruise, contusion, sprain, fracture; *pang*, twinge, stab, sting, cramp, stitch, gripe, colic.

adj. *painful*, sore, aching, tender, raw, uncomfortable; *distressing*, agonizing, excruciating, exquisite; *injured*, wounded, hurt, traumatized; *stinging*, itchy, smarting, throbbing, stabbing, shooting.

vb. *cause pain*, distress, agonize, torment; *injure*, wound, cut, gash, lacerate, sprain, wrench; *hurt*, ache, smart, burn, gnaw, sting, throb; *wince*, flinch, writhe, squirm.

338 TOUCH

n. *touch*, feel, contact, friction, pressure, squeeze; *handling*, manipulation, massage, reflexology; *light touch*, graze, brush, stroke, caress, pat, flick, tap; *sensation*, itch, scratch, tickle, tingle, prickly heat, pins and needles.

adj. *tactile*, touchable, tangible, palpable; *deft*, delicate, gentle, nimble, feathery; *firm*, tight, clumsy, heavy-handed, rough.

vb. *touch*, feel, finger, sense, fumble, grope, scrabble; *brush*, graze, skim, stroke, caress, pat, dab, paw, nuzzle; *handle*, manhandle, manipulate, massage, knead.

339 HEAT

n. *heat*, warmth, tepidness, lukewarmness, white heat, incandescence; *fever*, flush, glow, sweat, lather; *temperature*, boiling point, flashpoint, overheating, fever pitch; *fire*, flame, spark, blaze, bonfire, conflagration, inferno, holocaust; *heating*, burning, cauterization, combustion, ignition, incineration, cremation; *burn*, scald, scorch, brand, sunburn; *heater*, radiator, solar panel, space heater, geyser, boiler; *cooker*, stove, oven, hob, range, grate, fireplace, hearth; *furnace*, kiln, forge, incinerator, oasthouse.

adj. *hot*, red-hot, white-hot, incandescent, glowing; *feverish*, boiling, sweltering, baking, scorching, torrid, tropical, sultry; *warm*, tepid, lukewarm,

temperate, mild, balmy; *burning*, fiery, flaming, ablaze, aflame, afire, alight; *flammable*, inflammable, combustible, incendiary.

vb. *heat*, warm, boil, bake, scald, toast, scorch, fry, roast, grill; *burn*, kindle, flame, catch fire, flare up, blaze.

340 COLD

n. *cold*, coolness, chilliness, coldness, frostiness, iciness; *chill*, hypothermia, chilblains, frostbite; *wintriness*, snow, sleet, hail, frost, ice, black ice, hoarfrost, rime, icicle; *refrigeration*, glaciation, congelation, freezing; *refrigerator*, cooler, icebox, fridge, deep-freeze, freezer, cold storage.

adj. *cold*, stone-cold, ice-cold, frigid, chilly, parky (*colloq.*); *wintry*, icy, frosty, arctic, Siberian; *keen*, biting, piercing, raw, bitter, cutting; *frozen*, glacé, frappé, on the rocks.

vb. *chill*, cool, freeze, refrigerate, deep-freeze; *frost*, ice, ice up, sleet, hail, snow.

341 FUEL

n. *fuel*, kindling, firewood, tinder, faggot, log; *fossil fuel*, peat, coal, charcoal, coke, lignite, anthracite, petroleum, kerosene, paraffin, natural gas; *nuclear power*, solar energy, electricity, hydroelectricity; *lighter*, flint, firelighter, taper, spill, match, fuse, touchpaper.

adj. *combustible*, flammable, inflammable, incendiary, explosive.

vb. *fuel*, feed, stoke, power, add fuel to the flames; *light*, kindle, fire, catch.

342 TASTE

n. *taste*, flavour, savour, tang, bite, aftertaste, body, richness, tastiness; *sharpness*, sweetness, bitterness, saltiness, brackishness, piquancy, tanginess, spiciness; *appetite*, gusto, relish, zest, heartiness; *palate*, tongue, tastebuds, sweet tooth; *delicacy*, titbit, ambrosia, nectar, caviar.

adj. *tasty*, savoury, wholesome, flavourful, flavoursome; *sharp*, tangy, piquant, bitter, salty, peppery, spicy, sweet; *rich*, full-bodied, mellow, fruity.

delicious, tempting, appetizing, mouthwatering, delectable, palatable, moreish (*colloq.*), scrumptious (*colloq.*), yummy (*colloq.*).

vb. *taste*, sample, try, sip, lick; *savour*, relish, smack one's lips, come back for more, enjoy; *taste of*, savour of, smack of.

343 TASTELESSNESS

n. *tastelessness*, insipidity, blandness, staleness, flatness; *unwholesomeness*, unsavouriness, rankness, rottenness, rancidness; *gruel*, porridge, bread and water, slops, sawdust, dishwater, junk food.

adj. *tasteless*, flavourless, insipid, bland, thin, watery, wishy-washy, diluted; *unappetizing*, unwholesome, unpalatable, stale, overcooked, underdone, inedible; *unsavoury*, bitter, sour, rancid, rank, off, rotten, sickly, cloying, yukky (*colloq.*).

vb. *pall*, cloy, sicken, nauseate, repel, disgust, turn one's stomach.

344 PIQUANCY

n. *piquancy*, pungency, tastiness, bite, zest, tang, nip; *savouriness*, sharpness, tartness, sourness, saltiness, pepperiness, spiciness; *seasoning*, condiment, flavouring, additive, aromatic, herb, relish, spice, dressing; *ginger*, pepper, chilli, cayenne, curry, marinade.

adj. *piquant*, pungent, tasty, hot, tangy; *savoury*, salty, peppery, gingery, spicy, bitter, sour, tart, bittersweet, sweet-and-sour.

vb. *flavour*, season, spice, curry, ginger up, marinade.

345 SWEETNESS

n. *sweetness*, sugariness, saccharinity, sickliness; *sweetener*, sugar, saccharin, honey, nectar, mead, syrup, treacle, molasses; *confectionery*, candy, fudge, bonbon, sweetmeat, fondant, icing, frosting.

adj. *sweet*, sugary, sticky, saccharin, sickly, cloying, syrupy, treacly; *sugared*, honeyed, candied, crystallized, iced, glacé, frosted.

vb. *sweeten*, sugar, sugar-coat, candy, crystallize, ice, frost.

346 SOURNESS

n. *sourness*, tartness, astringency, acidity, acerbity, bitterness, sharpness; *acid*, vinegar, lemon, bitters, gall, alum, wormwood, acid drop.

adj. *sour*, sourish, unsweetened, tart, acid, astringent, acerbic, bitter; *green*, unripe, vinegary, sharp, unsweetened, dry.

vb. *sour*, turn, curdle, acidulate, set one's teeth on edge.

347 ODOUR

See also **349** (fragrance); **350** (stench).

n. *odour*, smell, aroma, scent, fragrance, bouquet, perfume; *stink*, stench, pong (*colloq.*); *exhalation*, breath, whiff, fumes, reek, vapour, effluvium; *redolence*, headiness, pungency, acridness.

adj. *odorous*, odoriferous, redolent, smelly; *scented*, perfumed, fragrant, heady, sweet-smelling; *foul*, stale, noxious, polluted, pungent, rank; *olfactory*, nasal.

vb. *smell*, exhale, give off, emit, stink, reek; *inhale*, sniff, nose, breathe in.

348 ODOURLESSNESS

n. *odourlessness*, lack of smell, freshness, sweetness, fresh air, unpollutedness, smokeless zone; *deodorization*, purification, fumigation, ventilation; *deodorant*, fumigant, disinfectant, air freshener.

adj. *odourless*, unscented, unperfumed, scentless; *deodorized*, pure, fresh, unpolluted, sweet-smelling.

vb. *deodorize*, freshen, clean, purify, ventilate, air, fumigate.

349 FRAGRANCE

See also **347** (odour).

n. *fragrance*, sweet smell, scent, bouquet, odour, aroma; *perfume*, toilet water, eau de cologne, aftershave, pomade; *pomander*, pot pourri, joss stick, air freshener; *essential oil*, fixative, civet, musk, ambergris, attar;

balm, spice, incense, sandalwood, camphor, honeysuckle, lavender, rose.
adj. *fragrant*, odorous, aromatic, redolent; *sweet-smelling*, perfumed, musky, flowery, spicy, fruity.
vb. *scent*, perfume, spice, sweeten.

350 STENCH
See also 347 (odour).
n. *stench*, stink, pong (*colloq.*), niff (*colloq.*), fetor, bad breath, halitosis, B.O.; *foulness*, rankness, putrefaction, rancidness, staleness, mustiness, fustiness; *atmospheric pollution*, fumes, smog, reek, miasma, fug, frowst; *stinker*, stinkbomb, skunk, bad egg, ammonia, sulphur.
adj. *smelly*, stinking, fetid, foul, offensive, noxious, pongy (*colloq.*), niffy (*colloq.*); *high*, gamy, off, putrid, rancid, rank, pungent, foxy; *stale*, stuffy, fuggy, frowsty, polluted, acrid, smoky.
vb. *stink*, reek, fume, smell, pong (*colloq.*), hum (*colloq.*), stink to high heaven.

351 HEARING
See also 353 (sound).
n. *hearing*, audition, auscultation, acoustics; *audibility*, distinctness, loudness, earshot, hearing distance; *overhearing*, eavesdropping, bugging, wiretapping; *listener*, auditor, hearer, audience; *headphones*, stethoscope, earpiece, hearing aid.
adj. *aural*, audiovisual, auditory, acoustic; *audible*, loud, distinct, clear.
vb. *hear*, listen, catch, be all ears (*colloq.*), hearken, heed, lend an ear, prick up one's ears; *overhear*, eavesdrop, listen in on, bug, wire-tap.

352 DEAFNESS
n. *deafness*, hardness of hearing, tonedeafness, deaf-mutism; *inaudibility*, indistinctness, faintness, softness; *lipreading*, sign language, deaf aid, ear trumpet.
adj. *deaf*, hard of hearing, deaf-mute, deaf and dumb, stone-deaf, deaf as a post; *inaudible*, indistinct, faint, muted; *tone-deaf*, tin-eared (*colloq.*),

cloth-eared (*colloq.*); *deafening*, earsplitting, earshattering.
vb. *deafen*, make one's ears ring; *go unheard*, fall on deaf ears, go unheeded; *not listen*, turn a deaf ear, ignore.

353 SOUND
See also 351 (hearing); 355 (loudness); 526 (voice).
n. *sound*, noise, utterance, speechsound; *resonance*, reverberation, sonority, loudness; *sound effect*, soundtrack, sound wave, voiceover; *tone*, pitch, level, timbre, intonation, cadence, lilt; *audibility*, distinctness, clarity; *recordplayer*, gramophone, hi-fi, stereo, sound system, music centre; *acoustics*, dynamics, phonetics.
adj. *sounding*, sonic, acoustic, dynamic, radiophonic; *audio*, mono, stereophonic, binaural, quadraphonic; *audible*, distinct, loud, clear, noisy, sonorous.
vb. *sound*, resound, ring out, reverberate, carry; *utter*, emit, speak, vocalize, voice.

354 SILENCE
See also 527 (voicelessness).
n. *silence*, noiselessness, soundlessness, stillness, hush, lull, peace and quiet; *muteness*, voicelessness, speechlessness, taciturnity; *silencer*, gag, muzzle, blackout.
adj. *silent*, noiseless, soundless, soundproof, hushed, still, quiet, peaceful; *mute*, unspoken, voiceless, speechless, tongue-tied, lost for words, monosyllabic, taciturn.
vb. *silence*, still, hush, quieten, lull; *mute*, tone down, subdue, quell; *muffle*, gag, muzzle, drown out.

355 LOUDNESS
See also 353 (sound); 357 (sudden sound); 359 (resonance).
n. *loudness*, distinctness, clarity, audibility; *volume*, crescendo, decibels, sonority; *noise*, report, bang, roar, crash, boom, reverberation; *stridency*, shrillness, vociferousness, noisiness, clamourousness; *shout*, yell, bellow, guffaw, cry, shriek, scream, screech,

blare, bray, catcall, boo; *din*, row, racket, clamour, outcry, hullabaloo, hubbub, caterwauling; *amplifier*, loud pedal, megaphone, loudhailer, loudspeaker, microphone, public-address system; *siren*, alarm, klaxon, foghorn, gong, trumpet.

adj. *loud*, audible, distinct, clear; *noisy*, clamorous, lusty, strident, vociferous, stentorian, loud-mouthed; *resonant*, sonorous, ringing, plangent; *shrill*, high-pitched, piercing, earsplitting, deafening.

vb. *be loud*, reverberate, resound, peal, swell, ring out, clang, blare, crash, thunder; *shout*, yell, bellow, roar, guffaw, cry out, screech, scream, shriek; *be noisy*, clamour, deafen, raise Cain, raise the roof (*colloq.*), make the rafters ring.

adv. *loudly*, at the top of one's voice, fortissimo.

356 FAINTNESS

See also 360 (mutedness).

n. *faintness*, softness, lowness, mutedness, indistinctness, inaudibility; *low sound*, whisper, undertone, sigh, murmur, mutter, mumble, hum, moan, groan, squeak; *tinkle*, rustle, swish, whirr, purr, lap, pad, patter.

adj. *faint*, soft, low, muted, murmured, soft-spoken, indistinct, inaudible; *quiet*, hushed, subdued, muffled, distant, far-off.

vb. *be faint*, die away, fade, weaken; *whisper*, murmur, croon, mutter, moan, groan, sigh; *tinkle*, chirr, whirr, purr, lap, swish, rustle, sough.

adv. *faintly*, under one's breath, sotto voce, piano, out of earshot.

357 SUDDEN SOUND

See also 355 (loudness).

n. *sudden sound*, report, pistol shot, gunfire, backfire, explosion, sonic boom, thunderclap; *bang*, crash, crack, peal, blast, burst, volley, salvo; *knock*, rap, tap, clap, rat-at-tat; *shout*, yell, whoop, hoot, screech, scream, shriek.

vb. *bang*, crash, thunder, crack, burst out; *explode*, backfire, erupt, go off,

ring out, peal; *cry out*, shout, scream, yelp, whoop, hoot.

358 REPEATED SOUND

n. *repeated sound*, reverberation, echo, roll, rumble; *rattle*, clatter, racket, chatter, babble, rhubarb, background noise; *drumming*, tattoo, thrumming, strumming, throbbing, pulse; *trill*, tremolo, vibrato, quaver; *buzz*, whirr, chirr, hum, drone.

vb. *roll*, rumble, grumble, reverberate, echo; *drum*, thrum, strum, beat, tick, throb; *trill*, vibrate, tremble, quaver; *rattle*, clatter, chatter, drone, hum, whirr.

359 RESONANCE

See also 355 (loudness).

n. *resonance*, reverberation, plangency, sonorousness, hollowness; *echo*, overtone, ring, ping, clang, twang, peal, chime; *tinkle*, clink, chink, clank, jangle, jingle; *bell*, gong, chimes, cymbals, tubular bells, glockenspiel, echo chamber.

adj. *resonant*, reverberant, plangent, sonorous, hollow, echoey, lingering, vibrant; *metallic*, tinkly, jingling, ringing, clanking.

vb. *resonate*, vibrate, carry, reverberate, echo; *peal*, chime, ring, ting, ping, twang, jingle, jangle; *clink*, clank, chink, tinkle.

360 MUTEDNESS

See also 356 (faintness).

n. *mutedness*, nonresonance, deadness, dullness, muffledness, indistinctness; *thud*, thump, thwack, clump, plonk, clonk, plop; *mute*, silencer, damper, soft pedal.

adj. *muted*, dead, dull, muffled, subdued, indistinct.

vb. *mute*, deaden, dull, soften; *subdue*, damp, stifle, muffle, tone down, lower; *thud*, thump, pound, clump, clonk, plonk, plop.

361 HISSING SOUND

adj. *hissing*, sibilant, fizzy, wheezy, splashy, sploshy.

vb. *hiss*, whisper, splash, swish, swash,

sigh, sough; *rustle*, rasp, whistle, wheeze; *buzz*, fizz, sizzle, spit, sputter.

362 HARSH SOUND
See also **366** (dissonance).

n. *harsh sound*, screech, squawk, croak, caw, skirl, shriek; *rasp*, cough, hawk, grate, scrape, scratch; *roughness*, hoarseness, huskiness, gruffness; *stridency*, shrillness, raucousness, braying; *discord*, dissonance, cacophony, jangle, clash.

adj. *harsh*, strident, shrill, raucous, brassy, tinny; *hoarse*, husky, gruff, throaty, growly, guttural; *rough*, rasping, grating, scratchy, rusty, creaky; *discordant*, jarring, cacophonous, dissonant, jangly, clashing.

vb. *shriek*, screech, squawk, croak, caw, bray, skirl, blare, clang; *scrape*, scratch, grate, rasp, saw, grind, creak; *jar*, clash, jangle, set one's teeth on edge.

363 HUMAN CRY
See also **355** (loudness).

n. *human cry*, shout, call, exclamation, ejaculation; *outcry*, clamour, raised voices, noise, din, hubbub; *yell*, yelp, whoop, hoot, halloo; *cheer*, hurrah, boo, catcall; *howl*, wail, roar, guffaw, bellow; *shriek*, scream, screech, squeal; *moan*, groan, grunt, whimper, gasp.

adj. *loud*, high-pitched, clamorous, noisy, vocal, vociferous, lusty, full-throated.

vb. *cry out*, call out, exclaim, ejaculate; *shout*, clamour, yell, bawl, holler (*colloq.*), howl, yowl, wail, caterwaul; *shriek*, screech, squeal, yelp; *chant*, chorus, cheer, whoop, boo, yodel; *roar*, rant, bellow, guffaw, hoot; *moan*, groan, whinge (*colloq.*), whimper, sob, gasp, grunt.

364 ANIMAL CRY
n. *animal cry*, call, birdcall, note, song.
vb. *cry*, call, caw, coo, quack, cluck, crow, cackle, honk, croak, gobble; *cheep*, peep, chirrup, tweet, whistle, warble, twitter, chatter; *squawk*, screech, squeal, scream; *bark*, yap, yelp, bay, bell, howl, whine; *grunt*,

growl, snarl, roar; *neigh*, bray, whinny, whicker, snort, snicker; *miaow*, mew, purr, hiss, spit; *bleat*, baa, moo, low, bellow; *hum*, drone, buzz, chirr.

365 MELODY
See also **367** (music).

n. *melody*, harmony, euphony, concord, tonality, consonance; *melodiousness*, tunefulness, musicality, mellifluousness, sweetness; *tune*, air, song, strain, refrain, ditty; *pitch*, intonation, register, key.

adj. *melodic*, tuneful, musical, true, in tune; *melodious*, harmonious, euphonious, sweet, mellifluous, dulcet, silvery, bell-like; *catchy*, lilting, memorable, singable, hummable.

vb. *be melodious*, harmonize, blend, chime in, chorus.

366 DISSONANCE
See also **362** (harsh sound).

n. *dissonance*, discord, disharmony, tone-deafness, atonality; *harshness*, raucousness, tonelessness, monotony; *cacophony*, caterwauling, Babel, row, racket, din.

adj. *dissonant*, discordant, atonal, out-of-tune, off-key, tone-deaf, flat, sharp; *inharmonious*, untuneful, unmusical, toneless, monotonous, singsong; *cacophonous*, raucous, harsh, jarring, jangling, grating.

vb. *be dissonant*, jangle, jar, grate, clash.

367 MUSIC
See also **365** (melody); **368** (musician).

n. *music*, harmony, melody, music-making, musicianship; *classical music*, chamber music, light music, Muzak (*tdmk.*); *pop music*, rock, blues, soul, disco, country and western, reggae, folk, punk, new wave, jazz, swing, trad, bop, jazz-rock; *performance*, recital, concert, gig (*colloq.*), jam session, recording session; *tune*, theme, signature, tune, backing, incidental music; *score*, libretto, lyrics, songbook, sheet music; *piece*, composition, work, opus, arrangement, setting, orchestration, improvisation; *song*, ballad, hymn, psalm, spiritual, aria, madrigal; *opera*, operetta, oratorio, chorale, mass, musical; *overture*, sonata, fugue, suite, concerto, symphony; *dance music*, jig, minuet, gavotte, mazurka, polka, waltz, foxtrot; *prelude*, intermezzo, impromptu, nocturne, scherzo, serenade, requiem, rondo.

adj. *musical*, tuneful, melodic, polyphonic, contrapuntal; *classical*, highbrow, straight, romantic, baroque; *popular*, lowbrow, middlebrow, bluesy, jazzy, hot (*colloq.*), cool (*colloq.*), funky (*colloq.*); *vocal*, operatic, choral, unaccompanied; *instrumental*, orchestral, symphonic, solo.

368 MUSICIAN
See also 367 (music).

n. *musician*, player, performer, soloist, accompanist, instrumentalist, artiste, virtuoso; *minstrel*, bard, troubadour, busker, one-man band; *singer*, vocalist, songster, chorister; prima donna, diva; *soprano*, mezzosoprano, contralto, treble, alto, countertenor, tenor, baritone, bass; *composer*, arranger, librettist, songwriter; *conductor*, maestro, leader, bandmaster, bandleader; *orchestra*, chamber orchestra, ensemble, group, band; *duo*, trio, quartet, quintet, sextet, octet.

vb. *play*, perform, execute, interpret, play by ear, sight-read, accompany; *sound*, pluck, bow, blow, beat, finger, tickle the ivories (*colloq.*); *sing*, vocalize, intone, carol, trill, chant, chorus; *arrange*, score, orchestrate, compose, set to music, transpose.

369 MUSICAL INSTRUMENT

n. *musical instrument*, synthesizer, record-player, tape-recorder, cassette deck, music centre, sound system; *record*, disc, album, cassette, tape, LP., EP., single, compact disc, digital record; *wind instrument*, brass, trumpet, trombone, bugle, flugelhorn, saxophone, French horn, tuba, euphonium, bagpipes; *woodwind*, oboe, bassoon, flute, clarinet; *stringed instrument*, double bass, cello, violin, fiddle (*colloq.*),

viola, harp; *guitar*, mandolin, lute, banjo, ukelele, cithar, zither, dulcimer; *keyboard instrument*, piano, grand, baby grand, upright, harpsichord, virginals, spinet, harmonium, organ, accordion; *percussion*, timpani, kettledrum, cymbal, triangle, tambourine, drum, vibraphone, marimba, xylophone, gong, chimes, glockenspiel, maracas, castanets.

370 VISION
See also 372 (visibility).

n. *vision*, seeing, sight, eyesight; *perception*, recognition, insight, imagination, mind's eye; *visual defect*, shortsightedness, myopia, long-sightedness, presbyopia, astigmatism, squint, strabismus, cast, colour blindness, cataract; *eye*, naked eye, peepers (*colloq.*), orbs (*colloq.*), glad eye (*colloq.*), sheep's eyes, evil eye; *look*, gaze, stare, glance, eye contact, glimpse, peek, peep, butcher's (*colloq.*), dekko (*colloq.*), once-over (*colloq.*), look-see (*colloq.*); *inspection*, scrutiny, reconnaissance, surveillance, watch, observation, lookout; *view*, sight, spectacle, eyesore, eyeful (*colloq.*), sight for sore eyes (*colloq.*); *survey*, perspective, overview, bird's eye view, outlook; *viewer*, spectator, observer, watcher, eye witness, onlooker, bystander, audience; *optical device*, telescope, binoculars, field glasses, microscope, magnifying glass; *spectacles*, glasses, specs (*colloq.*), goggles, contact lens, pince-nez, monocle, bifocals; *optical illusion*, mirage, will o' the wisp, ignis fatuus, trick photography, phantom.

adj. *visual*, ocular, optical, ophthalmic; *perceptive*, observant, clear-sighted, perspicacious; *sharp-eyed*, watchful, eagle-eyed, hawk-eyed, lynx-eyed; *short-sighted*, myopic, purblind, longsighted, presbyopic, colour-blind, cross-eyed, wall-eyed, astigmatic.

vb. *see*, behold, perceive, discern, make out, recognize; *glimpse*, catch sight of, spot, espy, clap eyes on; *look*, gaze, stare, gape, glare, peer, focus, fix, eye; *glance*, peek, peep, peer, wink, blink, squint, leer, ogle; *inspect*, scrutinize,

371 BLINDNESS

scan, peruse, look up and down, pore over; *watch*, observe, look out for, keep a weather eye open, keep one's eyes skinned/peeled (*colloq.*).

371 BLINDNESS

n. *blindness*, sightlessness, night-blindness, snow-blindness, colour-blindness, word-blindness, dyslexia; *blind spot*, blind side, tunnel vision; *blinkers*, blindfold, eye patch.
adj. *blind*, visually handicapped, blind as a bat, sightless, eyeless, unseeing; *blinded*, blindfold, blinkered, benighted; *blinding*, dazzling, flashing.
vb. *blind*, dazzle, blinker, blindfold, hoodwink; *go blind*, lose one's sight, be in the dark (*colloq.*), not see the wood for the trees.

372 VISIBILITY
See also **370** (vision).
n. *visibility*, conspicuousness, obviousness, prominence; *distinctness*, clarity, plainness, discernibility, perceptibility; *seeing distance*, field of vision, eyeshot, view.
adj. *visible*, discernible, perceptible, observable, detectable; *noticeable*, conspicuous, eye-catching, prominent; *apparent*, evident, obvious, plain, clear, crystal-clear, distinct, definite, clear-cut; *unmistakable*, glaring, blatant, flagrant, egregious.
vb. *be visible*, stand out, show up, leap to the eye, stick out like a sore thumb (*colloq.*); *appear*, come into view, loom, materialize.
adv. *visibly*, in full view, before one's very eyes, under one's nose.

373 INVISIBILITY
See also **376** (dimness); **469** (concealment).
n. *invisibility*, imperceptibility, indistinctness, vagueness, dimness; *poor visibility*, mistiness, haziness, fogginess; *concealment*, disguise, smokescreen, veil, curtain.
adj. *invisible*, unseen, imperceptible, indiscernible, unrecognizable; *inconspicuous*, microscopic, minute, faint; *indistinct*, unclear, vague, blurred,

hazy, misty, foggy; *hidden*, obscured, submerged, latent.
vb. *be invisible*, hide, lurk, escape notice, be lost to view; *disappear*, fade, vanish, submerge; *conceal*, veil, screen, curtain.
adv. *out of sight*, out of focus.

374 LIGHT
See also **377** (light source).
n. *light*, first light, dawn, broad daylight, sunlight, twilight, dusk, half-light, moonlight, starlight; *illumination*, lamplight, candlelight, artificial light; *brightness*, radiance, brilliance, luminosity; *shine*, lustre, gloss, sheen, iridescence, highlight; *ray*, beam, shaft, pencil, streak, chink; *flash*, glint, glitter, twinkle, sparkle, flicker; *gleam*, glimmer, shimmer, glow, nimbus, halo; *dazzle*, glare, blaze, flare; *luminescence*, fluorescence, phosphorescence, northern lights, aurora borealis; *play of light*, light and shade, dappling, chiaroscuro; *radiation*, X-ray, laser, hologram; *reflection*, refraction, diffraction.
adj. *light*, lit, floodlit, spotlit; *bright*, radiant, brilliant, effulgent; *gleaming*, lambent, flickering, shimmery; *sparkly*, glittery, glinting, twinkly, flashing, coruscating; *shiny*, lustrous, glossy, wet-look; *incandescent*, glowing, luminescent, phosphorescent, fluorescent, Day-glo (*tdmk.*).
vb. *shine*, blaze, dazzle, flash, sparkle, glitter, glint; *gleam*, glow, shimmer, flicker, twinkle; *radiate*, beam, reflect, refract, emit; *illuminate*, irradiate, light up, brighten.

375 DARKNESS
See also **376** (dimness); **384** (black).
n. *darkness*, blackness, murkiness, gloominess, night, nightfall; *dusk*, gloom, murk, shadow, silhouette; *blackout*, eclipse, fadeout, lights out.
adj. *dark*, black, inky, pitch-black, coal-black; *gloomy*, sombre, murky, shadowy, dingy; *nocturnal*, night-time, benighted, unlit, starless, moonless.
vb. *darken*, blacken, dim, fade out; *extinguish*, douse, switch off, snuff out;

befog, obscure, obfuscate, eclipse, overshadow.

376 DIMNESS
See also **373** (invisibility); **380** (opaqueness).

n. *dimness*, faintness, indistinctness, vagueness, fuzziness; *cloudiness*, mistiness, smokiness, haziness, opacity; *twilight*, half-light, gloaming, dusk, bad light; *murk*, gloom, shade, penumbra, shadow; *mist*, fog, haze, blur, film, cloud.

adj. *dim*, faint, indistinct, bleary, blurred, fuzzy; *vague*, nebulous, confused, grey; *filmy*, cloudy, opaque, obscured; *hazy*, misty, foggy, smoky; *shadowy*, twilit, gloomy, murky, dingy.

vb. *dim*, fade, wane, die away; *obscure*, bedim, befog, mist up, cloud, muddy; *blur*, smear, dirty, besmirch.

377 LIGHT SOURCE
See also **374** (light).

n. *light source*, naked light, flare, torch, bonfire; *fire*, coal, ember, brand, flame; *match*, lighter, taper, spill, candle; *lamp*, flashlight, lantern, headlamp, searchlight, floodlight; *light bulb*, fluorescent tube, strip lighting, strobe light, neon light, spotlight; *warning light*, sidelight, indicator, tail light, traffic light, lighthouse, beacon; *light fitting*, chandelier, electrolier, pendant, standard lamp.

adj. *luminous*, flaming, glowing, incandescent, dazzling, well-lit.

378 SCREEN
See also **202** (covering).

n. *screen*, shield, shelter, covering, shade; *awning*, canopy, windbreak, safety curtain; *sunscreen*, visor, sunglasses, eyeshade, parasol, umbrella; *blind*, shutter, jalousie, curtain, netting; *veil*, hood, mask, cloak, blindfold, blinkers.

adj. *screened*, shaded, protected, shuttered, blinkered; *shady*, sheltered, secluded.

vb. *screen*, shield, protect, shelter, shade; *conceal*, curtain, veil, cloak, blanket, hood, mask, shroud.

379 TRANSPARENCY
n. *transparency*, clearness, limpidity, pellucidity; *translucence*, thinness, fineness, gauziness, diaphanousness; *glass*, ice, water, crystal, cellophane, Perspex (*tdmk.*); *gauze*, lace, chiffon, gossamer.

adj. *transparent*, clear, limpid, pellucid, sheer, see-through; *translucent*, thin, fine, filmy, gauzy, lacy, diaphanous, revealing; *glassy*, crystalline, vitreous, crystal-clear.

380 OPAQUENESS
See also **376** (dimness).

n. *opaqueness*, opacity, filminess, cloudiness, muddiness, turbidity, murkiness; *opalescence*, milkiness, pearliness, frosting; *fog*, mist, film, smokescreen, smoked glass; *mattness*, thickness, density.

adj. *opaque*, filmy, cloudy, muddy, turbid, unclear, murky; *opalescent*, milky, pearly, matt, frosted; *foggy*, misty, smoky, hazy.

vb. *make opaque*, cloud, film, frost, smoke, darken, muddy, dim.

381 COLOUR
See also **490** (painting).

n. *colour*, hue, saturation, tone, brilliance, intensity; *chromaticism*, primary/secondary/complementary colour; *shade*, tint, tincture, dash, touch, tinge; *coloration*, colouring, pigmentation, colour scheme; *spectrum*, prism, rainbow, palette; *pigment*, paint, dye, stain, watercolour, wash, distemper; *colourfulness*, vividness, gaudiness, garishness.

adj. *coloured*, chromatic, tinted, dyed, colourfast; *colourful*, multicoloured, polychrome, variegated, technicoloured, psychedelic; *gaudy*, bright, vivid, garish, harsh, shocking, clashing, lurid, loud; *pale*, subdued, soft, subtle, pastel, muted; *deep*, rich, glowing, intense, brilliant.

vb. *colour*, tint, shade, tinge; *dye*, stain, wash, distemper, rouge; *paint*, pigment, enamel, crayon, daub.

382 COLOURLESSNESS
See also **383** (white).

383 WHITE

n. *colourlessness*, achromatism, neutrality, monochrome; *discoloration*, fading, bleaching, whitening; *pallor*, paleness, whiteness, bloodlessness, pastiness, sallowness, anaemia; *greyness*, drabness, insipidness, dullness, dinginess; *decolorant*, bleach, peroxide, whitener.

adj. *colourless*, achromatic, neutral, monochromatic; *natural*, undyed, bleached, faded, discoloured; *pale*, pallid, wan, pasty, sallow, washed out, anaemic, etiolated, livid, ashen; *fair*, ash-blond, mousy, albino; *grey*, dull, drab, dingy, insipid, lacklustre.

vb. *lose colour*, fade, run, discolour, pale; *decolorize*, bleach, whiten, blanch, etiolate.

383 WHITE

See also 382 (colourlessness).

n. *white*, ivory, magnolia, off white, broken white, ecru, cream; *whiteness*, paleness, creaminess, blondness, fairness; *milkiness*, pearliness, silverness, snowiness; *white heat*, incandescence, white light, white water, white horses, spume; *snow*, alabaster, milk, moonstone, hoarfrost, rime; *whitener*, whitewash, blanco, pipeclay, chalk; *white metal*, white gold, platinum, nickel.

adj. *white*, light, bright, dazzling; *pure white*, snow-white, lily-white, milk-white; *fair*, blond, ash-blond, flaxen, platinum-blond, albino; *white-haired*, hoary, silvery, snowy, grizzled; *whitish*, creamy, milky, pearly, chalky, floury, mealy, frosted; *white-skinned*, Caucasian, pale, ashen, waxen.

vb. *whiten*, lighten, fade, pale; *silver*, frost, rime, grizzle; *blanch*, bleach, whitewash.

384 BLACK

See also 375 (darkness).

n. *black*, ebony, sable, jet, ink, soot, carbon, coal, pitch; *blackness*, swarthiness, inkiness, sootiness; *Negro*, coloured, nigger (*derog.*), blackamoor.

adj. *black*, blackish, dirty, inky, sooty, fuliginous; *jet-black*, blue-black, pitch-black, coal-black, black as the ace of spades; *black-haired*, brunette, raven-haired; *dark-skinned*, swarthy, dusky, Negroid; *dark*, sombre, murky, gloomy, Stygian.

vb. *blacken*, darken, singe, char; *dirty*, smudge, tarnish, besmirch.

385 GREY

n. *grey*, taupe, pewter, lead, slate, gun-metal; *greyness*, dullness, drabness, colourlessness.

adj. *grey*, pearl-grey, dapple-grey, silver-grey, dove-grey, oyster; *dark grey*, blue-grey, slaty, steely, leaden; *opalescent*, pearly, silvery, frosted; *grey-haired*, greying, grizzled, pepper-and-salt, hoary; *greyish*, neutral, drab, smoky, hazy.

386 BROWN

n. *brown*, ochre, sepia, raw sienna, burnt umber, bistre; *bronze*, amber, copper, cinnamon, coffee, caramel, mocha, chocolate, mahogany; *brunette*, redhead, bay, roan, sorrel.

adj. *brown*, brownish, hazel, dun, nut-brown, tan, tawny, khaki; *light brown*, fawn, biscuit, beige, buff, oatmeal, café-au-lait; *reddish-brown*, coppery, chestnut, russet, liverish, auburn, peaty; *dark brown*, nigger-brown, swarthy, bronzed, tanned, sunburnt.

vb. *brown*, burn, scorch, toast, tan, bronze.

387 RED

n. *red*, carmine, vermilion, crimson lake, cochineal, rouge, henna; *redness*, rosiness, floridness, ruddiness, blush, flush, glow, high colour; *ruby*, garnet, coral, flame, blood, gore; *rose*, poppy, cherry, lobster, beetroot; *wine*, port, burgundy, claret.

adj. *red*, reddish, ruddy, rosy, apple-cheeked, rubicund, florid, sanguine; *blood-red*, bloody, gory, bloodshot; *red-hot*, glowing, flaming, warm; *bright red*, scarlet, crimson, pillarbox-red, brick-red, terracotta; *reddish-brown*, russet, rufous, oxblood; *red-gold*, titian, redheaded, strawberry blond; *light red*, pink, salmon-pink, shell pink, peachy, flesh-coloured, old rose; *dark red*, purplish, cerise, magenta, rose.

vb. *redden*, rouge, henna, raddle; *blush*, flush, glow, crimson, mantle, colour.

388 ORANGE

n. *orange*, amber, burnt orange, gamboge; *copper*, rust, bronze, ginger, henna; *tangerine*, apricot, peach, marmalade, marigold.

adj. *orange*, orangey, tan, russet; *coppery*, auburn, gingery, carroty.

389 YELLOW

n. *yellow*, chrome yellow, ochre, saffron, turmeric; *yellowness*, sallowness, biliousness, jaundice; *yellow metal*, gold, brass, ormolu; *lemon*, mustard, egg yolk, cream, butter; *primrose*, jonquil, daffodil, jasmine, mimosa, buttercup.

adj. *yellow*, yellowy, golden, blond, flaxen· *pale yellow*, creamy, honey-coloured, corn-coloured; *bright yellow*, lemon-yellow, primrose-yellow, canary-yellow, sulphur-yellow; *dark yellow*, old gold, mustardy, tawny, sandy, sallow.

390 GREEN

n. *green*, viridian, bice, verdigris, chlorophyll; *greenness*, greenery, verdure, leafiness, green belt, grass, turf; *emerald*, jade, aquamarine, beryl; *lime*, greengage, avocado, olive.

adj. *green*, greenish, glaucous, viridescent; *grassy*, leafy, mossy, verdant; *bright green*, grass-green, apple-green, pea-green, chartreuse, lime-green; *dark green*, sage-green, sea-green, celadon, moss-green, bottle-green, olive-green, khaki; *greenish-blue*, eau-de-Nil, turquoise.

391 BLUE

n. *blue*, cyan, cobalt blue, Prussian blue, ultramarine, indigo, woad; *sapphire*, lapis lazuli, turquoise, aquamarine; *forget-me-not*, cornflower, harebell, gentian, delphinium.

adj. *blue*, bluish, cerulean, sky-blue, azure; *light blue*, powder blue, duck-egg blue, Cambridge blue, Wedgwood blue; *bluey-green*, turquoise, kingfisher blue, peacock blue, electric blue;

bluey-grey, slaty, steely, gunmetal; *dark blue*, Oxford blue, royal blue, midnight blue, blue-black, navy.

392 PURPLE

n. *purple*, amethyst, gentian violet, Tyrian purple; *plum*, aubergine, mulberry, damson, cherry; *lilac*, heather, violet, lavender, heliotrope, fuchsia; *wine*, burgundy, claret, grape.

adj. *purple*, purplish, mauve, maroon, puce, magenta, cerise.

393 VARIEGATION

n. *variegation*, diversity, variety, nonuniformity, colourfulness; *patchwork*, motley, tartan, mosaic, chequerboard, marquetry; *kaleidoscope*, spectrum, rainbow, prism, coat of many colours; *iridescence*, shot silk, mother of pearl, tiger's eye, watered silk; *jasper*, agate, tortoiseshell, marble; *patch*, blotch, splotch, spot, dot, fleck, speck, freckle, speckle.

adj. *variegated*, multicoloured, polychromatic, colourful; *iridescent*, chatoyant, opalescent, pearly, nacreous, moiré; *patchy*, mottled, chequered, particoloured; *striped*, barred, marbled, veined, streaky; *pied*, grizzled, brindled, pepper-and-salt, piebald, skewbald; *spotted*, speckled, stippled, dotted, studded.

vb. *variegate*, diversify, chequer, patch, counterchange; *sprinkle*, pepper, dot, spangle, speckle, dapple; *stripe*, bar, vein, marble, streak, striate; *stain*, splash, blotch, mottle.

394 APPEARANCE

See also **464** (display).

n. *appearance*, phenomenon, manifestation, realization, materialization, embodiment; *aspect*, exterior, outside, externals, appearances; *front*, veneer, image, facade, pose, semblance, guise, first impressions; *look*, expression, countenance, mien, demeanour, air, bearing; *sight*, spectacle, panorama, display, exhibition; *apparition*, vision, mirage, hallucination, phantom, will o' the wisp.

adj. *apparent*, outward, external, superficial, visible, manifest; *seeming*, ostensible, specious, plausible, deceptive, meretricious.

vb. *appear*, seem, look, come over as; *show*, exhibit, display, manifest; *arise*, materialize, come into being, emerge, come to light, surface; *arrive*, turn up, show up, put in an appearance, pop up (*colloq.*), crop up.

adv. *apparently*, ostensibly, on the face of it, to all appearances; *superficially*, at face value, at first sight, prima facie; *on view*, on show, on display.

395 DISAPPEARANCE
See also **373** (invisibility).

n. *disappearance*, departure, flight, escape, elopement; *loss*, shrinkage, diminution, evaporation, dissolution; *extinction*, obliteration, erasure, cancellation, dispersal; *eclipse*, fadeout, blackout, disappearing trick; *evanescence*, transience, transitoriness, elusiveness.

adj. *disappearing*, vanishing, evanescent, transient, fleeting; *vanished*, missing, absentee, gone, lost to view, invisible.

vb. *disappear*, vanish, dematerialize, melt into thin air, sink without trace; *evaporate*, dissolve, dispel, disperse, scatter; *fade*, pale, shrink, dwindle; *depart*, escape, flee, elope, decamp, absent oneself, do a bunk (*colloq.*), play truant, go AWOL; *hide*, lurk, lie low, hide out; *obliterate*, erase, expunge, wipe out; *withdraw*, remove from the scene, carry off, kidnap, spirit away.

396 INTELLECT
See also **283** (nonmaterial world); **398** (thought).

n. *intellect*, mind, psyche, consciousness, awareness, self; *perception*, cognition, intuition, imagination, insight; *rationality*, reason, sense, understanding, comprehension, judgment, discernment, acumen; *intelligence*, I.Q., wits, senses, brains, grey matter, head, loaf (*colloq.*); *common sense*, nous (*colloq.*), savvy (*colloq.*), gumption, horse sense; *cleverness*, brilliance, braininess, high

I.Q., genius; *intellectual*, egghead (*colloq.*), blue stocking, highbrow, genius, brainbox (*colloq.*); *psychologist*, psychiatrist, psychoanalyst, psychotherapist, shrink (*colloq.*), trick cyclist (*colloq.*).

adj. *intellectual*, mental, conceptual, abstract, cerebral, theoretical; *cognitive*, perceptual, conscious, aware, intuitive, imaginative; *intelligent*, clever, brilliant, bright, gifted, forward, quick-witted, brainy (*colloq.*); *sensible*, rational, commonsensical, logical, reasoned; *psychic*, psychological, psychosomatic, subliminal, subconscious.

vb. *think*, conceive, imagine, reason, intellectualize, theorize, conceptualize; *perceive*, realize, understand, comprehend, discern, sense; *be intelligent*, use one's head, have one's wits about one, know a thing or two (*colloq.*).

397 LACK OF INTELLECT
See also **399** (lack of thought).

n. *lack of intellect*, instinct, intuition, unreason, unintellectuality; *unintelligence*, brainlessness, mindlessness, inanity, vacuity; *stupidity*, dullness, slowness, obtuseness, low I.Q.; *backwardness*, retardation, arrested development, mental deficiency, cretinism, imbecility, feeble-mindedness; *stupid person*, dullard, dunderhead, dunce, blockhead (*colloq.*), thicko (*colloq.*); *mental defective*, cretin, moron, idiot, half-wit, cabbage.

adj. *unintellectual*, intuitive, instinctive, animal, brute; *irrational*, unreasoning, illogical; *mindless*, brainless, vacuous, empty-headed, inane, scatterbrained; *unintelligent*, stupid, slow-witted, dim (*colloq.*), dull, obtuse, thick (*colloq.*), dense, boneheaded (*colloq.*), slow on the uptake; *mentally deficient*, backward, retarded, subnormal, feeble-minded, wanting, not all there, cretinous, moronic.

398 THOUGHT
See also **396** (intellect); **400** (reason).

n. *thought*, thinking, cogitation, concentration, cerebration, speculation, brainwork, intellectual exercise;

thoughtfulness, pensiveness, abstractedness, preoccupation, absorption, daydreaming, brown study; *consideration*, contemplation, deliberation, rumination, introspection, meditation, soul-searching; *reflection*, hindsight, afterthought, second thoughts; *forethought*, prudence, foresight, forward planning.

adj. *thinking*, deliberative, speculative, imaginative, cerebral, intellectual; *thoughtful*, pensive, studious, abstracted, preoccupied, engrossed, dreamy; *reflective*, meditative, introspective, contemplative.

vb. *think*, conceive, imagine, fancy; *cogitate*, ruminate, cerebrate, deliberate, rack one's brains; *consider*, contemplate, reflect, meditate, muse, brood, introspect, mull over, chew over; *think of*, invent, devise, dream up, think up; *speculate*, theorize, hypothesize, fantasize; *reconsider*, review, think again, have second thoughts; *preoccupy*, engross, absorb, obsess; *strike one*, come to mind, occur, cross one's mind.

adv. *on reflection*, on consideration, on second thoughts, with hindsight; *in mind*, on one's mind, on the brain.

399 LACK OF THOUGHT

See also 397 (lack of intellect); 401 (intuition).

n. *lack of thought*, intuition, spontaneity, instinct, flair, gut reaction, reflex, knee-jerk response; *thoughtlessness*, mindlessness, senselessness, irrationality, illogicality; *ignorance*, stupidity, empty-headedness, fatuousness, inanity.

adj. *unthinking*, unreflective, unimaginative, unoriginal; *intuitive*, spontaneous, instinctive, automatic, reflexive; *mindless*, thoughtless, ill-considered, senseless, irrational, illogical, half-baked (*colloq.*); *ignorant*, stupid, empty-headed, fatuous, inane, vacuous, blank.

vb. *not think about*, ignore, disregard, put out of one's mind, dismiss, laugh off, not give a second thought; *intuit*, sense, feel in one's bones.

400 REASON

See also 398 (thought).

n. *reason*, rationality, logic, ratiocination; *argumentation*, disputation, analysis, speculation, abstraction, rationalization; *induction*, deduction, lateral thinking, implication, inference; *premise*, hypothesis, postulate, assumption, supposition, thesis, theorem.

adj. *rational*, logical, conceptual, abstract, academic; *reasonable*, sensible, cogent, coherent, objective; *hypothetical*, theoretical, suppositional, putative, speculative; *analytical*, deductive, a priori, inductive, a posteriori.

vb. *reason*, argue, dispute, rationalize, intellectualize, philosophize; *theorize*, speculate, hypothesize, assume, presuppose; *infer*, deduce, conclude, imply, work out, put two and two together; *be logical*, follow, cohere, hang together, stand to reason, add up (*colloq.*), hold water, make sense.

401 INTUITION

See also 397 (lack of intellect); 455 (prediction).

n. *intuition*, instinct, feeling, insight, spontaneity, gut reaction; *irrationality*, illogicality, incoherence, unreason; *hypersensitivity*, sixth sense, extra-sensory perception, telepathy, second sight, clairvoyance; *presentiment*, hunch, guess, foreboding, premonition.

adj. *intuitive*, instinctive, visceral, spontaneous, impulsive; *irrational*, illogical, incoherent, subjective, impressionistic; *involuntary*, subconscious, subliminal, reflex, automatic, Pavlovian, mechanical, knee-jerk; *psychic*, clairvoyant, telepathic.

vb. *intuit*, guess, divine, sense, feel in one's bones; *use guesswork*, feel one's way, play it by ear (*colloq.*), follow one's nose (*colloq.*).

402 CURIOSITY

See also 414 (question).

n. *curiosity*, interest, concern, eagerness, inquiring mind; *inquisitiveness*, prying, officiousness, nosiness (*colloq.*); *morbid curiosity*, prurience, salaciousness, voyeurism, ghoulishness; *interro-*

gation, cross-examination, detection, quizzing, grilling, third degree (*colloq*.); *spy*, eavesdropper, voyeur, peeping Tom, ghoul, snooper (*colloq*.), rubberneck (*colloq*.), nosy parker (*colloq*.); *gossip*, scandalmonger, newsmonger, newshound, busybody.

adj. *curious*, interested, inquisitive, eager, agog; *prurient*, salacious, voyeuristic, ghoulish; *meddlesome*, interfering, officious, nosy (*colloq*.); *inquisitorial*, questioning, interrogatory.

vb. *be curious*, eavesdrop, listen in on, spy, snoop (*colloq*); *question*, interrogate, cross-examine, quiz; *enquire*, ask, seek to know; *meddle*, interfere, pry, poke/stick one's nose in.

403 LACK OF CURIOSITY

See also **405** (inattention); **756** (indifference).

n. *lack of curiosity*, unconcern, detachment, aloofness; *indifference*, nonchalance, insouciance, impassivity; *apathy*, inertia, boredom, listlessness.

adj. *incurious*, uninterested, unconcerned, detached, aloof; *indifferent*, nonchalant, insouciant, phlegmatic, impassive; *apathetic*, unenthusiastic, bored, blasé, listless.

404 ATTENTION

See also **406** (carefulness).

n. *attention*, notice, regard, heed; *mindfulness*, thoughtfulness, solicitude, consideration; *attentiveness*, concentration, alertness, watchfulness, vigilance; *observation*, inspection, scrutiny, surveillance; *preoccupation*, absorption, raptness, intentness, undivided attention; *studiousness*, application, diligence, assiduousness; *attention to detail*, meticulousness, scrupulousness, punctiliousness, conscientiousness.

adj. *attentive*, mindful, solicitous, considerate, thoughtful; *diligent*, studious, sedulous, assiduous; *meticulous*, scrupulous, punctilious, painstaking; *alert*, aware, conscious, watchful, observant, vigilant; *preoccupied*, absorbed, intent, rapt, engrossed, wrapped up in, riveted; *fixated*, obsessed, single-minded, brooding.

vb. *pay attention*, attend, heed, be on the ball (*colloq*.); *notice*, register, spot, take note, sit up and take notice, prick up one's ears; *observe*, watch, scrutinize, inspect, peruse; *concentrate*, drink in, lap up, hang on someone's words, be all ears (*colloq*.); *preoccupy*, engross, absorb, captivate; *draw attention to*, point out, mention, alert to.

405 INATTENTION

See also **403** (lack of curiosity); **407** (negligence).

n. *inattention*, negligence, carelessness, unawareness; *forgetfulness*, obliviousness, oversight, lapse, disregard; *thoughtlessness*, heedlessness, inconsiderateness, unconcern; *casualness*, offhandedness, desultoriness, cursoriness, vagueness; *absent-mindedness*, distractedness, abstraction, daydreaming, wool-gathering; *dreamer*, scatterbrain, butterfly mind.

adj. *inattentive*, negligent, careless, unmindful; *forgetful*, oblivious, absent-minded, unaware, unobservant; *thoughtless*, heedless, inconsiderate, cavalier; *casual*, offhand, desultory, cursory, superficial; *abstracted*, vague, pensive, dreamy, lost in thought, distracted; *flighty*, dizzy, mercurial, featherbrained, scatty (*colloq*.).

vb. *be inattentive*, overlook, neglect, disregard, miss, let slip; *forget*, lose track of, digress, lose the thread, wander; *daydream*, muse, moon, build castles in Spain; *distract*, disconcert, bewilder, put off.

406 CAREFULNESS

See also **404** (attention); **754** (caution).

n. *carefulness*, mindfulness, solicitude, consideration, attentiveness; *prudence*, circumspection, judiciousness, caution, vigilance; *care*, heed, concern, regard; *conscientiousness*, thoroughness, meticulousness, trouble, pains; *methodicalness*, orderliness, tidiness, neatness, fastidiousness; *accuracy*, precision, exactitude, rigour, perfectionism.

adj. *careful*, mindful, thoughtful, considerate, attentive, solicitous; *prudent*, cautious, circumspect, judicious, wary; *conscientious*, thorough, meticulous, scrupulous, painstaking; *methodical*, orderly, neat, tidy, fastidious, fussy; *exacting*, accurate, rigorous, perfectionist, pedantic.

vb. *be careful*, mind, heed, take into consideration; *watch out*, tread warily, mind one's step, mind one's P's and Q's; *beware of*, look out for, give a wide berth, steer clear of; *check up on*, keep tabs on, keep under surveillance.

407 NEGLIGENCE
See also **405** (inattention).

n. *negligence*, carelessness, forgetfulness, inattentiveness; *neglect*, oversight, dereliction, omission, lapse; *imprudence*, recklessness, impetuosity, indiscretion; *inexactitude*, inaccuracy, looseness, loose ends; *laxity*, slackness, sloppiness, untidiness, slovenliness.

adj. *negligent*, careless, forgetful, inattentive, remiss, neglectful; *casual*, lax, lackadaisical, slack, sloppy, slovenly, slipshod; *neglected*, untidy, unkempt, uncared-for; *reckless*, imprudent, indiscreet, off one's guard, impetuous.

vb. *neglect*, omit, miss, forget; *disregard*, ignore, overlook, turn a blind eye to; *discount*, dismiss, pooh-pooh (*colloq.*), laugh off; *avoid*, dodge, shirk, let slide, leave in the lurch; *gloss over*, scamp, skate over, skip; *procrastinate*, drift, freewheel, let the grass grow under one's feet.

408 IDEA
n. *idea*, notion, concept, abstraction, thought; *imagination*, fancy, invention, brainchild, wheeze (*colloq.*), wrinkle (*colloq.*); *theory*, hypothesis, conjecture, supposition, conception; *attitude*, opinion, viewpoint, stance; *fixed idea*, idée fixe, obsession, fixation, one-track mind.

adj. *ideal*, abstract, notional, conceptual; *theoretical*, hypothetical, conjectural, suppositional; *fanciful*, whimsical, imaginary, all in the mind.

409 TOPIC
n. *topic*, subject, concern, matter, food for thought; *theme*, message, burden, gist, content; *question*, problem, issue, thesis, point, argument, case; *proposal*, suggestion, motion, resolution; *news*, rumour, gossip, current events, current affairs.

adj. *topical*, current, actual, up-to-the-minute; *newsworthy*, thought-provoking, controversial, debatable.

adv. *on the agenda*, under discussion; *in the air*, on everyone's lips.

410 ARGUMENT
See also **635** (disagreement).

n. *argument*, discussion, dialogue, debate, exchange of views; *dispute*, quarrel, altercation, war of words, slanging match (*colloq.*); *controversy*, disputation, polemics, argumentation, dissension; *case*, thesis, grounds, premise, point at issue, pros and cons; *argumentativeness*, contentiousness, quarrelsomeness, combativeness.

adj. *argumentative*, disputatious, quarrelsome, litigious; *controversial*, contentious, polemical, provocative; *arguable*, debatable, questionable, controvertible, moot; *heated*, stormy, violent, ding-dong (*colloq.*); *well-argued*, cogent, coherent, logical, analytical, rational.

vb. *argue*, debate, discuss, bandy words; *quibble*, split hairs, chop logic, nit-pick, argue the toss; *quarrel*, dispute, wrangle, bicker, cross swords, have words, *attack*, pick holes in, outargue, shoot down in flames, demolish; *defend*, plead for, support, make out a case for.

411 SOPHISTRY
n. *sophistry*, false logic, illogicality, circularity; *casuistry*, speciousness, rationalization, doublethink; *ambiguity*, equivocation, mystification, obscurantism, woolliness; *quibbling*, hair-splitting, chicanery, choplogic; *fallacy*, contradiction in terms, non sequitur, inconsistency; *distortion*, perversion, newspeak, doubletalk.

adj. *sophistical*, casuistical, Jesuitical; *illogical*, unsound, circular, specious; *ambiguous*, equivocal, woolly, flimsy, waffly (*colloq.*); *fallacious*, contradictory, inconsistent, misleading; *captious*, hair-splitting, pettifogging, nit-picking.

vb. *reason falsely*, equivocate, quibble, cavil, split hairs; *mislead*, pervert, distort, mystify, bamboozle (*colloq.*), blind someone with science; *avoid the issue*, beat about the bush, miss the point, digress.

412 DEMONSTRATION
See also **417** (verification); **420** (evidence).

n. *demonstration*, proof, justification, validation, vindication, affirmation; *argument*, exposition, explanation, elucidation, illustration, clarification.

adj. *demonstrable*, arguable, justifiable, verifiable; *expository*, explanatory, elucidatory, illustrative; *affirmative*, conclusive, corroborative, irrefutable, incontrovertible, unanswerable.

vb. *demonstrate*, show, prove, establish, make out a case for, prove one's point; *affirm*, justify, vindicate, validate, substantiate, corroborate; *explain*, expound, illustrate, elucidate.

413 REFUTATION
See also **415** (answer); **421** (counterevidence).

n. *refutation*, confutation, disproof, rebuttal; *challenge*, disputation, contention, calling in question; *contradiction*, negation, denial, repudiation; *exposure*, invalidation, denunciation, criticism, hatchet job (*colloq.*).

adj. *refuted*, disproved, invalidated, demolished; *negatory*, contradictory, condemnatory, denunciatory.

vb. *refute*, rebut, invalidate, prove wrong, disprove; *contradict*, negate, deny, repudiate, gainsay, give the lie to; *challenge*, pick someone up on, take issue with, contend, disagree with; *expose*, show up, explode, denounce, condemn; *outargue*, puncture, deflate, squash, crush, shoot down in flames.

414 QUESTION
See also **402** (curiosity).

n. *question*, enquiry, query, request, petition; *interrogation*, examination,

investigation, inquisition, quiz; *exploration*, quest, probe, search, inquest, survey, fact-finding mission; *questionnaire*, poll, interview, canvass, vox pop; *review*, scrutiny, study, inspection, cross-examination, analysis; *riddle*, enigma, problem, brainteaser (*colloq.*), poser, 64 000 dollar question.

adj. *questioning*, enquiring, inquisitive, searching, quizzical, interrogative; *exploratory*, preliminary, investigative, detective; *problematical*, knotty, enigmatic, baffling, puzzling.

vb. *question*, ask, enquire, request; *probe*, look into, investigate, delve into, leave no stone unturned; *explore*, try out, test, put out feelers, take the temperature of; *survey*, scrutinize, inspect, screen, canvass, poll; *challenge*, badger, pester, heckle, lobby.

415 ANSWER
See also **413** (refutation).

n. *answer*, reply, reaction, response, acknowledgment, feedback; *retort*, rejoinder, riposte, comeback; *repartee*, backchat, lip (*colloq.*), badinage; *rebuttal*, countercharge, right of reply, counterblast, retaliation.

adj. *answering*, responsive, affirmative, positive; *negative*, contradictory, defensive, retaliatory.

vb. *answer*, reply, respond, take one's cue, acknowledge; *retort*, riposte, rebut, come back on; *react*, counter, parry, retaliate; *contradict*, negate, deny, disclaim.

416 EXPERIMENT
n. *experiment*, attempt, try-out, test, trial, dry run, practice shot, pilot scheme, rehearsal, audition, runthrough; *experimentation*, research, verification, proving; *speculation*, guesswork, trial and error, gamble, long shot, shot in the dark; *testing agent*, litmus test, benchmark, yardstick, criterion, touchstone; *subject*, guinea pig, control sample, sounding board.

adj. *experimental*, empirical, practical; *provisional*, tentative, probationary, unproven; *speculative*, hypothetical, exploratory, open-ended, hit-or-miss, random.

vb. *experiment*, test, sample, try out, research; *practise*, rehearse, audition, run through; *speculate*, hypothesize, gamble, fly a kite; *improvise*, feel one's way, play it by ear (*colloq.*), muddle through.

417 VERIFICATION

See also **412** (demonstration); **427** (certainty).

n. *verification*, demonstration, affirmation, validation, substantiation, authentication; *confirmation*, attestation, certification, corroboration, justification, vindication, proof; *check*, audit, inquest, post mortem, autopsy.

adj. *verified*, certified, attested, proven, tried and tested, authentic, genuine; *verifiable*, demonstrable, ascertainable, provable.

vb. *verify*, establish, prove, demonstrate, affirm, substantiate; *validate*, authenticate, attest, certify; *vindicate*, justify, confirm, corroborate, bear out; *check*, go over, cross-check, double check.

418 DISCRIMINATION

See also **18** (dissimilarity); **429** (judgment).

n. *discrimination*, discernment, circumspection, judgment, acumen; *distinction*, differentiation, nuance, nicety, shade of meaning; *perspicacity*, penetration, astuteness, shrewdness, insight, sensitivity; *appreciation*, refinement, connoisseurship, taste, flair, subtlety; *selectivity*, choosiness (*colloq.*), fussiness, fastidiousness.

adj. *discriminating*, perspicacious, judicious, circumspect, discerning; *fastidious*, selective, fussy, choosy (*colloq.*), picky (*colloq.*), difficult; *subtle*, delicate, fine, nice, nuanced; *critical*, exacting, rigorous, careful.

vb. *discriminate*, distinguish, differentiate, discern; *sort*, sift, tell apart, separate the sheep from the goats; *appraise*, judge, evaluate; *select*, choose, pick out, single out.

419 LACK OF DISCRIMINATION

n. *lack of discrimination*, unperceptiveness, insensitivity, coarseness; *crudeness*, randomness, inexactness, haphazardness; *confusion*, jumble, muddle, mixed bag, grist to the mill.

adj. *undiscriminating*, unselective, uncritical, unperceptive, insensitive; *unrefined*, crude, rough and ready, coarse, unpolished, unsubtle; *indiscriminate*, random, haphazard, hit-or-miss; *broad*, generalized, wholesale, blanket.

vb. *not discriminate*, lump together, roll into one, jumble, muddle, confuse, blur.

420 EVIDENCE

See also **412** (demonstration).

n. *evidence*, indication, sign, symptom; *data*, facts, information, dossier, documentation, file; *proof*, corroboration, verification, support, foundation, backing; *testimony*, witness, exhibit, statement, affidavit, attestation, deposition, allegation; *recommendation*, endorsement, reference, testimonial, credentials, warranty, seal of approval.

adj. *evidential*, indicative, symptomatic, suggestive, telling; *factual*, documentary, first-hand, straight from the horse's mouth; *corroborative*, reliable, affirmative, conclusive, irrefutable.

vb. *evidence*, show, indicate, reveal, suggest, betoken, evince; *give evidence*, attest, testify, bear witness; *recommend*, vouch for, guarantee, endorse; *support*, ratify, corroborate, confirm, bear out, verify.

421 COUNTEREVIDENCE

See also **413** (refutation).

n. *counterevidence*, contradiction, counterclaim; *rebuttal*, refutation, negation, denial; *conflicting evidence*, disproof, hostile witness, discrepancy.

adj. *contradictory*, negatory, conflicting, damaging.

vb. *contraindicate*, run counter to, point in the other direction, give the lie to, disprove; *refute*, rebut, contradict, negate, go against; *weaken*, damage, undermine, expose.

422 QUALIFICATION

n. *qualification*, reservation, proviso, condition, stipulation, prerequisite; *limitation*, specification, exception, restriction, modification; *exemption*, concession, allowance, mitigation, extenuation; *loophole*, escape clause, let-out, get-out.

adj. *qualifying*, restrictive, conditional, provisional, contingent, dependent; *mitigating*, extenuating, concessionary.

vb. *qualify*, modify, limit, restrict; *stipulate*, specify, lay down, insist on; *concede*, exempt, make allowance for, take into account; *mitigate*, moderate, extenuate, play down.

423 POSSIBILITY

See also **425** (probability).

n. *possibility*, eventuality, contingency, chance, off-chance, opportunity, likelihood; *potentiality*, virtuality, makings, possibilities, promise; *feasibility*, practicability, viability, capability.

adj. *possible*, potential, virtual, hypothetical; *attainable*, realizable, doable, achievable, obtainable; *practicable*, workable, viable, feasible; *credible*, reasonable, plausible, conceivable, likely, arguable.

vb. *make possible*, enable, facilitate, bring about; *have possibilities*, show promise, have the makings of, have potential.

adv. *possibly*, perhaps, maybe; *arguably*, potentially.

424 IMPOSSIBILITY

See also **426** (improbability).

n. *impossibility*, impracticability, hopelessness, absurdity; *impasse*, deadlock, dead end, blank wall, hopeless case, no-no (*colloq.*).

adj. *impossible*, impracticable, unworkable, not on (*colloq.*); *inconceivable*, unthinkable, unimaginable, implausible, unlikely, unreasonable; *insuperable*, insurmountable, insoluble, incurable, incorrigible; *unobtainable*, unavailable, unattainable, inaccessible.

vb. *be impossible*, be out of the question, be beyond the bounds of possibility; *make impossible*, rule out, prohibit, disallow, exclude; *attempt the impossible*, wish for the moon, find a needle in a haystack, get blood out of a stone, square the circle.

425 PROBABILITY

See also **423** (possibility).

n. *probability*, likelihood, expectation, prospect, promise; *predictability*, reliability, liability, fair chance, sporting chance; *conjecture*, assumption, educated guess, safe bet.

adj. *probable*, likely, foreseeable, predictable, liable, expected; *plausible*, reasonable, convincing, credible; *prospective*, hopeful, promising, rising.

vb. *be probable*, be on the cards, be in the offing; *foresee*, expect, predict, look forward to; *assume*, conjecture, guess, suppose.

adv. *probably*, in all likelihood, ten to one.

426 IMPROBABILITY

See also **424** (impossibility).

n. *improbability*, unlikelihood, doubtfulness, remote/outside/slim chance, long odds; *implausibility*, inconceivability, absurdity, ludicrousness; *forlorn hope*, pious hope, long shot, shot in the dark.

adj. *improbable*, unlikely, doubtful, dubious, uncertain; *implausible*, unconvincing, unbelievable, far-fetched, absurd.

427 CERTAINTY

See also **417** (verification); **434** (belief).

n. *certainty*, certitude, likelihood, inevitability, inexorability; *reliability*, dependability, infallibility, trustworthiness, unimpeachability; *assurance*, conviction, confidence, blind faith; *predictability*, definiteness, foregone conclusion, safe bet, dead cert (*colloq.*), sure thing (*colloq.*).

adj. *certain*, definite, sure, categorical; *unmistakable*, unequivocal, unambiguous, conclusive; *inevitable*, unavoidable, inexorable, ineluctable; *uncontrovertible*, undeniable, unquestionable, unimpeachable; *assured*, confident, convinced, unshakable; *reliable*, trustworthy, dependable, rock-solid; *infallible*, foolproof, failsafe, low-risk, gilt-edged.

vb. *know for certain*, feel sure of, put one's shirt on, bet one's bottom dollar; *rely on*, depend on, bank on, trust in; *make certain*, ensure, guarantee, confirm, check, double check; *finalize*, settle, firm up (*colloq.*), decide, clinch, wrap up (*colloq.*).

adv. *certainly*, doubtless, definitely, come rain or shine, no matter what, come hell or high water.

428 UNCERTAINTY
See also **435** (disbelief).
n. *uncertainty*, indefiniteness, doubtfulness, dubiousness; *ambiguity*, ambivalence, vagueness, borderline case, grey area; *indecision*, diffidence, hesitation, vacillation, irresolution; *unreliability*, fallibility, untrustworthiness, unpredictability, volatility, capriciousness; *doubt*, query, question mark, misgivings; *conjecture*, gamble, guess, toss-up (*colloq.*), unknown quantity, pig in a poke.

adj. *uncertain*, unsure, doubtful, dubious; *precarious*, chancy, risky, dodgy (*colloq.*), touch and go; *unpredictable*, unforeseeable, unknowable, fickle, volatile, capricious; *fallible*, untrustworthy, unreliable; *indefinite*, vague, ambivalent, ambiguous, undecided; *hesitant*, indecisive, diffident, unconfident, irresolute; *questionable*, arguable, debatable, moot.

vb. *be uncertain*, be in two minds, hesitate, waver, vacillate, shilly-shally (*colloq.*), dither (*colloq.*); *doubt*, disbelieve, wonder, suspect, challenge, query; *grope*, fumble, flounder, not know which way to turn; *hinge*, depend, hang in the balance, be in the lap of the gods.

429 JUDGMENT
See also **418** (discrimination).
n. *judgment*, discretion, discernment,

discrimination, acumen; *adjudication*, arbitration, umpirage, refereeing; *estimation*, evaluation, appraisal, assessment; *criticism*, opinion, comment, review, critique; *verdict*, ruling, decree, award, decision, settlement; *impartiality*, objectivity, fairness, justice; *judge*, umpire, referee, arbitrator, adjudicator, assessor.

adj. *judicial*, discretionary, judicatory; *judicious*, discerning, circumspect, shrewd; *judgmental*, critical, censorious, condemnatory; *approving*, appreciative, favourable, lenient; *impartial*, unbiased, objective, fair, just, broad-minded.

vb. *judge*, referee, umpire, adjudicate, arbitrate, decide, settle; *estimate*, appraise, assess, evaluate, size up, weigh up; *criticize*, review, pass judgment on, rule on; *pronounce*, decree, conclude, sum up.

430 MISJUDGMENT
See also **140** (tendency); **441** (error).
n. *misjudgment*, miscalculation, error, mistake, misconception; *wrongheadedness*, obstinacy, foolishness, fallibility; *partiality*, bias, partisanship, favouritism, one-sidedness, prejudice, bigotry; *injustice*, unfairness, discrimination, intolerance; *narrow-mindedness*, racism, chauvinism, sexism, colour prejudice, apartheid, segregation; *insularity*, parochialism, provincialism, closed mind.

adj. *mistaken*, misguided, wrong-headed, fallible; *partial*, biased, partisan, one-sided, unfair, unjust; *prejudiced*, bigoted, opinionated, dogmatic; *discriminatory*, sexist, racist, chauvinist; *insular*, parochial, provincial, narrow-minded, intolerant, hidebound, petty.

vb. *misjudge*, miscalculate, mistake, misconceive; *prejudice*, preconceive, presuppose, jump to conclusions; *bias*, predispose, warp, load, slant, skew, distort; *favour*, take sides, discriminate.

431 OVERESTIMATION
See also **482** (exaggeration).
n. *overestimation*, overvaluation, exces-

siveness, exorbitancy; *overstatement*, exaggeration, hyperbole, puff (*colloq.*), hype (*colloq.*), ballyhoo (*colloq.*); *over-confidence*, overoptimism, presumption, arrogance.

adj. *overrated*, overpraised, disappointing, not up to expectation; *over-valued*, overpriced, exorbitant, excessive; *overstated*, overdone, overemphasized, hyperbolic, over the top (*colloq.*); *overconfident*, overoptimistic, overenthusiastic, overambitious.

vb. *overestimate*, overshoot, overrate, overvalue; *overemphasize*, overpraise, exaggerate, hype (*colloq.*), build up, talk up (*colloq.*), lay it on with a shovel/trowel (*colloq.*); *maximize*, make much of, make a mountain out of a molehill.

432 UNDERESTIMATION
See also **483** (understatement).

n. *underestimation*, undervaluation, understatement, conservative estimate; *self-deprecation*, modesty, reticence, humility; *pessimism*, defeatism, despondency; *depreciation*, disparagement, belittlement.

adj. *underrated*, undervalued, neglected, overlooked, unsung; *modest*, self-effacing, self-deprecating, retiring; *pessimistic*, defeatist, despondent, gloomy; *disparaging*, derogatory, depreciative.

vb. *underestimate*, undervalue, underrate, underprice; *neglect*, overlook, do less than justice to, pass over; *minimize*, understate, play down, soft-pedal (*colloq.*); *disparage*, belittle, slight, pooh-pooh (*colloq.*), run down.

433 DISCOVERY
n. *discovery*, exploration, research, experimentation, excavation, prospecting; *encounter*, meeting, happening, coincidence; *realization*, revelation, inspiration, flash of insight; *invention*, find, results, findings, strike; *location*, identification, sighting, detection.

adj. *exploratory*, experimental, fact-finding; *probing*, investigative, detective.

vb. *discover*, invent, come up with, find out, learn; *happen on*, come across, hit upon, light upon, stumble across, encounter; *realize*, tumble to, see the light, catch on (*colloq.*), twig (*colloq.*); *unearth*, uncover, disinter, dig up, bring to light, ferret/nose out, detect; *find*, track down, locate, spot, sight, identify; *explore*, excavate, probe, investigate.

434 BELIEF
See also **427** (certainty); **868** (religion).

n. *belief*, credence, acceptance, conviction, assurance, certainty; *confidence*, faith, trust, reliance, expectation; *opinion*, persuasion, view, sentiment; *credo*, tenet, principle, creed, dogma, profession, ideology, doctrine, article of faith; *attitude*, position, viewpoint, standpoint, outlook, world-view; *prejudice*, dogmatism, bigotry, fanaticism; *credulity*, blind faith, superstition, naivety, gullibility; *credibility*, plausibility, likelihood.

adj. *believable*, credible, plausible, convincing, persuasive; *trustworthy*, dependable, reliable, trusty; *confident*, certain, sure, positive, convinced, assured; *opinionated*, dogmatic, doctrinaire, bigoted, fanatical; *credulous*, naive, gullible, superstitious, trusting, confiding.

vb. *believe*, maintain, hold, profess, avow; *trust*, rely, depend, count, bank, swear by, give credence; *adopt*, embrace, espouse, believe in; *think*, deem, allow, grant, be of the opinion; *be credulous*, fall for, take on trust, swallow (*colloq.*), buy (*colloq.*); *convince*, persuade, assure, win over, convert.

435 DISBELIEF
See also **428** (uncertainty); **869** (unbelief).

n. *disbelief*, incredulity, scepticism, cynicism; *doubt*, uncertainty, dubiety, unsureness; *unbelief*, agnosticism, atheism, heresy; *distrust*, mistrust, suspicion, wariness, misgiving, doubts, qualms, scruples; *recantation*, retraction, renunciation, disclaimer, apostasy; *derision*, scorn, mockery, ridicule.

adj. *disbelieving*, incredulous, sceptical, cynical, unconvinced; *doubtful*, dubious, unsure, uncertain; *unbelieving*, agnostic, atheistic, heretical, lapsed; *distrustful*, mistrustful, suspicious, wary, hesitant; *incredible*, unbelievable, inconceivable, implausible, unlikely; *untrustworthy*, unreliable, suspect, questionable; *derisive*, mocking, scornful.

vb. *disbelieve*, reject, call in question, challenge, discredit; *mock*, deride, scorn, laugh in the face of, laugh out of court; *mistrust*, distrust, suspect, have one's doubts about, hesitate; *recant*, retract, disclaim, renounce, change one's mind.

436 ASSENT
See also **19** (accord).

n. *assent*, agreement, concurrence, consent; *acceptance*, acknowledgment, acquiescence, submission, compliance; *sanction*, ratification, green light, go-ahead (*colloq.*); *approval*, approbation, thumbs-up (*colloq.*), endorsement, backing, support; *cooperation*, collaboration, unanimity, harmony, unison.

adj. *assenting*, consenting, agreeable, favourable, sympathetic; *accepting*, acquiescent, compliant, submissive; *cooperative*, collaborative, unanimous, likeminded; *approved*, unopposed, signed, carried.

vb. *assent*, consent, concur, agree, see eye to eye; *accept*, abide by, acquiesce, submit, comply, accede; *cooperate*, collaborate, meet half-way, fall in with; *admit*, concede, grant, allow, acknowledge; *sanction*, ratify, approve, welcome, applaud, okay (*colloq.*); *endorse*, support, back, second, go along with, sympathize with.

437 DISSENT

n. *dissent*, disagreement, discord, dissension; *dispute*, argument, quarrel, wrangle, controversy, difference of opinion; *negation*, contradiction, denial, repudiation, opposition, defiance; *disapproval*, dissatisfaction, dis-

content, disaffection, secession; *protest*, remonstration, objection, demurral, rejection, refusal; *disinclination*, reluctance, unwillingness, recalcitrance, disobedience.

adj. *dissenting*, dissident, recusant, disaffected, dissatisfied, discontented; *disinclined*, reluctant, unwilling, opposed, defiant, disobedient, bolshie (*colloq.*).

vb. *dissent*, disagree, agree to differ; *quarrel*, argue, fall out, wrangle, bicker; *dispute*, challenge, resist, oppose, defy, disobey; *refuse*, negate, reject, repudiate, deny; *object*, protest, demur, cavil, expostulate, remonstrate; *disapprove*, look askance at, frown on, hold no brief for.

438 KNOWLEDGE
See also **444** (wisdom); **624** (skill).

n. *knowledge*, wisdom, learning, erudition, scholarliness, pedantry; *awareness*, cognizance, understanding, comprehension, grasp, ken; *familiarity*, acquaintance, experience, dealings; *education*, schooling, instruction, enlightenment, information, illumination; *literacy*, numeracy, three Rs, rote-learning, book-learning; *skill*, accomplishment, expertise, proficiency, mastery, savvy (*colloq.*), know-how (*colloq*); *scholar*, student, intellectual, pedant, bookworm, polymath, Renaissance man, know-all (*colloq.*).

adj. *knowing*, wise, all-knowing, omniscient; *knowledgeable*, informed, well up on, au courant, au fait; *educated*, literate, numerate, well-read, lettered, enlightened, cultivated; *scholarly*, learned, bookish, erudite, donnish, academic, pedantic; *aware*, cognizant, conscious, familiar with, conversant, versed; *proficient*, skilful, accomplished, experienced.

vb. *know*, understand, comprehend, grasp; *get to know*, familiarize oneself with, acquaint oneself with, experience; *learn*, study, memorize, master; *know thoroughly*, know off pat, have at one's fingertips, know inside out, know backwards; *educate*, instruct, inform, enlighten.

439 IGNORANCE

See also **625** (unskilfulness).

n. *ignorance*, unknowingness, unawareness, incomprehension; *unfamiliarity*, inexperience, greenness, rawness; *inexpertness*, amateurishness, clumsiness, awkwardness, unskilfulness; *benightedness*, superstition, philistinism, illiteracy, stupidity, folly; *ignoramus*, dunce, booby, philistine, moron.

adj. *ignorant*, unknowing, uncomprehending, unwitting, unaware, unconscious; *unfamiliar*, inexperienced, raw, green, uninitiated; *uneducated*, uninformed, unenlightened, illiterate, philistine, crass, stupid; *inexpert*, unskilful, amateurish, clumsy, clueless (*colloq.*); *unknown*, uncharted, undiscovered, mysterious, enigmatic.

vb. *be ignorant*, not know, not have the foggiest idea, not have a clue (*colloq.*), not have an inkling; *mystify*, keep in the dark, baffle, perplex.

440 ACCURACY

See also **478** (truth).

n. *accuracy*, exactness, precision, exactitude; *correctness*, rightness, aptness, appropriateness; *meticulousness*, punctiliousness, rigour, pedantry, perfectionism; *fidelity*, truth, realism, authenticity, verisimilitude.

adj. *accurate*, precise, exact, spot on (*colloq.*), dead on (*colloq.*), bang on (*colloq.*), correct, right, apt, appropriate; *meticulous*, punctilious, rigorous, pedantic, perfectionist; *faithful*, true-to-life, factual, documentary, historical.

vb. *be accurate*, ring true, hit the nail on the head (*colloq.*); *prove accurate*, corroborate, substantiate, validate, bear out.

adv. *literally*, to the letter, verbatim, word for word.

441 ERROR

See also **430** (misjudgment); **479** (untruth).

n. *error*, mistake, miscalculation, misjudgment; *misunderstanding*, misconception, fallacy, misconstruction, misrepresentation, delusion; *inaccuracy*, imprecision, inexactness, carelessness, sloppiness; *wrongness*, unsoundness, falseness, misguidedness; *blunder*, oversight, gaffe, faux pas, lapse, howler (*colloq.*), bloomer (*colloq.*), clanger (*colloq.*); *misprint*, literal, erratum, corrigendum.

adj. *erroneous*, wrong, false, fallacious, delusory; *inaccurate*, incorrect, imprecise, inexact, wide of the mark; *misleading*, untrue, apocryphal, unfounded; *mistaken*, misguided, misinformed, misled; *erring*, fallible, wrong-headed, gone astray, off the rails (*colloq.*).

vb. *err*, be in the wrong, misjudge, miscalculate, blot one's copybook; *misunderstand*, misconceive, misinterpret, be at cross-purposes, bark up the wrong tree (*colloq.*); *blunder*, slip up, put one's foot in it (*colloq.*), boob (*colloq.*), make a balls-up/cockup (*vulg.*); *mislead*, misinform, deceive, delude, lead astray.

442 MAXIM

n. *maxim*, proverb, saying, adage, byword, saw, dictum; *epigram*, aphorism, apophthegm, witticism; *watchword*, slogan, catch phrase, motto; *moral*, golden rule, object lesson, cautionary tale; *truism*, cliché, platitude, bromide, chestnut (*colloq.*).

adj. *proverbial*, gnomic, aphoristic, epigrammatic; *pithy*, terse, witty, cryptic; *trite*, banal, hackneyed, commonplace, platitudinous, corny (*colloq.*).

443 NONSENSE

See also **445** (folly); **459** (lack of meaning); **772** (ridiculousness).

n. *nonsense*, silliness, foolishness, ridiculousness, absurdity; *senselessness*, meaninglessness, fatuousness, inanity; *rubbish*, drivel, gibberish, twaddle (*colloq.*), crap (*vulg.*), bullshit (*vulg.*), codswallop (*colloq.*).

adj. *nonsensical*, ridiculous, silly, foolish, laughable, ludicrous, absurd; *senseless*, meaningless, fatuous, asinine, inane; *crazy*, mad, preposterous, harebrained, crackpot (*colloq.*).

vb. *be absurd*, fool around, make a fool of oneself, act the fool; *rant*, rave, talk rot (*colloq.*), talk through a hole in one's head (*colloq.*).

444 WISDOM
See also **396** (intellect); **438** (knowledge).

n. *wisdom*, sagacity, sapience, profundity; *discernment*, perspicacity, penetration, acumen, insight; *understanding*, awareness, enlightenment, far-sightedness; *knowledge*, experience, learning, erudition, scholarliness; *common sense*, horse sense, level-headedness, sanity, realism, shrewdness, astuteness; *wise man*, sage, guru, mentor, pundit, thinker, Solomon.

adj. *wise*, sagacious, sapient, profound, deep; *perspicacious*, discerning, insightful, penetrating; *enlightened*, aware, understanding, far-sighted, long-headed; *knowledgeable*, experienced, learned, erudite, scholarly; *commonsensical*, realistic, level-headed, shrewd, astute.

vb. *be wise*, know the ways of the world, know what's what, have one's feet on the ground, have one's head screwed on (*colloq.*).

445 FOLLY
See also **397** (lack of intellect); **443** (nonsense); **447** (insanity).

n. *folly*, foolishness, silliness, stupidity; *futility*, pointlessness, fatuousness, meaninglessness, senselessness, absurdity; *imprudence*, indiscretion, recklessness, wildness; *lunacy*, madness, craziness, insanity, infatuation; *shallowness*, frivolity, levity, light-headedness, giddiness; *fool*, dolt, idiot, imbecile, moron, cretin, donkey, ass, goose (*colloq.*); *clown*, buffoon, simpleton, ninny, booby, sap, twit (*colloq.*), twerp (*colloq.*), berk (*colloq.*), prat (*colloq.*).

adj. *foolish*, stupid, silly, idiotic, asinine; *futile*, pointless, senseless, meaningless, absurd; *lunatic*, mad, crazy, insane; *unwise*, imprudent, indiscreet, irresponsible, reckless, wild; *shallow*, frivolous, light-headed, scatterbrained, giddy, scatty (*colloq.*); *puerile*, infantile, brainless, moronic, soft in the head.

vb. *be foolish*, look an idiot, make a fool of oneself, get one's fingers burned, never learn; *ramble*, burble, drivel, gibber, maunder, rabbit (*colloq.*); *go mad*, take leave of one's senses, be out of one's mind.

446 SANITY
n. *sanity*, saneness, rationality, coherence, reasonableness; *normality*, balance, stability, equilibrium; *common sense*, sobriety, lucidity, composure, clear-headedness, level-headedness.

adj. *sane*, rational, reasonable, coherent, sound; *normal*, balanced, stable, on an even keel; *lucid*, compos mentis, clear-headed, sober, calm, level-headed.

vb. *be sane*, be in one's right mind, be in possession of one's faculties; *see reason*, come to one's senses, calm down, compose oneself.

447 INSANITY
See also **58** (disturbance); **445** (folly).

n. *insanity*, mental illness, madness, lunacy, derangement; *maladjustment*, psychosis, neurosis, psychopathy, senility; *schizophrenia*, paranoia, hysteria, senile dementia, catatonia; *mania*, compulsion, obsession, phobia, fixation, complex, hangup (*colloq.*); *delusion*, hallucination, split personality, delirium, frenzy; *nervous breakdown*, neurasthenia, depression, baby blues (*colloq.*), melancholia; *eccentricity*, oddness, queerness, crankiness, weirdness; *lunatic*, madman, psychopath, schizophrenic, paranoiac, maniac, nutcase (*colloq.*), nut (*colloq.*), loony (*colloq.*); *eccentric*, crank, nutter (*colloq.*), oddball (*colloq.*), weirdo (*colloq.*).

adj. *insane*, mentally ill, mad, lunatic, disturbed, deranged, unbalanced, unhinged, senile, gaga (*colloq.*); *maladjusted*, autistic, neurotic, psychotic, schizoid, paranoid, hysterical, neurasthenic; *maniacal*, obsessive, fixated, compulsive, phobic, depressive, melancholic, manic-depressive; *crazed*, frenzied, delirious, raving, incoherent, demented, non compos mentis; *frantic*, distraught, possessed, wild, berserk; *crazy* (*colloq.*), screwy (*colloq.*), loony (*colloq.*), nuts (*colloq.*), bonkers (*colloq.*), crackers (*colloq.*), bananas (*colloq.*), cuckoo (*colloq.*); *touched*, wanting, barmy (*colloq.*), batty (*colloq.*), daft (*colloq.*), potty (*colloq.*), dotty (*colloq.*), not all there, not right in the head, certifiable; *eccentric*, odd, queer, weird, cranky; *perverted*, twisted, warped, sick, kinky (*colloq.*).

vb. *be insane*, rave, ramble, wander, see things, have a screw loose (*colloq.*); *go mad*, go out of one's mind, break down (*colloq.*), crack up (*colloq.*), flip one's lid (*colloq.*), lose one's marbles (*colloq.*), go off one's rocker (*colloq.*); *madden*, craze, unhinge, unbalance, drive up the wall/round the bend (*colloq.*).

448 MEMORY
See also **486** (record).

n. *memory*, recollection, reminiscence, remembrance, recall, evocation; *good memory*, retention, total recall, photographic memory; *nostalgia*, retrospection, hindsight, flashback, blast from the past (*colloq.*), golden oldie (*colloq.*); *souvenir*, memento, keepsake, reminder, memorial, monument, relic; *memorandum*, memo, aide-memoire, mnemonic, cue.

adj. *remembered*, fresh, vivid, distinct; *memorable*, unforgettable, indelible, haunting; *reminiscent*, evocative, redolent, nostalgic, retrospective, commemorative.

vb. *remember*, recollect, recall, bring to mind, evoke; *retain*, not forget, stamp/fix on one's memory; *reminisce*, recapture, relive, go down memory lane, hark back, cast one's mind back, dredge up, dig up; *remind*, prompt, jog the memory, refresh one's memory, call up, bring back, ring a bell; *memorize*, commit to memory, learn by heart, get off pat.

449 OBLIVION
See also **405** (inattention).

n. *oblivion*, unconsciousness, unawareness, blankness, limbo; *forgetfulness*, absent-mindedness, inattention, abstractedness; *loss of memory*, amnesia, mental block, blank; *obliteration*, effacement, erasure.

adj. *oblivious*, unconscious, unaware, heedless, unmindful; *forgetful*, absent-minded, abstracted, inattentive, amnesiac; *forgotten*, half-remembered, dim, hazy, indistinct.

vb. *forget*, misremember, clean forget, have a memory like a sieve; *be forgotten*, slip one's mind, go in one ear and out the other; *half-remember*, have on the tip of one's tongue, have at the back of one's mind; *efface*, obliterate, wipe out, erase; *forgive*, amnesty, bury the hatchet, let bygones be bygones.

450 EXPECTATION
See also **104** (future time); **453** (foresight).

n. *expectation*, expectancy, anticipation, suspense, curiosity; *optimism*, confidence, hope, trust, certainty; *pessimism*, apprehension, dread, anxiety; *forecast*, outlook, prospect, lookout.

adj. *expectant*, waiting, ready, prepared, forewarned; *eager*, curious, agog, itching; *optimistic*, hopeful, confident, sanguine; *pessimistic*, apprehensive, gloomy, anxious; *expected*, foreseen, hoped for, longed for; *prospective*, future, impending.

vb. *expect*, contemplate, foresee, forecast, predict, see coming, bargain for; *await*, stand by, be at the ready, be on the edge of one's seat, be on tenterhooks; *anticipate*, look forward to, hope for, long for; *rely on*, count on, bank on, have confidence in; *dread*, fear, have qualms/misgivings; *be expected*, be in store, loom, be on the cards.

adv. *expectantly*, with bated breath, in suspense.

451 SURPRISE
See also **454** (lack of foresight); **759** (wonder).

n. *surprise*, shock, astonishment, amazement, wonderment; *revelation*, eye-opener (*colloq.*), bombshell, bolt from the blue, windfall, stunner (*col-*

loq.); *unexpectedness*, suddenness, unpredictability, uncertainty.

adj. *surprised*, astonished, astounded, startled, stunned, thunderstruck, dumbfounded; *off-guard*, taken aback, caught unawares, caught napping/on the hop (*colloq.*); *unexpected*, unforeseen, unannounced, sudden, abrupt; *surprising*, amazing, shocking, staggering (*colloq.*).

vb. *not expect*, not suspect, be caught out, be wrong-footed; *ambush*, spring, pounce, trap; *amaze*, astound, astonish, startle, bowl over (*colloq.*), stun; *jolt*, electrify, galvanize, shock.

adv. *unexpectedly*, all of a sudden, out of the blue.

452 DISAPPOINTMENT

n. *disappointment*, disillusionment, disenchantment, false dawn, anticlimax, letdown, comedown (*colloq.*); *failure*, flash in the pan, damp squib, washout (*colloq.*); *setback*, blow, hitch, snag, hiccup (*colloq.*); *frustration*, dissatisfaction, disgruntlement, discontent; *discouragement*, despondency, gloom, chagrin, regret.

adj. *disappointed*, dissatisfied, disgruntled, discontented; *disillusioned*, disenchanted, disabused, jaundiced, embittered, soured; *foiled*, thwarted, baffled, frustrated; *discouraged*, despondent, regretful, let down, crestfallen, sick as a parrot (*colloq.*); *disappointing*, unsatisfactory, anticlimactic, not up to expectation, overrated.

vb. *disappoint*, fall short, leave something to be desired; *frustrate*, thwart, foil, get the better of; *disillusion*, disenchant, disabuse, bring down to earth with a bang; *betray*, let down (*colloq.*), jilt, leave in the lurch (*colloq.*); *be disappointed*, learn one's lesson, learn the hard way, find out to one's cost, have one's fingers burned.

453 FORESIGHT

See also **450** (expectation); **455** (prediction).

n. *foresight*, anticipation, forethought, premeditation, far-sightedness, vision; *preparedness*, readiness, provision, contingency plan; *foreknowledge*, forewarning, presentiment, foreboding, prediction; *prescience*, second sight, clairvoyance, precognition.

adj. *foresighted*, prescient, clairvoyant, prophetic, visionary; *far-sighted*, provident, prudent, prepared, ready; *anticipatory*, preemptive, premeditated.

vb. *foresee*, forecast, predict, prophesy, forewarn; *anticipate*, expect, preempt, forestall; *make provision*, prepare, premeditate, provide for, take precautions, plan ahead.

454 LACK OF FORESIGHT

See also **451** (surprise).

n. *lack of foresight*, unpreparedness, unreadiness, improvidence; *shortsightedness*, blindness, thoughtlessness, imprudence; *improvisation*, spontaneity, extemporization.

adj. *unprepared*, unready, unsuspecting, caught unawares; *improvident*, shiftless, thoughtless, imprudent, prodigal, happy-go-lucky; *improvised*, makeshift, extempore, unpremeditated, off-the-cuff.

vb. *lack foresight*, muddle through, live from day to day, live from hand to mouth; *improvise*, extemporize, think on one's feet.

455 PREDICTION

See also **453** (foresight); **877** (occultism).

n. *prediction*, prophesy, forecast, prognosis; *omen*, warning, sign, presage, portent; *ominousness*, portentousness, auspiciousness; *clairvoyance*, extra-sensory perception, prescience, precognition, foreknowledge; *astrology*, palmistry, divination, augury, fortune-telling; *horoscope*, I Ching, tarot, crystal ball; *prophet*, oracle, soothsayer, seer, astrologer, medium, clairvoyant, palmist; *forecaster*, futurologist, Cassandra, doom merchant.

adj. *predictive*, prophetic, apocalyptic, revelatory; *ominous*, portentous, oracular, auspicious; *clairvoyant*, prescient, psychic.

vb. *predict*, foresee, prophesy, foretell, forewarn; *forecast*, read the future,

456 SUPPOSITION

prognosticate; *foreshadow*, presage, prefigure, augur, spell, portend.

456 SUPPOSITION
See also 408 (idea).

n. *supposition*, assumption, premise, postulate; *idea*, suggestion, proposition, notion, fancy, conception; *theory*, hypothesis, conjecture, surmise, guess, inkling, hunch; *speculation*, guesswork, long shot, gamble.

adj. *suppositional*, hypothetical, conjectural, notional; *theoretical*, speculative, academic, armchair; *supposed*, alleged, so-called, putative.

vb. *suppose*, assume, presume, postulate, posit; *conjecture*, surmise, guess, divine, hazard a guess; *theorize*, hypothesize, speculate, imagine; *suggest*, propose, moot, put forward.

457 IMAGINATION
See also 4 (unreality); 479 (untruth).

n. *imagination*, creativity, inventiveness, originality, ingenuity; *mental image*, conception, visualization, projection, figment; *vision*, mind's eye, insight, empathy; *notion*, idea, whim, vagary, flight of fancy; *delusion*, hallucination, mirage, phantom; *fantasy*, fiction, escapism, make-believe, romance, daydreaming, wishful thinking, pipe dream, cloud-cuckoo-land.

adj. *imaginative*, creative, inventive, original, ingenious; *imaginary*, unreal, fictitious, make-believe, fabulous, legendary, mythological; *fanciful*, whimsical, fantastical, escapist, romantic, quixotic, idealistic.

vb. *imagine*, invent, create, devise, dream up, make up; *conceive*, think of, conjure up, visualize; *fantasize*, idealize, romanticize; *pretend*, make believe, daydream, build castles in Spain.

458 MEANING
See also 460 (intelligibility); 503 (clarity).

n. *meaning*, substance, essence, content, pith, matter; *sense*, import, force, tenor, drift, gist; *significance*, meaningfulness, point; *hidden meaning*, connotation, association, implication, suggestion, allusion; *figure of speech*, metaphor, simile, hyperbole; *symbolism*, allegory, parable, double meaning, ambiguity.

adj. *meaningful*, significant, pithy, meaty; *pointed*, telling, pregnant, revealing; *suggestive*, allusive, elliptical, implicit; *figurative*, metaphorical, allegorical, symbolic, connotative; *equivocal*, ambiguous, nebulous; *literal*, unambiguous, unequivocal, denotative; *synonymous*, equivalent, tautologous, tantamount; *semantic*, linguistic, philological.

vb. *mean*, denote, signify, designate; *symbolize*, stand for, connote, imply, suggest; *refer*, allude, mention, drive at, get at (*colloq.*); *convey*, express, communicate.

adv. *in a sense*, so to speak, as it were, that is to say.

459 LACK OF MEANING
See also 443 (nonsense); 461 (unintelligibility).

n. *lack of meaning*, meaninglessness, senselessness; *irrelevance*, insignificance, unimportance; *hollowness*, emptiness, triteness, banality, flatness; *unintelligibility*, illegibility, indecipherability, opaqueness; *nonsense*, gibberish, jargon, doubletalk, double Dutch (*colloq.*), gobbledygook (*colloq.*); *rubbish*, verbiage, twaddle (*colloq.*), claptrap (*colloq.*), piffle (*colloq.*), bunk (*colloq.*), flannel, hot air, eyewash (*colloq.*), guff (*colloq.*), waffle (*colloq.*).

adj. *meaningless*, senseless, expressionless, inscrutable, blank; *incomprehensible*, incoherent, unintelligible, opaque; *irrelevant*, insignificant, unimportant; *hollow*, empty, trivial, banal, trite; *nonsensical*, absurd, inane, fatuous; *verbose*, long-winded, waffly (*colloq.*).

vb. *mean nothing*, make no sense, not add up (*colloq.*); *talk nonsense*, prattle, babble, prate, rattle on, rabbit on (*colloq.*), blather; *jabber*, gibber, gabble, drivel, rant, rave.

460 INTELLIGIBILITY

See also **458** (meaning); **503** (clarity).

n. *intelligibility*, comprehensibility, legibility, readability, audibility; *clarity*, lucidity, limpidity, coherence; *simplicity*, straightforwardness, unambiguousness, explicitness; *simplification*, translation, explanation, demystification, popularization, vulgarization.

adj. *intelligible*, comprehensible, understandable, legible, readable, audible, decipherable; *clear*, lucid, limpid, coherent, transparent; *recognizable*, discernible, distinguishable, visible; *simple*, straight-forward, plain, explicit, unambiguous, forthright; *self-evident*, self-explanatory, obvious.

vb. *be intelligible*, make sense, add up (*colloq.*), speak for itself; *understand*, comprehend, penetrate, fathom; *take in*, take on board, cotton on, tumble to, twig (*colloq.*); *recognize*, discern, distinguish, make out; *clarify*, simplify, elucidate, decode, decipher, translate.

461 UNINTELLIGIBILITY

See also **459** (lack of meaning); **504** (obscurity).

n. *unintelligibility*, incomprehensibility, meaninglessness, incoherence; *difficulty*, obscurity, impenetrability, opaqueness; *illegibility*, indecipherability, unreadability, inaudibility, indistinctness; *jargon*, gibberish, mumbo-jumbo (*colloq.*), hocus-pocus (*colloq.*), double Dutch (*colloq.*); *equivocation*, pun, double entendre, weasel word, newspeak; *puzzlement*, perplexity, bafflement.

adj. *unintelligible*, incomprehensible, meaningless, incoherent; *impenetrable*, unfathomable, inscrutable, opaque; *obscure*, abstruse, esoteric, recondite, obfuscatory; *illegible*, indecipherable, unreadable, inaudible; *puzzling*, mysterious, enigmatic, cryptic; *ambiguous*, equivocal, paradoxical, evasive; *puzzled*, baffled, perplexed, nonplussed, flummoxed (*colloq.*), stumped (*colloq.*).

vb. *not understand*, make nothing of, not make head or tail of (*colloq.*), be at sea (*colloq.*); *be unintelligible*, baffle, perplex, puzzle, go over one's head, be beyond one; *equivocate*, prevaricate, fudge, obscure, obfuscate, complicate.

462 INTERPRETATION

n. *interpretation*, explanation, elucidation, clarification, illustration, exemplification; *account*, commentary, exposition, exegesis, explication, critique; *rendition*, version, paraphrase, adaptation; *annotation*, gloss, crib, translation, transcription; *application*, reading, construction, diagnosis, analysis.

adj. *interpretative*, explanatory, explicatory, elucidatory, illustrative; *critical*, analytical, diagnostic, evaluative.

vb. *interpret*, explain, expound, elucidate; *illuminate*, clarify, throw light on, account for; *read*, construe, understand, analyse, diagnose; *render*, reword, paraphrase, translate, transcribe, adapt; *comment on*, criticize, annotate, edit, gloss; *decipher*, decode, explain, solve, puzzle out, read between the lines.

adv. *namely*, to wit, that is, viz.

463 MISINTERPRETATION

n. *misinterpretation*, misunderstanding, misreading, misconstruction; *mistake*, misconception, misapprehension, error, delusion; *misrepresentation*, distortion, perversion, falsification; *travesty*, parody, caricature, mockery.

vb. *misinterpret*, misunderstand, misread, misconstrue, read into; *mistake*, confuse, get hold of the wrong end of the stick, get one's wires crossed; *falsify*, distort, twist, pervert, garble, scramble; *misrepresent*, travesty, parody, caricature.

464 DISPLAY

See also **394** (appearance); **785** (showiness).

n. *display*, presentation, demonstration, exhibition; *manifestation*, appearance, materialization, realization; *revelation*, disclosure, publication, exposure; *visibility*, prominence, conspicuousness, obviousness; *exhibit*, specimen, evidence, showpiece, collector's item; *show*, fair, exposition, market, parade, pageant; *showroom*, showcase, shop window, market place.

adj. *displayed*, conspicuous, prominent, noticeable, striking; *visible*, apparent, manifest, plain; *marked*, pronounced, evident, obvious, patent; *glaring*, flagrant, overt, eye-catching, blatant, public; *open*, candid, frank, above board.

vb. *display*, present, demonstrate, exhibit; *manifest*, show, evince, give signs of; *unfold*, reveal, unveil, divulge, disclose; *expose*, lay bare, unearth, unfurl, unsheathe; *emphasize*, highlight, spotlight, feature, throw into prominence/relief, foreground; *advertise*, publicize, proclaim, announce; *flaunt*, parade, show off, brandish, flourish.

adv. *on display*, on view, on show; *in public*, openly, for all to see.

465 LATENCY
See also **373** (invisibility); **467** (secret); **469** (concealment).

n. *latency*, dormancy, imperceptibility, invisibility; *concealment*, secrecy, hiddenness, obscurity; *insidiousness*, treacherousness, stealthiness, underhandedness; *undercurrent*, undertone, insinuation, hint, innuendo; *enigma*, unknown quantity, snake in the grass, nigger in the woodpile, mole (*colloq.*), secret agent.

adj. *latent*, dormant, quiescent, hidden, imperceptible; *invisible*, concealed, submerged, subterranean, underground; *inconspicuous*, unseen, obscure, unsung, backroom; *unspoken*, unsaid, tacit, implicit; *secret*, clandestine, covert, undercover; *insidious*, treacherous, underhand, stealthy; *indirect*, veiled, suggestive, allusive.

vb. *be latent*, hide, keep a low profile, lie low, lie doggo (*colloq.*); *steal*, creep, slink, lurk; *hint*, imply, suggest, insinuate.

466 INFORMATION
See also **470** (publication); **471** (news).

n. *information*, knowledge, intelligence, news, facts, data, statistics, info (*colloq.*), gen (*colloq.*), dope (*colloq.*), lowdown (*colloq.*); *communication*, report, message, statement, bulletin, communiqué, dispatch, press release, handout, update; *dissemination*, diffusion, transmission, broadcast, distribution, circulation; *announcement*, notification, intimation, warning, instruction, briefing; *hint*, clue, advice, tip-off (*colloq.*), word in one's ear; *informant*, reporter, messenger, spokesman, courier; *informer*, source, channel, grapevine (*colloq.*), little bird (*colloq.*), supergrass, mole (*colloq.*), nark (*colloq.*), stool pigeon, sneak, telltale.

adj. *informative*, instructive, helpful, enlightening; *communicative*, forthcoming, chatty, newsy, gossipy; *informed*, briefed, posted, apprised, primed, clued up (*colloq.*), genned up (*colloq.*), au courant.

vb. *inform*, apprise, acquaint, enlighten, fill someone in, put in the picture, wise up (*colloq.*); *instruct*, brief, notify, warn, advise, tip off (*colloq.*); *communicate*, convey, put across/over, transmit, diffuse, broadcast, circulate, put about; *be informed*, know the score (*colloq.*), be in the know (*colloq.*), know the state of play; *impart*, reveal, tell, leak, blab (*colloq.*), blow the gaff (*colloq.*), let the cat out of the bag (*colloq.*); *inform on*, betray, denounce, tell tales on, squeal (*colloq.*), rat (*colloq.*), shop (*colloq.*).

467 SECRET
See also **465** (latency).

n. *secret*, mystery, riddle, puzzle, enigma, code, cipher; *suppression*, concealment, censorship, misinformation, blackout, cover-up; *secrecy*, privacy, confidence, discretion, reticence; *secretiveness*, furtiveness, shiftiness, stealth.

adj. *secret*, top-secret, hush-hush (*colloq.*), confidential, classified; *covert*, clandestine, undercover, behind-the-scenes, anonymous, incognito; *underhand*, hole-and-corner, furtive, shifty, stealthy; *secretive*, unforthcoming, uncommunicative, buttoned-up, tight-lipped, close; *private*, discreet, reticent, cagey (*colloq.*).

vb. *keep secret*, keep under wraps, not let on, not breathe a word, hold one's tongue, clam up, keep one's counsel; *suppress*, gag, censor, whitewash; *conceal*, cover up, hush up, sweep under the carpet.

adv. *in secret*, in private, in camera, behind closed doors; *confidentially*, privately, between ourselves; *secretly*, on the sly, on the quiet.

468 DISCLOSURE
See also **203** (uncovering); **470** (publication).

n. *disclosure*, exposure, revelation, discovery, exposé; *publication*, announcement, proclamation, promulgation; *betrayal*, indiscretion, leak, give-away (*colloq.*); *confession*, admission, avowal, acknowledgment.

adj. *disclosed*, revealed, exposed, out, public; *revealing*, indiscreet, tell-tale, informative; *candid*, frank, open, forthcoming.

vb. *disclose*, divulge, reveal, uncover; *expose*, unveil, lay bare, unmask, blow someone's cover; *publish*, air, ventilate, take the lid off (*colloq.*); *announce*, declare, proclaim, promulgate; *confess*, admit, own up, come clean (*colloq.*), make a clean breast of it; *confide*, open up, bare one's soul, unburden oneself, tell all; *betray*, let slip, leak, give the game away, spill the beans (*colloq.*), let the cat out of the bag (*colloq.*).

469 CONCEALMENT
See also **465** (latency).

n. *concealment*, hiding, dissimulation, pretence, masquerade; *conspiracy*, intrigue, machinations, plotting; *disguise*, camouflage, subterfuge, smokescreen, anonymity, pseudonym; *mask*, cloak, veil, cover; *hiding-place*, hideout, hidey-hole (*colloq.*), cache, den, lair, retreat, refuge.

adj. *concealed*, latent, hidden, buried, gone to ground/earth; *disguised*, masked, anonymous, incognito; *clandestine*, secret, furtive, hole-and-corner; *conspiratorial*, cloak-and-dagger, backdoor, surreptitious, Machiavellian.

vb. *conceal*, hide, stow away, secrete, stash (*colloq.*), bury; *disguise*, dissimulate, camouflage, mask, cloak, veil, cover up; *hide*, lurk, skulk, lie low, steal, slink, creep; *ambush*, creep up on, lie in wait, waylay; *conspire*, intrigue, plot, contrive.

470 PUBLICATION
See also **466** (information); **468** (disclosure); **471** (news).

n. *publication*, proclamation, announcement, disclosure; *circulation*, dissemination, diffusion, broadcasting; *publicity*, promotion, advertising, hype (*colloq.*), ballyhoo (*colloq.*), media coverage; *public relations*, PR, image-making, soft sell, showmanship; *public place*, forum, arena, theatre, platform, rostrum, pulpit, soapbox; *public*, audience, readership, market, admass; *notice*, advertisement, placard, poster, puff (*colloq.*), blurb (*colloq.*); *slogan*, commercial, plug (*colloq.*), trailer; *publicist*, promoter, advertiser, adman, PR man; *herald*, announcer, messenger, town crier, barker, tout; *common knowledge*, open secret, public property, household name.

adj. *published*, broadcast, current, circulating, available; *public*, notorious, infamous, celebrated.

vb. *publish*, announce, proclaim, disclose; *distribute*, circulate, put about, disseminate, diffuse; *broadcast*, relay, pass on, spread the word, noise abroad, shout from the rooftops; *herald*, trumpet, blaze aboard, beat the drum; *publicize*, promote, sell, advertise, hype (*colloq.*), plug (*colloq.*), trail.

471 NEWS
See also **466** (information); **470** (publication).

n. *news*, current affairs, tidings, intelligence, word; *report*, story, newsflash, headlines, stop press, scoop, exclusive; *press*, fourth estate, journalism, Fleet Street; *newspaper*, daily, broadsheet, quality, heavy (*colloq.*), rag (*colloq.*), gutter press, yellow press, underground press; *organ*, journal, periodical, weekly, gazette, magazine, glossy; *rumour*, hearsay, buzz, canard, gossip, tittle-tattle, scandal, sensationalism; *reporter*, journalist, correspondent, newsman, newshound, gossip, scandal-monger, grapevine, bush telegraph.

adj. *newsworthy*, scandalous, sensational; *current*, abroad, topical, going round, rumoured, rife; *newsy*, chatty, gossipy, informative.

vb. *report*, publish, spread, noise abroad; *be newsworthy*, make news, hit the headlines, cause a sensation, make a splash.

472 COMMUNICATIONS

n. *communications*, signalling, semaphore, Morse code, telegraphy, telephony; *telecommunications*, telegram, cable, wire, walkie-talkie, intercom, bleeper, telephone, videophone, answering machine; *post*, mail, pigeon post, parcel post, recorded delivery, registered post; *media*, broadcasting, television, small screen, telly (*colloq.*), gogglebox (*colloq.*), videorecorder; *radio*, wireless, transmitter, crystal set, steam radio, transistor; *station*, channel, network, wavelength, frequency, airwaves; *broadcast*, transmission, relay, telecast, simulcast, outside broadcast; *programme*, recording, repeat, sitcom, docudrama, soap opera, chat show, quiz, phone-in, telethon; *broadcaster*, newsreader, presenter, announcer, commentator, anchorman.

473 AFFIRMATION
See also **436** (assent).

n. *affirmation*, declaration, assertion, pronouncement, statement; *profession*, admission, confession, avowal; *allegation*, claim, accusation, charge; *assurance*, confirmation, corroboration, support, endorsement, backing; *pledge*, promise, commitment, guarantee; *insistence*, emphasis, stress, vehemence.

adj. *affirmative*, positive, declarative; *definite*, categorical, unequivocal, express; *assertive*, peremptory, emphatic, insistent; *pledged*, committed, sworn, fully paid-up; *plain*, blunt, round, outspoken.

vb. *affirm*, state, express, declare, assert, pronounce; *profess*, admit, confess, avow, own up to; *allege*, claim, maintain, hold; *confirm*, assure, corroborate, second, endorse, support, back; *emphasize*, stress, reiterate, insist on, urge; *promise*, pledge, swear, engage, commit.

474 NEGATION
See also **437** (dissent).

n. *negation*, nay, negative, veto, refusal, rejection; *denial*, disavowal, repudiation, disclaimer, dissociation; *rebuttal*, refutation, challenge, contradiction; *renunciation*, abnegation, abjuration, retraction; *revocation*, repeal, cancellation, abrogation, annulment.

adj. *negative*, negatory, contrary, contradictory; *opposed*, antagonistic, dissident, recusant.

vb. *negate*, negative, veto, deny, refuse; *refute*, rebut, gainsay, contradict, reject; *repudiate*, disavow, disown, disclaim, dissociate oneself; *renounce*, forswear, abjure, abnegate; *revoke*, abrogate, cancel, annul, repeal.

475 TEACHING
See also **477** (school).

n. *teaching*, pedagogy, schooling, education, edification, enlightenment; *guidance*, instruction, tuition, coaching; *induction*, initiation, training, preparation; *inculcation*, indoctrination, brainwashing, propaganda; *lesson*, class, seminar, tutorial, clinic, workshop; *course*, curriculum, syllabus, timetable; *adult education*, night school, evening classes, day release, sandwich course, block release; *teacher*, instructor, coach, trainer, tutor, educationalist, pedagogue, master, mistress, mentor, guru.

adj. *educational*, pedagogic, scholastic, academic; *educative*, didactic, instructive; *extramural*, extracurricular, recreational; *vocational*, liberal, technical, practical.

vb. *teach*, instruct, tutor, lecture; *coach*, train, school, drill, exercise;

educate, guide, cultivate, edify, enlighten; *initiate*, induct, prepare, break in, show the ropes (*colloq.*); *instil*, inculcate, indoctrinate, din in, hammer in.

476 LEARNING

See also **438** (knowledge).

n. *learning*, lore, knowledge, skill; *wisdom*, erudition, scholarliness, learnedness; *apprenticeship*, tutelage, pupillage, novitiate, training; *self-improvement*, study, application, industry; *lesson*, assignment, project, homework, prep (*colloq.*), revision; *learner*, apprentice, disciple, beginner, recruit, tyro, novice, probationer; *scholar*, pupil, autodidact, student, tutee, undergraduate, swot (*colloq.*), bookworm.

adj. *studious*, industrious, diligent, motivated; *learned*, scholarly, lettered, academic, erudite, knowledgeable, wise.

vb. *learn*, find out, study, apply oneself; *train*, practise, get the hang of (*colloq.*), acquire the knack; *revise*, learn up, swot (*colloq.*), brush up (*colloq.*), burn the midnight oil, mug up (*colloq.*), bone up (*colloq.*).

477 SCHOOL

See also **476** (learning).

n. *school*, academy, institute, seminary, conservatoire; *primary school*, infant school, nursery, creche, kindergarten; *secondary school*, blackboard jungle, grammar/comprehensive/public/state/prep/boarding school, crammer, finishing school, sixth-form college; *further education*, college, campus, university, varsity (*colloq.*), polytechnic, poly (*colloq.*), Oxbridge, redbrick/plate-glass university, groves of academe, alma mater; *schoolroom*, classroom, lecture hall, amphitheatre, auditorium.

478 TRUTH

See also **440** (accuracy).

n. *truth*, plain/honest truth, facts of life, home truths; *truthfulness*, veracity, honesty, integrity, probity; *candour*, sincerity, openness, frankness; *straight-*forwardness, forthrightness, downrightness, bluntness; *ingenuousness*, naivety, artlessness, guilelessness.

adj. *truthful*, veracious, honest, upright; *reliable*, trustworthy, bona fide, honest-to-goodness, genuine; *candid*, sincere, open, frank, above board; *straightforward*, forthright, blunt, direct, bald, downright; *ingenuous*, naive, artless, guileless.

vb. *be truthful*, tell the truth, stick to the facts, give the true story; *speak one's mind*, speak up, make no bones about, call a spade a spade; *confess*, own up, open one's heart, make a clean breast of it.

479 UNTRUTH

See also **441** (error); **457** (imagination).

n. *untruth*, inaccuracy, falsehood, exaggeration, misrepresentation, distortion, perversion; *invention*, fabrication, fiction, romance, faction; *half-truth*, evasion, equivocation, ambiguity, white lie; *dishonesty*, disingenuousness, insincerity, falseness, duplicity, mendaciousness; *lie*, fib, whopper (*colloq.*), hoax, tall story, yarn (*colloq.*), cock and bull story, fairy tale, old wives' tale, superstition, fantasy.

adj. *untrue*, false, fictitious, unreal, imaginary; *fictional*, made-up, make-believe, fairy-tale, fabulous, legendary; *dishonest*, disingenuous, insincere, duplicitous, mendacious, lying; *evasive*, equivocal, ambiguous, hypocritical, two-faced; *spurious*, bogus, phoney, so-called.

vb. *lie*, pretend, dissemble, make believe; *invent*, fabricate, spin, weave, cook up; *exaggerate*, embellish, embroider, dress up.

480 DECEPTION

n. *deception*, dishonesty, duplicity, double-dealing, fraudulence; *deceitfulness*, artfulness, guile, craftiness, cunning; *treachery*, betrayal, perfidy, treason; *deceptiveness*, illusoriness, speciousness, meretriciousness; *trickery*, chicanery, sharp practice, sleight of hand, skulduggery (*colloq.*), hanky-panky (*colloq.*), jiggery-pokery (*colloq.*); *fraud*, racket, dodge, swindle, fiddle (*colloq.*), cheat, swiz (*colloq.*), rip-off (*colloq.*), con (*colloq.*); *trick*, ruse, stratagem, contrivance, wheeze (*colloq.*); *deceiver*, hypocrite, liar, impostor, traitor; *trickster*, cheat, fake, charlatan, quack, mountebank, rogue, swindler, con man (*colloq.*), shyster, wide boy (*colloq.*), spiv (*colloq.*), cowboy; *dupe*, fool, gull, soft touch, patsy (*colloq.*), mug (*colloq.*), fall guy (*colloq.*), sucker (*colloq.*).

adj. *deceitful*, dishonest, lying, duplicitous, treacherous, perfidious; *tricky*, artful, crafty, sly, wily, cunning; *fraudulent*, underhand, shifty, furtive; *deceptive*, illusory, specious, meretricious; *duped*, taken in, gulled, hoodwinked, taken for a ride (*colloq.*).

vb. *deceive*, defraud, cheat, fiddle (*colloq.*), wangle (*colloq.*), con (*colloq.*), swindle, fleece, diddle (*colloq.*), rip off (*colloq.*); *beguile*, delude, mislead, dupe, hoodwink, gull, bamboozle (*colloq.*), double-cross, put one over on (*colloq.*), lead up the garden path (*colloq.*); *be deceived*, be had (*colloq.*), fall for, get taken for a ride (*colloq.*).

481 FALSEHOOD
See also **479** (untruth).

n. *falsehood*, dishonesty, disingenuousness, insincerity, bad faith, mendaciousness; *hypocrisy*, cant, lip-service, cupboard love, crocodile tears; *deceitfulness*, duplicity, fraudulence, perjury, treason; *pretence*, dissimulation, playacting, trickery; *front*, facade, show, semblance, sham, bluff, simulation; *falsification*, counterfeiting, forgery, faking.

adj. *false*, dishonest, untrue, mendacious, lying; *hypocritical*, insincere, two-faced, disingenuous, mealy-mouthed; *deceitful*, shifty, sly, double-dealing, duplicitous, treacherous, perfidious; *falsified*, unfounded, trumped-up, rigged, framed, fixed; *seeming*, feigned, put on, assumed, pretended; *fake*, bogus, sham, phoney, counterfeit, simulated, fraudulent.

vb. *be false*, lie, fib, lie through one's teeth, perjure oneself, bear false witness; *falsify*, doctor, fiddle (*colloq.*), cook (*colloq.*), fix, rig, frame, nobble (*colloq.*); *fake*, forge, counterfeit, simulate; *pretend*, feign, dissimulate, dissemble, play-act, pass oneself off as.

482 EXAGGERATION
See also **431** (overestimation).

n. *exaggeration*, overemphasis, overstatement, overkill, overexposure; *extravagance*, excessiveness, exorbitance, outrageousness, flamboyance; *inflatedness*, bombast, pomposity, hyperbole, hot air (*colloq.*); *fuss*, to-do, ballyhoo (*colloq.*), storm in a teacup; *melodrama*, purple patch, sensationalism, hype (*colloq.*); *yarn* (*colloq.*), tall story (*colloq.*), fisherman's tale, flight of fancy.

adj. *exaggerated*, overstated, overdone, over the top (*colloq.*); *extravagant*, outrageous, flamboyant, preposterous; *excessive*, exorbitant, inordinate, disproportionate, astronomical; *inflated*, bombastic, pompous, high-flown, overblown; *melodramatic*, histrionic, sensational, highly coloured, overwritten, hyperbolic.

vb. *exaggerate*, overemphasize, overstate, overexpose, overdo, go too far, go to extremes; *inflate*, magnify, talk up, blow up, make mountains out of molehills; *dramatize*, embroider, play up, hype (*colloq.*), pile on the agony, lay it on thick (*colloq.*).

483 UNDERSTATEMENT
See also **432** (underestimation).

n. *understatement*, underemphasis, minimization, underestimation; *subtlety*, delicacy, restraint, refinement; *simplicity*, plainness, bareness, austereness; *reserve*, reticence, diffidence, modesty; *suggestion*, trace, suspicion, soupçon; *insipidness*, pallidness, tastelessness, wishy-washiness (*colloq.*).

adj. *understated*, underemphasized, underestimated, underrated; *simple*, plain, bare, stark, unadorned; *delicate*, subtle, restrained, pastel, watercolour; *insipid*, pallid, diluted, wishy-washy (*colloq.*); *reserved*, reticent, diffident, modest, unassuming; *imperceptible*, inconspicuous, unimpressive, underwhelming (*colloq.*).

vb. *understate*, underemphasize, underplay, underestimate, underrate; *moderate*, tone down, play down, water down, dilute; *deflate*, puncture, cut down to size, bring down to earth.

484 SIGN

n. *sign*, indication, mark, evidence, symptom; *image*, symbol, emblem, token; *hint*, pointer, clue, indicator, signpost, omen; *marker*, milestone, landmark, monument, memorial; *signal*, semaphore, tick-tack, warning sign, siren, alarm, beacon; *sign language*, mime, dumb show, charades, body language; *gesture*, nod, wink, shrug, nudge, wave; *applause*, clap, cheer, big hand (*colloq.*); *hiss*, boo, catcall, V-sign, raspberry, slow handclap; *badge*, insignia, coat of arms, crest, bearings, blazon; *uniform*, livery, dress, colours, tartan, old school tie; *flag*, ensign, standard, banner, pennant, tricolour, Union Jack/Flag, Blue Peter, skull and crossbones, Stars and Stripes.

adj. *indicative*, symptomatic, revealing, telling, significant; *symbolic*, token, emblematic, representational; *expressive*, suggestive, redolent.

vb. *indicate*, show, point to, signal, signpost; *reveal*, manifest, betoken, betray, attest to, evince; *symbolize*, stand for, represent, signify; *mark out*, designate, delimit, demarcate; *gesticulate*, mimic, act out, mime, copy; *gesture*, motion, wave, beckon, nod, shrug, point; *frown*, scowl, grimace, pout, smile.

485 IDENTIFICATION

n. *identification*, classification, designation, naming; *identity*, individuality, selfhood, particularity, idiosyncrasy; *identifying sign*, name, signature, autograph, fingerprint, initials, monogram; *proof of identity*, passport, I.D. card, visiting card; *trademark*, hallmark, brand name, imprint, logo, colophon; *marking*, track, spoor, footprint; *pass-*

word, watchword, shibboleth; *label*, nameplate, ticket, tag, docket, sticker; *seal*, stamp, counterfoil, stub, duplicate.

adj. *identifying*, classificatory, designatory; *characteristic*, typical, individual, idiosyncratic, quirky; *identifiable*, recognizable, distinguishable, discernable; *identified*, named, known, branded, earmarked.

vb. *identify*, name, classify, categorize, pin down, pigeonhole; *label*, ticket, tag, docket, stamp, number, letter; *sign*, seal, autograph, countersign, initial, brand, tattoo, earmark.

486 RECORD
See also **448** (memory).

n. *record*, register, roll, catalogue, inventory; *documentation*, file, dossier, case history, curriculum vitae; *account*, report, minutes, notes, jottings, memo; *diary*, journal, scrapbook, album, log, chronicle, archive, annals; *index card*, filing system, microfiche, tape recording, videotape, data bank; *monument*, statue, memorial, cairn, obelisk; *trace*, vestige, relic, remains; *trail*, track, path, swath, wake, wash, tidemark; *recorder*, registrar, clerk, amanuensis, scribe, secretary; *chronicler*, historian, diarist, archivist.

vb. *record*, register, document, catalogue, index, list, file; *report*, document, chronicle, set down, film, tape-record, photograph, video; *note*, minute, jot down, table, log; *score*, chalk up, mark up, notch up, tick off.

adv. *on record*, in black and white, on tape, in the can (*colloq.*).

487 OBLITERATION
See also **449** (oblivion).

n. *obliteration*, erasure, effacement, deletion; *cancellation*, annulment, revocation, repeal; *suppression*, censorship, blackout; *abolition*, elimination, liquidation, annihilation; *blank*, void, tabula rasa, clean slate; *rubber*, eraser, sponge, Snopake (*tdmk.*).

vb. *obliterate*, erase, efface, rub out, wipe out, blot out, snopake; *delete*, cross out, score out, strike out, scrub (*colloq.*); *cancel*, annul, revoke, repeal; *suppress*, quash, censor, blue-pencil, black out; *expunge*, eliminate, liquidate, annihilate; *bury*, submerge, cover up.

488 REPRESENTATION

n. *representation*, depiction, description, delineation; *enactment*, performance, rendering; *personification*, imitation, impersonation, characterization; *illustration*, exemplification, typification, symbolization, figuration; *impression*, likeness, portrayal, image; *portrait*, icon, effigy, statue, waxwork, dummy, photograph, painting, hologram; *reproduction*, facsimile, duplicate, copy; *design*, blueprint, sketch, outline, diagram; *plan*, map, chart, projection; *ornamental art*, fine arts, performing arts, photography, cinematography.

adj. *representative*, typical, exemplary, symbolic, emblematic, figurative; *descriptive*, graphic, vivid, evocative, impressionistic; *representational*, illustrative, pictorial, realistic, naturalistic, true-to-life.

vb. *represent*, stand for, symbolize, connote, mean, signify; *typify*, characterize, illustrate, exemplify; *personify*, epitomize, embody, incarnate; *enact*, perform, mime, impersonate, imitate; *depict*, describe, delineate, draw; *portray*, picture, figure, image, capture, evoke; *design*, sketch, draft, block out, map, chart, outline.

489 MISREPRESENTATION

n. *misrepresentation*, distortion, exaggeration, perversion, falsification; *travesty*, caricature, parody, mockery; *poor likeness*, daub, scrawl, botch, pale imitation, mere shadow; *misinterpretation*, misconstruction, misreading.

adj. *misrepresented*, falsified, distorted, inaccurate, misleading; *flat*, cardboard, unrealistic, infelicitous, inept.

vb. *misrepresent*, distort, exaggerate, pervert, falsify, mislead; *travesty*, caricature, parody, make a mockery of.

490 PAINTING

n. *painting*, art, fine art, graphics, illustration; *artistry*, composition, technique, draughtsmanship, brushwork, palette; *representation*, treatment, handling, rendering, depiction, portrayal; *artistic medium*, watercolour, oil, pastel, crayon, charcoal, tempera, gouache, acrylic; *picture*, mural, fresco, poster, canvas; *sketch*, line drawing, model, cartoon, maquette; *work of art*, old master, chef d'oeuvre, masterpiece; *studio*, atelier, gallery, museum; *portrait*, still life, collage, miniature, landscape, seascape, interior; *artist*, painter, draughtsman, designer, colourist.

adj. *artistic*, painterly, pictorial, picturesque, scenic, graphic; *representational*, realistic, figurative, Impressionist; *abstract*, nonrepresentational, nonobjective, Expressionist, Cubist, minimalist.

vb. *paint*, portray, depict, illustrate, limn, daub; *draw*, sketch, crayon, pencil; *colour*, shade, tint, wash, ink.

491 PHOTOGRAPHY

See also **525** (cinema).

n. *photography*, photojournalism, cinematography, radiography, holography; *photograph*, photo, X-ray, hologram, snapshot, snap, still, frame; *slide*, diapositive, transparency, print; *negative*, exposure, enlargement, blow-up, shot; *film*, filmstrip, microfilm, spool, reel, cassette, cartridge; *camera*, lens, viewfinder, flash, enlarger, projector, viewer, epidiascope, carousel.

adj. *photographic*, cinematographic, radiographic, holographic; *photogenic*, camera-shy, snap-happy (*colloq.*); *overexposed*, underexposed, fuzzy, grainy.

vb. *photograph*, take, snap, photostat, X-ray; *expose*, develop, print, process, enlarge, reproduce.

492 SCULPTURE

n. *sculpture*, plastic arts, modelling, carving, origami; *relief*, cameo, embossing, bas-relief, low relief, mezzo-relievo, high relief; *statue*, statuary, figurine, statuette, bust, head, torso, construction, mobile, stabile; *model*, maquette, death mask, cast, mould; *bronze*, stone, marble, clay, papier-mâché.

adj. *sculptured*, sculpted, graven, moulded, glyptic; *plastic*, mouldable, fictile, malleable; *embossed*, raised, repoussé.

vb. *sculpt*, sculpture, carve, hew, cut, chisel; *model*, fashion, mould, shape, cast; *raise*, emboss, undercut.

493 ENGRAVING

n. *engraving*, etching, intaglio, drypoint, line engraving, photogravure; *mezzotint*, aquatint, woodcut, linocut; *chasing*, fluting, chamfering, groove, line, channel, incision, glyph; *chisel*, burin, graver, needle.

adj. *engraved*, graven, etched; *incised*, carved, grooved, chased, sunk, recessed, fluted, chamfered.

vb. *engrave*, etch, chase, chamfer, chisel, incise; *impress*, stamp, recess.

494 LANGUAGE

See also **496** (word).

n. *language*, speech, tongue, talk, communication, body language, sign language; *style*, diction, parlance, vocabulary, idiom, phraseology, terminology, lingo (*colloq.*), patter, jargon; *natural language*, mother tongue, lingua franca, pidgin, creole, franglais; *artificial language*, Esperanto, Volapuk, computer language, BASIC, FORTRAN, COBOL; *usage*, Standard English, Queen's English, Received Pronunciation; *dialect*, vernacular, patois, Scouse, Brummie, Geordie, Mummerset; *regionalism*, accent, brogue, burr; *slang*, colloquialism, argot, cant, back slang, pig Latin, rhyming slang; *linguistics*, philology, grammar, semantics, phonetics.

adj. *linguistic*, philological, grammatical, semantic, phonetic; *idiomatic*, colloquial, slangy, racy, vulgar, demotic, common; *dialectal*, regional, local, broad, thick; *bilingual*, fluent, polyglot, multilingual.

495 LETTER

See also **513** (writing).

n. *letter*, character, sign, symbol, alphabet, ABC, syllabary; *picture writing*, ideogram, pictogram, hieroglyphic, cuneiform, rune; *lettering*, italic, copperplate, cursive, minuscule, capital, majuscule, uncial; *initial*, monogram, abbreviation, contraction, acronym, acrostic; *speech sound*, vowel, consonant, phoneme, syllable; *spelling*, orthography, transliteration, misspelling, cacography, dyslexia.

adj. *alphabetical*, hieroglyphic, runic, Cyrillic; *syllabic*, consonantal, vocalic; *capital*, upper-case, small, lower-case, italic, roman.

vb. *alphabetize*, syllabify, transliterate, spell; *initial*, letter, sign.

496 WORD

See also **494** (language).

n. *word*, expression, term, name, locution, phrase; *synonym*, antonym, homonym, homophone; *abbreviation*, contraction, acronym, portmanteau word, blend; *word origin*, etymology, root, derivative, folk etymology; *word-play*, pun, spoonerism, anagram, nonce word, neologism, coinage, weasel word; *slogan*, catch phrase, watchword, vogue word, buzzword, cliché; *swearword*, four-letter word, obscenity, oath, billingsgate, bad language; *long word*, polysyllable, mouthful, tongue twister; *barbarism*, corruption, malapropism, solecism; *word list*, glossary, vocabulary, lexicon, dictionary, thesaurus, index, concordance.

adj. *verbal*, lexical, terminological; *literal*, verbatim, word for word; *articulate*, fluent, expressive; *wordy*, verbose, sesquipedalian.

vb. *word*, state, formulate, phrase; *articulate*, express, put into words, verbalize.

497 NAME

n. *name*, designation, appellation, denomination; *epithet*, handle (*colloq.*), moniker (*colloq.*), nickname, pet name, sobriquet, pseudonym, pen name; *forename*, first/Christian/given name, middle name, surname, maiden name, last/family name, patronymic, metronymic; *place name*, toponym, eponym, namesake; *nomenclature*, terminology, classification, identification; *naming*, roll call, dubbing ceremony, christening, baptism; *title*, style, form of address, signature, label.

adj. *named*, titled, nee, alias, a.k.a., so-called; *nominal*, titular, in name only, named after, eponymous.

vb. *name*, call, term, designate, denominate; *title*, style, christen, baptize, dub, nickname; *classify*, identify, label, tag.

498 MISNOMER

n. *misnomer*, wrong name, pseudonym, pen name, nom de plume, alias, false name, nom de guerre; *nickname*, pet name, sobriquet, assumed name, stage name; *false identity*, impersonation, imposture, mistaken identity; *misnaming*, miscalling, malapropism, solecism; *anonymity*, namelessness, facelessness, no name, anon, so-and-so, A.N. Other, Mr X; *unnamed thing*, what's-its-name, thingummy (*colloq.*), thingamajig (*colloq.*), thingamabob (*colloq.*), thingie (*colloq.*).

adj. *misnamed*, pseudonymous, professed, so-called, self-styled, would-be; *anonymous*, nameless, faceless, unknown, unidentified, unnamed, incognito.

vb. *misname*, miscall, mistake; *impersonate*, pass oneself off as, go under the name of.

499 PHRASE

n. *phrase*, expression, turn of phrase, locution, construction, collocation, idiom; *set phrase*, saying, formula, proverb, catch phrase, cliché, motto; *inscription*, phrasing, wording, diction, parlance; *rephrasing*, rewording, restatement, paraphase, circumlocution.

vb. *phrase*, word, express, state, formulate, put into words; *rephrase*, reword, restate, paraphrase.

500 GRAMMAR

n. *grammar*, usage, syntax, word order, morphology, word formation; *declension*, inflection, conjugation, case, person, number, tense, voice, mood, agreement; *word class*, part of speech, noun, pronoun, adjective, modifier, verb, adverb, conjunction, article, determiner, preposition, interjection; *subject*, predicate, object, complement, apposition; *affix*, prefix, suffix, infix.

adj. *grammatical*, syntactic, morphological, correct, well-formed, standard, acceptable; *nominal*, adjectival, verbal, adverbial, prepositional, interjectional; *comparative*, superlative, absolute; *active*, passive, subjunctive.

vb. *parse*, analyse, construe, conjugate, inflect, decline; *qualify*, modify, govern, take, agree.

501 GRAMMATICAL ERROR

n. *grammatical error*, solecism, misusage, barbarism; *mistake*, slip of the tongue/pen, split infinitive, double negative, dangling participle; *ungrammaticality*, misconstruction, hypercorrection.

adj. *ungrammatical*, incorrect, hypercorrect, unacceptable; *nonstandard*, substandard, loose, sloppy, careless.

502 STYLE

n. *style*, mode, fashion, manner, idiom, vein, strain; *phraseology*, vocabulary, wording, diction, register, level, tone; *fluency*, mastery, articulacy, eloquence, word power, command, rhetoric, oratory; *elegance*, power, vigour, raciness; *inelegance*, awkwardness, clumsiness, stiltedness.

adj. *stylistic*, literary, rhetorical, oratorical; *mannered*, stylized, idiosyncratic, quirky; *elegant*, well crafted, well turned, fluent, articulate, eloquent; *inelegant*, infelicitous, stilted, clumsy, awkward, ponderous, flat, prosaic.

503 CLARITY

See also **460** (intelligibility).

n. *clarity*, clearness, lucidity, limpidity, transparency; *intelligibility*, perspicuity, straightforwardness, unambiguousness; *exactness*, preciseness, explicitness, directness; *simplicity*, plainness, unadornedness, baldness.

adj. *clear*, lucid, limpid, transparent; *intelligible*, perspicuous, understandable, straightforward, uncomplicated, unambiguous; *simple*, plain, uncluttered, unadorned; *exact*, precise, clearcut, explicit, direct, spelt out, in words of one syllable.

504 OBSCURITY

See also **461** (unintelligibility).

n. *obscurity*, unintelligibility, abstruseness, opaqueness; *complexity*, convolutedness, denseness, overcompression; *vagueness*, indefiniteness, ambiguity, obfuscation, obscurantism; *inexactness*, impreciseness, looseness, diffuseness, sloppiness; *wordiness*, verbosity, bombast, waffle (*colloq.*).

adj. *obscure*, unclear, unintelligible, opaque; *abstruse*, esoteric, recondite, recherché; *vague*, indefinite, ambiguous, obscurantist, obfuscatory; *complex*, involved, intricate, dense, compressed; *inexact*, imprecise, loose, woolly, sloppy, diffuse; *wordy*, verbose, overwritten, bombastic.

505 CONCISENESS

See also **179** (shortness); **520** (summary).

n. *conciseness*, concision, succinctness, brevity, pithiness; *terseness*, curtness, compression, economy, laconicism; *shorthand*, telegraphese, ellipsis; *condensation*, abridgment, summary, résumé.

adj. *concise*, succinct, brief, economical, short and sweet; *terse*, curt, monosyllabic, laconic, lapidary; *pithy*, epigrammatic, aphoristic, sententious; *compressed*, dense, compact, condensed, summarized; *crisp*, clipped, trenchant, incisive.

vb. *be concise*, come straight to the point, cut a long story short, not beat about the bush, cut the cackle (*colloq.*); *abbreviate*, contract, abridge, summarize; *compress*, condense, boil down, telescope.

adv. *in brief*, in a word, in a nutshell.

506 DIFFUSENESS

See also **530** (talkativeness).

n. *diffuseness*, wordiness, verbosity, long-windedness, prolixity; *discursiveness*, repetitiveness, padding, waffle (*colloq.*); *digression*, excursus, disquisition, peroration, harangue, tirade; *pleonasm*, tautology, redundancy, circumlocution.

adj. *diffuse*, verbose, wordy, long-winded, prosy, prolix; *repetitive*, redundant, tautologous, pleonastic, circumlocutous, roundabout; *protracted*, lengthy, tedious, long-drawn-out; *discursive*, digressive, rambling, off the point.

vb. *be diffuse*, enlarge, expand, dilate, amplify, elaborate, expatiate; *draw out*, spin out, pad, protract, filibuster; *discourse*, hold forth, harangue, perorate; *digress*, wander, ramble, rabbit (*colloq.*), blather (*colloq.*), gush, waffle (*colloq.*).

adv. *at length*, ad nauseam, on and on.

507 EMPHASIS

n. *emphasis*, stress, reiteration, insistence, vehemence; *force*, strength, power, vigour, punch (*colloq.*); *vividness*, raciness, verve, sparkle; *incisiveness*, trenchancy, pointedness, bite, edge, mordancy; *conviction*, fervour, passion, eloquence, cogency; *grandiloquence*, solemnity, weight, gravitas.

adj. *emphatic*, reiterative, insistent, vehement; *forceful*, powerful, cogent, vigorous, strongly worded, hard-hitting, punchy (*colloq.*); *vivid*, lively, sparkling, graphic, racy; *incisive*, trenchant, pointed, biting, cutting, mordant; *passionate*, fervent, convincing, persuasive, eloquent, effective; *serious*, weighty, measured, solemn, grave; *grandiloquent*, inspired, lofty, sublime.

vb. *emphasize*, stress, insist on, reiterate, underline, underscore, spell out, ram home, say in no uncertain terms; *persuade*, convince, carry weight, hit home.

508 LACK OF EMPHASIS

n. *lack of emphasis,* insipidness, vapidness, flatness; *prosiness,* turgidity, stiltedness, ponderousness; *dullness,* dryness, tediousness, jejuneness; *ineffectiveness,* feebleness, limpness, understatedness; *sentimentality,* mawkishness, schmaltz (*colloq.*).

adj. *unemphatic,* weak, insipid, colourless, flat; *prosy,* turgid, stilted, ponderous; *dull,* dry, thin, impoverished, jejune; *ineffective,* feeble, limp, understated; *prosaic,* pedestrian, clichéd, hackneyed, trite; *sentimental,* mawkish, novelettish, schmaltzy (*colloq.*), corny (*colloq.*).

509 SIMPLICITY

n. *simplicity,* straightforwardness, clarity, directness; *plainness,* naturalness, restraint, no frills, austerity, starkness, baldness; *unaffectedness,* unpretentiousness, homeliness, unsophistication, artlessness, naivety; *frankness,* candour, matter-of-factness, downrightness, bluntness.

adj. *simple,* straightforward, direct, uncomplicated, easy; *plain,* unadorned, unvarnished, uncluttered, natural, homespun; *austere,* restrained, stark, bare, bald; *unpretentious,* unaffected, unassuming, down-to-earth, no-nonsense, matter-of-fact; *unsophisticated,* artless, naive, innocent; *everyday,* workaday, homely, commonplace, humdrum.

vb. *speak plainly,* not mince one's words, spell it out, call a spade a spade, get down to brass tacks.

adv. *simply,* in plain English, in words of one syllable, not to put too fine a point on it.

510 ORNAMENT

See also **766** (decoration).

n. *ornament,* adornment, embellishment, enhancement; *ornamentation,* decoration, embroidery, frills, fuss, clutter; *ornateness,* preciousness, tweeness, floweriness, floridness, purple passage; *rhetoric,* bombast, fustian, pomposity, turgidity; *extravagance,* flamboyance, showiness, flashiness;

pretentiousness, affectation, sententiousness, grandioseness.

adj. *ornate,* elaborate, decorative, rich, lavish; *fussy,* frilly, cluttered, busy; *precious,* twee, flowery, florid; *extravagant,* flamboyant, showy, flashy; *rhetorical,* orotund, resonant, high-flown, grandiloquent; *inflated,* pompous, turgid, bombastic, pretentious, sententious.

vb. *decorate,* embellish, enhance, embroider, lay it on with a shovel/ trowel (*colloq.*).

511 ELEGANCE

n. *elegance,* taste, style, refinement, beauty, gracefulness; *restraint,* simplicity, classicism, proportion; *symmetry,* balance, flow, rhythm, harmony, smoothness, ease; *poise,* decorum, distinction, stateliness, dignity; *correctness,* propriety, appropriateness, felicity; *stylishness,* sophistication, smartness, polish, flair.

adj. *elegant,* tasteful, stylish, beautiful, graceful, refined; *restrained,* simple, understated, classical, symmetrical; *harmonious,* balanced, well-proportioned, flowing, rhythmic, smooth; *felicitous,* appropriate, well-put, correct, proper; *distinguished,* stately, dignified, poised, decorous; *sophisticated,* smart, polished, soigné, well-groomed.

vb. *make elegant,* beautify, refine, polish, finish, smarten up.

512 INELEGANCE

n. *inelegance,* gracelessness, ugliness, unsightliness, unshapeliness, lumpishness; *gaucheness,* awkwardness, clumsiness, ungainliness, unwieldiness; *artificiality,* stiffness, stiltedness, woodenness; *tastelessness,* vulgarity, impropriety, incorrectness, inappropriateness; *crudeness,* boorishness, uncouthness, coarseness.

adj. *inelegant,* graceless, gauche, awkward, clumsy, ungainly; *ugly,* unsightly, unshapely, lumpy; *artificial,* forced, contrived, laboured, stiff, stilted, wooden; *inappropriate,* infelicitous, jarring, grating, incorrect, improper; *tasteless,* vulgar, unrefined, common; *crude*, coarse, boorish, uncouth.

513 WRITING
See also **495** (letter); **515** (correspondence).

n. *writing*, composition, authorship, journalism, hackwork, Grub Street; *correspondence*, paperwork, documentation, bumf (*colloq.*), notes; *written matter*, script, copy, manuscript, typescript, transcript, minutes; *caption*, heading, legend, epigraph, inscription, rubric; *handwriting*, longhand, scribble, scrawl, cacography; *shorthand*, stenography, speedwriting, typewriting; *calligraphy*, penmanship, copperplate, pothook, flourish; *alphabet*, braille, code, cipher, hieroglyphics, pictogram, ideogram, cryptogram; *stationery*, vellum, parchment, papyrus, scroll.

adj. *written*, graphic, handwritten, manuscript, autograph, holograph; *italic*, roman, cursive, uncial; *bold*, round, flowing, spidery, cramped, crabbed.

vb. *write*, pen, trace, print, type, scribble, scrawl; *compose*, draft, put into writing, set down in black and white, put pen to paper; *copy*, transcribe, take down, jot, note, minute.

514 PRINT
n. *print*, type, newsprint, copy, text, printout; *publication*, impression, edition, offprint, reprint, print run; *printing*, lithography, offset, letterpress; *typesetting*, filmsetting, photocomposition, cold type, Monotype (*tdmk.*), Linotype (*tdmk.*), hot metal; *typography*, typeface, fount, upper/lower case, boldface, lightface, serif, sansserif; *page*, folio, proof, galley, revise, bromide; *printer's error*, correction, literal, typo; *printer*, typesetter, compositor, proofreader, copy editor, subeditor.

adj. *printed*, typographic, typeset, in/out of print.

vb. *print*, print off, run off, publish; *typeset*, photocompose, filmset.

515 CORRESPONDENCE
See also **513** (writing).

n. *correspondence*, communication, exchange, acknowledgment, reply, answer; *post*, mail, letters, postbag, delivery, dispatch; *letter*, epistle, missive, circular, chain letter, round robin, junk mail (*colloq.*); *greetings card*, postcard, love letter, Valentine, billet doux, poison pen letter; *correspondent*, addressee, sender, recipient, penfriend, penpal; *envelope*, s.a.e., cover, stamp, seal, postcode.

adj. *epistolary*, postal, air-mail.

vb. *correspond*, write, communicate, acknowledge, reply, drop a line to (*colloq.*); *post*, forward, mail, send; *address*, stamp, frank, seal.

516 BOOK
See also **518** (literature).

n. *book*, volume, tome, manuscript, MS, title; *bestseller*, classic, remainder, potboiler; *publication*, edition, impression, reprint, reissue; *text*, libretto, screenplay, scenario, lyrics; *library*, set, collection, anthology, series, compendium; *booklet*, pamphlet, leaflet, tract, brochure, prospectus; *bibliography*, catalogue, reading list, index; *cover*, dust jacket, binding, spine, boards; *page*, recto, verso, flyleaf, endpaper, frontispiece, appendix; *reader*, bookworm, bibliophile, librarian, bookseller.

adj. *hardback*, cased, softback, bound, looseleaf, paperback.

517 DESCRIPTION
See also **488** (representation).

n. *description*, account, exposition, delineation, portrayal, profile; *narration*, report, recital, tale, anecdote; *nonfiction*, reportage, documentary; biography, travelogue; *story*, narrative, plot, subplot, scenario, storyline; *history*, chronicle, annals, memoirs, case history, life story; *summary*, thumbnail sketch, cameo, vignette; *narrator*, story-teller, raconteur, historian, chronicler.

adj. *descriptive*, expository, narrative, graphic; *colourful*, vivid, scenic, picturesque; *true-to-life*, naturalistic, realistic, photographic; *expressive*, evocative, suggestive, impressionistic.

vb. *describe*, depict, delineate, characterize, represent; *draw*, paint, sketch, outline; *narrate*, recount, relate, tell, report, chronicle.

518 LITERATURE
See also **516** (book); **521** (poetry); **522** (prose).

n. *literature*, prose, poetry, classics, criticism, lit. crit; *novel*, drama, short story, novella; *nonfiction*, autobiography, biography, memoirs; *fiction*, romance, science fiction, sci-fi, detective story, thriller, whodunnit (*colloq.*); *pulp fiction*, trash, pap, novelette, penny dreadful, instant book, novelization; *bestseller*, blockbuster (*colloq.*), potboiler, classic; *writer*, author, dramatist, poet, novelist, litterateur, ghostwriter, wordsmith.
adj. *literary*, poetic, epic, heroic, mock-heroic, picaresque; *fictional*, romantic, cloak-and-dagger.
vb. *write*, author, compose, ghostwrite, compile, edit; *fictionalize*, dramatize, novelize, adapt.

519 DISSERTATION
n. *dissertation*, discourse, essay, treatise, thesis, monograph, paper; *exposition*, disquisition, examination, enquiry, survey, study, commentary, analysis, critique; *review*, notice, article, piece, write-up, editorial, leader.
adj. *discursive*, expository, critical, analytical.
vb. *dissertate*, treat, handle, discuss, examine; *develop*, amplify, go into, expatiate on, discourse on; *criticize*, comment, review, survey, write up.

520 SUMMARY
See also **505** (conciseness).

n. *summary*, résumé, precis, abstract, synopsis; *contents*, substance, gist, the long and short of it; *outline*, sketch, rundown, digest; *selection*, condensation, anthology, compilation, miscellany.
adj. *summarized*, abridged, condensed, potted; *concise*, brief, succinct, sketchy.
vb. *summarize*, sum up, precis, abstract; *condense*, conflate, abridge, boil down.

521 POETRY
See also **518** (literature).

n. *poetry*, poesy, verse, rhyme, alliteration, assonance; *poem*, verses, lines, epic, ode, hymn, elegy, lay; *light verse*, ballad, jingle, doggerel, limerick, clerihew, ditty; *verse form*, sonnet, haiku, couplet, triplet, quatrain, sestina, stanza, blank verse; *prosody*, versification, scansion, metrics; *metre*, foot, accent, beat, stress, rhythm, cadence; *poet*, bard, poet laureate, versifier, poetaster, rhymester, troubadour, minstrel.
adj. *poetic*, lyric, rhapsodic, epic, bardic, heroic, elegiac; *metrical*, prosodic, rhythmical, accented.
vb. *versify*, compose, scan, rhyme, elegize.

522 PROSE
See also **518** (literature).

n. *prose*, writing, running text, chapter, paragraph; *nonfiction*, history, biography, memoirs, reportage; *fiction*, novel, short story, essay, prose poem, stream of consciousness; *prosaicness*, plainness, prosiness, dullness, matter-of-factness; *speech*, address, talk, discourse, anecdote.
adj. *prosaic*, prosy, pedestrian, dull; *unaccented*, flat, unrelieved, uninspired; *historical*, factual, biographical.

523 DRAMA
n. *drama*, play, production, revival, spectacle, vehicle; *tragedy*, comedy, farce, melodrama, pantomime, revue skit; *vaudeville*, music hall, variety, musical comedy, cabaret, floor show; *theatre*, stage, footlights, West End, Broadway, theatreland, show business; *premiere*, opening night, preview, first night, sell-out, smash hit; *performance*, act, turn, role, part, bit/walk-on part, cameo, audition, rehearsal; *theatricals*, mime, charade, masque, dumb show; *stage directions*, exit, entrance, cue, prompt; *prologue*, epilogue, finale, final curtain, encore; *scenery*, set, props,

costume, wardrobe, greasepaint, make-up; *auditorium,* front of house, proscenium, apron, wings, flies, theatre-in-the-round; *balcony,* stalls, circle, gods (*colloq.*), stage door; *actor,* actress, leading lady/man, understudy, extra, trouper, thespian, entertainer, performer; *theatricality,* histrionics, staginess, ham (*colloq.*); *cast,* dramatis personae, company, troupe, chorus line.

adj. *dramatic,* theatrical, histrionic, stagy; *tragic,* straight, legitimate, melodramatic, blood-and-thunder, kitchen-sink; *comic,* farcical, burlesque, slapstick, knockabout (*colloq.*).

vb. *dramatize,* stage, present, put on, produce, direct; *perform,* play, act, enact, mime, tread the boards, go on stage, audition, rehearse; *overact,* play to the gallery, ham it up (*colloq.*), upstage, steal the limelight; *underact,* miss one's cue, fluff one's lines, dry (*colloq.*), corpse (*colloq.*), ad-lib.

524 DANCE

n. *dance,* ballet, tap dance, modern dance, folk dance; *choreography,* solo, pirouette, pas de deux, set; *minuet,* gavotte, mazurka, polka, polonaise; *ballroom dancing,* old-time dancing, waltz, foxtrot, quickstep, tango, bossa nova, rumba, cha-cha; *country dance,* jig, reel, hornpipe, morris dance, barn dance, square dance; *rock'n roll,* twist, jive, disco, Charleston, black bottom, boogie (*colloq.*); *ball,* hop, the dansant, knees-up (*colloq.*); *dancer,* ballerina, corps de ballet, chorus girl, hoofer (*colloq.*).

adj. *balletic,* graceful, stately, rhythmic, lively.

vb. *dance,* take the floor, shuffle, trip the light fantastic; *leap,* skip, spin, pirouette, cavort, cut a caper; *twist,* jive, bop (*colloq.*), disco, stomp (*colloq.*), jitterbug (*colloq.*), boogie (*colloq.*).

525 CINEMA

See also 491 (photography).

n. *cinema,* motion pictures, celluloid, silver/big screen, Hollywood; *cinematography,* animation, cartoon, montage,

soundtrack, Technicolor (*tdmk.*), Sensurround (*tdmk.*), Cinerama (*tdmk.*); *camerawork,* shot, still, tracking shot, special effects, close-up, fade-out, freeze-frame; *script,* screenplay, scenario, shooting script, continuity; *film,* movie, remake, silent, talkie, newsreel, trailer, short; *feature film,* B-movie, western, horse opera, spaghetti western, biopic, blue movie, skinflick (*colloq.*), blockbuster (*colloq.*), weepie (*colloq.*), tearjerker (*colloq.*); *studio,* picture house, picture palace, fleapit (*colloq.*), box office; *director,* star, co-star, screen idol, starlet.

adj. *cinematic,* cinematographic, photogenic, star-studded, bankable.

vb. *film,* shoot, roll, pan, track; *show,* project, screen, release; *script,* edit, produce, direct, cast, bankroll (*colloq.*).

526 VOICE

See also 353 (sound); 528 (speech).

n. *voice,* speech, utterance, tongue, exclamation, ejaculation; *articulation,* enunciation, delivery, pronunciation, elocution; *intonation,* modulation, inflection, pitch, tone, timbre; *accent,* burr, twang, drawl, lisp; *loud voice,* roar, shout, bellow, yell; *soft voice,* murmur, whisper, hiss.

adj. *vocal,* oral, phonetic, vocalic; *distinct,* aloud, clear, bell-like, fluting, sing-song; *loud,* shrill, strident, booming.

vb. *voice,* speak, utter, verbalize, vocalize, give voice/tongue, exclaim, ejaculate; *articulate,* enunciate, pronounce, elocute; *modulate,* inflect, intone, drone, drawl; *flute,* carol, warble, trill; *raise one's voice,* speak up, shout, boom, roar, bellow; *lower one's voice,* pipe down (*colloq.*), whisper, breathe, hiss.

527 VOICELESSNESS

See also 354 (silence); 531 (taciturnity).

n. *voicelessness,* silence, muteness, dumbness, speechlessness, inarticulacy; *hoarseness,* huskiness, gruffness, croakiness, breathiness, wheeziness.

adj. *voiceless,* speechless, silent, mute,

dumb; *inarticulate*, tongue-tied, dumb-struck, taciturn, mum; *hoarse*, husky, cracked, croaky, breathy, wheezy.

vb. *lose one's voice*, be mute, be struck dumb, be at a loss for words; *say nothing*, hold one's tongue (*colloq.*), shut up (*colloq.*), stick in one's throat, choke on; *silence*, gag, muffle, stifle, cut short, break in on.

528 SPEECH

See also **526** (voice); **532** (address).

n. *speech*, language, utterance, tongue, word of mouth; *articulacy*, fluency, eloquence, way with words, gift of the gab (*colloq.*); *discourse*, talk, conversation, dialogue, monologue, spiel, patter (*colloq.*); *rhetoric*, public speaking, oration, peroration, declamation, earful (*colloq.*); *comment*, remark, observation, aside, a word in edgeways; *speaker*, talker, lecturer, orator, spokesperson, mouthpiece.

adj. *spoken*, oral, verbal, vocal; *articulate*, fluent, eloquent, bilingual, polyglot; *rhetorical*, oratorical, declamatory, tub-thumping.

vb. *speak*, vocalize, voice, utter, say, articulate, verbalize; *speak up*, break one's silence, pipe up, find one's tongue, open one's mouth; *declare*, declaim, speak out, sound off, say one's piece, have one's say; *lecture*, orate, sermonize, pontificate, speechify, spout; *dictate*, trot out, reel off, recite.

529 SPEECH DEFECT

n. *speech defect*, aphasia, speech impediment, stammer, stutter, lisp, cleft palate; *inarticulacy*, indistinctness, mumbling, slur, drawl, twang.

adj. *inarticulate*, indistinct, thick, slurred; *nasal*, adenoidal, twangy, sibilant.

vb. *speak badly*, stammer, stutter, falter, hem and haw, hesitate; *mutter*, mumble, swallow one's words, gabble; *slur*, drawl, lisp, nasalize, speak with a plum in one's mouth.

530 TALKATIVENESS

See also **506** (diffuseness).

n. *talkativeness*, loquacity, garrulity, chattiness, fluency, volubility; *verbosity*, wordiness, prolixity, logorrhoea, verbal diarrhoea; *chatter*, prattle, jaw (*colloq.*), gossip, tittle-tattle, blather, gush, waffle (*colloq.*), gas (*colloq.*), hot air (*colloq.*); *chatterer*, chatterbox (*colloq.*), blatherskite (*colloq.*), windbag (*colloq.*), gasbag (*colloq.*).

adj. *talkative*, loquacious, voluble, garrulous; *verbose*, prolix, wordy, long-winded; *fluent*, glib, effusive, gushing, fulsome; *chatty*, gossipy, gabby (*colloq.*), gassy (*colloq.*).

vb. *be talkative*, chatter, prattle, run on, talk nineteen to the dozen, talk the hind leg off a donkey, rabbit on (*colloq.*), yak (*colloq.*); *jabber*, gabble, prate, blather, yap (*colloq.*); *digress*, ramble, wander, maunder, drone on, monopolize/hog the conversation; *expatiate*, sound off, spout (*colloq.*), outtalk, filibuster.

531 TACITURNITY

n. *taciturnity*, muteness, speechlessness, silence, quietness; *reserve*, reticence, uncommunicativeness, discretion; *curtness*, brusqueness, gruffness, terseness, laconism.

adj. *taciturn*, silent, mum, mute, speechless, tongue-tied; *reserved*, reticent, unforthcoming, uncommunicative, discreet, tight-lipped, close; *curt*, gruff, brusque, terse, laconic, monosyllabic.

vb. *be taciturn*, give nothing away, keep one's counsel, hold one's peace, hold one's tongue (*colloq.*), keep one's mouth shut, save one's breath, dry up, shut up (*colloq.*).

532 ADDRESS

See also **528** (speech).

n. *address*, apostrophe, aside, salutation, greeting; *speech*, public address, lecture, talk, oration, peroration, toast; *invocation*, appeal, interpellation, exhortation, pep talk (*colloq.*); *sermon*, homily, harangue, tirade; *addressee*, audience, captive audience, listener.

vb. *address*, apostrophize, greet, hail, salute, accost, buttonhole (*colloq.*); *orate*, perorate, speechify, pontificate;

invoke, appeal, exhort, interpellate;
preach, sermonize, harangue, lecture.

533 CONVERSATION

n. *conversation*, talk, dialogue, communication; *exchange*, banter, badinage, repartee, slanging match (*colloq.*); *chat*, tête à tête, heart-to-heart, natter (*colloq.*); *confab* (*colloq.*), chinwag (*colloq.*); *gossip*, chitchat, tittle-tattle, small talk; *conference*, parley, colloquy, symposium, summit, convention, pow-wow (*colloq.*); *consultation*, interview, audience; *discussion*, debate, talking shop (*colloq.*).

adj. *conversational*, chatty, newsy, forthcoming, communicative; *animated*, heated, quick-fire, ding-dong (*colloq.*).

vb. *converse*, talk, chat, pass the time of day, bandy words; *gossip*, tittle-tattle, natter (*colloq.*), chew the fat (*colloq.*); *confer*, parley, talk over, discuss, debate, go into a huddle.

534 SOLILOQUY

n. *soliloquy*, monologue, monody, aside, apostrophe; *solo*, one-man show, one-man band, one-hander.

vb. *soliloquize*, talk to oneself, think aloud, talk to a brick wall (*colloq.*), waste one's breath.

535 WILL

See also **537** (willingness); **539** (resolution).

n. *will*, volition, intention, purpose; *wish*, desire, inclination, preference, mind, disposition; *resolution*, determination, wilfulness, obstinacy; *will power*, assertiveness, self-control, self-determination, autonomy; *free will*, choice, option, discretion, free hand.

adj. *willing*, desirous, inclined, disposed, agreeable; *spontaneous*, unasked, unprompted, ready; *voluntary*, optional, discretionary, arbitrary; *autonomous*, independent, unconstrained, assertive, autocratic; *wilful*, self-willed, single-minded, determined; *intentional*, volitional, deliberate, willed, designed.

vb. *will*, wish, desire, want; *intend*, determine, purpose, plan; *be indepen-*

dent, know one's own mind, be one's own man, go one's own way; *assert oneself*, impose one's will, have one's own way; *choose*, opt for, plump for, favour.

adv. *at will*, ad libitum, as one pleases; *willingly*, voluntarily, of one's own accord, off one's own bat.

536 NECESSITY

See also **547** (predetermination).

n. *necessity*, compulsion, obligation, Hobson's choice, last resort; *determinism*, fatalism, force of circumstances, act of God; *inevitability*, unavoidability, destiny, fate, karma, lot; *prerequisite*, precondition, requirement, imperative, must; *instinct*, compulsion, reflex, Pavlovian reaction, knee-jerk reaction.

adj. *necessary*, required, requisite, imperative, indispensable; *compulsory*, obligatory, binding, mandatory, unavoidable, inescapable; *inevitable*, inexorable, ineluctable, preordained, fateful; *involuntary*, automatic, instinctive, mechanical.

vb. *necessitate*, oblige, dictate, compel; *require*, demand, insist, stipulate; *have no alternative/option*, bow to fate, take it or leave it, make a virtue of necessity; *preordain*, destine, doom, predetermine.

537 WILLINGNESS

See also **535** (will).

n. *willingness*, readiness, promptness, alacrity, zeal, eagerness; *inclination*, disposition, tendency, propensity, penchant; *goodwill*, cooperation, collaboration, helpfulness, spontaneity; *consent*, compliance, acquiescence, receptiveness; *obedience*, docility, tractability, pliability.

adj. *willing*, agreeable, acquiescent, compliant; *cooperative*, helpful, spontaneous, voluntary, unprompted; *prompt*, ready, eager, keen, zealous, enthusiastic; *inclined*, favourable, amenable, receptive, game; *obedient*, submissive, tractable, docile, manageable.

vb. *be willing*, feel like, have a mind to, desire to; *agree*, acquiesce, comply, consent; *cooperate*, collaborate, show willing, go along with, bend over backwards; *volunteer*, jump at, leap at, not hesitate.

adv. *willingly*, readily, gladly, voluntarily, with good grace, at the drop of a hat, like a shot.

538 UNWILLINGNESS
See also **542** (obstinacy).

n. *unwillingness*, reluctance, disinclination, hesitation; *doubt*, scruple, qualm, reservation; *disagreement*, disfavour, objection, demurral; *aversion*, repugnance, dislike, avoidance; *recalcitrance*, refractoriness, obstinacy, sullenness; *indifference*, apathy, abstention, dissociation.

adj. *unwilling*, reluctant, disinclined, loath; *half-hearted*, begrudging, forced, lukewarm; *averse*, opposed, unfavourable, hostile; *uncooperative*, unhelpful, sullen, bolshie (*colloq.*); *recalcitrant*, refractory, obstinate, awkward, disaffected; *hesitant*, tentative, cautious, unenthusiastic; *indifferent*, apathetic, uninterested, negligent.

vb. *be unwilling*, force oneself, not have the heart to, stick at, jib, balk, dig in one's heels; *object*, demur, cavil, protest; *hesitate*, scruple, hold off, hang back, drag one's feet; *recoil*, fight shy of, duck, shirk, slack, not pull one's weight.

adv. *unwillingly*, with bad grace, with heavy heart, under protest.

539 RESOLUTION
See also **43** (adhesion); **535** (will).

n. *resolution*, determination, resolve, firmness; *tenacity*, perseverance, staunchness, constancy; *will power*, relentlessness, ruthlessness, iron will; *drive*, energy, vigour, forcefulness; *commitment*, single-mindedness, devotion, dedication; *fortitude*, character, backbone, moral fibre; *spirit*, mettle, pluck, guts (*colloq.*).

adj. *resolute*, resolved, determined, single-minded, intent, set, bent on; *tenacious*, persevering, staunch, firm; *forceful*, energetic, driving, strong-willed; *uncompromising*, committed, whole-hearted, diehard; *ruthless*, grim, steely, implacable, indomitable; *intransigent*, inflexible, unbending, immovable, unshakable.

vb. *be resolute*, stand firm, stand one's ground, not budge, not give an inch; *resolve*, determine, make up one's mind, decide, will; *commit oneself*, set one's heart on, go all out for, not take no for an answer, put one's foot down (*colloq.*).

540 PERSEVERANCE
See also **43** (adhesion); **542** (obstinacy).

n. *perseverance*, persistence, tenacity, firmness; *steadfastness*, staunchness, constancy, dedication, devotion; *stamina*, staying power, patience, endurance; *tirelessness*, indefatigability, stalwartness, doggedness; *application*, assiduousness, sedulousness, diligence.

adj. *persevering*, persistent, tenacious, stubborn; *steadfast*, staunch, firm, stalwart, doughty; *constant*, devoted, dedicated, unwavering; *patient*, long-suffering, dogged, plodding; *undaunted*, unflagging, unfailing, tireless, indefatigable; *assiduous*, sedulous, industrious, diligent.

vb. *persevere*, persist, keep on, keep at it, never say die; *hold out*, hang on, stick it out, stay the course; *plod*, slog, beaver (*colloq.*), plug away (*colloq.*), peg away (*colloq.*).

adv. *to the bitter end*, come hell or high water, through thick and thin, come what may.

541 VACILLATION
See also **44** (nonadhesion); **544** (caprice).

n. *vacillation*, irresolution, indecision, uncertainty; *hesitation*, doubt, half-heartedness, apathy; *weakness*, faint-heartedness, gutlessness, spinelessness; *capriciousness*, fickleness, inconstancy, unpredictability; *suggestibility*, impressionability, malleability, pliancy.

adj. *vacillating*, indecisive, hesitant, wavering, changeable; *irresolute*, unresolved, uncertain, undecided; *capricious*, unstable, unpredictable, inconstant, fickle; *weak*, spineless, weak-kneed, faint-hearted, pusillanimous; *suggestible*, impressionable, malleable, pliable; *apathetic*, lukewarm, tepid, unenthusiastic.

vb. *vacillate*, fluctuate, waver, seesaw, blow hot and cold, shilly-shally (*colloq.*), dither; *hesitate*, falter, be in two minds, have second thoughts, hem and haw.

542 OBSTINACY
See also **538** (unwillingness); **540** (perseverence).

n. *obstinacy*, determination, perseverence, doggedness; *stubbornness*, obduracy, mulishness, pig-headedness; *intransigence*, inflexibility, toughness, hard line; *intractability*, incorrigibility, sullenness, dourness; *perverseness*, contrariness, bloody-mindedness (*colloq.*), cussedness (*colloq.*).

adj. *obstinate*, tenacious, persevering, dogged; *stubborn*, obdurate, self-willed, stiff-necked, pig-headed, mulish, dour; *intransigent*, tough, adamant, unyielding, inflexible, hard-line, immovable, unshakable; *dogmatic*, diehard, hidebound, opinionated, set in one's ways; *perverse*, contrary, cussed (*colloq.*), bloody-minded (*colloq.*); *intractable*, incorrigible, headstrong, wilful, unmanageable.

vb. *be obstinate*, persevere, persist, stick to one's guns; *resist*, hold out, dig in one's heels, put one's foot down.

adv. *over one's dead body* (*colloq.*), no way (*colloq.*).

543 EQUIVOCATION
n. *equivocation*, evasiveness, ambiguity, slipperiness, shiftiness; *uncertainty*, unpredictability, unreliability, untrustworthiness; *opportunism*, timeserving, hypocrisy, double-dealing; *infidelity*, disloyalty, treachery, perfidy; *defection*, desertion, apostasy, recantation; *reversal*, about-turn, U-turn, second thoughts, volte-face.

adj. *equivocal*, evasive, ambiguous, deceptive; *untrustworthy*, unreliable, shifty, slippery; *duplicitous*, hypocritical,

two-faced, timeserving; *capricious*, fickle, changeable, mercurial; *disloyal*, disaffected, apostate.

vb. *equivocate*, face both ways, say one thing and mean another, run with the hare and hunt with the hounds, have it both ways; *change one's mind/tune*, get cold feet, back out; *recant*, retract, go back on one's word, backtrack, backpedal; *desert*, defect, cross the floor, change sides.

544 CAPRICE
See also **541** (vacillation).

n. *caprice*, whim, fancy, impulse, notion; *humour*, mood, fad, craze, nine days' wonder; *capriciousness*, whimsicality, changeability, inconstancy, instability; *unreliability*, unpredictability, inconsistency, arbitrariness.

adj. *capricious*, whimsical, fanciful, irrational; *temperamental*, moody, changeable, mercurial; *fickle*, unpredictable, inconstant, volatile; *erratic*, wayward, irresponsible, feckless.

vb. *be capricious*, chop and change, blow hot and cold, act on impulse, take it into one's head.

545 SELECTION
n. *selection*, choice, option, alternative; *selectiveness*, eclecticism, choosiness, discrimination; *preference*, predilection, fancy, pick, favourite; *discretion*, first refusal, casting vote, veto; *vote*, ballot, poll, plebiscite, referendum.

adj. *selective*, eclectic, discriminating, fastidious, choosy (*colloq.*), particular; *optional*, discretionary, preferential, à la carte; *select*, choice, hand-picked, recherché.

vb. *select*, choose, pick, opt for, plump, settle on; *prefer*, fancy, favour, earmark, single out, reserve; *discriminate*, shop around, pick and choose, make up one's mind; *cull*, glean, sift, winnow, cream off.

546 REJECTION
n. *rejection*, dismissal, exclusion, veto; *disapproval*, dissatisfaction, fault-finding, captiousness; *refusal*, rebuff, disclaimer, denial, repudiation; *reject*,

discard, seconds, cast-off; *undesirability*, unsuitability, ineligibility, inadmissibility.

adj. *rejected*, unwanted, discarded, excluded; *undesirable*, unsuitable, ineligible, inadmissible.

vb. *reject*, turn down, decline, pass over; *refuse*, spurn, disdain, look a gift horse in the mouth; *discard*, scrap, ditch, junk (*colloq.*), throw out; *deny*, rebuff, repudiate, disown, disclaim; *dismiss*, rule out of court, give short shrift to, show the door; *exclude*, veto, blackball, cold-shoulder, give the brush-off (*colloq.*).

547 PREDETERMINATION

See also **536** (necessity); **559** (preparation).

n. *predetermination*, preordination, predestination, necessity; *preparation*, premeditation, prearrangement, rehearsal, forward planning; *agenda*, plan, order of the day, timetable, schedule; *foregone conclusion*, fix (*colloq.*), dead cert (*colloq.*), put-up job, frame-up (*colloq.*).

adj. *predetermined*, foreordained, premeditated, prearranged; *planned*, deliberate, preconceived, intentional, appointed.

vb. *predetermine*, predestine, foreordain, appoint; *premeditate*, preconceive, prepare, prearrange; *plan*, rehearse, schedule, timetable; *rig*, engineer, stage-manage, fix (*colloq.*).

548 IMPROVISATION

See also **560** (lack of preparation).

n. *improvisation*, extemporization, adlibbing, makeshift; *spontaneity*, impetuosity, impulsiveness, instinctiveness; *reflex*, impulse, snap decision, flash of inspiration, brainwave (*colloq.*).

adj. *improvised*, extempore, impromptu, makeshift, ad hoc; *spontaneous*, impulsive, impetuous, instinctive; *sudden*, unpremeditated, involuntary, automatic, unthinking, knee-jerk.

vb. *improvise*, act on impulse, extemporize, ad-lib, vamp, think on one's feet, play it by ear.

adv. *on the spur of the moment*, off-hand, off the cuff (*colloq.*), off the top of one's head (*colloq.*).

549 HABIT

See also **71** (rule); **72** (conformity).

n. *habit*, disposition, custom, wont, tendency, second nature; *familiarity*, force of habit, routine, regularity, daily round, groove, rut; *tradition*, precedent, orthodoxy, convention, mores, practice, usage; *protocol*, ritual, done thing, received wisdom; *habituation*, acclimatization, adjustment, conditioning.

adj. *habitual*, customary, regular, wonted, usual; *familiar*, conversant, known, accustomed, commonplace; *traditional*, orthodox, conventional, accepted; *long-standing*, time-honoured, hallowed, venerable; *ingrained*, deep-seated, deep-rooted, dyed-in-the-wool; *seasoned*, practised, inured, hardened, set in one's ways.

vb. *be in the habit of*, make a habit of, tend to; *adjust to*, accustom oneself to, get used to, get the hang/feel of; *habituate*, acclimatize, naturalize, condition.

550 UNACCUSTOMEDNESS

n. *unaccustomedness*, unwontedness, unfamiliarity, strangeness, novelty; *unconventionality*, unorthodoxy, nonconformity, irregularity; *neglect*, decay, rustiness, disuse.

adj. *unaccustomed*, unused, unfamiliar, novel, new, strange; *unusual*, unwonted, unprecedented, irregular; *unconventional*, unorthodox, nonconformist, radical; *neglected*, disused, rusty, decaying.

vb. *discontinue*, leave off, break with tradition, break the mould, turn over a new leaf; *wean*, cure, break the habit.

551 PERSUASION

See also **134** (motive); **139** (influence); **434** (belief).

n. *persuasion*, advertising, salesmanship, spiel (*colloq.*), honeyed words; *inducement*, incitement, pressure, carrot (*colloq.*); *persuadability*, credulity, credulousness, gullibility, susceptibility; *temptation*, bribery, enticement, encouragement; *persuader*, salesman, tempter; *pretext*, justification, plea, defence, pretence, allegation; *conviction*, conversion; *submission*, compliance; *concession*, agreement.

adj. *persuasive*, convincing, seductive, honey-tongued, plausible; *tempting*, enticing, seductive; *persuadable*, credulous, gullible, susceptible, easily swayed, submissive, compliant.

vb. *persuade*, advertise, get s.o. to do sth.; *goad*, cajole, wheedle, bully into, egg on (*colloq.*); *coerce*, push into, induce, brainwash, twist round one's little finger (*colloq.*); *incite*, stimulate, prick, prompt; *tempt*, bribe, entice, encourage; *plead*, claim, pretend, allege; *convince*, convert; *be persuaded*, succumb, yield, submit, comply; *concede*, agree.

552 DISSUASION

n. dissuasion, discouragement, no encouragement; *deterrence*, disincentive, intimidation; *deterrent*, killjoy, wet blanket (*colloq.*).

adj. *dissuasive*, discouraging; *deterrent*, intimidating, daunting; *cautionary*.

vb. *dissuade*, discourage, talk out of, advise against, put off, pour cold water on; *deter*, deflect, intimidate, daunt; *caution/warn against*.

553 INTENTION

See also **539** (resolution); **557** (plan); **755** (desire).

n. *intention*, intent, resolve, resolution, determination, threat; *project*, plan, design, calculation, meaning; *aim*, goal, objective, target, end; *destination*, terminus, station, port, airport.

adj. *intent/hell-bent on*; intentional, deliberate, voluntary, conscious.

vb. *intend*, resolve, decide, determine, threaten, look; *plan*, project, purpose, propose, undertake, mean, earmark; *aim*, go for; *hope*, expect, aspire, reckon on, calculate; *consider*, contemplate.

554 CHANCE

See also **135** (lack of motive).

n. *chance*, accident, fluke, coincidence, luck, luck of the draw, fate, the way the cookie crumbles (*colloq.*), toss-up (*colloq.*); *good luck*, bad luck, fortune, misfortune; *risk*, hazard, speculation, flutter, pig in a poke; *gambling*, gamble, bet, wager, stake; *horse-/greyhound-racing*, tote, football pools; *casino*, bingo, roulette, one-armed bandit; *lottery*, raffle, tombola, draw, premium bond; *stock exchange*, bear, bull, stag; *gambler*, speculator, punter, backer; *bookmaker*, bookie, turf accountant.

adj. *chance*, accidental, coincidental, lucky, fortuitous; *unintentional*, inadvertent, involuntary, unconscious; *haphazard*, random, happy-go-lucky; *risky*, hazardous, speculative, chancy.

vb. *gamble*, bet, wager, stake, game, punt, back; *risk*, hazard, speculate, have a flutter, run a risk, take risks, venture; *draw straws*, pick the short straw, spin a coin, toss for it.

adv. *by chance*, accidentally, coincidentally, as it happens, oddly enough; *on the off chance*.

555 PURSUIT

See also **414** (question); **761** (recreation).

n. *pursuit*, chase, prosecution, search, frisking, quest, enquiry; *exploration*, excavation, dig; *hunt*, stalk, trap, snare; *fishing*, ferreting, rabbitting, mousing; *pursuer*, seeker, searcher, search party, explorer; *hunter*, huntsman, fisherman, poacher, trapper, beater, stalker, tracker; *ratter*, rabbitter, mouser; *trawler*, drifter, whaler; *quarry*, prey; *steeplechase*, paperchase, treasure hunt.

adj. *pursuant*, in pursuit, on one's tail; *searching*, exploratory.

vb. *pursue*, follow, chase, seek, search, quest, look for, be after, enquire; *forage*, rummage, ferret, leave no stone unturned, sniff out (*colloq.*); *explore*, excavate, dig; *hunt*, stalk, beat, trail, track, poach, shoot, fish, trawl; *harry*, dog, shadow, tail.

556 AVOIDANCE

See also **605** (escape).

n. *avoidance,* sidestep, evasive action, dodge; *escape,* evasion; *forbearance,* moderation, abstinence; *refusal,* rejection, boycott; *nonparticipation,* noninvolvement, noncooperation; *avoider,* dodger, abstainer; *shirker,* idler, deserter, truant, coward.

adj. *avoiding,* evasive, shy, reluctant, elusive; *forbearing,* abstemious; *uncooperative,* reluctant, unwilling, reticent, unforthcoming; *avoidable,* unavoidable, inescapable.

vb. *avoid,* sidestep, dodge; *escape,* evade; *prevent,* avert; *eschew,* shun, fight shy of, give a miss, not go near, leave, let alone; *steer clear of,* give a wide berth to, not touch with a barge-pole (*colloq.*); *refuse,* reject, black (*colloq.*); *forbear,* refrain, abstain, forswear, hold back, do without; *shirk,* duck, cop out (*colloq.*), chicken out (*colloq.*).

557 PLAN

See also **488** (representation).

n. *plan,* project, proposal, suggestion, scheme, intention; *programme,* layout, design, blueprint, outline, recipe, organization; *diagram,* pattern, model, map, sketch, cartography; *strategy,* approach, course of action, agenda, schedule; *plot,* intrigue, conspiracy, (little) game (*colloq.*); *planner,* proposer, originator; *designer,* layout artist, map-maker, cartographer; *strategist,* plotter, conspirator.

adj. *planned,* projected, proposed; *schematic,* strategic; *plotting,* conspiratorial, scheming.

vb. *plan,* project, propose, suggest; *lay out,* draft, design, model, draw up, set out; *conceive,* hatch, dream up (*colloq.*); *organize,* schedule, approach, think ahead, orchestrate, engineer; *map,* sketch; *plot,* scheme, conspire, intrigue.

558 REQUIREMENT

See also **536** (necessity).

n. *requirement,* need, must, necessary, requisite; *necessity,* prerequisite, essential, sine qua non, stipulation; *want,* lack, demand, call for, shortage; *compulsion,* obligation.

adj. *required,* necessary, needed, indispensable; *essential,* vital; *wanted,* lacking, called for, in demand; *needy,* in need, deprived, destitute; *compulsory,* obligatory. **vb.** *require,* need, stand in need of, necessitate, stipulate; *want,* lack, call for, feel the lack of; *compel,* oblige, must.

adv. *in need,* in want; *of necessity,* necessarily.

559 PREPARATION

See also **57** (arrangement); **547** (predetermination).

n. *preparation,* making ready, getting ready, groundwork; *preliminaries,* tuning, priming, loading, approach, run-up; *acclimatization,* seasoning, hardening (off); *trial,* trial run, pilot (scheme), practice, rehearsal, dress rehearsal; *study,* prep, homework; *arrangement,* prearrangement, premeditation; *precaution,* provision, allowance, nest egg; *provisioning,* provisions, equipment; *preparedness,* readiness, fitness; *preparer,* trainer, pioneer, trailblazer, répétiteur, coach.

adj. *preparatory,* precautionary, preliminary, in preparation; *prepared,* ready (and waiting), standing by, fit, rehearsed, keyed up, primed, tuned, equipped, in readiness; *acclimatized,* seasoned, weathered, hardened (off); *ready-made,* off-the-peg, cooked, processed, oven-ready, ready to eat, instant.

vb. *prepare,* make ready, pave the way, lay the foundations, blaze a trail, prepare the ground, clear the decks, stand by, arrange (for); *prime,* load, tune, warm up, soften up, dig (over); *provide,* provision, equip, fit out; *acclimatize,* season, weather, harden (off); *rehearse,* practise, coach, train, groom, do one's homework, study; *allow for,* make provision for, put by (for a rainy day).

560 LACK OF PREPARATION
See also **111** (youth); **451** (surprise); **548** (improvisation).

n. *lack of preparation*, unpreparedness, unreadiness; *lack of rehearsal/training/ practice*; *rush*, haste; *improvisation*; *surprise*.

adj. *unprepared*, unready, caught napping/unawares/off one's guard, caught on the hop (*colloq.*), caught with one's pants/trousers down (*colloq.*); *unrehearsed*, untrained, unpractised; *rushed*, ill-equipped, disorganized, half-baked; *improvised*, impromptu, snap, extempore, extemporized, ad hoc; *unseasoned*, not weathered, not hardened (off); *raw*, uncooked.

vb. *be unprepared*, unready, etc., not prepare, plan, etc., live from day to day, cross that bridge when one comes to it, make no provision for; *improvise*, extemporize.

adv. *extempore*, off the cuff, off the top of one's head (*colloq.*).

561 ATTEMPT
n. *attempt*, try, essay, bid; *endeavour*, effort; *go* (*colloq.*), shot (*colloq.*), stab (*colloq.*), bash (*colloq.*), jab (*colloq.*), crack (*colloq.*).

adj. *game*, venturesome, tenacious, obstinate; *successful*, futile, desperate.

vb. *attempt*, try, essay, bid, seek; *endeavour*, make an effort, lift a finger; *strain*, struggle, strive, go all out, do one's best; *give it/have a go/shot/ stab/bash/jab/crack* (*colloq.*), give it a whirl (*colloq.*).

562 UNDERTAKING
See also **61** (beginning); **683** (promise).

n. *undertaking*, enterprise, business, task, job; *exercise*, operation, project, matter in hand, concern; *adventure*, quest, cause; *promise*, contract, agreement, obligation, commitment.

adj. *enterprising*, daring, adventurous, venturesome; *contracted*, obliged, committed.

vb. *undertake*, go in for, tackle, address oneself to; *take part in*, participate in, engage in, busy oneself

with; *embark on*, launch into, take up, assume, take on (oneself), get involved in, let oneself in for, get to grips with, get one's teeth into (*colloq.*); *promise*, contract, agree, commit oneself.

563 RELINQUISHMENT
See also **543** (equivocation); **696** (disposal).

n. relinquishment, giving up, abdication, renunciation, abandonment, castaway; *departure*, leaving, defection, desertion, walk-out, secession, retirement; *surrender*, handing over, ceding, cession, waiver.

adj. *relinquished*, abandoned, marooned, cast off.

vb. relinquish, give up, abdicate, renounce, forswear; *abandon*, maroon, cast away, forsake, ditch (*colloq.*); *depart*, leave, quit, defect, desert, withdraw, walk out, secede, retire, drop out; *surrender*, hand over, cede, waive, forgo; *resign*, give in, drop, chuck (*colloq.*).

564 USE
See also **566** (misuse); **578** (usefulness).

n. *use*, employment, utilization, exploitation; *application*, appliance, exercise, adoption, practice, usage; *con·umption*, wear, wear and tear; *usefulness*, applicability, benefit, practicality, purpose, point, pragmatism.

adj. *used*, in use, employed, utilized, applied, accepted, adopted; *worn*, used up, worn out, second-hand, nearly new (*colloq.*); *useful*, practical, pragmatic; *usable*, available, disposable.

vb. *use*, employ, put to use, put into service, utilize, make use of, avail oneself of, resort to; *exploit*, harness, capitalize on, take advantage of, cash in on (*colloq.*); *apply*, exercise, practise, put into practice, adopt; *consume*, expend, use up, wear, wear away/ down/out; *reuse*, recycle; *requisition*, commandeer, deploy.

565 NONUSE
See also **62** (end); **563** (relinquishment); **579** (uselessness).

n. nonuse, abeyance, unemployment; *discontinuance*, disuse, withdrawal, suspension, abolition; *rejection*, abandonment, scrapping; *abstinence*, avoidance; *store*, storage; *uselessness*.

adj. *unused*, unutilized, in abeyance, not in use, out of order; *new*, brand-new, pristine; *unemployed*, resting, idle; *discontinued*, withdrawn, suspended, abolished; *disused*, derelict, neglected, laid up, left to rot, in mothballs, mothballed; *extra*, spare, in hand, in reserve, surplus, superfluous; *useless*, impractical, pointless, senseless; *unusable*, unavailable.

vb. *not use*, etc, avoid, do without; *discontinue*, withdraw, suspend, abolish, dispense with; *reject*, abandon, scrap, ditch, drop, dump; *shelve*, lay/put aside, put in mothballs, mothball, put on a back burner.

566 MISUSE
See also **564** (use); **572** (waste).

n. misuse, abuse, maltreatment, mishandling, rough handling, malpractice, misapplication; *perversion*, prostitution, desecration; *wrong*, hurt; *overuse*, extravagance; *waste*.

vb. misuse, abuse, maltreat, mishandle, handle roughly, force, misapply; *pervert*, prostitute, desecrate; *wrong*, hurt; *misappropriate*, embezzle; *overuse*, overwork; *waste*, squander.

567 MEANS
See also **136** (operation); **568** (tool); **569** (materials).

n. *means*, method, way, device, medium; *ability*, knowledge, skill; *equipment*, wherewithal, materiel, provisions, facilities, tools, resources, channel; *money*, capital, necessary, credit; *manpower*.

vb. *enable*, provide the means, equip, resource; *finance*, back, raise the money; *be able*, manage, find a way.

568 TOOL
See also **138** (instrumentality); **567** (means).

n. *tool*, implement, utensil, gadget, instrument; *knife*, fork, spoon, tin-opener, bottle-opener, corkscrew, nutcracker; *nail*, hammer, screw, screwdriver; *drill*, bit, auger, brace, punch; *pliers*, pincers, tweezers, wrench, spanner, jemmy, crowbar, lever; *cutter*, chisel, plane, spokeshave, saw, router; *machine*, machinery, device, apparatus, mechanism, appliance; *wheel*, pulley, handle, block and tackle, clockwork, gears; *motor*, engine, petrol/diesel engine, internal combustion engine, steam engine, jet engine, rocket motor; *generator*, dynamo, turbine; *computer*, robot, calculator; *press*, mill.

adj. *mechanical*, mechanized, automatic.

569 MATERIALS
See also **197** (interweaving); **202** (covering); **567** (means).

n. *materials*, raw materials, building blocks; *mineral*, ore, sand, asbestos, clay, stone, marble, flint, masonry; *metal*, iron, gold, silver, copper, tin, nickel, lead, zinc; *alloy*, (stainless) steel, brass, bronze, gunmetal; *brick*, breeze block, glass, plaster, plasterboard, cement, (reinforced) concrete, mortar; *paving*, tarmac, asphalt, chippings, gravel, cobbles, flagstones; *tile*, slate, thatch, roofing felt; *wood*, timber, board, plank, rafter, joist, lath, plywood, chipboard, hardboard; *leather*, skin, hide; *paper*, rag, esparto grass, pulp, (card)board, millboard, pasteboard, strawboard, papier mâché; *bank*, bond, wove, laid; *cartridge paper*, art paper, (super)calendered paper, notepaper, carbon paper; *tissue paper*, tracing paper, crepe paper, newsprint; *plastic*, polythene, polystyrene, Perspex, PVC (polyvinyl chloride), Celluloid, Cellophane, fibreglass; *textile*, cloth, material, fabric, stuff; *cotton*, calico, poplin, shirting, towelling, terry, denim, gingham; *wool*, jersey, cashmere, angora; *suiting*, tweed, worsted, serge, mohair, felt, baize; *linen*, lawn, cambric, holland; *silk*, satin, taffeta, cheesecloth, chiffon, crêpe de chine, muslin, voile; *velvet*, corduroy, cord, velour, twill, flannelette; *nylon*, rayon, polyester, polycotton, Crimplene, Terylene, Dacron; *chintz*, damask, candlewick; *jute*, hessian, sacking, ticking, sailcloth, canvas, tapestry, mull.

570 STORE

See also **66** (assembly); **603** (preservation).

n. *store*, provision, stock, stock-in-trade, stockpile, backlog; *supply*, source, fount; *heap*, pile, load, mass, mound, collection, abundance, profusion, wine lake (*colloq.*), butter mountain (*colloq.*); *collection*, file, dictionary, thesaurus; *quarry*, mine, deposit, field, lode, vein, seam; *funds*, assets, reserves, nest egg, investment, holding; *horde*, treasure, cache; *bank*, account, deposit, savings, balance, credit; *dowry*, trousseau, bottom drawer; *storage*, warehousing, safekeeping; *warehouse*, stockroom, depot, garage, depository, repository, vault, magazine, arsenal; *battery*, accumulator; *cellar*, pantry, larder, storeroom, cupboard, loft, attic; *barn*, silo, granary, haystack, hayrick; *reservoir*, water tower, gasholder, gasometer, septic tank, cesspit; *refrigerator*, fridge, freezer; *trunk*, chest, safe; *computer*, microcomputer, microprocessor, word processor; *computing*, electronic data processing, DP, information retrieval; *hardware*, keyboard, terminal, VDU (visual display unit), disk drive, tape reader, CPU (central processing unit), printer; *software*, program, computer language, machine code/language, data, bit, byte, input, output, interface; *memory*, data base, data bank, punched cards, magnetic tape, (floppy) disk, disk pack, printout.

adj. *stored*, etc., in store; *in hand*, in reserve, in stock; *spare*.

vb. *store*, pile up, heap up, load up, stack (up); *store away*, put away, file (away), stash away (*colloq.*); *stock up*, stockpile, amass, accumulate, buy in, buy up, lay in, fuel (up); *save*, bank, invest, deposit; *save up*, hoard, squirrel away, put by for a rainy day; *garage*, warehouse, put in store; *lay up*, cocoon, put in mothballs, mothball;

preserve, pickle, bottle, preserve, salt, dry, refrigerate, freeze; *keep in reserve/hand*, put aside.

571 PROVISION

See also **453** (foresight); **559** (preparation); **685** (negotiation).

n. *provision*, supply, furnishing, delivery, purveying, fitting out, provisioning, catering; *provisions*, food, rations, supplies, stores, reserves, equipment; *budget*, management; *maintenance*, alimony, assistance; *provider*, supplier, purveyor, caterer; *storekeeper*, butler, quartermaster, housekeeper, cook; *shopkeeper*, merchant, grocer; *lender*, manager, purser, bursar, steward.

adj. *provided*, supplied, furnished, catered, all found, available, well-equipped.

vb. *provide*, supply, furnish, deliver, procure, purvey, fit out, arm, provision, cater; *feed*, serve, afford, give; *maintain*, board, put up (*colloq.*); *budget*, make provision, stock up, manage.

572 WASTE

See also **566** (misuse); **727** (extravagance).

n. *waste*, profligacy, wastefulness; *extravagance*, overspending, unnecessary expense; *consumption*, wear, attrition, erosion, atrophy, exhaustion, depletion; *leakage*, loss, escape, pollution; *overproduction*, superfluity, excess, misuse; *rubbish*, scrap, waste product, effluent.

adj. *wasteful*, profligate, extravagant, unnecessary; *superfluous*, disposable; *wasted*, lost, exhausted, misspent, futile, down the drain (*colloq.*).

vb. *waste*, squander, throw away, blow (*colloq.*); *misuse*, overwork; *consume*, wear, erode, deplete, exhaust; *leak*, escape, dissipate, pollute; *come to nothing*, go down the drain (*colloq.*).

573 SUFFICIENCY

See also **49** (completeness); **738** (satisfaction).

n. *sufficiency*, adequacy, acceptability, competence; *enough*, (bare) minimum, right amount, pass mark, quorum, what is acceptable, breadline, subsistence; *plenty*, abundance, copiousness; *a lot*, lashings (*colloq.*), bags (*colloq.*), oodles (*colloq.*); *profusion*, riot, feast; *lushness*, luxuriance.

adj. *sufficient*, adequate, enough, minimal, quorate; *satisfactory*, acceptable, competent, just right; *plentiful*, plenteous, abundant, copious; *wealthy*, affluent, generous, liberal; *profuse*, lush, luxuriant.

vb. *suffice*, be sufficient/enough; *satisfy*, fill the bill, do, pass muster, qualify; *be plentiful*, abound, swarm, proliferate; *teem/bristle with*, crawl with (*colloq.*).

574 INSUFFICIENCY

See also **50** (incompleteness); **273** (shortfall); **739** (dissatisfaction).

n. *insufficiency*, inadequacy, incompetence, failure; *not enough*, too little, too few, lack; *deficit*, shortfall, insufficient funds; *poverty*, need, starvation diet; *famine*, starvation, drought; *scarcity*, dearth, shortfall.

adj. *insufficient*, inadequate, not enough, too little, too few; *unsatisfactory*, unacceptable, incompetent; *poor*, disadvantaged, underprivileged, on supplementary benefit; *scarce*, in short supply, rare; *lacking*, deficient, light on (*colloq.*), thin, scant; *miserly*, mingy.

vb. *not suffice*, etc., be insufficient, etc., fall short, not come up to; *fail*, lack, want, require.

575 EXCESS

See also **272** (overstepping); **727** (extravagance); **844** (self-indulgence).

n. *excess*, too many, too much, overabundance, enough and to spare; *redundance*, redundancy, superfluity, glut, plethora, duplication, overkill; *flood*, inundation, saturation, congestion; *extra*, bonus, spare, surplus, balance; *overdoing it*, officiousness, ostentation, extravagance, obtrusiveness; *overindulgence*, too much of a good thing, overdose, overeating; *fat*, obes-

ity, flab (*colloq.*); *satiety*, engorgement, surfeit.

adj. *excessive*, too many, too much, overmuch, inordinate; *redundant*, superfluous, unnecessary; *flooded*, overflowing, saturated, stuffed; *extra*, spare, surplus; *officious*, ostentatious, extravagant, exorbitant, over the top (*colloq.*); *fat*, obese; *satiated*, sated, jaded, gorged.

vb. *be excessive*, etc., overstep, overdo it, go over the top (*colloq.*); *flood*, saturate, overflow; *overindulge*, overeat; *duplicate*, go begging; *satiate*, sate, jade, pall, gorge.

576 IMPORTANCE

See also **5** (essence); **31** (superiority); **774** (repute).

n. *importance*, significance, consequence; *substance*, matter, consideration, weight, value, moment, import, big deal (*colloq.*); *seriousness*, solemnity, gravity, no laughing matter; *prominence*, eminence; *heart of the matter*, cornerstone, linchpin, be-all and end-all; *urgency*, priority, emergency, matter of life and death; *VIP*, notable, personality, personage, magnate, tycoon, big gun (*colloq.*), bigwig (*colloq.*), big noise (*colloq.*).

adj. *important*, significant, big; *substantial*, considerable, weighty, urgent, momentous, eventful, earth-shattering; *serious*, solemn, grave; *leading*, notable, foremost, conspicuous; *central*, chief, basic, essential, major, main, fundamental, primary, principal; *influential*, formidable, illustrious, powerful; *exceptional*, imposing, outstanding, eminent, august, distinguished; *famous*, prominent, well-known.

vb. *be important*, etc., matter, count, carry weight, deserve attention; *make important*, promote, put on a pedestal; *stress*, underline, highlight, emphasize; *glorify*, honour, value, think a lot of, celebrate.

577 UNIMPORTANCE

See also **32** (inferiority); **187** (shallowness); **780** (humility).

n. *unimportance*, insignificance, triviality, frivolity, pettiness; *irrelevance*, immateriality, red herring; *the little man*, nonentity, figurehead, pawn, second fiddle; *trifle*, storm in a teacup, nothing to speak/write home about, technicality, small beer, pinprick.

adj. *unimportant*, ordinary, insignificant, inconsequential; *little*, negligible, wretched, paltry, measly (*colloq.*); *irrelevant*, immaterial, obscure, contemptible; *inessential*, unnecessary, fringe, peripheral.

vb. *be unimportant*, etc., not matter, not count, cut no ice, play second fiddle; *make light of*, think unimportant, play down.

578 USEFULNESS

See also **152** (fertility); **564** (use); **580** (convenience).

n. *usefulness*, utility, handiness, practicality; *adaptability*, suitability, applicability, efficacy; *convenience*, serviceability, availability, helpfulness; *value*, worth, advantage, profitability, productiveness, mileage (*colloq.*).

adj. *useful*, handy, practical, functional; *adaptable*, suitable, applicable, efficacious, effective; *convenient*, multipurpose, versatile, serviceable, available, helpful; *valuable*, invaluable, worthwhile, profitable, productive, economic; *pragmatic*.

vb. *be useful*, etc., be of use, come in handy (*colloq.*); *function*, work, serve, help.

579 USELESSNESS

See also **153** (infertility); **565** (nonuse); **581** (inconvenience).

n. *uselessness*, inutility; *unsuitability*, inefficacy, inadequacy, inconvenience, unavailability; *pointlessness*, futility, disadvantage, waste of time, wildgoose chase; *worthlessness*, waste, rubbish, dead duck.

adj. *useless*, unusable, unpractical; *unadaptable*, unsuitable, unemployable; *inconvenient*, unserviceable, unavailable, unhelpful, out of order, broken down; *pointless*, futile, vain; *worthless*, good-for-nothing, unprofitable, unrewarding; *ineffectual*, feckless.

vb. *be useless*, etc., not work, not function, not help, come to nothing; *flog a dead horse*, tilt at windmills; *make useless*, etc., sabotage, cripple, disable, spike.

580 CONVENIENCE

See also **115** (timeliness); **578** (usefulness); **629** (easiness).

n. *convenience*, ease, ease of use, easiness, facilitation, straightforwardness; *accessibility*, ease of access, closeness; *suitability*, pragmatism, expediency; *opportunism*, timeserving, utilitarianism, profit, advantage; *opportunity*, spare time, leisure; *freedom*, comfort, service, speed.

adj. *convenient*, easy to use, userfriendly; *accessible*, close, nearby, easy to reach, get-at-able (*colloq.*); *practical*, suitable, workable, pragmatic; *auspicious*, opportune, profitable, advantageous; *opportunist*, timeserving, utilitarian; *comfortable*, fast.

vb. *be convenient*, etc., not clash, suit, do work, fit; *benefit*, help, pay.

581 INCONVENIENCE

See also **116** (untimeliness); **579** (uselessness); **628** (difficulty).

n. *inconvenience*, difficulty, hindrance, drawback, handicap; *unsuitability*, previous engagement, awkwardness, unpleasantness; *discomfort*, disadvantage, inadvisability.

adj. *inconvenient*, difficult to use, cumbersome, unwieldy; *unsuitable*, unsatisfactory, inappropriate, awkward, unhappy; *inopportune*, untimely; *inadvisable*, disadvantageous, inexpedient.

vb. *be inconvenient*, etc., not do, not work, not help, not benefit; *inconvenience*, put out, incommode, bother, disrupt.

582 WORTH

See also **721** (price); **584** (perfection); **837** (virtue).

n. *worth*, goodness, excellence, greatness, quality, merit, virtue; *good quality*, redeeming feature, good point, saving grace; *value*, price; *pick*, élite, elect, chosen few, cream, crème de la crème; *superman*, superwoman, genius, ace, champion, paragon, cat's whiskers (*colloq.*), bee's knees (*colloq.*); *masterpiece*, plum, pièce de résistance, flagship; *hit*, knockout, blockbuster, best thing since sliced bread (*colloq.*); *classic*, all-time great.

adj. *good*, excellent, outstanding, fine, great, quality; *worthy*, commendable, creditable, admirable, praiseworthy; *choice*, handpicked, select; *superb*, wonderful, magnificent, fantastic, fabulous, glorious, marvellous, splendid, terrific, top-notch (*colloq.*); *super*, brill (*colloq.*), magic (*colloq.*), ace (*colloq.*), out of this world (*colloq.*); *best*, prime, premium, A-1, first-class, blue-chip, supreme; *classic*, vintage; *wholesome*, healthy, sound; *valuable*, priceless, good value; *not bad*, passable, tolerable, satisfactory, decent, acceptable, OK;

vb. *have value*, be worth it, rate, count; *do good*, improve, enhance, benefit.

583 WORTHLESSNESS

See also **604** (harm).

n. *worthlessness*, poor/low quality, shoddiness, mediocrity; *unworthiness*, wickedness, baseness, vileness, nastiness; *corruption*, depravity, obscenity, indecency, vulgarity.

adj. *worthless*, poor-/low-quality, second-rate, mediocre, indifferent; *shoddy*, low-grade, cheap, tacky, cheap and nasty, trashy; *lousy* (*colloq.*), rotten (*colloq.*), crummy (*colloq.*), ropy (*colloq.*); *awful*, dreadful, ghastly, wretched, horrid, horrible, terrible, beastly, grotty (*colloq.*); *wicked*, evil, base, vile, nasty, mean, shabby, vicious, villainous; *corrupt*, depraved, obscene, indecent, vulgar, sordid; *unworthy*, despicable, disgraceful, shameful, deplorable.

vb. *make worthless*, devalue, debase, cheapen, degrade; *do no good*, make things worse, be of no value.

584 PERFECTION

See also **49** (completeness); **188**
(summit); **582** (worth); **653** (completion).

n. *perfection*, faultlessness, flawlessness, impeccability; *correctness*, irreproachability, infallibility, integrity; *ideal*, sanspareil, paragon, model; *summit*, height, acme, peak; *example*, standard, pattern, showpiece.

adj. *perfect*, ideal, faultless, flawless, impeccable; *unbeatable*, unrivalled, beyond compare, matchless, peerless, supreme; *correct*, irreproachable, infallible; *immaculate*, pristine, spotless, stainless; *pure*, unadulterated, whole, entire, complete, one hundred per cent, sound.

vb. *perfect*, hone, polish, refine; *consummate*, crown, cap, seal, round off.

585 IMPERFECTION

See also **50** (incompleteness); **767** (blemish).

n. *imperfection*, faultiness, unsoundness; *immaturity*, underdevelopment, incompleteness, inadequacy, deficiency; *deformity*, disfigurement, discoloration, distortion, damage; *unevenness*, patchiness; *flaw*, fault, mistake, failing, defect, shortfall; *catch*, snag, drawback; *blemish*, mark, chip, crack, scratch, impurity.

adj. *imperfect*, faulty, unsound, flawed, defective; *immature*, underdeveloped, incomplete, inadequate, deficient, missing; *deformed*, disfigured, discoloured, distorted, damaged; *uneven*, patchy; *fair*, middling, could do better (*colloq.*); *blemished*, impure, marked, chipped, cracked, scratched, shop-soiled.

vb. *fall short*, not make the grade, be found wanting; *flaw*, mar, spoil.

586 CLEANNESS

See also **39** (purity); **590** (hygiene); **850** (morality).

n. *cleanness*, spotlessness, whiteness, shine, polish; *cleaning* (up), cleansing, washing (down/off/out/up), wiping (down/off/up), mopping up, scouring, scrubbing; *purge*, flush, dialysis, purification, filtration; *decontamination*, sterilization, delousing; *hygiene*, sanitation; *bath* (tub), public baths, shower, sauna, Turkish bath, jacuzzi, (wash)basin, bidet; *washing machine*, launderette, laundry, dishwasher; *soap* (flakes), shampoo, toothpaste, pumice (stone); *washing powder*, detergent, biological powder; *disinfectant*, bleach, antiseptic, cleanser; *polish*, shoe polish, wax, whitewash, blacking, blanco; *brush*, scrubbing brush, toothbrush, nailbrush, broom, mop, sponge, duster; *vacuum cleaner*, filter, mat; *cleaner*, washerwoman, launderer, char(lady), roadsweeper, dustman.

adj. *clean*, spotless, fresh, shiny, polished, neat, tidy; *sterile*, aseptic, antiseptic; *hygienic*, sanitary, disinfectant, detergent.

vb. *clean*, freshen, whiten, shine, polish; *cleanse*, wash (down/off/out/up), wipe (down/off/up), rinse, sluice, mop up, scour, scrub, sponge; *flush*, purify, dialyse, filter; *launder*, bleach, dry-clean; *bath*, bathe, shower; *sweep* (up), brush, dust, vacuum, springclean; *sanitize*, sterilize, disinfect, deodorize.

587 DIRTINESS

See also **591** (lack of hygiene); **851** (immorality).

n. *dirtiness*, uncleanness, uncleanliness, squalor; *contamination*, adulteration, pollution; *dirt*, filth, muck, mess; *mud*, slime, grease, dust, grime, oil, gunge (*colloq.*); *stain*, smear, patch, ring, mark, smudge, tarnish; *pigsty*, tip, slum, gutter, sewer; *slut*, pig (*colloq.*), mucky pup (*colloq.*).

adj. *dirty*, unclean, foul, squalid, filthy, mucky, messy, grotty (*colloq.*); *muddy*, slimy, greasy, dusty, grimy, oily, gungy (*colloq.*); *stained*, smeared, marked, smudged, tarnished; *contaminated*, adulterated, polluted.

vb. *dirty*, mess up, begrime, soil, muddy; *stain*, smear, mark, smudge, tarnish; *contaminate*, adulterate, pollute, foul.

588 HEALTH

See also **145** (vigour); **590** (hygiene).

n. *health*, healthiness, good condition, good health, convalescence, recovery; *fitness*, wellbeing, vitality, soundness; *salubrity*, wholesomeness, health food, fresh air, nonsmoker, health freak (*colloq.*).

adj. *healthy*, in good health, well; *convalescent*, on the mend, up and about, fully recovered; *fit* (as a fiddle), sound, robust, strapping, hale and hearty; *health-giving*, wholesome, nutritious, salubrious, nonsmoking, invigorating, beneficial, good for, therapeutic.

vb. *enjoy good health*, keep well, have a clean bill of health, feel fit, be in the pink (*colloq.*).

589 ILL HEALTH

See also **146** (inertness); **591** (lack of hygiene).

n. *ill health*, poor health, infirmity, indisposition; *illness*, sickness, disease, disorder, ailment, complaint, affliction, condition; *lack of fitness*, weakness, debility; *attack*, seizure, fit, stroke, breakdown; *infection*, epidemic, contagion, inflammation, fever, virus, bug (*colloq.*); *cold*, influenza, flu, fever, sore throat, headache, cough; *measles*, German measles, chicken pox, smallpox; *polio(myelitis)*, multiple sclerosis, muscular dystrophy, rheumatism, arthritis, ulcer, gangrene; *whooping cough*, pneumonia, tuberculosis, bronchitis, tonsillitis; *malaria*, typhoid, cholera, scarlet fever, hepatitis, leprosy; *diarrhoea*, dysentery, gastroenteritis, stomach upset; *heart disease*, allergy, anaemia; *cancer*, tumour, leukaemia; *diphtheria*, tetanus, rabies, venereal disease.

adj. *unhealthy*, in poor health, poorly, sickly, infirm, off colour (*colloq.*), under the weather (*colloq.*); *ill*, sick, diseased, ailing, indisposed, down with, laid up; *unfit*, weak, out of condition; *unwholesome*, poisonous, toxic, bad for, debilitating; *infectious*, contagious, catching, endemic, epidemic.

vb. *be unhealthy*, etc., not feel well, etc.; *suffer from*, ail, complain of; *sicken*, fall ill, catch, contract, go down with.

590 HYGIENE
See also **586** (cleanness); **588** (health).

n. *hygiene*, sanitation, cleanliness, public health, preventive medicine; *quarantine*, vaccination, inoculation, immunization; *disinfection*, sterilization, purification, pasteurization, chlorination, antisepsis; *hygienist*, sanitary inspector, sanitary engineer.

adj. *hygienic*, sanitary, germ-free; *disinfected*, sterilized, sterile, purified, pasteurized, chlorinated, antiseptic.

vb. *sanitize*, disinfect, sterilize, purify, boil, pasteurize, chlorinate; *vaccinate*, inoculate, immunize.

591 LACK OF HYGIENE
See also **587** (dirtiness); **589** (ill health).

n. *lack of hygiene*, lack of sanitation, no proper drainage, dirtiness; *epidemic*, outbreak, infestation, pollution, miasma.

adj. *unhygienic*, insanitary, dirty, germ-ridden, infected; *infested*, polluted, unfit for human habitation, condemned.

vb. *infect*, infest, pollute, condemn.

592 IMPROVEMENT
See also **253** (forward motion); **594** (repair).

n. *improvement*, amelioration, betterment; *development*, progress, advance; *reform*, modernization, new broom; *refinement*, enrichment, polish, enhancement; *advancement*, promotion; *upturn*, recovery, boom; *correction*, amendment, revision, editing, proofreading; *improver*, reformer, refiner, reviser, editor, proofreader.

adj. *improved*, better, reformed, amended, revised, edited; *developed*, advanced; *reforming*, reformatory, progressive.

vb. *improve*, get better; *better oneself*, turn over a new leaf, mend one's ways, pull one's socks up (*colloq.*); *develop*, progress, make progress, make advances; *improve upon*, elaborate on, go one better; *reform*, modernize, streamline, upgrade; *refine*, enrich, polish, enhance; *advance*, promote; *correct*, amend, revise, edit, proofread, rewrite.

593 DETERIORATION
See also **46** (disintegration); **142** (powerlessness); **150** (destruction); **254** (backward motion); **597** (blight).

n. *deterioration*, detriment, impairment, impoverishment, degeneration; *decline*, retrogression, slide, downturn, slump; *dilapidation*, disrepair, ruin; *decay*, rot, rotting, rust, erosion, corrosion, decomposition; *damage*, injury, wound, blemish, mark.

adj. *deteriorated*, impaired, impoverished, degenerate; *in decline*, retrogressive, failing; *dilapidated*, tumbledown, ruined; *decayed*, rotten, rusty, eroded, corroded, decomposed; *damaged*, injured, wounded, blemished, marked.

vb. *deteriorate*, worsen, get worse, degenerate, go downhill, go to the dogs (*colloq.*), go to pot (*colloq.*), decline, fall off, retrogress, slump, fail; *decay*, rot, rust, erode, eat away, corrode, decompose; *impair*, degrade, lower, coarsen, spoil; *damage*, injure, wound, blemish, mark.

594 REPAIR
See also **592** (improvement); **596** (remedy).

n. *repair*, mend, mending, remedy; *restoration*, renovation, refurbishment, reconditioning, refit, overhaul; *darn*, patch; *recuperation*, convalescence, recovery, healing; *cure*, refreshment, tonic, pick-me-up; *repairer*, mender, restorer, refurbisher, renovator, healer.

adj. *repaired*, mended, remedied, rectified; *restored*, renovated, refurbished, reconditioned, overhauled; *healed*, cured; *reparable*, mendable, restorable; *restorative*, curative, therapeutic, remedial, corrective.

vb. *repair*, mend, put right, fix, remedy, rectify; *restore*, renovate, refurbish, recondition, refit, overhaul; *heel*, sole, darn, patch; *heal*, cure; *recuperate*, convalesce, recover, get better.

595 DAMAGE

See also **604** (harm); **828** (disparagement).

n. *damage*, disrepair, injury, impairment, hurt, harm; *stain*, blemish, mark, foxing, discoloration, smudge; *tear*, dent, rip, scratch, disfigurement, scar; *corrosion*, rust, tarnish, rot, decay; *erosion*, weathering, wear and tear, battering; *wound*, cut, gash, bruise, sprain, strain.

adj. *damaged*, injured, impaired; *stained*, blemished, marked, foxed, discoloured, smudged; *torn*, scratched, scarred, disfigured, ravaged; *corroded*, rusty, tarnished, rotten, decayed; *eroded*, weathered, worn, frayed, battered; *wounded*, hurt, bruised, sprained, strained.

vb. *damage*, injure, impair, harm, spoil; *stain*, blemish, mark, discolour, smudge; *tear*, scratch, dent, rip, disfigure, deface; *corrode*, rust, tarnish, rot, decay; *erode*, eat away, weather, wear, batter; *wound*, hurt, cut, gash, bruise, sprain, strain.

596 REMEDY

See also **137** (counteraction); **594** (repair).

n. *remedy*, correction, corrective measure, cure, therapy; *help*, aid, first aid, relief; *atonement*, amends, redress; *medicine*, homeopathy, surgery, dentistry; *medicament*, medication, treatment, drug; *placebo*, panacea, quack remedy, patent medicine; *pill*, tablet, suppository, lozenge, capsule; *mixture*, linctus, ointment, balm; *antidote*, antacid, emetic, laxative; *plaster*, splint, dressing, bandage, poultice; *injection*, inoculation, vaccination, vaccine, jab (*colloq.*); *doctor*, physician, dentist, surgeon, nurse, therapist, healer.

adj. *remedial*, corrective, curative, healing, therapeutic; *soothing*, calming, emollient, anaesthetic; *medicinal*, medical, homeopathic, surgical.

vb. *remedy*, correct, cure, put right, fix, heal; *help*, aid, relieve, treat, tend, nurse; *soothe*, calm, drug, anaesthetize; *atone*, make amends, redress; *dress*, bathe, operate, set, inject.

597 BLIGHT

See also **593** (deterioration).

n. *blight*, rot, mould, mildew, fungus, rust; *infestation*, plague, pest, vermin, woodworm; *cancer*, canker, gangrene, necrosis; *bane*, curse, scourge, bugbear, cross, affliction; *nuisance*, annoyance, irritant, thorn in the flesh, pain (*colloq.*), pest (*colloq.*), pain in the arse/neck (*colloq.*); *poison*, toxin, carcinogen.

adj. *blighted*, rotten, mouldy, mildewed, wormeaten; *accursed*, afflicted, wretched; *pestilential*, infuriating, pesky (*colloq.*); *cancerous*, gangrenous, diseased; *poisonous*, toxic, carcinogenic.

598 SAFETY

See also **600** (refuge); **687** (security).

n. *safety*, preservation, security; *guarantee*, surety, warranty, insurance, failsafe; *protection*, shelter, defence, harbour, sanctuary, asylum; *immunity*, safe conduct, invulnerability, impregnability; *safekeeping*, custody, quarantine; *safety net*, lifebelt, lifeline, lifesaver; *precaution*, preventive measure, prophylaxis, immunization; *protector*, guardian, defender, security forces, police, vigilante; *guard*, gaoler, warder, patrol, watchman, bodyguard, minder, lifeguard; *warden*, curator, custodian, keeper, gamekeeper.

adj. *safe*, secure, sure; *guaranteed*, under warranty, insured; *immune*, invulnerable, impregnable; *hygienic*, non-toxic, childproof, unbreakable; *prophylactic*, preventive, protective; *unharmed*, safe and sound, in one piece, unscathed; *guarded*, locked up, under lock and key, behind bars, in quarantine.

vb. *be safe*, keep out of harm's way, keep a safe distance, give a wide berth, take precautions, be prepared; *safeguard*, immunize, protect, preserve; *defend*, shelter, shield, harbour, guard; *patrol*, police, watch over, have charge of, keep under surveillance.

599 DANGER
See also **425** (probability); **601** (trap).

n. *danger*, peril, hazard, black spot; *crisis*, flashpoint, trouble spot; *menace*, threat, sword of Damocles; *danger signal*, warning, red light, alarm; *danger zone*, no-go area, firing line, no man's land; *insecurity*, jeopardy, risk, precariousness.

adj. *dangerous*, perilous, hazardous, risky; *menacing*, threatening; *unsafe*, insecure, in jeopardy, precarious, dodgy (*colloq.*); *critical*, delicate; treacherous, slippery.

vb. *endanger*, put at risk, imperil, jeopardize; *menace*, threaten, loom; *hazard*, risk, expose, play with fire, tempt fate; *court danger*, skate on thin ice, sail too near the wind, enter the lions' den, run the gauntlet.

600 REFUGE
See also **469** (concealment); **598** (safety); **640** (defence).

n. *refuge*, retreat, asylum, sanctuary, haven, shelter, safe house; *air-raid shelter*, fallout shelter, bunker, dugout, trench, foxhole, bolthole; *central refuge*, central reservation, traffic island, emergency lane; *earth*, lair, den, burrow, nest; *fort*, castle, fortress, stockade, keep, stronghold, bastion; *screen*, cover, shield, windbreak; *refugee*, evacuee, displaced person, DP camp.

vb. *seek refuge*, run for cover, take shelter, make port.

601 TRAP
See also **242** (vehicle); **599** (danger); **668** (restraint).

n. *trap*, pitfall, snare, ambush; *mantrap*, gin, pit, noose, booby trap, mine; *decoy*, bait, blind, lure, diversion; *reef*, bar, sandbank, shoal, submerged rock, undertow, crevasse, quicksand.

vb. *trap*, ensnare, ambush, lie in wait.

602 WARNING
See also **484** (sign); **623** (advice); **678** (veto).

n. *warning*, caution, notice, lesson; *information*, nod, wink, word; *early warning*, advance notice, clue, hint, deterrent, warning shot; *admonishment*, rebuke, reprimand, telling-off, yellow card; *premonition*, presage, foreboding, omen, writing on the wall, harbinger of doom; *danger signal*, red flag, red light, fire alarm, foghorn; *horn*, hooter, klaxon, siren, tocsin; *alarm clock*, warning light, alarm bell, beacon; *SOS*, mayday, flare, distress signal.

adj. *cautionary*, warning, deterrent; ominous, symptomatic.

vb. *warn*, caution, give notice; *inform*, advise, notify, tip off, tip the wink (*colloq.*); *admonish*, reprove, rebuke, reprimand, tell off; *give/raise/sound the alarm*, dial 999, alert; *look out!*, watch your step!

603 PRESERVATION
See also **570** (store).

n. *preservation*, saving, safekeeping, maintenance; *conservation*, conservancy, protection; *game reserve*, bird sanctuary, nature reserve; *conservation area*, ancient monument, listed building; *refrigeration*, freezing, cold storage, drying, freeze-drying, canning, preserving, bottling; *embalming*, mummification, taxidermy; *preservative*, sugar, salt, brine, spice, pickle, water glass, ice, dry ice, formaldehyde.

adj. *preservative*, protective, preserving; *preserved*, salted, pickled, iced, frozen, dried, smoked, canned, tinned, potted, bottled; *well-preserved*, fresh, intact.

vb. *preserve*, save, maintain; *conserve*, protect, list; *paint*, varnish, creosote; *cure*, smoke, refrigerate, freeze, dry, can, bottle; *embalm*, mummify, stuff.

604 HARM
See also **583** (worthlessness); **595** (damage); **737** (unpleasantness).

n. *harm*, ill, hurt, damage, injury, detriment; *bad luck*, misfortune, disaster, destruction, ruin; *cruelty*, malevolence, viciousness, wrong, evil, persecution; *hurtfulness*, malice, spite, scandal, libel, slander, defamation; *unwholesomeness*, noxiousness, poison, toxin, pollution, radioactivity.

adj. *harmful*, damaging, injurious, pernicious, insidious, deleterious, detrimental; *disastrous*, destructive, ruinous; *harsh*, savage, fierce; *cruel*, malevolent, vicious, wrong, hurtful; *malicious*, spiteful, bitchy, libellous, slanderous, defamatory; *fatal*, lethal, deadly, poisonous, malignant, terminal; *toxic*, noxious, polluting, radioactive; *unwholesome*, infectious, unhygienic.

vb. *harm*, hurt, damage, injure, impair; *destroy*, ruin, wreck, undermine, play havoc with; *abuse*, ill-treat, wrong, persecute, victimize; *libel*, slander, defamate; *poison*, intoxicate, pollute, irradiate.

605 ESCAPE
See also **556** (avoidance); **606** (deliverance); **822** (exemption).

n. *escape*, flight, getaway, breakout, departure; *evasion*, avoidance, truancy, desertion, (moonlight) flit (*colloq.*); *rescue*, deliverance, freeing, letting off, reprieve; *withdrawal*, retreat, decampment, elopement; *get-out*, let-out, escape clause, loophole; *leak*, discharge, burst, seepage; *narrow escape*, close/near thing, close shave (*colloq.*); *way out*, (emergency) exit, egress, escape hatch, bolthole, fire escape, ejector seat; *escapee*, fugitive, runaway, deserter, truant.

adj. *escaped*, free, at large, truant, flown, AWOL.

vb. *escape*, flee, depart, take flight, break out; *evade*, elude, avoid, give the slip; *desert*, abscond, play truant, do a (moonlight) flit (*colloq.*); *rescue*, deliver, save, free, reprieve; *withdraw*, retreat, decamp, elope; *leak*, discharge, burst forth.

606 DELIVERANCE
See also **598** (safety); **605** (escape).

n. *deliverance*, rescue, saving, salvage; *extrication*, salvation, redemption, cure; *reprieve*, discharge, acquittal, pardon, liberation; *respite*, cease-fire, truce, stay of execution, remission, breather (*colloq.*); *rescuer*, deliverer, saviour, redeemer, liberator.

vb. *deliver*, rescue, free, save; *be the*

saving of, salvage, retrieve, extricate, redeem, cure; *reprieve*, discharge, acquit, let off, pardon, liberate.

607 ACTION
See also **523** (drama); **609** (activity); **645** (war); **856** (litigation).

n. *action*, doing, commission, perpetration, execution, performance; *step*, move, manoeuvre, initiative, measure, act, deed; *feat*, exploit, achievement, accomplishment; *activity*, work, job, task, occupation; *perpetrator*, executor, performer, doer, worker, activist.

adj. *acting*, active, in operation, operational, at work, employed, in the act, occupational.

vb. *do*, act, commit, conduct, perpetrate, execute, prosecute, perform, ply; *undertake*, put into effect, implement, enact, carry out; *accomplish*, achieve, bring about/off; *work*, function, be in operation, occupy oneself.

608 INACTION
See also **146** (inertness); **610** (inactivity).

n. *inaction*, inertness, passivity, failure/inability to act, abstention; *immobility*, paralysis, stasis; *rest*, idleness, unemployment, leisure; *suspension*, abeyance.

adj. *out of action*, inoperative, inert, passive; *immobile*, paralysed, static; *resting*, idle, unemployed; *suspended*, in abeyance.

vb. *do nothing*, fail to act, refrain, abstain, stay neutral, opt out, pass the buck; *shelve*, put on ice, mothball; *not act*, let sleeping dogs lie, wait and see, bide one's time, mark time, tick over, stand (idly) by, not lift a finger; *twiddle one's thumbs*, kick one's heels, be at a loose end.

609 ACTIVITY
See also **607** (action).

n. *activity*, movement; *nimbleness*, agility, liveliness, briskness; *life*, energy, vigour, get-up-and-go (*colloq.*); *business*, dealing, trading; *stir*, burst, fit, flurry; *bustle*, fuss, agitation, ado, bother, to-do, commotion; *readiness*, keenness, willingness, eagerness, alacrity; *enterprise*, enthusiasm, dynamism; *concentration*, diligence, industry; *determination*, tirelessness, perseverance; *hard worker*, slogger, busy bee (*colloq.*), eager beaver (*colloq.*); *enthusiast*, fanatic, militant, zealot.

adj. *active*, on the go, moving, in motion, working; *nimble*, agile, lively, brisk, busy; *keen*, willing, eager, enterprising, enthusiastic; *diligent*, industrious, energetic, vigorous, dynamic; *determined*, tireless, dogged, unflagging.

vb. *be active*, etc.; *rouse oneself*, make an effort, exert oneself, gird one's loins; *bustle*, hurry, get a move on, not hang about (*colloq.*), go for it (*colloq.*).

610 INACTIVITY

See also **146** (inertness); **608** (inaction); **619** (fatigue).

n. *inactivity*, inertia, torpor, listlessness; *quiet*, peace, calm, stillness; *laziness*, sloth, lethargy, apathy, indolence; *sleep*, rest, repose, nap, siesta, snooze, shut-eye (*colloq.*), kip (*colloq.*); *hibernation*, aestivation; *unconsciousness*, trance, coma, stupor; *strike*, lockout, shutdown; *laggard*, lazy-bones, slacker, loafer, passenger, sleeping partner; *layabout*, scrounger, good-for-nothing; *idle rich*, leisured classes.

adj. *inactive*, still, motionless, peaceful, calm; *slow-moving*, listless, sluggish, torpid; *idle*, slothful, indolent, lazy, leisured; *unenterprising*, apathetic, indifferent; *unconscious*, comatose, asleep; *tired*, weary, dopey, groggy, sleepy, somnolent.

vb. *be inactive*, etc., stagnate, drift, let things slide; *delay*, stall, drag one's feet, loiter, dawdle; *laze about*, lounge, loaf, idle, shirk, skive; *sleep*, doze, nap, slumber, rest; *hibernate*, aestivate.

611 WORK

See also **149** (production).

n. *work*, task, job, assignment, mission, undertaking, venture; *employment*, gainful employment, service; *post*, position, function, situation; *appoint*ment, vacancy, opening, headhunting; *profession*, occupation, line of work, career, trade, craft; *industry*, commerce, business, dealings, trade, affairs; *worker*, breadwinner, wage-earner, white-/blue-collar worker, professional (person), artisan, labourer.

adj. *working*, workaday, employed, self-employed, freelance, busy (with); *professional*, businesslike, efficient; *occupational*, industrial, commercial.

vb. *work*, do a job, work for, be engaged on, engage in, earn one's living; *apply for*, take a job; *employ*, take on, hire, appoint, engage, recruit, select, headhunt; *trade*, do/conduct/transact business, deal, negotiate.

612 LEISURE

See also **618** (ease); **761** (recreation).

n. *leisure*, free time, spare time, one's own time, time off, break, recess, retirement; *leisure activities*, recreation, relaxation, rest, sport, leisure centre; *holiday*, vacation, furlough, leave, leave of absence, R & R, sabbatical.

adj. *leisured*, unoccupied, retired, resting; *sabbatical*, on holiday.

vb. *take time off*, take a break, holiday, go on holiday; *relax*, take one's time, have all the time in the world; *retire*, give up work, drop out.

adv. *in one's own time*, at one's own pace, at one's leisure, at one's convenience.

613 WORKER

See also **149** (production).

n. *worker*, employee, self-employed person, freelance(r); *slave*, bondsman, menial, fag, coolie, bearer; *dogsbody*, skivvy, drudge, hewer of wood and drawer of water, chief cook and bottle-washer, factotum; *servant*, domestic (servant), maid, valet, tweeny, cook, chambermaid, housekeeper, butler, footman, groom, ostler; *dustman*, cleaner, char(lady), daily, help; *farmer*, farmhand, farm labourer, dairyman, shepherd; *forester*, nurseryman, gardener; *workman*, artisan, blue-collar worker, tradesman, craftsman, handyman, odd-job man, apprentice, (casual) labourer; *mechanic*, repairman, fitter; *factory worker*, steelworker, docker; *builder*, bricklayer, mason, plasterer, decorator, painter; electrician, glazier, tiler, slater, plumber; *carpenter*, cabinetmaker, joiner; *smith*, blacksmith, welder; *miner*, coalminer, collier; *jeweller*, goldsmith, silversmith, watchmaker, clockmaker; *tailor*, dressmaker; *author*, writer, journalist, photographer, editor, printer, proofreader, bookbinder; *businessman*, businesswoman, dealer, trader, merchant, middleman, wholesaler; *retailer*, shopkeeper, shop assistant, check-out girl; *employer*, industrialist, manufacturer; *manager*, supervisor, director, executive; *staff*, personnel, workforce, labour force, manpower, payroll; *office worker*, white-collar worker, clerk, secretary, shorthand typist, personal assistant, girl Friday, tealady, teaboy; *banker*, stockbroker, jobber; *lawyer*, solicitor, barrister; *engineer*, electrical/mechanical/civil engineer, architect, draughtsman, designer, town planner; *functionary*, operative, officer, executant, practitioner.

614 WORKSHOP
n. *workshop*, workplace, place of work; *workroom*, study, library, studio, atelier; *office*, bureau, shop, establishment, laboratory; *factory*, works, plant, installation; *yard*, site, industrial estate, depot, station, branch, dock; *shop floor*, production/assembly line; *mine*, quarry, foundry, refinery, laundry, kitchen, farm.

615 HASTE
See also **245** (speed); **753** (rashness).
n. *haste*, hurry, rush, bustle, scurry, scramble; *urgency*, pressure, deadline, rush job; *acceleration*, hastening, precipitation, recklessness, impatience; *dash*, burst of speed, push, spurt, sprint, race (against time).
adj. *hasty*, hurried, in a rush, fast, hustling; *urgent*, top-priority, hot off the press; *pressurized*, hard-pressed, hard-pushed; *rushed*, eleventh-hour, last-minute, skimped; *rash*, reckless, precipitate, impatient.
vb. *hurry*, rush, hustle, scurry, scramble, not waste time, lose no time; *throw together*, cobble together, whip up, hack out; *speed up*, hasten, dispatch, precipitate, expedite, railroad (*colloq.*); *hurry up*, goad, put a bomb under; *dash*, push, spurt, sprint, race, tear, zoom, whizz, bomb along (*colloq.*).

616 LACK OF HASTE
See also **246** (slowness); **406** (carefulness).
n. *lack of haste*, slowness, steadiness, deliberation; *leisure*, time to spare, no hurry; *dilatoriness*, hesitation, lack of enthusiasm, caution; *laziness*, procrastination, no sense of time, unpunctuality, mañana; *dawdle*, amble, saunter, stroll, trot, jog; *crawl*, snail's pace; *conscientiousness*, attention (to detail), thoroughness, accuracy; *consideration*, thoughtfulness; *dawdler*, crawler, plodder, slowcoach, Sunday-afternoon driver, late riser, lie-abed.
adj. *unhurried*, slow, steady, deliberate; *dilatory*, unenthusiastic, hesitant, cautious; *leisurely*, easygoing, phlegmatic, plodding; *lazy*, sluggish, slothful, languid; *late*, tardy, unpunctual; *painstaking*, conscientious, thorough, accurate; *considered*, thoughtout.
vb. *have all the time in the world*, take no note of time; *hesitate*, drawl, spin out, drag out; *not be hurried*, think over, weigh up, ponder, not rush into things, sleep on it; *dawdle*, amble, saunter, shamble, stroll, trot, jog; *crawl*, creep, inch; *linger*, loiter, (dilly-)dally.

617 EXERTION
n. *exertion*, effort, strain, muscle, elbow grease (*colloq.*); *force*, pressure, thrust, pull, tug, tension; *labour*, work, toil, hard graft, application; *hard work*, slog, fag (*colloq.*), grind; *trouble*, pains, sweat, bother, pain (*colloq.*); *exercise*, physical education, PE, physical training, PT, drill; *keep-fit*, jogging, aerobics, sport, games.

adj. *laborious*, gruelling, backbreaking, exhausting, arduous, uphill, killing; *industrious*, hard-working, dogged; *strenuous*, demanding, energetic.

vb. *exert oneself*, strive, try, make an/ the effort, endeavour, strain; *labour*, toil, sweat, work, hump; *grind*, plod, slog away, make heavy weather of; *apply oneself*, buckle down, knuckle down, set to, pull one's finger out; *go to great trouble*, bend over backwards, put oneself to a lot of bother, put oneself out, bust a gut (*colloq.*); *spare no effort*, do one's utmost, pull out all the stops.

adv. *laboriously*, with brute force, by the sweat of one's brow, the hard way; *with a vengeance*, all out, flat out, hammer and tongs (*colloq.*), tooth and nail (*colloq.*).

618 EASE
See also **612** (leisure); **629** (easiness); **740** (relief).

n. *ease*, repose, rest, relaxation; *comfort*, restfulness, peace and quiet, calm, tranquillity; *pause*, break, coffee/tea/lunch-break, lunch hour, recreation period; *holiday*, vacation, leave, furlough, day off, weekend, bank holiday.

adj. *at ease*, relaxed, casual, laid back (*colloq.*); *restful*, relaxing, comfortable, peaceful, quiet, calm, tranquil.

vb. *be at ease*, etc., take one's ease, rest, take it easy, relax, put one's feet up, lounge; *stop*, take a break, slow down, take time off; *take a holiday*, get away from it all, go on leave.

619 FATIGUE
See also **144** (weakness); **610** (inactivity).

n. *fatigue*, tiredness, weariness; *sleepiness*, somnolence, drowsiness, doziness; *weakness*, faintness, feebleness; *exhaustion*, prostration, collapse.

adj. *fatigued*, tired, weary; *sleepy*, somnolent, drowsy, dozy; *weak*, faint, feeble, drained; *exhausted*, worn out, all in, dead beat, dropping (*colloq.*), pooped (*colloq.*), whacked (*colloq.*), fagged out (*colloq.*), knackered (*colloq.*), shattered (*colloq.*); *fatiguing*, tir-

ing, punishing, knackering (*colloq.*), shattering (*colloq.*).

vb. *be tired*, etc.; *tire*, flag, wilt, droop; *fall asleep*, nod off, drop off, conk out (*colloq.*), flake out (*colloq.*), crash out (*colloq.*), go out like a light (*colloq.*); *collapse*, drop; *fatigue*, tire, weary, exhaust, wear out, tax, flog.

620 REFRESHMENT
See also **145** (vigour); **267** (ingestion); **740** (relief).

n. *refreshment*, recreation, renewal, recuperation, revival, recovery, restoration, relief; *invigoration*, stimulation, fillip; *food*, drink, stimulant, tonic.

adj. *refreshing*, reviving, restoring, restorative, recuperative; *cool*, invigorating, stimulating, bracing; *refreshed*, recovered.

vb. *refresh*, freshen, revive, restore; *reinvigorate*, stimulate, perk up, enliven; *be refreshed*, recover, recuperate, get one's second wind, get one's breath back; *take a breather*, cool off, stretch one's legs, freshen up, recharge one's batteries.

621 CONDUCT
See also **607** (action); **622** (management).

n. *conduct*, behaviour, comportment, actions; *customs*, way of life, moves; *style*, manner, air, attitude, demeanour; *way of speaking*, tone of voice, presentation; *good behaviour*, (good) manners, (good) breeding; *bad behaviour*, misbehaviour, misconduct, misdemeanours, rudeness; *past* (behaviour/history), background, (track) record; *practice*, methods, system, procedure, common practice, organization; *control*, guidance, supervision; *strategy*, plan, tactics, policy, programme.

adj. *behavioural*; *strategic*, tactical, planned.

vb. *behave*, conduct oneself/one's affairs, act, acquit oneself; *behave well*, be on one's best behaviour, behave oneself, set an example, mind one's P's and Q's; *behave badly*, misbehave, play up; *carry on*, run, manage, control, run, supervise.

622 MANAGEMENT

See also **57** (arrangement); **621** (conduct); **651** (success); **657** (authority); **665** (master).

n. *management*, direction, handling, running, administration, bureaucracy, organization, order; *authority*, command, charge, control, supervision, leadership; *government*, legislation, jurisdiction, power, regulation, politics, dictatorship, tyranny; *manager*, administrator, controller, coordinator, organizer, official, bureaucrat, executive, chairman, boss; *housekeeper*, steward, agent, deputy; *director*, inspector, chief, overseer, foreman, supervisor, board of directors; *legislator*, leader, politician, (prime) minister, premier, secretary of state, governor, statesman, prefect; *officer*, commander, captain; *chancellor*, vice-chancellor, governing body, warden, master, dean.

adj. *administrative*, organizational, bureaucratic, political; *managerial*, directorial, governmental, supervisory, legislative, governing, guiding; *authoritative*, in charge, commanding, leading, statesmanlike; *dictatorial*, tyrannical, despotic.

vb. *manage*, direct, handle, run, administer, organize, coordinate, order; *command*, be in charge of, head up, control, steer, supervise, lead, guide, be in the driving seat; *govern*, legislate, regulate, police.

623 ADVICE

See also **442** (maxim); **602** (warning).

n. *advice*, counsel, counselling, guidance; *recommendation*, tip, suggestion, hint, intimation, word in one's ear; *persuasion*, dissuasion, support, encouragement; *precept*, tenet, (golden) rule, guidelines; *instruction*, direction, ordinance, injunction, regulation, ruling, prescription; *warning*, caution, notice, criticism, admonition, admonishment; *adviser*, counsellor, guide, tutor, confidant(e), mentor; *consultant*,

lawyer, counsel, steering committee; *busybody*, back-seat driver.

adj. *advisory*, consultative, guiding, steering; *persuasive*, dissuasive, encouraging, supportive, cautionary; *prescriptive*, mandatory, statutory, binding.

vb. *advise*, counsel, advocate, recommend; *suggest*, submit, propose, hint, intimate; *persuade*, dissuade, encourage, enjoin, warn, guide; *consult*, call in, seek/take advice, consult counsel, see one's solicitor; *instruct*, prescribe, lay down.

624 SKILL

See also **141** (power); **438** (knowledge).

n. *skill*, facility, mastery, adeptness, adroitness, deftness; *ability*, competence, capability, capacity; *talent*, gift, genius, forte, flair, bent; *training*, experience, accomplishment, know-how; *expertise*, knack, touch, grip, technique; *skilled person*, man of many parts, master, veteran, old hand; *specialist*, professional, authority, expert; *genius*, talent; *craftsman*, artist, technician.

adj. *skilful*, skilled, apt, adept, adroit, deft, good at; *able*, competent, capable, talented, gifted; *professional*, authoritative, expert, businesslike; *trained*, experienced, accomplished, practised.

vb. *be skilful*, etc., excel, shine, play one's cards well, have a gift/talent, know the ropes, know one's way around.

625 UNSKILFULNESS

See also **142** (powerlessness); **439** (ignorance).

n. *unskilfulness*, clumsiness, awkwardness; *inexperience*, lack of experience/practice, rustiness; *inability*, incapacity, ineptitude, incompetence, inefficiency; *mismanagement*, mishandling, bungling, tactlessness, thoughtlessness; *mess*, hash, shambles, faux pas, pig's ear (*colloq.*), cockup (*colloq.*); *bungler*, bodger, amateur, jack of all trades and master of none, butterfingers.

adj. *unskilful*, clumsy, awkward, ham-fisted, bumbling; *inexperienced*, unqualified, unpractised, rusty; *inept*, incapable, incompetent, ineffectual, failed; *inefficient*, impractical, inexpert, unprofessional, unbusinesslike; *amateurish*, scratch, home-made, Heath Robinson, slapdash; *thoughtless*, tactless, ill-considered, foolish.

vb. *be unskilful*, etc., not have the knack, be no good at, bumble, fumble, flounder; *botch*, spoil, fluff, make a mess/hash of, bungle, mess up (*colloq.*), cock up (*colloq.*), make a pig's ear of (*colloq.*), fuck up (*vulg.*); *mismanage*, mishandle, blunder, blow it (*colloq.*).

626 CUNNING

See also **444** (wisdom); **480** (deception).

n. *cunning*, craft, craftiness, guile, slyness, artfulness, dishonesty, deceit, stealth, sleight of hand; *ingenuity*, resourcefulness, wisdom, shrewdness, cleverness; *ruse*, plot, intrigue, scheme, trick, deception, dodge, wiles, wrinkle, chicanery; *artful dodger*, snake in the grass, slyboots, plotter, schemer, cheat, trickster, con-man (*colloq.*), wide boy.

adj. *cunning*, crafty, sly, artful, wily, disingenuous, deceitful, scheming, shady; *ingenious*, resourceful, shrewd, clever, canny, sharp, smart (*colloq.*), not born yesterday (*colloq.*).

vb. *be cunning*, etc., plot, intrigue, scheme; *trick*, deceive, cheat, hoax, con (*colloq.*), put one over on (*colloq.*); *outwit*, outsmart, get the better of.

627 NAIVETY

See also **434** (belief); **439** (ignorance).

n. *naivety*, artlessness, innocence, simplicity, ingenuousness; *naturalness*, unsophistication, unaffectedness; *sincerity*, straightforwardness, frankness, candour, openness; *innocent*, child, ingènue, greenhorn, beginner, yokel, simpleton.

adj. *naive*, artless, green, innocent, wide-eyed, simple, ingenuous, unstudied; *natural*, unsophisticated, unaffected, childlike, unlearned; *sincere*, straightforward, frank, candid, open.

vb. *be naive*, etc., rush in where angels fear to tread, say what one thinks, speak one's mind, not mince one's words.

628 DIFFICULTY

See also **581** (inconvenience); **630** (hindrance).

n. *difficulty*, arduousness, laboriousness, awkwardness, inconvenience; *ordeal*, tall order, handful, uphill struggle, hard going, labours of Hercules, no picnic (*colloq.*); *trouble*, bother, hole (*colloq.*), scrape (*colloq.*), pickle (*colloq.*); *predicament*, dilemma, problem, fix; *puzzle*, teaser, poser, headache (*colloq.*); *obstacle*, impediment, stumbling block, complication, handicap.

adj. *difficult*, hard, arduous, laborious, tough, uphill, demanding; *awkward*, inconvenient, unmanageable, unwieldy; *troublesome*, bothersome; *problematic*, complex, complicated, involved, puzzling; *stubborn*, cussed, hard to shift, obstinate; *delicate*, ticklish, tricky, knotty.

vb. *be difficult*, etc., make things difficult, make difficulties for, plague; *trouble*, put to trouble/inconvenience, inconvenience, put out, perplex, bother, irk; *puzzle*, perplex, give one a headache, complicate matters; *hinder*, hamper, obstruct; *be in difficulty*, get into difficulties, run into trouble, flounder, get out of one's depth, come unstuck.

adv. *with difficulty*, uphill, the hard way, against the stream.

629 EASINESS

See also **580** (convenience); **631** (help).

n. *easiness*, ease, facility; *straightforwardness*, simplicity, convenience, feasibility; *facilitation*, simplification, deregulation; *sinecure*, cushy number (*colloq.*), soft option, easy way out, line of least resistance; *easy target*, easy meat, sitting duck; *no problem*, open-and-shut case, plain sailing, doddle (*colloq.*), picnic (*colloq.*), piece of cake (*colloq.*), money for jam/old rope (*colloq.*), child's play (*colloq.*), kid's stuff (*colloq.*), cinch (*colloq.*), pushover (*colloq.*), walkover (*colloq.*).

adj. *easy*, effortless, undemanding, painless, downhill, cushy (*colloq.*), nothing to it (*colloq.*); *straightforward*, simple, uncomplicated, convenient; *obvious*, clear, readable; *feasible*, manageable; *pleasant*, short, light; *helpful*, easy-going, willing.

vb. *be easy*, etc., present no difficulties, give no trouble, require no effort, make no demands; *go well*, go like clockwork, run smoothly; *have no trouble*, make short work of, sail through, cruise; *ease*, facilitate, smooth, oil the wheels, not stand in the way; *free*, unharness, unfetter; *simplify*, clarify, facilitate, deregulate.

adv. *easily*, readily, standing on one's head (*colloq.*), like falling off a log, with one hand tied behind one's back, blindfold (*colloq.*); *smoothly*, like clockwork (*colloq.*), like a dream (*colloq.*).

630 HINDRANCE

See also **114** (lateness); **628** (difficulty); **668** (restraint).

n. *hindrance*, impedance, impediment, nuisance, handicap, encumbrance; *obstructiveness*, picketing, boycott, blacking, filibustering; *restraint*, check, curb, resistance; *retardation*, drag, friction, headwind, tide; *prohibition*, bar, ban, embargo; *restriction*, limitation, control; *obstacle*, barrier, hurdle, hazard, bunker; *interruption*, intervention, interference; *hitch*, hold-up, setback, spanner in the works (*colloq.*); *obstruction*, blockage, constriction, jam, traffic jam, tailback, snarl-up (*colloq.*); *dam*, barrage, lock, weir; *bandage*, tourniquet, compress; *defence*, moat, wall, portcullis, drawbridge, fence, barricade, stockade; *gate*, tollgate, checkpoint, road block, stile, cattle-grid.

adj. *hindering*, obstructive; *unfavourable*, unhelpful; *restrictive*, limiting, controlling; *prohibitive*, preventive, preventive.

vb. *hinder*, impede, obstruct, hamper,

handicap, encumber; *restrain*, check, resist, retard, brake; *prohibit*, bar, ban; *restrict*, limit, curb, control, clamp down on; *repress*, quell, dam (up), cramp one's style; *constrict*, bandage, bind, cramp, hem in, hedge in; *interrupt*, intervene, interfere, meddle; *thwart*, frustrate, snooker, hamstring, stymie; *block/clog/jam (up)*, filibuster, stonewall, throw a spanner in the works (*colloq.*); *cripple*, paralyse, hobble, fetter; *picket*, boycott, black.

631 HELP

See also **138** (instrumentality); **578** (usefulness); **629** (easiness).

n. *help*, aid, assistance, succour, helping hand, charity; *relief*, easing, alleviation; *advice*, guidance, comfort, feedback; *encouragement*, moral support, backing; *medical assistance*, first aid, treatment, nursing; *financial help/aid/assistance*, foreign aid, loan, sponsorship; *grant*, bursary, scholarship, exhibition, allowance, honorarium; *subsidy*, maintenance, benefit, social security, subsistence, hand-out; *helper*, help, assistant, aide; *right-hand man*, henchman, sidekick (*colloq.*), girl/man Friday, aide-de-camp, lieutenant; *adviser*, counsellor, think-tank, tower of strength; *good Samaritan*, neighbour, fairy godmother; *sponsor*, supporter, champion, promoter.

adj. *helpful*, of assistance, auxiliary; *supportive*, encouraging, obliging.

vb. *help (out)*, aid, assist, succour, render assistance, do one a good turn, lend a hand (*colloq.*), give one a leg-up (*colloq.*), put in a word for; *relieve*, ease, alleviate, comfort; *advise*, guide, show the ropes; *encourage*, support, endorse, back, sustain; *treat*, minister to, nurse; *pay for*, finance, sponsor, subsidize, maintain, promote, patronize.

632 OPPOSITION

See also **14** (oppositeness); **137** (counteraction); **637** (defiance); **638** (resistance); **682** (protest).

n. *opposition*, antagonism, hostility; *noncooperation*, contrariness, recalcitrance, obstinacy; *denial*, counterargument, contradiction, objection; *disagreement*, dissension, dispute, conflict, clash; *defiance*, resistance, challenge; *competition*, struggle, rivalry; *opposite*, polarity, contrast, antithesis, dichotomy; *opponent*, adversary, antagonist, enemy; *contender*, contestant, rival, competitor, challenger, candidate.

adj. *opposing*, conflicting, antagonistic, adversarial, hostile, unfriendly, defiant; *uncooperative*, contrary, negative, bloody-minded, recalcitrant, obstinate, dissenting; *opposed to*, against, out of sympathy with.

vb. *oppose*, be dead against, disagree, dissent; *dispute*, deny, object, protest, argue against, contradict; *challenge*, resist, defy, fly in the face of, conflict with; *counter*, withstand, confront, hinder, obstruct; *compete against/with*, rival, contend, take up the cudgels.

633 COOPERATION

See also **40** (union); **43** (adhesion); **45** (combination).

n. *cooperation*, mutual assistance, fellowship, support; *working together*, joint/concerted effort, collaboration, teamwork, synergy, combined effort/operation; *merger*, amalgamation, union, coalition; *common aim*, solidarity, fellow feeling, sympathy; *league*, partnership, compact, treaty, alliance, détente; *concurrence*, unanimity, agreement, harmony, concert; *conspiracy*, collusion, connivance, complicity.

adj. *cooperative*, helpful, positive, constructive; *joint*, combined, mutual, bilateral; *sympathetic*, well-disposed, favourable, in sympathy with, concurrent; *in league*, synergic; *unanimous*, solid, united.

vb. *cooperate*, help one another, settle one's differences; *collaborate*, work together, combine/join forces, work in tandem, pull together; *help*, play ball, go along with, join in, muck in; *join together*, club together, team up, merge, amalgamate, unite, coalesce, combine; *agree*, concur, harmonize, see eye to eye; *conspire*, collude, connive, go into a huddle.

634 PARTY

See also **66** (assembly).

n. *party*, group, body, band; *member*, partner, adherent, follower, activist; *organization*, movement, political party, federation, association, society, circle, club; *council*, congress, parliament, legislature; *confederation*, alliance, Axis, coalition, league; *community*, fellowship, brotherhood, sisterhood, order; *confession*, church, religion, denomination, sect; *concern*, establishment, company, firm, corporation, partnership, syndicate, subsidiary, offshoot; *committee*, board of directors/governors, cabinet, junta, executive, administration; *faction*, splinter group, clique, in-group.

adj. *cooperative*, social, communal; *federal*, confederate, affiliated, associated; *corporate*, joint; *factional*, sectional, denominational, sectarian; *committed*, card-carrying, fully paid-up, militant.

vb. *join*, subscribe, enrol, sign on/up; *associate*, ally, federate, affiliate; *take sides*, side with, throw in one's lot with.

635 DISAGREEMENT

See also **18** (dissimilarity); **20** (disparity); **410** (argument); **437** (dissent); **643** (contention).

n. *disagreement*, nonagreement, difference of opinion; *dispute*, strife, contention, controversy, dissidence, dissent, dissension; *fight*, quarrel, squabble, wrangle, clash, row, tiff, feud, vendetta; *defiance*, rebellion, mutiny; *division*, split, breach, rift, schism, infighting; *disunity*, disharmony, discord, dissonance; *litigation*, legal battle, lawsuit, court action; *argument*, words, set-to, bickering, barney (*colloq.*), slanging match (*colloq.*); *bone of contention*, sore point, point at issue, talking point, hot potato (*colloq.*); *polemicist*, young Turk, rebel, firebrand, hothead.

adj. *disagreeing*, in disagreement, dissenting, nonconformist, at odds, at variance, at sixes and sevens, at loggerheads; *quarrelling*, warring, feuding, antagonistic, hostile; *contentious*, polemical, controversial, provocative, litigious, in dispute; *divided*, split, internecine; *rebellious*, mutinous, quarrelsome; *discordant*, disunited, dissonant; *conflicting*, clashing, divisive.

vb. *disagree*, differ, agree to differ, not go along with (*colloq.*), stick one's neck out; *dispute*, reject, contend, dissent, object, have a bone to pick with (*colloq.*), take issue with, clash; *fight*, quarrel, squabble, wrangle, row, feud; *divide*, split, go one's separate ways; *sue*, lodge a complaint, take to court; *argue*, bicker, fall out, have words.

636 AGREEMENT

See also **17** (similarity); **19** (accord); **436** (assent).

n. *agreement*, concurrence, consent; *contract*, compact, treaty, concordat, entente (cordiale), pact, convention, settlement; *approval*, acceptance, assent; *unanimity*, unity, solidarity, consensus, general agreement; *détente*, reconciliation; *peace*, harmony, accord, mutual understanding, rapport, sweetness and light; *consistency*, symmetry, match, coincidence, correspondence.

adj. *in agreement*, agreed, undisputed, concurring, of one mind, like-minded; *agreeable*, acquiescent, favourable, consenting; *unanimous*, united, allied, solid; *peaceful*, peaceable, harmonious, reconciled; *consistent*, symmetrical, matching, compatible, corresponding.

vb. *agree*, concur, accord, go along with (*colloq.*); *see eye to eye*, get along, hit it off (*colloq.*); *be reconciled*, bury the hatchet, make it up, mend one's fences; *consent*, acquiesce, accept; *assent*, approve, condone, give one's blessing; *correspond*, match, coincide, harmonize.

637 DEFIANCE

See also **632** (opposition); **662** (disobedience).

n. *defiance*, provocation, disobedience; *challenge*, dare, gauntlet, clenched fist; *revolt*, rebellion, mutiny, insubordination.

adj. *defiant*, provocative, challenging;

rebellious, mutinous, insubordinate, disobedient.

vb. *defy*, disobey, challenge, stand up to; *throw down the gauntlet*, provoke, dare; *scorn*, toss aside, snap one's fingers at; *revolt*, rebel, mutiny.

638 RESISTANCE

See also **137** (counteraction); **301** (friction); **632** (opposition).

n. *resistance*, stand, withstanding, retaliation; *objection*, opposition, protest, civil disobedience; *obstinacy*, reluctance, recalcitrance, unwillingness; *friction*, load, resistor.

adj. *resistant*, unyielding, proof; *obstinate*, reluctant, recalcitrant, unwilling.

vb. *resist*, withstand, stand up to, repel, hold off; *challenge*, not take lying down, put up a fight, not submit, hold out, stand one's ground, dig in one's heels, refuse to budge; *object*, protest, oppose, kick against; *frustrate*, stem, thwart, foil.

639 ATTACK

See also **147** (violence); **828** (disparagement).

n. *attack*, aggression, assault, first strike, offensive, onslaught; *push*, strike, charge, thrust, advance, storming, invasion, blitzkrieg, counterattack; *storming*, siege, blockade, bombardment, investment; *foray*, skirmish, sortie, sally; *raid*, air raid, blitz, barrage, broadside, volley, salvo; *mugging*, robbery with violence, grievous bodily harm, rape; *attacker*, aggressor, assailant; *besieger*, invader, raider, bomber; *terrorist*, gunman, mugger, rapist.

adj. *attacking*, aggressive, offensive.

vb. *attack*, assault, assail; *set upon*, go for, let fly at, fall upon, lay into (*colloq.*); *besiege*, lay siege to, blockade, invest; *bombard*, shell, bomb, strafe; *invade*, advance on, board, storm; *raid*, skirmish, foray, sortie, sally; *mug*, rape, beat up, jump on.

640 DEFENCE

See also **598** (safety); **600** (refuge); **649** (weapon).

n. *defence*, protection, safekeeping,

guard, preservation; *defensive measure*, safety precaution; *rampart*, bulwark, earthworks, wall, moat, bunker, trenches; *barbed wire*, minefield, tripwire, barrage balloon; *fort*, fortification, strongpoint, fortress, castle, keep, donjon, citadel, acropolis, barbican; *armour*, protective clothing, flak jacket, gas mask, helmet; *defender*, protector, champion; *armed forces*, security forces, civil defence, Home Guard; *guard*, sentry, patrol, watch, escort, convoy.

adj. *defensive*, protective, anti-aircract; *defended*, armed, armoured, dug in; *fortified*, barricaded, walled, bombproof.

vb. *defend*, protect, keep, safeguard, guard, preserve, shelter, screen; *garrison*, arm, munition, mobilize; *fortify*, reinforce, wall, fence; *fend off*, ward off, withstand, resist.

641 RETALIATION

n. *retaliation*, self-defence, counterattack, second strike, reprisal, backlash, boomerang; *revenge*, retribution, vengeance, recrimination; *punishment*, comeuppance, just deserts, a dose of one's own medicine; *vindictiveness*, revengefulness, spite; *tit for tat*, an eye for an eye and a tooth for a tooth, feud, vendetta, gangland killing; *rejoinder*, retort, riposte, repartee, counter, counterargument; *avenger*.

adj. *retaliatory*, second-strike; *recriminatory*, retributive, punitive; *vindictive*, revengeful, vengeful, spiteful.

vb. *retaliate*, counterattack, fight back, give as good as one gets; *take one's revenge*, get one's own back, avenge, get even with, pay back; *exact retribution/compensation*, punish, repay; *rejoin*, retort, riposte, counter; *get one's just deserts/comeuppance*, have had it coming to one, get what one deserved.

642 SUBMISSION

See also **72** (conformity); **663** (obedience); **782** (servility).

n. *submission*, compliance, acquiescence, acceptance; *surrender*, capitula-

tion, yielding; *subservience*, slavishness, deference, submissiveness; *fatalism*, resignation, defeatism; *docility*, humility, passivity, meekness.

adj. *submissive*, compliant, acquiescent, obedient; *amenable*, pliant, tractable; *subservient*, deferential, slavish, crawling; *fatalistic*, resigned, defeatist; *docile*, tame, humble, passive, meek.

vb. *submit*, comply, acquiesce, accept; *knuckle under*, bend, kow-tow, take it lying down (*colloq.*); *surrender*, capitulate, yield, give in, cave in, show the white flag, throw in the towel (*colloq.*); *admit defeat*, swallow one's pride, back down, eat humble pie; *defer to*, crawl, lick someone's boots (*colloq.*), lick someone's arse (*vulg.*).

643 CONTENTION

See also **635** (disagreement); **645** (war).

n. *contention*, conflict, clash, strife, dispute; *fighting*, force, combat, war, warfare, battle, hostilities; (*pitched*) *battle*, action, encounter, incident; *fracas*, affray, mêlée, fisticuffs, brawl, scuffle, scrap, punch-up (*colloq.*), dustup (*colloq.*), aggro (*colloq.*); *argument*, war of words, altercation, debate; *duel*, sparring match, joust, fencing; *boxing*, wrestling, judo, ju-jitsu, kung fu, karate, aikido; *contest*, competition, event, tournament, race; *game*, set, match, bout, round, rubber; *contender*, contestant, challenger, rival, competitor, candidate, nominee.

adj. *contending*, warring, competing, rival; *competitive*, sporting; *contentious*, aggressive, combative, pugnacious, bellicose, belligerent.

vb. *contend*, contest, confront, challenge, dispute, struggle, strive, tussle; *fight*, combat, battle, take on, do battle with, engage; *brawl*, spar, scrap, scuffle, come to blows; *compete*, rival, race.

644 PEACE

See also **235** (motionlessness); **354** (silence).

n. *peace*, freedom from war, absence of hostilities, peacetime, peace process;

truce, armistice, amnesty, ceasefire, lull; *cold war*, balance of power, peaceful, coexistence; *neutrality*, nonalignment, armed neutrality; *peace treaty/agreement*, nonaggression pact, nuclear freeze; *agreement*, friendship, cordiality; *pacifism*, nonviolence, nonaggression, appeasement, disarmament, nonintervention; *pacifist*, dove, conscientious objector, peacemaker, disarmer, neutral.

adj. *peaceful*, at peace, peacetime; *nonviolent*, bloodless; *neutral*, nonaligned, noninterventionist, peace-loving, peaceable; *friendly*, cordial.

vb. *keep the peace*, observe neutrality, call a truce, cease hostilities, make peace, disarm.

645 WAR

See also **643** (contention).

n. *war*, warfare, fighting, hostilities, armed conflict, combat, mobilization, call-up, conscription; *battle*, campaign, offensive, attack, strategy, tactics; *operation*, mission, invasion, raid, action; *world war*, global war, nuclear war, civil war, war of independence; *crusade*, holy war, jihad; *war of attrition*, trench/jungle/desert/guerrilla warfare, naval/submarine warfare, germ/chemical warfare; *psychological warfare*, war of nerves, propaganda war, cold war; *theatre of war*, battlefield, battleground, front (line), battle zone, no-man's land, arena; *belligerence*, hostility, aggressiveness, warmongering, sabre-rattling, aggression, militancy, militarism; *warmonger*, hawk, aggressor, belligerent.

adj. *warring*, hostile, at war, belligerent; *martial*, military, strategic, tactical; *armed*, under arms, on active service, mobilized; *bellicose*, militant, aggressive, hawkish, militaristic, warmongering.

vb. *wage war*, war, fight, battle, campaign; *attack*, raid, invade, engage; *declare war*, go to war, use force; *arm*, mobilize, call up, conscript, put on a war footing.

646 PACIFICATION

n. *pacification*, mollification, appeasement, peacemaking, conciliation, mediation; *agreement*, understanding, satisfaction, reparation, reconciliation; *truce*, armistice, ceasefire, amnesty; *treaty*, pact, convention; *disarmament*, demobilization, arms freeze, MBFR (Mutual Balanced Force Reduction), SALT (Strategic Arms Limitation Talks); *white flag*, peace offering, olive branch, overture, pipe of peace.

adj. *pacificatory*, placatory, conciliatory, propitiatory.

vb. *pacify*, mollify, appease, placate; *conciliate*, mediate, propitiate, reconcile; *force to negotiate*, bomb to the conference table; *agree*, settle one's differences; *disarm*, demobilize; *make peace*, bury the hatchet, shake hands, forgive and forget, let bygones be bygones; *sue for peace*, offer the hand of friendship, hold out the olive branch.

647 MEDIATION

See also **148** (moderation).

n. *mediation*, arbitration, good offices, shuttle diplomacy, interposition, intervention, intercession; *broking*, computer dating, matchmaking; *mediator*, intermediary, middleman, peacemaker, negotiator, broker, matchmaker, go-between; *arbiter*, arbitrator, umpire, referee, adjudicator, assessor, third party, neutral; *press officer/secretary*, public relations officer, spokesman, spokeswoman, spokesperson, intercessor, advocate, ombudsman.

adj. *mediatory*, intercessory.

vb. *mediate*, intercede, intervene, interpose; *arbitrate*, umpire, referee, adjudicate.

648 COMBATANT

n. *combatant*, soldier, conscript, volunteer, fighter, warrior, legionnaire, centurion; *gunner*, rifleman, sniper, bombardier, grenadier, artilleryman, infantryman; *seaman*, sailor, marine, submariner; *pilot*, navigator, bombaimer; *paratrooper*, commando; *guerrilla*, underground, freedom fighter, resistance fighter; *swordsman*, man-at-arms, knight, archer, lancer, hussar, cavalry; *reservist*, territorial, militia-man, irregular; *mercenary*, soldier of fortune, adventurer, freebooter, pirate; *private*, corporal, lance corporal, ser-geant, sergeant major, second lieuten-ant, lieutenant, captain, major, lieuten-ant colonel, colonel, brigadier, major general, lieutenant general, general, field marshal; *able seaman*, leading seaman, petty office, sublieutenant, lieutenant, lieutenant commander, commander, captain, rear admiral, vice admiral, admiral; *flight sergeant*, pilot officer, flying officer, flight lieutenant, squadron leader, wing commander, group captain, air commodore, air vice marshal, air marshal; *platoon*, com-pany, battalion, brigade, division, corps, regiment, unit, troop, squadron, flight, group, wing; *armed forces*, serv-ices, army, navy, air force, marines.

649 WEAPON

See also **640** (defence).

n. *weapon*, arms, armaments, weap-onry, arsenal, armoury; *club*, trun-cheon, cosh, mace, cudgel, shillelagh; *bow and arrow*, longbow, crossbow, bolt, javelin; *spear*, pike, lance, axe, sword, rapier, cutlass, sabre, scimitar, kukri, dagger, stiletto, bayonet, cold steel (*colloq.*); *explosive*, high explosive, TNT (trinitrotoluene), nitroglycerine, gunpowder, dynamite, cordite, gelig-nite, jelly (*colloq.*); *bomb*, atomic bomb, A-bomb, hydrogen bomb, H-bomb, nuclear bomb, neutron bomb, incendiary bomb, flying bomb, (hand) grenade, depth charge, torpedo, mine; *gun*, firearm, small arms, handgun, pistol, revolver, rifle, machine gun, sub-machine gun, shotgun, musket, shooter (*colloq.*); *field gun*, cannon, mortar, howitzer; *ammunition*, muni-tions, round, cartridge; *projectile*, rocket, shell, bullet, shot, slug, pellet, cannonball, grapeshot, shrapnel, flak, tracer; *guided missile*, cruise missile, ICBM (intercontinental ballistic mis-sile), MIRV (multiple independently targeted re-entry vehicle).

650 TROPHY

See also **448** (memory); **774** (repute); **859** (reward).

n. *trophy*, prize, award, reward, kudos; *cup*, plate, shield, badge, blue rosette, palm, laurels; *decoration*, medal, cross, star, ribbon, gong (*colloq.*); *mention* (in dispatches), honourable mention, cita-tion; *honour(s)*, title, order; *spoils*, plunder, loot, booty; *consolation prize*, booby prize, wooden spoon.

651 SUCCESS

See also **31** (superiority); **653** (com-pletion); **655** (prosperity).

n. *success*, happy/favourable outcome, happy ending, good fortune; *feat*, achievement, attainment, accomplish-ment, pass, graduation, good shot, (smash) hit (*colloq.*); *progress*, advance, lead; *good luck*, run of luck, lucky break, beginner's luck, fluke (*colloq.*); *flash in the pan*, nine days' wonder; *triumph*, victory, win, result, defeat, conquest, checkmate, game, set, and match, walkover, beating, thrashing (*colloq.*); *winner*, victor, conqueror, champion, prizewinner, roaring/run-away success, successful candidate, bestseller, blockbuster.

adj. *successful*, lucky, happy, fortunate; *profitable*, fruitful, beneficial, advanta-geous; *prosperous*, thriving, flourishing; *winning*, victorious, prizewinning, rec-ord-breaking, bestselling, conquering, triumphant, unbeaten, undisputed.

vb. *succeed*, achieve, accomplish, attain, fulfil; *pass*, graduate, make a success of, make a go of, pull off (*col-loq.*), bring off (*colloq.*); *bear fruit*, do well, pay off, work out, come off (*col-loq.*); *prosper*, profit, progress, advance, thrive, flourish, be/score a hit, make it big (*colloq.*), arrive (*colloq.*); *win*, be victorious, conquer, triumph, prevail, beat, defeat, trounce, crush, get the better of, thrash (*colloq.*), come out on top (*colloq.*).

652 FAILURE

See also **32** (inferiority); **654** (non-completion).

n. *failure*, lack of success, disaster,

débâcle, fiasco, bankruptcy, collapse, insolvency, flop (*colloq.*), washout (*colloq.*), damp squib (*colloq.*); *inefficacy*, ineffectiveness, breakdown, engine failure, fault; *negligence*, omission, neglect, oversight, faux pas, slip; *futility*, wasted effort, Pyrrhic victory, wild-goose chase; *defeat*, downfall, rout, overthrow, checkmate, beating, thrashing (*colloq.*); *loser*, no-hoper, unsuccessful candidate/competitor, underdog; *failure*, dud, lame duck, also-ran (*colloq.*), has-been (*colloq.*), bankrupt.

adj. *unsuccessful*, disastrous, abortive, miscarried, misfired, failed, would-be, manqué, insolvent, bankrupt; *unfortunate*, unlucky; *ineffectual*, ineffective, dud, defunct, kaput; *unprofitable*, futile, fruitless, bootless, (in) vain; *defeated*, beaten, overthrown, foiled, done for, hoist with one's own petard.

vb. *fail*, be unsuccessful, have no success; *not make the grade*, fall down, fall short, miss, flunk (*colloq.*), come a cropper (*colloq.*); *stop working*, malfunction, seize up, break down, falter, stall, get stuck, pack up (*colloq.*), conk out (*colloq.*); *fall flat*, come to nothing, come unstuck, fizzle out, fall through, flop (*colloq.*); *go down*, go under, go to the wall, go bankrupt, crash, go bust (*colloq.*); *lose*, be defeated, suffer defeat, come last, come second, be pipped at the post.

653 COMPLETION

See also **49** (completeness); **584** (perfection); **651** (success).

n. *completion*, finishing off, rounding off; *perfection*, realization, fulfilment, consummation, culmination; *end*, finish, ending, conclusion, termination; *achievement*, accomplishment; *readiness*, ripeness, maturity, fruition; *final stroke*, coup de grâce, finishing touch; *last straw*, breaking point, bitter end.

adj. *completed*, finished, fulfilled, done, sewn up (*colloq.*); *finishing*, concluding, conclusive, final, culminating, crowning.

vb. *complete*, finish off, round off, finalize; *perfect*, fulfil, consummate, put the finishing touches to, polish off,

wrap up (*colloq.*), see through, wind up; *end*, finish, conclude, culminate, terminate, come to a head; *achieve*, accomplish, realize, work out; *mature*, ripen.

654 NONCOMPLETION

See also **50** (incompleteness); **652** (failure).

n. *noncompletion*, nonfulfilment, job half-done, labour of Sisyphus, wild goose chase; *imperfection*, fault, blemish; *deficiency*, deficit, arrears, shortfall; *immaturity*, rawness, unripeness; *circular argument*, vicious circle; *stalemate*, draw; *postponement*, deferment, cold storage.

adj. *uncompleted*, unfinished, half-finished, half-done; *imperfect*, deficient, unrealized, not finalized, in the air, half-baked (*colloq.*); *immature*, unripe, underdone, parboiled; *never-ending*, endless, Sisyphean.

vb. *not complete*, leave undone, skimp, not follow through; *give up*, not stay the course, skip, drop out; *postpone*, defer, hold over, shelve, put on ice, put off.

655 PROSPERITY

See also **651** (success); **712** (wealth).

n. *prosperity*, success, welfare, wellbeing, happiness, good fortune; *milk and honey*, fat of the land, blessings, high life, life of Riley; *wealth*, riches, affluence, Easy Street, luxury, boom; *prime*, halcyon days, salad days, summer, golden age, heyday; *place in the sun*, bed of roses, clover.

adj. *prosperous*, successful, thriving, flourishing, booming, in clover; *wealthy*, affluent, fat, well-to-do, well-off, comfortable; *rising*, up and coming, on the up and up; *golden*, halcyon, sunny, rosy, blissful; *promising*, auspicious, cloudless, fair.

vb. *prosper*, do well, fare well, thrive, flourish, boom, do a roaring trade; *make a fortune*, make one's pile, grow fat, win the jackpot; *be on the up and up*, work one's way up, make it, blossom; *have it made*, never have had it so good, live like a lord, be rolling in money.

656 ADVERSITY

See also **628** (difficulty).

n. *adversity*, trouble, difficulty, struggle; *trial*, ordeal, adverse conditions, burden, pressure, opposition; *hardship*, hard/lean times, tough time, dark age, winter, cold wind, bad patch; *misfortune*, bad luck, hard lines; *misadventure*, disaster, accident, catastrophe; *evil influence*, curse, unlucky star, jinx.

adj. *adverse*, unfavourable, inauspicious; *opposed*, hostile, unfriendly, malign; *unfortunate*, unlucky, wretched; *troubled*, afflicted, burdened, plagued, beleaguered, bedevilled, stricken, fraught, hard pressed, up against it; *disastrous*, catastrophic, ruinous; *bleak*, cold, hard, lean.

vb. *be in trouble*, have a hard/thin time (of it), have been in the wars, go through it, be put through it, hit a bad patch, fall on hard times, feel the pinch, tighten one's belt.

657 AUTHORITY

See also **71** (rule); **622** (management); **661** (command); **672** (commission); **854** (jurisdiction).

n. *authority*, prestige, influence, sway, leadership; *power*, rule, jurisdiction, command, control, patronage, mandate, sovereignty; *right*, seniority, priority, prerogative; *supremacy*, ascendancy, hegemony, upper hand, dominion; *council*, panel, board, committee, cabinet, convocation, congress, convention, county/borough/town/parish council; *legislature*, legislative assembly, parliament, house, senate, administration, government; *democracy*, majority/minority rule, pluralism; *republicanism*, constitutional monarchy; *communism*, socialism; *dictatorship*, autocracy, tyranny, totalitarianism, police state, big brother; *officialdom*, bureaucracy, powers that be, they, them, Establishment, civil service; *councillor*, member of parliament, minister, statesman, parliamen-

tarian, senator, representative, delegate, congressman/-woman; *symbol of authority*, badge of office, insignia, regalia, crown, sceptre, standard, staff, wand, baton, crosier, mitre, bat; *uniform*, epaulette, tab, stripe, star, crown, gold braid, scrambled egg (*colloq.*).

adj. *authoritative*, influential, prestigious, commanding, leading, dominant; *empowered*, ruling, governing, constitutional, in command, in control, reigning, on the throne, sovereign, in power, in office; *democratic*, pluralist, republican, monarchical, communist, socialist; *governmental*, gubernatorial, bureaucratic, administrative, official.

vb. *rule*, have power over, hold sway, reign, have control, govern, control; *tyrannize*, dictate, oppress, lord it over, domineer, have the whip hand, call the tune; *take command*, assume control/command, accede to the throne, gain power, (be asked to) form a government; *seize power*, usurp, overthrow.

658 ANARCHY

See also **56** (disorder); **853** (illegality).

n. *anarchy*, lawlessness, breakdown of law and order, mob rule, rioting, civil disobedience, indiscipline, disruption; *disorder*, chaos, turmoil, pandemonium; *laissez-faire*, noninterference, nonintervention, permissiveness, indulgence, tolerance, licence; *laxity*, easing, relaxation, derestriction, deregulation, legalization, free-for-all.

adj. *anarchic*, lawless, uncontrolled, disruptive, undisciplined; *disordered*, chaotic, riotous; *permissive*, tolerant, indulgent, flexible, free-and-easy; *lax*, relaxed, loose, soft, negligent, easy, ineffectual.

vb. *take the law into one's own hands*, be a law unto oneself, kick over the traces, run amuck; *misgovern*, lose control, abdicate responsibility; *tolerate*, permit, indulge, not enforce, give free rein to, waive the rules, turn a blind eye to.

659 SEVERITY

See also **745** (seriousness).

n. *severity*, strictness, rigour, rigourousness; *discipline*, firmness, rod of iron, heavy hand; *harshness*, oppression, cruelty, draconian measures, tyranny, suppression; *intolerance*, bigotry, pedantry; *intransigence*, pound of flesh, no quarter, no compromise, inflexibility, full weight of the law, letter of the law; *austerity*, asceticism, self-denial, puritanism; *disciplinarian*, martinet, stickler, terror, scourge; *dictator*, despot, persecutor, oppressor; *extremist*, bigot, pedant, ascetic, puritan.

adj. *severe*, strict, rigorous, extreme; *disciplined*, firm, stern, uncompromising, hard-boiled, hard-headed; *harsh*, oppressive, cruel, draconian, drastic; *tyrannical*, autocratic, dictatorial, despotic; *intolerant*, bigoted, hidebound, pedantic, censorious; *inflexible*, unbending, rigid; *austere*, ascetic, puritanical.

vb. *be severe*, etc., tighten up on, clamp down on, crack down on; *discipline*, deal firmly with, get tough with, throw the book at, come down like a ton of bricks on (*colloq.*); *oppress*, tyrannize, suppress, intimidate, domineer, bully, persecute; *not tolerate*, not countenance, stand no nonsense; *insist*, put one's foot down, stand one's ground, hold out for.

660 LENIENCY

See also **813** (forgiveness).

n. *leniency*, mildness, softness, gentleness, kindness; *forgiveness*, pardon; *mercy*, clemency, quarter; *tolerance*, indulgence, sufferance, forbearance; *humanity*, compassion, sympathy, charity.

adj. *lenient*, mild, soft, gentle; *forgiving*, merciful, clement; *tolerant*, indulgent, enlightened, liberal, forbearing, easy-going, long-suffering; *humane*, compassionate, kindly, charitable, softhearted, sympathetic.

vb. *be lenient*, etc., pull one's punches, go easy on (*colloq.*), handle with kid gloves; *show forgiveness*, etc., overlook, forgive, pardon; *have mercy*, relent, take pity, spare the rod; *tolerate*, indulge, allow, put up with; *refrain*, forbear.

661 COMMAND

See also **622** (management); **657** (authority); **672** (commission); **681** (request).

n. *command*, order, direction, directive, instruction, (three-line) whip; *charge*, mandate, dictate; *decree*, proclamation, edict, papal bull, ordinance, prescription; *law*, act, injunction, writ, ruling; *summons*, subpoena, habeas corpus, order in council, sequestration; *(tax) demand*, requirement, passport.

adj. *mandatory*, compulsory, obligatory, statutory; *commanding*, imperative, peremptory, compelling.

vb. *command*, give/issue a command, etc., order, direct, instruct; *charge*, mandate, dictate, make compulsory, compel; *decree*, proclaim, ordain, prescribe, lay down; *rule*, enjoin, enforce, issue a writ, lay down the law; *summon*, subpoena, sequestrate; *demand*, require.

662 DISOBEDIENCE

See also **127** (revolution); **637** (defiance); **680** (refusal); **832** (improbity).

n. *disobedience*, refusal to obey, insubordination, noncompliance; *misbehaviour*, naughtiness, mischief; *awkwardness*, contrariness, cussedness, waywardness; *crime*, breach of the peace, disturbance, trespass, contempt of court, lawlessness; *violation*, transgression, infringement, delinquency; *mutiny*, rebellion, revolt, insurrection, defection, desertion, truancy; *defiance*, intractability, recalcitrance; *insurgence*, sedition, subversion, treason; *naughty child*, mischief-maker, trouble-maker, rascal, holy terror (*colloq.*), handful (*colloq.*); *criminal*, delinquent, hooligan, tearaway; *rebel*, mutineer, deserter; *revolutionary*, radical, insurrectionist, anarchist, hothead, firebrand; *insurgent*, subversive, rioter, terrorist.

adj. *disobedient*, insubordinate;

naughty, mischievous, unruly; *mutinous*, rebellious, riotous, dissident; *defiant*, intractable, awkward, difficult; *wayward*, contrary, bolshie, obstreperous, recalcitrant, refractory, bloodyminded; *traitorous*, treacherous, disloyal, duplicitous; *subversive*, disruptive, anarchic.

vb. *disobey*, defy, fail to comply, disregard; *misbehave*, play up, cause trouble; *violate*, break, transgress, infringe, trespass; *mutiny*, rebel, revolt, defect, desert, play truant.

663 OBEDIENCE

See also **642** (submission); **670** (subjection).

n. *obedience*, compliance, good behaviour, acquiescence; *deference*, slavishness, obsequiousness, submission, subservience, docility; *dutifulness*, devotion, loyalty, fidelity.

adj. *obedient*, compliant, acquiescent, law-abiding, well-behaved; *deferential*, slavish, obsequious, subservient; *docile*, submissive, tractable, meek, henpecked, under one's thumb (*colloq.*); *dutiful*, devoted, loyal, faithful.

vb. *obey*, comply, observe, heed, keep, acquiesce, agree; *behave*, do as one is told, submit, do one's duty, follow the party line, toe the line; *defer*, grovel, crawl, tug one's forelock, bow and scrape.

adv. *obediently*, quietly, with good grace, unquestioningly.

664 COMPULSION

See also **143** (strength); **536** (necessity); **558** (requirement).

n. *compulsion*, constraint, obligation, no choice; *pressure*, force, coercion, violence, duress, arm-twisting, strongarm tactics; *drive*, need, necessity, urgency; *threat*, blackmail, sanction, gunboat diplomacy; *conscription*, callup, impressment, draft; *forced labour*, slavery, servitude.

adj. *compulsory*, obligatory, mandatory, binding; *compelling*, compulsive, driving, coercive, irresistible; *necessary*, imperative, unavoidable.

vb. *compel*, oblige, constrain, leave no

choice; *force*, coerce, lean on, pressurize; *drive*, push, propel, urge; *require*, necessitate, dictate.

adv. *compulsorily*, bodily, under duress, under protest, of necessity.

665 MASTER

See also **31** (superiority); **622** (management).

n. *master*, mistress, lord, lady, lord of the manor, lady of the house; *director*, leader, governor, controller, overlord, superior, principal; *boss*, manager, supervisor, foreman, overseer, gaffer (*colloq.*), guv'nor (*colloq.*); *monarch*, sovereign, king, queen, prince, princess, regent, tsar, emperor, empress, grand duke; *president*, ruler, viceroy, potentate, chief, chieftain, margrave, elector, sheikh, sultan, proconsul, headman, maharajah, mogul, nawab; *despot*, tyrant, autocrat, Führer, Gauleiter, Duce, commissar; *official*, mayor, mayoress, provost, alderman, prefect, commissioner, civil servant, councillor, bureaucrat; *judge*, magistrate, sheriff, justice (of the peace), beak (*colloq.*).

666 SERVANT

See also **32** (inferiority).

n. *servant*, factotum, majordomo, butler, footman, flunky, maid, parlour maid, chambermaid; *nursery nurse*, nursemaid, nanny, ayah, wet nurse, au pair; *valet*, manservant, gentleman's gentleman, scout, lady's maid, lady-in-waiting, page; *steward*, stewardess, waiter, waitress; *housekeeper*, cook, kitchen maid, tweeny, skivvy; *daily* (woman), domestic, help, char(woman/lady), cleaning lady; *concierge*, doorman, porter, janitor, caretaker; *worker*, employee, staff, crew; *menial*, drudge, fag, dogsbody, handyman, odd-job man, chief cook and bottle-washer (*colloq.*); *slave*, serf, bondsman, villein, galley slave; *assistant*, secretary, amanuensis, aide, right-hand man, bodyguard, attendant, equerry, chaplain; *subaltern*, aide-de-camp, lieutenant, batman; *underling*, henchman, lackey, minion, junior.

adj. *serving*, in service, menial, below stairs; *working*, in employment.

vb. *serve*, wait on/upon, look after, minister to, attend, make oneself useful, work for, do for (*colloq.*).

667 FREEDOM

See also **669** (liberation); **677** (permission).

n. *freedom*, liberty, independence, freedom of action/choice, free will; *free speech*, civil rights, democracy, franchise, emancipation, universal suffrage, freedom of the press; *exemption*, immunity, special dispensation; *liberalism*, libertarianism, egalitarianism; *nonintervention*, autonomy, self-government, home rule; *free enterprise*, laissez-faire, market economy, free port, free trade; *room to manoeuvre*, play, Lebensraum, elbowroom, latitude, leeway, margin; *free hand*, blank cheque, carte blanche, free rein, licence; *freeman*, freedman, freedwoman, ex-convict, escapee; *independent*, freethinker, freelancer; *liberal*, libertarian, egalitarian; *gratuity*, free gift, freebie (*colloq.*), freesheet.

adj. *free*, at liberty, on the loose, at large; *independent*, self-governing, autonomous, democratic; *unattached*, self-employed, freelance; *exempt*, immune, unaffected; *emancipated*, enfranchised, liberated; *liberal*, libertarian, egalitarian; *unbiased*, unprejudiced, freethinking, enlightened; *free of charge*, gratis, complimentary; *unchecked*, unrestrained, unfettered, unshackled, unbridled, unhindered, uninhibited.

vb. *be free*, etc., have a free hand, be a free agent, please oneself, have the freedom/run of, make free with, feel free; *loosen up*, cut loose, let oneself go, let one's hair down (*colloq.*), let it all hang out (*colloq.*); *not interfere*, let alone, let be, live and let live, leave someone to their own devices.

668 RESTRAINT

See also **148** (moderation); **601** (trap); **630** (hindrance); **695** (retention); **843** (self-restraint).

n. *restraint*, prohibition, ban, bar, veto; *suppression*, repression, constraint, control, clampdown; *slowing*, deceleration, retardation, drag, curb, brake; *rein*, leash, bit, gag, muzzle, straitjacket; *arrest*, detention, remand, custody, house arrest; *imprisonment*, custodial sentence, incarceration, (solitary) confinement, internment, captivity, quarantine, care, time (*colloq.*), stretch (*colloq.*), porridge (*colloq.*); *restriction*, speed limit, curfew, roadblock; *boundary*, upper limit, ceiling, cut-off point; *economy*, freeze, cutback, credit squeeze, retrenchment, price control, prices and incomes policy; *price-fixing*, cartel, monopoly, closed shop, protectionism, tariff, restrictive practice; *gaoler*, jailer, (prison) warder/wardress, prison officer, (prison) governor, screw (*colloq.*); *keeper*, curator, custodian, attendant; *guard*, escort, bodyguard, garrison; *warden*, ranger, gamekeeper; *concierge*, porter, caretaker, housekeeper, janitor; *watchman*, coastguard, firewatcher, sentry, lookout, scout; *guardian*, foster/adoptive parent, tutor; *nanny*, nursery nurse, nursemaid, governess, childminder, baby-sitter.

adj. *restraining*, suppressive, repressive, restrictive, limiting; *restrained*, limited, controlled, disciplined; *inhibited*, straitlaced, reserved, uptight (*colloq.*); *custodial*, captive, imprisoned, under arrest, in detention, confined to barracks, gated; *in custody*, behind bars, in clink/jug (*colloq.*), inside (*colloq.*); *fettered*, handcuffed, manacled, in the stocks, in irons, bound, gagged; *protectionist*, monopolistic.

vb. *restrain*, limit, control, restrict; *prohibit*, ban, bar, veto; *suppress*, repress, clamp down on, inhibit; *subdue*, muzzle, silence, gag, censor; *slow*, decelerate, retard, curb, be a drag on, hold back, check; *fight back/down*, dam up, bottle up; *block*, hinder, impede, cramp, hamper; *arrest*, apprehend, detain, run in, pick up; *imprison*, remand in custody, put in prison, intern, incarcerate, confine, put behind bars (*colloq.*), put away (*colloq.*); *chain up*, fetter, manacle, handcuff, clap in irons; *economize*, freeze, cut back, control prices, tighten one's belt (*colloq.*), live within one's income.

669 LIBERATION
See also **606** (deliverance); **667** (freedom); **696** (disposal).

n. *liberation*, freeing, rescue, deliverance, salvation; *release*, discharge, acquittal, parole, bail; *demobilization*, disbanding; *extrication*, loosing, disengagement; *redemption*, forgiveness, absolution; *emancipation*, enfranchisement, liberalization, relaxation, easing.
vb. *liberate*, free, set free, turn loose, rescue, deliver, save; *release*, discharge, acquit, parole, bail; *demobilize*, disband, break up, demob (*colloq.*); *extricate*, disentangle, unravel, loose, disengage, unleash, let out, let off the lead; *redeem*, forgive, pardon, absolve; *emancipate*, enfranchise, give the vote, liberalize, relax, ease, deregulate.

670 SUBJECTION
See also **32** (inferiority); **663** (obedience).

n. *subjection*, subordination, subjugation, conquest, colonization, exploitation, annexation; *inferiority*, dependence; *allegiance*, nationality, subjecthood, service; *oppression*, hegemony, dominance, yoke; *enslavement*, slavery, servitude, bondage, feudalism; *slave labour*, forced labour, conscription, sweatshop.
adj. *subject*, subordinate; *inferior*, junior, subsidiary; *bound*, dependent, tied; *enslaved*, colonized, tributary, colonial; *oppressed*, downtrodden, under the yoke/jackboot, in the clutches of, under the sway of.
vb. *subjugate*, subject, conquer, subdue, reduce, subordinate, colonize, enslave, exploit; *oppress*, dominate, cow, have under one's thumb.

671 PRISON
See also **861** (means of punishment).

n. *prison*, gaol, jail, lockup, penitentiary, maximum-security prison, open prison, clink (*colloq.*), stir (*colloq.*), jug

(*colloq.*), nick (*colloq.*); *detention centre*, remand centre/home, internment camp, rehabilitation centre; *Borstal*, approved school, reformatory, reform school; *cell*, dungeon, guardroom, oubliette, cage; *condemned cell*, death row; *prisoner-of-war camp*, P.O.W. camp, concentration camp, death camp, gulag; *prisoner*, convict, inmate, jail/gaolbird (*colloq.*), con (*colloq.*), old lag (*colloq.*), guest of Her Majesty (*colloq.*), lifer (*colloq.*); *detainee*, accused, prisoner in the dock; *captive*, prisoner of war, P.O.W., political prisoner; *hostage*, kidnap victim.

672 COMMISSION
See also **657** (authority); **661** (command); **675** (delegate).

n. *commission*, mandate, charge, task, errand, assignment; *delegation*, deputation, legation, embassy, representation, mission, people's bureau; *appointment*, nomination, installation, induction, enthronement, ordination, consecration, coronation, inauguration, investment, investiture; *election*, return; *sequestration*, trusteeship, power of attorney, charter, licence, proxy; *regency*, protectorate.
adj. *commissioned*, deputed, empowered, entrusted, vicarious.
vb. *commission*, delegate, depute, mandate, charge, assign; *entrust*, commit, consign; *appoint*, nominate, install, induct, enthrone, anoint, ordain, consecrate, crown, inaugurate, invest; *authorize*, empower, charter, sanction, accredit, license; *elect*, return.

673 CANCELLATION
See also **474** (negation).

n. *cancellation*, cancelling, abrogation; *annulment*, nullification, invalidation; *revoking*, revocation, repudiation, retraction, rescission; *abolition*, dissolution, repeal, countermand, reprieve, reversal; *dismissal*, removal from office, unfrocking, suspension, sacking (*colloq.*), the sack (*colloq.*), the heave (*colloq.*), the boot (*colloq.*); *discharge*, court martial, recall, relief; *demotion*, downgrading; *redundancy*, natural wastage, layoff, job losses; *dethronement*, deposal, deposition, overthrow.

adj. *cancelled*, null and void, invalid, quashed.

vb. *cancel*, abrogate, scrub out; *annul*, nullify, invalidate, render null and void, void; *revoke*, repudiate, retract, rescind; *abolish*, dissolve, repeal, countermand, reprieve, reverse, quash, overrule, set aside; *dismiss*, remove from office, unfrock, strike off, suspend, give someone their cards, sack (*colloq.*), give someone notice, fire (*colloq.*), lay off, make redundant; *discharge*, cashier, court-martial, recall, relieve; *demote*, downgrade, kick upstairs, reduce to the ranks; *dethrone*, depose, unseat, overthrow.

674 RESIGNATION

See also **563** (relinquishment).

n. *resignation*, leaving, withdrawal, retirement, abdication, desertion; *renunciation*, relinquishment, abandonment; *pension*, golden handshake, superannuation, gold watch, redundancy money.

adj. *retiring*, outgoing; *retired*, ex-, former, sometime, one-time, emeritus.

vb. *resign*, leave, withdraw, retire, take early retirement, abdicate, stand down, not stand for re-election, tender one's resignation, apply for the Chiltern Hundreds, hand in one's notice, ask for one's cards; *renounce*, relinquish, abandon, desert, give up, throw up, quit.

675 DELEGATE

See also **672** (commission).

n. *delegate*, representative, consignee, deputy, agent; *delegation*, mission, deputation, committee, working party; *broker*, middleman, stockbroker, negotiator; *nominee*, appointee, proxy, stakeholder; *trustee*, executor, licensee; *legal representative*, advocate, attorney, counsel; *diplomat*, envoy, ambassador, plenipotentiary, consul, attaché, resident, high commissioner, chargé d'affaires; *mission*, embassy, legation, consulate, high commission; *legate*, nuncio.

676 DEPUTY

See also **128** (substitution).

n. *deputy*, second-in-command, right-hand man, lieutenant, assistant, second; *representative*, proxy, substitute, stand-in, agent, understudy, double; *spokesman*, spokeswoman, spokesperson, mouthpiece.

adj. *deputy*, vice-, pro-, acting.

vb. *deputize*, represent, act for, speak for, stand in for, substitute for, replace.

677 PERMISSION

See also **436** (assent); **667** (freedom); **852** (legality).

n. *permission*, authority, leave, freedom, liberty, consent; *authorization*, approval, clearance, sanction, legalization, go-ahead (*colloq.*), green light (*colloq.*); *dispensation*, concession, allowance; *free hand*, blank cheque, carte blanche; *permit*, licence, royal charter, franchise, certificate, grant; *pass*, passport, visa, safe-conduct, passbook, ticket, chit.

adj. *permissive*, tolerant, indulgent, lenient; *permitted*, allowed, free, permissible, printable; *licensed*, chartered, authorized, approved.

vb. *permit*, allow, let, consent, give permission, grant leave, vouchsafe; *authorize*, clear, sanction, pass, rubberstamp, legalize, decontrol; *license*, charter, certify, franchise; *approve*, give the go-ahead (*colloq.*), encourage; *tolerate*, brook, suffer.

678 VETO

See also **853** (illegality).

n. *veto*, prohibition, forbiddance, interdiction, (blanket) refusal, countermand, proscription, disqualification, taboo; *interference*, intervention; *ban*, bar, embargo, boycott, blacklist; *licensing laws*; *censorship*, suppression, news blackout, D-notice.

adj. *prohibitory*, prohibiting; *prohibitive*, restrictive; *prohibited*, forbidden, not allowed; *illegal*, unlawful, illicit, against the law; *banned*, barred, embargoed, blacked; *censored*, suppressed, blacked out, unprintable; *taboo*, frowned on.

vb. *veto*, prohibit, forbid, refuse, refuse permission, interdict, countermand, disqualify, restrict; *ban*, bar, boycott, embargo, proscribe, outlaw, black, blacklist; *debar*, shut out, blackball, exclude; *suppress*, censor, blue-pencil, cut.

679 OFFER

See also **537** (willingness).

n. *offer*, proffer, proffering; *bid*, tender; *proposal*, proposition, suggestion, submission, application; *approach*, advance, overture, invitation.

adj. *offered*, on offer, advertised; *for sale*, available, for hire, to let, on the market, up for grabs (*colloq.*).

vb. *offer*, proffer, make available; *bid*, tender; *propose*, suggest, put forward, submit, apply; *approach*, make advances/overtures, invite; *advertise*, put on the market, offer for sale, put up for auction, invite tenders; *offer one's services*, come forward, stand, run for, volunteer, run.

680 REFUSAL

See also **538** (unwillingness); **662** (disobedience); **682** (protest).

n. *refusal*, failure to obey/comply, noncompliance, reluctance, recalcitrance; *rejection*, thumb's-down, nonacceptance, denial, withholding, disallowance; *ban*, veto, prohibition; *rebuff*, snub, slap in the face.

adj. *noncompliant*, negative, recalcitrant, reluctant.

vb. *refuse*, fail to obey/comply; *reject*, decline, turn down, not accept, deny, withhold, disallow, not hear of; *ban*, veto, prohibit; *rebuff*, snub, cut, scorn, not listen, turn a deaf ear, ignore; *repel*, repulse, dismiss; *harden one's heart*, have nothing to do with, turn one's back on, wash one's hands of, set one's face against.

681 REQUEST

See also **661** (command).

n. *request*, appeal, plea, entreaty, begging; *demand*, requisition, ultimatum,

blackmail; *invitation*, invite, solicitation, canvassing; *petition*, call, application, claim, counterclaim; *prayer*, supplication, intercession, invocation; *suggestion*, proposal, motion, approach; *fund-raising*, begging letter, charity appeal, flag day, benefit game/performance; *advertising*, advertisement, circular, small ad, personal column; *petitioner*, lobby, lobbyist, pressure group; *appellant*, plaintiff, applicant, suppliant, claimant; *advertiser*, salesman, customer, enquirer; *canvasser*, solicitor, hawker, tout, barker, pedlar; *beggar*, scrounger, tramp, bum, sponger, hitch-hiker, mendicant.

adj. *supplicatory*, imprecatory, prayerful, suppliant, on bended knee, grovelling, with cap in hand, imploring, beseeching; *begging*, mendicant, charitable, fund-raising; *urgent*, insistent.

vb. *request*, ask for, call for, invite, express a wish, ask a favour; *demand*, requisition, blackmail; *petition*, appeal, apply, claim; *appeal for funds*, pass the hat round, have a whip-round (*colloq.*); *canvass*, solicit, hawk, tout, peddle; *beg*, entreat, plead, beseech, crave; *cadge*, sponge, scrounge, hitchhike, bum (*colloq.*), touch (*colloq.*); *pray*, supplicate, intercede, invoke, call on; *suggest*, propose, move, approach.

682 PROTEST

See also **538** (unwillingness); **632** (opposition); **680** (refusal).

n. *protest*, remonstration, deprecation, expostulation, dissent; *exception*, objection, demur, demurral; *murmur*, complaint, howl, squeal, raised voices, outcry, storm of protest, heckling; *demonstration*, protest meeting, sit-in, walkout, work-in, picket, secondary picketing, march, strike, civil disobedience, demo (*colloq.*); *disapproval*, dissatisfaction, raised eyebrows, jeers, slow handclap; *protester*, demonstrator, objecter, dissenter, heckler.

adj. *protesting*, dissatisfied, dissenting, protestant, deprecatory.

vb. *protest*, lodge/register a protest, remonstrate, deprecate, ask not to;

expostulate, take exception, raise objections, raise one's voice against; *object*, demur, kick, jib; *murmur*, complain, howl, squeal, grumble, moan, kick up a fuss, beef, heckle; *demonstrate*, march, go on strike, walk out, hold a sit-in, picket; *disapprove*, raise one's eyebrows, jeer, slow-handclap.

683 PROMISE
See also **473** (affirmation); **562** (undertaking); **684** (contract); **821** (duty).

n. *promise*, word (of honour), vow, pledge, credit, oath, troth, parole, assurance, signature; *profession*, declaration; *guarantee*, warranty, promissory note, banknote, bill, treasury note, IOU; *covenant*, bond, pact, contract, undertaking, agreement, commitment; *engagement*, betrothal.

adj. *promised*, pledged, covenanted, guaranteed, promissory; *committed*, on/under oath; *engaged*, betrothed, affianced.

vb. *promise*, give one's word, agree, engage, undertake, commit oneself, make a vow, pledge, swear; *profess*, declare, vow; *contract*, covenant, sign on the dotted line, set down in black and white; *guarantee*, assure, give an assurance; *get engaged*, exchange vows, plight one's troth.

684 CONTRACT
See also **562** (undertaking); **683** (promise).

n. *contract*, (binding) agreement, compact, conspiracy; *undertaking*, ratification, pact, covenant, arrangement, understanding; *settlement*, deal, bargain, compromise; *peace treaty*, convention, nonagression pact, concordat, entente, charter, alliance, league.

adj. *contractual*, binding; *contracted*, agreed (to), arranged, settled, negotiated, covenanted; *consenting*, agreeable.

vb. *contract*, agree (terms), enter into/make/sign a contract, strike a bargain, do/clinch/make a deal, shake hands, come to an arrangement, reach a compromise, covenant, ratify.

685 NEGOTIATION
See also **422** (qualification); **571** (provision); **707** (trade).

n. *negotiation*, bargaining, making terms, barter, collective bargaining, horse-trading, haggling, wheeler-dealing; *condition*, terms, small print, stipulation, frame of reference, contingency, provision, clause, proviso; *limitation*, strings, exclusion, exception, escape clause, loophole, catch, restriction, reservation, penalty.

adj. *conditional*, contingent, provisional, dependent, subject; *limiting*, qualifying, with strings attached.

vb. *negotiate*, bargain, haggle, barter, discuss, parley, treat; *propose conditions*, attach strings, stipulate, impose, hold out for, insist on, make demands, require.

686 COMPROMISE
See also **250** (middle way).

n. *compromise*, give and take, concessions on both sides, mutual concessions, compromise solution, working arrangement, modus vivendi, middle ground, middle course.

vb. *compromise*, give and take, make concessions, lower one's sights, meet halfway, back down, climb down; *split the difference*, split down the middle, go Dutch, go half and half; *steer a middle course*, make the best of a bad job, cut one's losses.

adv. *knock for knock*, fifty-fifty.

687 SECURITY
See also **598** (safety).

n. *security*, guarantee, warranty, surety; *bond*, pledge, covenant; *collateral*, mortgage, pawn, token, indemnity, cover, hostage, forfeit; *caution money*, deposit, down payment, bail, recognizance, stake; *guarantor*, mortgagor, backer, referee.

adj. *secured*, insured, covered; *pledged*, pawned, mortgaged, deposited, in hock (*colloq.*).

vb. *secure*, insure, cover; *guarantee*, warrant, indemnify, assure, underwrite, endorse; *pledge*, pawn, mortgage,

688 OBSERVANCE

deposit, pop (*colloq.*); *give security*, go bail, bail out, stand surety.

688 OBSERVANCE

See also **72** (conformity); **549** (habit).

n. *observance*, keeping, practice, habit, carrying out, performance, execution; *adherence*, conformity, orthodoxy, heeding, regard, respect, the done thing; *conscientiousness*, diligence, pedantry, scrupulousness, punctiliousness; *fidelity*, faithfulness, devotion, loyalty, dependability, compliance, obedience.

adj. *observant*, professing, practising, religious, orthodox, conformist; *conscientious*, diligent, pedantic, scrupulous, punctilious; *faithful*, loyal, devoted, dependable, responsible, compliant, obedient.

vb. *observe*, keep, practise, carry out, perform, execute; *heed*, respect, regard, pay due attention to; *conform*, abide by, follow, adopt, adhere; *be faithful to*, do one's duty, honour one's obligations, comply, obey, fulfil, keep faith, be as good as one's word.

689 NONOBSERVANCE

See also **73** (nonconformity); **407** (negligence).

n. *nonobservance*, nonperformance, nonfulfilment; *disregard*, disrespect, inattention, indifference; *nonconformity*, nonconformism; *unreliability*, negligence, neglect, laxity, omission, carelessness; *disobedience*, noncompliance, contravention, violation, transgression, infringement, sin, breach; *disloyalty*, unfaithfulness, infidelity, breach of faith.

adj. *nonobservant*, nonpractising; *inattentive*, indifferent; *nonconformist*, unorthodox; *unreliable*, negligent, lax, careless, irresponsible; *disobedient*, noncompliant, out of line, sinning; *disloyal*, unfaithful.

vb. *not observe*, disregard, omit, neglect; *disobey*, break, contravene, violate, transgress, infringe, sin, breach; *renege*, break faith, go back on one's word.

690 GAIN

See also **33** (increase); **35** (addition); **703** (taking); **719** (receipt).

n. *gain*, acquisition, obtaining, procurement, purchase, theft; *benefit*, yield, advantage, reward; *earnings*, income, earned income, pay, salary, wage(s), emolument, remuneration, stipend; *grant*, bursary, scholarship, exhibition, allowance, expenses, perks; *takings*, receipts, turnover, revenue, proceeds; *windfall*, jackpot, bonus, winnings, inheritance, legacy, bequest; *profit*, interest, dividend, yield, unearned income, return; *growth*, capital gain, savings, accumulation; *realization*, encashment, redemption, recouping.

adj. *gainful*, profitable, paid, salaried, paying, money-spinning, remunerative, lucrative, worthwhile, advantageous; *acquisitive*, on the make, covetous, greedy.

vb. *gain*, acquire, get, come by; *obtain*, procure, get hold of, lay one's hands on, appropriate, take possession of, buy, steal; *store up*, hoard, save, put by; *inherit*, come into, win; *pocket*, catch, net, land, secure; *earn*, make, benefit, glean, reap, accumulate, make money; *take*, turn over, gross, bring in; *profit*, capitalize on, cash in on (*colloq.*); *realize*, encash, redeem, recoup; *show a gain/profit*, pay a dividend, yield.

691 LOSS

See also **34** (decrease); **36** (subtraction).

n. *loss*, deprivation, lack, privation, bereavement; *forfeit*, forfeiture, eviction; *wastage*, leakage, shortfall, deficit, debit.

adj. *lost*, mislaid, missing, untraced; *deprived*, bereaved, bereft, shorn, denuded, stripped; *lacking*, wanting; *forfeit*, forfeited; *wasted*, down the drain (*colloq.*), irretrievable, irrecoverable.

vb. *lose*, miss, mislay; *let slip through one's fingers*, throw away, fritter away, say goodbye to, forfeit, squander; *go* *to waste*, leak, go down the drain (*colloq.*).

692 POSSESSION

See also **694** (property).

n. *possession*, ownership, proprietorship, custody, enjoyment; *mastery*, monopoly, domination, control, hold, grasp, clutches; *occupancy*, residence, tenancy, tenure, squatting, nine tenths of the law; *possessor*, owner, owneroccupier, proprietor, man of property, landowner, landlord, landlady, freeholder, leaseholder, lessee, householder; *occupier*, occupant, resident, tenant, squatter, lodger; *holder*, hirer.

adj. *proprietorial*, possessive, monopolistic; *propertied*, landed, to one's name.

vb. *possess*, be possessed of, own, have; *control*, monopolize, command, get one's hands on, grab, corner, hog (*colloq.*); *occupy*, fill, hold, enjoy.

693 JOINT POSSESSION

n. *joint possession*, joint ownership, co-ownership, partnership, participation; *public ownership*, nationalization, collectivism; *joint account*, (joint-stock) company, profit-sharing; *condominium*, time-sharing, housing association; *commune*, kibbutz, collective, kolkhoz, cooperative, coop; *common* (land), public property; *partner*, shareholder, stockholder, member, participant; *flatmate*, roommate; *communard*, kibbutznik, collectivist.

adj. *jointly owned*, joint, common, communal, participating, cooperative, collective; *public*, state-owned, nationalized.

vb. *share*, have a share in, have shares in, be in partnership with, go in with, participate, hold in common; *nationalize*, collectivize.

694 PROPERTY

See also **692** (possession).

n. *property*, possessions, belongings, impedimenta, trappings, accoutrements, goods and chattels, movables, effects, valuables, consumer durables, things, bits and pieces (*colloq.*), paraphernalia, clobber (*colloq.*), stuff (*colloq.*); *land*, real estate, realty, hereditament, immovables; *estate*, assets, means, capital, reserves, equity; *investment*, securities, stocks and shares, unit trusts; *rights*, interest, stake.

adj. *propertied*, landed; *proprietary*; *movable*, immovable, real, material.

695 RETENTION

See also **40** (union); **668** (restraint).

n. *retention*, holding, tenacity, adhesion; *hold*, grip, grasp, clasp, embrace, hug, bearhug, clinch; *clutches*, stranglehold, half-nelson, armlock.

adj. *retentive*, tenacious, tight, vicelike, fast; *sticky*, tacky, clinging, adhesive, fusible.

vb. *retain*, hold, keep a firm hold of, grip, grasp, clench, pin, clasp, embrace, hug, clinch; *secure*, fix, lock, clamp, fasten; *cling*, stick, adhere, fuse, hang on; *detain*, confine, withhold, contain.

696 DISPOSAL

See also **41** (separation); **563** (relinquishment); **669** (liberation).

n. *disposal*, abandonment, relinquishment, renunciation, alienation, cession; *release*, discharge, dumping, recycling, on the scrapheap; *refuse*, flotsam and jetsam, castoffs, waste.

adj. *abandoned*, derelict, cast-off; *disposable*, throwaway, soluble, biodegradable; *dispensable*, expendable, transferable, saleable.

vb. *dispose of*, throw away, discard, chuck out (*colloq.*); *pass on*, bequeath, part with; *sell off*, alienate, transfer; *jettison*, ditch, dump, drop, shed; *let go*, release, free, unhand, loose; *release*, discharge, lay off, pension off; *abandon*, relinquish, renounce, yield, cede; *do without*, forgo, dispense with, spare, waive; *disown*, disinherit, cut off without a penny.

697 TRANSFER OF PROPERTY

See also **239** (transfer); **707** (trade); **716** (payment).

n. *transfer of property*, assignment,

conveyancing, alienation, change of ownership, handover, consignment; *bequest*, inheritance, legacy, capital transfer, settlement, endowment; *purchase*, sale, lease, hire, letting, rental, exchange, barter, trade.

adj. *transferable*, alienable, exchangeable, negotiable.

vb. *transfer*, assign, convey, alienate, hand over, consign, sign over, make over, pass on; *bequeath*, will, leave, settle, endow, grant, hand down; *inherit*, succeed to, come into; *buy*, purchase, sell, lease, hire (out), let, rent, exchange, convert, barter, trade; *dispossess*, expropriate, nationalize; *change hands*, pass, revert.

698 GIVING
See also **725** (generosity).

n. *giving*, donation, conferral, bestowal; *charity*, alms, handout, food parcel, poor box; *gift*, present, presentation, golden handshake; *prize*, award, reward; *contribution*, subscription; *aid*, grant, subsidy, support, sponsorship; *tip*, gratuity, Christmas box; *bequest*, legacy, covenant; *largesse*, bounty, generosity; *offering*, sacrifice, church collection, offertory; *giver*, donor, contributor, subscriber, benefactor, tipper.

adj. *charitable*, votive, sacrificial; *bountiful*, generous, liberal, open-handed; *free*, gratis, complimentary.

vb. *give*, donate, confer, bestow, vouchsafe, render, afford, accord, allot, remit; *hand out*, distribute, dole out, share out; *present*, honour, award; *aid*, subsidize, support, sponsor, grant, endow; *contribute*, subscribe, help, shell out (*colloq.*), fork out (*colloq.*), put one's hand in one's pocket; *tip*; *bequeath*, leave; *offer*, sacrifice.

699 RECEIVING
See also **265** (admittance); **719** (receipt).

n. *receiving*, reception, admittance, admission, acceptance; *acquisition*, getting, gain, collection, assumption; *receipts*, winnings, proceeds, takings, income, gate; *toll*, tribute, tax, levy;

recipient, receiver, acceptor, accepting house; *trustee*, assignee, licensee, lessee, payee; *devisee*, legatee, heir(ess), inheritor, beneficiary; *winner*, grantee; *treasurer*, bursar, tax collector, exciseman, customs officer.

adj. *receptive*, welcoming, acquisitive.

vb. *receive*, acknowledge receipt of, admit, accept, be given, attract, land; *acquire*, obtain, derive, get, gain, win, collect, assume; *take in*, pocket, gross, net, make; *inherit*, succeed to, come into; *levy*, tax, charge; *be received*, come one's way, accrue, fall into one's lap.

700 ALLOCATION
See also **48** (part).

n. *allotment*, apportionment, distribution, administration, sharing, share-out, rationing; *division*, partition, demarcation, carve-up (*colloq.*); *share*, portion, allocation, quota, allowance; *ration*, dose, dosage, measure; *serving*, helping, slice, cut, whack (*colloq.*), dollop (*colloq.*); *lot*, parcel, batch.

vb. *allocate*, appoint, assign, detail; *allot*, apportion, distribute, administer, dispense, dole out, share (out), deal, farm out, dish out (*colloq.*); *ration*, dose, measure (out), mete out; *divide up*, divvy up, lot, parcel out, zone, partition, carve up (*colloq.*); *demarcate*, delimit.

adv. *proportionately*, pro rata, per head, per capita.

701 LENDING
See also **714** (credit).

n. *lending*, hiring, letting, subletting, leasing; *loan*, advance, mortgage, overdraft, bridging loan, pawnbroking, credit; *investment*, backing, finance, (start-up) capital; *let*, sublet, lease; *lender*, moneylender, creditor, usurer, Shylock (*colloq.*), loan shark (*colloq.*); *finance house*, credit institution, bank, building society; *investor*, financier, banker, mortgagee, pawnbroker.

vb. *lend*, hire out, let, sublet, lease; *loan*, advance, extend credit, put out at interest; *invest*, finance, back, subsidize, put money up, speculate.

702 BORROWING

See also **715** (debt).

n. *borrowing*, hire, rental, leasing, chartering; *mortgage*, loan, credit card, overdraft; *hire purchase*, HP, instalment plan, easy terms (*colloq.*), the never-never (*colloq.*); *pawn*, pledge; *copying*, plagiarism, imitation; *borrower*, mortgage, debtor, sponge, leech.
vb. *borrow*, hire, rent, lease, charter; *mortgage*, have an overdraft, be creditworthy, be in the red; *sponge*, cadge, bum (*colloq.*), touch (*colloq.*); *pawn*, pledge, pop (*colloq.*); *copy*, plagiarize, lift, crib (*colloq.*).

703 TAKING

See also **690** (gain); **705** (stealing).

n. *taking*, assumption, appropriation, exploitation, extortion, blackmail; *seizure*, grab, snatch, confiscation, impounding; *requisition*, requisitioning, commandeering, compulsory purchase, nationalization; *occupation*, settlement, colonization, annexation; *expropriation*, dispossession, exaction, disinheritance, distraint, foreclosure; *capture*, apprehension, arrest; *kidnap*, kidnapping, abduction, rape, slave trade; *receipt*, acceptance; *booty*, spoils, capture, haul, prize; *kidnapper*, abductor, rapist, captor, slaver; *predator*, parasite, bloodsucker, leech.
adj. *grasping*, grabbing, acquisitive, rapacious, predatory; *extortionate*, exploitative, parasitical.
vb. *take*, assume, take over, appropriate, grasp, grab, snatch, wrest, extort; *seize*, confiscate, impound; *bag*, pocket, net; *requisition*, commandeer, nationalize; *occupy*, settle, colonize, annex; *expropriate*, dispossess, deprive, exact, disinherit, divest; *capture*, take by storm, lead captive, apprehend, arrest, nab (*colloq.*); *kidnap*, abduct, rape, impress, press-gang; *receive*, accept.

704 GIVING BACK

See also **28** (compensation).

n. *giving back*, restitution, restoration, return; *repayment*, reimbursement, indemnification, refund, rebate; *amends*, reparation, compensation, recompense, damages; *reinstatement*, rehabilitation, privatization, denationalization; *recovery*, retrieval, repossession, clawback.
adj. *restitutory*, indemnificatory, compensatory.
vb. *give back*, restitute, make restitution, restore, return; *repay*, reimburse, indemnify, refund, rebate; *make amends*, make reparations, compensate, recompense; *reinstate*, rehabilitate, privatize, denationalize; *get back*, recover, retrieve, repossess, recoup, regain, claw back.

705 STEALING

See also **703** (taking).

n. *stealing*, theft, robbery, grand/petty larceny, kleptomania, pilfering; *burglary*, housebreaking, breaking and entering, safe-blowing/-breaking/-cracking, raid, smash-and-grab raid (*colloq.*), heist (*colloq.*); *shoplifting*, pickpocketing, bag-snatching, hold-up (*colloq.*), stick-up (*colloq.*), mugging, robbery with violence; *looting*, pillage, plunder, rustling, poaching; *hijack*, hijacking, skyjacking, kidnapping, abduction, piracy, body-snatching; *embezzlement*, misappropriation, tax evasion, smuggling, moonlighting, black economy, fiddle (*colloq.*); *fraud*, swindle, con (*colloq.*), diddle (*colloq.*), rip-off (*colloq.*); *thief*, robber, burglar, cat burglar, safe-blower/-breaker/-cracker, cracksman, raider; *shoplifter*, pickpocket, Artful Dodger, bag-snatcher, mugger; *highwayman*, bandit, brigand, footpad; *looter*, pillager, rustler, poacher; *hijacker*, skyjacker, kidnapper, abductor, pirate, body-snatcher; *embezzler*, tax evader, smuggler; *fraud*, swindler, con, crook, rogue, shark, fiddler (*colloq.*), rip-off merchant (*colloq.*).
adj. *thieving*, thievish, light-fingered, kleptomaniac, on the fiddle (*colloq.*); *marauding*, piratical, buccaneering.
vb. *steal*, thieve, rob, burgle, pilfer, filch, purloin, help oneself to, walk off with, nick (*colloq.*), pinch (*colloq.*), nobble (*colloq.*), swipe (*colloq.*), heist

(*colloq.*), snaffle (*colloq.*), knock off (*colloq.*), rip off (*colloq.*); *shoplift*, pick pockets, hold up, mug; *loot*, pillage, plunder, sack, raid, rustle, poach; *hijack*, skyjack, kidnap, abduct, shanghai; *embezzle*, misappropriate, smuggle, moonlight, fiddle (*colloq.*), cook the books (*colloq.*); *defraud*, cheat, swindle, con, diddle (*colloq.*), rook (*colloq.*), fleece (*colloq.*), rip off (*colloq.*); *fall off the back of a lorry* (*colloq.*).

706 BOOTY

See also **650** (trophy).

n. *booty*, loot, spoils, plunder, stolen goods, contraband, swag (*colloq.*), perks (*colloq.*); *haul*, catch, find, prize, winnings, ransom, treasure trove; *kidnap victim*, hostage.

707 TRADE

See also **685** (negotiation); **697** (transfer of property); **708** (purchase); **709** (sale); **710** (market).

n. *trade*, commerce, business; *trading*, barter, buying and selling, traffic, trafficking, dealing; *speculation*, brokerage, jobbing, transaction; *exchange*, swap, trade-in, payment in kind; *bargaining*, haggling, negotiations; *export*, import; *trader*, merchant, businessman, entrepreneur, trafficker, dealer, speculator, pedlar; *wholesaler*, middleman, retailer, shopkeeper, tradesman, chandler; *exporter*, importer; *broker*, jobber, stockbroker, estate agent; *business*, dealership, brokerage; *racketeer*, black marketeer, wheeler-dealer, slave trader, drug trafficker, fence (*colloq.*), tout (*colloq.*), cowboy (*colloq.*); *merchandise*, wares, goods, stock, supplies, stuff (*colloq.*); *article*, range, line, commodity; *durables*, consumer goods, consumer durables, perishables.

adj. *trading*, commercial, entrepreneurial, mercantile; *wholesale*, retail, marketable.

vb. *trade*, barter, merchandise, buy and sell, traffic, deal, transact; *exchange*, swap, trade in; *export*, import; *bargain*, negotiate, haggle,

wheel and deal, beat down; *racketeer*, profiteer, fence (*colloq.*), tout (*colloq.*).

708 PURCHASE

See also **707** (trade).

n. *purchase*, buying, shopping, mail order; *hire purchase*, easy terms, tick (*colloq.*), the never-never (*colloq.*); *shopping spree*, buy, bargain, impulse buy; *takeover*, merger, dawn raid; *purchaser*, buyer, highest bidder, consignee; *customer*, client, shopper, clientele, patron, market, consumer; *custom*, trade, patronage, goodwill.

vb. *purchase*, make a purchase, buy, shop, go shopping, window-shop, patronize; *invest in*, put one's money into, bid for, buy up; *take over*, buy out, corner, stockpile.

709 SALE

See also **697** (transfer of property).

n. *sale*, auction, selling; *clearance sale*, auction, stocktaking sale, closing-down sale, end-of-season sale, January sales, special purchase; *bazaar*, jumble/rummage sale, sale of work, fête, bring-and-buy sale; *dumping*; *boom*, sell-out, high turnover; *marketing*, merchandising, sales talk/pitch, high-pressure salesmanship, hard/soft sell, spiel (*colloq.*); *seller*, vendor, tout (*colloq.*); *shopkeeper*, retailer, trader, purveyor; *sales representative*, rep, commercial traveller; *salesman*, saleswoman, shop assistant, shop walker, shop girl; *booking clerk*, travel/ticket agent.

adj. *saleable*, marketable; for/on sale, available; *in demand*, called for, sought after; *sold out*, fresh out of (*colloq.*), off (*colloq.*).

vb. *sell*, make a sale, vend, auction, knock down, flog (*colloq.*); *market*, advertise, put up for sale, put on the market; *wholesale*, retail; *peddle*, hawk, tout (*colloq.*); *dump*, unload, sell off, clear out, remainder; *be sold off*, come under the hammer; *be in demand*, sell well, sell like hot cakes, do a roaring trade.

710 MARKET

See also **707** (trade).

n. *market*, bazaar, arcade, covered market, flea market; *mart*, exchange, entrepôt, depot, warehouse; *fair*, fayre, trade fair, show; *stall*, stand, kiosk, booth, barrow; *shop*, store, department store, chain store, boutique, emporium, supermarket, hypermarket, cash-and-carry, shopping centre/precinct, shopping mall; *free trade area*, market economy.

711 MONEY
See also **712** (wealth).

n. *money*, currency, Lsd, sterling, bullion, filthy lucre (*colloq.*), dough (*colloq.*), bread (*colloq.*), lolly (*colloq.*), brass (*colloq.*), shekels (*colloq.*); *cash*, small change, coin, banknote, treasury note, bill, hard cash, greenback, ready money, the ready (*colloq.*); *cheque*, credit card, postal order, money order, banker's order/draft, traveller's cheque, letter of credit, promissory note, IOU; *funds*, finances, capital, reserves, liquidity, bank account, bank balance, wherewithal (*colloq.*), the needful (*colloq.*); *pay*, salary, wages, remuneration, emolument, expenses, petty cash, pocket money, savings, nest egg; *cash flow*, turnover, profit; *forgery*, dud cheque (*colloq.*), rubber cheque (*colloq.*); *banker*, treasurer, keeper of the purse; *bursar*, purser, controller, comptroller, purse strings, paymaster; *cashier*, teller, croupier; *accountant*, bookkeeper; *bank*, savings bank, building society, cash dispenser; *treasury*, strongroom, vault, coffer, safe; *till*, cash register, checkout, gate; *money box*, piggybank, kitty, purse, wallet.

adj. *monetary*, financial, fiscal, pecuniary.

vb. *mint*, issue, coin, monetize, circulate; *cash*, encash, draw out, change; *forge*, counterfeit; *withdraw*, demonetize, call in; *finance*, capitalize, fund, bankroll (*colloq.*); *save*, amass, put by.

712 WEALTH
See also **655** (prosperity); **694** (property); **711** (money).

n. *wealth*, affluence, prosperity, comfort, ease, creditworthiness, high income bracket; *luxury*, opulence, fleshpots; *riches*, fortune, king's ransom, substance, assets, money, means, pile (*colloq.*), mint (*colloq.*), tidy sum (*colloq.*), packet (*colloq.*), pots of money (*colloq.*); *rich person*, multimillionnaire(ess), man/woman of means, Croesus, Midas, moneybags (*colloq.*), fat cat (*colloq.*), plutocrat, nouveau riche, new rich, idle rich, haves (*colloq.*).

adj. *rich*, wealthy, affluent, prosperous, well-off, comfortably off, comfortable, well-to-do, propertied, moneyed, well-heeled, born with a silver spoon in one's mouth, in the money, flush (*colloq.*), made of money, rolling in it (*colloq.*), filthy/stinking rich (*colloq.*), loaded (*colloq.*); *luxurious*, opulent, plush, palatial, up-market.

vb. *be rich*, have money to burn (*colloq.*), have a bob or two (*colloq.*); *afford*, make ends meet, keep the wolf from the door, do all right (*colloq.*), get by (*colloq.*); *get rich*, prosper, make money, come into money, rake it in (*colloq.*), laugh all the way to the bank (*colloq.*), make a bomb/fortune/packet/pile (*colloq.*), strike it rich (*colloq.*), line one's pocket (*colloq.*).

713 POVERTY
See also **558** (requirement).

n. *poverty*, impoverishment, impecuniousness; *beggary*, mendicancy, penury, destitution, pennilessness, indigence, privation, subsistence level, breadline (*colloq.*); *insolvency*, bankruptcy, ruin, collapse, queer street; *financial difficulty*, reduced/straitened circumstances, poverty trap; *pauper*, the poor, down-and-out, slum dweller, have-nots (*colloq.*); *beggar*, mendicant; *insolvent*, bankrupt.

adj. *poor*, impoverished, impecunious, poverty-stricken, penurious, straitened, on one's beam ends, on one's uppers, hard up (*colloq.*), short (*colloq.*); *destitute*, penniless, indigent, needy, on the breadline (*colloq.*), clean/flat/stony broke (*colloq.*), skint (*colloq.*); *deprived*, underprivileged, disadvantaged, underdeveloped, low-paid, underpaid, exploited; *insolvent*, bankrupt, ruined; *down at heel*, in rags, barefoot, starving, down and out.

vb. *be poor*, live from hand to mouth, have to watch the pennies, feel the pinch, fall on hard times, go broke/bust (*colloq.*); *impoverish*, beggar, ruin.

714 CREDIT

See also **701** (lending).

n. *credit*, loan, mortgage, credit facilities, credit account, charge account, credit card, credit note, hire purchase, deferred payment, easy terms, tick (*colloq.*); *creditworthiness*, reputation, trust, confidence, reliability; *creditor*, mortgagee, lender, investor, depositor.

vb. *credit*, allow/give credit, charge to one's account, credit one's account, lend, defer payment, grant a loan, put on the slate (*colloq.*), be in the black (*colloq.*); *take credit*, pay by credit card, keep an account with, borrow, mortgage.

715 DEBT

See also **702** (borrowing); **819** (entitlement).

n. *debt*, indebtedness, commitment, obligation, duty; *liability*, debit, mortgage, amount due/outstanding/owing, bill, arrears, back pay, bad debt; *debtor*, borrower, mortgagor, bad debtor.

adj. *indebted*, committed, obliged, bound, under an obligation; *in debt*, mortgaged, overdrawn, in the red (*colloq.*); *owed*, owing, outstanding, due, overdue, in arrears, unsettled, unpaid, payable, on credit.

vb. *owe*, be in debt, be overdrawn; *mortgage*, overdraw one's account, run up a debt/bill, get credit; *pay by credit card*, buy on hire purchase, buy on the never-never (*colloq.*), get on tick (*colloq.*).

716 PAYMENT

See also **697** (transfer of property).

n. *payment*, settlement, liquidation, reckoning, discharge; *remittance*, defrayment, disbursement, subsidy, subvention; *repayment*, reimbursement, recompense, restitution, refund, damages; *contribution*, subscription, donation, tribute; *deposit*, down payment, outlay, instalment; *pay*, wages, salary, emolument, honorarium, fee, remuneration, stipend, earnings, commission, pension; *payer*, paymaster, cashier, wages clerk.

vb. *pay*, settle, liquidate, reckon, discharge, honour, clear, square accounts with; *pay out*, foot the bill, pick up the tab (*colloq.*), bear the cost of, meet, stand, spend, expend, pay up, fork out (*colloq.*), shell out (*colloq.*), cough up (*colloq.*), stump up (*colloq.*); *remit*, defray, remunerate, disburse, subsidize; *repay*, reimburse, recompense, refund, pay damages; *contribute*, subscribe, donate, chip in (*colloq.*).

717 NONPAYMENT

n. *nonpayment*, default, failure to pay, withholding payment; *stoppage*, deduction; *tax evasion*, dishonoured/dud cheque; *insolvency*, run on a bank, crash, failure, collapse, bankruptcy, liquidation; *defaulter*, bankrupt, tax dodger.

adj. *defaulting*, in arrears, behind; *insolvent*, bankrupt, unable to pay, bust (*colloq.*), on the rocks (*colloq.*), washed up.

vb. *default*, fail to pay, fall into arrears; *stop*, deduct, dock, refuse/withhold payment; *welsh*, fiddle one's income tax, do a moonlight flit (*colloq.*); *stop a cheque*, refer to drawer, bounce, freeze, dishonour, repudiate; *fail*, crash, go under, go to the wall, fold, go bankrupt, go bust (*colloq.*); *bankrupt*, ruin; *go into liquidation*, be wound up; *wind up*, liquidate, put in the hands of a receiver.

718 EXPENDITURE

See also **716** (payment).

n. *expenditure*, spending, payment, outlay, disbursement, outgoings, investment; *extravagance*, overspend, spending spree, blowout (*colloq.*); *costs*, overheads, (out-of-pocket) expenses.

vb. *expend,* spend, pay, lay out, invest, disburse, bear the cost, meet, foot the bill; *incur,* run up; *stand,* treat; *draw on one's savings,* splash out, overspend, blow, get through, use up, consume.

719 RECEIPT

See also **690** (gain); **699** (receiving).

n. *receipt,* acknowledgment, ticket, voucher, chit, coupon, counterfoil, stub; *receipts,* income, revenue, takings, monies, proceeds, box office receipts, gate money, returns, royalty, rent; *income,* earnings, pay, salary, wages, remuneration, emolument; *dividend,* pension, annuity, capital gain; *grant,* scholarship, exhibition, bursary, maintenance, allowance, pocket money; *winnings,* prize, legacy, inheritance, windfall, bonus.

720 ACCOUNTS

See also **486** (record).

n. *accounts,* accounting, accountancy, auditing, audit; *creative accounting,* fiddling; *account,* profit-and-loss account, balance sheet, budget, budget forecast; *bookkeeping,* single entry, double entry, books, journal, day book, cash book, ledger, trial balance; *statement,* bill, manifest, invoice, receipt; *accountant,* actuary, chartered accountant, certified accountant, bookkeeper, auditor.

adj. *accounting,* budgetary, actuarial; *accountable.*

vb. *account,* keep accounts, keep the books, enter, debit, credit, post, book, balance; *present,* charge, invoice, bill; *budget,* cost; *falsify the accounts,* cook the books (*colloq.*), massage the figures; *audit,* examine, inspect.

721 PRICE

See also **582** (worth).

n. *price,* cost/selling price, quotation, estimate, price label/tag/ticket; *list price,* recommended retail price (RRP), retail price index (RPI), price control, price freeze; *toll,* entrance/admission charge, rent, hire charge, rental, ground rent, cover charge, postage, corkage; *interest rate,* commission,

introduction fee, retainer; *surcharge,* supplement, currency surcharge; *tax,* taxation, duty, levy, impost, tribute, tithe, direct/indirect taxation, inland revenue; *customs duty,* excise duty, tariff, purchase tax, sales tax, value-added tax (VAT); *capital gains tax* (CGT), capital transfer tax (CTT), stamp duty, estate duty, death duties, wealth tax; *income tax,* pay-as-you-earn (PAYE), National Insurance (NI), surtax, supertax, investment surcharge, tax credit, local income tax, corporation tax; *rates,* general rate, water rate, rating assessment, rateable value; *poll tax,* salt tax, window tax, danegeld.

adj. *taxable,* dutiable, gross.

vb. *price,* assess, cost, value, put a price on, estimate, quote, rate; *cost,* fetch, realize, go/sell for, change hands for, be priced at; *tax,* levy, impose, raise, put a tax on.

722 DISCOUNT

See also **36** (subtraction).

n. *discount,* reduction, rebate, deduction; *commission,* percentage, brokerage, cut, margin, mark-up, rake-off (*colloq.*); *concession,* special price/rate, bargain/cut price, special offer, bargain.

adj. *concessionary,* tax-free, duty-free, tax-deductible, net.

vb. *discount,* reduce, deduct, rebate, allow, knock off; *reduce,* cut, slash (*colloq.*).

723 DEARNESS

n. *dearness,* expensiveness, costliness, expense, sellers' market; *extravagance,* exorbitance, extortion, rip-off (*colloq.*), overcharging; *inflation,* inflationary spiral, rising/spiralling prices, sellers' market.

adj. *dear,* expensive, pricey, priceless, precious, up-market, extravagant, costly; *extortionate,* exorbitant, prohibitive, unreasonable, excessive, over-priced, stiff, steep; *inflationary,* rising, spiralling, soaring, climbing.

vb. *be dear,* cost a lot, cost a packet/pretty penny/fortune/the earth (*col-*

loq.); *extort*, profiteer, overcharge, short-change, exploit, sting, fleece, bleed, rip off (*colloq.*); *pay through the nose* (*colloq.*), be done (*colloq.*), be had (*colloq.*); *go up*, rise, soar, climb, rocket, go through the roof, appreciate; *put up*, increase, revalue, mark up.

724 CHEAPNESS

n. *cheapness*, inexpensiveness, reasonableness, competitiveness; *bargain*, good buy, snip (*colloq.*), good value, value for money, sale goods, rejects, seconds; *price reduction*, sale price, cheap rate, reduced rate, concessionary fare, cheap day return, package (holiday), excursion fare; *deflation*, slump, glut, buyers' market; *no charge*, free gift, labour of love, free delivery, Freepost, Freefone, reversed charges, complimentary tickets, comps (*colloq.*).
adj. *cheap*, inexpensive, reasonable, competitive, affordable, down-market; *reduced*, cut-price, cut, half-price, rock-bottom, knock-down, concessionary, marked down, to clear; *economical*, economy, budget, family-size, own-brand; *cheap and nasty*, shoddy, cheapo (*colloq.*); *free of charge*, gratis, complimentary, for nothing, on the house, tax-free, reply-paid, toll-free, collect (*US*).
vb. *be cheap*, go cheap, go for a song; *cheapen*, reduce, cut, mark down, slash; *fall in price*, depreciate, decline, slump, drop; *flood the market*, dump, undersell, undercut; *cost nothing*, be had for the asking; *economize*, budget, shop around, bulk-buy.

725 GENEROSITY
See also **698** (giving).
n. *generosity*, munificence, liberality, lavishness, free hand; *largesse*, bounty, gifts; *hospitality*, charity, open house, kind offer.
adj. *generous*, munificent, liberal, bounteous, bountiful, free-handed, open-handed; *lavish*, right royal, handsome, fit for a king/queen, slap-up (*colloq.*); *hospitable*, charitable, kind, philanthropic, big-hearted, unselfish, unstinting.

vb. *be generous*, give generously, spare no expense, not count the cost; *lavish*, not stint, heap/shower upon, do proud, push the boat out (*colloq.*), kill the fatted calf, do things in style.

726 THRIFT
n. *thrift*, economy, frugality; *care*, prudence, husbandry, careful management, good housekeeping, conservation; *savings*, cuts, cheeseparing, economies, retrenchment.
adj. *thrifty*, economical, frugal, meagre, sparing; *careful*, prudent, canny; *money-saving*, energy-saving, labour-saving.
vb. *be thrifty*, economize, keep costs down, live within one's means/income, make ends meet; *manage*, husband, save, conserve, recycle, waste nothing; *make savings*, cut costs, cut corners, cut back, retrench, tighten one's belt (*colloq.*)

727 EXTRAVAGANCE
See also **572** (waste), **575** (excess).
n. *extravagance*, wastefulness, profligacy, dissipation, improvidence, no thought for tomorrow; *lavishness*, prodigality, profusion, conspicuous consumption, money to burn; *over-spending*, permanent overdraft, deficit finance, splurge, spree; *squanderer*, wastrel, prodigal son, spendthrift, big spender.
adj. *extravagant*, wasteful, profligate, improvident, reckless, immoderate, spendthrift; *lavish*, prodigal, profuse, over-generous.
vb. *overspend*, overdraw, fritter away, dissipate, live beyond one's means; *blow/blue one's money*, splurge, lash out, not count the cost, hang the expense, spend money like water (*colloq.*), think money grows on trees (*colloq.*), spend money as if it were going out of fashion (*colloq.*); *squander*, waste, throw away, pour money down the drain, throw good money after bad.

728 MEANNESS
See also **834** (selfishness).

n. *meanness*, minginess, miserliness, stinginess, niggardliness, illiberality, cheeseparing, false economy; *skinflint*, miser, niggard, cheapskate, scrooge; *greed*, avarice, acquisitiveness, venality, voracity, avidity, covetousness, gluttony.

adj. *mean*, mingy, miserly, stingy, niggardly, illiberal, cheeseparing, penny-pinching, parsimonious, close, tight, tight-/close-fisted, grudging, sparing; *greedy*, avaricious, acquisitive, grasping, money-grubbing, mercenary, venal, voracious, avid, covetous, gluttonous, usurious, rapacious.

vb. *be mean*, begrudge; *scrimp*, scrape, skimp, do on the cheap (*colloq.*), pinch, stint, count the pennies; *be greedy*, hoard.

729 FEELING
See also **334** (sensation); **732** (strong emotion).

n. *feeling*, emotion, affection, sentiment, passion; *sensation*, experience, perception, sense of, consciousness, impression; *sympathy*, empathy, fellow feeling, vibes (*colloq.*), friendliness, understanding, appreciation, sensitivity, tenderness, warmth; *agitation*, commotion, trembling, tremor, tingling, quiver, flutter; *sentimentality*, emotion, lump in one's throat; *excitement*, thrill, kick (*colloq.*), buzz (*colloq.*); *enthusiasm*, vigour, ardour, zeal, fervour, fire, keenness, impatience, fanaticism, obsessiveness, mania.

adj. *feeling*, sentient, sensitive, sensible, sensuous, sensual; *sentimental*, romantic, passionate, emotional, affectionate, tender; *sympathetic*, understanding, appreciative, tender, warm; *agitated*, tense, nervous, edgy; *impressed*, influenced, affected, moved, stirred, touched, heart-felt; *enthusiastic*, vigorous, ardent, zealous, burning, keen, earnest, avid, impatient, fanatical, obsessive, manic; *excited*, worked up, keyed up, breathless, panting, exuberant, hysterical, overwrought, feverish, impassioned, dramatic.

vb. *feel*, sense, entertain, experience, endure, go through, undergo, bear,

taste, enjoy; *sympathize*, empathize, suffer with, feel for, commiserate, appreciate, know the feeling; *move*, affect, impress, touch, stir, influence, fire, quicken, excite; *respond*, react, warm to, catch, thrill.

730 SENSITIVITY
See also **334** (sensation).

n. *sensitivity*, sensibility, sensitiveness, awareness, responsiveness, alertness, consciousness; *susceptibility*, vulnerability, hypersensitivity; *touchiness*, prickliness, irritability, soft spot, sore point; *soft touch*, easy mark, softie (*colloq.*).

adj. *sensitive*, aware, conscious, sensible, responsive, alive, awake, alert, on one's toes; *susceptible*, vulnerable, impressionable, malleable; *compassionate*, tender-hearted, soft, romantic, emotional, soppy (*colloq.*); *tender*, bruised, painful, hypersensitive, delicate; *oversensitive*, touchy, prickly, thin-skinned; *nervous*, highly strung, irritable, impatient.

731 INSENSITIVITY
See also **335** (insensibility).

n. *insensitivity*, insensibility, unresponsiveness, unawareness, obliviousness, insentience, thick skin; *lethargy*, torpor, stupor, numbness, paralysis, coma, hypnosis; *calmness*, stolidness, imperturbability, impassiveness, coldness, sangfroid, detachment; *stupidity*, obtuseness, dullness; *callousness*, dourness, ruthlessness, brutality, no heart, heartlessness; *stoic*, ascetic, iceberg, robot, automaton.

adj. *insensitive*, unfeeling, insensible, unresponsive, unaware, oblivious, insentient, thick-skinned; *lethargic*, torpid, numb, paralysed, comatose, hypnotized, punchdrunk; *calm*, stolid, imperturbable, impassive, cold, unemotional, unruffled, expressionless, detached, stoical; *stupid*, obtuse, dull, bovine, unimaginative; *dead to*, blind to, deaf to, impervious; *hard-bitten*, hard-nosed, tough, inured, invulnerable; *callous*, dour, ruthless, brutal, hard-hearted, heartless, inhuman.

vb. *be unaffected*, feel no emotion,

leave cold, not turn a hair, not bat an eyelid; *harden oneself*, steel oneself, harden one's heart against, disregard, ignore, switch off (*colloq.*); *not see*, miss the point of; *benumb*, numb, deaden, toughen, harden, sear, stupefy, dull.

732 STRONG EMOTION
See also **729** (feeling).

n. *strong emotion*, excitement, animation, fever, frenzy, delirium; *hullabaloo*, to-do, flurry, fuss, scene, song and dance (*colloq.*); *exhilaration*, elation, euphoria, intoxication, abandon, thrill, ecstasy, ebullience, fever pitch, orgasm, high (*colloq.*); *anger*, rage, fury, temper, outburst, fit, hysterics, tantrum; *passion*, emotion, romanticism, lyricism, sensationalism, melodrama; *excitation*, agitation, stimulation, galvanization, activation, arousal; *inspiration*, invitation, incitement, appeal, provocation, encouragement; *fascination*, bewitching, interest, enchantment, captivation; *excitability*, impetuousness, impetuosity, restlessness, irritability, instability, explosiveness, hot blood, intolerance; *vehemence*, turbulence, boisterousness, recklessness, high spirits.

adj. *excited*, animated, thrilled, inspired, impassioned, stimulated, moved; *feverish*, delirious, effervescent, wound up, crazy, keyed up, a-quiver; *exhilarated*, elated, euphoric, intoxicated, ebullient, ecstatic, turned on (*colloq.*), high (*colloq.*); *angry*, furious, raging, in a temper, hysterical, on the rampage, on the warpath; *passionate*, emotional, romantic, lyrical; *exciting*, exhilarating, thrilling, stimulating, rousing; *stirring*, inspiring, moving, affecting, evocative; *gripping*, enthralling, heart-stopping, nerve-wracking, nail-biting; *interesting*, absorbing, fascinating, captivating, enchanting, bewitching, compelling; *dramatic*, momentous, sensational, melodramatic, mind-boggling; *provocative*, titillating, saucy, spicy, racy, tantalizing; *excitable*, volatile, mercurial, quicksilver, temperamental, turbulent;

highly strung, nervous, edgy, on edge, tense, jumpy, jittery, restless; *impetuous*, impulsive, hot-headed, headstrong; *impatient*, intolerant, irritable, quick-tempered; *enthusiastic*, keen, boisterous, high-spirited.

vb. *excite*, arouse, inflame, work up, wind up, incite, provoke, incense, impassion, fire, fuel, goad; *stimulate*, activate, awaken, animate, electrify, energize, galvanize, summon up, quicken, turn on (*colloq.*), switch on (*colloq.*); *enthuse*, inspire, stir, move, encourage, hearten, urge; *interest*, absorb, fascinate, intrigue, engage, captivate; *enthral*, enchant, bewitch, compel, delight, thrill; *anger*, enrage, make one's blood boil; *startle*, amaze, take one's breath away, arrest, impress; *get excited*, fret, fume, work oneself up, get on one's high horse, rage, explode, fly off the handle, create (*colloq.*), freak out (*colloq.*).

733 IMPASSIVITY
See also **148** (moderation); **335** (insensibility); **731** (insensitivity; **756** (indifference); **760** (lack of wonder).

n. *impassivity*, inexcitability, imperturbability, steadiness, level-headedness, sangfroid, phlegm; *calmness*, coolness, composure, self-control, self-restraint; *equanimity*, serenity, tranquillity, placidity; *mildness*, meekness, submissiveness, resignation, acquiescence; *detachment*, aloofness, nonchalance, dispassionateness; *apathy*, indifference, unconcern; *sobriety*, gravity, staidness, sedateness; *patience*, forbearance, stoicism, tolerance.

adj. *impassive*, inexcitable, imperturbable, phlegmatic, level-headed, unflappable (*colloq.*); *calm*, cool, collected, composed, self-possessed; *even-tempered*, serene, tranquil, placid, cool as a cucumber (*colloq.*); *mild*, meek, submissive, uncomplaining, resigned, acquiescent; *detached*, aloof, nonchalant, dispassionate, blasé; *apathetic*, indifferent, unconcerned, uninterested; *sober*, grave, staid, sedate, reserved;

patient, forbearing, long-suffering, stoical, tolerant, easy-going.
vb. *keep calm/cool*, keep one's temper, control oneself, master one's feelings, not excite oneself, keep a cool head, keep one's hair/shirt on (*colloq.*), keep one's cool (*colloq.*), not flap (*colloq.*), not bat an eyelid (*colloq.*); *resign oneself*, submit, swallow, take, stomach; *be patient*, tolerate, put up with, brook, abide, endure, support, suffer.

734 JOY
See also **336** (physical pleasure); **742** (cheerfulness); **746** (rejoicing).
n. *joy*, pleasure, delight, enjoyment, thrill, enchantment, kick (*colloq.*); *fun*, jollity, merriment, good time; *ecstasy*, rapture, elation, exhilaration, bliss, euphoria, exaltation; *glee*, relish, gusto, zest; *happiness*, gladness, felicity, satisfaction, fulfilment; *comfort*, ease, well-being, convenience, bed of roses, luxury, paradise; *indulgence*, self-indulgence, hedonism, self-gratification; *malice*, gloating, schadenfreude.
adj. *joyful*, happy, glad, delighted, pleased, satisfied, gratified, pleased as Punch; *joyous*, thrilled, excited, on top of the world; *ecstatic*, rapturous, elated, euphoric, overjoyed, enraptured, delirious, carried away, over the moon (*colloq.*), in seventh heaven; *jolly*, merry, cheery, gladsome; *pleasant*, enjoyable, comfortable, pleasurable, convenient, satisfying, cosy, welcome; *delightful*, adorable, blissful, divine (*colloq.*), heavenly (*colloq.*); *self-indulgent*, hedonistic, luxurious, palatial; *malicious*.
vb. *rejoice*, jump for joy, celebrate, congratulate oneself; *enjoy*, get pleasure from, take pleasure in, delight in, relish, have fun; *revel in*, bask in, adore, rave about, get a kick out of (*colloq.*), get off on (*colloq.*).

735 SORROW
See also **337** (physical pain); **743** (dejection); **747** (lamentation).
n. *sorrow*, sadness, melancholy, unhappiness, wretchedness, misery, gloom, woe; *despair*, distress, dejection,

despondency, depression, dolour, desolation; *torment*, heartache, agony, anguish, suffering; *mourning*, bereavement, grieving, grief, regret, remorse; *homesickness*, nostalgia, longing, yearning; *worry*, anxiety, care, disquiet, something on one's mind, concern, burden; *problem*, headache, bother, trouble; *phobia*, neurosis, hang-up (*colloq.*).
adj. *sorrowful*, sad, melancholy, unhappy, depressed, disconsolate; gloomy, woeful, down in the dumps (*colloq.*); *wretched*, miserable, pitiable, pathetic; *desperate*, despairing, dejected, despondent; *distressed*, upset, distraught, anguished; *troubled*, afflicted, vexed, burdened; *worried*, anxious, fretful; *sorrowing*, mournful, grief-stricken, heart-broken, cut up (*colloq.*); *homesick*, nostalgic; *distressing*, harrowing, agonizing, painful; *neurotic*, hung-up (*colloq.*), driven.
vb. *sorrow*, be unhappy, grieve, mourn, pine, yearn, eat one's heart out; *depress*, distress, upset, agonize; *worry*, trouble, torment, harrow.

736 PLEASANTNESS
See also **336** (physical pleasure).
n. *pleasantness*, pleasurableness, niceness, delightfulness, attractiveness, enjoyableness; *charm*, fascination, winsomeness, allure, loveliness, beauty; *amiability*, friendliness, affability; *treat*, joy, delight, fun, lark (*colloq.*); *melody*, harmony.
adj. *pleasant*, pleasurable, pleasing, genial, agreeable, nice, delightful, acceptable, welcome, enjoyable; *charming*, fascinating, winsome, ravishing, exquisite, lovely, beautiful, fetching; *good*, wonderful, marvellous, excellent; *amiable*, friendly, affable, likeable; *enchanting*, alluring, seductive, enticing, bewitching; *melodious*, harmonious, mellow, soothing; *delicious*, tasty, luscious, delectable, choice, refreshing.
vb. *please*, delight, give/afford pleasure, amuse, entertain, make happy, gladden; *comfort*, soothe, put at ease, stroke, pet; *attract*, interest, allure;

737 UNPLEASANTNESS

charm, bewitch, captivate, entrance; *gratify*, satisfy, indulge, pander to, pamper, coddle; *excite*, stimulate, thrill.

737 UNPLEASANTNESS

See also **337** (physical pain); **604** (harm).

n. *unpleasantness*, disagreeableness; *hatefulness*, loathsomeness, nastiness, ugliness; *disappointment*, difficulty, trouble, worry, thorn in the flesh; *persecution*, harassment, molestation; *soreness*, tenderness, inflammation; *bitterness*, unpalatability, sharpness, tastelessness, disgust; *annoyance*, nuisance, vexation, embarrassment; *curse*, pest, plague; *burden*, cross, load, affliction.

adj. *unpleasant*, disagreeable, undesirable, displeasing; *hateful*, repellent, loathsome, beastly, foul, nasty, obnoxious, disgusting, nauseating, revolting, offensive; *hideous*, ugly, dismal, dreary, grim, unattractive, uninviting, depressing, unappealing; *unpalatable*, tasteless; *painful*, inflamed, sore, tender; *annoying*, troublesome, bothersome, irritating, trying, tiresome, irksome, wearisome; *onerous*, burdensome, oppressive; *upsetting*, off-putting, disturbing.

vb. *displease*, dissatisfy, go against the grain, rub up the wrong way; *repel*, put one off, nauseate, disgust, sicken; *shock*, horrify, scandalize, offend; *trouble*, worry, afflict, upset, disturb, distress; *bother*, incommode, inconvenience, put out, put to trouble; *torment*, harass, bait, bully, persecute, victimize; *tease*, pester, annoy, irritate, vex, obsess, haunt, molest, peeve, needle.

738 SATISFACTION

See also **573** (sufficiency); **825** (approval).

n. *satisfaction*, contentment, ease of mind, peace of mind, happiness; *comfort*, snugness, rest, ease, tranquillity, serenity; *complacency*, self-satisfaction, smugness.

adj. *satisfied*, content, contented,

happy, carefree; *comfortable*, snug, relaxed, at ease, tranquil, serene, peaceful; *uncomplaining*, unenvious, easily pleased, undemanding; *complacent*, self-satisfied, smug, pleased with oneself; *satisfactory*, satisfying, acceptable, passable, unobjectionable.

vb. *be satisfied*, etc., have all that one could wish for, achieve one's heart's desire, have no complaints; *satisfy*, content, gratify, please, meet with approval, go down well, meet one's needs; *appease*, mollify, pacify, propitiate, reconcile.

739 DISSATISFACTION

See also **574** (insufficiency); **747** (lamentation); **826** (disapproval).

n. *dissatisfaction*, discontent, displeasure; *irritation*, resentment, regret, pique; *depression*, sadness, unhappiness, grief, vexation; *tension*, strain, unrest, uneasiness, restlessness, restiveness; *grudge*, ill will, grievance; *criticism*, fault-finding, nit-picking; *complaint*, murmur; *critic*, fault-finder, nit-picker; *dissident*, malcontent, angry young man, protester.

adj. *dissatisfied*, discontented, displeased, disgruntled, browned/cheesed off (*colloq.*); *uneasy*, restless, tense; *cross*, piqued, sulky, tetchy, peevish, testy; *critical*, querulous, hard to please, exacting, captious, censorious; *disconsolate*, disappointed; *grudging*, jealous, envious, resentful.

vb. *be dissatisfied*, etc., complain, harp, nag, grouse, grumble, moan (*colloq.*), beef (*colloq.*), bellyache (*colloq.*), mutter under one's breath; *criticize*, carp, split hairs, quibble.

740 RELIEF

See also **620** (refreshment).

n. *relief*, easing, alleviation, mitigation, abatement, assuagement; *help*, comfort, load off one's mind, consolation; *break in the clouds*, lull, respite, ray of sunshine; *painkiller*, sedative, analgesic, balm, anaesthetic; *remedy*, cure.

adj. *relieving*, easing, mitigating; *comforting*, consoling; *soothing*, analgesic, anodyne, anaesthetic; *remedial*, curative, restorative.

vb. *relieve*, ease, alleviate, mitigate, abate, assuage; *soften*, cushion, take the strain; *help*, comfort, console; *encourage*, buck, hearten; *lighten*, lift, unburden; *soothe*, deaden, still, lull, anaesthetize; *remedy*, cure; *be relieved*, feel relief, relieve oneself, feel better, take comfort, take heart; *breathe again*, heave a sigh of relief, thank one's lucky stars.

741 AGGRAVATION
See also **593** (deterioration).

n. *aggravation*, exacerbation, deterioration, worsening, degeneration; *augmentation*, intensification, strengthening, deepening, sharpening, heightening; *exasperation*, irritation, annoyance, embittering.

adj. *aggravated*, etc., unmitigated, unrelieved.

vb. *aggravate*, exacerbate, deteriorate, worsen, degenerate; *augment*, intensify, strengthen, deepen, sharpen, heighten, magnify, multiply; *exasperate*, irritate, annoy, embitter, sour, inflame, fuel, make matters worse.

742 CHEERFULNESS
See also **734** (joy); **748** (hope).

n. *cheerfulness*, cheeriness, high spirits, blitheness, light-heartedness, levity; *happiness*, satisfaction, contentment; *optimism*, hopefulness, positive thinking; *vitality*, animation, liveliness, joie de vivre, vivacity; *mirth*, merriment, glee, laughter, mischief, gaiety, jollity, good humour, jocularity, joviality; *good nature*, geniality, amiability, affability, life and soul of the party, conviviality.

adj. *cheerful*, cheery, high-spirited, blithe, sunny, light-hearted, chirpy, breezy, carefree, easy-going; *happy*, satisfied, content, on top of the world; *optimistic*, hopeful, sanguine, in good heart; *vital*, animated, lively, vivacious, radiant, sparkling, bouncy, ebullient, bright-eyed and bushy-tailed (*colloq.*), full of beans (*colloq.*); *merry*, mirthful, gleeful, mischievous, laughing, gay,

jolly, good-humoured, jocular, jovial; *good-natured*, genial, amiable, affable, convivial; *cheering*, warming, encouraging, heartening.

vb. *be cheerful*, etc., keep smiling, keep a stiff upper lip, put on a brave face, grin and bear it, keep one's chin/end/pecker up (*colloq.*); *cheer up*, perk up, take heart, pull oneself together, look on the bright side, snap out of it (*colloq.*); *cheer* (up), humour, jolly along, hearten, encourage; *console*, comfort.

743 DEJECTION
See also **735** (sorrow); **749** (hopelessness).

n. *dejection*, despondency, gloom, cheerlessness, low spirits, weltschmerz, the doldrums, the blues (*colloq.*); *despair*, defeatism, pessimism; *depression*, unhappiness, joylessness, misery, melancholy; *disappointment*, chagrin, disillusionment.

adj. *dejected*, despondent, sad, gloomy, cheerless, low, down, down in the mouth, morose, glum, blue (*colloq.*), down in the dumps (*colloq.*); *despairing*, defeatist, negative, pessimistic, downhearted; *depressed*, unhappy, suicidal, miserable, melancholy, dismal, world-weary, browned/cheesed off (*colloq.*); *disappointed*, dispirited, disheartened, disillusioned, crestfallen, hangdog, downcast, crushed; *upset*, put out, cut up (*colloq.*), pissed off (*colloq.*).

vb. *be dejected*, etc., mope, brood, languish, pine, moan, sulk, droop, pull a long face; *despair*, give up, lose heart, eat one's heart out; *depress*, dishearten, discourage, demoralize, dismay, sadden, get down; *dampen*, disappoint, put a damper on, pour cold water on.

744 HUMOUR
n. *humour*, sense of humour, wit, wittiness, jocularity; *satire*, burlesque, farce, spoof, take-off (*colloq.*); *sarcasm*, flippancy, facetiousness, irony, whimsy; *repartee*, banter, badinage, joking, buffoonery; *joke*, witticism, pun, play on words, jest, quip, wise-

745 SERIOUSNESS

crack, gag, one-liner, shaggy-dog story; *dirty joke*, double entendre, innuendo, sick joke, black comedy; *practical joke*, hoax; *cartoon*, comic strip, caricature; *comedy*, slapstick, situation comedy, sit com; *limerick*, clerihew, epigram, aphorism; *laughter*, mirth, gales/roar/shriek of laughter, giggle, the giggles, snigger, titter, chuckle, chortle, guffaw, cackle; *smile*, grin, smirk, simper; *humorist*, wit, wag, card (*colloq.*), satirist, comic writer, cartoonist; *joker*, practical joker, clown, buffoon, jester, comic, (stand-up) comedian, comedienne.

adj. *humorous*, funny, droll, amusing, comic, comical, farcical, funny ha-ha (*colloq.*); *witty*, satirical, sarcastic, ironic, sardonic; *ridiculous*, laughable, side-splitting, hilarious, uproarious, killing, killingly funny; *jocular*, jokey, joking, flippant, whimsical, facetious, tongue-in-cheek; *risqué*, near the bone, off-colour, blue.

vb. *joke*, jest, crack a joke, quip, pun, bring the house down (*colloq.*); *tease*, chaff, pull someone's leg, kid (*colloq.*); *ridicule*, make fun of, poke fun at, mock, caricature, satirize, lampoon, take off, ham up (*colloq.*), camp up (*colloq.*); *have a sense of humour*, see the funny side of, enjoy a joke; *laugh*, hoot, giggle, snigger, titter, chuckle, chortle, guffaw, cackle; *split one's sides*, roar with laughter, crease (*colloq.*), be in stiches, fall about, laugh like a drain, roll in the aisles (*colloq.*), nearly die (laughing) (*colloq.*); *smile*, grin, smirk, simper.

745 SERIOUSNESS

See also **659** (severity); **743** (dejection); **747** (lamentation); **762** (boredom).

n. *seriousness*, solemnity, earnestness, gravity, grimness; *sedateness*, sobriety, staidness, demureness, primness, sternness, puritanism; *dullness*, dryness, stuffiness, colourlessness; *killjoy*, sobersides, wet blanket (*colloq.*), spoilsport, party pooper (*colloq.*).

adj. *serious*, solemn, earnest, grave, unfunny; *grim*, forbidding, frowning, stern, po-faced; *sedate*, sober, stolid, staid, demure, prim, straitlaced, stern, puritanical; *straight-faced*, deadpan, poker-faced; *dull*, dry, stuffy, colourless, dreary.

vb. *take things (too) seriously*, not get the joke, not have a sense of humour, keep a straight face.

746 REJOICING

See also **734** (joy).

n. *rejoicing*, exultation, celebration, jubilation, triumph; *revelling*, revels, revelry, festivity, merrymaking, street party, carnival, thanksgiving; *clapping*, cheering, hallelujah, three cheers, hurrah, hooray.

adj. *rejoicing*, cock-a-hoop, over the moon (*colloq.*), exultant, jubilant; *celebratory*, triumphal, triumphant.

vb. *rejoice*, exult, celebrate, triumph; *revel*, make merry, carouse, dance/leap for joy, skip, dance in the streets, let one's hair down (*colloq.*), paint the town red (*colloq.*); *clap*, cheer, shout, whoop, yell; *gloat*, crow, rub one's hands.

747 LAMENTATION

See also **735** (sorrow); **739** (dissatisfaction); **745** (seriousness).

n. *lamentation*, mourning, wailing, weeping, sobbing, tears, gnashing of teeth; *cry*, sob, weep, whimper, bawl; *widow's weeds*, sackcloth and ashes, black; *grief*, regret, sorrow; *lament*, threnody, elegy, dirge, requiem, funeral march, wake.

adj. *lamenting*, mourning, grief-stricken, tearful, inconsolable; *mournful*, lugubrious, plaintive; *lamentable*, pathetic, woeful, pitiable.

vb. *lament*, mourn, keen, beat one's breast; *grieve*, sorrow, go into mourning, elegize; *bemoan*, regret, deplore; *condole*, commiserate, comfort; *weep*, wail, sob, cry, burst into tears, break down; *sob*, sigh, moan, whimper, groan.

748 HOPE

See also **742** (cheerfulness); **755** (desire).

n. *hope*, aspiration, ambition, high hopes; *dream*, pipe-dream, wishful thinking, heart's desire, promised land, utopia; *trust*, confidence, faith, reliance, optimism; *expectation*, assumption, presumption, anticipation; *promise*, good omen; *hopeful*, young hopeful, candidate, aspirant, competitor; *dreamer*, visionary, optimist.

adj. *hopeful*, aspiring, ambitious, would-be; *trusting*, confident, expectant, buoyant, optimistic, sanguine; *promising*, encouraging, favourable, auspicious, rosy.

vb. *hope*, aspire, set one's heart on, aim, long for; *trust*, rely, have faith, believe, feel confident, be in hopes of, rest assured; *expect*, assume, presume, anticipate; *look on the bright side*, live in hope, hope against hope, keep one's fingers crossed; *raise someone's hopes*, give to believe, encourage; *show promise*, have the makings of, augur well, bid fair, bode well.

749 HOPELESSNESS
See also **743** (dejection).

n. *hopelessness*, despondency, defeatism, despair, desperation, pessimism, cynicism, resignation, dashed hopes; *impossibility*, no chance, irrevocability; *hopeless case*, poor lookout, dead duck (*colloq.*), goner (*colloq.*); *pessimist*, Job's comforter, defeatist.

adj. *hopeless*, desperate, despondent, defeatist, pessimistic, cynical, resigned, past hoping; *vain*, futile, to no avail, impossible, irrevocable, irredeemable; *inauspicious*, unpropitious, unfavourable, ominous, bleak.

vb. *lose hope*, despair, give up, resign oneself, abandon hope, write off; *dash someone's hopes*, hold out no hope, discourage.

750 FEAR
See also **752** (cowardice).

n. *fear*, dread, awe, horror, fright, trepidation, terror, phobia, blue funk (*colloq.*); *panic*, alarm, scare, stampede; *intimidation*, threats, deterrence, sabre-rattling, reign of terror; *timidity*, timorousness, fearfulness, nervousness; *diffidence*, shyness, hesitation; *cold feet*, misgivings, qualms, apprehension, uneasiness, disquiet; *worry*, concern, anxiety; *tremor*, flutter, fear and trembling, adrenalin, cold sweat, butterflies (*colloq.*), heebie-jeebies (*colloq.*), collywobbles (*colloq.*), the creeps (*colloq.*), the willies (*colloq.*).

adj. *afraid*, frightened, terrified, petrified, horrified, scared (stiff), alarmed, panicky, panic-stricken, white as a sheet; *timid*, timorous, fearful, nervous, jittery, jumpy, uptight (*colloq.*); *diffident*, shy, hesitant, wary; *apprehensive*, uneasy; *worried*, concerned, anxious; *frightening*, frightful, alarming, awesome, horrifying, terrible, hair-raising, bloodcurdling, ghastly, grisly, gruesome, macabre; *creepy*, weird, scary, eerie.

vb. *fear*, be afraid, dread, stand in fear of; *get/have the wind up*, take fright, panic, lose one's nerve, break out in a cold sweat; *quake*, tremble, shake, quiver, shudder; *quail*, shrink, cower, funk, not be able to face, chicken out (*colloq.*); *freeze*, feel one's blood run cold/one's knees knock/one's hair stand on end; *frighten*, affright, scare, terrify, petrify, alarm; *intimidate*, menace, terrorize, put the fear of God into, browbeat, cow; *make nervous*, unnerve, put the wind up, shake, rattle, disquiet.

751 COURAGE
See also **539** (resolution).

n. *courage*, bravery, valour, heroism, fearlessness, intrepidity; *boldness*, audacity, daring, nerve, bottle (*colloq.*); *manliness*, prowess, chivalry, gallantry; *spirit*, dash, derring-do, pluck, mettle, backbone, guts (*colloq.*), spunk (*colloq.*); *fortitude*, resolution, morale, determination, courage of one's convictions; *hero*, heroine, brave, Amazon, daredevil, VC, lionheart.

adj. *courageous*, brave, valiant, heroic, ready for anything; *bold*, audacious, daring, spirited, dashing, plucky, spunky; *unafraid*, intrepid, fearless, dauntless, doughty, stout-hearted, unflinching; *manly*, chivalrous, gallant, macho.

vb. *be courageous*, have the courage/nerve to, venture, brave, beard, confront, face (the music), defy, dare to, show one's mettle, have what it takes, take it like a man, keep one's chin up (*colloq.*); *take courage*, pluck up courage, take heart, screw up one's courage, nerve oneself, brace oneself, put a brave face on; *hearten*, nerve, embolden, inspire, rally, boost, bolster, strengthen, give confidence, buck up.

752 COWARDICE
See also **541** (vacillation); **750** (fear).

n. *cowardice*, cowardliness, pusillanimity, faint-heartedness, timidity, weakness, spinelessness, white feather, yellow streak, funk (*colloq.*); quitting, defeatism; *boasting*, braggadocio, Dutch courage; *coward*, poltroon, dastard, cowardly custard (*colloq.*), rabbit (*colloq.*), chicken (*colloq.*), scaredy (*colloq.*), sissy (*colloq.*), *deserter*, quitter, defeatist, shirker, braggart.

adj. *cowardly*, craven, pusillanimous, faint-hearted, timid, lily-livered, gutless, spineless, yellow-bellied (*colloq.*), sissy (*colloq.*), yellow (*colloq.*), chicken (*colloq.*); *dastardly*, mean, cowering, defeatist.

vb. *lack courage*, not dare, have no stomach for, funk (*colloq.*); cringe, quail, shrink, cower, skulk; *panic*, desert, turn tail, slink away, cut and run; *get cold feet*, quit, lose one's nerve, bottle/chicken out (*colloq.*).

753 RASHNESS
See also **445** (folly); **615** (haste).

n. *rashness*, recklessness, carelessness, thoughtlessness, heedlessness, imprudence; *indiscipline*, irresponsibility, wildness, temerity, audacity; *folly*, indiscretion, foolhardiness, brinksmanship, gamble, a leap in the dark; *impulsiveness*, impetuosity, haste, hotheadedness; *daredevil*, hothead, tearaway, fire-eater, gambler, madcap, harum-scarum.

adj. *rash*, incautious, reckless, thoughtless, heedless, ill-considered, inconsiderate, unthinking; *undisciplined*, irresponsible, wild, buccaneering, trigger-happy; *careless*, slap-happy, hit-and-miss, devil-may-care; *foolish*, foolhardy, imprudent, indiscreet; *impulsive*, impetuous, overenthusiastic, hotheaded, headstrong, overhasty; *precipitous*, headlong, breakneck, do-or-die, suicidal.

vb. *be rash*, etc., not care, take the plunge, throw caution to the winds, damn the consequences, stick one's neck out; *rush into*, tempt providence, ask for trouble; *gamble*, take unnecessary risks, play with fire, risk one's neck, go out on a limb, dice with danger, court disaster.

754 CAUTION
See also **406** (carefulness); **453** (foresight).

n. *caution*, cautiousness, heed, heedfulness, wariness, care, safety first, prudence; *circumspection*, reverence, respect, discretion; *deliberation*, planning, forethought, foresight, precaution, prophylaxis, prophylactic; *vigilance*, watchfulness, alertness, suspicion.

adj. *cautious*, wary, careful, heedful, prudent; *circumspect*, gingerly, respectful, suspicious, nervous; *precautionary*, prophylactic; *vigilant*, watchful, alert, canny.

vb. *take care*, play safe, think twice, look before one leaps; *take preventive measures*, keep well out of, give a wide berth, keep one's head down; *look out*, watch one's step, tread warily, be on one's guard; *cover oneself*, see how the wind blows, feel one's way, leave nothing to chance.

755 DESIRE
See also **553** (intention); **681** (request); **748** (hope)

n. *desire*, wish, want, fancy; *requirement*, need; *longing*, yearning, hankering, yen, ambition, aspiration; *curiosity*, inquisitiveness, thirst for knowledge; *urge*, inclination, motivation, eagerness, keenness, itch, bug (*colloq.*); *craving*, covetousness, lust, mania, addiction, craze; *greed*, voracity, gluttony, rapacity; *hunger*, thirst, appetite, famine, starvation, drought; *object of one's desire*, desideratum, ambition, dream, fantasy.

adj. *desirous*, wishful; *aspiring*, would-be, hopeful, ambitious; *eager*, keen, avid, itching, bent on; *curious*, inquisitive; *covetous*, lusting, lecherous, crazy for; *greedy*, voracious, insatiable, rapacious; *hungry*, starving, ravenous, famished, empty, peckish (*colloq.*); *thirsty*, dry, parched; *desirable*, acceptable, welcome, enviable, appetizing, attractive.

vb. *desire*, wish, want, pray for; *welcome*, be glad of, fancy, could do with; *require*, need, must have; *long*, yearn, hanker, thirst, itch, set one's heart on, aspire, be dying for (*colloq.*); *covet*, lust after, crave, have designs on; *hunger*, thirst, starve, drool, could eat a horse (*colloq.*).

756 INDIFFERENCE

See also **403** (lack of curiosity); **733** (impassivity).

n. *indifference*, lack of interest, unconcern, apathy; *insensitivity*, coldness, impassivity; *half-heartedness*; *neutrality*, impartiality, disinterest; *promiscuousness*.

adj. *indifferent*, unconcerned, uninterested, apathetic, blasé, cool (*colloq.*); *insensitive*, cold, unimpressed, unmoved, uninvolved, impassive, unresponsive; *half-hearted*, lukewarm, not bothered, easy (*colloq.*); *neutral*, impartial, disinterested, impersonal, dispassionate; *unambitious*, easy-going, laid back (*colloq.*); *promiscuous*; *unwanted*, de trop, unwelcome, unasked, unbidden, uninvited; *undesirable*, unattractive.

vb. *not care* (less), not mind, be all the same to, can take it or leave it, not give a damn/hoot (*colloq.*); *leave one cold*, take no interest in, not care for, hold no brief for.

757 LIKING

See also **336** (physical pleasure); **795** (love).

n. *liking*, fondness, fancy, relish, weakness, partiality, sympathy, affinity, soft spot; *leaning*, inclination, penchant, propensity, proclivity; *preference*, predilection; *attraction*, fascination, appeal.

adj. *fond of*, partial to, keen on, sympathetic to; *likable*, popular, in favour, attractive, appealing, fetching, catchy.

vb. *like*, be fond of, care for, go for, fancy, relish, be partial to, have a weakness for, take pleasure in, be into (*colloq.*); *prefer*, favour, choose, incline.

758 DISLIKE

See also **796** (hate).

n. *dislike*, disinclination, distaste; *dissatisfaction*, displeasure; *repulsion*, repugnance, disgust, abhorrence, loathing; *aversion*, allergy, antipathy, prejudice; *bête noire*, bugbear, pet hate.

adj. *displeased*, dissatisfied, disenchanted, disgusted, fed up; *averse*, allergic, antipathetic, loath, anti; *undesirable*, disagreeable, objectionable, obnoxious; *repulsive*, repugnant, abhorrent, loathsome, rebarbative; *unpopular*, out of favour, unloved.

vb. *dislike*, not care for, not find to one's taste, have no time for, have no stomach for, not go for; *take a dislike to*, turn one's nose up at, not take kindly to; *shrink from*, shudder at, detest, abhor, loathe, can't abide/bear/stand; *displease*, antagonize, go against the grain, rub up the wrong way, put off, repel, disgust, make one's gorge rise.

759 WONDER

See also **451** (surprise).

n. *wonder*, wonderment, amazement, shock, astonishment, awe, fascination, stupefaction, bewilderment, bafflement, incredulity; *sensation*, drama, miracle, marvel, prodigy, phenomenon, seven wonders of the world; *oddity*, curiosity, rarity, freak, monster, monstrosity; *wizard*, miracle-worker, genius, child prodigy.

adj. *wondrous*, amazing, astonishing, astounding, remarkable, mind-boggling, breathtaking, stupefying, bewildering, baffling, unbelievable, out of this world; *sensational*, dramatic, miraculous, prodigious, phenomenal, extraordinary, unparalleled, monstrous, stupendous, fantastic, wonderful, fabulous, tremendous; *odd*, curious, strange, rare, freaky, freakish, weird, mysterious; *amazed*, astonished, astounded, rapt, spellbound, dumbfounded, struck dumb, speechless, open-mouthed, bewildered, stupefied, flabbergasted, bowled over, thunderstruck, transfixed.

vb. *wonder*, marvel, gasp, whistle, not get over; *stare*, gape, gaze, goggle, gawk, gawp, not believe one's eyes, rub one's eyes; *amaze*, astonish, astound; *bowl over*, stagger, take one's breath away, flabbergast, overwhelm, dumbfound; *confound*, baffle, bewilder.

760 LACK OF WONDER

See also **733** (impassivity); **756** (indifference).

n. *lack of wonder/astonishment*, etc., composure, blankness, impassivity; *expectation*, what one expected, just as one thought, nothing to write home about, nothing new under the sun, old hat (*colloq.*).

adj. *unsurprised*, unimpressed, unmoved, unperturbed; *expected*, foreseen, accustomed, common, usual.

vb. *not wonder*, not be surprised, see nothing remarkable, take in one's stride, not bat an eyelid, have seen it all before; *expect*, assume, take for granted, take as read.

761 RECREATION

See also **165** (habitat); **236** (land travel); **237** (water travel); **555** (pursuit); **612** (leisure).

n. *recreation*, amusement, pleasure, fun, leisure, spare time, diversion, relaxation, rest, (activity) holiday; *activity*, interest, pastime, hobby, pursuit, sport, game, play; *entertainment*, theatre, television, video, radio, music, opera, musical; *festival*, fiesta, carnival,

gala; *fair*, funfair, circus; *party*, house-warming party, bottle party, picnic, barbecue, street party, dinner, banquet, feast; *outing*, trip, day trip, excursion, jaunt; *camping*, pony-trekking, hiking, orienteering, mountaineering, rock-climbing; *athletics*, running, jogging, keep-fit, aerobics, cycling; *swimming*, diving, boating, rowing, sculling, canoeing, sailing, yachting, windsurfing, waterskiing, surfing; *skiing*, ski-jumping, tobogganning, skating, ice hockey; *flying*, gliding, parachuting, skydiving, parascending, hang-gliding; *equestrianism*, horseracing, showjumping, steeplechasing, dressage; *football*, soccer, rugby (football), volleyball, cricket, baseball, tennis, squash (rackets), badminton, golf, hockey, lacrosse, polo, croquet, snooker, billiards; *party game*, musical chairs, sardines, charades; *hopscotch*, leapfrog, hide-and-seek; *crossword*, jigsaw (puzzle), noughts and crosses, Rubik's cube, solitaire, video game; *chess*, draughts, checkers, backgammon, mah jong, ludo, snakes and ladders, Monopoly, Scrabble; *card game*, bridge, rummy, canasta, patience, whist, snap, pontoon, brag, poker; *roulette*, dice, bingo, tombola; *dancing*, ballet, folk/tap/morris/ballroom/old-time dancing; *waltz*, polka, mazurka, cancan, quickstep, foxtrot, flamenco, Charleston, cha-cha, conga, rumba, samba, jive, rock 'n' roll, twist, disco, breakdancing; *toy*, plaything, ball, balloon, rattle, bricks, marbles, water pistol, popgun, airgun, toy soldier; *doll*, teddy bear, golliwog, action man; *bicycle*, tricycle, fairy cycle, roller skates, skateboard, pedal car; *model railway*, train set, model, Meccano, Lego; *blood sport*, hunt, meet, fox-hunting, coursing, beagling, falconry, angling, fishing; *park*, gardens, playing field, recreation ground; *pitch*, ground, court, field, green, course; *theatre*, opera house, concert hall, dance hall, discotheque, night club, casino, bingo hall; *player*, sportsman, sportswoman, champion, grandmaster.

adj. *recreational*, sporting, sporty; *festive*, out to enjoy oneself, jovial, jolly;

amusing, entertaining, diverting, pleasant, enjoyable.

vb. *amuse*, entertain, divert, delight, cheer, make one laugh, tickle; *relax*, have fun, pursue, enjoy oneself, go on holiday; *have fun*, give/throw a party, have a good time, go out, celebrate, picnic, go dancing, let off steam (*colloq.*), paint the town red (*colloq.*), have a ball (*colloq.*); *camp*, climb, hike, ramble; *play games*, do sport, gamble, run, jump, jog, cycle, swim, dive, sail, ski, toboggan, skate; *hunt*, shoot, ride to hounds, course, fish, go fishing.

762 BOREDOM

See also **745** (seriousness).

n. *boredom*, tedium, monotony, sameness; *dreariness*, drabness, deadliness, dullness, banality; *stodginess*, flatness, colourlessness, heaviness, slowness; *weariness*, world-weariness, languor, ennui, time to kill; *bore*, bind, chore, grind, treadmill, daily round, drag (*colloq.*); *pub bore*, buttonholer, pain in the neck (*colloq.*).

adj. *boring*, tedious, monotonous, uneventful, repetitive, repetitious, same; *dreary*, drab, deadly, dull, unexciting, uninteresting, unfunny, unimaginative; *stodgy*, flat, colourless, heavy, ponderous, slow, turgid; *plain*, prosaic, mundane, humdrum, banal, commonplace, trite, pedestrian; *long-winded*, wordy, verbose, prolix; *wearisome*, tiresome, irksome; *bored*, at a loose end, twiddling one's thumbs; *sick of*, fed up to the back teeth; *weary*, world-weary, stale, cloyed, jaded.

vb. *bore stiff/rigid*, bore to tears/to death, go on and on, never vary; *weary*, try, irk; *pall*, cloy, jade, lose its novelty.

763 BEAUTY

See also **218** (symmetry); **511** (elegance); **765** (beautification).

n. *beauty*, pulchritude, loveliness, comeliness, prettiness, good looks, handsomeness, fairness, attractiveness, shapeliness; *glamour*, sex appeal, vital statistics, attractions; *grace*, charm,

elegance, chic; *grandeur*, magnificence, splendour, resplendence, radiance, brilliance, glory; *thing of beauty*, masterpiece, work of art, showpiece; *beauty spot*, view, landscape, seascape; *idol*, vision, dream, knockout, picture, fine figure of a man/woman, cheesecake (*colloq.*), beefcake (*colloq.*); *belle*, beauty queen, Venus, pin-up, stunner (*colloq.*), cracker (*colloq.*), dolly bird (*colloq.*), peach (*colloq.*), dish (*colloq.*), sight for sore eyes, dreamboat (*colloq.*), heartthrob (*colloq.*).

adj. *beautiful*, lovely, attractive, comely, fair; *pretty*, bonny, sweet, pretty as a picture; *good-looking*, handsome, husky, tall, dark, and handsome; *glamorous*, alluring, stunning, dishy (*colloq.*); *shapely*, well-formed, curvaceous, rounded, slim, slinky; *neat*, trim, well-kept, spruce, smart, natty, dapper; *graceful*, charming, exquisite, stylish, elegant, chic; *grand*, magnificent, splendid, resplendent, gracious, radiant, ravishing, gorgeous, brilliant, dazzling, glorious; *picturesque*, scenic, eye-catching.

764 UGLINESS

See also **219** (distortion); **512** (inelegance); **767** (blemish).

n. *ugliness*, hideousness, unsightliness, repulsiveness; *inelegance*, gracelessness, clumsiness; *deformity*, distortion, mutilation, defacement, disfigurement; *eyesore*, sight, fright (*colloq.*), blot on the landscape, horror, mess; *ugly duckling*, witch, scarecrow, no oil painting, plain Jane.

adj. *ugly*, hideous, unsightly, nasty, grotty (*colloq.*); *plain*, ill-favoured, frumpy, mousy; *repulsive*, horrible, ghastly, frightful, monstrous, loathsome, offensive; *deformed*, distorted, malformed, mutilated, defaced, disfigured, grotesque, misshapen; *unbecoming*, inelegant, graceless, unprepossessing, garish, gaudy; *coarse*, ungainly, cumbersome, clumsy, ill-fitting.

vb. *look a fright*, pull a face; *disfigure*, deface, mar, mutilate, distort.

765 BEAUTIFICATION

See also **510** (ornament); **763** (beauty); **766** (decoration).

n. *beautification*, face-lift, plastic surgery, skin graft, nose job (*colloq.*); *beauty treatment*, face mask, facial, manicure, pedicure; *tanning*, sun tan, sun bed, solarium; *grooming*, wash and brush-up; *hairdressing*, hair cut, trim, shave, styling, coiffure, hairdo; *short back and sides*, crewcut, pageboy, bouffant, Afro, Mohican, fringe, curls, ringlets, plait, pigtail, ponytail, bun; *shampoo and set*, perm, blow-dry, highlights, streaks; *beard*, goatee, imperial, moustache, toothbrush moustache, soup-strainer, handlebar moustache, muttonchops, sideboards, sideburns; *wig*, toupee, hairpiece, false eyelashes; *hairbrush*, comb, curlers, rollers, curling tongs, hairpin, hairgrip, kirby grip, slide, hairnet, hair dryer; *razor*, shaver, depilatory; *shampoo*, rinse, dye, henna, conditioner, hair spray, hair lacquer, hair cream; *make-up*, cosmetic, lipstick, lip gloss, eye shadow, eyeliner, mascara, rouge, blusher, foundation, moisturizer, face powder; *nail scissors*, nail clippers, nail file, nail polish; *beautician*, plastic surgeon, make-up artist, visagist, manicurist; *hairdresser*, barber, coiffeur, coiffeuse, stylist.

vb. *beautify*, prettify, improve the appearance of, dress up, primp, smarten, preen, groom, make up, titivate, doll up (*colloq.*), tart up (*colloq.*).

766 DECORATION

See also **510** (ornament); **765** (beautification).

n. *decoration*, adornment, ornamentation, embellishment, enrichment, finery; *interior decoration*, paint, wallpaper, furnishings; *flower arranging*, floral display, bouquet, posy, buttonhole, garland, wreath; *pattern*, design, detail, motif, tracery, scrollwork, check, pinstripe, herringbone, hound's tooth, polka dot, paisley; *needlework*, embroidery, tapestry, appliqué, smocking, broderie anglaise; *crochet*, lace, tatting, macramé, knitting; *trimming*,

frill, fringe, tassel, braid, bead, bow, bobble, ribbon, sequin, diamante; *jewellery*, bracelet, bangle, ring, engagement/wedding ring, signet ring, necklace, pendant, locket, charm, crucifix, earring, tiara, clasp, brooch, cameo, medallion; *jewel*, gem, precious stone, diamond, ruby, pearl, opal, sapphire, turquoise, emerald, beryl, garnet, amethyst, topaz, agate, onyx, coral, jet, mother of pearl, moonstone, lapis lazuli.

adj. *decorative*, ornamental, just for show, cosmetic; *ornate*, fancy, elaborate, intricate; *gaudy*, garish, florid; *decorated*, adorned, ornamented, embellished, patterned, inlaid, enamelled, engraved, tooled, embossed, studded; *worked*, embroidered, trimmed; *festooned*, garlanded, wreathed, hung; *bejewelled*, decked out, dressed to kill, sporting.

vb. *decorate*, ornament, adorn, embellish, enrich, enhance, set off, pick out, smarten up; *bedeck*, deck out, hang, trim, festoon; *paint*, wallpaper, varnish, whitewash, grain, lacquer; *embroider*, work, crochet; *inlay*, enamel, engrave, tool, emboss, gild.

767 BLEMISH

See also **219** (distortion); **585** (imperfection); **764** (ugliness).

n. *blemish*, flaw, defect, imperfection; *smudge*, smear, blur, tarnish, rust; *mark*, spot, daub, stain, speck, blot, blotch; *crack*, chip, dent; *mole*, birthmark, strawberry mark, freckle; *wart*, carbuncle, pimple, acne.

adj. *blemished*, flawed, defective, impaired, imperfect, shop-soiled; *smudged*, blurred, tarnished, rusty; *marked*, stained, foxed, spotted; *cracked*, dented, pitted.

vb. *blemish*, flaw, spoil, impair, mar, sully, deface; *smudge*, smear, blur, tarnish, rust; *mark*, daub, stain, speck, blot; *crack*, dent, pit, chip.

768 REFINEMENT

See also **418** (discrimination); **791** (courtesy).

n. *refinement*, tastefulness, good taste,

discrimination, discernment, good judgment; *connoisseurship*, epicureanism, palate, nose, flair; *tact*, tactfulness, euphemism, civility, courtesy, delicacy; *grace*, polish, sophistication, breeding, urbanity, manners, etiquette, culture, savoir faire; *decency*, propriety, decorum, respectability; *connoisseur*, epicurean, gourmet, sophisticate, cognoscente, dilettante, amateur, aesthete, critic.

adj. *refined*, discriminating, discerning, fastidious, epicurean; *tasteful*, in good taste, appreciative, aesthetic, critical; *tactful*, delicate, civil, decorous, seemly, respectable; *graceful*, dignified, polished, sophisticated, well-bred, urbane.

vb. *have good taste*, discriminate, criticize; *appreciate*, value.

769 VULGARITY

See also 419 (lack of discrimination); 785 (showiness); 792 (discourtesy).

n. *vulgarity*, tastelessness, bad/poor taste; *gaudiness*, garishness, brashness, loudness, ostentation; *tactlessness*, uncivility, discourtesy, rudeness, crassness, boorishness, shamelessness; *artificiality*, pretension, shoddiness, kitsch; *indecency*, impropriety, indecorum, indelicacy, obscenity; *bad form*, no breeding, commonness, incorrectness; *snob*, nouveau riche, parvenu, social climber, rough diamond, cad, lout, yob (*colloq.*).

adj. *vulgar*, tasteless, in bad/poor taste, non-U, naff (*colloq.*); *gaudy*, garish, brash, loud, meretricious, ostentatious, flash (*colloq.*); *tactless*, uncivil, discourteous, rude, crass, boorish, caddish, loutish, yobbish (*colloq.*); *artificial*, pretentious, shoddy, cheap and nasty, kitschy; *indecent*, indecorous, indelicate, obscene, improper; *unpolished*, gauche, unpresentable, uncultured, unsophisticated, common.

770 FASHION

See also 72 (conformity); 502 (style).

n. *fashion*, style, mode, trend, vogue; *craze*, fad, rage, cult; *latest fashion*, latest, last word, dernier cri; *fashionableness*, stylishness, chic, elegance; *society*, fashionable society, high society, smart set, jet set, bright young things, beautiful people; *upper crust*, cream, crème de la crème; *man/woman about town*, jetsetter, leader of fashion, trendsetter, swinger, playboy, swell, dandy, toff, peacock, blood, blade, beau, debutante, deb, deb's delight (*colloq.*).

adj. *fashionable*, modish, trendy, in vogue, all the rage, à la mode, up to the minute, with it (*colloq.*), groovy (*colloq.*), swinging (*colloq.*), in (*colloq.*); *stylish*, elegant, chic, exquisite, well-dressed; *posh*, smart, classy, swish (*colloq.*); *flashy*, dashing, foppish, rakish, snazzy (*colloq.*).

vb. *become popular*, find favour, catch on; *follow the fashion*, jump on the bandwagon, move with the times, follow the crowd, keep up with the Joneses, move in the right circles, get with it (*colloq.*); *lead the fashion*, set trends.

771 AFFECTATION

See also 480 (deception); 783 (vanity).

n. *affectation*, pretentiousness, pretension; *pose*, airs, act, image, façade, front, show, bluff; *artificiality*, mannerism, sham, humbug, insincerity, put-on (*colloq.*); *boast*, boastfulness, ostentation, bragging, swanking, self-glorification; *bravado*, bluster, bombast, hot air, grandiloquence; *charlatan*, humbug, impostor, bluffer, poser, poseur; *boaster*, braggart, big-mouth (*colloq.*), show-off.

adj. *affected*, pretentious, studied, mannered, contrived, stilted; *posing*, posturing, attitudinizing, for effect, ostentatious, poncy (*colloq.*); *superficial*, insincere, hypocritical, hollow, empty; *artificial*, sham, phoney, tongue-in-cheek; *self-righteous*, sanctimonious, mealy-mouthed, prim, stuck up, snobbish; *boastful*, big-mouthed (*colloq.*), loud-mouthed; *bombastic*, blustering, grandiloquent.

vb. *affect*, pretend, put on; *pose*, posture, attitudinize, put on airs, ponce around (*colloq.*); *fake*, sham, feign, make a show of, bluff; *overact*, ham it up, camp it up; *boast*, brag, vaunt, show off, swank, strut; *bluster*, rant.

772 RIDICULOUSNESS
See also **443** (nonsense); **744** (humour).

n. *ridiculousness*, ludicrousness, laughableness, risibility, absurdity; *extravagance*, exaggeration, caricature; *mimicry*, parody, travesty; *paradox*, catch-22 situation; *buffoonery*, fooling about/around, tomfoolery, horseplay, clowning; *escapade*, monkey tricks, nonsense, scrape.

adj. *ridiculous*, ludicrous, laughable, risible, farcical, mad, daft, silly; *absurd*, grotesque, bizarre, outlandish; *monstrous*, preposterous, outrageous; *contemptible*, derisory; *extravagant*, exaggerated, over the top (*colloq.*); *paradoxical*; *tomfool*, asinine, idiotic.

vb. *go from the sublime to the ridiculous*; *play the fool*, fool/lark about/around, clown, be a laughing stock, make an exhibition of oneself, go way over the top (*colloq.*); *caricature*, mimic, parody, make a fool of.

773 DERISION
See also **772** (ridiculousness); **824** (disrespect).

n. *derision*, ridicule, mockery, scoffing, scorn; *teasing*, ribbing, leg-pulling, ragging, banter; *snigger*, titter, smirk; *irony*, sarcasm, caricature, parody, lampoon, burlesque, spoof, send-up, take-off; *butt*, figure of fun, laughing stock, fair game; *stooge*, straight man, foil.

adj. *derisive*, mocking, scoffing, scornful; *ironic*, sarcastic, satirical.

vb. *deride*, ridicule, mock, scoff, scorn, jeer; *make fun of*, poke fun at, tease, rib, chaff, rag, twit; *snigger*, titter, smirk; *fool*, kid, pull someone's leg, take the mickey out of, have on (*colloq.*); *caricature*, satirize, lampoon, pillory, send up; *deflate*, debunk, puncture.

774 REPUTE
See also **650** (trophy); **778** (title); **823** (respect); **831** (probity).

n. *repute*, reputation, good standing, good name; *regard*, esteem, admiration, estimation; *favour*, good odour, popularity; *prestige*, glory, acclaim, honour, kudos, cachet, dignity, illustriousness; *eminence*, prominence, distinction, position, status; *renown*, fame, celebrity; *reliability*, respectability, trustworthiness, dependability; *worthy*, somebody, dignitary, pillar of society, doyen, leading light, celebrity, star, luminary, grand old man.

adj. *reputable*, of good repute, estimable, worthy, meritorious, admirable; *esteemed*, highly regarded, well thought of, highly acclaimed, celebrated, of note; *reliable*, trustworthy, dependable; *famous*, renowned, celebrated; *in favour*, popular; *illustrious*, eminent, prominent, distinguished, of distinction, leading, ranking, prestigious, august; *grand*, imposing, dignified, majestic, royal, regal, princely, lordly, superior, noble, aristocratic.

vb. *have a reputation*, have one's position to consider, command respect, be looked up to, go down in history; *gain a reputation*, do oneself credit, win one's spurs, gain recognition, make one's mark; *rank*, excel, shine, star; *outshine*, overshadow, eclipse; *respect*, pay respect to, regard, esteem, honour, look up to, admire; *praise*, acclaim, glorify, lionize, revere, put on a pedestal; *prize*, value, treasure; *reward*, crown, enthrone, ennoble, elevate to the peerage; *beatify*, canonize, deify, worship.

775 DISREPUTE
See also **824** (disrespect); **832** (improbity).

n. *disrepute*, ill repute, bad name, discredit; *notoriety*, infamy; *disfavour*, unpopularity, bad odour; *unreliability*, untrustworthiness; *disparagement*, slur, slight; *opprobrium*, disgrace, humiliation, shame, dishonour, ignominy, obloquy; *smear*, stain, tarnish, blot, slur; *scandal*, calumny, gossip, slander, defamation, libel.

adj. *disreputable*, shady, shifty; *notorious*, infamous; *unreliable*, untrustworthy; *questionable*, dubious, doubtful; *humiliating*, degrading, infra dig; *despised*, held in contempt; *despicable*, mean, base; *inglorious*, shameful, dishonourable, ignominious, disgraceful; *disgraced*, humiliated; *shabby*, squalid, scruffy; *obscure*, unknown, unheard-of.

vb. *bring into disrepute*, take away one's good name, disparage, tarnish, smear, cast aspersions on, blot, sully, mar, taint, blemish, dishonour, bring shame upon, disgrace, discredit, put to shame, expose, cut down to size (*colloq.*), take down a peg (*colloq.*); *fall into disrepute*, disgrace oneself, get a bad name, blot one's copybook, lose one's reputation, come down in the world, lose face; *stoop*, lower oneself, demean oneself, degrade oneself.

776 ARISTOCRAT

n. *aristocrat*, nobleman, noblewoman, noble, titled person, noble lord/lady, peer, peeress, peer of the realm, hereditary peer, life peer; *lords temporal*, duke, archduke, duchess, marquis, marquess, marchioness, earl, count, countess, viscount, viscountess, baron, baroness, baronet, dowager; *lords spiritual*, archbishop, bishop; *knight*, dame, don, squire, laird, Junker, boyar, grandee, patrician, grande dame; *king*, queen, prince, princess, monarch, sovereign, emperor, tsar, sultan, rajah, nawab, nabob, sheikh, emir, bey, khan; *aristocracy*, nobility, gentry, landed gentry, peerage, elite, privileged class, ruling class, establishment, high society, upper classes, upper crust (*colloq.*), toff (*colloq.*), nob (*colloq.*), Sloane Ranger, hooray Henry; *royalty*, court; *nobility*, high birth, blue blood, descent, ancestry, family, house, dynasty, caste, pedigree; *rank*, distinction, position, station, majesty, prerogative, privilege.

adj. *aristocratic*, noble, titled, in Burke's Peerage, ducal, baronial; *of*

high birth, well-born, blue-blooded, of good family, patrician; *royal*, regal, monarchical, majestic, kingly, queenly, princely, of royal blood; *upper-class*, respectable, top-drawer (*colloq.*), double-barrelled, posh, county, U.

777 COMMONER

n. *commoner*, pleb, plebeian, citizen; *ordinary person*, Joe Bloggs, John Doe, man in the street, man on the Clapham omnibus, common man; *worker*, housewife, blue-collar worker, white-collar worker; *nobody*, nonentity; *peasant*, yeoman, villein, serf, yokel, country bumpkin, country cousin; *tramp*, down-and-out, vagabond, bum, hobo, vagrant, outcast, untouchable; *commonality*, commons, bourgeoisie, citizenry, the people, populace, community, general public, the masses, the rank and file, hoi polloi, proletariat, Tom, Dick, and Harry; *rabble*, herd, mob, riffraff, scum, dregs of society, the great unwashed (*colloq.*); *middle class*, bourgeoisie, salaried classes, professional classes, yuppies (*colloq.*), intelligentsia; *lower classes*, working class, lower orders, have-nots, underdogs, poor whites, the underprivileged; *underworld*, demi-monde.

adj. *common*, average, ordinary; *working-class*, plebeian, proletarian; *middle-class*, (petit) bourgeois, upwardly mobile, suburban, provincial, gentrified; *lowly*, obscure, humble, mean, low, base.

778 TITLE

See also 774 (repute).

n. *title*, honorific, courtesy title, designation, handle (*colloq.*); *Majesty*, Royal Highness, Excellency, Grace, Lordship, Ladyship, my lord, my lady, Honourable, Right Honourable, Sir, Lady, Honour, Worship, Worshipful, Reverence; *Reverend*, Very Reverend, Right Reverend, Most Reverend, Monsignor, Holiness, padre; *Brother*, Sister, Reverend Father, Reverend Mother; *sir*, madam, ma'am, mister, Mr, mistress, Mrs, Miss, Ms; *monsieur*, madame, mademoiselle; *Herr*,

779 PRIDE

Frau, Fräulein; *señor*, *señora*, *señorita*; *signore*, signora, signorina; *sahib*, memsahib, bwana, effendi; *comrade*, brother, sister, tovarisch; *academic title*, bachelor, master, doctor, professor.

779 PRIDE
See also **783** (vanity).

n. *pride*, self-esteem, self-respect, self-regard, dignity, reputation; *haughtiness*, condescension, disdain, arrogance, insolence; *snobbery*, conceit, vainglory, self-glorification, big-headedness; *proud person*, snob, swank, prima donna, his nibs, Lord/Lady Muck.

adj. *proud*, self-respecting, house-proud; *lofty*, dignified, commanding, stately; *haughty*, condescending, patronizing, high-and-mighty; *disdainful*, arrogant, overbearing; *conceited*, vainglorious, big-headed, swollen-headed, strutting; *snobbish*, toffee-nosed (*colloq.*), stuck-up (*colloq.*), uppity (*colloq.*).

vb. *be proud*, etc., have one's pride, hold one's head high, stand erect, take pride in, pride oneself on; *be too proud*, give oneself airs, strut, be up on one's high horse; *disdain*, despise, condescend, patronize.

780 HUMILITY
See also **577** (unimportance); **782** (servility); **784** (modesty).

n. *humility*, humbleness, meekness, resignation; *self-abasement*, self-effacement, modesty, unpretentiousness; *lowliness*, inoffensiveness; *servility*, submissiveness, subservience, obedience.

adj. *humble*, meek, resigned; *self-abasing*, self-effacing, modest, unpretentious, unassuming; *lowly*, inoffensive, harmless; *servile*, submissive, subservient, obedient.

vb. *humble oneself*, resign oneself, turn the other cheek; *condescend*, deign, stoop, lower oneself, demean oneself; *submit*, crawl, eat humble pie, knuckle under.

781 INSOLENCE
See also **824** (disrespect).

n. *insolence*, effrontery, impudence, impertinence, rudeness, incivility; *nerve*, cheek (*colloq.*), gall, neck (*colloq.*), sauce (*colloq.*), lip (*colloq.*); *audacity*, temerity, boldness; *shamelessness*, blatancy, brazenness; *arrogance*, presumption; *disdain*, contempt; *upstart*, young pup (*colloq.*), whippersnapper, smart aleck, cheeky devil (*colloq.*).

adj. *insolent*, impudent, impertinent, rude, uncivil, impolite, offensive; *cheeky*, fresh, offhand, flippant, pert, familiar, cocky (*colloq.*), cocksure; *audacious*, bold, defiant; *shameless*, blatant, brazen; *arrogant*, presumptuous; *disdainful*, contemptuous, high-handed, imperious, snotty (*colloq.*).

vb. *get fresh*, have the cheek/nerve to, make bold to, make free with; *answer back*, cheek (*colloq.*); *get above oneself*, step out of line, presume, lord it, come the high and mighty with (*colloq.*); *express contempt*, snort, cock a snook, snap one's fingers at, give a V-sign.

782 SERVILITY
See also **642** (submission); **780** (humility).

n. *servility*, deference, compliance, subservience; *timeserving*, ingratiation, sycophancy, obsequiousness, fawning, crawling, bowing and scraping, boot-licking, arse-licking (*vulg.*), brown-nosing (*vulg.*); *sycophant*, toady, time-server, Uriah Heep, crawler, bootlicker, arse-licker (*vulg.*), yes-man, smoothie (*colloq.*), lapdog.

adj. *servile*, deferential, compliant, subservient; under the thumb (*colloq.*); *timeserving*, ingratiating, sycophantic, obsequious, smarmy (*colloq.*); *fawning*, crawling, whining, grovelling.

vb. *toady*, ingratiate oneself, fawn, crawl, grovel, curry favour, lick the boots of, suck up to (*colloq.*), lick the arse of (*vulg.*), brown-nose (*vulg.*); *comply*, kowtow, defer, tug one's forelock; *fetch and carry for*, stooge, pander to.

783 VANITY

See also **431** (overestimation); **771** (affectation); **779** (pride).

n. *vanity*, immodesty, conceit, self-importance, egotism, megalomania; *self-congratulation*, self-glorification, smugness, superciliousness, arrogance; *narcissism*, self-worship, self-love; *boastfulness*, boasting, showing off, exhibitionism; *egotist*, show-off, exhibitionist, peacock, Narcissus, God's gift to women (*colloq.*).

adj. *vain*, immodest, conceited, self-important, egotistical, megalomaniac; *self-satisfied*, complacent, smug, supercilious, arrogant, stuck-up (*colloq.*); *narcissistic*, full of oneself; *dogmatic*, opinionated; *cocky*, bumptious, pretentious, pompous, swollen-headed, big-headed, too big for one's boots (*colloq.*).

vb. *have a high opinion of oneself*, think a lot of oneself, be puffed up, think one knows it all, fish for compliments; *get above oneself*, get too big for one's boots (*colloq.*); *show off*, strut, put on airs, talk big, blow one's own trumpet; *go to one's head*, turn one's head.

784 MODESTY

See also **432** (underestimation); **780** (humility).

n. *modesty*, unpretentiousness, unassuming nature, unobtrusiveness, meekness, reserve, restraint; *shyness*, diffidence, timidity, bashfulness, reticence, reluctance; *prudishness*, demureness, coyness, inhibition; *chastity*, virtue; *mouse*, shrinking violet, doormat (*colloq.*).

adj. *modest*, unpretentious, unassuming, unobtrusive; *unassertive*, low-key, unimposing, unimpressive; *meek*, reserved, restrained, self-effacing; *shy*, diffident, timid, retiring, bashful, reticent, sheepish, reluctant, backward in coming forward (*colloq.*), wet (*colloq.*); *prudish*, blushing, demure, coy, inhibited; *chaste*, virtuous.

vb. *be modest*, efface oneself, hide one's light under a bushel, take a back seat, keep a low profile, keep in the background, play second fiddle, shun the limelight; *hang back*, hesitate, shrink, crawl into one's shell; *blush*, colour, flush, go red.

785 SHOWINESS

See also **464** (display); **769** (vulgarity).

n. *showiness*, ostentation, ostentatiousness, blatancy, flagrancy, exhibitionism, showmanship; *flashiness*, gaudiness, glitter, tinsel, garishness, flamboyance; *effect*, window-dressing, show; *splendour*, grandeur, magnificence, brilliance; *pomp*, majesty, pageantry, parade, spectacle; *pomposity*, extravagance, bombast, rhetoric; *dramatics*, histrionics, theatre, theatricality, sensationalism; *heroics*, bravado, stunt; *showman*, exhibitionist.

adj. *showy*, ostentatious, blatant, flagrant, shameless; *painted*, glorified, tarted up (*colloq.*); *flashy*, gaudy, glittering, garish, loud, flamboyant, lurid, conspicuous; *pompous*, extravagant, bombastic, pretentious; *splendid*, grandiose, magnificent, brilliant, splendiferous (*colloq.*); *sumptuous*, de luxe; *dramatic*, histrionic, spectacular, theatrical, stagy, for show, done for effect, cosmetic.

vb. *do for show*, do for effect, put on a show, flaunt, flourish, parade; *splurge*, make a splash, pull out all the stops; *play to the gallery*, show off, take the centre of the stage, upstage, grab the limelight, make an exhibition of oneself; *give oneself airs*, swank.

786 CELEBRATION

See also **746** (rejoicing).

n. *celebration*, festivity, festivities, festive occasion, fête, ceremony, function, occasion, party, beanfeast (*colloq.*), do (*colloq.*); *honouring*, keeping, commemoration, remembrance, observance, ceremonial, solemnization, performance, ritual; *coronation*, enthronement, installation, induction, inauguration; *anniversary*, jubilee, birthday, red-letter day, centenary; *salute*, drum roll, fanfare, fireworks; *cheering*, clapping, ovation, flag-waving, tribute, appreciation;

hero's welcome, red carpet, reception committee, ticker-tape parade; *congratulation(s)*, felicitation(s), toast, compliments, many happy returns, best wishes.

adj. *celebratory*, festive, commemorative, ceremonial; *anniversary*, centennial; *congratulatory*, welcoming, complimentary.

vb. *celebrate*, honour, keep, commemorate, remember, observe, mark; *solemnize*, perform; *crown*, enthrone, install, induct, inaugurate; *come out*, pass out, graduate; *welcome*, salute, fête, chair, lionize, garland; *cheer*, clap; *praise*, pay tribute to, sing the praises of; *throw a party*, kill the fatted calf, roll out the red carpet, hang out the flags; *congratulate*, toast, felicitate, raise one's glass to, drink to the health of.

787 FORMALITY

See also **791** (courtesy); **881** (ritual).

n. *formality*, ceremoniousness, stiffness, dignity, solemnity, etiquette, correct behaviour, the thing to do, protocol, form, ceremony; *ceremonial*, procedure, ritual, drill, practice, routine; *dress*, formal dress, black tie, regalia, formal attire, morning dress, evening dress, dinner jacket, lounge suit, long dress, best bib and tucker, Sunday best.

adj. *formal*, ceremonial, ceremonious, stiff, dignified, solemn, stately; *correct*, precise, punctilious, ritual, procedural.

vb. *observe the formalities*, stand on ceremony, do things by the book.

788 INFORMALITY

n. *informality*, lack of formality, lack of ceremony; *freedom*, licence, indulgence, toleration; *nonobservance*, nonadherence, breach of etiquette, bad form, gaffe; *casual dress*, shirtsleeves, mufti, civvies.

adj. *informal*, unconstrained, relaxed, unstuffy, unceremonious, casual; *unconventional*, lax, loose, tolerant, easy, free and easy.

vb. *not insist*, waive the rules, relax, show no respect for.

789 SOCIABILITY

See also **85** (accompaniment); **793** (friendship).

n. *sociability*, sociableness, gregariousness, friendliness, affability, cordiality, conviviality, geniality, heartiness, bonhomie; *compatibility*, togetherness, companionship, comradeship; *party*, social gathering, get-together, meeting, social, soirée, at home, reception, reunion, visit, date; *dinner party*, banquet, feast, bunfight, beano (*colloq.*), barbecue, picnic; *drinks party*, cocktail party, bottle party, wine-and-cheese party, coffee morning, tea party; *dance*, ball, disco, hop, knees-up (*colloq.*); *visitor*, caller, habitué, guest; *good companion*, good neighbour, good mixer, life and soul of the party; *host*, hostess, master of ceremonies; *gatecrasher*, unwelcome guest, freeloader.

adj. *sociable*, social, gregarious, clubbable, friendly, pally (*colloq.*), affable; *cordial*, convivial, genial, smiling, welcoming; *hospitable*, neighbourly; *compatible*, companionable, comradely; *extrovert*, outgoing, hearty.

vb. *like company*, make friends easily, mix well, get along/on well with; *invite*, entertain, host, throw a party, keep open house; *visit*, call on, drop in on; *go out*, get together, party, go nightclubbing; *gatecrash*, arrive uninvited.

790 UNSOCIABILITY

See also **41** (separation); **52** (exclusion).

n. *unsociability*, standoffishness, aloofness, unapproachability; *unfriendliness*, coolness; *introversion*, shyness; *uncommunicativeness*, reticence, taciturnity; *distance*, withdrawal, isolation, separation, retreat; *loneliness*, solitude, seclusion, retirement; *confinement*, quarantine, purdah; *exile*, banishment, deportation, expulsion, excommunication; *apartheid*, segregation; *ghetto*, enclave, reserve, reservation, homeland, bantustan, concentration camp, prison; *cloister*, ivory tower, desert island, den; *hermit*, loner, isolationist, recluse, stay-at-home, monk; *leper*, pariah, outsider, untouchable; *cast-away*, outcast, deportee, outlaw, displaced person, refugee, evacuee.

adj. *unsociable*, standoffish, distant, aloof, unapproachable, antisocial; *unfriendly*, cool, unneighbourly, unwelcoming; *uncommunicative*, reticent, taciturn, unforthcoming; *introverted*, shy, withdrawn, retiring, stay-at-home; *lonely*, friendless, desolate, solitary, unpopular; *secluded*, off the beaten track, isolated, out of the way, remote, deserted, cloistered.

vb. *keep oneself to oneself*, shun company, stay at home, shut oneself up, retire, take the veil; *cut dead*, cold-shoulder, ignore, snub, rebuff; *confine*, isolate, imprison, quarantine, segregate; *exclude*, blackball, expel, exile, outlaw, excommunicate, ostracize, send to Coventry.

791 COURTESY
See also **787** (formality); **823** (respect).

n. *courtesy*, politeness, good manners, civility, graciousness; *thoughtfulness*, consideration, generosity, decency, tact, discretion; *friendliness*, kindness, kindliness, amiability; *respect*, deference, obeisance; *chivalry*, gallantry, courtliness; *etiquette*, protocol, custom, convention; *culture*, breeding, gentility, correctness, refinement, urbanity, diplomacy; *condescension*, sycophancy, flattery, ingratiation; *act of courtesy*, salutation, salute, greeting, handshake, kiss, hug, embrace, smile, wave; *bow*, nod, curtsy; *presentation*, introduction, welcome, invitation, reception, compliment, acknowledgment, toast; *favour*, good turn.

adj. *courteous*, polite, civil, gracious, good-mannered, well-behaved, on one's best behaviour; *thoughtful*, considerate, generous, decent, tactful, discreet; *friendly*, kind, kindly, obliging, amiable; *respectful*, deferential; *chivalrous*, gallant, courtly; *cultured*, cultivated, well-bred, genteel, correct, refined, urbane, diplomatic, gentlemanly, ladylike; *condescending*, sycophantic, flattering, ingratiating.

vb. *behave oneself / well / properly*, oblige, mind one's P's and Q's, mind one's manners, not give offence; *salute*, greet, hail, raise one's hat, touch one's cap, present arms; *shake hands*, kiss, hug, embrace, smile, wave; *show respect*, bow, nod, curtsy, kiss hands; *present*, introduce, welcome, invite, receive, compliment, acknowledge, drink to, toast.

792 DISCOURTESY
See also **769** (vulgarity); **824** (disrespect).

n. *discourtesy*, impoliteness, bad manners, incivility; *rudeness*, disrespect, insolence, impudence, cheek; *act of discourtesy*, rebuff, insult, snub, abuse, rude word, rude gesture; *vulgarity*, boorishness, lack of refinement, ill breeding, coarseness; *rude person*, boor, lout, brute, yob (*colloq.*), yahoo; *unfriendliness*, brusqueness, unpleasantness, nastiness; *thoughtlessness*, lack of consideration, inattention; *misconduct*, bad behaviour.

adj. *discourteous*, impolite, bad-mannered, uncivil, unmannerly, ungracious; *rude*, disrespectful, insolent, impudent, saucy, cheeky, impertinent, obstreperous; *insulting*, abusive, offensive, crude; *vulgar*, coarse, boorish, unrefined, ill-bred, uncouth, uncultured, ungentlemanly; *brusque*, abrupt, gruff, curt, surly, churlish; *unfriendly*, unpleasant, nasty, unkind, disagreeable; *thoughtless*, tactless, inconsiderate, insensitive, cavalier, offhand.

vb. *be rude*, etc., insult, abuse, affront, outrage; *curse*, swear, damn; *snub*, ignore, cut dead, look right through, give the cold shoulder; *interrupt*, shout down; *frown*, scowl, pout.

793 FRIENDSHIP
See also **789** (sociability); **795** (love).

n. *friendship*, amity, comradeship, fraternity, fellowship, solidarity; *companionship*, togetherness, camaraderie, compatibility, intimacy, familiarity; *friendliness*, amicability, good terms, sociability, neighbourliness; *kindness*, hospitality, warmth, cordiality, sympathy, understanding; *act of friendship*, handshake, embrace, hug, kiss; *friend*, acquaintance, companion, comrade, crony, pal, mate, chum, buddy, girlfriend, boyfriend, best friend, bosom pal, intimate, confidant, classmate, roommate, playmate.

adj. *friendly*, amicable, sociable, affectionate, warm-hearted, well-meaning, kind, benevolent; *neighbourly*, brotherly, sisterly, fraternal; *intimate*, familiar, inseparable, close, pally (*colloq.*), matey (*colloq.*); *loyal*, faithful, staunch, trustworthy, true, devoted; *cordial*, congenial, hearty.

vb. *befriend*, make friends with, strike up an acquaintance, get to know; *be friendly*, keep company with, be in with (*colloq.*), go around with, be inseparable, be as thick as thieves; *court*, date, take out, go out with, make advances, woo; *be hospitable*, entertain, welcome, greet, embrace, introduce, present.

794 ENMITY

See also **796** (hate).

n. *enmity*, hostility, aggression, antagonism; *antipathy*, dislike, hatred, animosity; *ill feeling*, ill will, acrimony, bitterness, rancour, dissension; *alienation*, estrangement, separation, incompatibility; *hostile act*, conflict, hostilities, state of war, vendetta, feud; *enemy*, foe, traitor, antagonist, opponent, adversary, public enemy, arch enemy, aggressor, invader.

adj. *inimical*, hostile, antagonistic, aggressive; *unfriendly*, aloof, cool, chilly, cold, ill-disposed; *estranged*, irreconcilable, alienated, incompatible; *opposed*, at daggers drawn, at loggerheads, on bad terms; *rancorous*, bitter, acrimonious, grudging, resentful; *disloyal*, unfaithful, traitorous.

vb. *be hostile*, have one's hackles up, snap, snarl, growl; *oppose*, be opposed to, conflict, differ, be at odds with, clash, collide, be incompatible, be worlds apart; *antagonize*, provoke, estrange, alienate, make enemies; *fight*, battle, feud; *oppress*, persecute, hound.

795 LOVE

See also **757** (liking); **800** (endearment).

n. *love*, affection, fondness, attachment, devotion, true love; *adoration*, worship, admiration, fascination; *passion*, lust, desire, amorousness, rapture, ecstasy; *infatuation*, crush (*colloq.*), first love, calf love, puppy love; *Platonic love*, friendship, fellow feeling, sympathy; *predilection*, preference, fancy; *sentiment*, emotion, feeling; *romance*, love affair, relationship, amour, liaison, intrigue, flirtation; *lovableness*, charm, endearment, appeal, attractiveness, sex-appeal, coquetry; *love-making*, courtship, proposal, suit, gallantry; *lover*, flirt, philanderer, paramour, mistress, suitor, beau, escort; *boyfriend*, girlfriend, fiancé, fiancée, date, blind date, steady (*colloq.*), fella (*colloq.*), bird (*colloq.*); *admirer*, fan, aficionado, idol, hero, flame, heartthrob; *loved one*, soul mate, darling, intimate, sweetheart, valentine.

adj. *loving*, fond, affectionate, tender; *romantic*, sentimental, emotional; *devoted*, adoring, admiring; *passionate*, lustful, amorous, ardent; *infatuated*, besotted, crazy about, lovesick; *enamoured*, attracted, keen on, in love; *lovable*, endearing, adorable, lovely, appealing, attractive, seductive, desirable, captivating, enchanting; *beloved*, loved, cherished, adored, darling, pet; *erotic*, sexy, erogenous, amatory.

vb. *love*, like, be fond of, fancy, care for, be partial to, delight in; *cherish*, hold dear, treasure, prize, value, esteem; *adore*, worship, admire, revere; *be in love*, dote on, be crazy about, lose one's heart, be swept off one's feet, be infatuated, have a crush on; *desire*, long, yearn; *make love*, have intercourse, have sex, have it off (*colloq.*), sleep with, sleep together; *attract*, appeal, allure, bewitch, charm, enchant, captivate, fascinate, enrapture; *seduce*, woo, set one's cap at, flirt, philander; *rouse*, stir, excite, turn on (*colloq.*).

796 HATE

See also **758** (dislike); **794** (enmity).

n. *hate*, hatred, loathing, detestation, abhorrence; *repugnance*, revulsion, repulsion, disgust; *aversion*, antipathy, dislike, disfavour, odium; *animosity*, antagonism, hostility, ill feeling; *malevolence*, malice, spite, scorn, grudge; *phobia*, prejudice, bête noire, pet hate; *anathema*, abomination, menace, pest, bugbear.

adj. *hateful*, odious, detestable, obnoxious, loathsome, abhorrent, execrable, accursed, abominable; *repugnant*, revolting, repellent, disgusting, vile, nasty, horrid, beastly; *hostile*, antagonistic, averse, set against; *malicious*, malignant, malevolent, spiteful, vicious, vindictive, rancorous.

vb. *hate*, loathe, detest, abhor, abominate, recoil at; *reject*, spurn, refuse, object to, spit upon; *condemn*, denounce, execrate; *resent*, dislike, bear a grudge, have a down on, have it in for (*colloq.*); *antagonize*, alienate, estrange, set by the ears; *embitter*, poison, exacerbate, sour.

797 MARRIAGE

n. *marriage*, matrimony, conjugality, wedlock, union, alliance, match; *monogamy*, bigamy, polygamy, second marriage, open marriage, marriage of convenience, shotgun wedding, arranged marriage; *wedding*, nuptials, marriage ceremony, wedding service, civil marriage, church wedding, elopement; *reception*, wedding breakfast, marriage feast, honeymoon, anniversary; *bridal party*, best man, bridesmaid, matron of honour, page, attendant, usher; *married couple*, the happy couple, newlyweds, honeymooners, bridegroom, bride, spouse, partner, mate, husband, wife, better half (*colloq.*), trouble and strife (*colloq.*); old man, old lady, old dutch, common-law husband/wife; *matchmaker*, marriage bureau, lonely hearts column, computer dating.

adj. *matrimonial*, marital, conjugal, nuptial, connubial, premarital; *married*, wed, united, newlywed, engaged; *marriageable*, nubile, eligible, suitable.

vb. *marry*, wed, espouse, remarry, intermarry; *get married*, get spliced (*colloq.*), get hitched (*colloq.*), make an honest woman of (*colloq.*), become one, plight one's troth, say 'I do'; *join*, unite, pronounce man and wife; *give in marriage*, give away, marry off, matchmake; *honeymoon*, go away, elope, consummate; *marry well*, find a good match, marry into.

798 DIVORCE; WIDOWHOOD

n. *divorce*, annulment, dissolution of marriage, decree nisi, decree absolute, breakdown of marriage, broken marriage; *separation*, living apart, desertion; *divorce court*, maintenance, alimony, divorcee, corespondent, single parent, broken home; *widowhood*, widow, widower, survivor, relict, dowager, war widow, grass widow, golf widow.

adj. *divorced*, separated, on the rocks, living apart, widowed.

vb. *divorce*, get divorced, separate, split up; *leave*, walk out on, desert.

799 CELIBACY

n. *celibacy*, single state, bachelorhood, spinsterhood; *virginity*, maidenhood, chastity, purity; *celibate*, virgin, single person, bachelor, confirmed bachelor, misogynist, spinster, bachelor girl, old maid, maiden aunt; *monk*, nun, hermit, solitary.

adj. *celibate*, single, bachelor, unmarried, unwed, independent, free, unattached, eligible; *virginal*, chaste, pure, monastic, unconsummated.

vb. *be unmarried*, live alone, be on the shelf, take holy orders.

800 ENDEARMENT

See also **795** (love).

n. *endearment*, affection, fondness, attachment, love; *loving words*, blandishments, sweet nothings, flattery, compliments; *embrace*, hug, kiss, cuddle, stroke, caress, fondling, petting, necking (*colloq.*); *courtship*, suit, lovemaking, wooing, courting, dating; *flir-*

tation, familiarity, pass, advances, proposition; *love-letter*, valentine, proposal, offer of marriage, engagement; *darling*, dear, love, sweetheart, beloved, dearest, angel, pet, poppet, honey (*colloq.*), precious, treasure, jewel, duck (*colloq.*), chicken (*colloq.*), lamb (*colloq.*); *favourite*, teacher's pet, blue-eyed boy, apple of one's eye.

adj. *affectionate*, loving, sentimental, soppy (*colloq.*), lovey-dovey (*colloq.*).

vb. *cherish*, be fond of, love, coddle, cosset, pamper, pet, mother, spoil, spoonfeed, kill with kindness; *court*, woo, go out with, date, go steady, pursue, chase, make overtures; *make advances*, make passes, get fresh (*colloq.*), flirt, ogle, make eyes, leer, proposition; *hug*, embrace, cuddle, clasp, snuggle, nuzzle, kiss, neck (*colloq.*), snog (*colloq.*), smooch (*colloq.*), stroke, fondle, caress, pet; *trifle*, dally, toy, play fast and loose, philander; *propose*, pop the question (*colloq.*), get engaged.

801 CURSE

See also **806** (malevolence).

n. *curse*, malediction, evil eye, spell; *execration*, vilification, abuse, calumny, threat, vituperation, denunciation; *profanity*, oath, obscenity, swearword, four-letter word, expletive, imprecation, invective, bad language, billingsgate; *scurrility*, vulgarity, blasphemy, sacrilege, profanation.

adj. *maledictory*, vituperative, abusive; *scurrilous*, foul-mouthed, ribald, blue, indecent, obscene, vulgar, profane, blasphemous, sacrilegious; *cursed*, accursed, damned, execrable.

vb. *curse*, damn, condemn, wish ill, confound; *execrate*, fulminate, thunder against, inveigh against; *denounce*, abuse, call names, defame, vilify, vituperate, revile; *swear*, cuss, damn, blast, eff and blind (*colloq.*), swear like a trooper, blaspheme.

802 RESENTMENT; ANGER

n. *resentment*, bitterness, acrimony, rancour, spleen, gall; *displeasure*, ill humour, grudge, bone to pick, malice, animosity; *offence*, umbrage, hurt,

indignity, wrong, injustice, insult, affront; *anger*, rage, fury, passion, wrath, ire, vexation, indignation, exasperation, annoyance, irritation; *tantrum*, temper, tizzy (*colloq.*), paddy (*colloq.*), outburst, huff; *quarrel*, argument, tiff, fight; *frown*, scowl, glare, black look, snarl, growl.

adj. *resentful*, bitter, embittered, rancorous, acrimonious, smarting, hurt, sore; *grudging*, jealous, envious; *angry*, cross, irate, indignant, livid, furious, enraged, incensed, fuming, hopping mad (*colloq.*), beside oneself, up in arms; *irritated*, annoyed, peeved, vexed, exasperated, infuriated; *riled*, worked up, het up (*colloq.*), shirty (*colloq.*), ratty, hot under the collar (*colloq.*), impatient.

vb. *resent*, bear malice, bear a grudge, have a bone to pick; *take umbrage*, take offence, be insulted, take exception, take amiss; *get angry*, get cross, lose one's temper, lose one's rag (*colloq.*), go mad (*colloq.*), go spare (*colloq.*), see red, throw a tantrum, blow one's top (*colloq.*), hit the roof (*colloq.*), fly off the handle (*colloq.*), explode, go up the wall (*colloq.*), go off the deep end (*colloq.*); *be angry*, rage, fume, rant, roar, thunder, fulminate, seethe, boil, make a scene; *frown*, scowl, glare, glower, growl, snarl, snap, bite someone's head off (*colloq.*); *anger*, enrage, exasperate, madden, incense, infuriate, drive mad, make one's blood boil; *annoy*, irritate, upset, aggravate, needle, nettle, goad, rankle, rile, get on one's nerves, get one's dander up (*colloq.*), rub up the wrong way (*colloq.*); *vex*, bother, harass, pester, provoke, stir, ruffle; *antagonize*, offend, affront, insult.

803 IRASCIBILITY

n. *irascibility*, irritability, short temper, limited patience, temperament, sensitivity, touchiness; *shrew*, scold, virago, termagant, battleaxe, dragon, harridan, Tartar.

adj. *irascible*, choleric, querulous, irritable, prickly, touchy, edgy, short-tempered, tetchy, ratty (*colloq.*), shirty (*colloq.*); *peevish*, crotchety, testy, crusty, bilious, dyspeptic, cantankerous, gruff, grumpy; *sensitive*, thin-skinned, nervous, jumpy, uptight (*colloq.*); *temperamental*, moody, changeable, fractious, fretful; *snappy*, sharp, waspish, tart; *irritated*, annoyed, riled, nettled.

vb. *be irascible*, be short-tempered, be on a short fuse, snap, bark, fly at, turn on, jump down someone's throat (*colloq.*).

804 SULLENNESS
n. *sullenness*, ill humour, spleen, sourness, gruffness, sulkiness; *glumness*, discontent, melancholy, moroseness; *moodiness*, temperament, unsociability; *grimace*, pout, scowl, frown, glare, black look; *growl*, snarl, snap, snort.
adj. *sullen*, sulky, surly, churlish, curmudgeonly, cantankerous, unsociable; *disagreeable*, ill-humoured, sour, jaundiced, cross, crusty, crabby, grouchy, grumpy, stroppy (*colloq.*); *glum*, morose, mournful, melancholy, lugubrious, hangdog; *gloomy*, dismal, dark, sombre, cheerless; *moody*, temperamental, saturnine, dour; *gruff*, brusque, abrupt, irascible.
vb. *scowl*, glower, glare, lour, frown, grimace, pout, sulk; *snap*, snarl, growl, grunt; *grumble*, mutter, grouch, grouse, carp, complain; *mope*, be dejected, be unsociable.
adv. *sullenly*, with bad grace.

805 BENEVOLENCE
See also **807** (philanthropy); **809** (pity).
n. *benevolence*, kindness, kindheartedness, good will, benignity; *charity*, humanity, fellow feeling, philanthropy; *generosity*, magnanimity, altruism, selflessness; *consideration*, thoughtfulness; *pity*, sympathy, understanding, mercy, forgiveness; *good deed*, good turn, good works, service, favour, benefit; *kind person*, good Samaritan, Christian, good neighbour, philanthropist, altruist, humanitarian, reformer, well-wisher, do-gooder.
adj. *benevolent*, kind, charitable, benef-

icent, good, kindly, benign; *thoughtful*, considerate, well-meant, well-meaning, well-intentioned; *kindhearted*, warmhearted, compassionate, sympathetic; *helpful*, obliging, accommodating, neighbourly; *generous*, altruistic, unselfish, philanthropic, humanitarian; *loving*, tender, affectionate, motherly, fatherly; *merciful*, tolerant, forgiving; *gallant*, chivalrous, gracious, courteous.
vb. *be kind*, have a heart of gold, be kindness itself, mean well; *do good*, philanthropize, reform; *help*, oblige, do a good turn, do a favour, render a service; *give one's blessing*, wish well, support, encourage; *comfort*, show concern, relieve, mother, nurse.

806 MALEVOLENCE
See also **808** (misanthropy); **810** (pitilessness); **836** (evil); **838** (wickedness).
n. *malevolence*, ill will, wickedness, unkindness, malignity; *malice*, spite, gall, bitterness, acrimony, rancour; *hate*, animosity, enmity, bad blood; *inhumanity*, callousness, cruelty, barbarity, ferocity, sadism, brutality, savagery, monstrousness; *severity*, harshness, ruthlessness, relentlessness, hardheartedness; *harm*, misfortune, mischief, ill turn, catastrophe, disaster; *atrocity*, foul play, outrage, act of inhumanity, violence, torture, murder; *threat*, menace, intimidation, blackmail.
adj. *malevolent*, ill-natured, wicked, bad, evil, malign, malignant, baleful, hostile; *malicious*, spiteful, catty, caustic, bitter, acrimonious, vindictive; *unkind*, nasty, mean, beastly, ungracious, unfriendly, uncharitable; *cruel*, inhuman, merciless, savage, brutal, barbarous, truculent, fierce; *harsh*, severe, ruthless, cold, callous, hardhearted, cold-blooded, tough, intolerant; *maleficent*, venomous, treacherous; *fiendish*, devilish, diabolical, satanic, hellish, infernal; *threatening*, menacing, ominous, foreboding, impending, imminent.
vb. *be malevolent*, harm, abuse, maltreat, ill-treat, molest; *hurt*, injure, tor-

ture, torment; *victimize*, persecute, have it in for (*colloq.*), hound, harry, bully, oppress, tyrannize; *bear malice*, bear a grudge, spite; *rankle*, fester, poison; *threaten*, menace, intimidate, blackmail, hold to ransom, frighten, scare; *bode ill*, spell danger.

adv. *malevolently*, with evil intent; *spitefully*, out of spite; *threateningly*, on pain of death.

807 PHILANTHROPY
See also **805** (benevolence).

n. *philanthropy*, humanitarianism, utilitarianism; *benevolence*, humanity, altruism, dedication; public spiritedness, social conscience; *welfare state*, social work, social services, community service, voluntary work, charity, aid, benefit; *campaign*, crusade, worthy cause, good works; *philanthropist*, benefactor, humanitarian, do-gooder, missionary, voluntary worker; *altruist*, idealist, visionary, utopian; *patron*, founder, protector, guardian angel, supporter, fairy godmother, champion, backer; *kind person*, good neighbour, helper, good Samaritan, saint, angel.

adj. *philanthropic*, humanitarian, humane, altruistic, charitable; *enlightened*, liberal, reforming, public-spirited.

vb. *be charitable*, be public-spirited, do good, have a social conscience.

808 MISANTHROPY
n. *misanthropy*, hatred of mankind, misogyny, unsociability, cynicism; *selfishness*, egotism; *misanthrope*, misogynist, man-hater, woman-hater; *loner*, solitary, cynic, egotist.

adj. *misanthropic*, antisocial, unsociable, cynical.

vb. *misanthropize*, lose faith in human nature.

809 PITY
See also **805** (benevolence).

n. *pity*, compassion, charity, humanity, benevolence, soft-heartedness, warm-heartedness, understanding, tenderness; *sympathy*, empathy, condolence, fellow feeling, commiseration, comfort,

solace, consolation, relief; *mercy*, forbearance, forgiveness, clemency, grace, favour, quarter, second chance; *remorse*, compunction, regret.

adj. *pitying*, sympathetic, comforting, sorry, consoling; *compassionate*, kind, charitable, tender, understanding, soft-hearted; *merciful*, forbearing, forgiving, lenient, clement, gracious, generous, lax; *pitiful*, piteous, pitiable, pathetic, heart-rending.

vb. *pity*, sympathize, feel for, commiserate, grieve with, weep for, console, comfort, support; *show mercy*, pardon, forgive, spare, reprieve, give a second chance, take pity on, relent, unbend, relax; *ask for mercy*, plead with, move to pity, disarm, melt, thaw.

810 PITILESSNESS
See also **806** (malevolence).

n. *pitilessness*, hardness of heart, callousness, mercilessness, pound of flesh, heartlessness, inhumanity, cruelty, ruthlessness, implacability, relentlessness, remorselessness.

adj. *pitiless*, unfeeling, heartless, impassive, unmoved, cold, unsympathetic, cold-blooded; *relentless*, unrelenting, unbending, inflexible, inexorable, remorseless; *severe*, harsh, hard-hearted, stony-hearted, callous, brutal; *merciless*, unforgiving, unmerciful, barbarous, vindictive, vengeful, ruthless, implacable.

vb. *be pitiless*, harden one's heart, give no quarter, turn a deaf ear to, stop at nothing, persecute, avenge.

811 GRATITUDE
n. *gratitude*, gratefulness, thankfulness, appreciation, indebtedness, sense of obligation; *thanks*, thank-you, thank-you letter, leaving present, reward, tip; *acknowledgment*, tribute, credit, recognition, praise, vote of thanks; *thanksgiving*, blessing, benediction, grace, prayer.

adj. *grateful*, thankful, appreciative; *indebted*, obliged, beholden; *gratified*, pleased.

vb. *be grateful*, be in someone's debt, appreciate, receive with open arms, never forget; *thank*, say thank-you, reward, tip; *requite*, repay, return a favour; *acknowledge*, pay tribute, recognize, praise, applaud; *give thanks*, say grace.

adv. *gratefully*, with thanks.

812 INGRATITUDE

n. *ingratitude*, ungratefulness, lack of appreciation, thanklessness; *thoughtlessness*, selfishness, rudeness, grudging thanks, thankless task, ungrateful wretch.

adj. *ungrateful*, begrudging, unappreciative; *unmindful*, forgetful, selfish, rude, discourteous; *thankless*, unrewarding, unprofitable; *unthanked*, unrewarded, unacknowledged, without credit, unrequited.

vb. *be ungrateful*, show ingratitude, not thank, take for granted, presume upon.

813 FORGIVENESS

See also 660 (leniency); **809** (pity).

n. *forgiveness*, pardon, reprieve, amnesty, indemnity; *mercy*, grace, indulgence, forbearance, patience; *absolution*, remission, acquittal, release, discharge; *exoneration*, exculpation; *reconciliation*, redemption, rehabilitation, atonement.

adj. *forgiving*, merciful, lenient, forbearing, long-suffering, patient; *forgiven*, pardoned, absolved, acquitted, released, excused, let off; *reconciled*, restored, taken back, redeemed, rehabilitated, reinstated; *pardonable*, forgivable, excusable, venial.

vb. *forgive*, pardon, reprieve, grant amnesty to; *show mercy*, forbear, tolerate, bear with, relent, unbend, soften; *absolve*, remit, acquit, clear, discharge, excuse, justify; *exonerate*, exculpate; *ignore*, disregard, shut one's eyes to, wink at, overlook, condone, let pass; *be reconciled*, make it up, forgive and forget, bury the hatchet, let bygones be bygones, redeem; *ask forgiveness*, beg pardon, atone.

814 ATONEMENT

See also 641 (retaliation); 841 (penitence).

n. *atonement*, amends, reparation, indemnity, compensation, redress, satisfaction, repayment, restitution, requital, retribution; *propitiation*, reconciliation, appeasement, redemption, offering, sacrifice, scapegoat, substitute, representative; *expiation*, purgatory, penance, confession, shrift; *repentance*, apology, penitence.

adj. *atoning*, indemnificatory, compensatory, making amends; *propitiatory*, reconciliatory, appeasing, sacrificial, redemptive, representative, vicarious; *penitential*, penitentiary; *apologetic*, sorry, penitent, repentant.

vb. *atone*, make amends, make reparation, indemnify, compensate, redress, repay, requite, give satisfaction; *propitiate*, conciliate, reconcile, appease, apologize, beg pardon, satisfy, offer sacrifice; *expiate*, redeem, do penance, suffer purgatory.

815 JEALOUSY

n. *jealousy*, distrust, mistrust, suspicion, doubt, watchfulness, possessiveness; *envy*, resentment, hostility, unfaithfulness; *rivalry*, competition, competitiveness; *rival*, competitor, eternal triangle.

adj. *jealous*, suspicious, distrustful, possessive, watchful; *envious*, resentful, jaundiced, sour.

vb. *be jealous*, mistrust, distrust, suspect, doubt; *envy*, resent.

816 ENVY

n. *envy*, covetousness, desire, resentment, ill will, spite.
adj. *envious*, covetous, jealous, green with envy, grudging.
vb. *envy*, covet, desire, crave, lust after, hanker, grudge, begrudge.

817 RIGHT

n. *right*, rightfulness, what is right, obligation, duty; *lawfulness*, legality, legitimacy; *justice*, fairness, equity, impartiality, fair play, square deal, equality; *reward*, redress, retribution, just deserts, nemesis, poetic justice; *suitability*, fitness, propriety, etiquette, conformity; *morality*, virtue, decency, rectitude, integrity, probity.

adj. *right*, correct, accurate, precise, true, valid; *appropriate*, suitable, fitting, fit, apt, proper; *lawful*, legitimate, legal, rightful; *just*, fair, equitable, objective, unprejudiced, impartial, unbiased, disinterested, dispassionate, neutral, detached; *honest*, upright, straight, righteous, unimpeachable, straightforward, fair-minded, decent, sporting; *justifiable*, excusable, forgivable.

vb. *be just*, be fair, play the game, do the right thing, see fair play; *be in the right*, have grounds for, have cause to; *put right*, rectify, redress, remedy, mend, reform.

adv. *right*, rightly, equally, fairly, without distinction, without fear or favour.

818 WRONG

n. *wrong*, wrongness, wrongfulness, irregularity; *injustice*, inequity, unfairness; *partiality*, partisanship, prejudice, discrimination, bias, favouritism, preferential treatment, nepotism, old school tie; *grievance*, injury, mischief, foul play, raw deal; *disgrace*, shame, dishonour, slur; *sin*, vice, crime, misdeed, offence, trespass.

adj. *wrong*, wrongful, unreasonable, abnormal, irregular; *unfair*, unjust, inequitable, unsportsmanlike, not cricket (*colloq.*), below the belt; *partial*, partisan, biased, prejudiced, uneven, unbalanced, weighted, one-sided; *incorrect*, inaccurate, erroneous, imprecise, at fault; *injurious*, harmful; *unsuitable*, inappropriate, improper, unseemly; *illegal*, illegitimate, illicit, unlawful, criminal; *wicked*, sinful, bad, vicious, immoral; *unforgivable*, unjustifiable, inexcusable, reprehensible.

vb. *wrong*, harm, hurt, injure, maltreat; *err*, be in the wrong, be at fault; *do wrong*, break the law, transgress, infringe, trespass, cheat, not play fair, hit below the belt; *discriminate*, favour, show partiality, lean towards.

819 ENTITLEMENT

See also **715** (debt).

n. *entitlement*, dueness, due, right, privilege, prerogative; *merits*, deserts, just deserts, come-uppance, punishment, reward, compensation; *payment*, dues, fees, levy, contribution; *duty*, responsibility, obligation; *legal right*, claim, title, birthright, human rights; *bond*, security, title deed, patent, copyright; *warrant*, licence, charter, permit; *heir*, beneficiary, plaintiff.

adj. *entitled*, warranted, just, rightful, legitimate, lawful, legal, inviolable, inalienable; *due*, owing, payable, chargeable, unpaid, unsettled, in arrears, outstanding; *deserving*, worthy, meritorious, needy; *deserved*, merited, well-deserved; *fit*, fitting, right, proper, as it should be.

vb. *be entitled*, warrant, expect, have the right to; *claim*, lay claim to, insist on one's rights, exercise one's prerogative; *justify*, vindicate, exonerate, substantiate; *merit*, be worthy, deserve, earn, have it coming to one (*colloq.*), serve one right; *be due*, fall due, mature; *honour*, pay, discharge, meet an obligation; *assign*, attribute, give every man his due, acknowledge, credit, hand it to; *allot*, apportion, prescribe.

adv. *duly*, by right, by law.

820 LACK OF ENTITLEMENT

See also **272** (overstepping); **575** (excess).

n. *lack of entitlement*, absence of right, presumption, assumption, arrogation, violation; *undueness*, unfittingness, gratuitousness; *disentitlement*, dispossession, forfeiture, disqualification, disestablishment; *usurper*, pretender, impostor, squatter.

adj. *unentitled*, unqualified, unauthorized, presumptuous, without rights; *undue*, unwarranted, uncalled-for, unnecessary, gratuitous; *immoderate*, excessive; *undeserved*, unmerited, unjust, unfair; *undeserving*, unworthy; *improper*, unseemly, inappropriate; *spurious*, false, would-be, fictitious, bogus; *invalid*, forfeit, illicit, illegal, illegitimate.

vb. *not be entitled to*, have no right to, presume, arrogate, overstep the mark, take liberties, go too far; *usurp*, violate, trespass, encroach, infringe; *disentitle*, disqualify, invalidate, disfranchise, disestablish, expropriate, dispossess, depose.

821 DUTY

See also **683** (promise).

n. *duty*, obligation, responsibility, onus, liability, burden; *commitment*, pledge, promise, contract, engagement, debt, bond, tie, call of duty; *conscience*, sense of duty, moral obligation, moral imperative; *loyalty*, faithfulness, fealty, allegiance; *discharge of duty*, performance, acquittal, observance; *task*, commission, office, charge, station, profession; *precept*, code of duty, morality, ethics.

adj. *liable*, responsible, accountable, answerable, subject to; *obliged*, duty-bound, under obligation; *obligatory*, incumbent, mandatory, compulsory, binding, inescapable, unconditional, categorical; *dutiful*, conscientious, obedient, compliant, submissive, tractable; *ethical*, moral, honourable, decent.

vb. *be the duty of*, fall to, rest with, devolve on, be responsible for, should, ought, had better, behove; *commit oneself*, pledge oneself, engage, shoulder responsibility; *do one's duty*, discharge, fulfil, perform, acquit oneself, honour, pay; *oblige*, bind, saddle with, put under an obligation; *impose a duty*, require, detail, order, call upon, enjoin, look to, expect.

822 EXEMPTION

See also **605** (escape); **857** (acquittal).

n. *exemption*, immunity, nonliability, impunity; *exception*, privilege, special treatment; *freedom*, release, liberation, dispensation, absolution, acquittal, pardon; *permission*, leave, liberty, licence, charter, franchise.

adj. *exempt*, nonliable, immune, not subject to, free, clear; *privileged*, unaccountable, unaffected, independent; *unrestricted*, unbound, unrestrained, uncontrolled.

vb. *exempt*, free, clear, set apart, exclude; *excuse*, exonerate, exculpate, acquit, let off; *absolve*, pardon, forgive; *release*, lift restrictions, grant impunity, liberate; *be exempt*, get off scot-free, get away with it, get away with murder (*colloq.*); *shrug off*, shift the blame, pass the buck (*colloq.*), wash one's hands of.

823 RESPECT

See also **774** (repute); **791** (courtesy).

n. *respect*, regard, esteem, consideration, honour, high opinion, appreciation, favour; *repute*, high standing, authority; *admiration*, worship, veneration, adoration, hero-worship, awe; *praise*, reverence, homage, deference, humility, devotion; *respects*, regards, greeting, salutation, salute; *bow*, curtsy, red carpet, guard of honour.

adj. *respectful*, courteous, polite, ceremonious; *admiring*, awestruck; *reverential*, deferential, standing, kneeling, prostrate; *humble*, submissive, obsequious, servile; *respected*, well thought of, highly regarded, reputable, valued, appreciated, esteemed, venerable, time-honoured; *important*, impressive, imposing, authoritative.

vb. *respect*, think well of, regard highly, have a high opinion of, hold dear, value, appreciate, honour; *admire*, think the world of, take off one's hat to (*colloq.*), revere, look up to, hero-worship, put on a pedestal, pay homage, defer to; *praise*, extol, exalt, pay tribute, lionize; *pay one's respects*, greet, welcome, salute, drink to, toast; *show respect*, bow, curtsy, kneel, scrape, grovel, kowtow, be humble, submit; *command respect*, impress, impose, awe, overawe, overwhelm, humble.

824 DISRESPECT

See also **773** (derision); **781** (insolence); **792** (discourtesy).

n. *disrespect*, irreverence, discourtesy,

impoliteness; *dishonour*, disrepute; *contempt*, scorn, disdain, disparagement, low opinion, low esteem, disapprobation; *insult*, affront, slight, sneer, snub, rebuff, indignity, humiliation, degradation; *ridicule*, mockery, derision, taunt, jeer, hiss, catcall, boo.

adj. *disrespectful*, irreverent, discourteous, impolite, rude; *neglectful*, negligent; *dishonourable*, humiliating, degrading; *contemptible*, disreputable, despicable, worthless, shameful, base; *contemptuous*, scornful, supercilious, haughty, disdainful; *insulting*, offensive, pejorative, slighting, cutting; *impertinent*, cheeky, saucy, insolent, insubordinate; *offhand*, airy, breezy, cavalier.

vb. *have no respect for*, hold in contempt, have no time for; *underrate*, underestimate; *scorn*, despise, look down on, disdain, look down one's nose at (*colloq.*), disparage, denigrate, belittle; *taunt*, mock, scoff, deride, jeer at, sneer at, laugh at, ridicule; *insult*, offend, affront, slight, snub, rebuff, humiliate; *dishonour*, disgrace, put to shame; *show disrespect*, lack courtesy, jostle, tread on someone's toes, brush aside, ride roughshod over; *desecrate*, profane, cheapen, lower, degrade.

825 APPROVAL

See also **738** (satisfaction).

n. *approval*, approbation, satisfaction; *recognition*, acknowledgment, appreciation, gratitude; *permission*, agreement, sanction, acceptance, adoption, blessing, consent, assent, seal of approval, imprimateur; *admiration*, esteem, credit, prestige, honour, favour; *commendation*, compliment, bouquet, citation, favourable review, accolade, tribute; *praise*, adulation, eulogy, panegyric; *applause*, ovation, clapping, curtain call, encore, three cheers, acclaim; *supporter*, advocate, patron, admirer, fan.

adj. *approving*, satisfied, content, appreciative; *complimentary*, commendatory, laudatory, fulsome; *approved*, favourable, satisfactory; *commendable*, praiseworthy, laudable, meritorious,

estimable, creditable, admirable, unimpeachable; *approvable*, permissible, admissible, acceptable; *popular*, well thought of, in demand.

vb. *approve*, recognize, acknowledge, favour; *agree*, allow, permit, sanction, adopt; *accept*, pass, rubber-stamp, tick, endorse; *commend*, compliment, admire, take off one's hat to (*colloq.*), pay tribute, sing the praises of, speak well of, rave about, exalt, extol, boost, puff; *overrate*, exaggerate, overestimate, inflate; *applaud*, clap, cheer, stamp, whistle, hail, acclaim, welcome, drink to; *advocate*, recommend, support, back; *win praise*, gain credit, find favour, meet with approval, pass muster.

826 DISAPPROVAL

See also **739** (dissatisfaction).

n. *disapproval*, disapprobation, nonacceptance, rejection, refusal; *dissatisfaction*, discontent, displeasure, disfavour; *disagreement*, objection, opposition, contradiction; *criticism*, hostility, fault-finding, complaint, censure, critical review, attack, diatribe; *reprimand*, reproach, blame, rebuke, reproof, black mark, brickbat, rocket, admonition, telling-off, home truths, lecture, talking to, roasting (*colloq.*); *protest*, outcry, clamour, hiss, boo, catcall, raspberry; *taunt*, sneer, irony, sarcasm, dig; *blacklist*, boycott, bar, ban; *opponent*, critic, knocker (*colloq.*), anti.

adj. *disapproving*, hostile, critical, hypercritical, censorious; *reproving*, reproachful, stern, fault-finding, captious; *disparaging*, uncomplimentary, defamatory, deprecatory, unfavourable, opposed, against; *shocked*, not amused; *caustic*, trenchant, mordant, biting, venomous; *disapproved*, disreputable, insufficient, found wanting, not good enough; *reprehensible*, blameworthy, culpable, objectionable.

vb. *disapprove*, reject, not accept, object to, protest, demur; *disagree*, frown on, oppose, not hold with, take a dim view of; *regret*, deplore, lament; *disparage*, belittle, run down, denigrate, depreciate; *criticize*, complain, carp, find fault, pick holes, not think much of, censure, knock (*colloq.*), slam (*colloq.*), condemn, damn with faint praise; *reprove*, rebuke, reprimand, reprehend, upbraid, scold, chide, tell off, tick off, lecture, dress down (*colloq.*), tear off a strip (*colloq.*), haul over the coals (*colloq.*), carpet (*colloq.*), give a piece of one's mind; *punish*, castigate, chastise, rap over the knuckles; *reproach*, blame, incriminate, impeach; *boo*, hiss, whistle, heckle, lynch; *blacklist*, boycott, ban, bar; *be open to criticism*, get a bad name, get a bad press, incur blame, have a rough ride.

adv. *disapprovingly*, under protest, against one's better judgment.

827 FLATTERY
See also **782** (servility).
n. flattery, compliment, adulation, blandishments, blarney, soft soap (*colloq.*), flannel (*colloq.*); *insincerity*, false praise, hypocrisy, sham, eyewash (*colloq.*); *fawning*, cajolery, wheedling, obsequiousness; *flatterer*, hypocrite, toady, sycophant, yes-man, creep (*colloq.*), crawler (*colloq.*), hanger-on.
adj. *flattering*, complimentary, fulsome, adulatory; *insincere*, plausible, bland, mealy-mouthed, honeyed, sugary, saccharine; *smooth*, unctuous, smarmy (*colloq.*), slimy; *obsequious*, servile, ingratiating, sycophantic.
vb. *flatter*, compliment, praise, puff, boost, soft-soap (*colloq.*), lay it on thick (*colloq.*), overdo it; *cajole*, wheedle, coax, inveigle, suck up to (*colloq.*), sweet-talk, butter up (*colloq.*), massage someone's ego; *fawn*, court, curry favour, be servile, ingratiate oneself.

828 DISPARAGEMENT
See also **595** (damage); **639** (attack).
n. *disparagement*, depreciation, detraction, denigration, belittling; *degradation*, debasement, vilification; *defamation*, calumny, slander, libel, mud-slinging, smear campaign, character assassination; *criticism*, bad press, attack, hatchet job (*colloq.*), brickbat, knocking copy; *aspersion*, slur, stigma,

brand, smear, innuendo, insinuation; *scandal*, muck-raking, backbiting, gossip; *ridicule*, caricature, skit, satire, lampoon; *detractor*, critic, knocker (*colloq.*), mud-slinger; *slanderer*, libeller, defamer; *scandalmonger*, muck-raker, backbiter, gossip columnist, gutter press; *mocker*, scoffer, cynic, satirist.
adj. *disparaging*, deprecatory, derogatory, denigratory, pejorative; *defamatory*, slanderous, libellous; *contemptuous*, slighting, mocking, sarcastic, cynical, catty, snide; *caustic*, bitter, venomous, destructive.
vb. *disparage*, deprecate, detract, depreciate, belittle, play down, sell short, run down (*colloq.*); *discredit*, dishonour, defame, denigrate, blacken, vilify, malign, sully, defile, tarnish, smear, besmirch; *criticize*, slur, cast aspersions on, slight, knock (*colloq.*), pan, slate; *denounce*, decry, revile, expose, pillory; *slander*, libel, calumniate; *deride*, mock, ridicule, lampoon, satirize, guy, sneer at.

829 VINDICATION
n. *vindication*, justification, mitigation, extenuation, defence, apologia, excuse; *grounds*, right, basis, plea, alibi; *pretext*, whitewash, gloss; *exoneration*, exculpation, acquittal; *apologist*, witness, defendant, advocate, champion.
adj. *vindicating*, justifying, extenuating, mitigating, excusing; *justifiable*, arguable, defensible, plausible, allowable; *excusable*, pardonable.
vb. *vindicate*, justify, warrant, give grounds for, make excuses for; *whitewash*, varnish, gloss; *confirm*, bear out, support, show, demonstrate, prove; *uphold*, maintain, defend, plead; *exonerate*, exculpate, excuse, acquit, absolve, clear; *palliate*, mitigate, soften.

830 ACCUSATION
n. *accusation*, indictment, arraignment, prosecution, impeachment, denunciation; *charge*, allegation, complaint, imputation, incrimination, blame, censure; *insinuation*, slur, smear; *false*

charge, frame-up (*colloq.*), put-up job (*colloq.*), libel, slander, calumny, perjury; *action*, suit, case, count, plaint, citation, summons; *accuser*, plaintiff, prosecutor, accused, defendant, suspect, informer, witness.

adj. *accusing*, accusatory, condemnatory; *denunciatory*, incriminating; *defamatory*, calumnious; *accused*, charged, suspect; *accusable*, chargeable, liable to prosecution, inexcusable, indefensible.

vb. *accuse*, charge, bring charges, challenge, arraign, indict, impeach; *arrest*, book, prosecute, sue; *impute*, incriminate, blame, censure, point the finger at, lay at one's door; *denounce*, expose, inform, tell, blab (*colloq.*); *implicate*, involve; *complain*, find fault with, reprove; *slander*, libel, slur, calumniate, defame; *fabricate*, trump up, concoct, invent, frame (*colloq.*), perjure oneself, bear false witness.

831 PROBITY
See also **774** (repute); **837** (virtue).

n. *probity*, rectitude, uprightness, good character; *honesty*, integrity, truthfulness, genuineness, conscientiousness, good faith; *fidelity*, faithfulness, loyalty, reliability, constancy; *morality*, moral fibre, scruples, standards; *virtue*, goodness, purity; *honour*, nobility, chivalry; *principle*, point of honour; *honourable person*, man of honour, trusty soul, good sort, brick (*colloq.*); *good sport*, sportsman, fair play, good loser.

adj. *honourable*, upright, straight, erect, right, square; *honest*, truthful, law-abiding, incorruptible; *sincere*, frank, candid, straightforward; *loyal*, faithful, dependable, reliable, trusty, sterling, trustworthy, genuine, dutiful, conscientious; *moral*, principled, ethical, scrupulous, reputable, respectable; *fair*, just, equitable, impartial; *noble*, high-minded, idealistic, chivalrous, *virtuous*, good; *immaculate*, spotless, stainless, clean, pure; *innocent*, ingenuous, artless, guileless.

vb. *be honourable*, play fair, be in

good faith, keep faith, do the decent thing; *go straight* (*colloq.*), reform.

832 IMPROBITY
See also **662** (disobedience).

n. *improbity*, dishonesty, immorality, corruption, evil, wickedness; *guile*, cunning, artfulness, disingenuousness; *dishonour*, shame, disgrace, disrepute; *disloyalty*, infidelity, faithlessness, bad faith, double standard, duplicity, double-dealing, betrayal, sell-out; *perfidy*, treachery, treason, sedition, defection; *villainy*, roguery, foul play, skulduggery; *dishonest act*, racket, fiddle, wangle, dirty tricks.

adj. *immoral*, corrupt, evil, wicked, bad; *dishonest*, deceitful, fraudulent, criminal, bent (*colloq.*), crooked; *insincere*, two-faced, disingenuous, double-dealing; *unprincipled*, unscrupulous, unethical; *disreputable*, ignominious, ignoble; *unreliable*, faithless, unfaithful, inconstant; *perfidious*, treacherous, insidious; *sly*, underhand, crafty, devious, artful, foxy, cunning; *dubious*, shady, suspicious, questionable, fishy (*colloq.*), shifty; *base*, vile, mean, shabby, abject.

vb. *be dishonest*, deceive, lie, fib, cheat, swindle, defraud, double-cross, two-time (*colloq.*), do the dirty on (*colloq.*); *betray*, sell out, sell down the river.

833 DISINTERESTEDNESS

n. *disinterestedness*, selflessness, unselfishness, self-sacrifice, dedication, self-denial, altruism, martyrdom; *magnanimity*, generosity, liberality, nobility, philanthropy; *impartiality*, indifference; *neutrality*, objectivity, non-involvement, detachment, unconcern.

adj. *disinterested*, impartial, unbiased, unprejudiced, objective, fair, just; *indifferent*, unconcerned, dispassionate; *unselfish*, selfless, dedicated, self-sacrificing, self-effacing, humble; *magnanimous*, generous, liberal, unsparing; *noble*, high-minded, quixotic, chivalrous.

vb. *be disinterested*, put oneself last, take a back seat.

834 SELFISHNESS
See also **728** (meanness).

n. *selfishness*, self-interest, egoism, egotism, self-absorption, opportunism, individualism; *vanity*, narcissism, self-indulgence, self-worship; *greed*, meanness, avarice; *egoist*, egotist, narcissist, individualist, opportunist, gold-digger; *miser*, niggard.

adj. *selfish*, egocentric, self-centred, self-absorbed, self-seeking, egoistic, egotistic; *greedy*, miserly, mean, avaricious; *vain*, narcissistic, self-indulgent, conceited; *covetous*, envious, jealous, possessive, dog-in-the-manger.

vb. *be selfish*, put oneself first, look after number one; *monopolize*, hog, keep to oneself; *look out for oneself*, be on the make, have an eye for the main chance.

835 GOOD
See also **805** (benevolence); **837** (virtue).

n. *good*, benefit, advantage, interest; *good fortune*, providence, luck, boon, windfall, godsend, pennies from heaven, treasure trove; *gain*, profit, harvest, success, prosperity, wealth; *welfare*, wellbeing, fortune, weal; *improvement*, betterment, edification; *good turn*, help, service, favour, convenience; *common good*, public weal.

adj. *good*, beneficial, advantageous, gainful; *helpful*, useful, heaven-sent; *worthwhile*, valuable, profitable; *thriving*, successful, prosperous.

vb. *do good*, benefit, favour, bless; *be useful*, avail, serve, help; *make better*, edify, improve, do one a power of good; *do well*, flourish, thrive, prosper, succeed.

836 EVIL
See also **806** (malevolence); **838** (wickedness).

n. *evil*, ill; *accident*, tragedy, disaster, catastrophe, calamity, ruin; *nuisance*, trial, affliction; *misfortune*, ill luck, crying shame, raw deal; *harm*, mischief, damage, hurt, injury, pain, anguish, distress, trouble; *wrong*, disservice, dirty trick, foul play, outrage;

wickedness, corruption; *scourge*, pest, plague, bane; *disadvantage*, setback, hitch.

adj. *evil*, bad, ill, adverse, nefarious; *unfortunate*, catastrophic, disastrous, ruinous, calamitous; *distressing*, tragic, painful, hurtful; *wicked*, vicious, sinister, maleficent; *fatal*, fell, mortal, deadly.

vb. *do evil*, harm, damage, do mischief, do a disservice; *afflict*, ruin, trouble.

adv. *amiss*, awry, wrong.

837 VIRTUE
See also **582** (worth); **805** (benevolence); **831** (probity).

n. *virtue*, goodness, morality, uprightness, rectitude, righteousness, good behaviour; *kindness*, compassion, magnanimity; *honesty*, integrity, character, honour, probity; *temperance*, sanctity, saintliness, holiness; *purity*, chastity, innocence; *morals*, principles, ethics; *worth*, merit, saving grace; *good person*, good neighbour, salt of the earth, one in a million, good sort, brick (*colloq.*), pillar of society, saint, angel; *good example*, model, paragon.

adj. *virtuous*, good, upright, righteous, proper, moral, principled; *saintly*, angelic, holy; *kind*, kindly, generous, dutiful, conscientious, well-intentioned; *honest*, worthy, sterling, exemplary, unimpeachable; *perfect*, irreproachable, immaculate, impeccable, unblemished, excellent; *pure*, chaste, innocent.

vb. *be good*, behave oneself, have a clear conscience, set a good example, keep to the straight and narrow; *be virtuous*, resist temptation, go straight.

838 WICKEDNESS
See also **806** (malevolence); **810** (pitilessness); **836** (evil).

n. *wickedness*, vice, evil, unrighteousness, wrongdoing; *immorality*, corruption, depravity, wantonness, baseness; *iniquity*, sin, wrong, perversity, sin, transgression, trespass, offence; *outrage*, atrocity, enormity; *crime*, felony, underworld, den of vice; *malignity*, malevolence, villainy, roguery; *fault*, weakness, foible, bad habit, failing, demerit, shortcoming, peccadillo; *bad person*, wrongdoer, malefactor, evil-doer, sinner, miscreant, reprobate; *scoundrel*, wretch, villain, vagabond, rogue, rascal, knave, blackguard, bounder, blighter; *bad child*, terror, imp, scamp, monkey, scallywag; *bully*, ugly customer, nasty piece of work, ruffian, thug, lout, hoodlum, tough, yobbo (*colloq.*), brute, monster, beast, savage, barbarian; *idler*, loafer, wastrel, prodigal, good-for-nothing, ne'er-do-well, layabout, bad lot, riffraff, black sheep, troublemaker, mischief-maker; *crook*, liar, cheat, conman, twister, racketeer, impostor, traitor; *criminal*, felon, lawbreaker, offender, public enemy, thief, pickpocket, house-breaker, delinquent, vandal, pirate, gangster, desperado, murderer, assassin; *rake*, profligate, pimp, wanton, hussy; *cad*, rotter, heel (*colloq.*), bastard, worm, rat, louse, swine.

adj. *wicked*, evil, bad, wrong; *immoral*, corrupt, dissolute, degenerate, perverted, depraved, indecent, wanton; *naughty*, disobedient; *wayward*, perverse; *unscrupulous*, unprincipled; *mean*, despicable, base, vile, malevolent, callous, vicious, brutal, cruel; *outrageous*, shocking, scandalous, abominable, atrocious, heinous, monstrous, unforgivable, inexcusable; *offensive*, repugnant, distasteful; *hellish*, infernal, diabolic, fiendish; *criminal*, lawless, nefarious.

vb. *be wicked*, err, transgress, do wrong; *lapse*, stray, fall, backslide, degenerate, go off the rails (*colloq.*); *misbehave*, be naughty; *make wicked*, corrupt, pervert, lead astray, defile, tempt, seduce.

839 INNOCENCE

n. *innocence*, guiltlessness, blamelessness, irreproachability, faultlessness; *clear conscience*, clean hands, clean slate; *purity*, impeccability, stainlessness, virtue; *artlessness*, inexperience, unworldliness, naivety; *probity*, integrity, uprightness, incorruptibility; *innocent*, child, babe, lamb, dove; *innocent party*, injured party.

adj. *innocent*, not guilty, not responsible, guiltless, blameless, in the clear, acquitted; *pure*, clean, stainless, spotless, unsoiled, untainted, immaculate, undefiled; *perfect*, impeccable, faultless, above suspicion, sinless, unimpeachable, incorruptible; *ignorant*, simple, unsophisticated, inexperienced, naive, unworldly, green; *guileless*, artless; *harmless*, inoffensive, innocuous; *pardonable*, forgivable, excusable.

vb. *be innocent*, have a clear conscience, have nothing to confess; *mean no harm*, know no better.

840 GUILT

n. *guilt*, blame, culpability, charge, reproach; *responsibility*, liability, accountability *criminality*, delinquency, illegality, sinfulness; *guilty conscience*, bad conscience, remorse; *involvement*, complicity; *guilty act*, crime, offence, sin, transgression, trespass, misdemeanour; *misconduct*, misbehaviour, malpractice; *indiscretion*, peccadillo, impropriety; *error*, fault, lapse, slip, blunder.

adj. *guilty*, found guilty, condemned, judged, convicted, incriminated; *wrong*, at fault, to blame, culpable, reproachable; *suspected*, blamed, censured; *responsible*, liable, answerable, accountable; *red-handed*, caught in the act, caught in flagrante delicto; *sheepish*, shamefaced, embarrassed.

vb. *be guilty*, be caught in the act, plead guilty; *find guilty*, incriminate, charge, condemn.

841 PENITENCE

n. *penitence*, repentance, change of heart, contrition, compunction, confession; *remorse*, shame, self-reproach, regret; *self-accusation*, self-condemnation; *penance*, sackcloth and ashes, hair shirt; *apology*, atonement; *penitent*, prodigal son, reformed character, convert.

adj. *penitent*, repentant, contrite, remorseful, ashamed; *regretful*, full of regrets, sorry, apologetic; *conscience-stricken*, chastened, self-reproachful, self-accusing; *reformed*, converted.

vb. *repent*, feel shame, confess, acknowledge, own up, admit, plead guilty; *be penitent*, be contrite, regret, apologize, excuse oneself; *recant*, see the light, be converted, turn over a new leaf.

842 IMPENITENCE

n. *impenitence*, noncontrition, refusal to recant, obduracy, stubbornness; *hardness*, hardness of heart, heart of stone, pitilessness; *no regrets*, no apologies; *incorrigibility*, hardened sinner.

adj. *impenitent*, unrepentant, uncontrite, unashamed, unabashed, recusant; *hard*, obdurate, insensitive, callous, stubborn; *incorrigible*, irredeemable, hopeless, despaired of, lost.

vb. *be impenitent*, have no regrets, show no remorse, harden one's heart, refuse to recant, feel no compunction.

843 SELF-RESTRAINT

See also **668** (restraint).

n. *self-restraint*, self-control, self-discipline, restraint, asceticism, temperance, moderation, abstemiousness; *self-denial*, abstinence, continence, teetotalism, prohibitionism, vegetarianism, veganism; *abstainer*, total abstainer, teetotaller, prohibitionist, vegetarian, vegan, ascetic.

adj. *self-restrained*, self-controlled, ascetic, self-disciplined; *temperate*, moderate, restrained, measured, disciplined, careful, continent; *sparing*, plain, frugal, spartan; *abstemious*, sober.

vb. *be self-restrained*, restrain oneself, exercise self-control, control oneself, contain oneself, deny oneself, ration oneself, be moderate, abstain, refrain; *watch oneself*, know when to stop, know when one has had enough, keep within bounds; *give up*, swear off, go on a diet; *be sober*, keep sober, go on the wagon (*colloq.*).

844 SELF-INDULGENCE

See also **575** (excess).

n. *self-indulgence*, intemperance, immoderation, want of moderation, lack of restraint; *excess*, excessiveness, extravagance, overindulgence; *incontinence*, lack of self control, want of self control, indiscipline, addiction; *wastefulness*, waste; *sensuality*, voluptuousness, carnality, the fleshpots; *gluttony*, debauchery, dissoluteness, dissipation; *high living*, luxury, epicureanism, hedonism.

adj. *self-indulgent*, intemperate, immoderate, unrestrained; *excessive*, unlimited, overindulgent, extravagant; *incontinent*, uncontrolled, undisciplined; *wasteful*, spendthrift, uneconomical; *sensual*, sensuous, voluptuous, carnal, bodily, fleshly; *gluttonous*, debauched, dissolute, dissipated, hungover; *high-living*, pleasure-seeking, fun-loving, epicurean, hedonistic.

vb. *be self-indulgent*, indulge (oneself), be intemperate, be immoderate, luxuriate, wallow, deny oneself nothing; *have one's fling*, paint the town red (*colloq.*), sow one's wild oats; *overeat*, eat to excess, gorge, overindulge (oneself), binge; *drink too much*, drink to excess, go on a bender (*colloq.*); *not know when to stop*, burn the candle at both ends; *lack self-control*, lack discipline.

845 FASTING

n. *fasting*, abstinence from food, fast, bread and water, hunger strike; *starvation*, hunger, malnutrition, anorexia, famishment; *dieting*, slimming, diet, war rations; *fast day*, Lent, Ramadan, Yom Kippur.

adj. *fasting*, abstinent, abstaining, not eating; *starving*, hungry, famished; *underfed*, undernourished, poorly fed, half starved.

vb. *fast*, eat nothing, go without food; *starve*, go hungry, famish; *diet*, slim, reduce weight, lose weight, go on a diet; *go on hunger strike*, refuse food.

846 GLUTTONY

n. *gluttony*, greed, greediness, insatiability, voracity, intemperance, excess, overindulgence, overeating, insatiable appetite; *glutton*, gourmand, pig, hog, locust, gannet (*colloq.*), greedy pig,

greedy guts (*colloq.*); *gourmet*, gastronome, epicure; *feast*, blowout (*colloq.*).
adj. *gluttonous*, greedy, insatiable, overfed; *ravenous*, voracious, omnivorous; *gastronomic*, epicurean.
vb. *overeat*, stuff oneself, make a pig of oneself, eat like a horse, eat out of house and home; *guzzle*, gulp down, bolt down, wolf, scoff, demolish, polish off, gobble up, devour, gorge, cram, stuff.

847 SOBRIETY

n. *sobriety*, soberness, temperance, teetotalism, prohibition, abstinence; *sober person*, moderate drinker, teetotaller, abstainer, total abstainer, prohibitionist; *Band of Hope*, temperance society.
adj. *sober*, temperate, abstinent, abstemious; *teetotal*, on the wagon (*colloq.*); *clear-headed*, in one's right mind, in possession of one's senses, stone-cold sober, sober as a judge; *sobered*, sobered up, dried out.
vb. *be sober*, be temperate, drink moderately, not drink, not imbibe; *become teetotal*, give up alcohol, sign the pledge, go on the wagon (*colloq.*), dry out; *hold one's drink*, have a good head for drink; *sober up*, sleep it off (*colloq.*), get rid of a hangover, clear one's head.

848 DRUNKENNESS

n. *drunkenness*, intoxication, inebriation, insobriety, intemperance; *alcoholism*, drink problem, dipsomania, dt's, pink elephants; *tipsiness*, a drop too much, one over the limit, one too many; *drunkard*, drunk, heavy drinker, hard drinker, alcoholic, boozer (*colloq.*), inebriate, old soak, tippler, wino (*colloq.*), dypso (*colloq.*), lush (*colloq.*); *drinking bout*, pub-crawl, booze-up (*colloq.*), bender (*colloq.*), blind (*colloq.*); *Dutch courage*, a hair of the dog that bit you; *hangover*, head, headache, morning after the night before feeling.
adj. *drunk*, intoxicated, inebriated, under the influence, the worse for drink, boozed up (*colloq.*), dead drunk, blind drunk, drunk and disorderly;

tipsy, squiffy (*colloq.*), merry, high, befuddled, feeling no pain, sozzled (*colloq.*), sloshed (*colloq.*), tight (*colloq.*), pickled (*colloq.*), plastered (*colloq.*), woozy, stoned (*colloq.*), blotto (*colloq.*), canned (*colloq.*), legless (*colloq.*), pissed (*colloq.*), Brahms and Liszt; *seeing double*, glassy-eyed.
vb. *drink*, booze (*colloq.*), tipple, swig, guzzle, drink like a fish, hit the bottle, go pub-crawling, knock back a few, bend the elbow, drown one's sorrows, wet one's whistle (*colloq.*); *be drunk*, be merry, be tipsy, be under the influence of drink, have had one too many; *see double*, lurch, stagger, get stoned out of one's mind, pass out, crash out; *intoxicate*, inebriate, go to one's head.

849 DRUG-TAKING

n. *drug-taking*, smoking; *drug dependence*, drug addiction, drug abuse, habit, narcotism, solvent abuse, glue-sniffing; *drug*, narcotic, dope, hard drug; *joint*, reefer, shot, fix; *tobacco*, nicotine; *cannabis*, hemp, marijuana, hash, hashish, pot, grass, ganja; *cocaine*, coke, snow; *morphine*, opium, opium den; *heroin*, horse (*colloq.*), smack (*colloq.*), brown sugar (*colloq.*); *LSD*, acid, mescalin; *amphetamine*, speed (*colloq.*), bennies (*colloq.*); *high* (*colloq.*), buzz (*colloq.*), rush (*colloq.*).
adj. *drugged*, high (*colloq.*), stoned (*colloq.*); *stimulant*, opiate, narcotic, mind-blowing (*colloq.*).
vb. *drug* (oneself), smoke, turn on (*colloq.*), inject (oneself), mainline (*colloq.*), snort, sniff, pop (*colloq.*), take a trip.

850 MORALITY

See also **586** (cleanness); **831** probity); **837** (virtue).
n. *morality*, morals, virtue, decency, decorum, propriety, delicacy, chastity, virginity, continence, celibacy; *purity*, cleanness, cleanliness, spotlessness, untaintedness, immaculateness; *sinlessness*, perfection; *prudery*, primness, false shame, false modesty, prudishness; *prude*, prig, old maid; *Victorian*,

Puritan; *guardian of morality*, Mrs Grundy, censor; *celibate*, monk, nun.

adj. *moral*, good, virtuous, decent, honourable, decorous, demure, abstemious, platonic, continent; *pure*, clean, spotless, untainted, immaculate, innocent, sinless, perfect; *chaste*, celibate, virgin, virginal, white; *prudish*, prim, priggish, squeamish, shockable, narrow-minded, Victorian, straitlaced, puritanical, old-maidish.

vb. *moralize*, censor.

851 IMMORALITY

See also 587 (dirtiness).

n. *immorality*, indecency, shamelessness, immodesty, unchastity, looseness of morals, easy virtue, permissive society; *impurity*, imperfection, uncleanness, filthiness, taintedness, contamination, pollution, sinfulness; *lewdness*, lasciviousness, prurience, salaciousness, dissoluteness, dissipation, debauchery, licentiousness; *ribaldry*, bawdiness; *lust*, sensuality, eroticism, libido; *obscenity*, pornography, filth, smut, soft porn, blue film; *rape*, violation, indecent assault, sexual assault, incest; *promiscuity*, sleeping around (*colloq.*), dirty weekend (*colloq.*), free love, affair, extramarital relations, adultery, fornication, carnal knowledge, infidelity, unfaithfulness, eternal triangle; *prostitution*, street-walking, whoredom; *brothel*, house of ill repute, red-light district; *libertine*, lecher, womanizer, rake, playboy, stud; *whore*, harlot, tramp, trollop, slut, slag (*colloq.*), bint (*colloq.*); *voyeur*, pervert, flasher (*colloq.*), dirty old man (*colloq.*).

adj. *immoral*, amoral, indecent, wanton, shameless, immodest, unchaste, loose; *impure*, unclean, dirty, contaminated, polluted, sullied; *lewd*, lascivious, prurient, salacious, dissolute, lecherous, licentious, debauched, randy (*colloq.*); *sensual*, erotic, libidinous; *obscene*, filthy, smutty, dirty, lurid, pornographic, porno, blue; *vulgar*, coarse, risqué; *adulterous*, extramarital, illicit, unfaithful, incestuous.

vb. *be immoral*, sleep around (*colloq.*), commit adultery, fornicate, womanize;

seduce, debauch, take advantage of; *rape*, assault, violate.

852 LEGALITY

See also 677 (permission).

n. *legality*, lawfulness, permissibility, legitimacy; *legislation*, law-making, regulation, authorization, codification, sanction, enactment; *justice*, authority, right; *law*, body of law, statute book, constitution, charter, statute, legal code, code; *ordinance*, act, edict, regulation, rule, bylaw; *jurisprudence*, science of law, legal learning; *legislator*, law-maker, jurist.

adj. *legal*, lawful, legitimate, right, just; *permissible*, permitted, allowable, sanctioned, authorized, codified, statutory, within the law, constitutional; *jurisprudential*, nomothetic.

vb. *make legal*, enact, pass, put into effect.

adv. *legally*, by law, by order, legitimately, in the eyes of the law.

853 ILLEGALITY

See also 658 (anarchy); 678 (veto).

n. *illegality*, unlawfulness, unconstitutionality, miscarriage of justice, injustice, wrong verdict, loophole; *law-breaking*, breach of law, trespass, offence, wrong, violation, transgression, contravention, encroachment, infringement, foul play, malpractice; *criminal offence*, crime, misdemeanour, felony; *lawlessness*, street violence, crime wave, anarchy, terrorism, mob rule, gang rule; *riot*, rebellion, revolt, breakdown of law and order, chaos, disorder; *illegitimacy*, bastardy; *illegitimate child*, bastard, love child.

adj. *illegal*, unlawful, illicit, prohibited, banned, forbidden, not allowed, unauthorized, outside the law, contrary to the law, wrong; *contraband*, smuggled, hot (*colloq.*), stolen, black-market; *lawless*, anarchic, irresponsible, without law, riotous; *illegitimate*, bastard, born out of wedlock, born on the wrong side of the blanket.

vb. *be illegal*, break the law, do wrong, disobey, violate, transgress, contravene, infringe; *take the law into one's* *own hands*, be a law unto oneself, stand above the law; *suspend*, annul, cancel, nullify, abrogate, void.

adv. *illegally*, illicitly, unlawfully, criminally, illegitimately.

854 JURISDICTION

See also **657** (authority).

n. *jurisdiction*, authority, control, law and order, arm of the law, direction, supervision; *responsibility*, competence, capacity, power; *executive*, corporation, administration; *domain*, range, territory; *law officer*, judge, mayor, sheriff, legal administrator; *police*, police force, constabulary; *police officer*, policeman, policewoman, constable, cop (*colloq.*), copper (*colloq.*), bobby (*colloq.*), rozzer (*colloq.*), fuzz (*colloq.*), filth (*colloq.*); *traffic warden*, meter maid.

adj. *jurisdictional*, competent, executive, administrative, directive, judiciary, judicial.

vb. *administer*, direct, supervise; *judge*, administer/dispense justice, sit in judgment; *police*, keep order, control.

855 TRIBUNAL

n. *tribunal*, court, bench, board, judicial assembly, assizes, session, council; *throne*, woolsack, seat of justice; *dock*, witness box, bar, courthouse, lawcourt.

856 LITIGATION

n. *litigation*, going to law, judicature; *lawsuit*, case, suit, action, legal proceedings; *summons*, citation, subpoena, writ, search warrant, charge, indictment; *inquest*, inquiry, hearing, prosecution, defence, affidavit, examination, cross-examination, testimony, pleadings, arguments, reasoning, summing up; *ruling*, verdict, judgment, finding, decision; *acquittal*, favourable verdict; *condemnation*, unfavourable verdict; *appeal*, retrial, reversal of judgment; *litigant*, party, suitor, claimant, plaintiff, defendant, objector, accused, prisoner at the bar, accuser, prosecutor.

adj. *litigating*, suing, accusing, litigant; *going to law*, contesting, objecting, disputing, arguing, litigious.

vb. *litigate*, go to law, appeal to law, prosecute, sue, charge, indict, bring to trial, bring to justice, bring a suit, file a suit, file a claim, petition, bring an action against; *prepare a case*, prepare a brief; *try*, hear, give a hearing to, judge, rule, arbitrate, adjudicate; *sum up*, close the pleadings, charge the jury; *pass sentence*, sentence, return a verdict, rule, find, declare, pronounce, convict.

857 ACQUITTAL

n. *acquittal*, favourable verdict, verdict of not guilty, innocence; *discharge*, reprieve, release, remission, suspended sentence, pardon, clearance, case dismissed, exoneration, exculpation, let-off (*colloq.*).

adj. *acquitted*, not guilty, guiltless, innocent, in the clear, cleared, exonerated, exculpated, vindicated; *discharged*, set free, released, liberated; *reprieved*, forgiven.

vb. *acquit*, find not guilty, declare not guilty, prove innocent, vindicate, clear someone's name; *reprieve*, pardon, absolve, forgive, clear, dismiss, grant remission, discharge, let off (*colloq.*); *release*, set free.

858 CONVICTION

n. *conviction*, unfavourable verdict, condemnation, denunciation; *death sentence*, death warrant, condemned cell.

adj. *convicted*, found guilty, condemned, sentenced; *condemnatory*, damnatory.

vb. *convict*, find guilty, prove guilty, condemn, bring home the charge, judge, sentence, pass sentence on; *punish*, denounce, damn, curse; *sentence to death*, sign someone's death warrant, put on the black cap.

859 REWARD

See also **650** (trophy).

n. *reward*, award, prize, trophy, honour, decoration, accolade, bonus, premium, tribute; *recognition*, acknowledgment, thanks; *recompense*, compensation, remuneration, fee, pay, payment, guerdon, reparation, reimbursement; *profit*, return, gain; *tip*, gratuity, golden handshake, honorarium; *deserts*, just deserts; *reward for service*, pension; *bribe*, bait, kickback (*colloq.*).

adj. *rewarding*, profitable, worthwhile, advantageous, remunerative; *generous*, open-handed, charitable, unsparing, liberal.

vb. *reward*, award, honour, decorate, present, bestow a title, confer, grant; *recognize*, acknowledge, pay tribute, be grateful, thank, show one's gratitude; *recompense*, compensate, remunerate, pay, reimburse, redress, indemnify, make reparation; *bribe*, offer a bribe.

adv. *rewardingly*, profitably; *as a reward*, in compensation.

860 PUNISHMENT
See also **826** (disapproval).

n. *punishment*, chastisement, castigation, discipline, disciplinary action, reprimand, condemnation, reproof, correction, retribution; *penalty*, fine, damages, costs, liability; *banishment*, exile, expulsion, transportation; *prison sentence*, hard labour, solitary confinement, Borstal; *corporal punishment*, blow, clout, cane, rap, cuff, slap, smack, whip; *torture*, third degree; *capital punishment*, execution, death sentence, gallows, hanging, electrocution, decapitation, beheading, guillotining, garrotting, strangling, strangulation, impalement, crucifixion, drowning, burning; *mass execution*, mass murder, massacre, genocide, slaughter, annihilation; *martyrization*, martyrdom; *punisher*, chastiser, castigator, persecutor, torturer, inquisitor; *executioner*, hangman, firing squad.

adj. *punitive*, penal, castigatory, disciplinary, corrective; *punishable*, liable.

vb. *punish*, correct, chastise, castigate, discipline, reprimand, rebuke, sentence; *penalize*, fine, deprive, confiscate, take away, endorse one's licence; *demote*, suspend, downgrade, unfrock, cashier, reduce to the ranks; *slap*, smack, spank, wallop, cuff, clout, box on the ears, rap over the knuckles;

belt, beat, strap, tan, cane, birch, flog, whip, whack, thrash, thrash the living daylights out of, give a good hiding; *exile*, banish, deport, transport, expel; *isolate*, ostracize, send to Coventry, outlaw; *imprison*, jail, confine; *torture*, rack, break on the wheel, tar and feather, kneecap, martyr; *execute*, put to death, kill, crucify, stone to death, hang, hang draw and quarter, behead, decapitate, guillotine, garrotte, electrocute, gas, shoot, strangle, burn alive, impale, drown, poison; *massacre*, slaughter, annihilate; *be punished*, suffer punishment, face the music (*colloq.*), take one's medicine, pay the penalty, get one's just deserts.

861 MEANS OF PUNISHMENT
See also **671** (prison).

n. *scourge*, whip, horsewhip, belt, strap, cat o' nine tails, birch, cane, stick, rod, ruler; *pillory*, stocks, ducking stool, whipping post; *prison*, jail; *instrument of torture*, rack, wheel, thumbscrew, maiden, water torture, torture chamber; *scaffold*, gallows, gibbet, noose, rope, halter, garrotte, cross, stake, bullet, poison, guillotine, axe, electric chair, gas chamber, death chamber.

862 DIVINITY
n. *divinity*, divineness, deity; *God*, godhead, Spirit, Supreme Being, Creator, Providence, Preserver, prime mover, Alpha and Omega, the Eternal, Almighty, Allah, Brahma, Buddha; *Trinity*, three in one; *Father*, Lord, Yahweh, Jehovah, King of Kings, Lord of Lords, Lord of Hosts; *Jesus Christ*, Son of God, Son of Man, Emmanuel, Messiah, Saviour, Redeemer, Lamb of God, Good Shepherd, Friend, Prince of Peace; *Holy Spirit*, Holy Ghost, Comforter, Paraclete, Dove; *supreme deity*, the gods, Zeus, Jupiter, Apollo, Mars, Hermes, Mercury, Poseidon, Neptune, Bacchus, Hades, Pluto, Eros, Cupid, Venus, Pan; *object of worship*, god, goddess, idol, false god, golden calf, mumbo jumbo, cargo cult; *divine manifestation*,

theophany, incarnation, transfiguration, glory; *divine task*, creation, preservation, judgment, mercy, grace, salvation, propitiation, atonement, redemption, mediation, intercession.

adj. *divine*, godlike; *heavenly*, celestial, sublime, ineffable; *infinite*, supreme, absolute, omnipresent, sovereign; *transcendent*, immanent, self-existent, changeless; *eternal*, everlasting, immortal, timeless; *almighty*, omnipotent, all-powerful; *omniscient*, all-knowing, all-wise; *just*, merciful; *gracious*, loving, forgiving, providential; *holy*, godly, hallowed, sanctified, sacred; *religious*, mystical, spiritual, superhuman, supernatural, not of this world.

863 SAINT

See also **872** (holiness).

n. *saint*, believer, convert, man of prayer, man of God, holy man, patron saint; *the saints*, children of God, the righteous, the just, chosen people, the elect; *follower*, disciple, apostle; *saintliness*, sanctity, beatitude; *mystic*, holy person, fakir, dervish, ascetic; *good spirit*, angel, archangel, ministering spirit, guardian angel, seraph, cherub, (heavenly) host, principalities, authorities, powers, dominions.

adj. *saintly*, sanctified, beatified, blessed, holy, pious, righteous, just; *angelic*, ministering, guardian, heavenly, celestial.

864 DEVIL

see also **876** (sorcery); **877** (occultism).

n. *devil*, Satan, the Evil One, fallen angel, Mephistopheles, Beelzebub, Prince of Darkness, Lord of Misrule, Lucifer, serpent, Tempter, Accuser, Adversary, Antichrist, Old Harry (*colloq.*), Old Nick (*colloq.*); *evil spirit*, devil, demon, unclean spirit, succubus, incubus, fiend, powers of darkness; *devil worship*, demonism, Satanism, witchcraft, black magic, voodoo; *devil-worshipper*, Satanist.

adj. *satanic*, devilish, Mephistopholean; *wicked*, diabolical, fiendish; *infernal*, hellish.

865 FAIRY

n. *fairy*, spirit, little people, fairy godmother, fairy queen; *elf*, brownie, goblin, gnome, dwarf, pixie, sprite, hobgoblin, imp, puck, leprechaun, troll, gremlin; *genie*, centaur, satyr, faun, mermaid, Lorelei, nymph, yeti, Abominable Snowman, Green Man; *fairy tale*, fair story, folklore; *ghost*, spectre, phantom, spirit, poltergeist, spook (*colloq.*), dybbuk, wraith, visitant, departed spirit, presence, zombie; *apparition*, vision, appearance; *vampire*, ghoul, werewolf, ghoul, ogre, bogey (man).

adj. *fairylike*, elfish, impish; *mythical*, imaginary; *ghostly*, spooky (*colloq.*), eerie, haunted, weird, uncanny, supernatural, phantom, ghoulish, nightmarish.

vb. *haunt*, visit, walk, return from the dead.

866 HEAVEN

n. *heaven*, paradise, bliss, glory, Abraham's bosom, heavenly city, holy city, kingdom of heaven, kingdom of God, next world, the hereafter, world to come, eternal rest, celestial bliss, presence of God, new Jerusalem, kingdom come (*colloq.*), happy hunting grounds (*colloq.*), seventh heaven, cloud nine (*colloq.*), Elysium, Garden of Eden, nirvana; *resurrection*, afterlife, rapture, glorification, translation, ascension, assumption, millennium.

adj. *heavenly*, celestial, eternal, blessed, blissful, glorious, glorified.

867 HELL

n. *hell*, underworld, lower world, nether regions, abyss, bottomless pit, inferno, everlasting fire, hellfire, lake of fire and brimstone, place of departed spirits, Sheol, Gehenna, Hades, perdition, purgatory, limbo; *judgment*, punishment, darkness, separation, destruction, wrath, weeping and gnashing of teeth.

adj. *hellish*, infernal, damned.

868 RELIGION

See also **434** (belief).

n. *religion*, natural religion, revealed religion; *deism*, theism, monotheism, polytheism, pantheism, animism, gnosticism; *religious teaching*, Christianity, Judaism, Islam, Hinduism, Buddhism, Brahminism, Baha'ism, Zoroastrianism, Zen, Confucianism, Shintoism, Taoism; *revelation*, declaration, inspiration, illumination, prophecy; *sacred writings*, truth, word of God, Holy Writ, (Holy) Scriptures, (Holy) Bible, the Good Book (*colloq.*), canon, Old Testament, Talmud, Torah, Pentateuch, ten commandments, the Law and the Prophets, Psalms, Apocrypha, New Testament, Gospel, Good News, Acts (of the Apostles), Epistles, Revelation, Apocalypse, Koran, Vedas; *vision*, sign, miracle, theophany, incarnation, Word made flesh; *belief*, faith, teaching, doctrine, faith, creed, dogma, tenet, articles of faith, 39 Articles, confession; *study of religion*, theology, divinity, religious education, R.E., religious knowledge, R.K.; *religious teacher*, apostle, prophet, rabbi, preacher, lay-preacher, interpreter, commentator, expositor, evangelist, missionary, guru; *theologian*, scholar, divine.

adj. *religious*, holy, spiritual, divine, devout, godly; *revealed*, scriptural, holy, sacred, inspired, prophetic, biblical, canonical, apostolic, authoritative, infallible, trustworthy, evangelical, evangelistic, devotional; *theological*, doctrinal, dogmatic.

869 UNBELIEF
See also **435** (disbelief)

n. *unbelief*, atheism; *irreligion*, godlessness, unholiness, nothing sacred, profaneness, ungodliness; *wickedness*, sinfulness; *false religion*, idolatry, heresy; *heathenism*, paganism; *disbelief*, scepticism, doubt, agnosticism; *lack of faith*, lapse from faith; *freethinking*, rationalism, humanism, secularism, materialism, worldliness; *unbeliever*, dissenter, rationalist, freethinker, atheist; *agnostic*, sceptic, doubter, doubting Thomas; *idolater*, heretic; *materialist*,

worldling; *heathen*, pagan; *infidel*, apostate.

adj. *unbelieving*, atheistic; *irreligious*, godless, unholy, profane, ungodly, unspiritual; *wicked*, sinful; *disbelieving*, doubting, agnostic; *heathen*, pagan, idolatrous; *heretical*, unorthodox; *freethinking*, rationalistic, humanistic, secular, materialistic, worldly; *apostate*, unfaithful, lapsed, dissenting; *non-practising*, unconverted, lost.

870 ORTHODOXY

n. *orthodoxy*, strictness, soundness, fundamentalism; *heresy-hunting*, persecution, witch hunt; *conformist*, traditionalist, fundamentalist; *believer*, true believer; *the faithful*, congregation, flock, pillar of the church, communicant.

adj. *orthodox*, sound, pure, true, right-minded, non-heretical; *loyal*, devout, obedient; *practising*, committed, conforming, card-carrying (*colloq.*); *conventional*, traditional, conservative; *scriptural*, canonical, strict; *fundamentalist*, evangelical.

871 HETERODOXY

n. *heterodoxy*, unorthodoxy, wrong belief, modernism, liberalism; *sectarianism*, separatism, partisanship, schismatism, party spirit; *bigotry*, prejudice; *denominationalism*, nonconformism; *division*, dissociation, secession, separation, withdrawal, excommunication; *heresy*, divergence, distortion, perversion; *sect*, schism, division, split, faction, branch, offshoot; *denomination*, tradition; *separatist*, rebel, dissident, dissenter, nonconformist, heretic.

adj. *heterodox*, unorthodox, unsound, unconventional, nonconformist, unauthorized; *heretical*, divergent, perverted; *sectarian*, partisan, schismatic, breakaway, exclusive, denominational.

vb. *declare heretical*, condemn, excommunicate; *secede*, separate, withdraw, break away.

872 HOLINESS
See also **863** (saint).

n. *holiness*, sanctity, consecration, godliness, saintliness, sacredness, goodness, spirituality, unworldliness, piety, devotion; *loyal* ⁊, dutifulness, faithfulness, zeal, commitment, dedication, perseverance, allegiance, earnestness; *reverence*, worship, awe, fear of God, humility, prayerfulness, meditation, contemplation, communion, mysticism; *sanctimoniousness*, pietism, show of piety, religiosity, formalism; *fanaticism*, fundamentalism, bibliolatry; *the saints*, the righteous, the just, man of prayer, believer; *fanatic*, zealot, bigot, Pharisee, scribe, fundamentalist, Bible puncher (*colloq.*), hot-gospeller (*colloq.*), missionary, evangelical, revivalist, pilgrim.

adj. *holy*, pious, devout, consecrated, godly, saintly, sacred, solemn, spiritual, unworldly, otherworldly; *loyal*, faithful, zealous, committed, practising, dedicated, earnest; *reverent*, worshipful, prayerful, humble, meek, pure in heart, God-fearing; *meditative*, contemplative; *sanctimonious*, self-righteous, holier-than-thou, goody-goody (*colloq.*); *fanatical*, fundamentalist, Pharisaic, evangelical, born-again, crusading, fervent, enthusiastic.

vb. *be holy*, fear God, worship, praise, pray, say one's prayers, go to church, persevere, keep the faith, fight the good fight (*colloq.*); *become holy*, repent and believe, be converted, see the error of one's ways, see the light; *make holy*, sanctify, consecrate, dedicate, hallow; *bring to God*, convert, proselytize; *canonize*, beatify.

873 PROFANITY

n. *profanity*, impiety, godlessness, irreverence; *blasphemy*, sacrilege, desecration, violation, defilement; *scoffing*, derision; *worldliness*, materialism; *hypocrisy*, false piety, self-righteousness, cant, lip service; *profane person*, blasphemer, sinner, reprobate; *scoffer*, mocker; *worldling*, materialist; *hypocrite*; *unbeliever*, backslider, apostate.

adj. *profane*, unholy; *impious*, godless, ungodly, unrighteous, sinful, irreverent, irreligious, worldly, earthbound; *hardened*, brazen; *blasphemous*, sacrilegious, swearing; *hypocritical*, self-righteous, insincere, deceitful; *apostate*, unregenerate.

vb. *profane*, desecrate, violate, defile, commit sacrilege; *blaspheme*, swear, take the name of the Lord in vain; *backslide*, apostasize, harden one's heart.

874 WORSHIP

n. *worship*, honour, reverence, homage, respect, adoration, veneration, exaltation, devotion, praise; *act of worship*, service, rite, liturgy; *prayer*, prayer for the day, intercession, vigils, rogation, supplication, litany, benediction, collect, blessing, grace, petition, request, invocation, thanksgiving; *private devotion*, meditation, quiet time, prayer; *hymn*, song, song of praise, psalm, chant, anthem, canticle, chorus; *worshipper*, adorer, venerator; *churchgoer*, Christian, communicant; *congregation*, church, flock, assembly; *supplicant*, intercessor, petitioner, man of prayer.

adj. *worshipping*, devoted, reverent, supplicant, devout, prayerful, religious; *worshipful*, reverential, solemn, sacred, holy, devotional, liturgical; *meditating*, praying, interceding, communicating, kneeling; *worshipped*, revered, adored.

vb. *worship*, revere, honour, adore, venerate, exalt, praise, glorify, respect, do worship to, pay homage to, homage, laud, humble oneself, prostrate oneself, kneel, genuflect; *pray*, say a prayer, say one's prayers, meditate; *give thanks*, thank, bless; *petition*, supplicate, intercede, entreat, ask, invoke, beseech; *idolize*, deify; *sing hymns*, sing psalms, chant.

875 IDOLATRY

n. *idolatry*, false worship, idolism, idol-worship, image-worship, iconolatry; *heathenism*, paganism, irreligion, fetishism, anthropomorphism, demonism, demonolatry, devil-worship, sun-worship, hero-worship, animal-worship, mumbo jumbo, hocus-pocus, sorcery; *idolization*, apotheosis, deification; *idol*, graven image, false god, image, icon, statue, fetish, totem; *idolater*, idol-worshipper, pagan, heathen, idolizer, fetishist, demonist, devil-worshipper; *idol-maker*, image-maker.

adj. *idolatrous*, heathen, pagan, fetishistic, idol-worshipping, devil-worshipping.

vb. *idolatrize*, worship idols, worship the golden calf; *enshrine*, deify, apotheosize; *idolize*, worship, put on a pedestal, sing the praises of, dote on, treasure.

876 SORCERY

See also **864** (devil).

n. *sorcery*, witchcraft, wizardry, magic, superstition, occultism, diabolism, black magic, black art; *miracle-working*, thaumaturgy; *witch-doctoring*, voodooism; *exorcism*, ghost-laying; *magic rite*, invocation, incantation, spell; *enchantment*, bewitchment, curse, hoodoo, evil eye, jinx, influence, possession, trance; *magic word*, hocus-pocus, abracadabra, open sesame, mumbo jumbo; *charm*, fetish, amulet, talisman, mascot, lucky charm; *sorcerer*, witch, wizard, enchanter, spellbinder; *magician*, conjuror, juggler, illusionist; *witch-doctor*, medicine-man, shaman, voodoo; *seer*, soothsayer, wise man, diviner, clairvoyant; *astrologer*, alchemist; *miracle worker*, thaumaturgist; *spiritualist*, medium, spirit raiser, occultist, necromancer, exorcist; *spiritism*, spiritualism, spirit communication; *séance*, ouija board, planchette, automatic writing, table-turning.

adj. *sorcerous*, devilish, diabolic, occult, necromantic; *magical*, spellbinding, enchanting, supernatural, uncanny, weird, eerie; *bewitched*, enchanted, spellbound, charmed; *cursed*, under the evil eye.

vb. *practise sorcery*, do magic, divine, conjure; *exorcise*, lay ghosts; *raise spirits*, call up spirits; *recite a spell*, recite an incantation, wave a wand; *bewitch*, enchant, charm, fascinate, spellbind; *possess*, curse, put under a curse; *hold a séance*.

877 OCCULTISM

See also **455** (prediction); **864** (devil).

n. *occultism*, mysticism, religion, occult lore; *astrology*, alchemy, divination, prediction; *hypnotism*, hypnosis; *spiritualism*, spirit communication, sitting, séance; *spirit manifestation*, ghost, automatic writing, spirit message; *psychics*, parapsychology, psychic science, ESP, clairvoyance, intuition, second sight, telepathy, psychokinesis, spoon-bending; *mystic*, yogi, esoteric; *fortune-teller*, crystal-gazer, palmist; *spiritualist*, medium; *psychic*, clairvoyant, telepathist, mind-reader; *seer*, prophet, oracle.

adj. *occult*, cabbalistic, religious, mystic, mysterious, dark, transcendental, supernatural, paranormal; *psychic*, psychical, telepathic, clairvoyant, fey.

vb. *practise occultism*, alchemize, astrologize, transform, divine; *practise spiritualism*, study spiritualism; *hold a séance*, attend a séance; *materialize*, dematerialize; *hypnotize*, mesmerize.

878 ECCLESIASTICISM

n. *ecclesiasticism*, churchdom, the church, ministry; *call*, vocation, mission; *holy orders*, ordination, induction, appointment, installation; *Holy Office*, priesthood, pastorship, papacy, primacy, incumbency; *parish*, diocese, bishopric, see; *preaching*, spiritual guidance, pastoral care, confession, absolution, ministration; *prayer*, fellowship, communion; *synod*, convocation, council, chapter, tribunal.

adj. *ecclesiastical*, orthodox, authoritative, apostolic, spiritual; *priestly*, sacerdotal, ministerial, pastoral, pontifical, papal, episcopal, clerical.

vb. *ordain*, order, enthrone, frock; *consecrate*, sanctify; *take holy orders*, be ordained.

879 CLERGY

n. *clergy*, hierarchy, clerical order; *clergyman*, servant of God, preacher, minister, pastor, vicar, parson, rector, parish priest; *curate*, chaplain, cleric, padre; *priest*, prelate, bishop, arch-

880 LAITY

bishop, deacon, archdeacon, dean, canon, prior, primate, patriarch, cardinal; *pope*, pontiff, Holy Father; *monk*, friar, prior, abbot, superior, Trappist, Benedictine; *nun*, sister, bride of Christ, abbess, Mother Superior; *missionary*, evangelist; *rabbi*, imam, lama.
adj. *clerical*, ordained, pastoral, episcopal, papal, monastic.
vb. *be ordained*, enter the ministry, take holy orders, take the veil.

880 LAITY

n. *laity*, layman, lay people, lay brethren; *parish*, flock, sheep, fold, community, church, congregation, assembly; *parishioner*, church member, elder, deacon, lay-preacher, lay-reader, novice, altar boy, chorister, beadle, verger, sexton.
adj. *lay*, laical, secular, non-clerical, unordained; *temporal*, of the world, civil; *irreligious*, unholy, profane, unsacred, unconsecrated.
vb. *laicize*, secularize, deconsecrate.

881 RITUAL

See also 787 (formality).

n. *ritual*, custom, institution, observance, practice; *order*, form, litany, liturgy, ordinance; *rite*, ceremony, celebration; *service*, divine worship, matins, evensong, vespers, mass, prayer meeting, Bible study, Sunday School; *sacrament*, Holy Communion, Lord's Supper, Eucharist, baptism, christening, marriage service, nuptial mass, requiem mass; *ritual object*, cross, crucifix, altar, candle, chalice, incense, holy water, sacred relics, prayer wheel, prayer book, hymn book, psalter; *clerical dress*, canonicals, surplice, vestment, cassock, chasuble, cope, mitre, staff, crook, crosier; *holy day*, feast day, festival, Sabbath, Lord's Day, Advent, Christmas, Epiphany, Lent, Shrove Tuesday, Ash Wednesday, Easter, Good Friday, Whitsun, Pentecost, Passover.
adj. *ritual*, formal, solemn, ceremonial, customary, liturgical.
vb. *perform ritual*, celebrate, observe, keep; *officiate*, minister, baptize, confirm, ordain, excommunicate; *worship*, pray, take communion; *bless*, dedicate, consecrate; *kneel*, genuflect, bow, cross oneself.

882 TEMPLE

n. *temple*, shrine, sanctuary, pantheon, place of worship, house of prayer, holy place; *church*, house of God, kirk,. chapel, tabernacle, meeting-house, mission; *cathedral*, minster, abbey; *synagogue*, mosque; *monastery*, friary, priory, nunnery, convent; *parsonage*, presbytery, rectory, manse, vicarage, deanery, Vatican; *cemetery*, graveyard, churchyard; *altar*, font, pulpit, lectern, pew; *nave*, aisle, transept, chancel, choir, vestry, crypt; *tower*, steeple, belfry, buttress, cloister, lych-gate.

A

A-1 *adj* 31, 582
abacus *n* 75
abandon *n* 732, *vb* 163, 563, 565, 674, 696
abandoned *adj* 163, 563, 696
abandon hope *vb* 749
abandonment *n* 563, 565, 674, 696
abate *vb* 34, 740
abatement *n* 34, 148, 171, 740
abbess *n* 879
abbey *n* 882
ábbot *n* 879
abbreviate *vb* 30, 36, 171, 179, 505
abbreviation *n* 36, 171, 495, 496
ABC *n* 495
abdicate *vb* 563, 674
abdicate responsibility *vb* 658
abdication *n* 563, 674
abduct *vb* 703, 705
abduction *n* 703, 705
abductor *n* 703, 705
aberrant *adj* 73, 252
aberration *n* 73, 252
abeyance *n* 123, 565, 608
abhor *vb* 758, 796
abhorrence *n* 758, 796
abhorrent *adj* 758, 796
abide *vb* 1, 93, 122, 733
abide by *vb* 436, 688
abiding *adj* 1, 93
ability *n* 141, 567, 624
abject *adj* 832
abjuration *n* 474
abjure *vb* 474
ablaze *adj* 339
able *adj* 141, 624
able-bodied *adj* 143
able seaman *n* 648
abnegate *vb* 474
abnegation *n* 474
abnormal *adj* 73, 219, 818
abnormality *n* 73, 219
aboard *adv* 237
abode *n* 158, 165
abolish *vb* 2, 150, 565, 673
abolished *adj* 565
abolition *n* 150, 487, 565, 673
A-bomb *n* 649
abominable *adj* 796, 838
Abominable Snowman *n* 865
abominate *vb* 796

abomination *n* 796
aboriginal *adj* 61, 164
aborigine *n* 164
abort *vb* 153
abortion *n* 153, 323
abortive *adj* 652
abound *vb* 29, 573
about-face *vb* 254
about-turn *n* 121, 126, 196, 254, 543
above *adv* 184
above all *adv* 31, 59, 70
above average *adv* 31
above board *adj* 464, 478
above par *adv* 31
above suspicion *adj* 839
ab ovo *adv* 22, 61
abracadabra *n* 876
abrade *vb* 36, 291, 301
Abraham's bosom *n* 866
abrasion *n* 36, 300, 301, 337
abrasive *adj* 301
abreast *adv* 25, 176, 194, 214
abridge *vb* 30, 36, 171, 179, 505, 520
abridged *adj* 171, 179, 520
abridgment *n* 30, 36, 171, 179, 505
abroad *adj* 471, *adv* 54, *n* 54
abrogate *vb* 474, 673, 853
abrogation *n* 474, 673
abrupt *adj* 96, 190, 451, 792, 804
abruptness *n* 96
abscond *vb* 262, 605
absence *n* 2, 163
absence of hostilities *n* 644
absence of right *n* 820
absent *adj* 2, 163
absentee *adj* 395, *n* 163
absenteeism *n* 163
absent-minded *adj* 405, 449
absent-mindedness *n* 405, 449
absent oneself *vb* 163, 395
absolute *adj* 49, 500, 862
absolutely *adv* 49
absolution *n* 669, 813, 822, 878
absolve *vb* 669, 813, 822, 829, 857
absolved *adj* 813
absorb *vb* 166, 199, 265, 309, 398, 404, 732
absorbed *adj* 404
absorbent *adj* 232, 265, *n* 309
absorbing *adj* 732
absorption *n* 45, 51, 72, 199, 265, 398, 404
abstain *vb* 556, 608, 843
abstainer *n* 556, 843, 847

abstaining *adj* 845
abstemious *adj* 556, 843, 847, 850
abstemiousness *n* 843
abstention *n* 538, 608
abstinence *n* 556, 565, 843, 847
abstinence from food *n* 845
abstinent *adj* 845, 847
abstract *adj* 2, 4, 283, 396, 400, 408,
   490, *n* 520, *vb* 520
abstracted *adj* 398, 405, 449
abstractedness *n* 398, 449
abstraction *n* 400, 405, 408
abstractness *n* 4
abstruse *adj* 461, 504
abstruseness *n* 504
absurd *adj* 426, 443, 445, 459, 772
absurdity *n* 424, 426, 443, 445, 772
abundance *n* 29, 152, 182, 570, 573
abundant *adj* 29, 86, 152, 182, 573
abuse *n* 566, 792, 801, *vb* 566, 604,
   792, 801, 806
abusive *adj* 792, 801
abut *vb* 173, 176
abyss *n* 89, 186, 867
academic *adj* 400, 438, 456, 475, 476
academic title *n* 778
academy *n* 477
accede *vb* 436
accede to the throne *vb* 657
accelerate *vb* 33, 245
acceleration *n* 33, 245, 615 '
accent *n* 494, 521, 526
accented *adj* 521
accept *vb* 265, 436, 636, 642, 699,
   703, 825
acceptability *n* 265, 573
acceptable *adj* 265, 500, 573, 582,
   736, 738, 755, 825
acceptance *n* 265, 434, 436, 636, 642,
   699, 703, 825
accepted *adj* 549, 564
accepting *adj* 436
accepting house *n* 699
acceptor *n* 699
access *n* 240, 263, 265, 271
accessibility *n* 232, 265, 580
accessible *adj* 173, 232, 261, 265, 580
accession *n* 261
accessories *n* 35
accessory *adj* 35, 85, *n* 53, 85
accident *n* 135, 554, 656, 836
accidental *adj* 135, 554
accidental death *n* 323
accidentally *adv* 135, 554

acclaim *n* 774, 825, *vb* 774, 825
acclimatization *n* 72, 549, 559
acclimatize *vb* 549, 559
acclimatized *adj* 559
accolade *n* 825, 859
accommodate *vb* 19, 51, 156
accommodating *adj* 19, 805
accommodation *n* 19, 156, 165
accompaniment *n* 35, 85, 162
accompanist *n* 368
accompany *vb* 85, 368
accompanying *adj* 85, 162
accomplish *vb* 149, 607, 651, 653
accomplished *adj* 438, 624
accomplishment *n* 438, 607, 624, 651,
   653
accord *n* 15, 19, 636, *vb* 9, 17, 19, 72,
   636, 698
according to the rules *adv* 71
accordion *n* 369
accost *vb* 532
account *n* 462, 486, 517, 570, 720, *vb*
   720
accountability *n* 134
accountable *adj* 134, 720, 821, 840
accountancy *n* 720
accountant *n* 75, 711, 720
account for *vb* 134, 462
accounting *adj* 720, *n* 720
accounts *n* 720
accoutrements *n* 694
accredit *vb* 672
accretion *n* 33, 35, 43
accrue *vb* 33, 699
accumulate *vb* 33, 66, 287, 570, 690
accumulation *n* 33, 690
accumulator *n* 570
accuracy *n* 406, 440, 616
accurate *adj* 406, 440, 616, 817
accursed *adj* 597, 796, 801
accusable *adj* 830
accusation *n* 473, 830
accusatory *adj* 830
accuse *vb* 830
accused *adj* 830, *n* 671, 830, 856
accuser *n* 830, 856
Accuser *n* 864
accusing *adj* 830, 856
accustomed *adj* 549, 760
accustom oneself to *vb* 549
AC/DC *adj* 73
ace *adj* 582, *n* 79, 582
acerbic *adj* 346
acerbity *n* 346

ache *vb* 337
achievable *adj* 423
achieve *vb* 149, 607, 651, 653
achievement *n* 261, 607, 651, 653
achieve one's heart's desire *vb* 738
Achilles' heel *n* 144
aching *adj* 337
achromatic *adj* 382
achromatism *n* 382
acid *adj* 346, *n* 346, 849
acid drop *n* 346
acidity *n* 346
acidulate *vb* 346
acknowledge *vb* 415, 436, 515, 791,
  811, 819, 825, 841, 859
acknowledge receipt of *vb* 699
acknowledgment *n* 415, 436, 468, 515,
  719, 791, 811, 825, 859
acme *n* 31, 49, 188, 584
acne *n* 767
acoustic *adj* 351, 353
acoustics *n* 351, 353
acquaint *vb* 466
acquaintance *n* 438, 793
acquaint oneself with *vb* 438
acquiesce *vb* 436, 537, 636, 642, 663
acquiescence *n* 436, 537, 642, 663,
  733
acquiescent *adj* 436, 537, 636, 642,
  663, 733
acquire *vb* 690, 699
acquire the knack *vb* 476
acquisition *n* 690, 699
acquisitive *adj* 690, 699, 703, 728
acquisitiveness *n* 728
acquit *vb* 606, 669, 813, 822, 829, 857
acquit oneself *vb* 621, 821
acquittal *n* 606, 669, 813, 821, 822,
  829, 856, 857
acquitted *adj* 813, 839, 857
acrid *adj* 350
acridness *n* 347
acrimonious *adj* 794, 802, 806
acrimony *n* 794, 802, 806
acronym *n* 495, 496
acropolis *n* 640
across *adv* 180
across-the-board *adj* 69
across the board *adv* 15, 51
acrostic *n* 495
acrylic *n* 490
act *n* 523, 607, 661, 771, 852, *vb* 138,
  523, 607, 621
act for *vb* 676

acting *adj* 607, 676
action *n* 136, 138, 607, 643, 645, 830,
  856
action man *n* 761
actions *n* 621
activate *vb* 136, 141, 732
activation *n* 732
active *adj* 136, 141, 500, 607, 609
activist *n* 607, 634
activity *n* 234, 607, 609, 761
act of courtesy *n* 791
act of discourtesy *n* 792
act of friendship *n* 793
act of God *n* 536
act of inhumanity *n* 806
act of worship *n* 874
act on *vb* 136
act on impulse *vb* 96, 544, 548
actor *n* 523
act out *vb* 484
actress *n* 523
Acts *n* 868
act the fool *vb* 443
actual *adj* 1, 3, 101, 282, 409
actuality *n* 1, 3
actualization *n* 1
actualize *vb* 3
actually *adv* 1
actuarial *adj* 75, 720
actuary *n* 75, 720
acuity *n* 296
acumen *n* 396, 418, 429, 444
acute *adj* 296
acuteness *n* 296
adage *n* 442
adagio *adv* 246
Adam *n* 332
adamant *adj* 542
adamantine *adj* 289
adapt *vb* 19, 72, 121, 125, 462, 518
adaptability *n* 125, 130, 578
adaptable *adj* 19, 69, 72, 125, 130,
  578
adaptation *n* 19, 72, 121, 462
adapter *n* 121
add *vb* 33, 35, 75
addendum *n* 35
add fuel to the flames *vb* 341
addiction *n* 755, 844
addition *n* 33, 35, 75
additional *adj* 33, 35
additive *n* 35, 344
add on *vb* 35
address *n* 158, 522, 532, *vb* 515, 532

addressee *n* 515, 532
address oneself to *vb* 562
address the question *vb* 9
add up *vb* 400, 460
adenoidal *adj* 529
adept *adj* 624
adeptness *n* 624
adequacy *n* 573
adequate *adj* 27, 141, 573
adhere *vb* 43, 181, 688, 695
adherence *n* 43, 688
adherent *n* 634
adhering *adj* 43
adhesion *n* 43, 695
adhesive *adj* 40, 43, 318, 695, *n* 42, 43, 318
adhesiveness *n* 318
ad hoc *adj* 94, 101, 121, 548, 560
ad hominem *adv* 70
adieu *n* 262
ad infinitum *adv* 89
adipose *adj* 319
adjacent *adj* 176
adjectival *adj* 500
adjective *n* 500
adjoin *vb* 173, 176
adjoining *adj* 173, 176
adjourn *vb* 114
adjournment *n* 62, 114
adjudicate *vb* 429, 647, 856
adjudication *n* 429
adjudicator *n* 429, 647
adjunct *n* 35
adjust *vb* 19, 72, 121
adjustment *n* 19, 121, 549
adjust to *vb* 549
ad-lib *vb* 96, 523, 548
ad-libbing *n* 548
ad libitum *adv* 535
adman *n* 470
admass *n* 69, 470
administer *vb* 622, 700, 854
administer/dispense justice *vb* 854
administration *n* 136, 622, 634, 657, 700, 854
administrative *adj* 136, 622, 657, 854
administrator *n* 622
admirable *adj* 582, 774, 825
admiral *n* 648
admiration *n* 774, 795, 823, 825
admire *vb* 774, 795, 823, 825
admirer *n* 795, 825
admiring *adj* 795, 823
admissibility *n* 51, 265

admissible *adj* 265, 825
admission *n* 51, 263, 265, 468, 473, 699
admit *vb* 51, 263, 265, 436, 468, 473, 699, 841
admit defeat *vb* 642
admittance *n* 265, 699
admixture *n* 35, 38
admonish *vb* 602
admonishment *n* 602, 623
admonition *n* 623, 826
ad nauseam *adv* 88, 506
ado *n* 609
adolescence *n* 111
adolescent *adj* 111, *n* 111
adopt *vb* 12, 43, 265, 434, 564, 688, 825
adopted *adj* 564
adoption *n* 12, 564, 825
adorable *adj* 734, 795
adoration *n* 795, 823, 874
adore *vb* 734, 795, 874
adored *adj* 795, 874
adorer *n* 874
adoring *adj* 795
adorn *vb* 766
adorned *adj* 766
adornment *n* 510, 766
a dose of one's own medicine *n* 641
adrenalin *n* 750
adroit *adj* 624
adroitness *n* 624
a drop too much *n* 848
adulation *n* 825, 827
adulatory *adj* 827
adult *adj* 112, *n* 112
adult education *n* 475
adulterate *vb* 38, 121, 144, 288, 305, 587
adulterated *adj* 587
adulteration *n* 288, 587
adulterous *adj* 851
adultery *n* 851
adulthood *n* 112
advance *adj* 212, *n* 33, 234, 253, 259, 261, 592, 639, 651, 679, 701, *vb* 33, 124, 138, 212, 234, 253, 592, 651, 701
advanced *adj* 102, 113, 253, 592
advancement *n* 253, 592
advance notice *n* 602
advance on *vb* 639
advances *n* 800
advancing *adj* 259, 261

advantage *n* 26, 31, 578, 580, 690, 835
advantageous *adj* 115, 580, 651, 690, 835, 859
advent *n* 104, 261
Advent *n* 881
adventure *n* 562
adventurer *n* 648
adventurous *adj* 562
adverb *n* 500
adverbial *adj* 500
adversarial *adj* 14, 632
adversary *n* 632, 794
Adversary *n* 864
adverse *adj* 215, 656, 836
adverse conditions *n* 656
adversity *n* 656
advertise *vb* 59, 464, 470, 551, 679, 709
advertised *adj* 679
advertisement *n* 470, 681
advertiser *n* 470, 681
advertising *n* 470, 551, 681
advice *n* 466, 623, 631
advise *vb* 466, 602, 623, 631
advise against *vb* 552
adviser *n* 623, 631
advisory *adj* 623
advocate *n* 647, 675, 825, 829, *vb* 623, 825
aeon *n* 90, 92
aerate *vb* 304, 306
aerated *adj* 306
aeration *n* 306
aerator *n* 286
aerial *adj* 184, 238, 306
aerobatic *adj* 238
aerobatics *n* 238
aerobics *n* 617, 761
aerodrome *n* 238
aerodynamic *adj* 238
aerodynamics *n* 238
aeronaut *n* 238
aeronautic *adj* 238
aeronautical *adj* 244
aeronautics *n* 238
aeroplane *n* 244
aerosol *n* 304
aerospace *n* 238
aesthete *n* 768
aesthetic *adj* 768
aestival *adj* 108
aestivate *vb* 610
aestivation *n* 610

aetiology *n* 132
afar *adv* 172
affability *n* 736, 742, 789
affable *adj* 736, 742, 789
affair *n* 101, 851
affairs *n* 611
affect *vb* 136, 138, 729, 771
affectation *n* 510, 771
affected *adj* 729, 771
affecting *adj* 732
affection *n* 173, 729, 795, 800
affectionate *adj* 173, 729, 793, 795, 800, 805
affianced *adj* 683
affidavit *n* 420, 856
affiliate *vb* 43, 634
affiliated *adj* 634
affiliation *n* 9, 43
affinity *n* 9, 17, 42, 757
affirm *vb* 143, 412, 417, 473
affirmation *n* 412, 417, 473
affirmative *adj* 412, 415, 420, 473
affix *n* 500, *vb* 35
afflict *vb* 737, 836
afflicted *adj* 597, 656, 735
affliction *n* 589, 597, 737, 836
affluence *n* 655, 712
affluent *adj* 573, 655, 712
afford *vb* 571, 698, 712
affordable *adj* 724
afforest *vb* 327
affray *n* 56, 643
affright *vb* 750
affront *n* 802, 824, *vb* 792, 802, 824
aficionado *n* 795
afire *adj* 339
aflame *adj* 339
afloat *adv* 237
aforementioned *adj* 59
afraid *adj* 750
afresh *adv* 106
Afro *n* 765
aft *adv* 213
after *adv* 100
aftereffect *n* 37, 60, 100, 133
afterlife *n* 104, 323, 866
aftermath *n* 37, 60, 100, 133
afternoon *n* 110
afters *n* 60, 267
aftershave *n* 349
aftertaste *n* 342
afterthought *n* 35, 60, 100, 114, 398
afterwards *adv* 60, 100
afterword *n* 60

again and again *adv* 88, 117
against *adj* 632, 826, *adv* 215
against one's better judgment *adv* 826
against the clock *adv* 97
against the law *adj* 678
against the stream *adv* 628
agape *adj* 232
agate *n* 393, 766
age *n* 90, 92, 107, 112, *vb* 107
aged *adj* 107, 112
age group *n* 66, 101, 103
ageing *adj* 112
ageless *adj* 91, 95, 111
agelessness *n* 91, 95
agency *n* 136, 138
agenda *n* 57, 76, 97, 547, 557
agent *n* 63, 128, 622, 675, 676
agent provocateur *n* 139
age-old *adj* 107
ages *n* 93
agglomerate *vb* 66
agglomeration *n* 35, 43
agglutination *n* 35
aggrandizement *n* 170
aggravate *vb* 741, 802
aggravated *adj* 741
aggravation *n* 741
aggregate *adj* 47, *n* 47, 74
aggression *n* 639, 645, 794
aggressive *adj* 145, 147, 639, 643, 645, 794
aggressiveness *n* 145, 645
aggressor *n* 639, 645, 794
aggro *n* 56, 147, 643
agile *adj* 245, 609
agility *n* 609
agitate *vb* 58
agitated *adj* 58, 281, 729
agitation *n* 58, 234, 280, 281, 609, 729, 732
agitator *n* 121
agitprop *n* 58, 127
agnate *adj* 12
agnostic *adj* 435, 869, *n* 869
agnosticism *n* 435, 869
agog *adj* 402, 450
agonize *vb* 337, 735
agonizing *adj* 337, 735
agony *n* 337, 735
agrarian *adj* 328
agree *vb* 9, 17, 19, 72, 436, 500, 537, 551, 562, 633, 636, 646, 663, 683, 684, 825

agreeable *adj* 336, 436, 535, 537, 636, 684, 736
agreed *adj* 636, 684
agreeing *adj* 19
agreement *n* 9, 13, 15, 19, 72, 436, 500, 551, 562, 633, 636, 644, 646, 683, 684, 825
agree to differ *vb* 437, 635
agricultural *adj* 328
agriculture *n* 328
agronomic *adj* 328
agronomist *n* 328
agronomy *n* 328
a hair of the dog that bit you *n* 848
ahead *adj* 104, *adv* 59, 212, 253
ahead of time *adv* 98
aid *n* 138, 596, 631, 698, 807, *vb* 596, 631, 698
aide *n* 631, 666
aide-de-camp *n* 631, 666
aide-memoire *n* 448
aikido *n* 643
ail *vb* 589
ailing *adj* 589
ailment *n* 589
aim *n* 249, 553, *vb* 249, 553, 748
aim for *vb* 249
air *n* 286, 304, 306, 316, 365, 394, 621, *vb* 306, 316, 348, 468
airborne *adj* 238
air bubble *n* 306
airbus *n* 244
air commodore *n* 648
air-condition *vb* 316
air-conditioning *n* 306
aircraft *n* 244
aircraft carrier *n* 243
airfield *n* 238
air force *n* 648
air freshener *n* 348, 349
airgun *n* 761
airiness *n* 286, 306
airing *n* 306
airlane *n* 238
airlift *n* 238
airline *n* 238
airliner *n* 244
air-mail *adj* 515
airman/woman *n* 238
air marshal *n* 648
air pipe *n* 316
airport *n* 238, 553
air raid *n* 639
air-raid shelter *n* 600

airs *n* 771
airship *n* 244
airstream *n* 316
airstrip *n* 238
airtight *adj* 233
air travel *n* 238
air vice marshal *n* 648
airwaves *n* 472
airway *n* 316
airworthy *adj* 238
airy *adj* 304, 306, 316, 824
aisle *n* 240, 882
ajar *adj* 232
akimbo *adj* 220
akin *adj* 17
à la *adv* 17
alabaster *n* 383
à la carte *adj* 545
alacritous *adj* 245
alacrity *n* 96, 245, 537, 609
à la mode *adj* 770
alarm *n* 97, 355, 484, 599, 750, *vb* 750
alarm bell *n* 602
alarm clock *n* 602
alarmed *adj* 750
alarming *adj* 750
albino *adj* 382, 383
album *n* 369, 486
albumen *n* 318
alchemist *n* 876
alchemize *vb* 877
alchemy *n* 121, 125, 877
alcohol *n* 267
alcoholic *n* 848
alcoholism *n* 848
alcove *n* 158, 227
alderman *n* 665
a leap in the dark *n* 753
alert *adj* 404, 730, 754, *vb* 602
alertness *n* 404, 730, 754
alert to *vb* 404
alexandrine *n* 84
al fresco *adj* 306, *adv* 198, 232
algebra *n* 75
algebraic *adj* 75
alias *adj* 497, *n* 498
alibi *n* 829
alien *adj* 6, 10, 54, 54, 284, *n* 54, 54
alienable *adj* 697
alienate *vb* 696, 697, 794, 796
alienated *adj* 794
alienation *n* 696, 697, 794
alienness *n* 6, 54

alight *adj* 339, *vb* 261, 275
align *vb* 15, 19, 55, 103, 222
alignment *n* 19, 55, 222
alike *adj* 15
alimentation *n* 267
alimony *n* 571, 798
alive *adj* 37, 730
alive and kicking *adj* 322
Allah *n* 862
all anyhow *adv* 16, 56
all around *adv* 206
allay *vb* 148
all but *adv* 50
allegation *n* 420, 473, 551, 830
allege *vb* 473, 551
alleged *adj* 456
allegiance *n* 670, 821, 872
allegorical *adj* 458
allegory *n* 458
all-embracing *adj* 47, 49, 51
allergic *adj* 334, 758
allergy *n* 334, 589, 758
alleviate *vb* 148, 631, 740
alleviation *n* 148, 631, 740
alley *n* 240
all found *adj* 571
alliance *n* 40, 45, 633, 634, 684, 797
allied *adj* 40, 45, 636
all-in *adj* 51
all in *adj* 142, 619
all in all *adv* 27
all-inclusive *adj* 69
all in the mind *adj* 408
alliteration *n* 17, 88, 521
all-knowing *adj* 438, 862
allocate *vb* 700
allocation *n* 700
all of a sudden *adv* 451
allot *vb* 23, 698, 700, 819
allotment *n* 165, 329, 700
all out *adv* 617
all over *adv* 49, 156
allow *vb* 434, 436, 660, 677, 722, 825
allow/give credit *vb* 714
allowable *adj* 829, 852
allowance *n* 28, 422, 559, 631, 677, 690, 700, 719
allowed *adj* 677
allow for *vb* 28, 559
alloy *n* 38, 45, 321, 569, *vb* 45
all-powerful *adj* 141, 862
all present and correct *adv* 55
all-round *adj* 16, 49
all-rounder *n* 49, 80

219

all shipshape and Bristol fashion *adj* 55

all the rage *adj* 770

all the same *adv* 17

all the world and his wife *n* 47

all things being equal *adv* 11

all things considered *adv* 27

all-time great *n* 582

all together *adv* 66

all told *adv* 47

allude *vb* 458

allure *n* 257, 736, *vb* 736, 795

alluring *adj* 736, 763

allusion *n* 458

allusive *adj* 458, 465

alluvial *adj* 37, 311

alluvium *n* 311

all-wise *adj* 862

ally *n* 193, *vb* 40, 45, 634

alma mater *n* 477

almanac *n* 76, 97

almighty *adj* 862

Almighty *n* 862

almost *adv* 30, 50, 173

alms *n* 698

aloft *adv* 184

alone *adj* 41, 79

aloneness *n* 79

alongside *adv* 194, 214

aloof *adj* 41, 44, 172, 403, 733, 790, 794

aloofness *n* 44, 172, 403, 733, 790

alopecia *n* 203

a lot *n* 573

aloud *adj* 526

alp *n* 184

alpha *n* 61

alpha and omega *n* 49

Alpha and Omega *n* 862

alphabet *n* 495, 513

alphabetical *adj* 495

alphabetize *vb* 57, 495

alpine *adj* 184, 329

alpinism *n* 274

alpinist *n* 274

also-ran *n* 32, 652

altar *n* 881, 882

altar boy *n* 880

alter *vb* 121

alterant *n* 121

alteration *n* 121

altercation *n* 410, 643

alter ego *n* 11, 13

alternate *adj* 65, *vb* 11, 65, 92, 119, 280

alternately *adv* 119

alternating *adj* 11, 119, 280

alternation *n* 11, 65, 119, 280

alternative *adj* 128, *n* 545

alternative date *n* 102

altitude *n* 23, 184

alto *n* 368

altogether *adv* 47

altruism *n* 805, 807, 833

altruist *n* 805, 807

altruistic *adj* 805, 807

alum *n* 346

a.m. *adv* 109

amalgam *n* 38, 45

amalgamate *vb* 38, 40, 45, 633

amalgamation *n* 633

amanuensis *n* 486, 666

amass *vb* 66, 570, 711

amateur *n* 625, 768

amateurish *adj* 439, 625

amateurishness *n* 439

amatory *adj* 795

amaze *vb* 451, 732, 759

amazed *759*

amazement *n* 451, 759

amazing *adj* 451, 759

amazon *n* 143, 751

amazonian *adj* 143

ambassador *n* 675

amber *n* 386, 388

ambergris *n* 349

ambidexterity *n* 81

ambidextrous *adj* 81, 214

ambience *n* 206

ambient *adj* 206

ambiguity *n* 81, 411, 428, 458, 479, 504, 543

ambiguous *adj* 81, 411, 428, 458, 461, 479, 504, 543

ambition *n* 748, 755, 755

ambitious *adj* 748, 755

ambivalence *n* 81, 428

ambivalent *adj* 81, 428

amble *n* 246, 616, *vb* 234, 236, 246, 616

ambrosia *n* 267, 342

ambulance *n* 242

ambulant *adj* 234, 236

ambush *n* 601, *vb* 451, 469, 601

amelioration *n* 592

amenable *adj* 537, 642

amend *vb* 592

amended *adj* 592
amendment *n* 592
amends *n* 28, 596, 704, 814
amethyst *n* 392, 766
amiability *n* 736, 742, 791
amiable *adj* 736, 742, 791
amicability *n* 793
amicable *adj* 793
amidst *adv* 38, 63
amiss *adv* 836
amity *n* 793
ammonia *n* 350
ammunition *n* 649
amnesia *n* 449
amnesiac *adj* 449
amnesty *n* 123, 644, 646, 813, *vb* 449
amoeba *n* 217
among *adv* 38, 63
amoral *adj* 851
amorous *adj* 795
amorousness *n* 795
amorphous *adj* 217
amorphousness *n* 217
amount *n* 23
amount due/outstanding/owing *n* 715
amount to *vb* 74
amour *n* 795
amphetamine *n* 849
amphibian *adj* 326, *n* 326
amphibious *adj* 81
amphitheatre *n* 210, 477
ample *adj* 23, 29, 86, 180, 182
ampleness *n* 182
amplification *n* 170
amplifier *n* 355
amplify *vb* 170, 506, 519
amplitude *n* 23, 29, 168, 180
amply *adv* 29
amputate *vb* 36
amputation *n* 36
amulet *n* 876
amuse *vb* 736, 761
amusement *n* 761
amusing *adj* 744, 761
anachronism *n* 98
anachronistic *adj* 98, 102
anacoluthon *n* 65
anaemia *n* 144, 382, 589
anaemic *adj* 144, 382
anaesthesia *n* 335
anaesthetic *adj* 596, 740, *n* 335, 740
anaesthetize *vb* 335, 596, 740
anaesthetized *adj* 335
anagram *n* 196, 496

analgesic *adj* 740, *n* 148, 335, 740
analogous *adj* 9, 13, 17, 194, 218
analogue *n* 13
analogy *n* 9, 17, 194, 218
analyse *vb* 46, 462, 500
analysis *n* 41, 46, 400, 414, 462, 519
analytical *adj* 400, 410, 462, 519
anarchic *adj* 56, 658, 662, 853
anarchist *n* 662
anarchistic *adj* 127
anarchy *n* 56, 658, 853
anathema *n* 796
anatomical *adj* 298
anatomization *n* 46
anatomize *vb* 46, 48
anatomy *n* 298
ancestor *n* 59
ancestors *n* 323
ancestral *adj* 12, 154
ancestry *n* 12, 59, 132, 154, 776
anchor *n* 131, *vb* 131, 160
anchorage *n* 160
anchorman *n* 472
ancient *adj* 105, 107
ancient history *n* 105
ancient monument *n* 105, 603
ancillary *adj* 32, 35
androgyne *n* 38
androgynous *adj* 38, 332
android *n* 330
anecdote *n* 517, 522
anew *adv* 106
an eye for an eye and a tooth for a
 tooth *n* 641
angel *n* 800, 807, 837, 863
angelic *adj* 837, 863
anger *n* 732, 802, *vb* 732, 802
angle *n* 195, 220, *vb* 195, 220
angled *adj* 195
angling *n* 761
angora *n* 569
angry *adj* 732, 802
angry young man *n* 73, 739
anguish *n* 337, 735, 836
anguished *adj* 735
angular *adj* 220
animal *adj* 326, 397, *n* 320, 326
animal cry *n* 364
animal husbandry *n* 328
animal-worship *n* 875
animate *vb* 143, 145, 322, 732
animated *adj* 145, 322, 533, 732, 742
animation *n* 322, 525, 732, 742
animism *n* 868

animosity n 794, 796, 802, 806
ankh n 197
anklet n 223
annals n 97, 486, 517
annex vb 35, 703
annexation n 670, 703
annexe n 35
annihilate vb 2, 150, 324, 487, 860
annihilation n 2, 150, 324, 487, 860
anniversary adj 786, n 92, 119, 786, 797
annotate vb 462
annotation n 462
announce vb 59, 464, 468, 470
announcement n 466, 468, 470
announcer n 470, 472
annoy vb 737, 741, 802
annoyance n 597, 737, 741, 802
annoyed adj 802, 803
annoying adj 737
annual adj 92, 327
annuity n 719
annul vb 2, 474, 487, 673, 853
annular adj 223
annulment n 2, 474, 487, 673, 798
a nobody n 4
anodyne adj 148, 740
anoint vb 302, 319, 672
anomalous adj 73
anomaly n 73
anon n 498
anonymity n 469, 498
anonymous adj 467, 469, 498
anorexia n 183, 845
anorexic adj 183, n 183
another matter/story n 18
another time n 102
a nothing n 4
answer n 415, 515, vb 137, 415
answerable adj 821, 840
answer back vb 781
answering adj 415
answering machine n 472
antacid n 596
antagonism n 14, 632, 794, 796
antagonist n 632, 794
antagonistic adj 14, 474, 632, 635, 794, 796
antagonize vb 14, 758, 794, 796, 802
antarctic adj 215
antecedence n 59, 99
antecedent adj 59, 99, n 59, 99
antedate vb 59, 98
antediluvian adj 105, 107

ante meridiem adv 109
antenatal adj 152
antenna n 183, 228
anterior adj 59, 99, 212
anteriority n 99
anteroom n 212
anthem n 874
anthology n 45, 66, 516, 520
anthracite n 341
anthropoid adj 330
anthropological adj 330
anthropomorphism n 875
anti adj 758, n 826
anti-aircraft adj 640
Antichrist n 864
anticipate vb 59, 99, 104, 450, 453, 748
anticipation n 113, 450, 453, 748
anticipatory adj 99, 113, 453
anticlimactic adj 452
anticlimax n 452
anticlockwise adj 14, 214, adv 97, 254
anticyclone n 307
antidote n 14, 137, 596
antipathetic adj 14, 258, 758
antipathy n 14, 758, 794, 796
antipodean adj 14, 172, 215
antipodes n 14
antiquarianism n 105
antiquated adj 105, 107
antique adj 107, n 105, 107
antiquity n 105, 107
antisemitism n 331
antisepsis n 39, 590
antiseptic adj 39, 586, 590, n 586
antisocial adj 790, 808
antithesis n 14, 215, 632
antithetical adj 14, 215
antonym n 14, 496
anxiety n 450, 735, 750
anxious adj 281, 450, 735, 750
apace adv 245
apart adj 41, adv 41, 44, 46
apartheid n 41, 52, 430, 790
apartment n 165
apathetic adj 44, 146, 403, 538, 541, 610, 733, 756
apathy n 44, 146, 403, 538, 541, 610, 733, 756
ape n 21, vb 21
apeman n 330
aperient n 232
aperitif n 59
aperture n 232

apex *n* 188
aphasia *n* 529
aphorism *n* 442, 744
aphoristic *adj* 442, 505
apiary *n* 165, 326
apocalypse *n* 62
Apocalypse *n* 868
apocalyptic *adj* 62, 455
Apocrypha *n* 868
apocryphal *adj* 441
apogee *n* 188
Apollo *n* 862
apologetic *adj* 814, 841
apologia *n* 829
apologist *n* 829
apologize *vb* 814, 841
apology *n* 814, 841
apophthegm *n* 442
apostasize *vb* 873
apostasy *n* 435, 543
apostate *adj* 543, 869, 873, *n* 125,
    869, 873
a posteriori *adj* 400
apostle *n* 863, 868
apostolic *adj* 868, 878
apostrophe *n* 532, 534
apostrophize *vb* 532
apotheosis *n* 49, 188, 875
apotheosize *vb* 875
apparatchik *n* 53, 72
apparatus *n* 568
apparel *n* 204
apparent *adj* 372, 394, 464
apparently *adv* 394
apparition *n* 394, 865
appeal *n* 532, 681, 732, 757, 795, 856,
    vb 532, 681, 795
appeal for funds *vb* 681
appealing *adj* 757, 795
appeal to law *vb* 856
appear *vb* 61, 261, 372, 394
appearance *n* 162, 198, 216, 261, 394,
    464, 865
appearances *n* 394
appease *vb* 148, 646, 738, 814
appeasement *n* 148, 644, 646, 814
appeasing *adj* 814
appellant *n* 681
appellation *n* 497
append *vb* 35
appendage *n* 35, 48, 60, 85
appendix *n* 35, 516
appetite *n* 342, 755
appetizer *n* 59, 267

appetizing *adj* 267, 342, 755
applaud *vb* 436, 811, 825
applause *n* 484, 825
apple-cheeked *adj* 387
apple-green *adj* 390
apple of one's eye *n* 800
apple-pie order *n* 55
appliance *n* 564, 568
applicability *n* 564, 578
applicable *adj* 136, 578
applicant *n* 681
application *n* 136, 404, 462, 476, 540,
    564, 617, 679, 681
applied *adj* 564
appliqué *n* 766
apply *vb* 564, 679, 681
apply for *vb* 611
apply for the Chiltern Hundreds *vb*
    674
apply oneself *vb* 476, 617
appoint *vb* 547, 611, 672, 700
appointed *adj* 547
appointee *n* 675
appointment *n* 611, 672, 878
apportion *vb* 23, 700, 819
apportionment *n* 700
apposite *adj* 9
appositeness *n* 9
apposition *n* 500
appraisal *n* 177, 429
appraise *vb* 418, 429
appreciate *vb* 33, 723, 729, 768, 811,
    823
appreciated *adj* 823
appreciation *n* 33, 177, 418, 729, 786,
    811, 823, 825
appreciative *adj* 429, 729, 768, 811,
    825
apprehend *vb* 668, 703
apprehension *n* 450, 703, 750
apprehensive *adj* 450, 750
apprentice *n* 61, 106, 476, 613
apprenticeship *n* 476
apprise *vb* 466
apprised *adj* 466
approach *n* 104, 240, 259, 261, 557,
    559, 679, 681, *vb* 173, 259, 261, 557,
    679, 681
approachable *adj* 261
approaching *adj* 104, 261
approbation *n* 436, 825
appropriate *adj* 9, 19, 440, 511, 817,
    vb 690, 703
appropriateness *n* 19, 440, 511

appropriation *n* 703
approvable *adj* 825
approval *n* 436, 636, 677, 825
approve *vb* 436, 636, 677, 825
approved *adj* 436, 677, 825
approved school *n* 671
approving *adj* 429, 825
approximate *adj* 17, 173, *vb* 9, 173
approximately *adv* 23, 173
approximation *n* 17, 128
appurtenance *n* 85
apricot *n* 388
a priori *adj* 400
apron *n* 523
apropos *adj* 9
apt *adj* 19, 140, 440, 624, 817
aptitude *n* 140, 141
aptness *n* 19, 440
aquamarine *n* 390, 391
aquarium *n* 326
aquatic *adj* 237, 305
aquatics *n* 237
aquatint *n* 493
aqueduct *n* 42, 240, 315
aqueous *adj* 305
aquiline *adj* 220
a-quiver *adj* 732
arable *adj* 328
arbiter *n* 647
arbitrariness *n* 10, 135, 544
arbitrary *adj* 10, 135, 535
arbitrate *vb* 429, 647, 856
arbitration *n* 19, 63, 429, 647
arbitrator *n* 63, 148, 429, 647
arboreal *adj* 327
arboretum *n* 329
arboriculture *n* 329
arbour *n* 165
arc *n* 221
arcade *n* 221, 710
arch *adj* 49, *n* 42, 221, 226, *vb* 221, 225, 226
archaeology *n* 105
archaic *adj* 105, 107
archaism *n* 105, 107
archangel *n* 863
archbishop *n* 776, 879
archdeacon *n* 879
archduke *n* 776
arched *adj* 221, 226
arch enemy *n* 794
archer *n* 255, 648
archery *n* 255
archetypal *adj* 22

archetype *n* 22
archipelago *n* 311
architect *n* 132, 149, 613
architectural *adj* 216, 298
architecture *n* 216, 298
archive *n* 105, 486
archivist *n* 486
arctic *adj* 215, 340
ardent *adj* 729, 795
ardour *n* 729
arduous *adj* 617, 628
arduousness *n* 628
area *n* 23, 156, 157, 168
arena *n* 157, 210, 470, 645
Argie *n* 331
argot *n* 494
arguable *adj* 410, 412, 423, 428, 829
arguably *adv* 423
argue *vb* 400, 410, 437, 635
argue against *vb* 632
argue the toss *vb* 410
arguing *adj* 856
argument *n* 409, 410, 412, 437, 635, 643, 802
argumentation *n* 400, 410
argumentative *adj* 410
argumentativeness *n* 410
arguments *n* 856
arhythmic *adj* 120
aria *n* 367
arid *adj* 153, 309
aridity *n* 153, 309
arise *vb* 1, 61, 101, 133, 276, 394
aristocracy *n* 776
aristocrat *n* 776
aristocratic *adj* 774, 776
arithmetic *n* 75
arithmetical *adj* 75
arm *n* 35, *vb* 571, 640, 645
armaments *n* 649
armchair *adj* 456
armed *adj* 640, 645
armed conflict *n* 645
armed forces *n* 640, 648
armed neutrality *n* 644
armful *n* 23
arm in arm *adv* 40, 176
armistice *n* 123, 644, 646
armlock *n* 695
arm of the law *n* 854
armour *n* 202, 289, 640
armoured *adj* 640
armoury *n* 649
arms *n* 649

arms freeze *n* 646
arm-twisting *n* 664
army *n* 86, 648
aroma *n* 347, 349
aromatic *adj* 349, *n* 344
around the clock *adv* 95, 97
arousal *n* 336, 732
arouse *vb* 334, 336, 732
arpeggio *n* 64
arraign *vb* 830
arraignment *n* 830
arrange *vb* 55, 57, 298, 368, 559
arranged *adj* 57, 684
arranged marriage *n* 797
arrange in succession *vb* 64
arrangement *n* 55, 57, 298, 367, 559, 684
arranger *n* 368
arrant *adj* 49
array *n* 55, *vb* 57, 204
arrears *n* 654, 715
arrest *n* 668, 703, *vb* 123, 668, 703, 732, 830
arrested development *n* 397
arrival *n* 261
arrive *vb* 261, 322, 394, 651
arrive uninvited *vb* 789
arriving *adj* 261
arrogance *n* 431, 779, 781, 783
arrogant *adj* 779, 781, 783
arrogate *vb* 820
arrogation *n* 820
arrow *n* 255
arrowhead *n* 220
arse *n* 213
arse-licker *n* 782
arse-licking *n* 782
arsenal *n* 570, 649
arson *n* 150
arsonist *n* 150
arsy versy *adv* 56
art *n* 490
artefact *n* 149
artery *n* 240
artful *adj* 480, 626, 832
artful dodger *n* 626, 705
artfulness *n* 480, 626, 832
arthritis *n* 589
article *n* 282, 500, 519, 707
article of faith *n* 434
articles of faith *n* 868
articulacy *n* 502, 528
articulate *adj* 496, 502, 528, *vb* 496, 526, 528

articulation *n* 526
artificial *adj* 17, 21, 149, 512, 769, 771
artificial insemination *n* 12, 152
artificiality *n* 512, 769, 771
artificial language *n* 494
artificial light *n* 374
artificial respiration *n* 322
artillery *n* 255
artilleryman *n* 648
artisan *n* 149, 611, 613
artist *n* 490, 624
artiste *n* 368
artistic *adj* 490
artistic medium *n* 490
artistry *n* 490
artless *adj* 478, 509, 627, 831, 839
artlessness *n* 478, 509, 627, 839
art paper *n* 569
as a result *adv* 60, 133
as a result of *prep* 132
as a reward *adv* 859
as a rule *adv* 27, 69
as a whole *adv* 47
asbestos *n* 569
ascend *vb* 184, 274
ascendancy *n* 31, 139, 141, 657
ascendant *n* 284
ascending *adj* 274
ascending/descending order *n* 55
ascension *n* 274, 866
ascent *n* 184, 234, 274
ascertainable *adj* 417
ascetic *adj* 659, 843, *n* 659, 731, 843, 863
asceticism *n* 659, 843
a screw loose *n* 58
ascribable *adj* 134
ascribe *vb* 134
aseptic *adj* 586
ash *n* 300
ashamed *adj* 841
ash-blond *adj* 382, 383
ashen *adj* 382, 383
ashes *n* 37
Ash Wednesday *n* 881
Asian *n* 331
aside *n* 252, 528, 532, 534
asinine *adj* 443, 445, 772
as it happened *adv* 8
as it happens *adv* 554
as it should be *adj* 819
as it were *adv* 17, 458
ask *vb* 402, 414, 874

ask a favour *vb* 681
askew *adj* 26, 219
ask for *vb* 681
ask forgiveness *vb* 813
ask for mercy *vb* 809
ask for one's cards *vb* 674
ask for trouble *vb* 753
ask not to *vb* 682
aslant *adj* 195
asleep *adj* 610
as much again *adv* 81
as new *adv* 106
as one *adv* 66, 79
as one man *adv* 40
as one pleases *adv* 535
aspect *n* 394
asperity *n* 291
aspersion *n* 828
asphalt *n* 202, 569
aspirant *n* 748
aspirate *vb* 270
aspiration *n* 270, 748, 755
aspire *vb* 553, 748, 755
aspiring *adj* 104, 748, 755
as regards *prep* 9
ass *n* 445
assail *vb* 639
assailant *n* 639
assassin *n* 147, 150, 324, 838
assassinate *vb* 150, 324
assassination *n* 150, 324
assault *n* 147, 639, *vb* 147, 639, 851
assemble *vb* 45, 53, 66, 149, 259, 298
assembled *adj* 66
assembly *n* 66, 259, 874, 880
assembly line *n* 64, 149
assent *n* 436, 636, 825, *vb* 436, 636
assenting *adj* 436
assert *vb* 143, 473
assertion *n* 473
assertive *adj* 143, 473, 535
assertiveness *n* 143, 535
assert oneself *vb* 535
assess *vb* 177, 429, 721
assessment *n* 177, 429
assessor *n* 429, 647
assets *n* 570, 694, 712
assiduous *adj* 404, 540
assiduousness *n* 404, 540
assign *vb* 134, 672, 697, 700, 819
assignable *adj* 134
assignee *n* 699
assignment *n* 476, 611, 672, 697

assimilate *vb* 17, 51, 54, 72, 125, 166, 199, 265
assimilation *n* 17, 45, 51, 72, 199
assimilative *adj* 265
assist *vb* 631
assistance *n* 138, 571, 631
assistant *n* 32, 631, 666, 676
assist at *vb* 162
assizes *n* 855
associate *n* 53, *vb* 40, 43, 45, 85, 634
associated *adj* 40, 43, 85, 634
association *n* 9, 40, 42, 43, 45, 458, 634
assonance *n* 17, 88, 521
assorted *adj* 16, 38
assortment *n* 16, 38
assuage *vb* 148, 740
assuagement *n* 740
assume *vb* 134, 400, 425, 456, 562, 699, 703, 748, 760
assume control/command *vb* 657
assumed *adj* 134, 481
assumed name *n* 498
assumption *n* 134, 400, 425, 456, 699, 703, 748, 820, 866
assurance *n* 427, 434, 473, 683
assure *vb* 434, 473, 683, 687
assured *adj* 427, 434
astern *adv* 213
asteroid *n* 284
asteroidal *adj* 284
as the crow flies *adv* 222
as thick as thieves *adv* 40, 40
as things stand *adv* 7, 8
asthma *n* 316
asthmatic *adj* 316
astigmatic *adj* 370
astigmatism *n* 370
astonish *vb* 451, 759
astonished *adj* 451, 759
astonishing *adj* 759
astonishment *n* 451, 759, 760
astound *vb* 451, 759
astounded *adj* 451, 759
astounding *adj* 759
astral *adj* 284
astringency *n* 346
astringent *adj* 171, 346
astrologer *n* 455, 876
astrological sign *n* 284
astrologize *vb* 877
astrology *n* 455, 877
astronaut *n* 238
astronomical *adj* 168, 284, 482

astronomy *n* 284
astrophysical *adj* 284
astrophysics *n* 284
astute *adj* 444
astuteness *n* 418, 444
asunder *adj* 41, *adv* 41, 44, 46
asylum *n* 598, 600
asymmetrical *adj* 10, 26, 219
asymmetry *n* 10, 18, 26, 219
as you were *adv* 126
at a bad time *adv* 116
at a disadvantage *adv* 26
at a discount *adv* 36
at a distance *adv* 172
at a loose end *adj* 762
at a loss *adv* 36
at an advantage *adv* 26
at an angle *adv* 195
at anchor *adv* 160
at arm's length *adv* 172
at a stroke *adv* 47, 96
atavism *n* 105, 126
atavistic *adj* 105
at bottom *adv* 5, 186, 189
at cross-purposes *adv* 20, 56
at daggers drawn *adj* 794
at different times *adv* 18
at ease *adj* 618, 738, *adv* 19
atelier *n* 490, 614
at face value *adv* 394
at fault *adj* 818, 840
at first *adv* 61
at first light *adv* 109
at first sight *adv* 198, 394
at full speed *adv* 245
at full tilt *adv* 147
at hand *adv* 104, 162, 173
at heart *adv* 5, 199
atheism *n* 435, 869
atheist *n* 869
atheistic *adj* 435, 869
athletic *adj* 143
athleticism *n* 143
athletics *n* 761
at home *adv* 19, 162, 199, *n* 789
at intervals *adv* 65, 119, 174
at large *adj* 605, 667
at last *adv* 62, 114
at length *adv* 93, 178, 506
at liberty *adj* 667
at loggerheads *adj* 635, 794
atmosphere *n* 206, 284, 304, 306
atmospheric *adj* 206, 304, 307
atmospheric pollution *n* 350

at no time *adv* 91
at odds *adj* 635, *adv* 20
atoll *n* 311
atom *n* 30, 78, 79, 169, 282
atomic bomb *n* 649
atomic power *n* 141
atomization *n* 46, 304
atomize *vb* 46, 304
atomizer *n* 304
atonal *adj* 366
atonality *n* 366
at once *adv* 96
atone *vb* 28, 596, 813, 814
atonement *n* 28, 596, 813, 814, 841, 862
at one's convenience *adv* 612
at one's leisure *adv* 612
at one's own pace *adv* 612
at one time *adv* 90, 102, 105
atoning *adj* 814
A to Z *n* 49
at peace *adj* 644
at present *adv* 90, 101
at regular intervals *adv* 119
at rest *adv* 160
atrocious *adj* 838
atrocity *n* 806, 838
atrophy *n* 142, 572, *vb* 142
at sea *adv* 237
at sixes and sevens *adj* 635, *adv* 56
attach *vb* 35, 40
attaché *n* 675
attaché case *n* 167
attachment *n* 35, 53, 795, 800
attach oneself to *vb* 85
attach strings *vb* 685
attack *n* 145, 589, 639, 645, 826, 828, *vb* 145, 410, 639, 645
attacker *n* 639
attacking *adj* 639
attain *vb* 261, 651
attainable *adj* 261, 423
attainment *n* 261, 651
attar *n* 349
attempt *n* 416, 561, *vb* 561
attempt the impossible *vb* 424
attend *vb* 85, 101, 162, 404, 666
attendance *n* 162
attendant *adj* 85, 162, *n* 85, 666, 668, 797
attend a séance *vb* 877
attention *n* 404, 616
attention to detail *n* 404
attentive *adj* 404, 406

attentiveness *n* 404, 406
attenuate *vb* 171, 183, 288
attenuation *n* 171, 288
attest *vb* 417, 420
attestation *n* 417, 420
attested *adj* 417
attest to *vb* 484
at the core *adv* 200
at the crack of dawn *adv* 109
at the double *adv* 245
at the drop of a hat *adv* 96, 537
at the end of the day *adv* 27, 62, 93
at the heart *adv* 200
at the last minute *adv* 114
at the moment *adv* 1, 101
at the outset *adv* 61
at the right moment *adv* 115
at the same time *adv* 17, 103
at the top of one's voice *adv* 355
at the top of the tree *adv* 188
at the very least *adv* 30
at the wrong moment *adv* 116
attic *n* 167, 184, 570
at times *adv* 90, 92
attire *n* 204
attitude *n* 7, 408, 434, 621
attitudinize *vb* 771
attitudinizing *adj* 771
attorney *n* 675
attract *vb* 256, 257, 699, 736, 795
attracted *adj* 795
attraction *n* 256, 257, 757
attractions *n* 763
attractive *adj* 256, 257, 755, 757, 763, 795
attractiveness *n* 736, 763, 795
attributable *adj* 134
attribute *n* 5, 70, 85, *vb* 134, 819
attribution *n* 134
attrition *n* 34, 36, 300, 301, 572
at variance *adj* 635, *adv* 20
at war *adj* 645
at will *adv* 535
at work *adj* 607
aubergine *n* 392
auburn *adj* 386, 388
au courant *adj* 438, 466
auction *n* 709, 709, *vb* 709
audacious *adj* 751, 781
audacity *n* 751, 753, 781
audibility *n* 351, 353, 355, 460
audible *adj* 351, 353, 355, 460
audience *n* 162, 351, 370, 470, 532, 533

audio *adj* 353
audiovisual *adj* 351
audit *n* 417, 720, *vb* 720
auditing *n* 720
audition *n* 351, 416, 523, *vb* 416, 523
auditor *n* 351, 720
auditorium *n* 477, 523
auditory *adj* 351
au fait *adj* 438
auger *n* 232, 568
augment *vb* 33, 35, 170, 741
augmentation *n* 33, 170, 741
augur *vb* 455
augur well *vb* 748
augury *n* 455
august *adj* 29, 576, 774
auld lang syne *n* 105
aunt *n* 12
au pair *n* 164, 666
aural *adj* 351
aureole *n* 223
Aurora *n* 109
aurora borealis *n* 374
auscultation *n* 351
auspicious *adj* 115, 455, 580, 655, 748
auspiciousness *n* 455
austere *adj* 509, 659
austereness *n* 483
austerity *n* 509, 659
authentic *adj* 3, 22, 417
authenticate *vb* 3, 417
authentication *n* 417
authenticity *n* 3, 22, 440
author *n* 132, 149, 518, 613, *vb* 518
authoritative *adj* 29, 141, 622, 624, 657, 823, 868, 878
authorities *n* 863
authority *n* 29, 141, 622, 624, 657, 677, 823, 852, 854
authorization *n* 677, 852
authorize *vb* 677, 677
authorized *adj* 677, 852
authorship *n* 513
autistic *adj* 447
autobiography *n* 518
autocracy *n* 657
autocrat *n* 665
autocratic *adj* 535, 659
auto-da-fe *n* 324
autodidact *n* 476
autograph *adj* 513, *n* 485, *vb* 485
automate *vb* 75, 141
automated *adj* 141
automatic *adj* 399, 401, 536, 548, 568

automatic writing *n* 876, 877
automation *n* 149
automaton *n* 731
automobile *n* 242
automotive *adj* 234, 242
autonomous *adj* 535, 667
autonomy *n* 535, 667
autopsy *n* 323, 417
autumn *n* 108
autumnal *adj* 108
autumn equinox *n* 108
auxiliary *adj* 32, 35, 631, *n* 32, 35
avail *vb* 835
availability *n* 162, 578
available *adj* 162, 470, 564, 571, 578, 679, 709
avail oneself of *vb* 564
avalanche *n* 275
avant-garde *adj* 59, *n* 59, 106, 212
avarice *n* 728, 834
avaricious *adj* 728, 834
avenge *vb* 641, 810
avenger *n* 641
avenue *n* 240
average *adj* 27, 63, 72, 148, 777, *n* 27, 63, 69, 250
averageness *n* 27
average out *vb* 27
averse *adj* 538, 758, 796
aversion *n* 538, 758, 796
avert *vb* 556
aviary *n* 165, 326
aviate *vb* 238
aviation *n* 238
aviational *adj* 244
aviator *n* 238
aviatrix *n* 238
avid *adj* 728, 729, 755
avidity *n* 728
avocado *n* 390
avoid *vb* 251, 407, 556, 565, 605
avoidable *adj* 556
avoidance *n* 538, 556, 565, 605
avoider *n* 556
avoiding *adj* 556
avoid the issue *vb* 10, 411
avoirdupois *adj* 177
avow *vb* 434, 473
avowal *n* 468, 473
avuncular *adj* 12
await *vb* 450
awake *adj* 730
awaken *vb* 334, 732

award *n* 429, 650, 698, 859, *vb* 698, 859
aware *adj* 334, 396, 404, 438, 444, 730
awareness *n* 334, 396, 438, 444, 730
awash *adj* 305
away *adj* 163
awe *n* 750, 759, 823, 872, *vb* 823
awesome *adj* 750
awestruck *adj* 823
awful *adj* 583
awkward *adj* 116, 285, 502, 512, 538, 581, 625, 628, 662
awkward age *n* 111
awkwardness *n* 439, 502, 512, 581, 625, 628, 662
awning *n* 202, 378
AWOL *adj* 605
a word in edgeways *n* 528
awry *adj* 26, 219, *adv* 836
axe *n* 649, 861, *vb* 34, 36
axeman *n* 147, 324
axis *n* 200
Axis *n* 634
axle *n* 193, 200, 279
ayah *n* 666
azure *adj* 39

B

baa *vb* 364
Babbitry *n* 72
babble *n* 358, *vb* 314, 459
babbling *adj* 314
babe *n* 839
babe in arms *n* 111
Babel *n* 56, 366
baby *adj* 169, *n* 169
baby blues *n* 447
baby boom *n* 152
baby grand *n* 369
babyhood *n* 111
babyish *adj* 111, 144
baby-sitter *n* 668
Bacchus *n* 862
bachelor *adj* 799, *n* 79, 332, 778, 799
bachelor girl *n* 79, 333, 799
bachelorhood *n* 799
back *adj* 62, 213, *n* 213, *vb* 193, 213, 254, 436, 473, 554, 567, 631, 701, 825
back and forth *adv* 280
back and forwards *adv* 119
backbiter *n* 828

balanced *adj* 19, 131, 218, 446, 511
balance of power *n* 25, 644
balance of terror *n* 25
balance out *vb* 27
balance sheet *n* 720
balcony *n* 191, 523
bald *adj* 203, 478, 509
baldness *n* 203, 503, 509
bale *n* 66
baleful *adj* 806
bale out *vb* 264
balk *vb* 538
ball *n* 223, 225, 524, 761, 789, *vb* 225
ballad *n* 367, 521
ballast *n* 25, 28, 131, 285
ballcock *n* 233
ballerina *n* 524
ballet *n* 524, 761
balletic *adj* 524
ballistic *adj* 255
ballistics *n* 255
balloon *n* 225, 244, 761, *vb* 170, 225, 238
ballooning *n* 238
balloonist *n* 238
ballot *n* 545
ballroom dancing *n* 524
balls *n* 152
balls-up *n* 56
balls up *vb* 56
ballyhoo *n* 431, 470, 482
balm *n* 148, 302, 349, 596, 740
balmy *adj* 339
balustrade *n* 193
Bamboo Curtain *n* 52
bamboozle *vb* 411, 480
ban *n* 52, 630, 668, 678, 680, 826, *vb* 52, 630, 668, 678, 680, 826
banal *adj* 117, 442, 459, 762
banality *n* 117, 459, 762
bananas *adj* 447
band *n* 66, 175, 368, 634
bandage *n* 202, 596, 630, *vb* 202, 630
bandit *n* 705
bandleader *n* 368
bandmaster *n* 368
Band of Hope *n* 847
band together *vb* 45, 66
bandy *adj* 219
bandy-legged *adj* 221
bandy words *vb* 129, 410, 533
bane *n* 150, 597, 836
bang *n* 247, 355, 357, *vb* 247, 357
bangle *n* 766

bang on *adj* 440
banish *vb* 52, 161, 198, 266, 860
banishment *n* 52, 161, 266, 790, 860
banister *n* 193
banjo *n* 369
bank *n* 195, 569, 570, 701, 711, *vb* 195, 434, 570
bankable *adj* 525
bank account *n* 711
bank balance *n* 711
banker *n* 613, 701, 711
banker's order/draft *n* 711
bank holiday *n* 618
banknote *n* 683, 711
bank on *vb* 427, 450
bankroll *vb* 525, 711
bankrupt *adj* 652, 713, 717, *n* 652, 713, 717, *vb* 717
bankruptcy *n* 652, 713, 717
banned *adj* 678, 853
banner *n* 484
banquet *n* 267, 761, 789
bantamweight *adj* 286
banter *n* 533, 744, 773
bantustan *n* 790
baptism *n* 61, 265, 497, 881
baptismal *adj* 59, 61, 265
baptism of fire *n* 59
baptize *vb* 59, 61, 265, 497, 881
bar *n* 233, 601, 630, 668, 678, 826, 855, *vb* 41, 233, 393, 630, 668, 678, 826
barb *n* 296, *vb* 296
barbarian *n* 54, 147, 330, 838
barbarism *n* 496, 501
barbarity *n* 806
barbarous *adj* 806, 810
barbecue *n* 761, 789
barbed *adj* 296
barbed wire *n* 640
barber *n* 765
barbican *n* 640
bard *n* 368, 521
bardic *adj* 521
bare *adj* 203, 205, 483, 509
barefoot *adj* 713
barefooted *adj* 205
barelegged *adj* 205
barely *adv* 30
bareness *n* 203, 483
bare one's soul *vb* 468
bargain *n* 684, 708, 722, 724, *vb* 685, 707
bargain/cut price *n* 722

beagling *n* 761
be a goner *vb* 323
beak *n* 212, 228, 665
beaker *n* 167
be a laughing stock *vb* 772
be a law unto oneself *vb* 658, 853
be-all and end-all *n* 576
be all ears *vb* 351, 404
be all the same to *vb* 756
beam *n* 193, 374, *vb* 374
bean *n* 30
beanfeast *n* 267, 786
be angry *vb* 802
beano *n* 267, 789
beanpole *n* 183
bear *n* 554, *vb* 193, 241, 729
bear a grudge *vb* 796, 802, 806
beard *n* 765, *vb* 751
bearer *n* 241, 613
bear false witness *vb* 481, 830
bear fruit *vb* 651
bearhug *n* 695
bearing *n* 9, 234, 394
bearings *n* 159, 249, 484
bearish *adj* 275
bear malice *vb* 802, 806
bear out *vb* 417, 420, 440, 829
bear the cost *vb* 718
bear the cost of *vb* 716
bear with *vb* 813
bear witness *vb* 420
be as good as one's word *vb* 688
beast *n* 147, 326, 838
be as thick as thieves *vb* 793
beastly *adj* 583, 737, 796, 806
beast of burden *n* 241
beat *n* 88, 119, 158, 280, 521, *vb* 119,
   247, 280, 281, 358, 368, 555, 651,
   860
beat about the bush *vb* 411
be at a loose end *vb* 608
be at a loss for words *vb* 527
be at cross-purposes *vb* 441
be at death's door *vb* 323
beat down *vb* 707
be at ease *vb* 618
beaten *adj* 652
beater *n* 555
be at fault *vb* 818
beatified *adj* 863
beatify *vb* 774, 872
beating *n* 651, 652
beat it *vb* 262
beatitude *n* 863

be at odds *vb* 18
be at odds with *vb* 794
beat one's breast *vb* 747
be at sea *vb* 461
beat the drum *vb* 470
be at the ready *vb* 450
beat up *vb* 147, 639
be at variance *vb* 18
beau *n* 770, 795
beautician *n* 765
beautification *n* 765
beautiful *adj* 511, 736, 763
beautiful people *n* 770
beautify *vb* 511, 765
beauty *n* 511, 736, 763
beauty queen *n* 763
beauty spot *n* 763
beauty treatment *n* 765
beaver *vb* 540
be behind the times *vb* 98
be beyond one *vb* 461
be beyond the bounds of possibility
   vb 424
be born *vb* 322
be brittle *vb* 295
becalmed *adj* 235
be capricious *vb* 544
be careful *vb* 406
be caught in the act *vb* 840
be caught out *vb* 451
be caught short *vb* 268
because of *prep* 132, 134
be charitable *vb* 807
be cheap *vb* 724
be cheerful *vb* 742
beck *n* 314
beckon *vb* 484
become dense *vb* 287
become holy *vb* 872
become one *vb* 79, 797
become popular *vb* 770
become small *vb* 30
become teetotal *vb* 847
be concise *vb* 505
be consecutive *vb* 64
be conspicuous *vb* 162
be conspicuous by one's absence *vb*
   163
be contrite *vb* 841
be convenient *vb* 580
be converted *vb* 125, 841, 872
be convex *vb* 226
be courageous *vb* 751
be crazy about *vb* 795

be had for the asking *vb* 724
behave *vb* 621, 663, 791
behave badly *vb* 621
behave oneself *vb* 621, 837
behave well *vb* 621
behaviour *n* 621
behavioural *adj* 621
behead *vb* 36, 179, 324, 860
beheading *n* 860
behind *adj* 717, *adv* 60, 213, *n* 213
behind bars *adj* 598, 668
behind closed doors *adv* 467
behindhand *adj* 98, 114
behind one's back *adv* 163
behind-the-scenes *adj* 467
behind the times *adj* 102
behold *vb* 370
beholden *adj* 811
be holy *vb* 872
be honourable *vb* 831
be horizontal *vb* 191
be hospitable *vb* 793
be hostile *vb* 794
behove *vb* 821
be humble *vb* 823
be identical *vb* 13
beige *adj* 386
be ignorant *vb* 439
be illegal *vb* 853
be immoderate *vb* 844
be immoral *vb* 851
be impenitent *vb* 842
be important *vb* 576
be impossible *vb* 424
be in a class of one's own *vb* 70
be inactive *vb* 610
be inattentive *vb* 405
be in charge of *vb* 622
be in clover *vb* 336
be incompatible *vb* 794
be incomplete *vb* 50
be inconvenient *vb* 581
be in debt *vb* 715
be in demand *vb* 709
be independent *vb* 44, 73, 535
be in difficulty *vb* 628
be inert *vb* 146
be infatuated *vb* 795
be inferior *vb* 32
be in fine fettle *vb* 145
be infinite *vb* 89
be informed *vb* 466
being *adj* 1, *n* 1, 320, 322
be in good faith *vb* 831

be inherited *vb* 12
be in hopes of *vb* 748
be in love *vb* 795
be innocent *vb* 839
be in one's right mind *vb* 446
be in on the ground floor *vb* 61
be in operation *vb* 607
be in order *vb* 55
be in partnership with *vb* 693
be in possession of one's faculties *vb* 446
be insane *vb* 447
be inseparable *vb* 793
be in someone's debt *vb* 811
be in stiches *vb* 744
be in store *vb* 450
be instrumental *vb* 138
be insufficient etc *vb* 574
be insulted *vb* 802
be intelligent *vb* 396
be intelligible *vb* 460
be intemperate *vb* 844
be in the air *vb* 101
be in the black *vb* 714
be in the blood *vb* 12
be in the dark *vb* 371
be in the driving seat *vb* 622
be in the habit of *vb* 549
be in the know *vb* 466
be in the land of the living *vb* 322
be in the lap of the gods *vb* 428
be in the offing *vb* 425
be in the pink *vb* 588
be in the red *vb* 702
be in the right *vb* 817
be in the right ballpark *vb* 173
be in the wind *vb* 101
be in the wrong *vb* 441, 818
be into *vb* 757
be in trouble *vb* 656
be in two minds *vb* 44, 428, 541
be invisible *vb* 373
be in with *vb* 793
be irascible *vb* 803
be irregular *vb* 120
be irrelevant *vb* 6
be irresolute *vb* 44
be jealous *vb* 815
bejewelled *adj* 766
be just *vb* 817
be just around the corner *vb* 104
be kind *vb* 805
be kindness itself *vb* 805
be late *vb* 114

be on the ball *vb* 404
be on the cards *vb* 425, 450
be on the edge of one's seat *vb* 450
be on the make *vb* 834
be on the same wavelength *vb* 19
be on the shelf *vb* 799
be on the up and up *vb* 655
be on the wrong track *vb* 252
be open to criticism *vb* 826
be opposed to *vb* 794
be opposite *vb* 14, 215
be ordained *vb* 878, 879
be out in front *vb* 212
be out of one's element *vb* 54
be out of one's mind *vb* 445
be out of the ordinary *vb* 70
be out of the question *vb* 424
be over and done with *vb* 2
be overdrawn *vb* 715
be parallel *vb* 194
be part and parcel of *vb* 5, 53
be partial to *vb* 757, 795
be past *vb* 105
be patient *vb* 733
be penitent *vb* 841
be periodic *vb* 92
be permanent *vb* 122
be persuaded *vb* 551
be pipped at the post *vb* 652
be pitiless *vb* 810
be plentiful *vb* 573
be poor *vb* 713
be possessed of *vb* 692
be prepared *vb* 598
be present *vb* 1, 101, 162
be priced at *vb* 721
be probable *vb* 425
be proud *vb* 779
be public-spirited *vb* 807
be puffed up *vb* 783
be punished *vb* 860
be put through it *vb* 656
bequeath *vb* 696, 697, 698
bequest *n* 690, 697, 698
be rash *vb* 753
be real *vb* 3
bereaved *adj* 323, 691
bereavement *n* 323, 691, 735
be received *vb* 699
be reconciled *vb* 636, 813
be redolent of *vb* 17
be refreshed *vb* 620
bereft *adj* 691
be related *vb* 9

be related to *vb* 12
be relevant *vb* 9
be relieved *vb* 740
be resolute *vb* 539
be responsible for *vb* 821
be rhythmic *vb* 119
be rich *vb* 712
berk *n* 445
Berlin Wall *n* 52
be rolling in money *vb* 655
berserk *adj* 447
berth *n* 160, *vb* 160, 237
be rude *vb* 792
beryl *n* 321, 390, 766
be safe *vb* 598
be sane *vb* 446
be satisfied *vb* 738
beseech *vb* 681, 874
beseeching *adj* 681
be self-indulgent *vb* 844
be selfish *vb* 834
be self-restrained *vb* 843
be servile *vb* 827
be severe *vb* 659
be shallow *vb* 187
be short-tempered *vb* 803
beside oneself *adj* 802
beside the point *adv* 6, 10
besiege *vb* 210, 639
besieger *n* 639
be similar *vb* 17
be situated *vb* 1, 7
be skilful *vb* 624
be slain *vb* 323
be slow *vb* 114
be slow off the mark *vb* 98
besmirch *vb* 376, 384, 828
be sober *vb* 843, 847
be sold off *vb* 709
besotted *adj* 795
be spared *vb* 322
bespoke *adj* 70, 204
best *adj* 29, 582, *vb* 31
be stable *vb* 131
best bib and tucker *n* 204, 787
best friend *n* 793
bestial *adj* 326
best man *n* 797
best of both worlds *n* 27
bestow *vb* 698
bestowal *n* 698
bestow a title *vb* 859
be struck dumb *vb* 527
bestseller *n* 516, 518, 651

bestselling *adj* 651
best thing since sliced bread *n* 582
best wishes *n* 786
be sufficient/enough *vb* 573
be superior *vb* 31
be swept off one's feet *vb* 795
bet *n* 554, *vb* 554
be taciturn *vb* 531
be talkative *vb* 530
be tantamount to *vb* 13
be temperate *vb* 847
bête noire *n* 758, 796
be the duty of *vb* 821
be the same *vb* 13
be the saving of *vb* 606
be thrifty *vb* 726
be tipsy *vb* 848
be tired *vb* 619
betoken *vb* 420, 484
bet one's bottom dollar *vb* 427
be too proud *vb* 779
be tough *vb* 294
betray *vb* 452, 466, 468, 484, 832
betrayal *n* 468, 480, 832
betrothal *n* 683
betrothed *adj* 683
be truthful *vb* 478
better *adj* 592, *vb* 253
better days *n* 102
better half *n* 797
betterment *n* 253, 592, 835
better oneself *vb* 592
between ourselves *adv* 467
between Scylla and Charybdis *adv* 63
between the devil and the deep blue
   sea *adv* 63
be unaffected *vb* 731
be uncertain *vb* 428
be uncommitted *vb* 44
be under the influence of drink *vb*
   848
be unequal *vb* 26
be ungrateful *vb* 812
be unhappy *vb* 735
be unhealthy *vb* 589
be unimportant *vb* 577
be unintelligible *vb* 461
be unlike *vb* 18
be unmarried *vb* 799
be unprepared *vb* 560
be unproductive *vb* 153
be unreal *vb* 4
be unrelated *vb* 10
be unskilful *vb* 625

be unsociable *vb* 804
be unsuccessful *vb* 652
be unwilling *vb* 538
be up on one's high horse *vb* 779
be upstanding *vb* 190, 276
be useful *vb* 578, 835
be useless *vb* 579
bevel *n* 195, *vb* 195
bevelled *adj* 209
beverage *n* 267
be vertical *vb* 190
be victorious *vb* 651
be vigorous *vb* 145
be violent *vb* 147
be virtuous *vb* 837
be visible *vb* 372
bevy *n* 66
beware of *vb* 406
be wicked *vb* 838
bewilder *vb* 405, 759
bewildered *adj* 759
bewildering *adj* 759
bewilderment *n* 759
be willing *vb* 537
be wise *vb* 444
bewitch *vb* 139, 732, 736, 795, 876
bewitched *adj* 876
bewitching *adj* 139, 732, 736, *n* 732
bewitchment *n* 876
be worlds apart *vb* 794
be worth it *vb* 582
be worthy *vb* 819
be wound up *vb* 717
be wrong-footed *vb* 451
bey *n* 776
beyond compare *adj* 584
biannual *adj* 81, 92
bias *n* 26, 140, 195, 219, 430, 818, *vb*
   26, 140, 219, 430
biased *adj* 26, 140, 219, 430, 818
Bible puncher *n* 872
Bible study *n* 881
biblical *adj* 868
bibliography *n* 76, 516
bibliolatry *n* 872
bibliophile *n* 516
bice *n* 390
bicentenary *n* 84, 92
bicker *vb* 410, 437, 635
bickering *n* 635
bicycle *n* 81, 242, 761
bid *n* 561, 679, *vb* 561, 679
bide one's time *vb* 90, 608
bidet *n* 586

bid fair *vb* 748
bid farewell *vb* 262
bid for *vb* 708
biennial *adj* 81, 92, 327
bier *n* 325
bifocals *n* 370
bifurcate *vb* 81
bifurcation *n* 81, 260
big *adj* 29, 168, 576
bigamy *n* 797
big battalions *n* 31, 141
big boys *n* 31
big brother *n* 657
big cat *n* 326
big deal *n* 576
big gun *n* 576
big guns *n* 31
big hand *n* 484
big-headed *adj* 779, 783
big-headedness *n* 779
big-hearted *adj* 725
bight *n* 221, 310
big-mouth *n* 771
big-mouthed *adj* 771
bigness *n* 168
big noise *n* 576
bigot *n* 659, 872
bigoted *adj* 181, 430, 434, 659
bigotry *n* 181, 430, 434, 659, 871
big spender *n* 727
bigwig *n* 576
bilateral *adj* 81, 633
bilingual *adj* 81, 494, 528
bilingualism *n* 81
bilious *adj* 803
biliousness *n* 389
bill *n* 228, 683, 711, 715, 720, *vb* 720
billet *n* 165, *vb* 158
billet doux *n* 515
billiards *n* 761
billingsgate *n* 496, 801
billion *n* 84
billionth *adj* 84
bill of fare *n* 76
billow *n* 310, *vb* 226
billy *n* 332
Billy Bunter *n* 168
bin *n* 167
binary *adj* 74, 81
binaural *adj* 81, 353
bind *n* 762, *vb* 40, 66, 171, 630, 821
binding *adj* 171, 536, 623, 664, 684, 821, *n* 516
binge *vb* 844

bingo *n* 554, 761
bingo hall *n* 761
binoculars *n* 370
bint *n* 851
biochemical *adj* 320
biochemistry *n* 320
biodegradable *adj* 46, 125, 696
biographical *adj* 522
biography *n* 517, 518, 522
biological *adj* 320
biological powder *n* 586
biology *n* 320
biomass *n* 327
bionic *adj* 38
biopic *n* 525
biorhythms *n* 119
biotechnology *n* 320
bipartite *adj* 81
biped *n* 326
biplane *n* 81, 244
birch *n* 861, *vb* 860
bird *n* 326, 333, 795
birdcall *n* 364
birdlime *n* 318
bird of passage *n* 94
bird of prey *n* 326
bird sanctuary *n* 603
birds and the bees *n* 152
bird's eye view *n* 47, 184, 370
birds of a feather *n* 17
birth *n* 61, 322
birth control *n* 153
birthday *n* 92, 119, 786
birthday suit *n* 205
birthing *n* 152
birthmark *n* 767
birth pangs *n* 61
birthplace *n* 165
birthright *n* 819
biscuit *adj* 386
bisect *vb* 48, 63, 81
bisection *n* 81
bisexual *adj* 38, 73, 81, *n* 38, 73
bisexuality *n* 81
bishop *n* 776, 879
bishopric *n* 878
bistre *n* 386
bistro *n* 165
bit *n* 79, 568, 570, 668
bit/walk-on part *n* 523
bit by bit *adv* 24, 48
bitch *n* 326, 333
bitchy *adj* 604

bite *n* 30, 48, 267, 296, 342, 344, 507, *vb* 296
bite someone's head off *vb* 802
bite the dust *vb* 275
biting *adj* 296, 340, 507, 826
bits and pieces *n* 694
bitter *adj* 340, 342, 343, 344, 346, 794, 802, 806, 828
bitter end *n* 653
bitterness *n* 342, 346, 737, 794, 802, 806
bitters *n* 346
bittersweet *adj* 344
bittiness *n* 50
bitty *adj* 48, 50
bivouac *n* 165
bizarre *adj* 772
blab *vb* 466, 830
black *adj* 375, 384, *n* 331, 384, 747, *vb* 52, 556, 630, 678
blackamoor *n* 384
black art *n* 876
black as the ace of spades *adj* 384
blackball *vb* 41, 52, 546, 678, 790
blackballing *n* 41
blackboard jungle *n* 477
black bottom *n* 524
black comedy *n* 744
black economy *n* 705
blacked *adj* 678
blacked out *adj* 678
blacken *vb* 375, 384, 828
blackguard *n* 838
black-haired *adj* 384
black hole *n* 284
black ice *n* 307, 340
blacking *n* 586, 630
blackish *adj* 384
blackleg *n* 73
blacklist *n* 41, 76, 678, 826, *vb* 41, 52, 678, 826
black look *n* 802, 804
black magic *n* 864, 876
blackmail *n* 664, 681, 703, 806, *vb* 681, 806
Black Maria *n* 242
black mark *n* 826
black-market *adj* 853
black marketeer *n* 707
blackness *n* 375, 384
blackout *n* 335, 354, 375, 395, 467, 487
black out *vb* 335, 487
black sheep *n* 54, 838

blacksmith *n* 613
black spot *n* 599
black tie *n* 787
blade *n* 296, 770
blame *n* 134, 826, 830, 840, *vb* 134, 826, 830
blamed *adj* 840
blameless *adj* 839
blamelessness *n* 839
blameworthy *adj* 826
blanch *vb* 382, 383
blanco *n* 383, 586
bland *adj* 148, 343, 827
blandishments *n* 800, 827
blandness *n* 148, 343
blank *adj* 2, 163, 399, 459, *n* 77, 449, 487
blank cheque *n* 667
blanket *adj* 47, 69, 419, *n* 202, *vb* 202, 378
blanket coverage *n* 51, 69
blankness *n* 2, 163, 449, 760
blank verse *n* 521
blank wall *n* 424
blare *n* 355, *vb* 355, 362
blarney *n* 827
blasé *adj* 403, 733, 756
blaspheme *vb* 801, 873
blasphemer *n* 873
blasphemous *adj* 801, 873
blasphemy *n* 801, 873
blast *n* 306, 316, 357, *vb* 306, 316, 801
blast from the past *n* 105, 448
blastoff *n* 238, 262
blast off *vb* 61, 238
blatancy *n* 781, 785
blatant *adj* 372, 464, 781, 785
blather *n* 530, *vb* 459, 506, 530
blatherskite *n* 530
blaze *n* 339, 374, *vb* 339, 374
blaze aboard *vb* 470
blaze a trail *vb* 59, 61, 559
blazon *n* 484
bleach *n* 382, 586, *vb* 382, 383, 586
bleached *adj* 382
bleaching *n* 382
bleak *adj* 108, 656, 749
bleary *adj* 376
bleat *vb* 364
bleed *vb* 264, 723
bleeding *adj* 303
bleeper *n* 42, 472

blue-chip *adj* 31, 582
blue-collar worker *n* 613, 777
blue-eyed boy *n* 800
blue film *n* 851
blue funk *n* 750
blue-grey *adj* 385
blue movie *n* 525
blue-pencil *vb* 36, 487, 678
Blue Peter *n* 484
blueprint *n* 22, 488, 557, *vb* 22
blue rosette *n* 650
blues *n* 367
blue skies *n* 307
blue stocking *n* 396
bluesy *adj* 367
bluey-green *adj* 391
bluey-grey *adj* 391
bluff *n* 184, 190, 481, 771, *vb* 771
bluffer *n* 771
bluish *adj* 391
blunder *n* 116, 441, 840, *vb* 441, 625
blunt *adj* 179, 297, 473, 478, *vb* 144, 148, 297
bluntness *n* 297, 478, 509
blur *n* 217, 376, 767, *vb* 4, 217, 376, 419, 767
blurb *n* 470
blurred *adj* 217, 373, 376, 767
blush *n* 387, *vb* 387, 784
blusher *n* 765
blushing *adj* 784
bluster *n* 771, *vb* 316, 771
blustering *adj* 771
blustery *adj* 307, 316
B-movie *n* 525
boar *n* 326, 332
board *n* 289, 569, 657, 855, *vb* 571, 639
boarder *n* 164, 199
board of directors *n* 622
board of directors/governors *n* 634
boards *n* 202, 516
boast *n* 771, *vb* 771
boaster *n* 771
boastful *adj* 771
boastfulness *n* 771, 783
boasting *n* 752, 783
boat *n* 243
boating *n* 237, 761
boatman *n* 237
boatswain *n* 237
bob *n* 192, 277, 280, 286, *vb* 277
bobble *n* 766
bobby *n* 854

bode ill *vb* 806
bode well *vb* 748
bodge *vb* 50
bodger *n* 625
bodily *adj* 282, 334, 844, *adv* 664
bodkin *n* 232
body *n* 182, 282, 287, 324, 330, 342, 634
body and soul *adv* 47, 49
body building *n* 143
body fluid *n* 303
body forth *vb* 3, 6, 198, 282
bodyguard *n* 85, 598, 666, 668
body language *n* 334, 484, 494
body of law *n* 852
bodypart *n* 48
body-snatcher *n* 705
body-snatching *n* 705
bodywork *n* 298
bog *n* 308
bogey *n* 865
boggy *adj* 308
bogus *adj* 479, 481, 820
Bohemian *adj* 73, *n* 73
boil *n* 226, *vb* 267, 281, 339, 590, 802
boil down *vb* 171, 505, 520
boiler *n* 339
boiling *adj* 307, 339
boiling point *n* 339
boisterous *adj* 147, 732
boisterousness *n* 732
bold *adj* 513, 751, 781
boldface *n* 514
boldness *n* 751, 781
bole *n* 225, 327
bollocks *n* 152
bolshie *adj* 127, 437, 538, 662
bolster *n* 193, *vb* 33, 193, 751
bolt *n* 42, 66, 233, 649, *vb* 40, 96, 233, 245, 262, 267
bolt down *vb* 846
bolted *adj* 233
bolt from the blue *n* 451
bolthole *n* 232, 600, 605
bolt upright *adv* 190
bomb *n* 649, *vb* 639
bomb-aimer *n* 648
bomb along *vb* 615
bombard *vb* 255, 639
bombardier *n* 648
bombardment *n* 150, 255, 639
bombast *n* 170, 482, 504, 510, 771, 785
bombastic *adj* 482, 504, 510, 771, 785

bomber *n* 244, 639
bombproof *adj* 640
bombshell *n* 451
bomb site *n* 232
bomb to the conference table *vb* 646
bona fide *adj* 22, 478
bonbon *n* 345
bonce *n* 188
bond *n* 9, 40, 42, 569, 683, 687, 819, 821, *vb* 40
bondage *n* 32, 670
bondsman *n* 613, 666
bone *n* 289
bone-dry *adj* 309
boneheaded *adj* 397
bone of contention *n* 635
bone to pick *n* 802
bone up *vb* 476
bonfire *n* 339, 377
bonhomie *n* 789
bonkers *adj* 447
bonny *adj* 763
bonus *n* 33, 35, 575, 690, 719, 859
bony *adj* 289
boo *n* 355, 363, 484, 824, 826, *vb* 363, 826
boob *vb* 441
boobs *n* 226
booby *n* 439, 445
booby prize *n* 60, 650
booby trap *n* 601
boogie *n* 524, *vb* 524
book *n* 516, *vb* 113, 720, 830
bookbinder *n* 613
bookie *n* 554
booking clerk *n* 709
bookish *adj* 438
bookkeeper *n* 711, 720
bookkeeping *n* 720
book-learning *n* 438
booklet *n* 516
bookmaker *n* 554
books *n* 720
bookseller *n* 516
bookworm *n* 438, 476, 516
boom *n* 33, 192, 355, 592, 655, 709, *vb* 526, 655
boomerang *n* 248, 641, *vb* 248
booming *adj* 526, 655
boon *n* 835
boor *n* 792
boorish *adj* 512, 769, 792
boorishness *n* 512, 769, 792

boost *n* 33, 145, 276, *vb* 33, 141, 145, 751, 825, 827
booster *n* 255
booth *n* 710
bootless *adj* 652
bootlicker *n* 782
bootlicking *n* 782
booty *n* 650, 703, 706
booze *n* 267, *vb* 267, 848
boozed up *adj* 848
boozer *n* 165, 848
booze-up *n* 848
bop *n* 367, *vb* 524
border *n* 173, 176, 208, 209, 211, *vb* 173, 176, 209, 211, 214
bordering *adj* 211
borderline *adj* 209, *n* 211
borderline case *n* 63, 428
bore *n* 232, 314, 762, *vb* 227, 232
bored *adj* 403, 762
boredom *n* 403, 762
borehole *n* 227
bore stiff/rigid *vb* 762
bore to tears/to death *vb* 762
boring *adj* 762
born-again *adj* 106, 125, 151, 872
born on the wrong side of the blanket *adj* 853
born out of wedlock *adj* 853
born with a silver spoon in one's mouth *adj* 712
borough *n* 157
borrow *vb* 21, 54, 702, 714
borrowed *adj* 54
borrower *n* 702, 715
borrowing *n* 702
Borstal *n* 671, 860
bosky *adj* 327
bosom *n* 226
bosom pal *n* 793
bosomy *adj* 226
boss *n* 31, 223, 226, 622, 665, *vb* 31
bossa nova *n* 524
botanical *adj* 320, 327
botanical gardens *n* 329
botanize *vb* 327
botany *n* 320
botch *n* 489, *vb* 56, 625
both *adj* 81
bother *n* 281, 609, 617, 628, 735, *vb* 581, 628, 737, 802
bothersome *adj* 628, 737
bottle *n* 143, 145, 167, 751, *vb* 570, 603

bottle/chicken out *vb* 752
bottled *adj* 603
bottle-green *adj* 390
bottleneck *n* 123, 181
bottle-opener *n* 568
bottle party *n* 761, 789
bottle up *vb* 668
bottling *n* 603
bottom *adj* 189, *n* 32, 189
bottom drawer *n* 570
bottomless *adj* 89, 186
bottomless pit *n* 867
bottom line *n* 3
bottom of the heap *n* 32
bottom out *vb* 32, 189
bouffant *adj* 226, *n* 765
bough *n* 327
boulder *n* 311
boulevard *n* 240
bounce *n* 248, 293, *vb* 293, 717
bounce back *vb* 248
bouncer *n* 266
bouncy *adj* 248, 293, 742
bound *adj* 516, 668, 670, 715, *n* 274,
   vb 211, 274
boundary *n* 62, 206, 207, 209, 211,
   668
bounder *n* 838
bound for *adj* 249
boundless *adj* 86, 89
boundlessness *n* 89
bounteous *adj* 725
bountiful *adj* 698, 725
bounty *n* 698, 725
bouquet *n* 66, 347, 349, 766, 825
bourgeois *adj* 72
bourgeoisie *n* 777
bout *n* 92, 643
boutique *n* 710
bovine *adj* 326, 731
bovver *n* 147
bow *n* 212, 221, 226, 255, 766, 791,
   823, *vb* 32, 185, 219, 221, 226, 368,
   791, 823, 881
bow and arrow *n* 649
bow and scrape *vb* 663
bowdlerization *n* 36
bowdlerize *vb* 36
bowed *adj* 185, 219
bowel movement *n* 268
bowels *n* 166, 186, 199
bowing and scraping *n* 782
bowl *n* 167, 227, 255, *vb* 255
bowled over *adj* 759

bow-legged *adj* 221
bowler *n* 255
bowl over *vb* 451, 759
bow out *vb* 262
bow to fate *vb* 536
bow-wow *n* 326
box *n* 167, *vb* 202
Box and Cox *adv* 11
boxing *n* 643
box office *n* 525
box office receipts *n* 719
box on the ears *vb* 860
boxroom *n* 167
boy *n* 332
boyar *n* 776
boycott *n* 41, 52, 556, 630, 678, 826,
   vb 52, 630, 678, 826
boyfriend *n* 332, 793, 795
brace *n* 81, 193, 568, *vb* 143, 193
bracelet *n* 223, 766
brace oneself *vb* 751
bracing *adj* 145, 620
bracket *n* 40, 42, 193, *vb* 40, 207
bracket together *vb* 9
brackishness *n* 342
bradawl *n* 232
brag *n* 761, *vb* 771
braggadocio *n* 752
braggart *n* 752, 771
bragging *n* 771
Brahma *n* 862
Brahminism *n* 868
Brahms and Liszt *adj* 848
braid *n* 197, 766, *vb* 197
braille *n* 513
brainbox *n* 396
brainchild *n* 149, 408
brain death *n* 323
braininess *n* 396
brainless *adj* 397, 445
brainlessness *n* 397
brains *n* 396
brainteaser *n* 414
brainwash *vb* 72, 551
brainwashing *n* 139, 475
brainwave *n* 548
brainwork *n* 398
brainy *adj* 396
braise *vb* 267
brake *n* 148, 246, 668, *vb* 235, 246,
   630
branch *n* 41, 48, 81, 155, 220, 327,
   614, 871, *vb* 48, 67, 220, 260
branching *adj* 67, 260, *n* 67, 260

branch line *n* 240
branch out *vb* 16
brand *n* 68, 339, 377, 828, *vb* 68, 485
branded *adj* 485
brandish *vb* 464
brand name *n* 485
brand-new *adj* 106, 565
brash *adj* 769
brashness *n* 769
brass *n* 369, 389, 569, 711
brasserie *n* 165
brass tacks *n* 3
brassy *adj* 362
brat *n* 111
bravado *n* 771, 785
brave *adj* 751, *n* 751, *vb* 212, 751
bravery *n* 751
brawl *n* 56, 147, 643, *vb* 643
brawn *n* 143
brawny *adj* 143
bray *n* 355, *vb* 362, 364
braying *n* 362
brazen *adj* 781, 873
brazenness *n* 781
breach *n* 41, 50, 65, 174, 232, 272, 635, 689, *vb* 41, 272, 689
breach of etiquette *n* 788
breach of faith *n* 689
breach of law *n* 853
breach of the peace *n* 56, 662
bread *n* 711
bread and water *n* 343, 845
breadline *n* 573, 713
breadth *n* 23, 180, 182, 191
breadwinner *n* 611
break *n* 41, 50, 65; 115, 123, 174, 232, 612, 618, *vb* 41, 147, 295, 662, 689
breakability *n* 295
breakable *adj* 295
break and enter *vb* 263
breakaway *adj* 41, 871
break away *vb* 871
breakaway group *n* 41
breakdancing *n* 761
breakdown *n* 46, 589, 652
break down *vb* 46, 125, 447, 652, 747
breakdown of law and order *n* 658, 853
breakdown of marriage *n* 798
breaker *n* 310
break faith *vb* 689
break in *vb* 475
breaking and entering *n* 705

breaking point *n* 653
break in on *vb* 116, 527
break in the clouds *n* 740
breakneck *adj* 245, 753
break new ground *vb* 61
break off *vb* 50, 65, 123
break one's silence *vb* 528
break on the wheel *vb* 860
breakout *n* 264, 605
break out *vb* 264, 605
break out in a cold sweat *vb* 750
break ranks *vb* 73
break the habit *vb* 550
break the ice *vb* 61
break the law *vb* 818, 853
break the mould *vb* 73, 550
break through *vb* 307
breakup *n* 41, 46, 67
break up *vb* 46, 48, 67, 150, 669
break wind *vb* 316
break with tradition *vb* 550
breast *n* 226, *vb* 212, 274
breath *n* 316, 322, 347
breathe *vb* 1, 316, 322, 526
breathe again *vb* 740
breathe in *vb* 347
breathe new life into *vb* 322
breather *n* 123, 606
breathiness *n* 527
breathing *adj* 322, *n* 316
breathless *adj* 729
breathtaking *adj* 759
breathy *adj* 527
bred-in-the-bone *adj* 5
breed *n* 5, 68, *vb* 149, 151, 152, 328
breeder *n* 149
breeding *n* 768, 791
breeding ground *n* 132
breeze *n* 306, 316
breeze block *n* 569
breeze in *vb* 263
breezy *adj* 306, 316, 742, 824
brevity *n* 94, 179, 505
brew *n* 267, *vb* 38, 307
bribe *n* 859, *vb* 551, 859
bribery *n* 551
brick *n* 289, 569, 831, 837
brickbat *n* 826, 828
bricklayer *n* 613
brick-red *adj* 387
bricks *n* 761
bridal party *n* 797
bride *n* 333, 797
bridegroom *n* 332, 797

broken reed *n* 4, 142
broken white *n* 383
broker *n* 42, 63, 647, 675, 707
brokerage *n* 707, 722
broking *n* 647
bromide *n* 442, 514
bronchitis *n* 589
bronze *n* 386, 388, 492, 569, *vb* 386
bronzed *adj* 386
brooch *n* 42, 766
brood *n* 66, 86, 155, *vb* 398, 743
brooding *adj* 404
broody *adj* 152
brook *n* 314, *vb* 677, 733
broom *n* 586
brothel *n* 851
brother *n* 12, 778
Brother *n* 778
brotherhood *n* 40, 634
brotherly *adj* 12, 793
brougham *n* 242
brow *n* 188, 212
browbeat *vb* 750
brown *adj* 386, *n* 386, *vb* 386
browned/cheesed off *adj* 739, 743
brownie *n* 865
brownish *adj* 386
brown-nose *vb* 782
brown-nosing *n* 782
brown study *n* 398
brown sugar *n* 849
bruise *n* 337, 595, *vb* 300, 595
bruised *adj* 595, 730
Brummie *n* 494
brunch *n* 267
brunette *adj* 384, *n* 386
brunt *n* 247
brush *n* 338, 586, *vb* 173, 187, 338,
  586
brush aside *vb* 824
brush-off *n* 258
brush up *vb* 476
brushwork *n* 490
brusque *adj* 531, 792, 804
brusqueness *n* 531, 792
brutal *adj* 147, 731, 806, 810, 838
brutality *n* 147, 731, 806
brute *adj* 217, 397, *n* 147, 792, 838
brute force *n* 143
brutish *adj* 326
bubble *n* 4, 94, 225, 286, *vb* 281, 306
bubble up *vb* 314
bubbly *adj* 304, 306
buccaneering *adj* 705, 753

buck *n* 332, *vb* 740
bucket *n* 167, 227
bucketful *n* 23
buckle *n* 42, *vb* 219, 227
buckled *adj* 219
buckle down *vb* 617
buck-toothed *adj* 228
buck up *vb* 751
bucolic *adj* 328
bud *n* 61, 226, 327
Buddha *n* 862
Buddhism *n* 868
budding *adj* 61, 100, 104, 106
buddy *n* 85, 332, 793
budge *vb* 234
budget *adj* 724, *n* 571, 720, *vb* 571,
  720, 724
budgetary *adj* 720
budget forecast *n* 720
buff *adj* 386, *vb* 292, 301
buffer *n* 63, 207, 332, *vb* 290
buffet *n* 165, *vb* 316
buffoon *n* 445, 744
buffoonery *n* 744, 772
bug *n* 589, 755, *vb* 351
bugbear *n* 597, 758, 796
bugging *n* 351
buggy *n* 242
bugle *n* 369
build *n* 216, *vb* 276, 298
build castles in Spain *vb* 405, 457
builder *n* 613
building *n* 298
building block *n* 53
building blocks *n* 569
building society *n* 701, 711
buildup *n* 33
build up *vb* 431
built-in *adj* 5, 53
built-up *adj* 165
built-up area *n* 157
bulb *n* 223, 225, 327
bulbous *adj* 170, 225
bulge *n* 33, 225, 226, *vb* 225, 226, 228
bulging *adj* 49, 228
bulk *n* 23, 29, 168, 182, 285, 287,
  vb 29
bulk-buy *vb* 724
bulkhead *n* 207
bulk large *vb* 3
bulk up *vb* 170, 182
bulky *adj* 23, 29, 168, 182, 285, 287
bull *n* 326, 332, 554
bulldoze *vb* 150, 247

bulldozer *n* 150, 191, 247
bullet *n* 225, 255, 649, 861
bulletin *n* 466
bullion *n* 711
bullish *adj* 274
bullock *n* 326
bull's eye *n* 200
bullshit *n* 4, 443
bully *n* 147, 838, *vb* 659, 737, 806
bully into *vb* 551
bulwark *n* 640
bum *n* 213, 681, 777, *vb* 681, 702
bumble *vb* 625
bumbling *adj* 625
bumf *n* 513
bump *n* 226, 228, 247, *vb* 247
bumper *adj* 86
bumper to bumper *adv* 64, 176
bump off *vb* 324
bumptious *adj* 783
bumpy *adj* 226, 291
bun *n* 765
bunch *n* 66, *vb* 43, 66
bundle *n* 23, 66, *vb* 66
bunfight *n* 267, 789
bung *n* 202, 233, *vb* 233, 255
bungalow *n* 165
bungle *vb* 625
bungler *n* 625
bungling *n* 625
bunion *n* 226
bunk *n* 459
bunker *n* 167, 600, 630, 640
buoy *n* 286
buoyancy *n* 286, 293, 306
buoyant *adj* 274, 286, 293, 306, 748
buoy up *vb* 193
bur *n* 43
burble *vb* 445
burden *n* 285, 409, 656, 735, 737, 821, *vb* 285
burdened *adj* 656, 735
burdensome *adj* 285, 737
bureau *n* 614
bureaucracy *n* 622, 657
bureaucrat *n* 622, 665
bureaucratic *adj* 622, 657
burgeon *vb* 33, 152
burgeoning *adj* 108
burglar *n* 263, 705
burglary *n* 705
burgle *vb* 263, 705
burgundy *n* 387, 392
burial *n* 325

buried *adj* 186, 325, 469
burin *n* 493
burlesque *adj* 523, *n* 21, 744, 773, *vb* 21
burly *adj* 143
burn *n* 314, 339, *vb* 337, 339, 386
burn alive *vb* 860
burning *adj* 339, 729, *n* 339, 860
burnish *vb* 301
burn the candle at both ends *vb* 844
burn the midnight oil *vb* 114, 476
burnt orange *n* 388
burnt-out *adj* 144, 150
burnt umber *n* 386
burp *n* 316, *vb* 316
burr *n* 494, 526
burrow *n* 165, 227, 232, 600, *vb* 227
bursar *n* 571, 699, 711
bursary *n* 631, 690, 719
burst *n* 357, 605, 609, *vb* 147, 232
burst forth *vb* 605
bursting at the seams *adj* 49
burst into tears *vb* 747
burst of speed *n* 615
burst out *vb* 357
bury *vb* 186, 269, 325, 469, 487
bury the hatchet *vb* 449, 636, 646, 813
bus *n* 242
bush *n* 327
bush telegraph *n* 471
business *n* 562, 609, 611, 707
businesslike *adj* 611, 624
businessman *n* 613, 707
businesswoman *n* 613
busker *n* 368
bust *adj* 717, *n* 226, 492
bust a gut *vb* 617
bustle *n* 234, 281, 609, 615, *vb* 609
busty *adj* 226
busy *adj* 510, 609, 611
busy bee *n* 609
busybody *n* 402, 623
busy oneself with *vb* 562
butch *adj* 332
butcher *n* 147, 150, 324, *vb* 150, 324
butcher's *n* 370
butchery *n* 324
butler *n* 571, 613, 666
butt *n* 773, *vb* 176, 247
butter *n* 290, 319, 389, *vb* 319
buttercup *n* 389
butterfingers *n* 625
butterflies *n* 281, 750

butterfly mind *n* 405
butter mountain *n* 570
butter up *vb* 827
buttery *adj* 319
butt in *vb* 65, 263
buttocks *n* 213
button *n* 226
buttoned-up *adj* 467
buttonhole *n* 766, *vb* 532
buttonholer *n* 762
buttress *n* 131, 143, 193, 228, 882, *vb* 131, 143, 193
buxom *adj* 168, 226
buy *n* 708, *vb* 434, 690, 697, 708
buy and sell *vb* 707
buyer *n* 708
buyers' market *n* 724
buy in *vb* 570
buying *n* 708
buying and selling *n* 707
buy on hire purchase *vb* 715
buy on the never-never *vb* 715
buy out *vb* 708
buy up *vb* 570, 708
buzz *n* 358, 471, 729, 849, *vb* 361, 364
buzz off *vb* 262
buzzword *n* 496
bwana *n* 778
by/in comparison *adv* 9
by and large *adv* 69
by chance *adv* 135, 554
by degrees *adv* 24, 65
by fits and starts *adv* 65
bygone *adj* 105, 107
bygone days *n* 105
bylaw *n* 71, 852
by law *adv* 819, 852
by leaps and bounds *adv* 253
by means of *prep* 138
by night *adv* 110
by oneself *adv* 79
by order *adv* 852
bypass *n* 214, 240, 251, 278, *vb* 214, 251
by-product *n* 37, 60, 133, 149
by proxy *adv* 128
byre *n* 165, 328
by right *adv* 819
by road *adv* 236
bystander *n* 162, 370
byte *n* 570
by the book *adv* 71
by-the-by *adj* 269

by the same token *adv* 13, 17, 25
by the sweat of one's brow *adv* 617
by the way *adv* 10
byword *n* 442

C

cab *n* 242
cabal *n* 45
cabaret *n* 523
cabbage *n* 397
cabbage patch *n* 329
cabbalistic *adj* 877
cabin *n* 165
cabinet *n* 167, 634, 657
cabinetmaker *n* 613
cable *n* 42, 472
cache *n* 469, 570
cachet *n* 774
cackle *n* 744, *vb* 364, 744
cacography *n* 495, 513
cacophonous *adj* 362, 366
cacophony *n* 362, 366
cad *n* 769, 838
cadaver *n* 324
cadaverous *adj* 324
caddish *adj* 769
caddy *n* 167
cadence *n* 353, 521
cadge *vb* 681, 702
caesura *n* 65
cafe *n* 165
café-au-lait *adj* 386
cafeteria *n* 165
cage *n* 671, *vb* 210
cagey *adj* 467
caique *n* 243
cairn *n* 486
cajole *vb* 551, 827
cajolery *n* 827
cake *n* 43, 287, *vb* 43, 287
caked *adj* 287
cakehole *n* 232
calamitous *adj* 836
calamity *n* 836
calculate *vb* 75, 177, 553
calculation *n* 75, 177, 553
calculator *n* 75, 568
calculus *n* 75
calendar *n* 97
calendar month *n* 92
calf *n* 326
calf love *n* 795
calibrate *vb* 24, 177

calibration n 24
calico n 569
call n 363, 364, 681, 878, vb 364, 497
call a spade a spade vb 478, 509
call a truce vb 644
called for adj 558, 709
caller n 789
call for n 558, vb 558, 681
calligraphy n 513
call in vb 623, 711
calling in question n 413
call in question vb 435
callipers n 177
call it a day vb 62
call names vb 801
call of duty n 821
call of nature n 268
call on vb 681, 789
callous adj 289, 335, 731, 806, 810, 838, 842
callousness n 289, 335, 731, 806, 810
call out vb 363
callow adj 50, 106, 111
callowness n 50, 106, 111
call the tune vb 139, 657
call-up n 645, 664
call up vb 448, 645
call upon vb 821
call up spirits vb 876
calm adj 55, 131, 148, 314, 446, 610, 618, 731, 733, n 55, 235, 610, 618, vb 148, 596
calm down vb 446
calming adj 596
calmness n 148, 731, 733
calumniate vb 828, 830
calumnious adj 830
calumny n 775, 801, 828, 830
Calvary n 325
camaraderie n 793
camber n 26, 226, vb 195
cambric n 569
Cambridge blue adj 391
cameo n 228, 492, 517, 523, 766
camera n 491
camera-shy adj 491
camerawork n 525
camouflage n 17, 21, 469, vb 17, 469
camp n 160, 165, 671, vb 160, 165, 761
campaign n 645, 807, vb 645
camper n 242
camp follower n 85
camphor n 349

camping n 761
camp it up vb 771
camp up vb 744
campus n 477
can n 167, vb 603
canal n 314, 315
canard n 471
canary-yellow adj 389
canasta n 761
cancan n 761
cancel vb 2, 474, 487, 673, 853
cancellation n 2, 395, 474, 487, 673
cancelled adj 673
cancelling n 673
cancel out vb 137, 150
cancer n 150, 589, 597
cancerous adj 597
candid adj 464, 468, 478, 627, 831
candidate n 632, 643, 748
candied adj 345
candle n 377, 881
candlelight n 374
candlewick n 569
candour n 478, 509, 627
candy n 345, vb 345
cane n 193, 860, 861, vb 860
canine adj 326
canister n 167
canker n 150, 597
cannabis n 849
canned adj 603, 848
cannibalize vb 48
canning n 603
cannon n 247, 248, 649, vb 247, 248
cannonade n 255
cannonball n 255, 649
canny adj 626, 726, 754
canoe n 243, vb 237
canoeing n 237, 761
canon n 71, 868, 879
canonical adj 71, 868, 870
canonicals n 881
canonize vb 774, 872
canopy n 202, 378
cant n 195, 481, 494, 873, vb 195
can't abide/bear/stand vb 758
can take it or leave it vb 756
cantankerous adj 803, 804
canteen n 165
canticle n 874
canvas n 490, 569
canvass n 414, vb 414, 681
canvasser n 681
canvassing n 681

cap *n* 188, 202, 233, *vb* 188, 202, 584
capability *n* 141, 423, 624
capable *adj* 141, 624
capacious *adj* 23, 29, 156
capacity *n* 23, 156, 624, 854
capillary *n* 183
capital *adj* 495, *n* 495, 567, 694, 701, 711
capital gain *n* 690, 719
capital gains tax *n* 721
capitalize *vb* 711
capitalize on *vb* 115, 564, 690
capital punishment *n* 324, 860
capital transfer *n* 697
capital transfer tax *n* 721
capitulate *vb* 642
capitulation *n* 642
capon *n* 332
caprice *n* 120, 544
capricious *adj* 120, 130, 428, 541, 543, 544
capriciousness *n* 120, 130, 428, 541, 544
capsizal *n* 196
capsize *vb* 26, 196
capstone *n* 188
capsule *n* 167, 244, 596
captain *n* 31, 237, 622, 648, 648, *vb* 31, 237
caption *n* 513
captious *adj* 411, 739, 826
captiousness *n* 546
captivate *vb* 139, 257, 404, 732, 736, 795
captivating *adj* 732, 795
captivation *n* 732
captive *adj* 668, *n* 671
captive audience *n* 532
captivity *n* 668
captor *n* 703
capture *n* 703, *vb* 488, 703
car *n* 242
carafe *n* 167
caramel *n* 386
carapace *n* 202, 289
caravan *n* 64, 165
carbon *n* 384
carbonate *vb* 304
carbonated *adj* 304
carbon copy *n* 13, 21
carbon paper *n* 569
carborundum *n* 296
carboy *n* 167
carbuncle *n* 226, 767

carcass *n* 324
carcinogen *n* 597
carcinogenic *adj* 597
card *n* 73, 330, 485, 744
cardboard *adj* 489
card-carrying *adj* 43, 634, 870
card game *n* 761
cardinal *adj* 3, 74, *n* 879
cardinal point *n* 249
care *n* 406, 668, 726, 735, 754
careen *vb* 195, 247
career *n* 611, *vb* 245
career woman *n* 333
care for *vb* 757, 795
carefree *adj* 738, 742
careful *adj* 406, 418, 726, 754, 843
careful management *n* 726
carefulness *n* 406
careless *adj* 56, 405, 407, 501, 689, 753
carelessness *n* 405, 407, 441, 689, 753
caress *n* 338, 800, *vb* 338, 800
caretaker *n* 666, 668
cargo *n* 166, 239, 285
cargo cult *n* 862
caricature *n* 21, 463, 489, 744, 772, 773, 828, *vb* 21, 463, 489, 744, 772, 773
caricaturist *n* 21
carmine *n* 387
carnage *n* 147, 324
carnal *adj* 282, 844
carnality *n* 844
carnal knowledge *n* 40, 851
carnival *n* 746, 761
carnivore *n* 326
carnivorous *adj* 267, 326
carol *vb* 368, 526
carouse *vb* 746
carousel *n* 279, 491
carp *vb* 739, 804, 826
carpenter *n* 613
carpet *vb* 826
carriage *n* 234, 239, 242
carried *adj* 436
carried away *adj* 734
carrier *n* 241
carrier bag *n* 241
carrot *n* 134, 551
carroty *adj* 388
carry *vb* 172, 193, 241, 353, 359
carrying out *n* 688
carry off *vb* 395
carry on *vb* 124, 621

carry out *vb* 136, 607, 688
carry the day *vb* 31
carry weight *vb* 139, 507, 576
cart *n* 242, *vb* 241
cartage *n* 239
carte blanche *n* 667, 677
cartel *n* 45, 52, 79, 668
carter *n* 241
cartilage *n* 294
cartilaginous *adj* 294
cartographer *n* 557
cartographic *adj* 284
cartography *n* 284, 557
carton *n* 167
cartoon *n* 490, 525, 744
cartoonist *n* 744
cartridge *n* 491, 649
cartridge paper *n* 569
cartwheel *n* 196
carve *vb* 216, 492
carved *adj* 493
carve-up *n* 700
carve up *vb* 700
carving *n* 492
cascade *n* 275, 314, *vb* 275, 314
case *n* 167, 202, 210, 409, 410, 500, 830, 856
cased *adj* 516
case dismissed *n* 857
case-hardened *adj* 289
case history *n* 486, 517
cash *n* 711, *vb* 711
cash-and-carry *n* 710
cash book *n* 720
cash dispenser *n* 711
cash flow *n* 711
cashier *n* 711, 716, *vb* 277, 673, 860
cash in on *vb* 564, 690
cashmere *n* 569
cash register *n* 711
casino *n* 554, 761
cask *n* 167
casket *n* 167
Cassandra *n* 455
cassette *n* 369, 491
cassette deck *n* 369
cassock *n* 881
cast *n* 68, 140, 255, 370, 492, 523, *vb* 149, 203, 216, 255, 492, 525
castanets *n* 369
cast aspersions on *vb* 775, 828
cast away *adj* 311
castaway *n* 563, 790
cast away *vb* 563

caste *n* 776
castigate *vb* 826, 860
castigation *n* 860
castigator *n* 860
castigatory *adj* 860
casting vote *n* 26, 139, 545
castle *n* 600, 640
castle in Spain *n* 4
cast-off *adj* 563, 696, *n* 546
cast off *vb* 237
cast-offs *n* 204, 696
cast one's mind back *vb* 448
castrate *vb* 36, 153
castration *n* 36, 153
castrato *n* 153
casual *adj* 405, 407, 618, 788
casual dress *n* 788
casualness *n* 405
casualty *n* 323
casual wear *n* 205
casuistical *adj* 411
casuistry *n* 411
casus belli *n* 132
cat *n* 326
cataclysm *n* 147, 150
cataclysmic *adj* 147, 150
catacombs *n* 325
catafalque *n* 325
catalepsy *n* 335
cataleptic *adj* 335
catalogue *n* 57, 76, 486, 516, *vb* 57, 76, 486
catalyst *n* 121
catamaran *n* 243
catapult *n* 255, *vb* 255
cataract *n* 314, 370
catarrh *n* 268
catastrophe *n* 150, 656, 806, 836
catastrophic *adj* 150, 656, 836
catatonia *n* 335, 447
catatonic *adj* 335
cat burglar *n* 705
catcall *n* 355, 363, 484, 824, 826
catch *n* 585, 685, 706, *vb* 235, 341, 351, 589, 690, 729
catch-22 situation *n* 772
catch-all *adj* 47, *n* 51, 69
catch fire *vb* 339
catching *adj* 589
catch on *vb* 433, 770
catch phrase *n* 442, 496, 499
catch sight of *vb* 370
catchy *adj* 365, 757
categorical *adj* 427, 473, 821

categorization *n* 57
categorize *vb* 68, 485
category *n* 48, 68
cater *vb* 571
catered *adj* 571
caterer *n* 571
catering *n* 571
caterwaul *vb* 363
caterwauling *n* 355, 366
cathartic *adj* 266, 268, *n* 39
cathedral *n* 882
catholic *adj* 38, 51
catholicity *n* 51, 69
cat o' nine tails *n* 861
cat's cradle *n* 197
cat's whiskers *n* 582
cattle *n* 326
cattle-grid *n* 630
catty *adj* 806, 828
catwalk *n* 240
Caucasian *adj* 383
caucus *n* 66
caught in flagrante delicto *adj* 840
caught in the act *adj* 840
caught napping/on the hop *adj* 451
caught napping/unawares/off one's guard *adj* 560
caught on the hop *adj* 560
caught unawares *adj* 451, 454
caught with one's pants/trousers down *adj* 560
cauldron *n* 167
caulk *vb* 233
causal *adj* 132
causality *n* 64, 132
cause *n* 132, 562, *vb* 132, 134
cause and effect *n* 64
cause a sensation *vb* 471
caused *adj* 134
causeless *adj* 135
cause pain *vb* 337
cause trouble *vb* 662
causeway *n* 42, 240
caustic *adj* 806, 826, 828
cauterization *n* 339
caution *n* 406, 602, 616, 623, 754, *vb* 602
caution/warn against *vb* 552
cautionary *adj* 552, 602, 623
cautionary tale *n* 442
caution money *n* 687
cautious *adj* 406, 538, 616, 754
cautiousness *n* 754
cavalier *adj* 405, 792, 824

cavalry *n* 648
cave *n* 227
cave in *vb* 227, 642
caver *n* 275
cavern *n* 227
cavernous *adj* 186, 227
caviar *n* 342
cavil *vb* 411, 437, 538
caving *n* 275
cavity *n* 227, 232
cavort *vb* 524
caw *n* 362, *vb* 362, 364
cayenne *n* 344
cease *vb* 62, 123, 235
ceasefire *n* 123
cease-fire *n* 606
ceasefire *n* 644, 646
cease hostilities *vb* 644
ceaseless *adj* 95
cease to exist *vb* 2
cede *vb* 563, 696
ceding *n* 563
ceiling *n* 29, 49, 184, 188, 211, 668
celadon *adj* 390
celebrate *vb* 576, 734, 746, 761, 786, 881
celebrated *adj* 29, 470, 774, 774
celebration *n* 746, 786, 881
celebratory *adj* 746, 786
celebrity *n* 29, 774, 774
celestial *adj* 284, 862, 863, 866
celestial bliss *n* 866
celestial body *n* 284
celibacy *n* 79, 799, 850
celibate *adj* 79, 799, 850, *n* 799, 850
cell *n* 320, 671
cellar *n* 167, 186, 570
cello *n* 369
cellophane *n* 379
Cellophane *n* 569
cellular *adj* 320
celluloid *n* 525
Celluloid *n* 569
cement *n* 43, 289, 569
cement *vb* 40, 43
cemetery *n* 325, 882
censor *n* 850, *vb* 36, 467, 487, 668, 678, 850
censored *adj* 678
censorious *adj* 429, 659, 739, 826
censorship *n* 467, 487, 678
censure *n* 826, 830, *vb* 826, 830
censured *adj* 840
census *n* 75

cent *n* 30
centaur *n* 865
centenarian *n* 84
centenary *n* 92, 786
centennial *adj* 84, 92, 786
central *adj* 63, 199, 200, 250, 576
centrality *n* 200
centralize *vb* 200
central refuge *n* 600
central reservation *n* 250, 600
centre *n* 63, 166, 199, 200, 250, 259, *vb* 259
centre of attraction *n* 200, 257
centre on *vb* 200
centrepiece *n* 200
centrifugal *adj* 67, 260
centripetal *adj* 66, 200, 257, 259
centrist *n* 148
centurion *n* 648
century *n* 84, 90, 92
ceramics *n* 149
cerebral *adj* 396, 398
cerebrate *vb* 398
cerebration *n* 398
ceremonial *adj* 786, 787, 881, *n* 786, 787
ceremonious *adj* 787, 823
ceremoniousness *n* 787
ceremony *n* 786, 787, 881
cerise *adj* 387, 392
certain *adj* 427, 434
certainly *adv* 427
certainty *n* 427, 434, 450
certifiable *adj* 447
certificate *n* 677
certification *n* 417
certified *adj* 417
certified accountant *n* 720
certify *vb* 417, 677
certitude *n* 427
cerulean *adj* 391
cervix *n* 152
cessation *n* 62, 123, 235
cession *n* 563, 696
cesspit *n* 570
cha-cha *n* 524, 761
chafe *vb* 291, 301
chaff *n* 37, *vb* 744, 773
chagrin *n* 452, 743
chain *n* 42, 60, 64
chain letter *n* 515
chain reaction *n* 133
chain store *n* 710
chain up *vb* 668

chair *vb* 786
chairman *n* 622
chalet *n* 165
chalice *n* 167, 881
chalk *n* 300, 311, 383
chalk and cheese *n* 14
chalk up *vb* 486
chalky *adj* 300, 311, 383
challenge *n* 413, 474, 632, 637, *vb* 14, 215, 413, 414, 428, 435, 437, 632, 637, 638, 643, 830
challenger *n* 632, 643
challenging *adj* 637
chambermaid *n* 613, 666
chamber music *n* 367
chamber orchestra *n* 368
chameleon *n* 130
chamfer *vb* 195, 231, 493
chamfered *adj* 493
chamfering *n* 493
champaign *n* 313
champion *adj* 31, *n* 31, 582, 631, 640, 651, 761, 807, 829
chance *adj* 10, 135, 554, *n* 115, 135, 423, 554, *vb* 135
chancel *n* 882
chancellor *n* 622
chancy *adj* 428, 554
chandelier *n* 192, 377
chandler *n* 707
change *n* 121, *vb* 120, 121, 125, 130, 307, 711
changeability *n* 16, 94, 130, 217, 544
changeable *adj* 16, 94, 120, 130, 541, 543, 544, 803
changeableness *n* 130
changeable thing *n* 130
change for the better/worse *n* 121, *vb* 121
change hands *vb* 697
change hands for *vb* 721
changeless *adj* 862
change of direction *n* 121
change of heart *n* 841
change of life *n* 112
change of mind *n* 121
change of ownership *n* 697
change one's mind *vb* 125, 435, 543
change one's tune *vb* 121, 543
changeover *n* 121, 125, 196
changeround *n* 128
change round *vb* 121, 128, 196
change sides *vb* 543
change the face of *vb* 127

changing *adj* 121
channel *n* 42, 227, 231, 240, 310, 315, 466, 472, 493, 567, *vb* 227, 231
channelled *adj* 227
chant *n* 874, *vb* 103, 363, 368, 874
chaos *n* 56, 150, 217, 658, 853
chaotic *adj* 56, 217, 658
chap *n* 332
chapel *n* 882
chaperon *n* 85, *vb* 85
chaplain *n* 666, 879
chapter *n* 522, 878
chapter of accidents *n* 101
char *n* 586, 613, 666, *vb* 384
charabanc *n* 242
character *n* 5, 73, 74, 330, 495, 539, 837
character assassination *n* 150, 828
characteristic *adj* 70, 485, *n* 70
characterization *n* 488
characterize *vb* 5, 488, 517
charade *n* 523
charades *n* 484, 761
charcoal *n* 341, 490
charge *n* 245, 247, 255, 473, 622, 639, 661, 672, 821, 830, 840, 856, *vb* 141, 147, 247, 661, 672, 699, 720, 830, 840, 856
chargeable *adj* 819, 830
charge account *n* 714
charged *adj* 285, 830
chargé d'affaires *n* 675
charger *n* 167
charge the jury *vb* 856
charge to one's account *vb* 714
charisma *n* 29, 139, 256
charismatic *adj* 29, 139, 256
charitable *adj* 660, 681, 698, 725, 805, 807, 809, 859
charity *n* 631, 660, 698, 725, 805, 807, 809
charity appeal *n* 681
charlatan *n* 21, 480, 771
Charleston *n* 524, 761
charm *n* 66, 139, 257, 736, 763, 766, 795, 876, *vb* 139, 736, 795, 876
charmed *adj* 876
charming *adj* 139, 257, 736, 763
Charon *n* 237
chart *n* 57, 488, *vb* 488
charter *n* 71, 238, 672, 684, 819, 822, 852, *vb* 672, 677, 702
chartered *adj* 677
chartered accountant *n* 720

chartering *n* 702
chartreuse *adj* 390
chase *n* 231, 555, *vb* 231, 258, 493, 555, 800
chased *adj* 493
chasing *n* 493
chasm *n* 41, 174, 186
chassis *n* 193
chaste *adj* 784, 799, 837, 850
chastened *adj* 841
chastise *vb* 826, 860
chastisement *n* 860
chastiser *n* 860
chastity *n* 784, 799, 837, 850
chasuble *n* 881
chat *n* 533, *vb* 533
chateau *n* 165
chatoyant *adj* 393
chat show *n* 472
chatter *n* 358, 530, *vb* 358, 364, 530
chatterbox *n* 530
chatterer *n* 530
chattiness *n* 530
chatty *adj* 466, 471, 530, 533
chauvinism *n* 331, 430
chauvinist *adj* 331, 430
cheap *adj* 583, 724
cheap and nasty *adj* 583, 724, 769
cheap day return *n* 724
cheapen *vb* 583, 724, 824
cheapness *n* 724
cheapo *adj* 724
cheap rate *n* 724
cheapskate *n* 728
cheat *n* 480, 480, 626, 838, *vb* 480, 626, 705, 818, 832
check *n* 123, 148, 417, 630, 766, *vb* 123, 137, 148, 235, 417, 427, 630, 668
checkers *n* 761
checklist *n* 57, 76
checkmate *n* 123, 651, 652, *vb* 123
checkout *n* 711
check-out girl *n* 613
checkpoint *n* 271, 630
checks and balances *n* 137
check up on *vb* 406
cheek *n* 781, 792, *vb* 781
cheek by jowl *adv* 43, 176
cheeky *adj* 781, 792, 824
cheeky devil *n* 781
cheep *vb* 364
cheer *n* 363, 484, *vb* 363, 742, 746, 761, 786, 825

cheerful *adj* 742
cheerfulness *n* 742
cheeriness *n* 742
cheering *adj* 742, *n* 746, 786
cheerless *adj* 743, 804
cheerlessness *n* 743
cheer up *vb* 742
cheery *adj* 734, 742
cheesecake *n* 333, 763
cheesecloth *n* 569
cheeseparing *adj* 728, *n* 726, 728
cheetah *n* 245
chef d'oeuvre *n* 149, 490
chemistry *n* 125
cheque *n* 711
chequer *vb* 16, 393
chequerboard *n* 393
chequered *adj* 16, 393
chequered career *n* 16
cherish *vb* 795, 800
cherished *adj* 795
cherry *n* 387, 392
cherub *n* 863
chess *n* 761
chest *n* 167, 570
chestnut *adj* 386, *n* 88, 442
chesty *adj* 316
chevron *n* 195, 220
chew *vb* 267
chewiness *n* 294
chewing *n* 267
chew over *vb* 398
chew the fat *vb* 533
chewy *adj* 294
chiaroscuro *n* 374
chic *adj* 763, 770, *n* 763, 770
chicanery *n* 411, 480, 626
chick *n* 326, 333
chicken *adj* 752, *n* 752, 800
chicken out *vb* 556, 750
chicken pox *n* 589
chide *vb* 826
chief *adj* 31, 576, *n* 31, 141, 622, 665
chief cook and bottle-washer *n* 613, 666
chiefly *adv* 31
chieftain *n* 665
chiffon *n* 183, 379, 569
chilblains *n* 340
child *n* 111, 627, 839
childbearing *n* 152
childbirth *n* 152
childhood *n* 111
childish *adj* 111

childless *adj* 153
childlike *adj* 627
childminder *n* 668
child prodigy *n* 759
childproof *adj* 598
children of God *n* 863
child's play *n* 629
chill *n* 340, *vb* 340
chilli *n* 344
chilliness *n* 340
chilly *adj* 340, 794
chime *n* 359, *vb* 103, 119, 359
chime in *vb* 19, 365
chimera *n* 4, 38
chimerical *adj* 4
chimes *n* 97, 359, 369
chimney *n* 181, 232
Chinese boxes *n* 175
chink *n* 181, 231, 232, 359, 374, *vb* 359
chink in someone's armour *n* 144
chinook *n* 316
chintz *n* 569
chinwag *n* 533
chip *n* 48, 75, 585, 767, *vb* 41, 295, 300, 767
chipboard *n* 569
chip in *vb* 35, 65, 716
chip off the old block *n* 13
chipped *adj* 585
chippings *n* 569
chirpy *adj* 742
chirr *n* 358, *vb* 356, 364
chirrup *vb* 364
chisel *n* 493, 568, *vb* 216, 492, 493
chit *n* 677, 719
chitchat *n* 533
chivalrous *adj* 751, 791, 805, 831, 833
chivalry *n* 751, 791, 831
chlorinate *vb* 590
chlorinated *adj* 590
chlorination *n* 590
chlorophyll *n* 390
chock-a-block *adj* 49, 66
chocolate *n* 386
choice *adj* 545, 582, 736, *n* 535, 545
choir *n* 882
choke *n* 233, *vb* 233
choke on *vb* 527
cholera *n* 589
choleric *adj* 803
choose *vb* 418, 535, 545, 757
choosiness *n* 418, 545
choosy *adj* 18, 418, 545

chop *vb* 36, 41
chop and change *vb* 121, 544
choplogic *n* 411
chop logic *vb* 410
chopper *n* 244
choppy *adj* 314
choral *adj* 367
chorale *n* 367
chore *n* 762
choreography *n* 524
chorister *n* 368, 880
chortle *n* 744, *vb* 744
chorus *n* 19, 88, 103, 119, 874, *vb* 19, 21, 88, 103, 363, 365, 368
chorus girl *n* 524
chorus line *n* 523
chosen few *n* 31, 582
chosen people *n* 863
chow *n* 267
christen *vb* 59, 61, 497
christening *n* 59, 61, 497, 881
Christian *n* 805, 874
Christianity *n* 868
Christmas *n* 108, 881
Christmas box *n* 698
chromatic *adj* 381
chromaticism *n* 381
chrome yellow *n* 389
chromosomal *adj* 320
chromosome *n* 12, 320
chronicle *n* 97, 486, 517, *vb* 97, 486, 517
chronicler *n* 486, 517
chronological *adj* 97
chronology *n* 97
chronometer *n* 97
chronometrical *adj* 97
chronometry *n* 97
chubby *adj* 168
chuck *vb* 255, 563
chucker-out *n* 266
chuckle *n* 744, *vb* 744
chuck out *vb* 266, 696
chug *vb* 234
chum *n* 793
chunk *n* 48
church *n* 634, 874, 880, 882
church collection *n* 698
churchdom *n* 878
churchgoer *n* 874
church member *n* 880
church wedding *n* 797
churchyard *n* 325, 882
churlish *adj* 792, 804

churn *vb* 281
churn out *vb* 151
chute *n* 275
cinch *n* 629
cinema *n* 525
cinematic *adj* 525
cinematographic *adj* 234, 491, 525
cinematography *n* 488, 491, 525
cinema vérité *n* 3
Cinerama *n* 525
cinnamon *n* 386
cipher *n* 74, 77, 467, 513
circa *adv* 173
circle *n* 66, 223, 278, 523, 634, *vb* 206, 223, 278
circlet *n* 223
circuit *n* 75, 119, 127, 223, 251, 278, *vb* 251, 278, 279
circuitous *adj* 195, 214, 251, 278
circular *adj* 223, 225, 278, 411, *n* 69, 515, 681
circular argument *n* 654
circularity *n* 223, 225, 411
circulate *vb* 223, 271, 466, 470, 711
circulating *adj* 470
circulation *n* 223, 271, 278, 466, 470
circulatory *adj* 223
circumference *n* 6, 156, 198, 206, 208, 223
circumlocution *n* 251, 499, 506
circumlocutious *adj* 251, 506
circumnavigate *vb* 237
circumnavigation *n* 237, 278
circumscribe *vb* 198, 206, 211, 223, 278
circumscription *n* 211
circumspect *adj* 406, 418, 429, 754
circumspection *n* 406, 418, 754
circumstances *n* 7, 8
circumstantial *adj* 6, 8
circus *n* 240, 761
cirrus *n* 307
cistern *n* 167
citadel *n* 640
citation *n* 650, 825, 830, 856
cite *vb* 70
cithar *n* 369
citizen *n* 164, 777
citizenry *n* 777
city *n* 157
city centre *n* 157
city slicker *n* 164
civet *n* 349
civic *adj* 330

civil *adj* 768, 791, 880
civil defence *n* 640
civil disobedience *n* 638, 658, 682
civility *n* 768, 791
civilization *n* 330
civil marriage *n* 797
civil rights *n* 667
civil servant *n* 665
civil service *n* 657
civil war *n* 645
civvies *n* 205, 788
clad *adj* 202, 204
cladding *n* 201
claim *n* 473, 681, 819, *vb* 473, 551,
  681, 819
claimant *n* 681, 856
clairvoyance *n* 401, 453, 455, 877
clairvoyant *adj* 401, 453, 455, 877, *n*
  455, 876, 877
clamminess *n* 318
clammy *adj* 308, 318
clamorous *adj* 355, 363
clamour *n* 355, 363, 826, *vb* 355, 363
clamourousness *n* 355
clamp *vb* 40, 695
clampdown *n* 668
clamp down on *vb* 630, 659, 668
clam up *vb* 467
clan *n* 12, 52, 66, 330
clandestine *adj* 465, 467, 469
clang *n* 359, *vb* 355, 362
clanger *n* 116, 441
clank *n* 359, *vb* 359
clanking *adj* 359
clannish *adj* 52
clannishness *n* 52
clap *n* 247, 357, 484, *vb* 746, 786, 825
clap eyes on *vb* 370
clap in irons *vb* 668
clapped out *adj* 62, 107
clapping *n* 746, 786, 825
claptrap *n* 459
claret *n* 387, 392
clarification *n* 39, 412, 462
clarify *vb* 39, 460, 462, 629
clarinet *n* 369
clarity *n* 353, 355, 372, 460, 503, 509
clash *n* 14, 103, 362, 632, 635, 643,
  vb 20, 103, 362, 366, 635, 794
clashing *adj* 362, 381, 635
clash with *vb* 14
clasp *n* 42, 695, 766, *vb* 43, 695, 800
class *n* 24, 48, 68, 475, *vb* 24, 68

classic *adj* 22, 91, 95, 582, *n* 516, 518,
  582
classical *adj* 218, 367, 511
classical music *n* 367
classicism *n* 511
classics *n* 518
classification *n* 57, 68, 485, 497
classificatory *adj* 68, 485
classified *adj* 57, 467
classify *vb* 55, 68, 485, 497
classmate *n* 793
classroom *n* 477
classy *adj* 770
clatter *n* 358, *vb* 358
clause *n* 685
clawback *n* 704
claw back *vb* 704
clay *n* 290, 311, 492, 569
clayey *adj* 311
clean *adj* 39, 586, 831, 839, 850, *adv*
  49, *vb* 39, 348, 586
clean/flat/stony broke *adj* 713
cleaner *n* 586, 613
clean forget *vb* 449
clean hands *n* 839
cleaning *n* 586
cleaning lady *n* 666
cleanliness *n* 39, 590, 850
cleanness *n* 586, 850
cleanse *vb* 586
cleanser *n* 586
cleanse the Augean stables *vb* 39
clean-shaven *adj* 203, 292
cleansing *n* 586
clean slate *n* 127, 487, 839
clean sweep *n* 127
clear *adj* 232, 307, 351, 353, 355, 372,
  379, 460, 503, 526, 629, 822, *vb* 266,
  274, 677, 716, 813, 822, 829, 857
clearance *n* 156, 174, 266, 677, 857
clearance sale *n* 709
clear conscience *n* 839
clear-cut *adj* 372, 503
cleared *adj* 857
clear-headed *adj* 446, 847
clear-headedness *n* 446
clearing *n* 232
clearness *n* 379, 503
clear off *vb* 262
clear one's head *vb* 847
clear out *vb* 264, 709
clear-sighted *adj* 370
clear someone's name *vb* 857
clear the decks *vb* 559

clear up *vb* 307
cleavage *n* 41
cleave *vb* 41, 43, 81, 181
cleaver *n* 296
cleft *adj* 41, *n* 41, 181
cleft palate *n* 529
clemency *n* 660, 809
clement *adj* 660, 809
clench *vb* 171, 695
clenched fist *n* 637
clergy *n* 879
clergyman *n* 879
cleric *n* 879
clerical *adj* 878, 879
clerical dress *n* 881
clerical order *n* 879
clerihew *n* 521, 744
clerk *n* 486, 613
clever *adj* 396, 626
cleverness *n* 396, 626
cliché *n* 88, 442, 496, 499
clichéd *adj* 508
client *n* 708
clientele *n* 708
cliff *n* 184, 190, 311
cliffhanger *n* 25
climacteric *n* 112
climactic *adj* 188
climate *n* 206, 307
climatic *adj* 206, 307
climatologist *n* 307
climax *n* 62, 184, 188, *vb* 31, 188
climb *n* 33, 184, 274, *vb* 33, 184, 274, 723, 761
climb down *vb* 686
climber *n* 274
climbing *adj* 723, *n* 274
climes *n* 157
clinch *n* 695, *vb* 49, 427, 695
clincher *n* 49, 62
cling *vb* 43, 181, 695
clinging *adj* 43, 181, 695
clinging vine *n* 43
clinic *n* 475
clink *n* 359, 671, *vb* 359
clinker-built *adj* 175
clip *n* 48, *vb* 41, 229
clipped *adj* 505
clipper *n* 243
clique *n* 45, 52, 66, 634
cliquey *adj* 52
cliquishness *n* 52
cloak *n* 202, 378, 469, *vb* 202, 378, 469

cloak-and-dagger *adj* 469, 518
cloaked *adj* 202
cloakroom *n* 167
clobber *n* 204, 694, *vb* 247
cloche *n* 329
clock *n* 97
clock in *vb* 61
clockmaker *n* 613
clock off *vb* 62
clock up *vb* 97
clockwatching *n* 97
clockwise *adj* 214, *adv* 97
clockwork *n* 568
clod *n* 43
clog *vb* 233
cloister *n* 790, 882
cloistered *adj* 790
clone *n* 13, 17, 21, *vb* 13, 17, 21
clonk *n* 360, *vb* 360
close *adj* 43, 173, 173, 308, 467, 531, 580, 728, 793, *n* 240, *vb* 233
close/near thing *n* 605
closed *adj* 233
closed door *n* 52
closed mind *n* 430
closedown *n* 62, 123
close down *vb* 62
closed shop *n* 52, 668
close-fitting *adj* 19
close in *vb* 259
closeness *n* 173, 173, 580
close of play *n* 62
close quarters *n* 173
close range *n* 173
close ranks *vb* 173
close season *n* 108
close-set *adj* 40
close shave *n* 115, 605
closet *n* 167
close the pleadings *vb* 856
close to *adv* 162, 173
close-up *n* 525
close up *vb* 173
closing-down sale *n* 709
closing time *n* 62
closure *n* 123, 233
clot *n* 43, 287, *vb* 182, 287, 317
cloth *n* 299, 569
clothe *vb* 204
cloth-eared *adj* 352
clothier *n* 204
clothing *n* 204
clotted *adj* 182, 287, 317
clottedness *n* 182

cloud *n* 304, 307, 376, *vb* 4, 376, 380
cloudburst *n* 307
cloud cover *n* 307
cloud-cuckoo-land *n* 457
cloudiness *n* 376, 380
cloudless *adj* 655
cloud nine *n* 866
cloudy *adj* 304, 307, 376, 380
clout *n* 139, 860, *vb* 247, 860
cloven *adj* 41, 81
clover *n* 655
cloverleaf *n* 240
clown *n* 445, 744, *vb* 772
clowning *n* 772
cloy *vb* 343, 762
cloyed *adj* 762
cloying *adj* 343, 345
club *n* 247, 634, 649
clubbable *adj* 789
club together *vb* 85, 633
cluck *vb* 364
clue *n* 466, 484, 602
clued up *adj* 466
clueless *adj* 439
clump *n* 43, 66, 360, *vb* 66, 360
clumsiness *n* 439, 502, 512, 625, 764
clumsy *adj* 285, 338, 439, 502, 512, 625, 764
cluster *n* 43, 66, *vb* 43, 66, 259
clutch *n* 43, 66, *vb* 43
clutches *n* 692, 695
clutter *n* 56, 510
cluttered *adj* 510
coach *n* 242, 475, 559, *vb* 475, 559
coaching *n* 475
coagulate *vb* 43, 182, 287
coagulated *adj* 317
coagulation *n* 40, 287
coal *n* 321, 341, 377, 384
coal-black *adj* 375, 384
coalesce *vb* 13, 40, 633
coalescence *n* 40
coalition *n* 40, 633, 634
coal measures *n* 321
coalminer *n* 613
coarse *adj* 50, 291, 419, 512, 764, 792, 851
coarse-grained *adj* 299
coarsen *vb* 291, 593
coarseness *n* 291, 419, 512, 792
coast *vb* 234, 292
coastal *adj* 310, 311
coastguard *n* 237, 668
coastline *n* 209, 310

coat *n* 175, *vb* 175, 187, 201, 202
coating *n* 201, 202
coat of arms *n* 484
coat of many colours *n* 16, 393
coax *vb* 827
cobalt blue *n* 391
cobbles *n* 569
cobblestones *n* 202
cobble together *vb* 149, 615
COBOL *n* 494
cobweb *n* 4, 183
cocaine *n* 849
cochineal *n* 387
cock *n* 152, 326, 332, *vb* 190, 228
cock-a-hoop *adj* 746
cock and bull story *n* 4, 479
cock a snook *vb* 781
cockcrow *n* 109
cock of the walk *n* 31
cockshut *n* 110
cocksure *adj* 781
cocktail *n* 38, 110, 267
cocktail party *n* 789
cock-up *n* 56, 625
cock up *vb* 56, 625
cocky *adj* 781, 783
cocoon *n* 167, 202, *vb* 202, 570
coda *n* 35, 60
coddle *vb* 736, 800
code *n* 71, 467, 513, 852
code of duty *n* 821
codger *n* 332
codicil *n* 35
codification *n* 852
codified *adj* 852
codswallop *n* 443
coefficient *n* 74
coerce *vb* 551, 664
coercion *n* 664
coercive *adj* 664
coeval *adj* 103, *n* 103
coexist *vb* 1
coexistence *n* 1, 85, 103, 644
coexistent *adj* 85, 103
coextension *n* 194
coextensive *adj* 25, 194
coffee *n* 386
coffee/tea/lunch-break *n* 618
coffee morning *n* 789
coffer *n* 167, 711
coffin *n* 325
cogency *n* 141, 507
cogent *adj* 141, 400, 410, 507
cog in the wheel *n* 53

colours *n* 484
colour scheme *n* 381
colt *n* 326, 332
coltish *adj* 111
column *n* 64, 190
columnar *adj* 225
coma *n* 335, 610, 731
comatose *adj* 142, 335, 610, 731
comb *n* 229, 765
combat *n* 643, 645, *vb* 137, 643
combatant *n* 648
combative *adj* 643
combativeness *n* 410
combination *n* 38, 40, 45
combine *n* 45, *vb* 38, 40, 45, 79, 633
combine/join forces *vb* 633
combined *adj* 38, 40, 45, 633
combined effort/operation *n* 633
combustible *adj* 339, 341
combustion *n* 339
come about *vb* 1, 101
come a cropper *vb* 652
come across *vb* 433
come after *vb* 60
come and go *vb* 120
comeback *n* 415
come back for more *vb* 342
come back on *vb* 415
come between *vb* 63, 207
come by *vb* 690
come clean *vb* 468
comedienne *n* 744
comedown *n* 275, 452
come down *vb* 238
come down in the world *vb* 775
come down like a ton of bricks on *vb* 659
come down on the side of *vb* 43
comedy *n* 523, 744
come forward *vb* 679
come full circle *vb* 196
come hell or high water *adv* 427, 540
come in handy *vb* 578
come in the wake of *vb* 60
come into *vb* 690, 697, 699
come into being *vb* 1, 216, 394
come into money *vb* 712
come into the world *vb* 322
come into view *vb* 372
come last *vb* 60, 652
comeliness *n* 763
comely *adj* 763
come off *vb* 651
come off second best *vb* 32

come one's way *vb* 699
come out *vb* 123, 786
come out on top *vb* 651
come over as *vb* 394
come rain or shine *adv* 427
come round *vb* 92
come round again *vb* 119
come second *vb* 652
comestibles *n* 267
come straight to the point *vb* 505
comet *n* 284
come the high and mighty with *vb* 781
come to *vb* 74
come to a halt *vb* 235
come to a head *vb* 653
come to an arrangement *vb* 684
come to an end *vb* 62
come to blows *vb* 643
come together *vb* 103, 259
come to light *vb* 394
come to mind *vb* 398
come to nothing *vb* 572, 579, 652
come to one's senses *vb* 446
come to pass *vb* 60
come to the fore *vb* 212
come to the same thing *vb* 13
come under the hammer *vb* 709
come unstuck *vb* 628, 652
comeuppance *n* 641, 819
come up with *vb* 433
come what may *adv* 540
comfort *n* 336, 580, 618, 631, 712, 734, 738, 740, 809, *vb* 631, 736, 740, 742, 747, 805, 809
comfortable *adj* 336, 580, 618, 655, 712, 734, 738
comfortably off *adj* 712
Comforter *n* 862
comforting *adj* 740, 809
comic *adj* 523, 744, *n* 744
comedian *n* 744
comical *adj* 744
comic strip *n* 744
comic writer *n* 744
coming *adj* 104, *n* 261
coming into being *n* 1
command *n* 502, 622, 657, 661, *vb* 622, 661, 692
commandeer *vb* 564, 703
commandeering *n* 703
commander *n* 31, 622, 648
commanding *adj* 622, 657, 661, 779
commando *n* 648

command respect *vb* 774, 823
commemorate *vb* 786
commemoration *n* 786
commemorative *adj* 448, 786
commence *vb* 61
commencement *n* 61
commend *vb* 825
commendable *adj* 582, 825
commendation *n* 825
commendatory *adj* 825
commensurate *adj* 9, 19
comment *n* 429, 528, *vb* 519
commentary *n* 462, 519
commentator *n* 472, 868
comment on *vb* 462
commerce *n* 611, 707
commercial *adj* 611, 707, *n* 470
commercial traveller *n* 709
commiserate *vb* 729, 747, 809
commiseration *n* 809
commissar *n* 665
commission *n* 607, 672, 716, 721, 722, 821, *vb* 672
commissioned *adj* 672
commissioner *n* 665
commit *vb* 473, 607, 672
commit adultery *vb* 851
commitment *n* 43, 473, 539, 562, 683, 715, 821, 872
commit oneself *vb* 43, 539, 562, 683, 821
commit sacrilege *vb* 873
commit suicide *vb* 324
committed *adj* 43, 473, 539, 562, 634, 683, 715, 870, 872
committee *n* 634, 657, 675
commit to memory *vb* 448
commodious *adj* 156
commodity *n* 707
common *adj* 32, 69, 117, 494, 512, 693, 760, 769, 777, *n* 313, 693
common aim *n* 633
commonality *n* 777
common carrier *n* 241
commoner *n* 777
common fraction *n* 74
common good *n* 835
common knowledge *n* 470
common-law husband/wife *n* 797
commonly *adv* 117
common man *n* 27, 777
commonness *n* 117, 769
common or garden *adj* 72
common people *n* 69

commonplace *adj* 27, 442, 509, 549, 762
common practice *n* 621
common run *n* 27, 69
commons *n* 777
common sense *n* 148, 396, 444, 446
commonsensical *adj* 396, 444
commonwealth *n* 331
commotion *n* 56, 281, 609, 729
communal *adj* 40, 45, 330, 634, 693
communard *n* 693
commune *n* 164, 693
communicable *adj* 239
communicant *n* 870, 874
communicate *vb* 458, 466, 515
communicating *adj* 874
communication *n* 40, 466, 494, 515, 533
communications *n* 472
communicative *adj* 466, 533
communion *n* 872, 878
communiqué *n* 466
communism *n* 657
communist *adj* 657
community *n* 164, 330, 634, 777, 880
community service *n* 807
commute *vb* 119, 236
commuter *n* 164, 236
compact *adj* 23, 40, 43, 287, 505, *n* 633, 636, 684, *vb* 171
compact disc *n* 369
compacted *adj* 171
compaction *n* 40, 171
compactness *n* 287
companion *n* 85, 793
companionable *adj* 789
companionship *n* 85, 789, 793
companionway *n* 42
company *n* 66, 85, 523, 634, 648, 693
company man *n* 72
comparability *n* 17
comparable *adj* 9, 17, 194
comparative *adj* 24, 500
comparatively *adv* 9
compare *vb* 9, 17, 194
comparison *n* 9, 194
compartment *n* 48, 158, 167, 232
compartmentalize *vb* 57
compartmentalized *adj* 48
compass *n* 156, 177, 249
compassion *n* 660, 809, 837
compassionate *adj* 660, 730, 805, 809
compass point *n* 249
compatibility *n* 19, 72, 789, 793

compatible *adj* 19, 72, 636, 789
compel *vb* 558, 661, 664, 732
compelling *adj* 661, 664, 732
compendium *n* 45, 66, 516
compensate *vb* 25, 28, 137, 704, 814, 859
compensation *n* 28, 137, 704, 814, 819, 859
compensatory *adj* 28, 137, 704, 814
compete *vb* 643
compete against/with *vb* 632
competence *n* 141, 573, 624, 854
competent *adj* 141, 573, 624, 854
competing *adj* 643
competition *n* 632, 643, 815
competitive *adj* 643, 724
competitiveness *n* 724, 815
competitor *n* 632, 643, 748, 815
compilation *n* 45, 66, 520
compile *vb* 53, 518
complacency *n* 738
complacent *adj* 738, 783
complain *vb* 682, 739, 804, 826, 830
complain of *vb* 589
complaint *n* 589, 682, 739, 826, 830
complement *n* 500, *vb* 85
complementarity *n* 9, 11
complementary *adj* 9, 11
complete *adj* 47, 584, *vb* 49, 62, 653
complete change *n* 127
completed *adj* 653
completely *adv* 49
completeness *n* 47, 49
completion *n* 62, 653
complex *adj* 56, 197, 224, 504, 628, *n* 47, 197, 447
complexion *n* 5, 68
complexity *n* 224, 504
compliance *n* 436, 537, 551, 642, 663, 688, 782
compliant *adj* 72, 436, 537, 551, 642, 663, 688, 782, 821
complicate *vb* 56, 461
complicated *adj* 628
complicate matters *vb* 628
complication *n* 628
complicity *n* 633, 840
compliment *n* 791, 825, 827, *vb* 791, 825, 827
complimentary *adj* 667, 698, 724, 786, 825, 827
complimentary tickets *n* 724
compliments *n* 786, 800

comply *vb* 436, 537, 551, 642, 663, 688, 782
component *adj* 53, *n* 48, 53, 282
components *n* 166
comportment *n* 621
compose *vb* 53, 368, 513, 518, 521
composed *adj* 131, 148, 733
compose oneself *vb* 446
composer *n* 149, 368
composite *adj* 38, 40
composition *n* 45, 57, 149, 298, 367, 490, 513
compositor *n* 514
compos mentis *adj* 446
composure *n* 131, 148, 446, 733, 760
compound *n* 38, 158, 210, *vb* 40
comprehend *vb* 51, 396, 438, 460
comprehensibility *n* 460
comprehensible *adj* 460
comprehension *n* 396, 438
comprehensive *adj* 47, 49, 51, 69
comprehensiveness *n* 47, 49, 51, 69
compress *n* 233, 630, *vb* 66, 171, 179, 287, 505
compressed *adj* 171, 181, 504, 505
compression *n* 171, 179, 181, 505
compressor *n* 171
comprise *vb* 51, 53
comprising *adj* 51
compromise *n* 63, 250, 684, 686, *vb* 63, 686
compromise solution *n* 686
comps *n* 724
comptroller *n* 711
compulsion *n* 447, 536, 536, 558, 664
compulsive *adj* 447, 664
compulsorily *adv* 664
compulsory *adj* 71, 536, 558, 661, 664, 821
compulsory purchase *n* 703
compunction *n* 809, 841
computation *n* 75, 177
computational *adj* 75
compute *vb* 75, 177
computer *n* 75, 568, 570
computer dating *n* 647, 797
computerize *vb* 75
computer language *n* 494, 570
computing *n* 75, 570
comrade *n* 85, 778, 793
comradely *adj* 789
comradeship *n* 789, 793
con *n* 38, 480, 483, 671, 705, *vb* 480, 626, 705

concatenation *n* 35
concave *adj* 221, 227
concavity *n* 221, 227
conceal *vb* 166, 202, 373, 378, 467, 469
concealed *adj* 465, 469
concealment *n* 373, 465, 467, 469
concede *vb* 422, 436, 551
conceit *n* 779, 783
conceited *adj* 779, 783, 834
conceivable *adj* 423
conceive *vb* 22, 149, 152, 396, 398, 457, 557
concentrate *n* 39, *vb* 39, 200, 259, 287, 404
concentrated *adj* 287
concentration *n* 259, 287, 398, 404, 609
concentration camp *n* 671, 790
concept *n* 408
conception *n* 152, 408, 456, 457
conceptual *adj* 396, 400, 408
conceptualize *vb* 283, 396
concern *n* 101, 402, 406, 409, 562, 634, 735, 750, *vb* 9
concerned *adj* 750
concerning *prep* 9
concert *n* 19, 367, 633
concerted *adj* 19
concert hall *n* 761
concertina *vb* 230
concerto *n* 367
concession *n* 422, 551, 677, 722
concessionary *adj* 422, 722, 724
concessionary fare *n* 724
concessions on both sides *n* 686
concierge *n* 666, 668
conciliate *vb* 646, 814
conciliation *n* 646
conciliator *n* 148
conciliatory *adj* 19, 646
concise *adj* 179, 505, 520
conciseness *n* 179, 505
concision *n* 505
conclude *vb* 62, 62, 123, 400, 429, 653
concluding *adj* 62, 653
conclusion *n* 62, 123, 653
conclusive *adj* 412, 420, 427, 653
conclusively *adv* 62
concoct *vb* 149, 830
concoction *n* 38, 149
concomitant *adj* 85, 133, 162, *n* 85
concord *n* 19, 365
concordance *n* 496

concordat *n* 636, 684
Concorde *n* 244
concourse *n* 259
concrete *adj* 1, 3, 282, 287, *n* 569
concreteness *n* 1, 3, 282, 287
concretion *n* 40
concretization *n* 198, 287
concur *vb* 19, 436, 633, 636
concurrence *n* 103, 259, 436, 633, 636
concurrent *adj* 103, 633
concurrently *adv* 103
concurring *adj* 636
condemn *vb* 413, 591, 796, 801, 826, 840, 840, 858, 871
condemnation *n* 856, 858, 860
condemnatory *adj* 413, 429, 830, 858
condemned *adj* 591, 840, 858
condemned cell *n* 671, 858
condensation *n* 36, 179, 270, 287, 303, 305, 308, 505, 520
condense *vb* 36, 171, 179, 270, 287, 303, 505, 520
condensed *adj* 171, 179, 287, 505, 520
condenser *n* 304
condescend *vb* 779, 780
condescending *adj* 779, 791
condescension *n* 779, 791
condiment *n* 344
condition *n* 7, 422, 589, 685, *vb* 549
conditional *adj* 7, 8, 422, 685
conditionally *adv* 8
conditioner *n* 765
conditioning *n* 549
conditions *n* 8
condole *vb* 747
condolence *n* 809
condominium *n* 693
condone *vb* 636, 813
conducive *adj* 136, 138, 140
conduct *n* 621, *vb* 607
conduction *n* 239
conduct oneself/one's affairs *vb* 621
conductor *n* 368
conduit *n* 315
cone *n* 225
confab *n* 533
confection *n* 38
confectionery *n* 345
confederate *adj* 634
confederation *n* 45, 634
confer *vb* 533, 698, 859
conference *n* 40, 66, 533
conferral *n* 698
confess *vb* 468, 473, 478, 841

confession *n* 468, 473, 634, 814, 841, 868, 878
confidant(-e) *n* 623, 793
confide *vb* 468
confidence *n* 427, 434, 450, 467, 714, 748
confident *adj* 427, 434, 450, 748
confidential *adj* 467
confidentially *adv* 467
confiding *adj* 434
configuration *n* 216
confine *vb* 181, 199, 210, 211, 668, 695, 790, 860
confined *adj* 30, 181
confined to barracks *adj* 668
confinement *n* 152, 181, 668, 790
confines *n* 209
confirm *vb* 131, 417, 420, 427, 473, 829, 881
confirmation *n* 131, 417, 473
confirmed bachelor *n* 799
confiscate *vb* 703, 860
confiscation *n* 703
conflagration *n* 339
conflate *vb* 520
conflict *n* 14, 632, 643, 794, *vb* 18, 20, 794
conflicting *adj* 421, 632, 635
conflicting evidence *n* 421
conflict with *vb* 14, 632
confluence *n* 40, 259
confluent *adj* 259
conform *vb* 72, 688
conforming *adj* 870
conformist *adj* 72, 688, *n* 72, 870
conformity *n* 15, 19, 72, 688, 817
confound *vb* 759, 801
confront *vb* 212, 215, 632, 643, 751
confrontation *n* 215, 259
Confucianism *n* 868
confuse *vb* 56, 217, 419, 463
confused *adj* 56, 58, 281, 376
confusedly *adv* 56
confusion *n* 56, 281, 419
confutation *n* 413
conga *n* 761
congeal *vb* 43, 182, 287, 317
congelation *n* 340
congenial *adj* 793
congenital *adj* 12
congested *adj* 66
congestion *n* 287, 575
conglomeration *n* 40, 66
congratulate *vb* 786

congratulate oneself *vb* 734
congratulation(s) *n* 786
congratulatory *adj* 786
congregate *vb* 66, 259
congregated *adj* 66
congregation *n* 66, 259, 870, 874, 880
congress *n* 40, 259, 634, 657
congressman/-woman *n* 657
congruence *n* 13
congruent *adj* 13, 19
congruity *n* 19
conical *adj* 225
coniferous *adj* 327
conjectural *adj* 408, 456
conjecture *n* 408, 425, 428, 456, *vb* 425, 456
conjoin *vb* 40
conjoined *adj* 40
conjugal *adj* 797
conjugality *n* 797
conjugate *vb* 500
conjugation *n* 500
conjunction *n* 40, 85, 500
conjunctive *adj* 40
conjure *vb* 876
conjure up *vb* 457
conjuror *n* 876
conk *n* 228
conk out *vb* 619, 652
con man *n* 480
con-man *n* 626
conman *n* 838
connect *vb* 9, 40
connected *adj* 9
connection *n* 9, 40, 42
connective *adj* 40
connivance *n* 633
connive *vb* 633
connoisseur *n* 267, 768
connoisseurship *n* 418, 768
connotation *n* 458
connotative *adj* 458
connote *vb* 458, 488
connubial *adj* 797
conquer *vb* 651, 670
conquering *adj* 651
conqueror *n* 651
conquest *n* 32, 651, 670
consanguineous *adj* 12
conscience *n* 821
conscience-stricken *adj* 841
conscientious *adj* 406, 616, 688, 821, 831, 837

conscientiousness *n* 404, 406, 616, 688, 831
conscientious objector *n* 644
conscious *adj* 396, 404, 438, 553, 730
consciousness *n* 396, 729, 730
conscript *n* 648, *vb* 645
conscription *n* 645, 664, 670
consecrate *vb* 672, 872, 878, 881
consecrated *adj* 872
consecration *n* 672, 872
consecutive *adj* 60, 64
consecutively *adv* 64
consecutiveness *n* 64
consensus *n* 15, 19, 636
consent *n* 436, 537, 636, 677, 825, *vb* 19, 436, 537, 636, 677
consenting *adj* 436, 636, 684
consequence *n* 60, 133, 576
consequent *adj* 133
consequently *adv* 133, 134
conservancy *n* 603
conservation *n* 603, 726
conservation area *n* 603
conservatism *n* 72, 122
conservative *adj* 72, 870, *n* 122
conservative estimate *n* 432
conservatoire *n* 477
conservatory *n* 165, 329
conserve *vb* 95, 122, 124, 603, 726
consider *vb* 398, 553
considerable *adj* 29, 168, 576
considerably *adv* 29
considerate *adj* 404, 406, 791, 805
consideration *n* 398, 404, 406, 576, 616, 791, 805, 823
considered *adj* 616
consign *vb* 239, 672, 697
consignee *n* 675, 708
consignment *n* 239, 697
consistency *n* 15, 19, 72, 182, 287, 636
consistent *adj* 15, 19, 72, 636
consist in *vb* 53
consisting of *adj* 51
consolation *n* 740, 809
consolation prize *n* 650
console *vb* 740, 742, 809
consolidation *n* 40, 43, 287
consoling *adj* 740, 809
consonance *n* 365
consonant *adj* 19, 72, *n* 495
consonantal *adj* 495
consort *n* 85, *vb* 85

conspicuous *adj* 162, 228, 372, 464, 576, 785
conspicuous consumption *n* 727
conspicuousness *n* 162, 228, 372, 464
conspiracy *n* 45, 469, 557
conspiracy *n* 633, 684
conspirator *n* 557
conspiratorial *adj* 469, 557
conspire *vb* 469, 557, 633
constable *n* 854
constabulary *n* 854
constancy *n* 15, 119, 122, 124, 131, 539, 540, 831
constant *adj* 15, 117, 119, 122, 124, 131, 540
constantly *adv* 117
constellation *n* 66, 284
constipation *n* 268
constituent *adj* 53, *n* 48, 53, 282
constitute *vb* 53
constitution *n* 5, 71, 298, 852
constitutional *adj* 5, 657, 852, *n* 236
constitutional monarchy *n* 657
constrain *vb* 664
constraint *n* 664, 668
constrict *vb* 171, 181, 630
constricted *adj* 171, 181
constricting *adj* 171
constriction *n* 171, 181, 630
constrictor *n* 171
construct *vb* 53, 298
construction *n* 149, 298, 462, 492, 499
constructional *adj* 298
constructive *adj* 149, 633
construe *vb* 462, 500
consul *n* 675
consulate *n* 675
consult *vb* 623
consultant *n* 623
consultation *n* 533
consultative *adj* 623
consult counsel *vb* 623
consume *vb* 150, 267, 564, 572, 718
consumer *n* 708
consumer durables *n* 694, 707
consumer goods *n* 707
consummate *vb* 584, 653, 797
consummation *n* 653
consumption *n* 267, 564, 572
contact *n* 176, 338
contact lens *n* 370
contagion *n* 239, 589
contagious *adj* 239, 589
contain *vb* 51, 156, 166, 206, 211, 695

container *n* 167, 239
containerize *vb* 166
containing *adj* 51
containment *n* 166
contain oneself *vb* 843
contaminate *vb* 587
contaminated *adj* 587, 851
contamination *n* 587, 851
contemplate *vb* 398, 450, 553
contemplation *n* 398, 872
contemplative *adj* 398, 872
contemporaneous *adj* 85, 101, 103
contemporaneousness *n* 101
contemporaneusness *n* 103
contemporary *adj* 101, 103, *n* 101, 103
contempt *n* 781, 824
contemptible *adj* 577, 772, 824
contempt of court *n* 662
contemptuous *adj* 781, 824, 828
contend *vb* 413, 632, 635, 643
contender *n* 632, 643
contending *adj* 643
content *adj* 738, 742, 825, *n* 409, 458, *vb* 738
contented *adj* 738
contention *n* 413, 635, 643
contentious *adj* 41, 410, 635, 643
contentiousness *n* 410
contentment *n* 336, 738, 742
contents *n* 166, 520
contest *n* 643, *vb* 643
contestant *n* 632, 643
contesting *adj* 856
context *n* 8
contextual *adj* 8
contextualize *vb* 7
contiguity *n* 176
contiguous *adj* 176, 207
continence *n* 843, 850
continent *adj* 268, 843, 850, *n* 311
continental *adj* 311
Continental *n* 331
contingency *n* 6, 423, 685
contingency plan *n* 453
contingent *adj* 6, 8, 133, 422, 685
continual *adj* 90, 117, 124
continually *adv* 117, 124
continuance *n* 1, 93
continuation *n* 124
continue *vb* 1, 64, 90, 93, 117, 124
continuing *adj* 93, 122, 253
continuity *n* 15, 64, 90, 122, 124, 292, 525

continuous *adj* 15, 64, 124, 292
continuously *adv* 64, 124
continuum *n* 64
contort *vb* 219, 224
contorted *adj* 219, 224
contortion *n* 219, 224
contour *n* 208, 216
contraband *adj* 853, *n* 706
contraception *n* 153
contract *n* 562, 636, 683, 684
contract *n* 821, *vb* 30, 34, 171, 179, 181, 183, 505, 562, 589, 683, 684
contracted *adj* 171, 562, 684
contraction *n* 30, 34, 36, 171, 181, 495, 496
contractual *adj* 684
contradict *vb* 14, 20, 413, 415, 421, 474, 632
contradiction *n* 14, 260, 413, 421, 437, 474, 632, 826
contradiction in terms *n* 411
contradictory *adj* 14, 411, 413, 415, 421, 474
contraflow *n* 14
contraindicate *vb* 421
contralto *n* 368
contraposition *n* 14, 215
contrapuntal *adj* 14, 367
contrariety *n* 14, 215, 260
contrariness *n* 542, 632, 662
contrariwise *adv* 215
contrary *adj* 14, 137, 215, 474, 542, 632, 662
contrary to the law *adj* 853
contrast *n* 16, 18, 73, 632, *vb* 9, 14, 16, 18
contrasting *adj* 18, 73
contravene *vb* 14, 689, 853
contravention *n* 689, 853
contribute *vb* 698, 716
contribution *n* 698, 716, 819
contributor *n* 698
contributory *adj* 138
contrite *adj* 841
contrition *n* 841
contrivance *n* 138, 480
contrive *vb* 149, 469
contrived *adj* 512, 771
control *n* 621, 622, 630, 657, 668, 692, 854, *vb* 55, 621, 622, 630, 657, 668, 692, 854
controlled *adj* 668
controller *n* 622, 665, 711
controlling *adj* 630

control oneself *vb* 733, 843
control prices *vb* 668
control sample *n* 416
controversial *adj* 41, 409, 410, 635
controversy *n* 410, 437, 635
controvertible *adj* 410
contusion *n* 337
conurbation *n* 157, 165
convalesce *vb* 594
convalescence *n* 588, 594
convalescent *adj* 588
convection *n* 239
convene *vb* 66
convenience *n* 115, 138, 162, 578, 580, 629, 734, 835
convenience food *n* 267
convenient *adj* 115, 138, 162, 578, 580, 629, 734
conveniently *adv* 115
convent *n* 882
convention *n* 66, 72, 533, 549, 636, 646, 657, 684, 791
conventional *adj* 71, 72, 549, 870
conventional wisdom *n* 72
converge *vb* 40, 181, 200, 259
convergence *n* 40, 259
convergent *adj* 200, 257, 259
converging *adj* 66
conversant *adj* 438, 549
conversation *n* 528, 533
conversational *adj* 533
converse *adj* 14, *n* 14, *vb* 533
conversely *adv* 11, 14
conversion *n* 121, 125, 551
convert *n* 125, 841, 863, *vb* 121, 125, 434, 551, 697, 872
converted *adj* 125, 841
convertibility *n* 125
convertible *adj* 125, 126, 129, *n* 242
convex *adj* 221, 225, 226, 228
convexity *n* 221, 225, 226, 228
convey *vb* 234, 239, 241, 458, 466, 697
conveyance *n* 234, 239, 242
conveyancing *n* 697
conveyor belt *n* 15, 64, 241
convict *n* 671, *vb* 856, 858
convicted *adj* 840, 858
conviction *n* 427, 434, 507, 551, 858
convince *vb* 139, 434, 507, 551
convinced *adj* 427, 434
convincing *adj* 139, 425, 434, 507, 551
convivial *adj* 742, 789
conviviality *n* 742, 789

convocation *n* 657, 878
convoke *vb* 66
convoluted *adj* 56, 219, 224
convolutedness *n* 224, 504
convolution *n* 219, 224
convoy *n* 85, 640, *vb* 85
convulse *vb* 147, 281
convulsion *n* 58, 127, 147, 281
convulsive *adj* 147, 281
coo *vb* 364
cook *n* 571, 613, 666, *vb* 267, 481
cooked *adj* 559
cooker *n* 339
cookery *n* 267
cook the books *vb* 705, 720
cook up *vb* 479
cool *adj* 367, 620, 733, 756, 790, 794, *vb* 340
cool as a cucumber *adj* 733
cooler *n* 340
cool-headedness *n* 148
coolie *n* 241, 613
cooling-off period *n* 123
coolness *n* 340, 733, 790
cool off *vb* 620
cool one's heels *vb* 114
coon *n* 331
coop *n* 165, 328, 693
cooperate *vb* 19, 436, 537, 633
cooperation *n* 19, 40, 45, 129, 436, 537, 633
cooperative *adj* 19, 40, 45, 129, 436, 537, 633, 634, 693, *n* 40, 45, 693
coordinate *vb* 622
coordinated *adj* 40
coordinates *n* 204
coordination *n* 40, 55
coordinator *n* 622
co-ownership *n* 693
cop *n* 854
cope *n* 881
coping *n* 188
copious *adj* 152, 573
copiousness *n* 573
cop out *vb* 556
copper *n* 386, 388, 569, 854
copperplate *n* 495, 513
coppery *adj* 386, 388
copse *n* 327
copulate *vb* 40
copulation *n* 40
copulative *adj* 40
copy *n* 13, 17, 21, 151, 488, 513, 514,

costliness *n* 723
costly *adj* 723
cost nothing *vb* 724
costs *n* 28, 718, 860
costume *n* 204, 523
costumier *n* 204
cosy *adj* 734
coterie *n* 52, 66
coterminous *adj* 176, 207, 211
cottage *n* 165
cottage industry *n* 149
cottager *n* 164
cotton *n* 569
cotton on *vb* 460
cottony *adj* 299
couchant *adj* 191
cough *n* 316, 362, 589
cough up *vb* 716
could do better *adj* 585
could do with *vb* 755
could eat a horse *vb* 755
council *n* 634, 657, 855, 878
councillor *n* 657, 665
counsel *n* 623, 623, 675, *vb* 623
counselling *n* 623
counsellor *n* 623, 631
count *n* 75, 776, 830, *vb* 74, 139, 434, 576, 582
countdown *n* 238
countenance *n* 212, 394
counter *adj* 14, 137, 215, *n* 193, 641, *vb* 126, 137, 415, 632, 641
counteract *vb* 14, 137
counteraction *n* 137
counteractive *adj* 137
counterargument *n* 632, 641
counterattack *n* 137, 258, 639, 641, *vb* 641
counterbalance *n* 137, *vb* 28, 137
counterblast *n* 137, 415
counterchange *vb* 393
countercharge *n* 415
counterclaim *n* 421, 681
countercurrent *n* 14
counterevidence *n* 421
counterfeit *adj* 21, 481, *n* 21, *vb* 21, 481, 711
counterfeiter *n* 21
counterfeiting *n* 481
counterfoil *n* 485, 719
countermand *n* 673, 678, *vb* 673, 678
counterpart *n* 11, 17, 25
counterpoint *n* 14
counterpoise *n* 285

counterproductive *adj* 137
counterrevolution *n* 137
counterrevolutionary *adj* 137
countersign *vb* 485
counterstroke *n* 258
countertenor *n* 368
countervailing *adj* 137
counterweight *n* 25, 28, 131, 137, 285
countess *n* 776
count in *vb* 51
countless *adj* 86, 89
count on *vb* 450
count out *vb* 52
countrified *adj* 165
country and western *n* 367
country bumpkin *n* 164, 777
country cousin *n* 777
country dance *n* 524
count the pennies *vb* 728
county *adj* 776, *n* 157
county/borough/town/parish council *n* 657
coup *n* 161
coup de grâce *n* 62, 653
coup d'état *n* 127
coupé *n* 242
couple *n* 81, *vb* 40, 40
couplet *n* 81, 521
coupling *n* 40, 40
coupon *n* 719
courage *n* 751
courage of one's convictions *n* 751
courageous *adj* 751
courier *n* 241, 466
course *n* 64, 90, 124, 140, 175, 234, 240, 249, 253, 315, 475, 761, *vb* 314, 761
course of action *n* 557
coursing *n* 761
court *n* 210, 761, 776, 855, *vb* 793, 800, 827
court action *n* 635
court danger *vb* 599
court disaster *vb* 753
courteous *adj* 791, 805, 823
courtesy *n* 768, 791
courtesy of *prep* 138
courtesy title *n* 778
courthouse *n* 855
courting *n* 800
courtliness *n* 791
courtly *adj* 791
court martial *n* 673
court-martial *vb* 673

courtship *n* 795, 800
courtyard *n* 158
cousin *n* 12
couturier *n* 204
cove *n* 221, 310, 330
covenant *n* 683, 684, 687, 698, *vb* 683, 684
covenanted *adj* 683, 684
cover *n* 28, 167, 202, 204, 210, 212, 233, 469, 515, 516, 600, 687, *vb* 40, 51, 156, 198, 202, 687
coverage *n* 156, 172
cover charge *n* 721
covered *adj* 202, 687
covered market *n* 710
covering *n* 202, 378
cover oneself *vb* 28, 754
covert *adj* 465, 467
cover-up *n* 467
cover up *vb* 467, 469, 487
cover up for *vb* 128
covet *vb* 755, 816
covetous *adj* 690, 728, 755, 816, 834
covetousness *n* 728, 755, 816
covey *n* 66
cow *n* 326, *vb* 670, 750
coward *n* 556, 752
cowardice *n* 752
cowardliness *n* 752
cowardly *adj* 752
cowardy custard *n* 752
cowboy *n* 480, 707
cower *vb* 185, 750, 752
cowering *adj* 752
cowshed *n* 165, 328
coy *adj* 784
coyness *n* 784
CPU *n* 570
crabbed *adj* 513
crabby *adj* 804
crabwise *adv* 195, 214
crack *n* 41, 174, 181, 231, 232, 357, 561, 585, 767, *vb* 41, *vb* 46, *vb* 174, 295, 357, 767
crack a joke *vb* 744
crack down on *vb* 659
cracked *adj* 527, 585, 767
cracker *n* 763
crackers *adj* 447
crackpot *adj* 443
crack shot *n* 255
cracksman *n* 705
crack up *vb* 46, 447

cradle *n* 61, 111, 132, 165, 280, *vb* 193
craft *n* 149, 243, 611, 626, *vb* 149
craftiness *n* 480, 626
craftsman *n* 149, 613, 624
crafty *adj* 480, 626, 832
crag *n* 228, 311
cragginess *n* 291
craggy *adj* 228, 291
cram *vb* 49, 66, 166, 846
crammed *adj* 49
crammer *n* 477
cramp *n* 337, *vb* 171, 181, 630, 668
cramped *adj* 30, 181, 513
crampedness *n* 181
cramp one's style *vb* 630
cramp someone's style *vb* 142
crane *n* 192, 276
crank *n* 73, 447
crankiness *n* 447
cranky *adj* 447
cranny *n* 181, 220, 231
crap *n* 268, 443, *vb* 268
crappy *adj* 268
crash *n* 34, 123, 150, 247, 355, 357, 717, *vb* 34, 147, 150, 165, 238, 247, 275, 355, 357, 652, 717
crashland *vb* 238
crash-landing *n* 238
crash out *vb* 619, 848
crass *adj* 182, 439, 769
crassness *n* 182, 769
crate *n* 167, 244
crater *n* 186, 227
crave *vb* 681, 755, 816
craven *adj* 752
craving *n* 755
crawl *n* 616, *vb* 29, 86, 185, 246, 616, 642, 663, 780, 782
crawler *n* 616, 782, 827
crawling *adj* 29, 66, 642, 782, *n* 782
crawl into one's shell *vb* 784
crawl with *vb* 573
crayon *n* 490, *vb* 381, 490
craze *n* 544, 755, 770, *vb* 447
crazed *adj* 447
craziness *n* 445
crazy *adj* 443, 445, 447, 732
crazy about *adj* 795
crazy for *adj* 755
crazy paving *n* 65
creak *vb* 362
creaky *adj* 362

cream *n* 302, 319, 383, 389, 582, 770,
  vb 302, 319
creaminess *n* 383
cream off *vb* 270, 545
creamy *adj* 319, 383, 389
crease *n* 230, *vb* 171, 744
creased *adj* 230
create *vb* 22, 132, 149, 216, 457, 732
creation *n* 1, 3, 149, 216, 284, 322,
  862
creative *adj* 22, 132, 149, 457
creative accounting *n* 720
creativity *n* 22, 457
creator *n* 22, 132, 149
Creator *n* 862
creature *n* 32, 320, 322, 326, 330
creature comforts *n* 336
creche *n* 477
credence *n* 434
credentials *n* 420
credibility *n* 434
credible *adj* 423, 425, 434
credit *n* 134, 567, 570, 683, 701, 714,
  811, 825, *vb* 714, 720, 819
creditable *adj* 582, 825
credit account *n* 714
credit card *n* 702, 711, 714
credit facilities *n* 714
credit institution *n* 701
credit note *n* 714
credit one's account *vb* 714
creditor *n* 701, 714
credits *n* 76
credit squeeze *n* 668
creditworthiness *n* 712, 714
credo *n* 434
credulity *n* 434, 551
credulous *adj* 434, 551
credulousness *n* 551
creed *n* 434, 868
creek *n* 310, 312
creel *n* 167
creep *n* 827, *vb* 246, 465, 469, 616
creep up on *vb* 469
creepy *adj* 750
creepy-crawly *n* 326
cremate *vb* 325
cremation *n* 325, 339
crematorium *n* 325
crème de la crème *n* 31, 582, 770
crenellated *adj* 174, 229
crenellation *n* 229
creole *n* 38, 494
creosote *vb* 603

crêpe de chine *n* 569
crepe paper *n* 569
crepuscular *adj* 110
crescendo *n* 33, 355
crescent *n* 221, 240
crest *n* 184, 188, 484, *vb* 188
crestfallen *adj* 452, 743
cretin *n* 397, 445
cretinism *n* 397
cretinous *adj* 397
crevasse *n* 41, 227, 601
crevice *n* 174, 181, 231
crew *n* 66, 237, 666
crewcut *n* 765
crib *n* 462, *vb* 21, 702, 702
cricket *n* 761
crime *n* 662, 818, 838, 840, 853
crime wave *n* 853
criminal *adj* 818, 832, 838, *n* 662, 838
criminality *n* 840
criminally *adv* 853
criminal offence *n* 853
crimp *vb* 224, 229
crimped *adj* 224
Crimplene *n* 569
crimson *adj* 387, *vb* 387
crimson lake *adj* 387
cringe *vb* 752
crinkle *n* 230, *vb* 224, 230
crinkled *adj* 230
crinkly *adj* 224
cripple *vb* 142, 144, 219, 579, 630
crippled *adj* 219
crisis *n* 8, 101, 115, 599
crisp *adj* 295, 505
crispness *n* 295
crispy *adj* 295
criss-cross *adj* 174, 197, *vb* 174, 197
criss-crossing *n* 197
crit *n* 518
criterion *n* 71, 416
critic *n* 739, 768, 826, 828
critical *adj* 418, 429, 462, 519, 599,
  739, 768, 826
critical path *n* 57
critical point *n* 115
critical review *n* 826
criticism *n* 413, 429, 518, 623, 739,
  826, 828
criticize *vb* 429, 462, 519, 739, 768,
  826, 828
critique *n* 429, 462, 519
croak *n* 362, *vb* 323, 362, 364

croakiness *n* 527
croaky *adj* 527
crochet *n* 149, 766, *vb* 766
crocodile *n* 64, 178
crocodile tears *n* 481
Croesus *n* 712
croft *n* 328
crofter *n* 164, 328
crone *n* 112
crony *n* 793
crook *n* 220, 705, 838, 881, *vb* 220
crooked *adj* 219, 832
croon *vb* 356
crop *n* 133, 149, 328
crop up *vb* 61, 88, 101, 394
croquet *n* 761
crosier *n* 657, 881
cross *adj* 739, 802, 804, *n* 38, 197,
    597, 650, 737, 861, 881, *vb* 137, 197,
    271
crossbow *n* 649
crossbred *adj* 38, 328
cross-check *vb* 417
cross-country *n* 236
crossdresser *n* 73
crossed line *n* 20
cross-examination *n* 402, 414, 856
cross-examine *vb* 402
cross-eyed *adj* 370
crossing *n* 237, 271
crossing point *n* 271
cross oneself *vb* 881
cross one's mind *vb* 398
cross out *vb* 487
cross-purposes *n* 20
cross-refer *vb* 9, 57
cross-reference *n* 9
crossroads *n* 8, 40, 197, 207, 260
cross swords *vb* 410
cross that bridge when one comes to
    it *vb* 560
cross the floor *vb* 543
cross the threshold *vb* 263
crosswind *n* 316
crossword *n* 761
crotchety *adj* 803
crouch *n* 277, *vb* 185, 277
crouched *adj* 185
croupier *n* 711
crow *vb* 364, 746
crowbar *n* 568
crowd *n* 66, 86, *vb* 66, 86, 173, 287
crowded *adj* 66, 86, 173

crown *n* 188, 223, 657, 657, *vb* 188,
    584, 672, 774, 786
crowning *adj* 188
crowning glory *n* 49
crow's feet *n* 230
crow's nest *n* 184
crucial *adj* 3, 200
crucible *n* 38, 125
crucifix *n* 197, 766, 881
crucifixion *n* 860
cruciform *adj* 197
crucify *vb* 860
crude *adj* 50, 217, 291, 419, 512, 792
crudeness *n* 419, 512
crudity *n* 50, 291
cruel *adj* 604, 659, 806, 838
cruelty *n* 604, 659, 806, 810
cruise *n* 237, *vb* 234, 237, 238, 629
cruise missile *n* 649
cruiser *n* 243
cruising *n* 237
crumb *n* 30, 48, 169, 300
crumble *vb* 46, 107, 295, 300
crumbliness *n* 295, 300
crumbling *adj* 46, 107
crumbly *adj* 295, 300
crummy *adj* 32, 583
crumpet *n* 333
crumple *vb* 219
crumpled *adj* 230
crunch *n* 3, 115
crunchiness *n* 295
crunchy *adj* 295
crusade *n* 645, 807
crusading *adj* 125, 872
crush *n* 66, 86, 795, *vb* 66, 147, 300,
    413, 651
crushed *adj* 230, 743
crusher *n* 300
crushing *adj* 285
crust *n* 202
crustacean *n* 326
crusty *adj* 803, 804
crutch *n* 193, 220
crux *n* 115
cry *n* 355, 747, *vb* 364, 747
crying shame *n* 836
cry out *vb* 355, 357, 363
cry out for *vb* 273
crypt *n* 186, 325, 882
cryptic *adj* 442, 461
cryptogram *n* 513
crystal *n* 379
crystal ball *n* 455

crystal-clear *adj* 372, 379
crystal-gazer *n* 877
crystal-gazing *n* 104
crystalline *adj* 289, 321, 379
crystallization *n* 125, 287
crystallize *vb* 125, 287, 289, 345
crystallized *adj* 345
crystal set *n* 472
cube *n* 220, *vb* 75, 82
cubicle *n* 158
Cubist *adj* 490
cuboid *adj* 220
cuckoo *adj* 447
cuckoo in the nest *n* 54
cuddle *n* 800, *vb* 800
cudgel *n* 247, 649
cue *n* 448, 523
cuff *n* 230, 247, 860, *vb* 247, 860
cul de sac *n* 233
culinary *adj* 267
cull *n* 324, *vb* 545
culminate *vb* 31, 653
culminating *adj* 653
culmination *n* 49, 188, 653
culpability *n* 840
culpable *adj* 134, 826, 840
cult *n* 770
cultivate *vb* 149, 152, 327, 328, 329, 475
cultivated *adj* 438, 791
cultural *adj* 330
culture *n* 330, 768, 791
cultured *adj* 17, 21, 791
culvert *n* 315
cumbersome *adj* 285, 581, 764
cumulative *adj* 33
cumulus *n* 307
cuneiform *adj* 220, *n* 495
cunning *adj* 480, 626, 832, *n* 480, 626, 832
cunt *n* 152
cup *n* 167, 226, 227, 650
cupboard *n* 167, 570
cupboard love *n* 481
cupful *n* 23
Cupid *n* 862
cupola *n* 226
cur *n* 326
curate *n* 879
curate's egg *n* 50
curative *adj* 137, 594, 596, 740
curator *n* 598, 668
curb *n* 148, 246, 630, 668, *vb* 148, 211, 630, 668

curd *n* 182, 317
curdle *vb* 182, 287, 317, 346
curdled *adj* 287, 317
cure *n* 137, 594, 596, 606, 740, *vb* 137, 550, 594, 596, 603, 606, 740
cure-all *n* 69
cured *adj* 594
curfew *n* 110, 668
curiosity *n* 402, 450, 755, 759
curious *adj* 402, 450, 755, 759
curl *n* 224, *vb* 224
curlers *n* 765
curlicue *n* 224
curling tongs *n* 765
curls *n* 765
curly *adj* 224
curmudgeonly *adj* 804
currency *n* 101, 106, 711
currency surcharge *n* 721
current *adj* 1, 90, 101, 106, 409, 470, 471, *n* 124, 140, 234, 253, 314, 316
current affairs *n* 101, 409, 471
current events *n* 409
currently *adv* 1, 90
curriculum *n* 475
curriculum vitae *n* 486
curry *n* 344, *vb* 344
curry favour *vb* 782, 827
curse *n* 597, 656, 737, 801, 876, *vb* 792, 801, 858, 876
cursed *adj* 801, 876
cursive *adj* 513, *n* 495
cursoriness *n* 50, 187, 273, 405
cursory *adj* 50, 94, 187, 273, 405
curt *adj* 179, 505, 531, 792
curtail *adj* 36, *vb* 30, 34, 171, 179
curtailed *adj* 179
curtailment *n* 36, 171
curtain *n* 192, 202, 207, 373, 378, *vb* 373, 378
curtain call *n* 825
curtain-raiser *n* 59
curtness *n* 505, 531
curtsy *n* 277, 791, 823, *vb* 277, 791, 823
curvaceous *adj* 221, 226, 763
curvature *n* 221, 226
curve *n* 221, 226, *vb* 221, 225, 226
curved *adj* 221, 225, 226
curvedness *n* 223, 225
curvilinear *adj* 221
curvy *adj* 221
cushion *n* 148, 193, 290, *vb* 144, 193, 290, 740

cushiony *adj* 290
cushy *adj* 336, 629
cushy number *n* 629
cuss *vb* 801
cussed *adj* 542, 628
cussedness *n* 542, 662
custodial *adj* 668
custodial sentence *n* 668
custodian *n* 598, 668
custody *n* 598, 668, 692
custom *n* 107, 122, 549, 708, 791, 881
customary *adj* 549, 881
customer *n* 330, 681, 708
custom-made *adj* 70, 204
customs *n* 621
customs duty *n* 721
customs officer *n* 699
cut *adj* 179, 179, 724, *n* 48, 229, 296,
   337, 595, 700, 722, *vb* 34, 36, 179,
   229, 337, 492, 595, 678, 680, 722,
   724
cut a caper *vb* 524
cut across *vb* 197
cut a long story short *vb* 505
cut and run *vb* 752
cut back *vb* 36
cutback *n* 34, 36, 668
cut back *vb* 34, 668, 726
cut corners *vb* 726
cut costs *vb* 726
cut dead *vb* 790, 792
cut down *vb* 41
cut down to size *vb* 483, 775
cut in *vb* 65
cutlass *n* 649
cut loose *vb* 667
cut no ice *vb* 577
cut off *vb* 41
cut-off point *n* 211, 668
cut off without a penny *vb* 696
cut one's losses *vb* 686
cut-price *adj* 724
cuts *n* 726
cut short *vb* 179, 527
cutter *n* 568
cut the cackle *vb* 505
cutthroat *n* 324
cutting *adj* 296, 340, 507, 824
cutting edge *n* 296
cut up *adj* 735, 743
cyan *n* 391
cybernetics *n* 75
cycle *n* 88, 92, 119, 223, 279, *vb* 761
cyclic *adj* 223, 279

cyclical *adj* 88, 92, 119
cyclically *adv* 119
cycling *n* 761
cyclone *n* 279, 307
cylinder *n* 225
cylindrical *adj* 223, 225
cymbal *n* 369
cymbals *n* 359
cynic *n* 808, 828
cynical *adj* 435, 749, 808, 828
cynicism *n* 435, 749, 808
cynosure *n* 200, 257
Cyrillic *adj* 49

D

dab *vb* 338
dabble *vb* 187, 308
da capo *adv* 88
Dacron *n* 569
dad *n* 154
daffodil *n* 389
daft *adj* 447, 772
dagger *n* 649
dago *n* 331
daily *adj* 92, *n* 471, 613, 666
daily round *n* 15, 119, 549, 762
dainty *adj* 169
dairyman *n* 613
dais *n* 184
dally *vb* 616, 800
dam *n* 312, 630, *vb* 233, 630
damage *n* 150, 585, 593, 595, 604,
   836, *vb* 150, 421, 593, 595, 604, 836
damaged *adj* 585, 593, 595
damages *n* 28, 704, 716, 860
damaging *adj* 421, 604
damask *n* 569
dame *n* 333, 776
damn *vb* 792, 801, 801, 858
damnatory *adj* 858
damned *adj* 801, 867
damn the consequences *vb* 753
damn with faint praise *vb* 826
damp *adj* 308, *vb* 360
dampen *vb* 148, 308, 743
damper *n* 148, 233, 360
dampness *n* 305, 308
dampproof *adj* 309
damp squib *n* 452, 652
damsel *n* 333
damson *n* 392
dam up *vb* 668
dance *n* 524, 789, *vb* 130, 524

dance/leap for joy *vb* 746
dance attendance on *vb* 85
dance hall *n* 761
dance in the streets *vb* 746
dance music *n* 367
dancer *n* 524
dancing *n* 761
dandy *n* 770
danegeld *n* 721
danger *n* 599
dangerous *adj* 599
danger signal *n* 599, 602
danger zone *n* 599
dangle *vb* 44, 192
dangling *adj* 192
dangling participle *n* 501
dank *adj* 308
dankness *n* 308
dapper *adj* 55, 763
dapple *vb* 393
dappled *adj* 38
dapple-grey *adj* 385
dappling *n* 374
Darby and Joan *n* 112
dare *n* 637, *vb* 637
daredevil *n* 751, 753
dare to *vb* 751
daring *adj* 562, 751, *n* 751
dark *adj* 110, 375, 384, 804, 877
dark age *n* 656
Dark Ages *n* 105
dark blue *adj* 391
dark brown *adj* 386
darken *vb* 186, 375, 380, 384
dark-green *adj* 390
dark grey *adj* 385
darkie *n* 331
darkness *n* 110, 375, 867
dark red *adj* 387
dark-skinned *adj* 384
dark yellow *adj* 389
darling *adj* 795, *n* 795, 800
darn *n* 594, *vb* 197, 594
dart *n* 255, *vb* 96, 130, 245
Darwinism *n* 320
dash *n* 30, 38, 145, 245, 381, 615,
  751, *vb* 96, 147, 234, 245, 314, 615
dashed hopes *n* 749
dashing *adj* 751, 770
dash someone's hopes *vb* 749
dastard *n* 752
dastardly *adj* 752
data *n* 420, 466, 570
data bank *n* 486, 570

data base *n* 570
data processing *n* 75
date *n* 789, 795, *vb* 793, 800
date-expired *adj* 105
dateless *adj* 91
datelessness *n* 91
dateline *n* 97, 211
dating *n* 800
daub *n* 489, 767, *vb* 302, 381, 490,
  767
daughter *n* 12
daunt *vb* 552
daunting *adj* 552
dauntless *adj* 751
dawdle *n* 246, 616, *vb* 60, 93, 114,
  246, 610, 616
dawdler *n* 616
dawn *n* 61, 109, 374
dawn chorus *n* 109
dawn raid *n* 708
day *n* 92
day and night *n* 14
day book *n* 720
day boy *n* 198
daybreak *n* 109
daydream *vb* 4, 405, 457
daydreaming *n* 398
day-dreaming *n* 405
daydreaming *n* 457
Day-glo *adj* 374
day in day out *adv* 64
daylight saving *n* 97
day off *n* 618
day release *n* 198, 475
days gone by *n* 102
days of yore *n* 105
daystar *n* 284
days to come *n* 102
daytime *adj* 109
day trip *n* 761
dazzle *n* 374, *vb* 371, 374
dazzling *adj* 371, 377, 383, 763
deacon *n* 879, 880
dead *adj* 2, 323, 335, 360
dead and buried *adj* 325
dead and gone *adj* 2, 323
dead as a doornail *adj* 323
dead beat *adj* 619
dead cert *n* 427, 547
dead drunk *adj* 848
dead duck *n* 579, 749
deaden *vb* 148, 335, 360, 731, 740
dead end *n* 233, 424
dead heat *n* 25, 103

dead letter *n* 105
deadline *n* 62, 211, 615
deadliness *n* 762
deadlock *n* 25, 123, 233, 235, 424
deadly *adj* 150, 323, 324, 604, 762, 836
dead march *n* 325
deadness *n* 335, 360
dead of night *n* 110
dead on *adj* 440
deadpan *adj* 745
dead ringer *n* 13
dead to *adj* 731
deaf *adj* 352
deaf aid *n* 352
deaf and dumb *adj* 352
deaf as a post *adj* 352
deafen *vb* 352, 355
deafening *adj* 352, 355
deaf-mute *adj* 352
deaf-mutism *n* 352
deafness *n* 352
deaf to *adj* 731
deal *n* 684, *vb* 611, 700, 707
dealer *n* 613, 707
dealership *n* 707
deal firmly with *vb* 659
dealing *n* 609, 707
dealings *n* 438, 611
dean *n* 622, 879
deanery *n* 882
dear *adj* 723, *n* 800
dearest *n* 800
dearness *n* 723
dearth *n* 153, 273, 574
death *n* 2, 62, 323
deathbed *adj* 114, *n* 323
death blow *n* 62
death camp *n* 671
death certificate *n* 323
death chamber *n* 861
death duties *n* 721
death knell *n* 323
deathless *adj* 95
deathly *adj* 323, 324
death mask *n* 492
death notice *n* 323
death rattle *n* 323
death row *n* 671
death sentence *n* 858, 860
death throes *n* 323
death toll *n* 323
death warrant *n* 858
deb *n* 770

débâcle *n* 275, 652
debar *vb* 678
debarred *adj* 52
debarring *adj* 52
debase *vb* 277, 583
debasement *n* 277, 828
debasing *adj* 277
debatable *adj* 409, 410, 428
debate *n* 410, 533, 643, *vb* 410, 533
debauch *vb* 851
debauched *adj* 336, 844, 851
debauchery *n* 336, 844, 851
debilitate *vb* 144
debilitated *adj* 142
debilitating *adj* 589
debility *n* 142, 144, 589
debit *n* 691, 715, *vb* 720
debouch *vb* 264
debriefing *n* 100
debris *n* 37
deb's delight *n* 770
debt *n* 715, 821
debtor *n* 702, 715
debunk *vb* 773
debut *n* 61, 261
debutante *n* 770
decade *n* 84, 92
decagon *n* 84
decalogue *n* 84
decamp *vb* 262, 395, 605
decampment *n* 262, 605
decanter *n* 167
decapitate *adj* 36, *vb* 324, 860
decapitation *n* 36, 324, 860
decathlon *n* 84
decay *n* 2, 46, 107, 108, 550, 593, 595, *vb* 2, 46, 107, 593, 595
decayed *adj* 593, 595
decaying *adj* 46, 550
decease *n* 323
deceased *adj* 323
deceit *n* 626
deceitful *adj* 480, 481, 626, 832, 873
deceitfulness *n* 480, 481
deceive *vb* 4, 441, 480, 626, 832
deceiver *n* 480
decelerate *vb* 34, 246, 668
deceleration *n* 34, 246, 668
decency *n* 768, 791, 817, 850
decent *adj* 204, 582, 791, 817, 821, 850
decentralization *n* 67
decentralize *vb* 67
deception *n* 480, 626

278

deceptive *adj* 394, 480, 543
deceptiveness *n* 480
decibels *n* 355
decide *vb* 132, 427, 429, 539, 553
deciduous *adj* 327
decimal *adj* 74, 84, *n* 74, 84
decimalize *vb* 84
decimate *vb* 34, 84, 87, 150, 324
decimation *n* 150
decipher *vb* 460, 462
decipherable *adj* 460
decision *n* 429, 856
deck *vb* 175
decked out *adj* 766
deckle edge *n* 229
deckle-edged *adj* 209
deck out *vb* 204, 766
declaim *vb* 528
declamation *n* 528
declamatory *adj* 528
declaration *n* 473, 683, 868
declarative *adj* 473
declare *vb* 468, 473, 528, 683, 856
declare heretical *vb* 871
declare not guilty *vb* 857
declare war *vb* 645
declension *n* 500
decline *n* 34, 107, 108, 171, 185, 254,
275, 593, *vb* 34, 144, 275, 500, 546,
593, 680, 724
declining *adj* 275
declining years *n* 112
decoction *n* 303
decode *vb* 460, 462
décolleté *adj* 205
decolorant *n* 382
decolorize *vb* 382
decompose *vb* 2, 41, 46, 593
decomposed *adj* 46, 593
decomposition *n* 41, 46, 593
deconsecrate *vb* 880
decontamination *n* 586
decontrol *vb* 677
decorate *vb* 510, 766, 859
decorated *adj* 766
decoration *n* 510, 650, 766, 859
decorative *adj* 510, 766
decorator *n* 613
decorous *adj* 511, 768, 850
decorum *n* 511, 768, 850
decoy *n* 212, 257, 601
decrease *adj* 36, *n* 30, 34, 171, *vb* 30,
34, 171
decreasing *adj* 34

decreasingly *adv* 34
decree *n* 429, 661, *vb* 71, 429, 661
decree absolute *n* 798
decree nisi *n* 798
decrement *n* 36
decrepit *adj* 144
decrepitude *n* 144
decrescendo *n* 34
decry *vb* 828
dedicate *vb* 872, 881
dedicated *adj* 43, 540, 833, 872
dedication *n* 43, 539, 540, 807, 833,
872
deduce *vb* 400
deduct *adj* 36, *vb* 34, 717, 722
deduction *n* 34, 36, 400, 717, 722
deductive *adj* 400
deed *n* 607
deem *vb* 434
deep *adj* 23, 186, 381, 444
deep down *adv* 186, 199
deepen *vb* 186, 741
deep end *n* 186
deepening *n* 741
deep-freeze *n* 340, *vb* 340
deeply *adv* 186
deep-rooted *adj* 5, 131, 186, 549
deep-sea *adj* 186, 237, 310
deep-seated *adj* 5, 131, 186, 199, 549
deep thought *n* 186
deface *vb* 595, 764, 767
defaced *adj* 764
defacement *n* 764
defamate *vb* 604
defamation *n* 604, 775, 828
defamatory *adj* 604, 826, 828, 830
defame *vb* 801, 828, 830
defamer *n* 828
default *n* 717, *vb* 717
defaulter *n* 717
defaulting *adj* 717
defeat *n* 651, 652, *vb* 31, 651
defeated *adj* 652
defeatism *n* 432, 642, 743, 749, 752
defeatist *adj* 432, 642, 743, 749, 752,
n 749, 752
defecate *vb* 268
defecation *n* 268
defect *n* 144, 273, 585, 767, *vb* 125,
163, 543, 563, 662
defection *n* 44, 163, 543, 563, 662,
832
defective *adj* 32, 50, 273, 585, 767
defectiveness *n* 50

deliquescence *n* 303
deliquescent *adj* 303
delirious *adj* 447, 732, 734
delirium *n* 447, 732
deliver *vb* 571, 605, 606, 669
deliverance *n* 605, 606, 669
deliverer *n* 606
delivery *n* 152, 239, 515, 526, 571
delousing *n* 586
delphinium *n* 391
delta *n* 310, 313
delude *vb* 4, 441, 480
deluge *n* 66, 307, *vb* 305, 314
delusion *n* 4, 441, 447, 457, 463
delusory *adj* 4, 441
de luxe *adj* 785
delve into *vb* 414
demand *n* 558, 681, *vb* 536, 661, 681
demanding *adj* 617, 628
demarcate *vb* 52, 207, 211, 484, 700
demarcated *adj* 211
demarcation *n* 41, 176, 211, 700
dematerialize *vb* 2, 283, 395, 877
demeaning *adj* 277
demean oneself *vb* 775, 780
demeanour *n* 394, 621
demented *adj* 447
demerit *n* 838
demijohn *n* 167
demilitarized zone *n* 52
demi-monde *n* 777
demise *n* 62, 323
demo *n* 682
demob *vb* 669
demobilization *n* 41, 67, 646, 669
demobilize *vb* 67, 646, 669
democracy *n* 25, 657, 667
democratic *adj* 25, 657, 667
demolish *vb* 2, 147, 150, 277, 410, 846
demolished *adj* 413
demolition *n* 150, 277
demon *n* 864
demonetize *vb* 711
demonism *n* 864, 875
demonist *n* 875
demonolatry *n* 875
demonstrable *adj* 412, 417
demonstrate *vb* 412, 417, 464, 682, 829
demonstration *n* 412, 417, 464, 682
demonstrator *n* 682
demoralize *vb* 743
demote *vb* 161, 277, 673, 860
demotic *adj* 494

demotion *n* 161, 275, 277, 673
demur *n* 682, *vb* 437, 538, 682, 826
demure *adj* 745, 784, 850
demureness *n* 745, 784
demurral *n* 437, 538, 682
demystification *n* 460
den *n* 165, 469, 600, 790
denationalization *n* 704
denationalize *vb* 704
denature *vb* 121
denial *n* 413, 421, 437, 474, 546, 632, 680
denigrate *vb* 824, 826, 828
denigration *n* 828
denigratory *adj* 828
denim *n* 569
denizen *n* 164
den of vice *n* 838
denominate *vb* 497
denomination *n* 497, 634, 871
denominational *adj* 634, 871
denominationalism *n* 871
denominator *n* 74
denotative *adj* 458
denote *vb* 458
denouement *n* 62
denounce *vb* 413, 466, 796, 801, 828, 830, 858
dense *adj* 40, 43, 182, 285, 287, 397, 504, 505
denseness *n* 504
density *n* 43, 182, 285, 287, 380
dent *n* 227, 595, 767, *vb* 227, 595, 767
dented *adj* 227, 767
dentist *n* 596
dentistry *n* 596
denudation *n* 203
denude *vb* 203
denuded *adj* 203, 691
denunciation *n* 413, 801, 830, 858
denunciatory *adj* 413, 830
deny *vb* 413, 415, 437, 474, 546, 632, 680
deny oneself *vb* 843
deny oneself nothing *vb* 844
deodorant *n* 348
deodorization *n* 348
deodorize *vb* 348, 586
deodorized *adj* 348
depart *vb* 163, 262, 395, 563, 605
departed *adj* 323
departed spirit *n* 865
depart from *vb* 18

deserve attention *vb* 576
deserved *adj* 819
deserving *adj* 819
desiccate *vb* 309
desiccated *adj* 309
desiccation *n* 309
desideratum *n* 755
design *n* 216, 488, 553, 557, 766, *vb* 149, 216, 488, 557
designate *adj* 100, *vb* 458, 484, 497
designation *n* 485, 497, 778
designatory *adj* 485
designed *adj* 535
designer *n* 149, 204, 490, 557, 613
desirable *adj* 755, 795
desire *n* 535, 755, 795, 816, *vb* 535, 755, 795, 816
desire to *vb* 537
desirous *adj* 535, 755
desist *vb* 123
desolate *adj* 790
desolation *n* 153, 735
despair *n* 735, 743, 749, *vb* 743, 749
despaired of *adj* 842
despairing *adj* 735, 743
despatch *vb* 49
desperado *n* 838
desperate *adj* 561, 735, 749
desperation *n* 749
despicable *adj* 583, 775, 824, 838
despise *vb* 779, 824
despised *adj* 775
despoil *vb* 150
despondency *n* 432, 452, 735, 743, 749
despondent *adj* 432, 452, 735, 743, 749
despot *n* 659, 665
despotic *adj* 622, 659
dessert *n* 60, 267
destabilize *vb* 26
destination *n* 211, 236, 249, 261, 553
destine *vb* 536
destiny *n* 104, 536
destitute *adj* 558, 713
destitution *n* 713
destroy *vb* 150, 324, 604
destroyed *adj* 150
destroyer *n* 150, 243
destruction *n* 150, 324, 604, 867
destructive *adj* 2, 150, 324, 604, 828
destructiveness *n* 150
desultoriness *n* 405
desultory *adj* 56, 65, 130, 405

detached *adj* 41, 165, 403, 731, 733, 817
detachedness *n* 44, 172
detachment *n* 403, 731, 733, 833
detail *n* 48, 79, 766, *vb* 70, 700, 821
details *n* 70
detain *vb* 668, 695
detainee *n* 671
detect *vb* 433
detectable *adj* 372
detection *n* 402, 433
detective *adj* 414, 433, *n* 203
detective story *n* 518
détente *n* 633, 636
detention *n* 668
detention centre *n* 671
deter *vb* 552
detergent *adj* 586, *n* 586
deteriorate *vb* 121, 593, 741
deteriorated *adj* 593
deterioration *n* 121, 150, 593, 741
determinant *adj* 132, *n* 132
determination *n* 535, 539, 542, 553, 609, 751
determine *vb* 132, 535, 539, 553
determined *adj* 535, 539, 609
determiner *n* 500
determinism *n* 132, 536
deterrence *n* 552, 750
deterrent *adj* 552, 602, *n* 552, 602
detest *vb* 758, 796
detestable *adj* 796
detestation *n* 796
dethrone *vb* 161, 673
dethronement *n* 673
detour *n* 221, 240, 251, 252
detract *vb* 828
detraction *n* 828
detractor *n* 828
detriment *n* 593, 604
detrimental *adj* 604
detritus *n* 37
de trop *adj* 756
deuce *n* 81
deus ex machina *n* 138
devalue *vb* 583
devastate *vb* 150, 203
devastation *n* 150
develop *vb* 33, 133, 149, 216, 253, 491, 519, 592
developed *adj* 592
develop fan out *vb* 170
development *n* 33, 101, 133, 170, 253, 320, 592

deviant *adj* 20, 73, 252, *n* 73
deviate *vb* 18, 73, 214, 220, 251, 252
deviation *n* 121, 195, 221, 25J, 252, 260
deviationism *n* 73
deviationist *adj* 73
device *n* 138, 567, 568
devil *n* 864, 864
devilish *adj* 806, 864, 876
devil-may-care *adj* 753
devil worship *n* 864
devil-worship *n* 875
devil-worshipper *n* 864, 875
devil-worshipping *adj* 875
devious *adj* 832
devise *vb* 22, 149, 216, 398, 457
devisee *n* 699
deviser *n* 22
devoid *adj* 163
devolve on *vb* 821
devoted *adj* 540, 663, 688, 793, 795, 874
devotion *n* 539, 540, 663, 688, 795, 823, 872, 874
devotional *adj* 868, 874
devour *vb* 150, 267, 846
devout *adj* 868, 870, 872, 874
dew *n* 308
dewlap *n* 192
dewy *adj* 308
dextral *adj* 214
dhow *n* 243
diabolic *adj* 838, 876
diabolical *adj* 806, 864
diabolism *n* 876
diagnose *vb* 462
diagnosis *n* 462
diagnostic *adj* 462
diagonal *adj* 195, *n* 195
diagram *n* 57, 208, 488, 557
diagrammatic *adj* 57
dial *n* 97, 212
dial 999 *vb* 602
dialect *n* 494
dialectal *adj* 494
dialogue *n* 129, 410, 528, 533
dialyse *vb* 586
dialysis *n* 586
diamante *n* 766
diameter *n* 180, 200, 250
diametrically opposite *adj* 14
diametric opposites *n* 14
diamond *n* 220, 289, 766
diaphanous *adj* 183, 286, 379

diaphanousness *n* 379
diaphragm *n* 207
diapositive *n* 491
diarist *n* 486
diarrhoea *n* 268, 589
diary *n* 97, 486
diaspora *n* 41, 67
diatribe *n* 826
dice *n* 761
dice with danger *vb* 753
dichotomy *n* 41, 81, 632
dick *n* 152
dictate *n* 661, *vb* 528, 536, 657, 661, 664
dictator *n* 659
dictatorial *adj* 622, 659
dictatorship *n* 622, 657
diction *n* 494, 499, 502
dictionary *n* 76, 496, 570
dictum *n* 442
didactic *adj* 475
diddle *n* 705, *vb* 480, 705
die *n* 216, *vb* 2, 62, 94, 216, 323
die aborning *vb* 153
die away *vb* 356, 376
die down *vb* 235
diehard *adj* 539, 542, *n* 122
die in harness *vb* 323
die out *vb* 2, 105, 323
diet *n* 845, *vb* 845
dietary *adj* 267
dietetics *n* 267
dieting *n* 845
differ *vb* 18, 20, 635, 794
difference *n* 18, 20, 26, 260
difference of opinion *n* 437, 635
different *adj* 18, 20, 26
differential *n* 20, 24
differentiate *vb* 18, 418
differentiation *n* 18, 418
different kettle of fish *n* 18
different time *n* 102
difficult *adj* 418, 628, 662
difficult to use *adj* 581
difficulty *n* 461, 581, 628, 656, 737
diffidence *n* 428, 483, 750, 784
diffident *adj* 428, 483, 750, 784
diffraction *n* 374
diffuse *adj* 504, 506, *vb* 67, 260, 466, 470
diffuseness *n* 504, 506
diffusion *n* 67, 466, 470
dig *n* 555, 826, *vb* 186, 328, 555, 559
digest *n* 520, *vb* 265, 267

digestible *adj* 267
digestion *n* 267
digestive *adj* 265
digger *n* 270
dig in *vb* 131, 160
dig in one's heels *vb* 538, 542, 638
dig in one's toes *vb* 122
digit *n* 74
digital *adj* 74
digital record *n* 369
digital watch *n* 97
dignified *adj* 511, 768, 774, 779, 787
dignitary *n* 774
dignity *n* 511, 774, 779, 787
digress *vb* 6, 10, 65, 214, 251, 252, 405, 411, 506, 530
digression *n* 65, 214, 251, 252, 506
digressive *adj* 65, 252, 506
digs *n* 165
dig up *vb* 270, 325, 433, 448
dilapidated *adj* 46, 107, 593
dilapidation *n* 2, 46, 107, 593
dilate *vb* 170, 506
dilated *adj* 170
dilation *n* 170
dilatoriness *n* 114, 616
dilatory *adj* 98, 114, 246, 616
dilemma *n* 628
dilettante *n* 768
diligence *n* 404, 540, 609, 688
diligent *adj* 404, 476, 540, 609, 688
dilly-dally *vb* 114, 246
dilute *adj* 144, 183, 305, *vb* 38, 144, 183, 288, 305, 483
diluted *adj* 343, 483
dilution *n* 288, 305
dim *adj* 376, 397, 449, *vb* 375, 376, 380
dime *n* 30
dimensions *n* 23, 156, 168
diminish *vb* 30, 34, 171
diminishing *adj* 34
diminuendo *n* 34
diminution *n* 30, 34, 171, 395
diminutive *adj* 23, 30, 169
diminutiveness *n* 30, 169
dimness *n* 373, 376
dimple *n* 227
dimpled *adj* 227
din *n* 355, 363, 366
dine *vb* 267
diner *n* 165, 267
dingdong *adj* 11, 25
ding-dong *adj* 410, 533

dinghy *n* 243
dinginess *n* 382
dingy *adj* 375, 376, 382
din in *vb* 475
din into *vb* 88
dinky *adj* 169
dinner *n* 761
dinner jacket *n* 787
dinner party *n* 789
dinosaur *n* 105
diocese *n* 878
dip *n* 34, 185, 227, 275, 305, *vb* 34, 185, 275
diphtheria *n* 589
diplomacy *n* 791
diplomat *n* 675
diplomatic *adj* 791
dipsomania *n* 848
diptych *n* 81
direct *adj* 222, 250, 297, 478, 503, 509, *adv* 222, 249, *vb* 31, 159, 249, 523, 525, 622, 661, 854
direct/indirect taxation *n* 721
directed *adj* 249
direction *n* 140, 159, 240, 249, 622, 623, 661, 854
directional *adj* 159
direction finder *n* 249
directive *adj* 854, *n* 661
directness *n* 222, 297, 503, 509
director *n* 525, 613, 622, 665
directorial *adj* 622
directory *n* 57, 76
direct route *n* 222
dirge *n* 325, 747
dirigible *n* 244
dirt *n* 587
dirtiness *n* 587, 591
dirty *adj* 384, 587, 591, 851, 851, *vb* 376, 384, 587
dirty joke *n* 744
dirty old man *n* 851
dirty trick *n* 836
dirty tricks *n* 832
dirty weekend *n* 851
disable *vb* 142, 144, 579
disabled *adj* 142, 144, 235
disablement *n* 142
disabuse *vb* 452
disabused *adj* 452
disadvantage *n* 26, 32, 579, 581, 836, *vb* 26
disadvantaged *adj* 574, 713
disadvantageous *adj* 116, 581

disaffected *adj* 437, 538, 543
disaffection *n* 437
disagree *vb* 437, 632, 635, 826
disagreeable *adj* 737, 758, 792, 804
disagreeableness *n* 737
disagreeing *adj* 635
disagreement *n* 73, 437, 538, 632, 635, 826
disagree with *vb* 413
disallow *vb* 424, 680
disallowance *n* 680
disallowed *adj* 52
disappear *vb* 2, 94, 373, 395
disappearance *n* 163, 395
disappearing *adj* 395
disappearing trick *n* 395
disappoint *vb* 273, 452, 743
disappointed *adj* 452, 739, 743
disappointing *adj* 431, 452
disappointment *n* 452, 737, 743
disapprobation *n* 824, 826
disapproval *n* 437, 546, 682, 826
disapprove *vb* 437, 682, 826
disapproved *adj* 826
disapproving *adj* 826
disapprovingly *adv* 826
disarm *vb* 142, 144, 644, 646, 809
disarmament *n* 644, 646
disarmer *n* 644
disarray *n* 56
disaster *n* 150, 604, 652, 656, 806, 836
disaster area *n* 150
disastrous *adj* 150, 604, 652, 656, 836
disavow *vb* 474
disavowal *n* 474
disband *vb* 41, 46, 48, 67, 669
disbanding *n* 669
disbandment *n* 41, 46, 67
disbar *vb* 266
disbarment *n* 266
disbelief *n* 435, 869
disbelieve *vb* 428, 435
disbelieving *adj* 435, 869
disburse *vb* 716, 718
disbursement *n* 716, 718
disc *n* 223, 369
discard *n* 54, 546, *vb* 286, 546, 696
discarded *adj* 546
discern *vb* 370, 396, 418, 460
discernable *adj* 485
discernibility *n* 372
discernible *adj* 372, 460
discerning *adj* 18, 418, 429, 444, 768

discernment *n* 396, 418, 429, 444, 768
discharge *n* 255, 264, 266, 268, 605, 606, 669, 673, 696, 716, 813, 857, *vb* 255, 264, 266, 268, 605, 606, 669, 673, 696, 716, 813, 819, 821, 857
discharged *adj* 857
discharge of duty *n* 821
disciple *n* 21, 476, 863
disciplinarian *n* 659
disciplinary *adj* 860
disciplinary action *n* 860
discipline *n* 55, 659, 860, *vb* 55, 659, 860
disciplined *adj* 55, 659, 668, 843
disclaim *vb* 415, 435, 474, 546
disclaimer *n* 435, 474, 546
disclose *vb* 203, 464, 468, 470
disclosed *adj* 468
disclosure *n* 203, 464, 468, 470
disco *n* 367, 524, 761, 789, *vb* 524
discography *n* 76
discoid *adj* 223
discoloration *n* 382, 585, 595
discolour *vb* 382, 595
discoloured *adj* 382, 585, 595
discomfort *n* 337, 581
discompose *vb* 58
disconcert *vb* 58, 405
disconcerted *adj* 58
disconnected *adj* 65
disconnectedness *n* 65
disconsolate *adj* 735, 739
discontent *n* 437, 452, 739, 804, 826
discontented *adj* 437, 452, 739
discontinuance *n* 565
discontinuation *n* 123
discontinue *vb* 62, 65, 123, 550, 565
discontinued *adj* 107, 565
discontinuity *n* 16, 65
discontinuous *adj* 16, 65
discontinuously *adv* 65
discord *n* 20, 362, 366, 437, 635
discordant *adj* 20, 362, 366, 635
discotheque *n* 761
discount *n* 36, 722, *vb* 407, 722
discourage *vb* 552, 743, 749
discouraged *adj* 452
discouragement *n* 452, 552
discouraging *adj* 552
discourse *n* 519, 522, 528, *vb* 506
discourse on *vb* 519
discourteous *adj* 769, 792, 812, 824
discourtesy *n* 769, 792, 824
discover *vb* 433

discovery n 433, 468
discredit n 775, vb 435, 775, 828
discreet adj 467, 531, 791
discrepancy n 18, 20, 26, 421
discrete adj 41, 65
discretion n 429, 467, 531, 535, 545, 754, 791
discretionary adj 429, 535, 545
discriminate vb 18, 418, 430, 545, 768, 818
discriminating adj 18, 418, 545, 768
discrimination n 18, 26, 418, 429, 430, 545, 768, 818
discriminatory adj 26, 430
discursive adj 252, 506, 519
discursiveness n 506
discuss vb 410, 519, 533, 685
discussion n 410, 533
disdain n 779, 781, 824, vb 546, 779, 824
disdainful adj 779, 781, 824
disease n 589
diseased adj 589, 597
disembark vb 237, 261
disembarkation n 261
disembodied adj 283
disembody vb 283
disenchant vb 452
disenchanted adj 452, 758
disenchantment n 452
disencumber vb 286
disengage vb 669
disengaged adj 41
disengagement n 669
disentangle vb 669
disentitle vb 820
disentitlement n 820
disestablish vb 820
disestablishment n 820
disfavour n 538, 775, 796, 826
disfigure vb 219, 595, 764
disfigured adj 585, 595, 764
disfigurement n 219, 585, 595, 764
disfranchise vb 820
disgorge vb 266
disgrace n 775, 818, 832, vb 775, 824
disgraced adj 775
disgraceful adj 583, 775
disgrace oneself vb 775
disgruntled adj 452, 739
disgruntlement n 452
disguise n 17, 21, 202, 373, 469, vb 17, 202, 469
disguised adj 469

disgust n 737, 758, 796, vb 343, 737, 758
disgusted adj 758
disgusting adj 737, 796
dish n 227, 267, 763
dishabille n 205
disharmony n 366, 635
dishearten vb 743
disheartened adj 743
dishevel vb 56, 291
dishevelled adj 56, 291
dishonest adj 479, 480, 481, 832
dishonest act n 832
dishonesty n 479, 480, 481, 626, 832
dishonour n 775, 818, 824, 832, vb 717, 775, 824, 828
dishonourable adj 775, 824
dishonoured/dud cheque n 717
dish out vb 700
dish up vb 267
dishwasher n 586
dishwater n 343
dishy adj 763
disillusion vb 452
disillusioned adj 452, 743
disillusionment n 452, 743
disincentive n 552
disinclination n 437, 538, 758
disinclined adj 437, 538
disinfect vb 39, 586, 590
disinfectant adj 586, n 348, 586
disinfected adj 590
disinfection n 590
disingenuous adj 479, 481, 626, 832
disingenuousness n 479, 481, 832
disinherit vb 696, 703
disinheritance n 703
disintegrate vb 2, 41, 46, 48, 67, 283, 295
disintegrated adj 46
disintegration n 2, 41, 46
disinter vb 325, 433
disinterest n 756
disinterested adj 756, 817, 833
disinterestedness n 833
disjointed adj 65
disjointedness n 65
disk drive n 570
disk memory n 570
disk pack n 570
dislike n 538, 758, 794, 796, vb 758, 796
dislocate vb 58, 161
dislocated adj 58, 161

287

dissident *adj* 41, 73, 437, 474, 662, *n* 73, 739, 871
dissimilar *adj* 18, 20
dissimilarity *n* 16, 18, 20
dissimulate *vb* 469, 481
dissimulation *n* 17, 469, 481
dissipate *vb* 572, 727
dissipated *adj* 336, 844
dissipation *n* 336, 727, 844, 851
dissociate *vb* 41
dissociate oneself *vb* 474
dissociation *n* 10, 41, 474, 538, 871
dissolute *adj* 838, 844, 851
dissoluteness *n* 844, 851
dissolution *n* 41, 46, 62, 67, 303, 395, 673
dissolution of marriage *n* 798
dissolve *vb* 4, 41, 46, 48, 67, 217, 290, 303, 305, 395, 673
dissolved *adj* 303
dissonance *n* 20, 362, 366, 635
dissonant *adj* 20, 362, 366, 635
dissuade *vb* 552, 623
dissuasion *n* 552, 623
dissuasive *adj* 552, 623
distaff side *n* 12, 333
distance *n* 172, 790, *vb* 172
distant *adj* 172, 356, 790
distant future *n* 102
distaste *n* 758
distasteful *adj* 838
distemper *n* 381, *vb* 381
distend *vb* 170, 225
distended *adj* 170, 170, 226
distension *n* 170
distil *vb* 39, 270, 304
distillate *n* 39, 270
distillation *n* 39, 270, 304
distinct *adj* 41, 65, 351, 353, 355, 372, 448, 526
distinction *n* 18, 29, 418, 511, 774, 776
distinctive *adj* 18, 70
distinctiveness *n* 70
distinctness *n* 351, 353, 355, 372
distinguish *vb* 18, 70, 418, 460
distinguishable *adj* 460, 485
distinguished *adj* 29, 511, 576, 774
distort *vb* 4, 217, 219, 411, 430, 463, 489, 764
distorted *adj* 10, 219, 489, 585, 764
distortion *n* 10, 219, 411, 463, 479, 489, 585, 764, 871
distract *vb* 405

distracted *adj* 405
distractedness *n* 405
distraint *n* 703
distraught *adj* 447, 735
distress *n* 337, 735, 836, *vb* 337, 735, 737
distressed *adj* 107, 735
distressing *adj* 337, 735, 836
distress signal *n* 602
distribute *vb* 23, 57, 67, 470, 698, 700
distribution *n* 57, 67, 466, 700
district *n* 157
distrust *n* 435, 815, *vb* 435, 815
distrustful *adj* 435, 815
disturb *vb* 58, 161, 281, 737
disturbance *n* 56, 58, 161, 281, 662
disturbed *adj* 58, 161, 281, 447
disturbing *adj* 737
disunited *adj* 635
disunity *n* 635
disuse *n* 550, 565
disused *adj* 107, 550, 565
ditch *n* 210, 231, 315, *vb* 238, 546, 563, 565, 696
dither *vb* 428, 541
ditto *adv* 13, 21
ditty *n* 365, 521
diuretic *adj* 268
diurnal *adj* 109
diva *n* 368
dive *n* 186, 275, *vb* 186, 245, 275, 761
diver *n* 275
diverge *vb* 18, 20, 41, 67, 73, 195, 252, 260
divergence *n* 18, 20, 41, 67, 195, 252, 260, 871
divergent *adj* 18, 20, 67, 260, 871
divers *adj* 16, 80
diverse *adj* 16, 18
diversify *vb* 16, 121, 393
diversion *n* 121, 214, 252, 601, 761
diversity *n* 16, 18, 393
divert *vb* 214, 761
diverting *adj* 761
divest *vb* 203, 703
divest oneself *vb* 205
divide *n* 207, *vb* 41, 48, 68, 75, 207, 635
divided *adj* 48, 635
divide fifty-fifty *vb* 63
dividend *n* 690, 719
divide up *vb* 700
dividing line *n* 176
divination *n* 104, 455, 877

divine *adj* 734, 862, 868, *n* 868, *vb*
104, 401, 456, 876, 877
divine manifestation *n* 862
divineness *n* 862
diviner *n* 876
divine task *n* 862
divine worship *n* 881
diving *n* 237, 761
divinity *n* 862, 868
division *n* 41, 68, 75, 635, 648, 700,
871, 871
divisive *adj* 41, 635
divorce *n* 41, 798, *vb* 41, 798
divorce court *n* 798
divorced *adj* 798
divorcee *n* 798
divot *n* 327
divulge *vb* 203, 464, 468
divvy up *vb* 700
dizzy *adj* 405
DNA *n* 12, 320
D-notice *n* 678
do *n* 786, *vb* 573, 607
do/clinch/make a deal *vb* 684
do/conduct/transact business *vb* 611
doable *adj* 423
do a bunk *vb* 395
do a disservice *vb* 836
do a favour *vb* 805
do a flit *vb* 605
do a good turn *vb* 805
do a job *vb* 611
do all right *vb* 712
do a moonlight flit *vb* 717
do a roaring trade *vb* 655, 709
do as one is told *vb* 663
do battle with *vb* 643
docile *adj* 55, 537, 642, 663
docility *n* 537, 642, 663
dock *adj* 36, *n* 614, 855, *vb* 41, 160,
179, 237, 238, 261, 717
docker *n* 613
docket *n* 485, *vb* 485
docking *n* 238
doctor *n* 596, 778, *vb* 121, 481
doctrinaire *adj* 434
doctrinal *adj* 868
doctrine *n* 434, 868
docudrama *n* 472
document *vb* 486, 486
documentary *adj* 420, 440, *n* 3, 517
documentation *n* 420, 486, 513
dodder *vb* 144
doddering *adj* 112

doddle *n* 629
dodecahedron *n* 84
dodge *n* 480, 556, 626, *vb* 195, 407,
556
dodger *n* 556
dodgy *adj* 428, 599
doe *n* 333
doer *n* 607
do evil *vb* 836
do for *vb* 666
do for effect *vb* 785
do for show *vb* 785
dog *n* 326, 332, *vb* 555
dog days *n* 108
dog-eared *adj* 230
dogged *adj* 540, 542, 609, 617
doggedness *n* 540, 542
doggerel *n* 521
dog-in-the-manger *adj* 834
dog-leg *n* 220
dogma *n* 434, 868
dogmatic *adj* 430, 434, 542, 783, 868
dogmatism *n* 434
dogood *vb* 582
do good *vb* 805, 807, 835
do-gooder *n* 805, 807
dogsbody *n* 613, 666
dog someone's footsteps *vb* 60, 173
dog the footsteps of *vb* 85
do in *vb* 150, 324
doing *n* 607
dole out *vb* 698, 700
do less than justice to *vb* 432
doll *n* 333, 761
dolled up *adj* 204
dollop *n* 700
doll up *vb* 765
dolly bird *n* 333, 763
dolour *n* 735
dolt *n* 445
do magic *vb* 876
domain *n* 157, 854
dome *n* 223, 225, 226, *vb* 221
domed *adj* 221, 226
domestic *adj* 164, 199, 326, *n* 613,
666
domestic animal *n* 326
domesticated *adj* 328
domestic science *n* 267
domicile *n* 165
dominance *n* 139, 141, 670
dominant *adj* 139, 141, 657
dominate *vb* 29, 139, 141, 670
domination *n* 31, 692

dominer *vb* 657, 659
dominion *n* 157, 657
dominions *n* 863
domino theory *n* 64
do mischief *vb* 836
don *n* 776, *vb* 204
donate *vb* 698, 716
donation *n* 698, 716
done *adj* 653
done for *adj* 150, 323, 652
done for effect *adj* 785
done thing *n* 72, 549
donjon *n* 640
donkey *n* 241, 445
donkey's years *n* 93
donnish *adj* 438
do no good *vb* 583
donor *n* 12, 154, 698
do nothing *vb* 608
don't knows *n* 27, 44
doodle *n* 217
doom *vb* 536
doomed *adj* 104
doom merchant *n* 455
doomsday *n* 62, 104
do one a good turn *vb* 631
do one a power of good *vb* 835
do one's best *vb* 561
do one's duty *vb* 663, 688, 821
do oneself credit *vb* 774
do oneself in *vb* 324
do one's homework *vb* 559
do one's own thing *vb* 44, 73, 79
do one's utmost *vb* 49, 617
do on the cheap *vb* 728
door *n* 232, 263
do-or-die *adj* 753
doorman *n* 666
doormat *n* 144, 784
doorstep *n* 209
dope *n* 466, 849, *vb* 335
do penance *vb* 814
dopey *adj* 610
Doppelganger *n* 13
do proud *vb* 725
dormancy *n* 146, 465
dormant *adj* 146, 465
dormitory *n* 165
dormitory town *n* 157
dorsal *adj* 213
dosage *n* 700
dose *n* 23, 700, *vb* 700
do sport *vb* 761
doss down *vb* 165

dosshouse *n* 165
dossier *n* 420, 486
dot *n* 169, 393, *vb* 87, 288, 393
dotage *n* 112
dote on *vb* 795, 875
do the decent thing *vb* 831
do the dirty on *vb* 832
do the right thing *vb* 817
do the rounds *vb* 271
do things by the book *vb* 787
do things in style *vb* 725
dotted *adj* 288, 393
dotted about *adj* 67, 87
dotty *adj* 447
double *adj* 81, *n* 13, 81, 676, *vb* 81
double back *vb* 213, 254
double-barrelled *adj* 81, 776
double bass *n* 369
double-book *vb* 103
double check *vb* 417, 427
double chin *n* 192
double-cross *vb* 480, 832
double-dealing *adj* 81, 481, 832, *n* 81, 480, 543, 832
double-decker *n* 81, 175, 242
double Dutch *n* 459, 461
double-edged *adj* 81
double entendre *n* 461, 744
double entry *n* 720
double figures *n* 84
double meaning *n* 458
double negative *n* 501
double-quick *adj* 245
double standard *n* 832
doublet *n* 81
double take *n* 248
doubletalk *n* 411, 459
doublethink *n* 411
doubling *n* 81
doubly *adv* 81
doubt *n* 428, 435, 538, 541, 815, 869, *vb* 428, 815
doubter *n* 869
doubtful *adj* 426, 428, 435, 775
doubtfulness *n* 426, 428
doubting *adj* 869
doubting Thomas *n* 869
doubtless *adv* 427
doubts *n* 435
douche *n* 305
dough *n* 290, 711
doughiness *n* 290
doughty *adj* 143, 540, 751
doughy *adj* 290

dour *adj* 542, 731, 804
dourness *n* 542, 731
douse *vb* 305, 375
dove *n* 644, 839
Dove *n* 862
dove-grey *adj* 385
dovetail *vb* 19, 40, 176
dowager *n* 333, 776, 798
dowel *n* 42
do well *vb* 651, 655, 835
do without *vb* 556, 565, 696
down *adj* 743, *adv* 36, *n* 290, *vb* 267
down and out *adj* 713
down-and-out *n* 713, 777
down at heel *adj* 713
downcast *adj* 743
downdraught *n* 316
downer *n* 148
downfall *n* 275, 652
downgrade *vb* 277, 673, 860
downgrading *n* 277, 673
downhearted *adj* 743
downhill *adj* 275, 629
down in the dumps *adj* 735, 743
down in the mouth *adj* 275, 743
down-market *adj* 69, 724
down payment *n* 48, 687, 716
downpipe *n* 315
downpour *n* 307
downright *adj* 49, 478, *adv* 49
downrightness *n* 478, 509
downs *n* 313
downstage *adv* 212
downstairs *adv* 185
down the drain *adj* 572, 691
down-to-earth *adj* 3, 509
down tools *vb* 123
down to the ground *adv* 49
downtrodden *adj* 670
downturn *n* 121, 275, 593
downward *adj* 275
down with *adj* 589
downy *adj* 290
do work *vb* 580
do worship to *vb* 874
do wrong *vb* 818, 838, 853
dowry *n* 570
doyen *n* 107, 112, 774
doyenne *n* 112
doze *vb* 146, 610
dozen *n* 84
doziness *n* 619
dozy *adj* 619
DP *n* 570

DP camp *n* 600
drab *adj* 15, 382, 385, 762
drabness *n* 15, 382, 385, 762
draconian *adj* 127, 659
draconian measures *n* 659
draft *n* 664, *vb* 216, 488, 513, 557
drag *n* 137, 256, 301, 630, 668, 762, *vb* 234, 256
drag in *vb* 269
dragnet *n* 69, 256
dragon *n* 803
drag one's feet *vb* 246, 538, 610
drag out *vb* 124, 178, 616
drain *n* 264, 315, *vb* 142, 309, 328
drainage *n* 309
drained *adj* 619
drainpipe *n* 315
drake *n* 332
dram *n* 267
drama *n* 518, 523, 759
dramatic *adj* 523, 729, 732, 759, 785
dramatics *n* 785
dramatis personae *n* 76, 523
dramatist *n* 518
dramatize *vb* 482, 518, 523
drape *vb* 192, 230
drapery *n* 192
drastic *adj* 659
draught *n* 256, 267, 316
draught horse *n* 241
draughts *n* 761
draughtsman *n* 490, 613
draughtsmanship *n* 490
draughty *adj* 316
draw *n* 25, 257, 554, 654, *vb* 25, 234, 256, 257, 488, 490, 517
draw a parallel *vb* 194
draw a parallel between *vb* 9, 17
draw attention to *vb* 404
draw a veil over *vb* 202
drawback *n* 581, 585
draw breath *vb* 322
drawbridge *n* 240, 630
draw in *vb* 256
drawing power *n* 256
drawl *n* 526, 529, *vb* 526, 529, 616
drawn *adj* 171
draw near *vb* 259
draw nigh *vb* 104
draw on one's savings *vb* 718
draw out *vb* 178, 506, 711
draw straws *vb* 554
draw up *vb* 261, 557
dray *n* 242

dread *n* 450, 750, *vb* 450, 750
dreadful *adj* 583
dream *n* 748, 755, 763
dreamboat *n* 763
dreamer *n* 405, 748
dreamlike *adj* 4
dream up *vb* 22, 398, 457, 557
dream world *n* 4
dreamy *adj* 398, 405
dreariness *n* 762
dreary *adj* 737, 745, 762
dredge *vb* 256, 270
dredger *n* 243, 270
dredge up *vb* 448
dregs *n* 32, 37
dregs of society *n* 777
drench *vb* 305
drenched *adj* 305
dress *n* 204, 484, 787, *vb* 204, 596
dressage *n* 761
dress down *vb* 826
dressed *adj* 204
dressed to kill *adj* 766
dressed up to the nines *adj* 204
dressing *n* 344, 596
dressing-up *n* 204
dressmaker *n* 613
dress rehearsal *n* 559
dress up *vb* 204, 479, 765
drey *n* 165
dribble *n* 30, *vb* 308, 314
dried *adj* 603
dried out *adj* 847
dried-up *adj* 309
drift *n* 234, 249, 458, *vb* 67, 234, 238, 407, 610
drifter *n* 236, 243, 555
drifting *adj* 94, 234
drill *n* 71, 232, 568, 617, 787, *vb* 15, 232, 328, 475
drink *n* 267, 310, 620, *vb* 267, 848
drinkable *adj* 267
drink in *vb* 404
drinking bout *n* 848
drink like a fish *vb* 848
drink moderately *vb* 847
drink problem *n* 848
drinks party *n* 789
drink to *vb* 791, 823, 825
drink to excess *vb* 844
drink too much *vb* 844
drink to the health of *vb* 786
drip *n* 144, *vb* 246
drip-dry *vb* 309

dripping *adj* 305, *n* 319
drippy *adj* 144
drive *n* 141, 141, 145, 240, 247, 255, 539, 664, *vb* 136, 141, 145, 234, 247, 255, 664
drive at *vb* 458
drive away *vb* 258
drive insane *vb* 58
drivel *n* 443, *vb* 445, 459
drive mad *vb* 802
driven *adj* 735
drive round the bend *vb* 58
drive up the wall/round the bend *vb* 447
driving *adj* 539, 664
driving force *n* 134, 141
drizzle *n* 307, 308
drizzly *adj* 307, 308
droll *adj* 744
drone *n* 358, *vb* 358, 364, 526
drone on *vb* 530
drool *vb* 268, 755
droop *n* 192, *vb* 192, 619, 743
droopiness *n* 192
droopy *adj* 192, 275
drop *n* 30, 34, 48, 169, 185, 225, 275, *vb* 34, 62, 123, 152, 275, 563, 565, 619, 696, 724
drop a brick *vb* 116
drop a brick/clanger *vb* 20
drop a line to *vb* 515
drop anchor *vb* 237
drop dead *vb* 323
drop in *vb* 261, 263
drop in on *vb* 789
drop in the ocean *n* 30
drop like a stone *vb* 190
drop off *vb* 619
dropout *n* 73
drop out *vb* 73, 563, 612, 654
dropping *adj* 619
droppings *n* 268
dross *n* 37
drought *n* 307, 309, 574, 755
drove *n* 66
drown *vb* 49, 150, 275, 860
drowning *n* 860
drown one's sorrows *vb* 848
drown out *vb* 354
drowsiness *n* 619
drowsy *adj* 619
drudge *n* 613, 666
drug *n* 596, 849, *vb* 335, 596, 849
drug abuse *n* 849

dusky *adj* 384
dust *n* 300, 587, *vb* 300, 586
dustbowl *n* 153, 309
duster *n* 586
dustiness *n* 300
dust jacket *n* 202, 516
dustman *n* 586, 613
dustsheet *n* 202
dustup *n* 56, 147, 643
dust up *vb* 147
dusty *adj* 300, 309, 587
Dutch courage *n* 752, 848
dutiable *adj* 721
dutiful *adj* 663, 821, 831, 837
dutifulness *n* 663, 872
duty *n* 715, 721, 817, 819, 821
duty-bound *adj* 821
duty-free *adj* 722
dwarf *adj* 30, *n* 169, 865, *vb* 171
dwarfish *adj* 169, 185
dwarfishness *n* 185
dwell *vb* 165
dweller *n* 164
dwelling *n* 165
dwindle *vb* 34, 144, 395
dwindling *adj* 34
dybbuk *n* 865
dye *n* 381, 765, *vb* 381
dyed *adj* 381
dyed-in-the-wool *adj* 49, 549
dying *adj* 323
dying breath *n* 323
dying day *n* 323
dyke *n* 73
dynamic *adj* 132, 143, 234, 353, 609
dynamics *n* 353
dynamism *n* 141, 145, 145, 609
dynamite *n* 255, 649
dynamo *n* 132, 141, 568
dynasty *n* 64, 155, 330, 776
dypso *n* 848
dysentery *n* 268, 589
dyslexia *n* 371, 495
dyspeptic *adj* 80

E

eager *adj* 402, 450, 537, 609, 755
eager beaver *n* 609
eagerness *n* 402, 537, 609, 755
eagle-eyed *adj* 370
earful *n* 528
earl *n* 776
earlier *adj* 99, *adv* 102

earliness *n* 113
early *adj* 98, 113
early bird *n* 99, 109
early on *adv* 61, 113
early riser *n* 109
early warning *n* 602
earmark *vb* 485, 545, 553
earmarked *adj* 485
earn *vb* 690, 819
earned income *n* 690
earnest *adj* 729, 745, 872
earnestness *n* 745, 872
earnings *n* 690, 716, 719
earn one's living *vb* 611
earpiece *n* 351
earring *n* 192, 766
earshattering *adj* 352
earshot *n* 351
earsplitting *adj* 352, 355
earth *n* 3, 165, 284, 311, 600
earthbound *adj* 284, 873
earthly *adj* 284
earth mother *n* 154
earthquake *n* 147, 150
earth sciences *n* 284
earth-shattering *adj* 576
earthworks *n* 640
ear trumpet *n* 352
ease *n* 336, 511, 580, 618, 629, 712,
  734, 738, *vb* 290, 302, 629, 631, 669,
  740
easel *n* 193
ease of access *n* 580
ease off *vb* 246
ease of mind *n* 738
ease of use *n* 580
easily *adv* 629
easily pleased *adj* 738
easily swayed *adj* 551
easiness *n* 580, 629
easing *adj* 740, *n* 148, 631, 658, 669,
  740
Easter *n* 881
easy *adj* 336, 509, 629, 658, 756, 788
easy-going *adj* 19, 616, 629, 660, 733,
  742, 756
easy mark *n* 730
easy meat *n* 629
Easy Street *n* 655
easy target *n* 629
easy terms *n* 702, 708, 714
easy to reach *adj* 580
easy to use *adj* 580
easy virtue *n* 851

easy way out *n* 629
eat *vb* 267
eat away *vb* 593, 595
eater *n* 267
eat humble pie *vb* 642, 780
eat like a horse *vb* 846
eat nothing *vb* 845
eat one's heart out *vb* 735, 743
eat out of house and home *vb* 846
eat to excess *vb* 844
eau de cologne *n* 349
eau-de-nil *adj* 390
eavesdrop *vb* 351, 402
eavesdropper *n* 402
eavesdropping *n* 351
ebb *n* 34, 254, *vb* 34
ebb and flow *n* 119, 280
ebony *n* 384
ebullience *n* 732
ebullient *adj* 732, 742
eccentric *adj* 20, 70, 73, 447, *n* 20,
   73, 447
eccentricity *n* 73, 447
ecclesiastical *adj* 878
ecclesiasticism *n* 878
ecdysiast *n* 205
echelon *n* 64
echo *n* 21, 248, 358, 359, *vb* 13, 17,
   21, 81, 88, 248, 358, 359
echo chamber *n* 248, 359
echoey *adj* 248, 359
echt *adj* 22
eclectic *adj* 38, 51, 545
eclecticism *n* 69, 545
eclecticness *n* 51
eclipse *n* 375, 395, *vb* 31, 375, 774
ecological *adj* 320
ecology *n* 320
economic *adj* 578
economical *adj* 505, 724, 726
economies *n* 726
economize *vb* 668, 724, 726
economy *adj* 724, *n* 505, 668, 726
ecru *n* 383
ecstasy *n* 336, 732, 734, 795
ecstatic *adj* 732, 734
ectoplasm *n* 4
ecumenicalism *n* 69
ecumenicism *n* 51
eddy *n* 279, 314, *vb* 314
edge *n* 31, 173, 208, 209, 211, 214,
   507, *vb* 195, 209, 211, 214, 296
edgeways *adv* 195
edginess *n* 281

edging *adj* 211, *n* 209
edgy *adj* 281, 729, 732, 803
edible *adj* 267
edict *n* 71, 661, 852
edification *n* 475, 835
edifice *n* 298
edify *vb* 475, 835
edit *vb* 462, 518, 525, 592
edited *adj* 592
editing *n* 592
edition *n* 514, 516
editor *n* 592, 613
editorial *n* 519
educate *vb* 438, 475
educated *adj* 438
educated guess *n* 425
education *n* 438, 475
educational *adj* 475
educationalist *n* 475
educative *adj* 475
eerie *adj* 750, 865, 876
efface *vb* 449, 487
effacement *n* 449, 487
efface oneself *vb* 32, 784
eff and blind *vb* 801
effect *n* 60, 133, 136, 785
effective *adj* 136, 138, 141, 507, 578
effectiveness *n* 141
effects *n* 694
effeminacy *n* 144
effeminate *adj* 144, 332
effendi *n* 778
effervesce *vb* 281
effervescence *n* 281, 304
effervescent *adj* 281, 304, 732
effete *adj* 144
effeteness *n* 144
efficacious *adj* 141, 578
efficacy *n* 578
efficient *adj* 611
effigy *n* 488
efflorescence *n* 300
effluent *n* 264, 572
effluvium *n* 347
effort *n* 561, 617
effortless *adj* 629
effrontery *n* 781
effulgent *adj* 374
effusive *adj* 530
egalitarian *adj* 25, 667, *n* 667
egalitarianism *n* 25, 667
egghead *n* 396
egg on *vb* 551
eggshell *n* 183, 295

egg yolk *n* 389
egocentric *adj* 834
egoism *n* 70, 834
egoist *n* 834
egoistic *adj* 834
egotism *n* 199, 783, 808, 834
egotist *n* 783, 808, 834
egotistic *adj* 834
egotistical *adj* 70, 783
ego-trip *n* 70
egregious *adj* 372
egress *n* 264, 605
eight *n* 84
eighth *adj* 84
eighty *n* 84
ejaculate *vb* 363, 526
ejaculation *n* 363, 526
eject *vb* 198, 238, 258, 266, 268
ejection *n* 198, 266, 268
ejector *n* 266
ejector seat *n* 605
elaborate *adj* 510, 766, *vb* 506
elaborate on *vb* 592
elan *n* 145
elapse *vb* 90, 105
elastic *adj* 170, 248, 290, 293
elastic band *n* 293
elasticity *n* 170, 290, 293, 294
elated *adj* 732, 734
elation *n* 732, 734
elbow *n* 220, *vb* 173
elbow grease *n* 301, 617
elbowroom *n* 667
elder *adj* 31, 59, *n* 31, 112, 880
elderly *adj* 112
elder statesman *n* 112
eldest *n* 59, 99
elect *adj* 100, *n* 52, 582, *vb* 672
election *n* 672
elector *n* 665
electrical/mechanical/civil engineer *n* 613
electric blue *adj* 391
electric chair *n* 861
electrician *n* 613
electricity *n* 141, 341
electrify *vb* 141, 145, 451, 732
electrocute *vb* 324, 860
electrocution *n* 324, 860
electrolier *n* 377
electronic data processing *n* 570
elegance *n* 502, 511, 763, 770
elegant *adj* 502, 511, 763, 770
elegiac *adj* 325, 521

elegize *vb* 521, 747
elegy *n* 325, 521, 747
element *n* 48, 53, 282
elemental *adj* 132, 189
elementary *adj* 61
elements *n* 307
elevate *vb* 184, 276
elevated *adj* 184, 276
elevate to the peerage *vb* 774
elevation *n* 184, 276, 298
eleven *n* 84
elevenses *n* 109, 267
eleventh-hour *adj* 615
eleventh hour *n* 114
elf *n* 865
elfish *adj* 865
elicit *vb* 132, 270
eligibility *n* 51
eligible *adj* 797, 799
eliminate *vb* 36, 87, 266, 487
elimination *n* 36, 266, 487
elite *n* 31, 582, 776
ellipsis *n* 179, 195, 505
elliptical *adj* 179, 195, 458
elocute *vb* 526
elocution *n* 526
elongate *vb* 178
elongated *adj* 178
elongation *n* 178
elope *vb* 262, 395, 605, 797
elopement *n* 262, 395, 605, 797
eloquence *n* 502, 507, 528
eloquent *adj* 502, 507, 528
elucidate *vb* 412, 460, 462
elucidation *n* 412, 462
elucidatory *adj* 412, 462
elude *vb* 605
elusive *adj* 4, 556
elusiveness *n* 395
Elysium *n* 866
emaciated *adj* 183
emaciation *n* 183
emanate from *vb* 133
emanation *n* 264
emancipate *vb* 669
emancipated *adj* 667
emancipation *n* 667, 669
emasculate *vb* 153
embalm *vb* 95, 325, 603
embalming *n* 603
embargo *n* 41, 52, 235, 630, 678, *vb* 678
embargoed *adj* 678
embark *vb* 237, 262

embarkation *n* 262
embark on *vb* 61, 562
embarrassed *adj* 840
embarrassment *n* 737
embassy *n* 672, 675
embed *vb* 131, 160, 186, 269
embedded *adj* 186
embellish *vb* 479, 510, 766
embellished *adj* 766
embellishment *n* 510, 766
ember *n* 377
embezzle *vb* 566, 705
embezzlement *n* 705
embezzler *n* 705
embitter *vb* 741, 796
embittered *adj* 452, 802
embittering *n* 741
emblem *n* 484
emblematic *adj* 484, 488
embodiment *n* 5, 198, 282, 394
embody *vb* 3, 5, 198, 282, 488
embolden *vb* 751
emboss *vb* 492, 766
embossed *adj* 226, 492, 766
embossing *n* 228, 492
embrace *n* 695, 791, 793, 800, *vb* 51, 199, 206, 265, 434, 695, 791, 793, 800
embrocation *n* 319
embroider *vb* 149, 479, 482, 510, 766
embroidered *adj* 766
embroidery *n* 149, 510, 766
embroil *vb* 56, 197, 224
embryo *n* 61, 132, 208, 217
embryonic *adj* 61, 132, 217
emerald *n* 390, 766
emerge *vb* 61, 133, 264, 394
emergence *n* 261
emergency *n* 101, 115, 576
emergency lane *n* 600
emeritus *adj* 674
emery board *n* 291
emery paper *n* 301
emetic *adj* 266, *n* 596
emigrant *adj* 264
emigrate *vb* 67, 262, 264
emigration *n* 67, 262, 264
emigratory *adj* 262
eminence *n* 29, 228, 276, 576, 774
eminent *adj* 29, 276, 576, 774
emir *n* 776
emission *n* 264
emit *vb* 264, 266, 347, 353, 374
Emmanuel *n* 862

emollient *adj* 596, *n* 148, 302
emolument *n* 690, 711, 716, 719
emotion *n* 729, 729, '732, 795
emotional *adj* 729, 730, 732, 795
empathize *vb* 729
empathy *n* 457, 729, 809
emperor *n* 665, 776
emphasis *n* 473, 507
emphasize *vb* 143, 464, 473, 507, 576
emphatic *adj* 473, 507
Empire State Building *n* 184
empirical *adj* 3, 416
empiricism *n* 3
emplacement *n* 160
employ *vb* 564, 611
employed *adj* 564, 607, 611
employee *n* 613, 666
employer *n* 613
employment *n* 564, 611
emporium *n* 710
empower *vb* 672
empowered *adj* 657, 672
empress *n* 665
emptiness *n* 2, 163, 459
empty *adj* 2, 163, 459, 755, 771, *vb* 266
empty-headed *adj* 397, 399
empty-headedness *n* 399
empty promise *n* 4
empty talk *n* 4
empyreal *adj* 284
empyrean *n* 284
emulate *vb* 17, 21
emulation *n* 21
emulator *n* 21
emulsifier *n* 182
emulsify *vb* 317
emulsion *n* 317
enable *vb* 423, 567
enact *vb* 488, 523, 607, 852
enactment *n* 488, 852
enamel *n* 202, *vb* 202, 381, 766
enamelled *adj* 766
enamoured *adj* 795
encamp *vb* 160
encampment *n* 160
encapsulate *vb* 51, 199, 202, 269
encase *vb* 202, 210, 269
encash *vb* 690, 711
encashment *n* 690
enchant *vb* 732, 795, 876
enchanted *adj* 876
enchanter *n* 876
enchanting *adj* 732, 736, 795, 876

enchantment *n* 732, 734, 876
encircle *vb* 206, 210, 223
enclave *n* 41, 157, 790
enclose *vb* 156, 166, 198, 199, 202, 206, 210
enclosure *n* 158, 210
encompass *vb* 51, 156, 206, 210
encore *n* 35, 88, 523, 825
encounter *n* 433, 643, *vb* 101, 433
encourage *vb* 132, 138, 145, 193, 551, 623, 631, 677, 732, 740, 742, 748, 805
encouragement *n* 132, 193, 551, 623, 631, 732
encouraging *adj* 623, 631, 742, 748
encroach *vb* 263, 272, 820
encroaching *adj* 272
encroachment *n* 263, 272, 853
encrust *vb* 201
encrustation *n* 201, 291
encrusted *adj* 291
encumber *vb* 285, 630
encumbrance *n* 285, 630
encyclopedic *adj* 49
encyclopedicity *n* 51
end *n* 62, 123, 211, 553, 653, *vb* 62, 123, 653
endanger *vb* 599
endangered species *n* 326
end-date *n* 123
endearing *adj* 795
endearment *n* 795, 800
endeavour *n* 561, *vb* 561, 617
ended *adj* 62
endemic *adj* 69, 199, 589
ending *n* 62, 653
endless *adj* 64, 86, 89, 95, 654
endless band *n* 64
endless belt *n* 221
endlessly *adv* 95
end-of-season sale *n* 709
end of the road *n* 62, 123
endorse *vb* 420, 436, 473, 631, 687, 825
endorsement *n* 420, 436, 473
endorse one's licence *vb* 860
endow *vb* 697, 698
endowment *n* 697
endpaper *n* 516
end point *n* 62
end-product *n* 149
end result *n* 60, 62, 133
end to end *adv* 64, 176
end up in *vb* 261

endurance *n* 1, 93, 95, 122, 143, 540
endure *vb* 1, 37, 64, 93, 122, 124, 729, 733
enduring *adj* 1, 93, 122
enemy *n* 632, 794
energetic *adj* 143, 145, 539, 609, 617
energize *vb* 141, 143, 145, 322, 732
energy *n* 141, 141, 143, 145, 322, 539, 609
energy-saving *adj* 726
energy source *n* 141
enervate *vb* 144
en famille *adv* 199
enfeeble *vb* 144
enfold *vb* 199, 210
enforce *vb* 661
enfranchise *vb* 669
enfranchised *adj* 667
enfranchisement *n* 669
engagé *adj* 43
engage *vb* 473, 611, 643, 645, 683, 732, 821
engaged *adj* 683, 797
engage in *vb* 562, 611
engagement *n* 683, 800, 821
engagement/wedding ring *n* 766
engender *vb* 152
engine *n* 141, 568
engineer *n* 149, 613, *vb* 132, 149, 547, 557
engine failure *n* 652
engorgement *n* 575
engrave *vb* 493, 766
engraved *adj* 493, 766
engraving *n* 493
engross *vb* 398, 404
engrossed *adj* 398, 404
engulf *vb* 150
enhance *vb* 29, 276, 510, 582, 592, 766
enhancement *n* 510, 592
enigma *n* 414, 465, 467
enigmatic *adj* 414, 439, 461
enjoin *vb* 623, 661, 821
enjoy *vb* 40, 336, 342, 692, 729, 734
enjoyable *adj* 336, 734, 736, 761
enjoyableness *n* 736
enjoy a joke *vb* 744
enjoy good health *vb* 588
enjoyment *n* 336, 692, 734
enjoy oneself *vb* 761
enlarge *vb* 33, 170, 491, 506
enlargement *n* 33, 170, 491
enlarger *n* 491

enlighten *vb* 438, 466, 475
enlightened *adj* 438, 444, 660, 667, 807
enlightening *adj* 466
enlightenment *n* 438, 444, 475
enlist *vb* 76, 263, 265
enlistment *n* 263
enliven *vb* 143, 145, 322, 620
en masse *adv* 47, 66, 86
enmesh *vb* 197, 224
enmity *n* 794, 806
ennoble *vb* 774
ennui *n* 762
enormity *n* 29, 168, 838
enormous *adj* 29, 168
enormously *adv* 29
enough *adj* 573, *n* 573
enough and to spare *n* 575
enquire *vb* 402, 414, 555
enquirer *n* 681
enquiring *adj* 414
enquiry *n* 414, 519, 555
enrage *vb* 147, 732, 802
enraged *adj* 802
enrapture *vb* 795
enraptured *adj* 734
enrich *vb* 592, 766
enrichment *n* 592, 766
enrol *vb* 43, 76, 263, 265, 634
enrolment *n* 43, 263, 265
en route *adv* 234, 239
ensconced *adj* 160
ensemble *n* 47, 204, 368
enshrine *vb* 325, 875
ensign *n* 484
enslave *vb* 670
enslaved *adj* 670
enslavement *n* 670
ensnare *vb* 56, 257, 601
ensue *vb* 60
ensuing *adj* 60, 133
ensure *vb* 427
entail *vb* 132
entangle *vb* 56, 197
entente *n* 636, 684
enter *vb* 76, 232, 263, 271, 720
enter into/make/sign a contract *vb* 684
enterprise *n* 145, 562, 609
enterprising *adj* 145, 253, 562, 609
entertain *vb* 729, 736, 761, 789, 793
entertainer *n* 523
entertaining *adj* 761
entertainment *n* 761

enter the lions' den *vb* 599
enter the ministry *vb* 879
enthral *vb* 257, 732
enthralling *adj* 732
enthrone *vb* 672, 774, 786, 878
enthronement *n* 672, 786
enthuse *vb* 732
enthusiasm *n* 145, 609, 729
enthusiast *n* 609
enthusiastic *adj* 145, 537, 609, 729, 732, 872
entice *vb* 551
enticement *n* 551
enticing *adj* 551, 736
entire *adj* 47, 49, 584
entirely *adv* 47, 49
entirety *n* 47, 49
entitled *adj* 819
entitlement *n* 819
entity *n* 1, 47, 79
entomb *vb* 186, 325
entombment *n* 325
entrails *n* 166, 199
entrance *n* 212, 232, 240, 261, 263, 271, 523, *vb* 736
entrance/admission charge *n* 721
entrant *n* 263
entreat *vb* 681, 874
entreaty *n* 681
entree *n* 267
entrench *vb* 122, 131, 186, 272
entrenched *adj* 131, 160, 186
entrenchment *n* 272
entrepôt *n* 710
entrepreneur *n* 707
entrepreneurial *adj* 707
entresol *n* 189
entrust *vb* 672
entrusted *adj* 672
entry *n* 263
entryism *n* 127, 139
entryist *adj* 127
entwine *vb* 224
enumerate *vb* 70, 74
enunciate *vb* 526
enunciation *n* 526
enuresis *n* 268
envelop *vb* 202, 206, 210
envelope *n* 167, 202, 210, 515
enveloped *adj* 202
enviable *adj* 755
envious *adj* 739, 802, 815, 816, 834
environment *n* 8, 206
environmental *adj* 8, 206

environs *n* 157, 173, 206
envoy *n* 675
envy *n* 815, 816, *vb* 815, 816
enzyme *n* 121, 320
EP *n* 369
epaulette *n* 657
ephemeral *adj* 4, 94, 322
epic *adj* 518, 521, *n* 521
epicentre *n* 200
epicure *n* 267, 846
epicurean *adj* 768, 844, 846, *n* 768
epicureanism *n* 267, 768, 844
epidemic *adj* 589, *n* 589, 591
epidermis *n* 202
epidiascope *n* 491
epigram *n* 442, 744
epigrammatic *adj* 442, 505
epigraph *n* 513
epilogue *n* 35, 60, 523
Epiphany *n* 881
episcopal *adj* 878, 879
episode *n* 8, 101
episodic *adj* 65
epistle *n* 515
Epistles *n* 868
epistolary *adj* 515
epitaph *n* 325
epithet *n* 497
epitome *n* 5
epitomize *vb* 5, 488
epoch *n* 90, 92
eponym *n* 497
eponymous *adj* 497
equal *adj* 25, 218, *n* 25
equal footing *n* 25
equality *n* 25, 817
equalize *vb* 17, 25
equalizer *n* 25
equally *adv* 25, 817
equal opportunity *n* 25
equal rights *n* 25
equanimity *n* 733
equate *vb* 194
equation *n* 17, 25
equator *n* 63, 211, 223
equerry *n* 666
equestrianism *n* 761
equidistance *n* 194
equidistant *adj* 25, 63, 194, 250
equilateral *adj* 25
equilibrium *n* 25, 131, 218, 235, 446
equine *adj* 326
equinoctial *adj* 108
equip *vb* 559, 567

equipment *n* 559, 567, 571
equipped *adj* 559
equitable *adj* 25, 817, 831
equity *n* 694, 817
equivalence *n* 13, 17, 25, 218
equivalent *adj* 11, 13, 17, 128, 129, 458, *n* 11, 128
equivocal *adj* 411, 458, 461, 479, 543
equivocate *vb* 411, 461, 543
equivocation *n* 411, 461, 479, 543
eradicate *vb* 150, 266
eradication *n* 150
erase *vb* 150, 395, 449, 487
eraser *n* 301, 487
erasure *n* 395, 449, 487
erect *adj* 190, 276, 831, *vb* 190, 228, 276, 298
erection *n* 276, 298
erectness *n* 190
erode *vb* 36, 46, 150, 301, 572, 593, 595
eroded *adj* 593, 595
erogenous *adj* 795
Eros *n* 862
erosion *n* 34, 36, 46, 107, 150, 300, 301, 572, 593, 595
erotic *adj* 795, 851
eroticism *n* 851
err *vb* 441, 818, 838
errand *n* 672
errant *adj* 236
erratic *adj* 120, 130, 544
erratum *n* 441
erring *adj* 441
erroneous *adj* 441, 818
error *n* 430, 441, 463, 840
ersatz *adj* 17, 21, 128
erstwhile *adj* 99, 105
erudite *adj* 438, 444, 476
erudition *n* 438, 444, 476
erupt *vb* 147, 264, 357
eruption *n* 147, 264
escalate *vb* 33
escalating *adj* 33
escalation *n* 33
escalator *n* 274, 276
escapade *n* 772
escape *n* 262, 395, 556, 572, 605, *vb* 262, 264, 395, 556, 572, 605
escape clause *n* 422, 605, 685
escaped *adj* 605
escapee *n* 605, 667
escape hatch *n* 605
escapement *n* 97

escape notice *vb* 373
escape route *n* 264
escaping *adj* 264
escapism *n* 457
escapist *adj* 457
escarpment *n* 184, 190, 311
eschatological *adj* 62
eschew *vb* 556
escort *n* 85, 332, 640, 668, 795, *vb* 85
esoteric *adj* 70, 461, 504, *n* 877
ESP *n* 877
esparto grass *n* 569
especially *adv* 70
Esperanto *n* 494
espouse *vb* 43, 434, 797
esprit de corps *n* 43
espy *vb* 370
essay *n* 519, 522, 561, *vb* 561
essence *n* 1, 5, 39, 270, 458
essential *adj* 5, 53, 558, 576, *n* 558
essentially *adv* 5
essential oil *n* 349
essential part *n* 5
establish *vb* 122, 131, 132, 160, 189, 412, 417
establishment *n* 160, 614, 634, 776
Establishment *n* 139, 657
estate *n* 7, 328, 694
estate agent *n* 707
estate duty *n* 721
esteem *n* 774, 823, 825, *vb* 774, 795
esteemed *adj* 774, 823
estimable *adj* 774, 825
estimate *n* 721, *vb* 23, 75, 177, 429, 721
estimation *n* 75, 177, 429, 774
estrange *vb* 794, 796
estranged *adj* 794
estrangement *n* 794
estuary *n* 310
etch *vb* 231, 493
etched *adj* 231, 493
etching *n* 231, 493
eternal *adj* 89, 91, 95, 862, 866
eternally *adv* 89, 95
eternal rest *n* 866
eternal triangle *n* 815, 851
eternity *n* 89, 91, 95, 323
ether *n* 284, 304, 306
ethereal *adj* 283, 284, 304, 306
ethical *adj* 821, 831
ethics *n* 821, 837
ethnic *adj* 54, 164, 331
ethnicity *n* 54, 331

ethnic minority *n* 331
ethnological *adj* 330
etiolate *vb* 4, 382
etiolated *adj* 382
etiquette *n* 768, 787, 791, 817
etymology *n* 132, 496
Eucharist *n* 881
eulogy *n* 825
eunuch *n* 153
euphemism *n* 768
euphonious *adj* 365
euphonium *n* 369
euphony *n* 365
euphoria *n* 336, 732, 734
euphoric *adj* 732, 734
euthanasia *n* 323
evacuate *vb* 161, 262, 264, 266, 268
evacuation *n* 161, 262, 266, 268
evacuee *n* 161, 600, 790
evade *vb* 556, 605
evaluate *vb* 418, 429
evaluation *n* 429
evaluative *adj* 462
evanescence *n* 94, 395
evanescent *adj* 4, 94, 395
evangelical *adj* 125, 868, 870, 872, *n* 872
evangelist *n* 868, 879
evangelistic *adj* 868
evangelize *vb* 125
evaporate *vb* 2, 94, 125, 304, 309, 395
evaporation *n* 34, 125, 304, 309, 395
evasion *n* 479, 556, 605
evasive *adj* 461, 479, 543, 556
evasive action *n* 556
evasiveness *n* 543
eve *n* 110
Eve *n* 333
even *adj* 15, 25, 74, 119, 191, 218, 292, *vb* 191, 292
evening *n* 110
evening classes *n* 475
evening dress *n* 204, 787
evening of one's life *n* 112
even keel *n* 25, 131
evenness *n* 15, 218, 292
even off *vb* 15
even out *vb* 25, 27, 222
evensong *n* 110, 881
event *n* 8, 643
even-tempered *adj* 131, 733
even-temperedness *n* 131
eventful *adj* 576
eventide *n* 110

eventuality *n* 423
eventually *adv* 104
Everest *n* 31, 184
evergreen *adj* 91, 93, 95, 106, 327
everlasting *adj* 89, 95, 862
everlasting fire *n* 867
everlastingness *n* 89, 91
eversion *n* 196
everyday *adj* 509
everyman *n* 69
every man Jack *n* 69
every now and then *adv* 118
everyone *n* 47
everything *n* 47
everything but the kitchen sink *n* 16, 38, 49
evict *vb* 52, 198, 266
eviction *n* 52, 161, 198, 266, 691
evidence *n* 420, 464, 484, *vb* 420
evident *adj* 372, 464
evidential *adj* 420
evil *adj* 583, 806, 832, 836, 838, *n* 604, 832, 836, 838
evildoer *n* 838
evil eye *n* 370, 801, 876
evil hour *n* 116
evil influence *n* 656
evil spirit *n* 864
evince *vb* 420, 464, 484
evocation *n* 448
evocative *adj* 448, 488, 517, 732
evoke *vb* 17, 132, 448, 488
evolution *n* 253, 320
evolve *vb* 1, 133, 253
ewe *n* 326, 333
ewer *n* 167
ex- *adj* 674
exacerbate *vb* 741, 796
exacerbation *n* 741
exact *adj* 440, 503, *vb* 703
exacting *adj* 406, 418, 739
exaction *n* 703
exactitude *n* 406, 440
exactness *n* 440, 503
exact retribution/compensation *vb* 641
exaggerate *vb* 272, 431, 479, 482, 489, 825
exaggerated *adj* 272, 482, 772
exaggeration *n* 219, 272, 431, 479, 482, 489, 772
exalt *vb* 276, 823, 825, 874
exaltation *n* 66, 734, 874
examination *n* 414, 519, 856
examine *vb* 519, 720

example *n* 59, 584
exasperate *vb* 147, 741, 802
exasperated *adj* 802
exasperation *n* 741, 802
excavate *vb* 186, 227, 270, 433, 555
excavated *adj* 227
excavation *n* 186, 270, 433, 555
excavator *n* 270
exceed *vb* 272
excel *vb* 70, 272, 624, 774
excellence *n* 31, 582
Excellency *n* 778
excellent *adj* 31, 582, 736, 837
except *vb* 52
excepting *adv* 52
exception *n* 70, 73, 422, 682, 685, 822
exceptional *adj* 29, 70, 73, 576
excerpt *n* 48
excess *n* 572, 575, 844, 846
excessive *adj* 272, 431, 482, 575, 723, 820, 844
excessiveness *n* 272, 431, 482, 844
exchange *n* 11, 11, 28, 128, 129, 515, 533, 697, 707, 710, *vb* 11, 128, 129, 697, 707
exchangeable *adj* 697
exchanged *adj* 129
exchange of views *n* 410
exchange vows *vb* 683
excise *vb* 36, 270
excise duty *n* 721
exciseman *n* 699
excision *n* 36, 270
excitability *n* 732
excitable *adj* 732
excitation *n* 732
excite *vb* 336, 729, 732, 736, 795
excited *adj* 729, 732, 734
excitement *n* 336, 729, 732
exciting *adj* 732
exclaim *vb* 363, 526
exclamation *n* 363, 526
exclude *vb* 41, 52, 198, 424, 546, 678, 790, 822
excluded *adj* 52, 546
excluding *adj* 52, *adv* 52
exclusion *n* 41, 52, 198, 546, 685
exclusion zone *n* 52, 157
exclusive *adj* 52, 70, 871, *n* 106, 471
exclusiveness *n* 52
excommunicate *vb* 52, 266, 790, 871, 881
excommunication *n* 52, 266, 790, 871
ex-convict *n* 667

excrement *n* 37, 268
excremental *adj* 268
excrescence *n* 226, 228
excreta *n* 268
excrete *vb* 268
excretion *n* 268
excretory *adj* 266, 268
excruciating *adj* 337
exculpate *vb* 813, 822, 829
exculpated *adj* 857
exculpation *n* 813, 829, 857
excursion *n* 236, 761
excursion fare *n* 724
excursus *n* 506
excusable *adj* 813, 817, 829, 839
excuse *n* 134, 829, *vb* 813, 822, 829
excused *adj* 813
excuse oneself *vb* 841
excusing *adj* 829
execrable *adj* 796, 801
execrate *vb* 796, 801
execration *n* 801
executant *n* 613
execute *vb* 136, 324, 368, 607, 688, 860
execution *n* 136, 324, 607, 688, 860
executioner *n* 324, 860
executive *adj* 136, 854, *n* 613, 622, 634, 854
executor *n* 607, 675
exegesis *n* 462
exemplary *adj* 488, 837
exemplification *n* 462, 488
exemplify *vb* 22, 488
exempt *adj* 667, 822, *vb* 422, 822
exemption *n* 422, 667, 822
exercise *n* 562, 564, 617, *vb* 475, 564
exercise one's prerogative *vb* 819
exercise self-control *vb* 843
exertion *n* 617
exert oneself *vb* 609, 617
exhalation *n* 304, 316, 347
exhale *vb* 304, 316, 347
exhaust *vb* 142, 572, 619
exhausted *adj* 142, 572, 619
exhausting *adj* 617
exhaustion *n* 142, 572, 619
exhaustive *adj* 47, 49
exhaustiveness *n* 49
exhibit *n* 420, 464, *vb* 394, 464
exhibition *n* 394, 464, 631, 690, 719
exhibitionism *n* 783, 785
exhibitionist *n* 205, 783, 785
exhilarated *adj* 732

exhilarating *adj* 732
exhilaration *n* 732, 734
exhort *vb* 532
exhortation *n* 532
exhumation *n* 105
exhume *vb* 105, 325
exile *n* 52, 161, 266, 790, 860, *vb* 52, 161, 266, 790, 860
exist *vb* 1, 101, 322
existence *n* 1, 3, 162, 322
existent *adj* 1, 162
existential *adj* 1
existentialism *n* 1
existing *adj* 1, 3, 101, 322
exit *n* 262, 264, 323, 523, 605, *vb* 264
exodus *n* 67, 262, 264
exonerate *vb* 813, 819, 822, 829
exonerated *adj* 857
exoneration *n* 813, 829, 857
exorbitance *n* 482, 723
exorbitancy *n* 431
exorbitant *adj* 431, 482, 575, 723
exorcise *vb* 876
exorcism *n* 876
exorcist *n* 876
exotic *adj* 54, 73, 172, 329
exotica *n* 54
expand *vb* 33, 170, 178, 293, 506
expandable *adj* 170, 293
expanded *adj* 170
expandibility *n* 293
expanse *n* 156, 178, 180, 313
expansion *n* 33, 170
expansive *adj* 156, 180
expatiate *vb* 506, 530
expatiate on *vb* 519
expatriate *n* 54
expect *vb* 425, 450, 453, 553, 748, 760, 819, 821
expectancy *n* 450
expectant *adj* 450, 748
expectantly *adv* 450
expectation *n* 104, 425, 434, 450, 748, 760
expected *adj* 425, 450, 760
expecting *adj* 152
expectorate *vb* 268
expectoration *n* 266, 268
expediency *n* 115, 580
expedient *adj* 115, *n* 128
expedite *vb* 113, 615
expedition *n* 236
expeditious *adj* 245

expel *vb* 41, 52, 161, 198, 266, 268, 790, 860
expellant *adj* 266
expend *vb* 564, 716, 718
expendable *adj* 696
expenditure *n* 718
expense *n* 723
expenses *n* 690, 711, 718
expensive *adj* 723
expensiveness *n* 723
experience *n* 107, 438, 444, 624, 729, *vb* 101, 438, 729
experienced *adj* 438, 444, 624
experiment *n* 416, *vb* 416
experimental *adj* 416, 433
experimentation *n* 416, 433
expert *adj* 624, *n* 112, 624
expertise *n* 438, 624
expiate *vb* 814
expiation *n* 814
expiatory *adj* 28
expiration *n* 316
expire *vb* 62, 94, 105, 123, 316, 323
expiry *n* 62, 123
explain *vb* 134, 412, 462, 462
explanation *n* 132, 134, 412, 460, 462
explanatory *adj* 412, 462
expletive *n* 801
explication *n* 462
explicatory *adj* 462
explicit *adj* 460, 503
explicitness *n* 460, 503
explode *vb* 46, 94, 147, 232, 357, 413, 732, 802
exploit *n* 607, *vb* 115, 149, 564, 670, 723
exploitation *n* 564, 670, 703
exploitative *adj* 703
exploited *adj* 713
exploration *n* 236, 414, 433, 555
exploratory *adj* 59, 414, 416, 433, 555
explore *vb* 59, 61, 236, 414, 433, 555
explorer *n* 555
explosion *n* 33, 147, 357
explosive *adj* 147, 341, *n* 255, 649
explosiveness *n* 732
exponent *n* 74
export *n* 707, *vb* 239, 707
exportation *n* 239
exporter *n* 241, 707
expose *vb* 4, 203, 306, 413, 421, 464, 468, 491, 599, 775, 828, 830
exposé *n* 468
exposed *adj* 316, 334, 468

exposition *n* 412, 462, 464, 517, 519
expositor *n* 868
expository *adj* 412, 517, 519
expostulate *vb* 437, 682
expostulation *n* 682
exposure *n* 203, 306, 413, 464, 468, 491
expound *vb* 412, 462
express *adj* 473, *n* 242, *vb* 216, 270, 458, 473, 496, 499
express a wish *vb* 681
express contempt *vb* 781
expression *n* 74, 216, 270, 394, 496, 499
Expressionist *adj* 490
expressionless *adj* 459, 731
expressive *adj* 484, 496, 517
ex-prisoner *n* 198
expropriate *vb* 697, 703, 820
expropriation *n* 703
expulsion *n* 52, 161, 198, 266, 268, 790, 860
expulsive *adj* 255, 266
expunge *vb* 150, 395, 487
expurgate *vb* 36
expurgation *n* 36
exquisite *adj* 337, 736, 763, 770
extant *adj* 1, 37, 101
extempore *adj* 454, 548, 560, *adv* 560
extemporization *n* 454, 548
extemporize *vb* 96, 454, 548, 560
extemporized *adj* 560
extend *vb* 64, 124, 156, 172, 178, 180, 191, 222, 293
extend credit *vb* 701
extended *adj* 178
extended family *n* 12
extensibility *n* 170, 293
extensible *adj* 170, 293
extension *n* 23, 35, 156, 178
extensive *adj* 23, 156, 180
extensively *adv* 29, 156
extent *n* 24, 156, 168, 172, 178, 180
extenuate *vb* 144, 422
extenuating *adj* 422, 829
extenuation *n* 422, 829
exterior *adj* 6, 198, *n* 6, 198, 394
exteriority *n* 6
exterminate *vb* 150, 324
extermination *n* 150, 324
external *adj* 6, 198, 394
externality *n* 6
externalization *n* 6, 198
externalize *vb* 6, 198

externals *n* 394
extinct *adj* 2, 105, 323
extinction *n* 2, 150, 323, 395
extinguish *vb* 2, 150, 375
extirpate *vb* 150
extirpation *n* 150
extol *vb* 823, 825
extort *vb* 270, 703, 723
extortion *n* 270, 703, 723
extortionate *adj* 703, 723
extra *adj* 33, 35, 565, 575, *n* 33, 523, 575
extract *n* 39, 48, 149, 270, *vb* 270
extraction *n* 154, 270
extractor *n* 270
extracurricular *adj* 475
extradite *vb* 52, 266
extradition *n* 52, 266
extramarital *adj* 851
extramarital relations *n* 851
extramural *adj* 198, 475
extraneous *adj* 6, 10, 54, 198
extraneous element *n* 54
extraneousness *n* 6, 10, 54
extraordinary *adj* 29, 759
extras *n* 35
extra-sensory perception *n* 283, 401, 455
extraterrestrial *adj* 54, 284, *n* 54
extravagance *n* 482, 510, 566, 572, 575, 718, 723, 727, 772, 785, 844
extravagant *adj* 482, 510, 572, 575, 723, 727, 772, 785, 844
extreme *adj* 127, 659
extremism *n* 127
extremist *adj* 127, *n* 127, 659
extremity *n* 62, 209, 211
extricate *vb* 270, 606, 669
extrication *n* 270, 606, 669
extroversion *n* 198
extrovert *adj* 198, 789
extrude *vb* 171, 178
extruded *adj* 178
extrusion *n* 178
exuberant *adj* 729
exudate *n* 305
exudation *n* 264, 268
exude *vb* 264, 268
exult *vb* 746
exultant *adj* 746
exultation *n* 746
eye *n* 370, *vb* 370
eyeball to eyeball *adv* 173
eye-catching *adj* 162, 372, 464, 763

eye contact *n* 370
eyeful *n* 370
eyeless *adj* 371
eyelet *n* 232
eyeliner *n* 765
eye of heaven *n* 284
eye-opener *n* 451
eye patch *n* 371
eyeshade *n* 378
eye shadow *n* 765
eyeshot *n* 372
eyesight *n* 370
eyesore *n* 370, 764
Eyetie *n* 331
eyewash *n* 459, 827
eye-witness *n* 162, 37

F

fabric *n* 197, 282, 298, 299, 569
fabricate *vb* 149, 479, 830
fabrication *n* 149, 479
fabulous *adj* 457, 479, 582, 759, *n* 771
facade *n* 187, 198, 212, 394, 481, 771
face *n* 97, 198, 212, *vb* 187, 201, 212, 215, 751
face both ways *vb* 44, 543
faceless *adj* 498
facelessness *n* 498
face-lift *n* 106, 765
face mask *n* 765
face powder *n* 765
face the music *vb* 860
facetious *adj* 744
facetiousness *n* 744
face to face *adv* 173
facial *adj* 198, *n* 765
facilitate *vb* 423, 629, 629
facilitation *n* 580, 629
facilities *n* 567
facility *n* 624, 629
facing *adj* 212, *n* 201, 212
facsimile *n* 13, 21, 488
fact *n* 1, 3
fact-finding *adj* 433
fact-finding mission *n* 414
faction *n* 41, 479, 634, 871
factional *adj* 634
factor *n* 48, 74, 132
factory *n* 614
factory farming *n* 149, 328
factory ship *n* 243
factory worker *n* 613
factotum *n* 613, 666

facts *n* 420, 466
facts of life *n* 3, 152, 478
factual *adj* 1, 3, 420, 440, 522
fad *n* 544, 770
fade *vb* 2, 4, 94, 107, 144, 323, 356, 373, 376, 382, 383, 395
fade away *vb* 105
faded *adj* 382
fadeout *n* 375, 395, 525
fade out *vb* 62, 375
fading *n* 382
faecal *adj* 268
faeces *n* 268
fag *n* 613, 617, 666
fag end *n* 37
fagged out *adj* 619
faggot *n* 341
fail *vb* 123, 273, 574, 593, 652, 717
failed *adj* 625, 652
failing *adj* 112, 593, *n* 585, 838
failsafe *adj* 427, *n* 28, 598
fail to act *vb* 608
fail to comply *vb* 662
fail to obey/comply *vb* 680
fail to pay *vb* 717
failure *n* 123, 275, 452, 574, 652, 652, 717
failure/inability to act *n* 608
failure to obey/comply *n* 680
failure to pay *n* 717
faint *vb* 335, *adj* 352, 356, 373, 376, 619, *n* 335
faint-hearted *adj* 541, 752
faint-heartedness *n* 541, 752
faintly *adv* 356
faintness *n* 352, 356, 376, 619
fair *adj* 25, 307, 382, 383, 429, 585, 655, 763, 817, 831, 833, *n* 464, 710, 761
fair chance *n* 425
fair game *n* 773
fairly *adv* 817
fair-minded *adj* 817
fairness *n* 383, 429, 763, 817
fair play *n* 817, 831
fair sex *n* 333
fair story *n* 865
fairy *n* 73, 865
fairy cycle *n* 761
fairy godmother *n* 631, 807, 865
fairy gold *n* 4
fairylike *adj* 865
fairy queen *n* 865

fairy-tale *adj* 479
fairy tale *n* 479, 865 .
faith *n* 434, 748, 868
faithful *adj* 440, 663, 688, 793, 831, 872
faithfulness *n* 688, 821, 831, 872
faithless *adj* 832
faithlessness *n* 832
fake *adj* 21, 128, 481, *n* 21, 480, *vb* 21, 481, 771
faking *n* 481
fakir *n* 863
falconry *n* 761
fall *n* 34, 108, 185, 192, 275, *vb* 34, 152, 185, 192, 275, 323, 838
fall about *vb* 744
fallacious *adj* 411, 441
fallacy *n* 411, 441
fall apart *vb* 46
fall asleep *vb* 323, 619
fall away *vb* 121
fall back *vb* 254
fall between two stools *vb* 63
fall down *vb* 652
fall due *vb* 819
fallen angel *n* 864
fall flat *vb* 652
fall for *vb* 434, 480
fall guy *n* 480
fallibility *n* 428, 430
fallible *adj* 428, 430, 441
fall ill *vb* 589
fall in *vb* 66
falling *adj* 275
falling/shooting star *n* 284
falling-off *n* 171
fall in price *vb* 724
fall into arrears *vb* 717
fall into disrepute *vb* 775
fall into line *vb* 72
fall into one's lap *vb* 699
fall in with *vb* 436
fall off *n* 254, *vb* 593
fall off the back of a lorry *vb* 705
fall on deaf ears *vb* 352
fall on hard times *vb* 656, 713
fallout *n* 37, 60, 100, 133
fall out *vb* 67, 437, 635
fallout shelter *n* 600
fallow *adj* 146, 153
falls *n* 314
fall short *vb* 26, 32, 50, 273, 452, 574, 585, 652

fall through *vb* 273, 652
fall to *vb* 821
fall upon *vb* 639
false *adj* 21, 441, 479, 481, 820
false charge *n* 830
false dawn *n* 4, 452
false economy *n* 728
false eyelashes *n* 765
false god *n* 862, 875
falsehood *n* 479, 481
false identity *n* 498
false logic *n* 411
false modesty *n* 850
false name *n* 498
falseness *n* 441, 479
false note *n* 20
false piety *n* 873
false praise *n* 827
false religion *n* 869
false shame *n* 850
false worship *n* 875
falsification *n* 463, 481, 489
falsified *adj* 481, 489
falsify *vb* 4, 463, 481, 489
falsify the accounts *vb* 720
Falstaff *n* 168
Falstaffian *adj* 168
falter *vb* 246, 280, 529, 541, 652
fame *n* 29, 774
familial *adj* 12, 154, 155, 330
familiar *adj* 88, 117, 549, 781, 793
familiarity *n* 88, 117, 438, 549, 793, 800
familiarize oneself with *vb* 438
familiar with *adj* 438
family *n* 12, 66, 154, 330, 776
family man *n* 332
family planning *n* 153
family relationships *n* 12
family-size *adj* 724
family tree *n* 64
famine *n* 153, 273, 574, 755
famish *vb* 845
famished *adj* 755, 845
famishment *n* 845
famous *adj* 29, 576, 774
fan *n* 795, 825, *vb* 316
fanatic *n* 127, 609, 872
fanatical *adj* 434, 729, 872
fanaticism *n* 434, 729, 872
fanciful *adj* 408, 457, 544
fancy *adj* 766, *n* 408, 456, 544, 545, 755, 757, 795, *vb* 398, 545, 755, 757, 795

fancy dress *n* 204
fanfare *n* 786
fang *n* 296
fanlight *n* 232
fanny *n* 152
fan out *vb* 67, 260
fantasize *vb* 4, 398, 457
fantastic *adj* 4, 582, 759
fantastical *adj* 457
fantasy *n* 4, 457, 479, 755
far *adj* 172
far afield *adv* 172
far and wide *adv* 49, 156, 172
far-away *adj* 172
farce *n* 523, 744
farcical *adj* 523, 744, 772
fare *n* 267
farewell *adj* 262, *n* 262
fare well *vb* 655
far-fetched *adj* 272, 426
far-flung *adj* 67, 172
farinaceous *adj* 300
farm *n* 328, 614, *vb* 149, 328
farmer *n* 149, 328, 613
farmhand *n* 328, 613
farming *n* 328
farm labourer *n* 613
farm out *vb* 700
farmstead *n* 328
farness *n* 172
far-off *adj* 172, 356
far off *adv* 172
farrago *n* 38
far-reaching *adj* 127, 156, 180
farrow *vb* 152
far-sighted *adj* 444, 453
far-sightedness *n* 444, 453
fart *n* 316, *vb* 316
farthest *adj* 172
fascia *n* 212
fascinate *vb* 139, 732, 795, 876
fascinating *adj* 139, 732, 736
fascination *n* 139, 257, 732, 736, 757, 759, 795
fashion *n* 204, 502, 770, *vb* 53, 149, 216, 492
fashionable *adj* 106, 204, 770
fashionableness *n* 770
fashionable society *n* 770
fast *adj* 131, 245, 580, 615, 695, *n* 845, *vb* 845
fast day *n* 845
fasten *vb* 40, 233, 695
fastener *n* 42

fiddler *n* 705
fiddling *n* 720
fidelity *n* 440, 663, 688, 831
fidgetiness *n* 130, 281
fidgety *adj* 130, 281
field *n* 157, 158, 313, 570, 761
field glasses *n* 370
field gun *n* 649
field marshal *n* 648
field of vision *n* 372
fiend *n* 864
fiendish *adj* 806, 838, 864
fierce *adj* 147, 604, 806
fiery *adj* 339
fiesta *n* 761
fifth *adj* 84
fifth column *n* 127
fifty *n* 84
fifty-fifty *adj* 25, *adv* 686
fight *n* 147, 635, 802, *vb* 635, 643, 645, 794
fight back *vb* 641
fight back/down *vb* 668
fighter *n* 244, 648
fighting *n* 643, 645
fight shy of *vb* 538, 556
fight the good fight *vb* 872
figment *n* 457
figment of the imagination *n* 4
figuration *n* 488
figurative *adj* 458, 488, 490
figure *n* 74, 208, 216, 330, *vb* 488
figurehead *n* 212, 577
figure-hugging *adj* 181
figure of eight *n* 197, 221
figure of fun *n* 773
figure of speech *n* 458
figurine *n* 492
filament *n* 183, 299
filamentous *adj* 183
filch *vb* 705
file *n* 57, 76, 167, 178, 291, 292, 296, 301, 420, 486, 570, *vb* 57, 76, 296, 301, 486, 570
file a claim *vb* 856
file a suit *vb* 856
filial *adj* 12, 155
filibuster *vb* 93, 114, 506, 530, 630
filibustering *n* 93, 506, 630
filigree *adj* 174, *n* 197, 232
filing system *n* 486
fill *vb* 49, 201, 692
filler *n* 124
filling *n* 35, 166, 201, 269

fillip *n* 145, 620
fill someone in *vb* 466
fill the bill *vb* 573
filly *n* 326, 333
film *n* 376, 380, 491, 525, *vb* 380, 486, 525
filminess *n* 380
filmography *n* 76
filmset *vb* 514
filmsetting *n* 514
filmstrip *n* 491
filmy *adj* 376, 379, 380
filter *n* 586, *vb* 39, 586
filth *n* 587, 851, 854
filthiness *n* 851
filthy *adj* 587, 851
filthy/stinking rich *adj* 712
filthy lucre *n* 711
filtration *n* 39, 586
final *adj* 62, 653, *n* 62
final curtain *n* 523
finale *n* 62, 523
finality *n* 62
finalize *vb* 427, 653
finally *adv* 62
final offer *n* 62, 211
final stroke *n* 653
finance *n* 701
finance *vb* 567, 631, 701, 711
finance house *n* 701
finances *n* 711
financial *adj* 711
financial difficulty *n* 713
financial help/aid/assistance *n* 631
financier *n* 701
find *n* 433, 706, *vb* 433, 856
find a good match *vb* 797
find a needle in a haystack *vb* 424
find a way *vb* 567
find fault *vb* 826
find fault with *vb* 830
find favour *vb* 770, 825
find guilty *vb* 840, 858
finding *n* 856
findings *n* 433
find not guilty *vb* 857
find one's tongue *vb* 528
find out *vb* 433, 476
find out to one's cost *vb* 452
fine *adj* 288, 379, 418, 582, *n* 860, *vb* 860
fine art *n* 490
fine arts *n* 488
fine figure of a man/woman *n* 763

311

fineness *n* 144, 183, 288, 295, 379
finery *n* 204, 766
finespun *adj* 183, 299
fine-tune *vb* 19
fine tuning *n* 19
finger *vb* 338, 368
fingerprint *n* 485
finish *n* 292, 299, 653, *vb* 62, 123, 292, 511, 653
finished *adj* 62, 653
finished article *n* 149
finished with *adj* 105
finishing *adj* 653
finishing/last touch *n* 49
finishing line *n* 211
finishing off *n* 653
finishing school *n* 477
finishing touch *n* 653
finish off *vb* 49, 62, 653
finite *adj* 322
fiord *n* 310, 312
fire *n* 145, 339, 377, 729, *vb* 161, 255, 266, 341, 673, 729, 732
fire alarm *n* 602
firearm *n* 255, 649
fire away *vb* 61
firebrand *n* 147, 635, 662
fire-eater *n* 753
fire escape *n* 264, 605
firelighter *n* 341
fireplace *n* 339
fireside *n* 165
firewatcher *n* 668
firewood *n* 341
fireworks *n* 786
firing line *n* 212, 599
firing squad *n* 860
firm *adj* 40, 43, 122, 131, 289, 338, 539, 540, 659, *n* 634
firmament *n* 284
firmness *n* 122, 131, 289, 539, 540, 659
firm up *vb* 427
first *adj* 61, 99, *adv* 59
first/Christian/given name *n* 497
first aid *n* 596, 631
first and foremost *adv* 59
first base *n* 61, 189
firstborn *n* 59, 99
first-class *adj* 31, 582
first come first served *n* 59, 99
first-hand *adj* 420
first impressions *n* 394
first lady *n* 31

first lap *n* 61
first light *n* 374
first love *n* 795
firstly *adv* 61
first night *n* 61, 523
first principles *n* 61
first-rate *adj* 31
first refusal *n* 545
first round *n* 61
first strike *n* 639
first thing *adv* 113
firth *n* 310
fiscal *adj* 711
fish *n* 326, *vb* 555, 761
fisherman *n* 555
fisherman's tale *n* 482
fish for compliments *vb* 783
fishing *n* 555, 761
fishing boat *n* 243
fish out of water *n* 20, 54
fishy *adj* 832
fissile *adj* 46
fission *n* 41, 46
fissure *n* 41, 174
fisticuffs *n* 643
fit *adj* 143, 559, 588, 817, 819, *n* 281, 589, 609, 732, *vb* 9, 19, 580
fit for a king/queen *adj* 725
fitful *adj* 65, 120, 130, 281
fitfulness *n* 120
fitness *n* 19, 143, 559, 588, 817
fit out *vb* 559, 571
fitted *adj* 53
fitter *n* 613
fit the bill *vb* 19
fitting *adj* 19, 817, 819
fitting out *n* 571
five *n* 84
fivefold *adv* 84
fivefold etc *adj* 84
fiver *n* 84
five-star *adj* 31
fix *n* 547, 628, 849, *vb* 122, 131, 160, 267, 370, 481, 547, 594, 596, 695
fixated *adj* 404, 447
fixation *n* 408, 447
fixative *n* 43, 349
fixed *adj* 122, 131, 481
fixed idea *n* 408
fixity *n* 122, 131
fixture *n* 53
fizz *vb* 306, 361
fizziness *n* 304
fizzle out *vb* 62, 123, 652

fizzy *adj* 304, 306, 361
flab *n* 168, 575
flabbergast *vb* 759
flabbergasted *adj* 759
flabbiness *n* 144, 290
flabby *adj* 144, 290
flaccid *adj* 144, 290
flaccidity *n* 144, 290
flag *n* 484, *vb* 144, 175, 619
flag day *n* 681
flagon *n* 167
flagrancy *n* 785
flagrant *adj* 372, 464, 785
flagship *n* 582
flagstones *n* 569
flag-waving *n* 786
flair *n* 140, 399, 418, 511, 624, 768
flak *n* 649
flake *n* 48, 175, 300, *vb* 175, 295, 300
flake out *vb* 619
flakiness *n* 295, 300
flak jacket *n* 640
flaky *adj* 175, 295, 300
flamboyance *n* 482, 510, 785
flamboyant *adj* 482, 510, 785
flame *n* 339, 377, 387, 795, *vb* 339
flamenco *n* 761
flaming *adj* 339, 377, 387
flammable *adj* 339, 341
flange *n* 209
flank *n* 214, *vb* 214
flannel *n* 459, 827
flannelette *n* 569
flap *n* 202, 232, 281, *vb* 44, 192
flare *n* 94, 374, 377, 602, *vb* 94, 170, 180
flared *adj* 170, 180
flare up *vb* 339
flash *adj* 769, *n* 374, 491, *vb* 94, 96, 245, 374
flashback *n* 448
flasher *n* 205, 851
flash flood *n* 314
flashiness *n* 510, 785
flashing *adj* 371, 374
flash in the pan *n* 94, 452, 651
flashlight *n* 377
flash of insight *n* 433
flash of inspiration *n* 548
flashpoint *n* 339, 599
flashy *adj* 510, 770, 785
flat *adj* 185, 191, 292, 297, 366, 489, 502, 508, 522, 762, *n* 165
flatmate *n* 693

flatness *n* 185, 191, 292, 297, 343, 459, 508, 762
flat out *adj* 185, *adv* 245, 617
flats *n* 185, 191, 313
flatten *vb* 150, 171, 185, 191, 222, 277, 292, 297
flattened *adj* 277
flatter *vb* 827
flatterer *n* 827
flattering *adj* 791, 827
flattery *n* 791, 800, 827
flatulence *n* 316
flaunt *vb* 464, 785
flavour *n* 342, *vb* 344
flavourful *adj* 342
flavouring *n* 344
flavourless *adj* 343
flavour of the month *n* 106
flavoursome *adj* 342
flaw *n* 50, 144, 585, 767, *vb* 585, 767
flawed *adj* 585, 767
flawless *adj* 47, 584
flawlessness *n* 584
flaxen *adj* 383, 389
flay *vb* 203
flea *n* 169
flea market *n* 710
fleapit *n* 525
fleck *n* 169, 393
fled *adj* 163
fledgling *n* 106, 326
flee *vb* 262, 395, 605
fleece *n* 202, *vb* 480, 705, 723
fleet *n* 86, 237
fleet-footed *adj* 245
fleeting *adj* 4, 94, 179, 234, 395
fleetingness *n* 179
Fleet Street *n* 471
flesh and blood *n* 282
flesh-coloured *adj* 387
fleshiness *n* 168
fleshly *adj* 282, 844
flesh out *vb* 33, 35
fleshpots *n* 712
flex *vb* 221, 290, 293
flexibility *n* 125, 130, 290, 293
flexible *adj* 19, 72, 125, 130, 290, 293, 658
flexion *n* 221
flexitime *n* 90
flick *n* 247, 338
flicker *n* 30, 94, 374, *vb* 94, 120, 130, 281, 374
flickering *adj* 374

flier *n* 238

flies *n* 523

flight *n* 238, 254, 262, 395, 605, 648, *vb* 276

flight/gaggle/skein *n* 66

flight lieutenant *n* 648

flight of fancy *n* 457, 482

flight sergeant *n* 648

flighty *adj* 130, 405

flimsiness *n* 144, 286, 295

flimsy *adj* 4, 144, 183, 286, 295, 411

flinch *vb* 337

fling *vb* 147, 247, 255

flint *n* 289, 341, 569

flinty *adj* 289, 311

flip one's lid *vb* 447

flippancy *n* 744

flippant *adj* 744, 781

flipside *n* 213

flirt *n* 795, *vb* 795, 800

flirtation *n* 795, 800

flit *n* 605, *vb* 96, 130, 245

float *n* 242, 286, *vb* 192, 237, 286

floating *adj* 192

floating vote *n* 27, 44

floaty *adj* 286

flock *n* 66, 870, 874, 880, *vb* 66, 86

flog *vb* 619, 709, 860

flog a dead horse *vb* 579

flood *n* 29, 66, 150, 253, 314, 575, *vb* 86, 147, 305, 314, 575

flooded *adj* 575

floodgate *n* 315

floodlight *n* 377

floodlit *adj* 374

floodplain *n* 308, 311

flood the market *vb* 724

floor *n* 30, 175, 185, 189, 193, *vb* 191, 202, 277

flooring *n* 202

floor show *n* 523

flop *n* 652, *vb* 290, 652

floppiness *n* 290

floppy *adj* 44, 290

floppy disk *n* 75

flora *n* 320, 327

floral *adj* 327, 329

floral display *n* 766

floret *n* 327

florid *adj* 387, 510, 766

floridness *n* 387, 510

flotilla *n* 237

flotsam and jetsam *n* 696

flounce *n* 230

flounder *vb* 428, 625, 628

flour *n* 300, *vb* 300

flourish *n* 224, 513, *vb* 145, 152, 464, 651, 655, 785, 835

flourishing *adj* 651, 655

floury *adj* 300, 383

flow *n* 64, 121, 124, 234, 303, 314, 511, *vb* 44, 64, 303, 314

flow chart *n* 57

flower *n* 327

flower arranging *n* 766

flowerhead *n* 327

floweriness *n* 510

flowery *adj* 349, 510

flow gently *vb* 314

flowing *adj* 124, 314, 511, 513

flown *adj* 163, 605

flu *n* 589

fluctuate *vb* 11, 44, 65, 120, 121, 130, 280, 541

fluctuating *adj* 280

fluctuation *n* 120, 121, 130, 234, 280

flue *n* 232

fluency *n* 502, 528, 530

fluent *adj* 494, 496, 502, 528, 530

fluff *n* 286, *vb* 625

fluffiness *n* 286

fluff one's lines *vb* 523

fluffy *adj* 286

flugelhorn *n* 369

fluid *adj* 121, 130, 183, 217, 303, 305, *n* 303, 305

fluidity *n* 130, 217, 303

fluke *n* 10, 135, 554, 651

flummoxed *adj* 461

flunk *vb* 652

flunky *n* 666

fluorescence *n* 374

fluorescent *adj* 374

fluorescent tube *n* 377

flurry *n* 316, 609, 732

flush *adj* 191, 712, *n* 339, 387, 586, *vb* 387, 586, 784

flush out *vb* 39

fluster *n* 281, *vb* 58

flustered *adj* 281

flute *n* 369, *vb* 231, 526

fluted *adj* 231, 493

fluting *adj* 526, *n* 231, 493

flutter *n* 280, 554, 729, 750, *vb* 280, 281

fluttery *adj* 281

fluvial *adj* 314

flux *n* 121, 234, 303

foray *n* 639, *vb* 639
forbear *n* 99, *vb* 556, 660, 813
forbearance *n* 556, 660, 733, 809, 813
forbearing *adj* 556, 660, 733, 809, 813
forbid *vb* 678
forbiddance *n* 678
forbidden *adj* 678, 853
forbidding *adj* 745
force *n* 66, 136, 143, 147, 247, 285, 458, 507, 617, 643, 664, *vb* 247, 270, 329, 566, 664
forced *adj* 512, 538
forced labour *n* 664, 670
forceful *adj* 141, 143, 145, 147, 507, 539
forcefully *adv* 143
forcefulness *n* 141, 539
force of circumstances *n* 536
force of habit *n* 549
force oneself *vb* 538
forceps *n* 270
force to negotiate *vb* 646
ford *n* 187, 271, *vb* 271
fore *n* 212
foreboding *adj* 806, *n* 401, 453, 602
forecast *n* 59, 104, 450, 455, *vb* 59, 450, 453, 455
forecaster *n* 455
foreclosure *n* 703
forecourt *n* 212
forefathers *n* 323
for effect *adj* 771
forefront *n* 59, 212
foregoing *adj* 59
foregone conclusion *n* 427, 547
foreground *n* 173, 212, *vb* 464
forehead *n* 212
foreign *adj* 6, 10, 54, 172
foreign aid *n* 631
foreign body *n* 54
foreigner *n* 54, 331
foreignness *n* 6, 54
foreign parts *n* 54
foreknowledge *n* 453, 455
foreman *n* 31, 622, 665
foremost *adj* 31, 59, 212, 576
forename *n* 497
forenoon *n* 109
foreordain *vb* 547
foreordained *adj* 547
forerunner *n* 59
foresee *vb* 104, 425, 450, 453, 455
foreseeable *adj* 425
foreseen *adj* 450, 760

foreshadow *vb* 99, 104, 455
foreshorten *vb* 179
foreshortened *adj* 179
foresight *n* 99, 113, 398, 453, 754
foresighted *adj* 453
forest *n* 86, 327
forestall *vb* 52, 59, 99, 113, 453
forester *n* 613
foretaste *n* 59
foretell *vb* 59, 455
forethought *n* 398, 453, 754
forever *adv* 62, 89, 95, 122
n 95
for ever and a day *adv* 95
forewarn *vb* 453, 455
forewarned *adj* 450
forewarning *n* 99, 453
foreword *n* 59, 61
forfeit *adj* 691, 820, *n* 687, 691, *vb* 691
forfeited *adj* 691
forfeiture *n* 691, 820
forgather *vb* 66
forge *n* 339, *vb* 21, 149, 216, 481, 711
forge ahead *vb* 212, 253
forger *n* 21
forgery *n* 21, 481, 711
forget *vb* 405, 407, 449
forgetful *adj* 405, 407, 449, 812
forgetfulness *n* 405, 407, 449
forget-me-not *n* 391
forgivable *adj* 813, 817, 839
forgive *vb* 449, 660, 669, 809, 813, 822, 857
forgive and forget *vb* 646, 813
forgiven *adj* 813, 857
forgiveness *n* 660, 669, 805, 809, 813
forgiving *adj* 660, 805, 809, 813, 862
forgo *vb* 563, 696
for good *adv* 62, 95, 122
for good and all *adv* 95
forgotten *adj* 449
for hire *adj* 679
fork *n* 81, 220, 260, 568, *vb* 48, 220, 260
forked *adj* 220, 260
for keeps *adv* 95
fork out *vb* 698, 716
forlorn hope *n* 426
form *n* 7, 71, 216, 298, 787, 881, *vb* 216, 298
form a government *vb* 657
formal *adj* 298, 787, 881

formal attire *n* 787
formaldehyde *n* 603
formal dress *n* 787
formalism *n* 872
formality *n* 787
format *n* 216
formation *n* 149, 216
formative *adj* 132, 216
formative years *n* 111
former *adj* 59, 99, 105, 674
formerly *adv* 105
formidable *adj* 576
formless *adj* 217
formlessness *n* 217
form of address *n* 497
formula *n* 74, 499
formulaic *adj* 71
formulate *vb* 216, 496, 499
formulation *n* 216
fornicate *vb* 851
fornication *n* 851
for nothing *adj* 724
forsake *vb* 163, 563
for sale *adj* 679
for show *adj* 785
forswear *vb* 474, 556, 563
fort *n* 600, 640
forte *n* 624
forthcoming *adj* 466, 468, 533
for the most part *adv* 29
for the present *adv* 101
for the sake of *prep* 138
for the time being *adv* 90, 94, 101
forthright *adj* 460, 478
forthrightness *n* 478
forthwith *adv* 96
fortification *n* 640
fortified *adj* 640
fortify *vb* 143, 640
fortissimo *adv* 355
fortitude *n* 539, 751
fortnight *n* 92
fortnightly *adj* 92
FORTRAN *n* 494
fortress *n* 600, 640
fortuitous *adj* 115, 135, 554
fortuitousness *n* 135
fortunate *adj* 651
fortune *n* 135, 554, 712, 835
fortune-teller *n* 877
fortune-telling *n* 455
forum *n* 470
forward *adj* 113, 212, 253, 396, *adv*
212, 253, *vb* 239, 241, 515

forward-looking *adj* 253
forward motion *n* 253
forwardness *n* 113
forward planning *n* 113, 398, 547
fossil *n* 37, 105, 107, 321
fossil fuel *n* 141, 321, 341
fossilization *n* 289
fossilize *vb* 289
fossilized *adj* 321
foster *vb* 12, 132, 138
foster/adoptive parent *n* 668
fostering *n* 12
foster parent *n* 154
foul *adj* 347, 350, 587, 737, *vb* 268,
587
foul-mouthed *adj* 801
foulness *n* 350
foul play *n* 323, 806, 818, 832, 836,
853
foul up *vb* 56
found *vb* 61, 132, 189
foundation *n* 61, 131, 189, 193, 420,
765
foundation garment *n* 193
founder *n* 132, 149, 807
found guilty *adj* 840, 858
foundry *n* 614
found wanting *adj* 826
fount *n* 132, 514, 570
fountain *n* 314
fountainhead *n* 132
four *n* 83
fourfold *adj* 83, *adv* 83
four-in-hand *n* 83
four-letter word *n* 83, 496, 801
four-poster *n* 83
foursome *n* 83
foursquare *adj* 83, *adv* 83
fourth *n* 83
fourth estate *n* 471
fowl *n* 326
foxed *adj* 595, 767
foxhole *n* 232, 600
fox-hunting *n* 761
foxing *n* 595
foxtrot *n* 367, 524, 761
foxy *adj* 350, 832
fracas *n* 56, 643
fraction *n* 30, 48, 74, 78
fractional *adj* 48, 78
fractionally *adv* 78
fractious *adj* 803
fracture *n* 41, 337, *vb* 41, 46, 295
fragile *adj* 94, 144, 183, 295

fragility *n* 94, 144, 295
fragment *n* 48, 78, *vb* 41, 46, 48, 295
fragmentary *adj* 48, 50, 78
fragmentation *n* 41, 46
fragmented *adj* 46
fragrance *n* 347, 349
fragrant *adj* 347, 349
frail *adj* 142, 144, 295
frailness *n* 142
frailty *n* 144, 295
frame *n* 167, 206, 208, 209, 491, *vb* 149, 193, 208, 481, 830
framed *adj* 481
frame of mind *n* 7
frame of reference *n* 685
frame-up *n* 547, 830
framework *n* 216, 298
franchise *n* 667, 677, 822, *vb* 677
frangibility *n* 295
frangible *adj* 295
franglais *n* 494
frank *adj* 297, 464, 468, 478, 627, 831, *vb* 515
frankness *n* 297, 478, 509, 627
frantic *adj* 147, 447
frappé *adj* 340
fraternal *adj* 12, 793
fraternity *n* 793
Frau *n* 778
fraud *n* 480, 705, 705
fraudulence *n* 480, 481
fraudulent *adj* 480, 481, 832
fraught *adj* 656
Fräulein *n* 778
fray *vb* 301
frayed *adj* 595
freak *n* 20, 73, 759
freakish *adj* 20, 759
freak out *vb* 732
freaky *adj* 759
freckle *n* 393, 767
free *adj* 41, 44, 605, 667, 677, 698, 799, 822, *vb* 44, 605, 606, 629, 669, 696, 822
free and easy *adj* 658, 788
freebie *n* 667
freebooter *n* 648
free delivery *n* 724
freedman *n* 667
freedom *n* 580, 667, 677, 788, 822
freedom fighter *n* 127, 648
freedom from war *n* 644
freedom of action/choice *n* 667

freedom of the press *n* 667
freedwoman *n* 667
free enterprise *n* 667
free-floating *adj* 44, 192
Freefone *n* 724
free-for-all *n* 56, 658
free gift *n* 667, 724
free hand *n* 535, 667, 677, 725
free-handed *adj* 725
free-hanging *adj* 192
freeholder *n* 692
freeing *n* 605, 669
freelance *n* 613
freelance *adj* 611, 667
freelancer *n* 667
freeloader *n* 789
free love *n* 851
freeman *n* 667
freemartin *n* 153
freemasonry *n* 52, 139
free of charge *adj* 667, 724
free port *n* 667
Freepost *n* 724
free rein *n* 667
freesheet *n* 667
free speech *n* 667
free spirit *n* 44
free-standing *adj* 41
freethinker *n* 73, 667, 869
freethinking *adj* 73, 667, 869, *n* 869
free time *n* 612
free trade *n* 263, 667
free trade area *n* 710
freewheel *vb* 234, 407
free will *n* 535, 667
freeze *n* 34, 123, 235, 668, *vb* 34, 95, 123, 287, 289, 307, 340, 570, 603, 668, 717, 750
freeze-dry *vb* 309
freeze-drying *n* 603
freeze-frame *n* 525
freezer *n* 340, 570
freezing *adj* 307, *n* 340, 603
freight *n* 166, 239, 285, *vb* 166
freighter *n* 243
French horn *n* 369
French leave *n* 163
frenzied *adj* 147, 447
frenzy *n* 147, 447, 732
frequency *n* 24, 117, 178, 472
frequent *adj* 117, *vb* 85, 158, 165
frequently *adv* 117
fresco *n* 490

fresh *adj* 106, 111, 306, 348, 448, 586, 603, 781
fresh air *n* 306, 348, 588
fresh-air fiend *n* 198
freshen *vb* 316, 348, 586, 620
freshen up *vb* 106, 620
freshet *n* 314
freshness *n* 22, 106, 111, 348
fresh out of *adj* 709
fresh water *n* 305
fret *vb* 301, 732
fretful *adj* 735, 803
fretwork *n* 197, 232
friability *n* 295, 300
friable *adj* 295, 300
friar *n* 879
friary *n* 882
friction *n* 137, 256, 301, 338, 630, 638
frictional *adj* 301
fridge *n* 340, 570
friend *n* 85, 793
Friend *n* 862
friend at court *n* 139
friendless *adj* 790
friendliness *n* 729, 736, 789, 791, 793
friendly *adj* 644, 736, 789, 791, 793
friendship *n* 85, 644, 793, 795
frigate *n* 243
fright *n* 750, 764
frighten *vb* 750, 806
frightened *adj* 750
frightening *adj* 750
frightful *adj* 750, 764
frigid *adj* 340
frill *n* 209, 230, 766, *vb* 230
frills *n* 35, 510
frilly *adj* 230, 510
fringe *adj* 73, 209, 577, *n* 209, 214, 765, 766, *vb* 176, 209
frisking *n* 555
fritter *vb* 90
fritter away *vb* 691, 727
frivolity *n* 445, 577
frivolous *adj* 445
frizz *n* 224
frizzy *adj* 224
frock *vb* 878
Frog *n* 331
from A to Z *adv* 51
from east to west *adv* 191
from north to south *adv* 190
from now on *adv* 104
from scratch *adv* 22, 61
from side to side *adv* 191, 280

from stem to stern *adv* 178
from the beginning *adv* 22, 61
from the word go *adv* 61
from time to time *adv* 90, 92
from top to toe *adv* 49, 178, 190
front *n* 212, 394, 481, 645, 771, *vb* 31, 59, 212
frontage *n* 212
frontal *adj* 212
frontier *n* 172, 207, 211
frontier post *n* 271
frontispiece *n* 59, 516
front line *n* 212
front man *n* 212
front of house *n* 523
front of the queue *n* 59
frost *n* 307, 340, *vb* 340, 345, 380, 383
frostbite *n* 340
frosted *adj* 345, 380, 383, 385
frostiness *n* 340
frosting *n* 300, 345, 380
frosty *adj* 340
froth *n* 286, 306, *vb* 306
frothy *adj* 286, 306
frown *n* 230, 231, 802, 804, *vb* 219, 484, 792, 802, 804
frowned on *adj* 678
frowning *adj* 745
frown on *vb* 437, 826
frowst *n* 350
frowsty *adj* 350
frozen *adj* 340, 603
frugal *adj* 726, 843
frugality *n* 726
fruit *n* 133
fruitful *adj* 149, 152, 651
fruition *n* 653
fruitless *adj* 153, 652
fruitlessness *n* 153
fruity *adj* 342, 349
frumpy *adj* 764
frustrate *vb* 452, 630, 638
frustrated *adj* 452
frustration *n* 452
fry *vb* 339
fuchsia *n* 392
fuck *vb* 40
fucking *n* 40
fuck up *vb* 625
fudge *n* 345, *vb* 4, 219, 461
fuel *n* 141, 341, *vb* 341, 570, 732, 741
fug *n* 350
fuggy *adj* 350

fugitive *n* 605
fugue *n* 367
Führer *n* 665.
fulcrum *n* 63, 193, 200
fulfil *vb* 651, 653, 688, 821
fulfilled *adj* 653
fulfilment *n* 261, 653, 734
fuliginous *adj* 384
full *adj* 47, 49, 182
full-blown *adj* 49
full-bodied *adj* 342
full circle *n* 127
full-frontal *adj* 212
full-grown *adj* 168
full-length *adj* 49, 178
fullness *n* 47, 49, 182
full of beans *adj* 742
full of oneself *adj* 783
full of regrets *adj* 841
full-scale *adj* 49
full steam ahead *adv* 145
full-throated *adj* 363
full throttle *n* 245
full-time *adj* 49
full weight of the law *n* 659
fully *adv* 47, 49
fully paid-up *adj* 473, 634
fully recovered *adj* 588
fulminate *vb* 801, 802
fulsome *adj* 530, 825, 827
fumble *vb* 338, 428, 625
fume *vb* 147, 304, 350, 732, 802
fumes *n* 304, 347, 350
fumigant *n* 348
fumigate *vb* 304, 348
fumigation *n* 348
fuming *adj* 147, 802
fun *n* 734, 736, 761
function *n* 74, 136, 611, 786, *vb* 55, 136, 578, 607
functional *adj* 136, 578
functionary *n* 613
fund *vb* 711
fundamental *adj* 3, 5, 61, 132, 189, 576
fundamentalism *n* 870, 872
fundamentalist *adj* 870, 872, *n* 870, 872
fundamentally *adv* 5
fundamentals *n* 3
fund-raising *adj* 681, *n* 681
funds *n* 570, 711
funeral *adj* 325, *n* 325

funeral march *n* 747
funeral parlour *n* 325
funerary *adj* 325
funfair *n* 761
fungus *n* 597
funicular *n* 240
funk *n* 752, *vb* 750, 752
funky *adj* 367
fun-loving *adj* 844
funnel *n* 181, 232, *vb* 181
funny *adj* 744
funny ha-ha *adj* 744
fur *n* 202, *vb* 201
furious *adj* 732, 802
furl *vb* 225, 230
furlough *n* 163, 612, 618
furnace *n* 339
furnish *vb* 571
furnished *adj* 571
furnishing *n* 571
furnishings *n* 766
furore *n* 147
furring *n* 201
furrow *n* 227, 230, 231, *vb* 230, 231
furrowed *adj* 227, 231
further *vb* 253
furtherance *n* 253
further education *n* 477
furthermore *adv* 35
furtive *adj* 467, 469, 480
furtiveness *n* 467
fury *n* 147, 732, 802
fuse *n* 341, *vb* 38, 40, 45, 79, 695
fusible *adj* 695
fusion *n* 38, 40, 45
fuss *n* 281, 482, 510, 609, 732
fussiness *n* 418
fussing *adj* 281
fussy *adj* 406, 418, 510
fustian *n* 510
fustiness *n* 350
futile *adj* 445, 561, 572, 579, 652, 749
futility *n* 153, 445, 579, 652
future *adj* 100, 104, 450, *n* 102, 104
future time *n* 104
futurism *n* 106
futuristic *adj* 54, 102
futurity *n* 104
futurologist *n* 455
futurology *n* 104
fuzz *n* 854
fuzziness *n* 217, 376
fuzzy *adj* 217, 376, 49

G

gabble *vb* 459, 529, 530
gabby *adj* 530
gadget *n* 282, 568
gaffe *n* 441, 788
gaffer *n* 31, 665
gag *n* 233, 354, 668, 744, *vb* 233, 354, 467, 527, 668
gaga *adj* 107, 112, 447
gagged *adj* 668
gaiety *n* 742
gain *n* 35, 690, 699, 835, 859, *vb* 261, 690, 699
gain admittance *vb* 263
gain a reputation *vb* 774
gain credit *vb* 825
gainful *adj* 690, 835
gainful employment *n* 611
gain ground *vb* 253
gain power *vb* 657
gain recognition *vb* 774
gainsay *vb* 413, 474
gait *n* 234
gala *n* 761
galactic *adj* 284
galaxy *n* 66, 86, 284
gale *n* 307
gales/roar/shriek of laughter *n* 744
gall *n* 346, 781, 802, 806
gallant *adj* 751, 791, 805
gallantry *n* 751, 791, 795
galleon *n* 243
gallery *n* 490
galley *n* 514
galley slave *n* 666
gallimaufry *n* 38
gallop *n* 245, *vb* 234, 245
gallows *n* 192, 860, 861
galore *adj* 86
galvanization *n* 732
galvanize *vb* 141, 145, 451, 732
gamble *n* 416, 428, 456, 554, 753, *vb* 416, 554, 753, 761
gambler *n* 554, 753
gambling *n* 554
gamboge *n* 388
game *adj* 537, 561, *n* 326, 643, 761, *vb* 554
gamekeeper *n* 598, 668
game reserve *n* 326, 603
games *n* 617
game set and match *n* 651

gamut *n* 49
gamy *adj* 350
gander *n* 332
gang *n* 66
gangland killing *n* 641
gangly *adj* 184
gangrene *n* 589, 597
gangrenous *adj* 597
gang rule *n* 853
gangster *n* 838
gang up *vb* 66, 85
gangway *n* 240
ganja *n* 849
gannet *n* 846
gaol *n* 671
gaoler *n* 598, 668
gap *n* 20, 50, 65, 163, 174, 232
gape *vb* 174, 232, 370, 759
gaping *adj* 170, 186, 227
gap-toothed *adj* 174
garage *n* 570, 160, *vb* 570
garb *n* 204, *vb* 204
garble *vb* 463
garden *n* 329, *vb* 327, 329
garden centre *n* 329
gardener *n* 329, 613
Garden of Eden *n* 866
gardens *n* 165, 761
gargantuan *adj* 168
garish *adj* 381, 764, 766, 769, 785
garishness *n* 381, 769, 785
garland *n* 223, 766, *vb* 786
garlanded *adj* 766
garment *n* 204
garnet *n* 387, 766
garrison *n* 668, *vb* 640
garrotte *n* 324, 861, *vb* 324, 860
garrotting *n* 860
garrulity *n* 530
garrulous *adj* 530
gas *n* 141, 303, 304, 306, 530, *vb* 324, 860
gasbag *n* 530
gas chamber *n* 861
gaseous *adj* 303, 304, 306
gaseousness *n* 304
gash *n* 229, 231, 337, 595, *vb* 41, 231, 337, 595
gasholder *n* 570
gasify *vb* 304
gas mask *n* 640
gasometer *n* 570
gasp *n* 316, 363, *vb* 316, 363, 759
gassy *adj* 304, 530

gastroenteritis *n* 589
gastronome *n* 267, 846
gastronomic *adj* 267, 846
gastronomy *n* 267
gate *n* 232, 263, 630, 699, 711
gatecrash *vb* 54, 263, 789
gatecrasher *n* 54, 263, 789
gated *adj* 668
gate money *n* 719
gather *n* 230, *vb* 230, 259
gathered *adj* 66, 230
gather in *vb* 328
gathering *n* 40
gauche *adj* 512, 769
gaucheness *n* 512
gaudiness *n* 381, 769, 785
gaudy *adj* 381, 764, 766, 769, 785
gauge *n* 24, 177, *vb* 177
Gauleiter *n* 665
gaunt *adj* 183
gauntlet *n* 637
gauze *n* 183, 286, 379
gauziness *n* 379
gauzy *adj* 286, 379
gavotte *n* 367, 524
gawk *vb* 759
gawp *vb* 759
gay *adj* 73, 742, *n* 73
gaze *n* 370, *vb* 370, 759
gazebo *n* 165
gazelle *n* 245
gazette *n* 471
gazetteer *n* 76
gear *n* 204
gears *n* 568
gee-gee *n* 326
geezer *n* 332
Gehenna *n* 867
Geiger counter *n* 177
gel *vb* 182
gelatine *n* 318
geld *vb* 36, 153
gelding *n* 153
gelignite *n* 649
gem *n* 766
gemstone *n* 321
gen *n* 466
gene *n* 12, 320
genealogical *adj* 12
genealogy *n* 12
general *adj* 69, *n* 648
general agreement *n* 636
generality *n* 69
generalize *vb* 69

generalized *adj* 419
generally *adv* 69, 117
general public *n* 69, 777
general rate *n* 721
generate *vb* 22, 61, 132, 149
generation *n* 66, 92, 103, 149
generative *adj* 132, 149
generator *n* 141, 568
generic *adj* 68, 69
generosity *n* 182, 698, 725, 791, 805, 833
generous *adj* 29, 182, 573, 698, 725, 791, 805, 809, 833, 837, 859
genesis *n* 61, 132
genetic *adj* 12, 133, 155, 320
genetic engineering *n* 12, 320
genetics *n* 320
genial *adj* 736, 742, 789
geniality *n* 742, 789
genie *n* 865
genitals *n* 152
genius *n* 396, 396, 582, 624, 624, 759
genned up *adj* 466
genocide *n* 150, 324, 860
genteel *adj* 791
gentian *n* 391
gentian violet *n* 392
gentility *n* 791
gentle *adj* 148, 290, 338, 660
gentleman *n* 332
gentlemanly *adj* 791
gentleman of the road *n* 236
gentleman's gentleman *n* 666
gentleness *n* 148, 290, 660
gentrified *adj* 777
gentry *n* 776
genuflect *vb* 277, 874, 881
genuflection *n* 277
genuine *adj* 22, 417, 478, 831
genuine article *n* 22
genuineness *n* 22, 831
genus *n* 68
geographical *adj* 159, 284
geography *n* 159, 284
geological *adj* 284, 321
geology *n* 284, 321
geometric *adj* 75
geometry *n* 75, 177
Geordie *n* 494
geriatric *adj* 107, 112
geriatrics *n* 112
germ *n* 61, 132, 169, 208, 320
germ/chemical warfare *n* 645
germane *adj* 9

German measles *n* 589
germ-free *adj* 590
germinate *vb* 327
germ-ridden *adj* 591
gerontocracy *n* 112
gerontology *n* 112
gestation *n* 152
gesticulate *vb* 484
gesture *n* 484, *vb* 484
get *vb* 690, 699
get/have the wind up *vb* 750
get a bad name *vb* 775, 826
get a bad press *vb* 826
get above oneself *vb* 781, 783
get a kick out of *vb* 734
get along *vb* 19, 636
get along/on well with *vb* 789
get a move on *vb* 245, 609
get angry *vb* 802
get at *vb* 458
get-at-able *adj* 261, 580
getaway *n* 262, 605
get away from it all *vb* 618
get away with it *vb* 822
get away with murder *vb* 822
get back *vb* 704
get better *vb* 592, 594
get blood out of a stone *vb* 270, 424
get by *vb* 712
get cold feet *vb* 543, 752
get credit *vb* 715
get cross *vb* 802
get divorced *vb* 798
get down *vb* 275, 743
get down to brass tacks *vb* 509
get engaged *vb* 683, 800
get even with *vb* 641
get excited *vb* 732
get fresh *vb* 781, 800
get hitched *vb* 40, 797
get hold of *vb* 690
get hold of the wrong end of the
  stick *vb* 463
get in first *vb* 113
get into difficulties *vb* 628
get involved in *vb* 562
get married *vb* 797
get off on *vb* 734
get off pat *vb* 448
get off scot-free *vb* 822
get one's breath back *vb* 620
get one's dander up *vb* 802
get one's fingers burned *vb* 445
get one's hands on *vb* 692

get one's just deserts *vb* 860
get one's just deserts/comeuppance *vb*
  641
get one's leg over *vb* 40
get one's oats *vb* 40
get one's own back *vb* 641
get one's second wind *vb* 620
get one's skates on *vb* 245
get one's teeth into *vb* 562
get one's wires crossed *vb* 463
get on one's high horse *vb* 732
get on one's nerves *vb* 802
get on tick *vb* 715
get-out *n* 422, 605
get out of hand *vb* 56
get out of one's depth *vb* 628
get pleasure from *vb* 734
get rich *vb* 712
get rid of a hangover *vb* 847
get s.o. to do sth. *vb* 551
get sidetracked *vb* 10, 252
get somewhere *vb* 253
get spliced *vb* 40, 797
get stoned out of one's mind *vb*
  848
get stuck *vb* 652
get taken for a ride *vb* 480
get the better of *vb* 452, 626, 651
get the go-ahead *vb* 253
get the hang/feel of *vb* 549
get the hang of *vb* 476
get through *vb* 718
getting *n* 699
getting on *adj* 112
getting ready *n* 559
get to *vb* 261
get together *vb* 45, 66, 789
get-together *n* 66, 789
get to grips with *vb* 562
get to know *vb* 438, 793
get too big for one's boots *vb* 783
get tough with *vb* 659
get under way *vb* 61, 262
get-up-and-go *n* 145, 609
get used to *vb* 549
get weaving/cracking *vb* 61, 245
get what one deserved *vb* 641
get with it *vb* 770
get worse *vb* 593
geyser *n* 314, 339
ghastly *adj* 583, 750, 764
ghetto *n* 41, 157, 790
ghettoism *n* 41
ghost *n* 4, 865, 877

give up alcohol *vb* 847
give up the ghost *vb* 323
give up work *vb* 612
give voice/tongue *vb* 526
giving *n* 698
giving back *n* 704
giving up *n* 563
glacé *adj* 340, 345
glaciation *n* 340
glad *adj* 734
gladden *vb* 736
glade *n* 232
glad eye *n* 370
gladly *adv* 537
gladness *n* 734
glad rags *n* 204
gladsome *adj* 734
glamorous *adj* 763
glamour *n* 763
glance *n* 370, *vb* 370
glare *n* 374, 802, 804, *vb* 370, 802, 804
glaring *adj* 372, 464
glass *n* 292, 295, 307, 379, 569
glasses *n* 370
glasshouse *n* 165, 329
glassiness *n* 292
glassy *adj* 289, 292, 314, 321, 379
glassy-eyed *adj* 848
glaucous *adj* 390
glaze *n* 202, 292, 318, *vb* 202, 292
glazier *n* 613
gleam *n* 374, *vb* 374
gleaming *adj* 374
glean *vb* 545, 690
gleanings *n* 37
glee *n* 734, 742
gleeful *adj* 742
glib *adj* 530
glide *vb* 90, 238, 292, 314
glider *n* 244
gliding *n* 238, 761
glimmer *n* 374, *vb* 281
glimpse *n* 370, *vb* 370
glint *n* 374, *vb* 374
glinting *adj* 374
glitter *n* 374, 785, *vb* 374
glittering *adj* 785
glittery *adj* 374
gloaming *n* 110, 376
gloat *vb* 746
gloating *n* 734
global *adj* 47, 69, 156, 284
global war *n* 645

globe *n* 47, 223, 225, 284
globe-trotter *n* 236
globe-trotting *adj* 236, *n* 236
globose *adj* 225
globular *adj* 223, 225
globule *n* 225
glockenspiel *n* 359, 369
gloom *n* 375, 376, 452, 735, 743
gloominess *n* 375
gloomy *adj* 375, 376, 384, 432, 450, 735, 743, 804
glorification *n* 866
glorified *adj* 785, 866
glorify *vb* 576, 774, 874
glorious *adj* 582, 763, 866
glory *n* 763, 774, 862, 866
gloss *n* 187, 292, 374, 462, 829, *vb* 187, 292, 462, 829
glossary *n* 76, 496
gloss over *vb* 407
glossy *adj* 292, 374, *n* 471
glow *n* 339, 374, 387, *vb* 374, 387
glower *vb* 802, 804
glowing *adj* 339, 374, 377, 381, 387
glue *n* 42, 43, 318, *vb* 43
glue-sniffing *n* 849
gluey *adj* 43, 318
glum *adj* 743, 804
glumness *n* 804
glut *n* 152, 328, 575, 724
glutinousness *n* 318
glutton *n* 846
gluttonous *adj* 267, 728, 844, 846
gluttony *n* 267, 728, 755, 844, 846
glyph *n* 493
glyptic *adj* 492
gnarled *adj* 219, 291
gnashing of teeth *n* 747
gnat *n* 169
gnaw *vb* 337
gnome *n* 865
gnomic *adj* 442
gnosticism *n* 868
go *n* 561, *vb* 234
go/sell for *vb* 721
goad *vb* 147, 551, 615, 732, 802
go against *vb* 421
go against the grain *vb* 737, 758
go-ahead *adj* 145, 253, *n* 436, 677
goal *n* 62, 249, 261, 553
go all out *vb* 49, 561
go all out for *vb* 539
go along with *vb* 436, 537, 633, 636
go around with *vb* 793

gossamer *n* 4, 183, 286, 379
gossip *n* 402, 409, 471, 471, 530, 533, 775, 828, *vb* 533
gossip columnist *n* 828
gossipy *adj* 466, 471, 530
go steady *vb* 800
go straight *vb* 831, 837
go the way of all flesh *vb* 323
go the whole hog *vb* 49
go through *vb* 101, 729
go through it *vb* 656
go through the floor *vb* 32, 189
go through the roof *vb* 188, 723
go through the roof/ceiling *vb* 31
go to and fro *vb* 119
go to church *vb* 872
go to extremes *vb* 482
go together *vb* 85
go to great trouble *vb* 617
go to law *vb* 856
go too far *vb* 272, 482, 820
go to one's head *vb* 783, 848
go to pieces *vb* 46
go to pot *vb* 593
go to rack and ruin *vb* 2, 150
go to the dogs *vb* 150, 593
go to the wall *vb* 150, 652, 717
go to war *vb* 645
go to waste *vb* 691
got up *adj* 204
gouache *n* 490
gouge *vb* 227
gouge out *vb* 186
go under *vb* 275, 652, 717
go under/down *vb* 150
go under the name of *vb* 498
go unheard *vb* 352
go unheeded *vb* 352
go up *vb* 723
go up the wall *vb* 802
gourmand *n* 846
gourmandise *n* 267
gourmet *n* 267, 768, 846
govern *vb* 141, 500, 622, 657
governess *n* 668
governing *adj* 622, 657
governing body *n* 622
government *n* 622, 657
governmental *adj* 622, 657
governor *n* 31, 332, 622, 665, 668
go way over the top *vb* 772
go well *vb* 629
go west *vb* 323
go without food *vb* 845

grab *n* 703, *vb* 692, 703
grabbing *adj* 703
grab the limelight *vb* 785
grace *n* 763, 768, 809, 811, 813, 862, 874
Grace *n* 778
graceful *adj* 511, 524, 763, 768
gracefulness *n* 511
graceless *adj* 512, 764
gracelessness *n* 512, 764
gracious *adj* 763, 791, 805, 809, 862
graciousness *n* 791
gradation *n* 24, 55
gradational *adj* 24, 55
grade *vb* 15, 24, 57, 68
graded *adj* 57
gradient *n* 184, 195, 274
gradual *adj* 24, 64
gradual decrease *n* 34
gradually *adv* 24, 148
graduate *vb* 24, 177, 651, 786
graduation *n* 651
graft *vb* 35, 329
grain *n* 30, 169, 299, 300, *vb* 766
grainy *adj* 291, 300, 491
grammar *n* 494, 500
grammar/comprehensive/public/state/ prep/boarding school *n* 477
grammatical *adj* 494, 500
grammatical error *n* 501
gramophone *n* 353
granary *n* 570
grand *adj* 29, 763, 774, *n* 84, 369
grand/petty larceny *n* 705
grandad *n* 112
grand duke *n* 665
grande dame *n* 112, 776
grandee *n* 776
grandeur *n* 29, 763, 785
grandfather *n* 112
grandfather clock *n* 97
grandiloquence *n* 507, 771
grandiloquent *adj* 507, 510, 771
grandiose *adj* 785
grandioseness *n* 510
grandmaster *n* 761
grandmother *n* 112
grand old man *n* 112, 774
grandparent *n* 12
grange *n* 165
granite *n* 289, 311
granny *n* 112
granny flat *n* 112, 165

grant *n* 631, 677, 690, 698, 719, *vb*
  434, 436, 697, 698, 859
grant a loan *vb* 714
grant amnesty to *vb* 813
grantee *n* 699
grant impunity *vb* 822
grant leave *vb* 677
grant remission *vb* 857
granulate *vb* 300
granulated *adj* 299, 300
granule *n* 30, 48, 169, 300
grape *n* 392
grapeshot *n* 69, 649
grapevine *n* 466, 471
graph *n* 24, 57
graphic *adj* 488, 490, 507, 513, 517
graphics *n* 490
grasp *n* 43, 141, 438, 692, 695, *vb* 43,
  438, 695, 703
grasping *adj* 703, 728
grass *n* 327, 390, 849
grass-green *adj* 390
grassland *n* 313
grassroots *n* 69
grass widow *n* 798
grassy *adj* 327, 390
grate *n* 339, 362, *vb* 20, 291, 301, 362,
  366
grateful *adj* 811
gratefully *adv* 811
gratefulness *n* 811
gratification *n* 336
gratified *adj* 734, 811
gratify *vb* 736, 738
gratifying *adj* 336
grating *adj* 20, 291, 301, 362, 366,
  512, *n* 301
gratis *adj* 667, 698, 724
gratitude *n* 811, 825
gratuitous *adj* 135, 820
gratuitousness *n* 135, 820
gratuity *n* 667, 698, 859
grave *adj* 285, 507, 576, 733, 745, *n*
  325
gravel *n* 311, 569
gravelly *adj* 291, 311
graven *adj* 492, 493
graven image *n* 875
graver *n* 493
graveyard *n* 325, 882
gravid *adj* 152
gravitas *n* 285, 507
gravitate *vb* 140
gravitational *adj* 257

gravity *n* 257, 285, 576, 733, 745
gravy *n* 303
graze *n* 187, 301, 338, *vb* 173, 187,
  301, 338
grease *n* 302, 319, 587, *vb* 292, 302,
  319
grease paint *n* 523
greasiness *n* 292, 302, 319
greasy *adj* 292, 302, 319, 587
great *adj* 29, 582
great-aunt *n* 12
greatest *adj* 29
greatest part *n* 29
greatly *adv* 29
great-nephew *n* 12
greatness *n* 29, 582
great-niece *n* 12
great outdoors *n* 198, 306
great quantity *n* 29
great-uncle *n* 12
greed *n* 728, 755, 834, 846
greediness *n* 846
greedy *adj* 690, 728, 755, 834, 846
greedy guts *n* 846
greedy pig *n* 846
green *adj* 50, 106, 111, 346, 390, 439,
  627, 839, *n* 390, 761
greenback *n* 711
green belt *n* 157, 313, 390
greenery *n* 327, 390
greengage *n* 390
greenhorn *n* 106, 627
greenhouse *n* 329
greenish *adj* 390
greenish-blue *adj* 390
green light *n* 436, 677
Green Man *n* 865
greenness *n* 50, 106, 390, 439
greensward *n* 313
green with envy *adj* 816
greenwood *n* 327
greet *vb* 261, 532, 791, 793, 823
greeting *n* 261, 532, 791, 823
greetings card *n* 515
gregarious *adj* 789
gregariousness *n* 789
gremlin *n* 865
grenade *n* 649
grenadier *n* 648
grey *adj* 63, 376, 382, 385, *n*
  385
grey area *n* 63, 428
greybeard *n* 112
grey eminence *n* 139

grey-haired *adj* 385
greyhound *n* 245
greying *adj* 385
greyish *adj* 385
grey matter *n* 396
greyness *n* 382, 385
grid *n* 24, 177, 197
grief *n* 735, 739, 747
grief-stricken *adj* 735, 747
grievance *n* 739, 818
grieve *vb* 735, 747
grieve with *vb* 809
grieving *n* 735
grievous bodily harm *n* 147, 639
grill *vb* 267, 339
grille *n* 197, 232
grilling *n* 402
grim *adj* 539, 737, 745
grimace *n* 804, *vb* 219, 484, 804
grime *n* 587
grimness *n* 745
grimy *adj* 587
grin *n* 744, *vb* 744
grin and bear it *vb* 742
grind *n* 617, 762, *vb* 296, 300, 301, 362, 617
grind down *adj* 36
grinder *n* 300
grinding *n* 300
grindstone *n* 296
grip *n* 43, 167, 624, 695, *vb* 43, 695
gripe *n* 337
gripping *adj* 732
grisly *adj* 750
gristle *n* 294
gristly *adj* 294
grist to the mill *n* 419
grit *n* 143, 289, 300
gritty *adj* 289, 300, 311
grizzle *vb* 383
grizzled *adj* 383, 385, 393
groan *n* 356, 363, *vb* 356, 363, 747
grocer *n* 571
groggy *adj* 610
groom *n* 613, *vb* 55, 559, 765
groomed *adj* 55, 204
grooming *n* 765
groove *n* 15, 158, 227, 230, 231, 493, 549, *vb* 227, 230, 231
grooved *adj* 227, 231, 493
groovy *adj* 770
grope *vb* 338, 428
gross *adj* 47, 49, 721, *n* 84, *vb* 690, 699

grotesque *adj* 764, 772
grotto *n* 227
grotty *adj* 583, 587, 764
grouch *vb* 804
grouchy *adj* 804
ground *adj* 300, *n* 132, 185, 189, 193, 210, 311, 761, *vb* 189, 191, 277
ground floor *n* 189
groundless *adj* 135
ground rent *n* 721
grounds *n* 37, 134, 313, 410, 829
groundwork *n* 61, 559
group *n* 66, 68, 368, 634, 648, *vb* 57, 68
group captain *n* 648
grouse *vb* 739, 804
grove *n* 327
grovel *vb* 663, 782, 823
grovelling *adj* 681, 782
groves of academe *n* 477
grow *vb* 33, 149, 327, 328, 329
grower *n* 149
grow fat *vb* 655
growing *adj* 33
growing pains *n* 61, 111
growl *n* 802, 804, *vb* 364, 794, 802, 804
growly *adj* 362
grown-up *adj* 112, *n* 112
grow old *vb* 107
growth *n* 33, 226, 253, 322, 690
grub *n* 267, 326
Grub Street *n* 513
grudge *n* 739, 796, 802, *vb* 816
grudging *adj* 728, 739, 794, 802, 816
grudging thanks *n* 812
gruel *n* 317, 343
gruelling *adj* 617
gruesome *adj* 750
gruff *adj* 362, 531, 792, 803, 804
gruffness *n* 362, 527, 531, 804
grumble *vb* 358, 682, 739, 804
grumpy *adj* 803, 804
grunt *n* 363, *vb* 363, 364, 804
guano *n* 268
guarantee *n* 473, 598, 683, 687, *vb* 420, 427, 683, 687
guaranteed *adj* 598, 683
guarantor *n* 687
guard *n* 598, 640, 640, 668, *vb* 598, 640
guarded *adj* 598
guardian *adj* 863, *n* 154, 598, 668
guardian angel *n* 807, 863

guardian of morality *n* 850
guard of honour *n* 823
guardroom *n* 671
gubernatorial *adj* 657
guerdon *n* 859
guerrilla *n* 127, 648
guess *n* 401, 428, 456, *vb* 401, 425, 456
guesswork *n* 416, 456
guest *n* 789
guest of Her Majesty *n* 671
guest worker *n* 161
guff *n* 459
gufflaw *n* 355, 363, 744, *vb* 355, 363, 744
guidance *n* 475, 621, 623, 631
guide *n* 59, 85, 623, *vb* 85, 249, 475, 622, 623, 631
guided missile *n* 649
guideline *n* 71
guidelines *n* 623
guiding *adj* 622, 623
guild *n* 40, 66
guile *n* 480, 626, 832
guileless *adj* 831, 839
guilelessness *n* 478
guiless *adj* 478
guillotine *n* 296, 861, *vb* 179, 324, 860
guillotining *n* 860
guilt *n* 840
guiltless *adj* 839, 857
guiltlessness *n* 839
guilty *adj* 840
guilty act *n* 840
guilty conscience *n* 840
guinea pig *n* 416
guise *n* 394
guitar *n* 369
gulag *n* 671
gulf *n* 174, 310
gull *n* 480, *vb* 480
gulled *adj* 480
gullet *n* 232
gullibility *n* 434, 551
gullible *adj* 434, 551
gully *n* 181, 227, 231, 315
gulp *n* 267, *vb* 267
gulp down *vb* 846
gum *n* 43, 318, *vb* 40, 43
gummy *adj* 43, 318
gumption *n* 396
gun *n* 649
gunboat diplomacy *n* 664
gunfire *n* 357

gunge *n* 318, 587
gungy *adj* 318, 587
gunman *n* 639
gunmetal *adj* 391, *n* 385, 569
gunner *n* 255, 648
gunnery *n* 255
gunpowder *n* 649
gurgle *vb* 306, 314
gurgling *adj* 314
guru *n* 444, 475, 868
gush *n* 530, *vb* 147, 264, 314, 506
gushing *adj* 530
gust *n* 306, *vb* 306, 307, 316
gusto *n* 145, 342, 734
gusty *adj* 306, 316
gutless *adj* 144, 752
gutlessness *n* 541
gut reaction *n* 399, 401
guts *n* 53, 143, 145, 166, 199, 539, 751
gutter *n* 209, 231, 315, 587, *vb* 130, 281
gutter press *n* 471, 828
guttural *adj* 362
guv'nor *n* 665
guy *n* 332, *vb* 828
guzzle *vb* 267, 846, 848
gymnastics *n* 143
gynaecological *adj* 333
gyrate *vb* 223
gyration *n* 223, 279
gyratory *adj* 223, 279
gyre *n* 27

H

habeas corpus *n* 661
habit *n* 122, 549, 688, 849
habitat *n* 158, 165
habitation *n* 162
habitual *adj* 549
habituate *vb* 549
habituation *n* 549
habitué *n* 789
hack *n* 326, *vb* 41
hackney carriage *n* 242
hackneyed *adj* 88, 442, 508
hack out *vb* 615
hackwork *n* 513
had better *vb* 821
Hades *n* 323, 862, 867
haemorrhage *n* 303
hag *n* 112

handle with kid gloves *vb* 660
handling *n* 136, 338, 490, 622
hand-me-downs *n* 204
handout *n* 466, 631, 698
hand out *vb* 698
handover *n* 129, 697
hand over *vb* 129, 563, 697
hand-picked *adj* 545, 582
handrail *n* 193
handshake *n* 261, 791, 793
handsome *adj* 725, 763
handsomeness *n* 763
handwriting *n* 513
handwritten *adj* 513
handy *adj* 115, 138, 162, 173, 578
handyman *n* 613, 666
hang 192, *vb* 44, 133, 192, 324, 766, 860
hang back *vb* 32, 538, 784
hangdog *adj* 743, 804
hang draw and quarter *vb* 860
hanger *n* 192
hanger-on *n* 85, 827
hang fire *vb* 114
hang-glider *n* 244
hang-gliding *n* 238, 761
hanging *adj* 192, *n* 192, 192, 324, 860
hang in the balance *vb* 428
hangman *n* 324, 860
hang on *vb* 124, 540, 695
hang on someone's words *vb* 404
hang-out *n* 165
hang out at *vb* 165
hang out the flags *vb* 786
hangover *n* 37, 60, 848
hang the expense *vb* 727
hang together *vb* 400
hangup *n* 447, 735
hank *n* 66
hanker *vb* 755, 816
hankering *n* 755
hanky-panky *n* 480
hansom *n* 242
haphazard *adj* 56, 135, 419, 554
haphazardness *n* 135, 419
happen *vb* 101
happening *n* 8, 101, 433
happen on *vb* 433
happiness *n* 655, 734, 738, 742
happy *adj* 651, 734, 738, 742
happy/favourable outcome *n* 651
happy ending *n* 651
happy event *n* 152
happy few *n* 31

happy-go-lucky *adj* 454, 554
happy hunting grounds *n* 323, 866
happy medium *n* 27, 63, 148, 250
hara kiri *n* 324
harangue *n* 506, 532, *vb* 506, 532
harass *vb* 737, 802
harassment *n* 737
harbinger *n* 59
harbinger of doom *n* 602
harbour *n* 598, *vb* 598
hard *adj* 143, 287, 289, 294, 321, 628, 656, 842, *adv* 145
hard/lean times *n* 656
hard/soft sell *n* 709
hardback *adj* 516
hard-bitten *adj* 731
hardboard *n* 569
hard-boiled *adj* 659
hard cash *n* 711
hard drinker *n* 848
hard drug *n* 849
harden *vb* 287, 289, 294, 559, 731
hardened *adj* 289, 549, 559, 873
hardened sinner *n* 842
hardening *n* 559
harden off *vb* 329
harden oneself *vb* 731
harden one's heart *vb* 680, 810, 842, 873
harden one's heart against *vb* 731
hard going *n* 628
hard graft *n* 617
hard-headed *adj* 659
hard-hearted *adj* 289, 731, 806, 810
hard-heartedness *n* 289
hard-heartedness *n* 806
hard-hitting *adj* 141, 507
hard labour *n* 860
hard-line *adj* 542
hard line *n* 542
hard lines *n* 656
hardly *adv* 30
hardness *n* 143, 289, 294, 842
hardness of hearing *n* 352
hardness of heart *n* 810, 842
hard-nosed *adj* 731
hard of hearing *adj* 352
hard-pressed *adj* 615, 656
hard-pushed *adj* 615
hardship *n* 656
hard shoulder *n* 209
hard stuff *n* 267
hard substance *n* 289
hard to please *adj* 739

have at the back of one's mind *vb* 449
have a weakness for *vb* 757
have a whip-round *vb* 681
have been in the wars *vb* 656
have being *vb* 1
have cause to *vb* 817
have charge of *vb* 598
have confidence in *vb* 450
have control *vb* 657
have designs on *vb* 755
have faith *vb* 748
have fun *vb* 734, 761
have good taste *vb* 768
have grounds for *vb* 817
have had it coming to one *vb* 641
have had its day *vb* 105
have had one too many *vb* 848
have influence *vb* 139
have intercourse *vb* 795
have it both ways *vb* 81, 543
have it coming to one *vb* 819
have it in for *vb* 796, 806
have it made *vb* 655
have it off *vb* 795
have it off with *vb* 40
have many irons in the fire *vb* 16
have many strings to one's bow *vb* 16
have mercy *vb* 660
have money to burn *vb* 712
haven *n* 165, 600
have nine lives *vb* 93, 322
have no alternative/option *vb* 536
have no bearing on *vb* 10
have no complaints *vb* 738
have no regrets *vb* 842
have no respect for *vb* 824
have no right to *vb* 820
have no stomach for *vb* 752, 758
have no success *vb* 652
have nothing to confess *vb* 839
have nothing to do with *vb* 10, 680
have no time for *vb* 758, 824
have no trouble *vb* 629
have-nots *n* 713, 777
have on *vb* 773
have one foot in the grave *vb* 323
have one's cake and eat it *vb* 81
have one's doubts about *vb* 435
have one's feet on the ground *vb* 444
have one's fingers burned *vb* 452
have one's fling *vb* 844
have one's hackles up *vb* 794
have one's head screwed on *vb* 444

have one's own way *vb* 535
have one's position to consider *vb* 774
have one's pride *vb* 779
have one's roots in *vb* 133
have one's say *vb* 528
have one's wits about one *vb* 396
have on the tip of one's tongue *vb* 449
have possibilities *vb* 423
have potential *vb* 423
have power over *vb* 657
have qualms/misgivings *vb* 450
haversack *n* 167
have run its course *vb* 105
haves *n* 712
have second thoughts *vb* 44, 398, 541
have seen better days *vb* 105
have seen it all before *vb* 760
have sex *vb* 795
have sex with *vb* 40
have shares in *vb* 693
have the best of both worlds *vb* 81
have the cheek/nerve to *vb* 781
have the courage/nerve to *vb* 751
have the ear of *vb* 139
have the freedom/run of *vb* 667
have the makings of *vb* 423, 748
have the right to *vb* 819
have the whip hand *vb* 657
have to watch the pennies *vb* 713
have under one's thumb *vb* 139, 670
have value *vb* 582
have what it takes *vb* 751
have words *vb* 410, 635
having said that *adv* 28
hawk *n* 122, 362, 645, *vb* 268, 681, 709
hawker *n* 681
hawk-eyed *adj* 370
hawkish *adj* 645
hayrick *n* 570
haystack *n* 570
haywire *adv* 56
hazard *n* 135, 554, 599, 630, *vb* 554, 599
hazard a guess *vb* 456
hazardous *adj* 554, 599
haze *n* 307, 376
hazel *adj* 386
haziness *n* 373, 376
hazy *adj* 4, 307, 373, 376, 380, 385, 449
H-bomb *n* 649
he *n* 332

head *adj* 212, *n* 188, 396, 492, 848, *vb* 31, 59, 159
headache *n* 589, 628, 735, 848
head and shoulders *adv* 49
head boy/girl *n* 31
head-count *n* 75
headed *adj* 249
headfirst *adv* 147
head for *vb* 249
headgear *n* 204
headhunt *vb* 611
headhunting *n* 611
headiness *n* 347
heading *n* 513
headlamp *n* 377
headland *n* 228, 311
headless *adj* 179
headlines *n* 471
headlong *adj* 245, 753, *adv* 147
headman *n* 665
head off *vb* 258
head-on *adj* 212
head over heels *adv* 196
headphones *n* 351
headquarters *n* 165
headrest *n* 193
headroom *n* 156, 174
heads *n* 212
head start *n* 26, 31, 59, 113
headstrong *adj* 542, 732, 753
head up *vb* 212, 622
headway *n* 234, 253
headwind *n* 316, 630
heady *adj* 347
heal *vb* 594, 596
healed *adj* 594
healer *n* 594, 596
healing *adj* 596, *n* 594
health *n* 143, 588
health food *n* 39, 267, 588
health freak *n* 588
health-giving *adj* 588
healthiness *n* 588
healthy *adj* 143, 582, 588
heap *n* 66, 570, *vb* 66
heap/shower upon *vb* 725
heaps *n* 29
heap up *vb* 570
hear *vb* 334, 351, 856
hear/see things *vb* 4
hearer *n* 351
hearing *n* 351, 856
hearing aid *n* 351
hearing distance *n* 351

hearken *vb* 351
hearsay *n* 471
hearse *n* 242, 325
heart *n* 5, 63, 199, 200, 322
heartache *n* 735
heart-broken *adj* 735
heart disease *n* 589
hearten *vb* 143, 732, 740, 742, 751
heartening *adj* 742
heart-felt *adj* 729
hearth *n* 165, 339
heartiness *n* 342, 789
heartland *n* 157, 199
heartless *adj* 731, 810
heartlessness *n* 731, 810
heart of stone *n* 842
heart of the matter *n* 576
heart-rending *adj* 809
heart's desire *n* 748
heart-shaped *adj* 221
heart-stopping *adj* 732
heartthrob *n* 763, 795
heart-to-heart *n* 533
heartwood *n* 199
hearty *adj* 789, 793
heat *n* 339, *vb* 339
heated *adj* 410, 533
heater *n* 339
heath *n* 313, 327
heathen *adj* 869, 875, *n* 869, 875
heathenism *n* 869, 875
heather *n* 392
Heath Robinson *adj* 625
heating *n* 339
heatwave *n* 307
heave *n* 256, *vb* 241, 256, 281
heave a sigh of relief *vb* 740
heaven *n* 323, 866
heavenly *adj* 284, 734, 862, 863, 866
heavenly city *n* 866
heavens *n* 184, 284
heaven-sent *adj* 115, 835
heavier-than-air *adj* 244
heaviness *n* 23, 285, 762
heavy *adj* 146, 285, 762, *n* 266, 471
heavy drinker *n* 848
heavy hand *n* 659
heavy-handed *adj* 338
heavy object *n* 285
heavyweight *adj* 285, *n* 31
hebdomadal *adj* 92
heckle *vb* 414, 682, 826
heckler *n* 682
heckling *n* 682

hedge *n* 28, 210, *vb* 28
hedge in *vb* 630
hedge one's bets *vb* 44
hedonism *n* 336, 734, 844
hedonistic *adj* 336, 734, 844
heebie-jeebies *n* 281, 750
heed *n* 404, 406, 754, *vb* 351, 404,
  406, 663, 688
heedful *adj* 754
heedfulness *n* 754
heeding *n* 688
heedless *adj* 405, 449, 753
heedlessness *n* 405, 753
heel *n* 838, *vb* 594
hefty *adj* 29, 143, 168
hegemony *n* 31, 139, 141, 657, 670
heifer *n* 326, 333
height *n* 23, 184, 228, 276, 584
heighten *vb* 184, 741
heightening *n* 741
heights *n* 184
heinous *adj* 838
heir *n* 37, 100, 155, 699, 819
heiress *n* 155
heirloom *n* 107
heist *n* 705, *vb* 705
held in contempt *adj* 775
helical *adj* 224
helicopter *n* 244
heliotrope *n* 392
helix *n* 224
hell *n* 323, 867
hellfire *n* 867
hell for leather *adv* 245
hellish *adj* 806, 838, 864, 867
hell-raising *adj* 56
helmet *n* 640
help *n* 596, 613, 631, 666, 740,
  835, *vb* 138, 578, 580, 596, 633, 698,
  740, 805, 835
helper *n* 631, 807
helpful *adj* 138, 466, 537, 578, 629,
  631, 633, 805, 835
helpfulness *n* 138, 537, 578
helping *n* 23, 700
helping hand *n* 631
helpless *adj* 142, 144
helplessness *n* 142, 144
helpmate *n* 193
help one another *vb* 633
help oneself to *vb* 705
help (out) *vb* 631
helter skelter *adv* 245
hem *n* 209, *vb* 176, 206, 209

he-man *n* 143, 332
hem and haw *vb* 529, 541
hem in *vb* 210, 630
hemisphere *n* 81, 223, 225, 226
hemispherical *adj* 221, 226
hemp *n* 849
hen *n* 326, 333
hence *adv* 133, 134
henceforth *adv* 104
henchman *n* 32, 631, 666
henna *n* 387, 388, 765, *vb* 387
henpecked *adj* 663
hepatitis *n* 589
heptad *n* 84
heptagon *n* 84
Heptateuch *n* 84
herald *n* 470, *vb* 59, 470
herb *n* 327, 344
herbaceous *adj* 327, 329
herbaceous border *n* 329
herbal *adj* 329
herbarium *n* 329
herbivore *n* 326
herbivorous *adj* 267, 326
Hercules *n* 143
herd *n* 66, 72, 777, *vb* 66
herd instinct *n* 330
hereafter *n* 104
here and now *n* 101
here and there *adv* 67, 174
hereditament *n* 694
hereditary *adj* 12, 133, 155
hereditary peer *n* 776
heredity *n* 12
heresy *n* 73, 435, 869, 871
heresy-hunting *n* 870
heretic *n* 73, 869, 871
heretical *adj* 73, 435, 869, 871
hermaphrodite *n* 38, 73, 153
hermaphroditic *adj* 38
Hermes *n* 862
hermetically sealed *adj* 233
hermit *n* 790, 799
hero *n* 751, 795
heroic *adj* 518, 521, 751
heroics *n* 785
heroin *n* 849
heroine *n* 751
heroism *n* 751
hero's welcome *n* 786
hero-worship *n* 823, 875, *vb* 823
Herr *n* 778
herringbone *n* 195, 766

hesitant *adj* 130, 246, 280, 428, 435, 538, 541, 616, 750
hesitate *vb* 130, 280, 428, 435, 529, 538, 541, 616, 784
hesitation *n* 130, 246, 280, 428, 538, 541, 616, 750
hessian *n* 569
heterodox *adj* 871
heterodoxy *n* 871
heterogeneity *n* 16
heterogeneous *adj* 16, 38
het up *adj* 802
hew *vb* 216, 492
hewer of wood and drawer of water *n* 613
hexad *n* 84
hexagon *n* 84, 220
hexagonal *adj* 220
hexameter *n* 84
Hexateuch *n* 84
heyday *n* 111, 655
hiatus *n* 50, 65, 232
hibernal *adj* 108
hibernate *vb* 146, 610
hibernation *n* 108, 146, 610
hiccup *n* 123, 316, 452, *vb* 316
hidden *adj* 373, 465, 469
hidden meaning *n* 458
hiddenness *n* 465
hide *n* 202, 569, *vb* 373, 395, 465, 469, 469
hide-and-seek *n* 761
hidebound *adj* 430, 542, 659
hide one's light under a bushel *vb* 784
hideous *adj* 737, 764
hideousness *n* 764
hideout *n* 469
hide out *vb* 395
hidey-hole *n* 469
hiding *n* 469
hiding-place *n* 469
hierarchical *adj* 24, 55, 68
hierarchy *n* 24, 55, 57, 64, 68, 879
hieroglyphic *adj* 495, *n* 495
hieroglyphics *n* 513
hi-fi *n* 353
higgledy-piggledy *adv* 16, 38, 56
high *adj* 23, 184, 228, 350, 732, 848, 849, *n* 307, 732, 849
high/low rise *adj* 165
high/low season *n* 108
high and dry *adj* 311
high and low *adv* 49, 156

high-and-mighty *adj* 779
high birth *n* 776
highbrow *adj* 367, *n* 396
high calibre *n* 31
high colour *n* 387
high commission *n* 675
high commissioner *n* 675
high-density *adj* 86
highest *adj* 188
highest bidder *n* 708
high explosive *n* 649
high fashion *n* 204
high-flier *n* 31
high-flown *adj* 276, 482, 510
high-handed *adj* 781
high hopes *n* 748
high income bracket *n* 712
high IQ *n* 396
high jump *n* 274
high-jumper *n* 274
highland *n* 184, 311
high life *n* 655
highlight *n* 374, *vb* 70, 464, 576
highlights *n* 765
high-living *adj* 844
high living *n* 844
highly¹ acclaimed *adj* 774
highly coloured *adj* 482
highly regarded *adj* 774, 823
highly strung *adj* 730, 732
high-minded *adj* 831, 833
high noon *n* 109
high opinion *n* 823
high-pitched *adj* 355, 363
high point *n* 29, 184, 188
high-powered *adj* 145
high-pressure salesmanship *n* 709
high profile *n* 212, 228
high relief *n* 228, 492
high-rise *adj* 184
high seas *n* 310
high society *n* 770, 776
high-speed *adj* 245
high-speed train *n* 242
high-spirited *adj* 732, 742
high spirits *n* 732, 742
high standing *n* 823
high summer *n* 108
high time *n* 114
high turnover *n* 709
high-water mark *n* 188
highway *n* 240
highwayman *n* 705
high wind *n* 307

hijack *n* 705, *vb* 705
hijacker *n* 705
hijacking *n* 705
hike *n* 236, *vb* 236, 761
hiker *n* 236
hiking *n* 761
hilarious *adj* 744
hill *n* 274
hind *adj* 213, *n* 333
hinder *vb* 628, 630, 632, 668
hindering *adj* 630
hindmost *adj* 60, 62, 213
hindquarters *n* 213
hindrance *n* 581, 630
hindsight *n* 100, 105, 398, 448
Hinduism *n* 868
hinge *n* 40, 42, 132, 200, *vb* 40, 133, 279, 428
hinge on *vb* 200
hint *n* 38, 465, 466, 484, 602, 623, *vb* 465, 623
hinterland *n* 157, 213, 311
hippie *n* 73
hire *n* 697, 702, *vb* 611, 697, 702
hire charge *n* 721
hireling *n* 32
hire out *vb* 701
hire purchase *n* 702, 708, 714
hirer *n* 692
hiring *n* 701
hirsute *adj* 291
his nibs *n* 779
hiss *n* 484, 526, 824, 826, *vb* 361, 364, 526, 826
hissing *adj* 361
historian *n* 486, 517
historical *adj* 3, 97, 107, 440, 522
historicity *n* 3
history *n* 517, 522
histrionic *adj* 482, 523, 785
histrionics *n* 523, 785
hit *n* 247, 582, *vb* 247
hit a bad patch *vb* 656
hit-and-miss *adj* 753
hit bedrock *vb* 189
hit below the belt *vb* 818
hitch *n* 123, 452, 630, 836, *vb* 40, 192
hitch-hike *vb* 681
hitch-hiker *n* 681
hitherto *adv* 101
hit home *vb* 507
hit it off *vb* 19, 636
hitman *n* 150, 324
hit-or-miss *adj* 416, 419

hit rock bottom *vb* 32
hit the bottle *vb* 848
hit the headlines *vb* 471
hit the nail on the head *vb* 440
hit the roof *vb* 802
hit upon *vb* 135, 433
hive off *vb* 41, 67
hoard *vb* 570, 690, 728
hoarfrost *n* 340, 383
hoarse *adj* 362, 527
hoarseness *n* 362, 527
hoary *adj* 107, 383, 385
hoax *n* 479, 744, *vb* 626
hob *n* 339
hobble *vb* 40, 181, 246, 630
hobby *n* 761
hobgoblin *n* 865
hobnob *vb* 85
hobo *n* 777
Hobson's choice *n* 536
hockey *n* 761
hocus-pocus *n* 461, 875, 876
hoe *vb* 328
hog *n* 326, 846, *vb* 52, 692, 834
hog's back *n* 226
hoi polloi *n* 777
hoist *n* 276, *vb* 276
hoist with one's own petard *adj* 652
hold *n* 692, 695, *vb* 166, 434, 473, 692, 695
holdall *n* 167
hold a séance *vb* 876, 877
hold a sit-in *vb* 682
hold back *vb* 556, 668
hold dear *vb* 795, 823
holder *n* 167, 692
hold forth *vb* 506
hold in common *vb* 693
hold in contempt *vb* 824
holding *n* 570, 695
hold no brief for *vb* 437, 756
hold off *vb* 123, 538, 638
hold one's drink *vb* 847
hold one's head high *vb* 779
hold one's peace *vb* 531
hold one's tongue *vb* 467, 527, 531
hold out *vb* 43, 540, 542, 638
hold out for *vb* 659, 685
hold out no hope *vb* 749
hold out the olive branch *vb* 646
hold over *vb* 123, 654
hold sway *vb* 141, 657
hold the centre *vb* 63
hold to ransom *vb* 806

holdup *n* 114, 123, 246, 630, 705
hold up *vb* 98, 705
hold water *vb* 400
hole *n* 50, 158, 174, 227, 232, 628, *vb* 227, 232
hole-and-corner *adj* 467, 469
holey *adj* 232
holiday *n* 163, 612, 618, *vb* 612
holier-than-thou *adj* 872
holiness *n* 837, 872
Holiness *n* 778
holistic *adj* 47
holland *n* 569
holler *vb* 363
hollow *adj* 4, 163, 227, 359, 459, 771, *n* 186, 227, 231, *vb* 186, 227
hollow man *n* 4
hollowness *n* 359, 459
Hollywood *n* 525
holocaust *n* 62, 150, 324, 339
hologram *n* 374, 488, 491
holograph *adj* 513
holographic *adj* 491
holography *n* 491
holster *n* 202
holt *n* 165
holy *adj* 837, 862, 863, 868, 868, 872, 874
holy city *n* 866
Holy Communion *n* 881
holy day *n* 881
Holy Father *n* 879
Holy Ghost *n* 862
holy man *n* 863
Holy Office *n* 878
holy orders *n* 878
holy person *n* 863
holy place *n* 882
Holy Spirit *n* 862
holy terror *n* 662
holy war *n* 645
holy water *n* 881
Holy Writ *n* 868
homage *n* 823, 874, *vb* 874
home *adj* 164, 199, *n* 165
homebody *n* 199
home economics *n* 267
Home Guard *n* 640
home in *vb* 158, 259
home in on *vb* 200
homeland *n* 790
homeless *adj* 161
homelessness *n* 161
homeliness *n* 509

home-loving *adj* 235
homely *adj* 509
home-made *adj* 625
homemaker *n* 333
homeopathic *adj* 596
homeopathy *n* 596
home rule *n* 667
homesick *adj* 735
homesickness *n* 735
homespun *adj* 509
homestead *n* 165
home stretch *n* 62
home town *n* 165
home truths *n* 3, 478, 826
homework *n* 476, 559
homeworking *n* 149
homicidal *adj* 150, 324
homicide *n* 147, 324
homily *n* 532
hominid *n* 330
hominoid *adj* 330
homoeostasis *n* 131
homoeostatic *adj* 25, 131
homogeneity *n* 15, 39
homogeneous *adj* 15, 39
homogenize *vb* 15, 17, 38, 45
homonym *n* 496
homophone *n* 496
homo sapiens *n* 330
homosexual *adj* 73, *n* 73, 332
homunculus *n* 169
hone *vb* 296, 584
honest *adj* 478, 817, 831, 837
honest-to-goodness *adj* 478
honesty *n* 478, 831, 837
honey *n* 318, 345, 800
honey-coloured *adj* 389
honeycomb *n* 197
honeycombed *adj* 232
honeyed *adj* 345, 827
honeyed words *n* 551
honeymoon *n* 61, 797, *vb* 797
honeymooners *n* 797
honeysuckle *n* 349
honey-tongued *adj* 551
honk *vb* 364
honorarium *n* 631, 716, 859
honorary *adj* 4
honorific *n* 778
honour *n* 774, 823, 825, 831, 837, 859, 874, *vb* 576, 698, 716, 774, 786, 819, 821, 823, 859, 874
Honour *n* 778
honourable *adj* 821, 831, 850

Honourable *n* 778
honourable mention *n* 650
honourable person *n* 831
honouring *n* 786
honour one's obligations *vb* 688
honour(s) *n* 650
hooch *n* 267
hood *n* 202, 378, *vb* 202, 378
hoodlum *n* 838
hoodoo *n* 876
hoodwink *vb* 371, 480
hoodwinked *adj* 480
hoofer *n* 524
hoof it *vb* 236
hook *n* 192, 220, *vb* 40, 192, 220
hooked *adj* 220
hook, line, and sinker *adv* 47, 49
hookup *n* 40, 42
hooligan *n* 147, 662
hooliganism *n* 147
hooray *n* 746
hooray Henry *n* 776
hoot *n* 357, 363, *vb* 357, 363, 744
hooter *n* 97, 602
hop *n* 274, 524, 789, *vb* 274
hop, step, and jump *n* 173
hope *n* 450, 748, *vb* 553, 748
hope against hope *vb* 748
hoped for *adj* 450
hope for *vb* 450
hopeful *adj* 425, 450, 742, 748, 755, *n* 748
hopefulness *n* 742
hopeless *adj* 749, 842
hopeless case *n* 424, 749
hopelessness *n* 424, 749
hopper *n* 167
hopping mad *adj* 802
hopscotch *n* 761
horde *n* 86, 570
horizon *n* 172, 191, 211
horizontal *adj* 191, 222, *n* 222
horizontality *n* 191, 222
horizontally *adv* 191
horn *n* 228, 289, 602
horn of plenty *n* 152
hornpipe *n* 524
horny *adj* 289
horological *adj* 97
horology *n* 97
horoscope *n* 104, 284, 455
horrible *adj* 583, 764
horrid *adj* 583, 796
horrified *adj* 750

horrify *vb* 737
horrifying *adj* 750
horror *n* 750, 764
hors de combat *adv* 142
hors d'oeuvres *n* 267
horse *n* 326, 849
horse-/greyhound-racing *n* 554
horse opera *n* 525
horseplay *n* 772
horsepower *n* 141
horseracing *n* 761
horse sense *n* 396, 444
horseshoe *n* 221
horse-trading *n* 685
horsewhip *n* 861
horticultural *adj* 327, 329
horticulturalist *n* 329
horticulture *n* 329
hose down *vb* 305
hospice *n* 165
hospitable *adj* 261, 265, 725, 789
hospitality *n* 261, 265, 725, 793
host *n* 29, 66, 86, 789, 863, *vb* 789
hostage *n* 671, 687, 706
hostel *n* 165
hostelry *n* 165
hostess *n* 789
hostile *adj* 14, 258, 538, 632, 635, 645, 656, 794, 796, 806, 826
hostile act *n* 794
hostile witness *n* 421
hostilities *n* 643, 645, 794
hostility *n* 14, 632, 645, 794, 796, 815, 826
hot *adj* 307, 339, 344, 367, 853
hot air *n* 4, 459, 482, 530, 771
hot and bothered *adj* 281
hotbed *n* 132
hot blood *n* 732
hotchpotch *n* 38, 419
hotel *n* 165
hot-foot it *vb* 245
hot-gospeller *n* 872
hothead *n* 147, 635, 662, 753
hot-headed *adj* 732, 753
hot-headedness *n* 753
hothouse *n* 329
hot line *n* 42
hot metal *n* 514
hot off the press *adj* 106, 615
hot potato *n* 635
hot under the collar *adj* 802
hot up *vb* 33
hound *n* 326, *vb* 794, 806

hound's tooth *n* 766
hour *n* 90, 92
hourglass *n* 97, 181
house *n* 165, 284, 330, 657, 776, *vb* 160
house arrest *n* 668
houseboat *n* 165
housebound *adj* 235
housebreaker *n* 263, 838
housebreaking *n* 705
household *adj* 164, *n* 164
householder *n* 164, 692
household name *n* 470
househusband *n* 332
housekeeper *n* 571, 613, 622, 666, 668
house of cards *n* 144
house of God *n* 882
house of ill repute *n* 851
house of prayer *n* 882
house-proud *adj* 779
housetrained *adj* 268, 326
housewarming *n* 61
house-warming party *n* 761
housewife *n* 333, 777
housing *n* 165
housing association *n* 693
housing estate/scheme *n* 165
hovel *n* 165
hover *vb* 184, 238, 286
hovercraft *n* 243
howitzer *n* 649
howl *n* 363, 682, *vb* 363, 364, 682
howler *n* 441
HP *n* 702
hub *n* 63, 199, 200, 259
hubbub *n* 56, 355, 363
huddle *n* 66, *vb* 66, 173
hue *n* 5, 68, 381
huff *n* 802, *vb* 306
hug *n* 43, 695, 791, 793, 800, *vb* 43, 173, 181, 695, 791, 800
huge *adj* 29, 168
hugely *adv* 29
hugeness *n* 168
hulk *n* 168
hulking *adj* 29, 168
hullabaloo *n* 56, 355, 732
hum *n* 356, 358, *vb* 350, 358, 364
human *adj* 322, 330, *n* 322
human being *n* 330
human condition *n* 322
human cry *n* 363
humane *adj* 660, 807
humanism *n* 869

humanistic *adj* 869
humanitarian *adj* 805, 807, *n* 805, 807
humanitarianism *n* 807
humanity *n* 330, 660, 805, 807, 809
humankind *n* 330
humanoid *adj* 330, *n* 330
human race *n* 330
human rights *n* 819
humble *adj* 30, 642, 777, 780, 823, 833, 872, *vb* 277, 823
humbleness *n* 780
humble oneself *vb* 780, 874
humbug *n* 771, 771
humdrum *adj* 509, 762
humid *adj* 308
humidify *vb* 308
humidity *n* 308
humilation *n* 277
humiliate *vb* 824
humiliated *adj* 775
humiliating *adj* 277, 775, 824
humiliation *n* 775, 824
humility *n* 432, 642, 780, 823, 872
hummable *adj* 365
humorist *n* 744
humorous *adj* 744
humour *n* 5, 544, 744, *vb* 742
hump *n* 225, 226, 228, *vb* 241, 617
hump-back *n* 221
humped *adj* 228
hunch *n* 277, 401, 456, *vb* 185, 277
hunch-backed *adj* 219
hunched *adj* 185
hundred *n* 84
hundredfold *adv* 84
hundredweight *n* 23
hung *adj* 766
hunger *n* 755, 845, *vb* 755
hunger strike *n* 845
hung jury *n* 25
hungover *adj* 844
hungry *adj* 755, 845
hung-up *adj* 735
hunk *n* 48
hunt *n* 555, 761, *vb* 555, 761
hunter *n* 97, 326, 555
huntsman *n* 555
hurdle *n* 630, *vb* 274
hurdler *n* 274
hurl *vb* 147, 247, 255
hurrah *n* 363, 746
hurricane *n* 147, 307, 316
hurried *adj* 615
hurry *n* 245, 615, *vb* 245, 609, 615

hurry up *vb* 615
hurt *adj* 337, 595, 802, *n* 337, 566,
 595, 604, 802, 836, *vb* 337, 566, 595,
 604, 806, 818
hurtful *adj* 604, 836
hurtfulness *n* 604
hurtle *vb* 147, 245
husband *n* 332, 797, *vb* 726
husbandry *n* 726
hush *n* 235, 354, *vb* 354
hushed *adj* 354, 356
hush-hush *adj* 467
hush up *vb* 467
husk *n* 37, 202, *vb* 203
huskiness *n* 362, 527
husky *adj* 362, 527, 763
hussar *n* 648
hussy *n* 838
hustle *vb* 234, 245, 615
hustling *adj* 615
hutch *n* 165, 328
hybrid *adj* 38, 328, *n* 38
hydrant *n* 305
hydrate *vb* 305
hydrated *adj* 305
hydration *n* 305
hydroelectricity *n* 141, 341
hydrofoil *n* 243
hydrogen bomb *n* 649
hydrography *n* 284, 310
hydrology *n* 310
hydrotherapy *n* 305
hygiene *n* 39, 586, 590
hygienic *adj* 39, 586, 590, 598
hygienist *n* 590
hymn *n* 367, 521, 874
hymn book *n* 881
hype *n* 431, 470, 482, *vb* 431, 470,
 482
hyperbole *n* 272, 431, 458, 482
hyperbolic *adj* 431, 482
hypercorrect *adj* 501
hypercorrection *n* 501
hypercritical *adj* 826
hypermarket *n* 710
hypersensitive *adj* 334, 730
hypersensitivity *n* 334, 401, 730
hypnosis *n* 731, 877
hypnotic *adj* 139
hypnotism *n* 139, 877
hypnotize *vb* 139, 877
hypnotized *adj* 731
hypocrisy *n* 481, 543, 827, 873
hypocrite *n* 480, 827, 873

hypocritical *adj* 479, 481, 543, 771,
 873
hypothermia *n* 340
hypothesis *n* 134, 400, 408, 456
hypothesize *vb* 134, 398, 400, 416, 456
hypothetical *adj* 134, 400, 408, 416,
 423, 456
hysteria *n* 447
hysterical *adj* 147, 447, 729, 732
hysterics *n* 73

I

ICBM *n* 649
ice *n* 305, 340, 379, 603, *vb* 340, 345
iceberg *n* 731
icebox *n* 340
ice-cold *adj* 340
iced *adj* 345, 603
ice hockey *n* 761
ice up *vb* 340
I Ching *n* 455
icicle *n* 192, 340
iciness *n* 340
icing *n* 345
icon *n* 488, 875
iconoclasm *n* 73
iconoclast *n* 73
iconoclastic *adj* 73
iconolatry *n* 875
icy *adj* 340
ID *n* 271, 485
idea *n* 408, 456, 457
ideal *adj* 2, 4, 283, 408, 584, *n* 584
idealism *n* 283
idealist *n* 807
idealistic *adj* 457, 831
idealize *vb* 4, 283, 457
ideally *adv* 4
idée fixe *n* 408
identical *adj* 13, 15, 25
identifiable *adj* 485
identification *n* 433, 485, 497
identified *adj* 485
identify *vb* 68, 433, 485, 497
identifying *adj* 485
identifying sign *n* 485
identikit *adj* 72
identity *n* 13, 15, 25, 485
ideogram *n* 495, 513
ideology *n* 434
idiom *n* 494, 499, 502
idiomatic *adj* 70, 494
idiosyncrasy *n* 70, 485

idiosyncratic *adj* 70, 485, 502
idiot *n* 397, 445
idiotic *adj* 445, 772
idle *adj* 146, 235, 565, 608, 610, *vb* 90, 136, 146, 610
idleness *n* 608
idler *n* 556, 838
idle rich *n* 610, 712
idol *n* 763, 795, 862, 875
idolater *n* 869, 875
idolatrize *vb* 875
idolatrous *adj* 869, 875
idolatry *n* 869, 875
idolism *n* 875
idolization *n* 875
idolize *vb* 874, 875
idolizer *n* 875
idol-maker *n* 875
idol-worship *n* 875
idol-worshipper *n* 875
idol-worshipping *adj* 875
ignis fatuus *n* 4, 370
ignition *n* 339
ignoble *adj* 832
ignominious *adj* 775, 832
ignominy *n* 775
ignoramus *n* 439
ignorance *n* 399, 439
ignorant *adj* 399, 439, 839
ignore *vb* 352, 399, 407, 680, 731, 790, 792, 813
ilk *n* 68
ill *adj* 589, 836, *n* 604, 836
ill-assorted *adj* 20
ill-bred *adj* 792
ill breeding *n* 792
ill-considered *adj* 399, 625, 753
ill-digested *adj* 50
ill-disposed *adj* 794
illegal *adj* 678, 818, 820, 853
illegality *n* 840, 853
illegally *adv* 853
illegibility *n* 459, 461
illegible *adj* 461
illegitimacy *n* 12, 155, 853
illegitimate *adj* 818, 820, 853
illegitimate child *n* 853
illegitimately *adv* 853
ill-equipped *adj* 560
ill-favoured *adj* 764
ill feeling *n* 794, 796
ill-fitting *adj* 764
ill health *n* 589
ill humour *n* 802, 804

ill-humoured *adj* 804
illiberal *adj* 728
illiberality *n* 728
illicit *adj* 678, 818, 820, 851, 853
illicitly *adv* 853
illiteracy *n* 439
illiterate *adj* 439
ill luck *n* 836
ill-matched *adj* 20
ill-natured *adj* 806
illness *n* 337, 589
illogical *adj* 397, 399, 401, 411
illogicality *n* 399, 401, 411
ill repute *n* 775
ill-starred *adj* 116
ill-treat *vb* 604, 806
ill turn *n* 806
illuminate *vb* 374, 462
illumination *n* 374, 438, 868
illusion *n* 4
illusionist *n* 876
illusoriness *n* 480
illusory *adj* 4, 480
illustrate *vb* 412, 488, 490
illustration *n* 412, 462, 488, 490
illustrative *adj* 412, 462, 488
illustrious *adj* 576, 774
illustriousness *n* 774
ill will *n* 739, 794, 806, 816
image *n* 394, 484, 488, 771, 875, *vb* 488
image-maker *n* 875
image-making *n* 470
image-worship *n* 875
imaginary *adj* 4, 408, 457, 479, 865
imagination *n* 22, 370, 396, 408, 457
imaginative *adj* 22, 396, 398, 457
imagine *vb* 4, 22, 396, 398, 456, 457
imago *n* 326
imam *n* 879
imbalance *n* 10, 20, 26, 219
imbecile *n* 445
imbecility *n* 397
imbibe *vb* 267
imbibing *n* 267
imbue *vb* 38, 162, 269
imitate *vb* 17, 21, 488
imitation *adj* 17, 128, *n* 17, 21, 128, 488, 702
imitative *adj* 21
imitator *n* 21
immaculate *adj* 39, 584, 831, 837, 839, 850
immaculateness *n* 39, 850

344

immanent *adj* 5, 862
immaterial *adj* 10, 283, 577
immateriality *n* 577
immature *adj* 50, 106, 111, 113, 585, 654
immaturity *n* 50, 106, 111, 113, 585, 654
immeasurable *adj* 89
immeasurably *adv* 89
immediacy *n* 96, 113
immediate *adj* 96, 113, 245
immediately *adv* 96, 101
immense *adj* 29, 168
immensely *adv* 29
immensity *n* 29, 89, 168
immerse *vb* 269, 305
immersion *n* 186
immigrant *adj* 261, 263, *n* 54, 161, 164, 263, 331
immigration *n* 263
imminence *n* 104
imminent *adj* 104, 261, 806
immobile *adj* 122, 131, 146, 235, 608
immobility *n* 122, 131, 146, 235, 608
immobilize *vb* 235
immoderate *adj* 727, 820, 844
immoderation *n* 844
immodest *adj* 783, 851
immodesty *n* 783, 851
immoral *adj* 818, 832, 838, 851
immorality *n* 832, 838, 851
immortal *adj* 89, 91, 95, 862
immortality *n* 89, 91, 95
immortalize *vb* 95
immovable *adj* 40, 122, 131, 235, 539, 542, 694
immovable feast *n* 119
immovableness *n* 122
immovables *n* 694
immune *adj* 598, 667, 822
immunity *n* 598, 667, 822
immunization *n* 590, 598
immunize *vb* 590, 598
immure *vb* 210
immutability *n* 91, 122
immutable *adj* 91, 122
imp *n* 838, 865
impact *n* 141, 247
impair *vb* 593, 595, 604, 767
impaired *adj* 593, 595, 767
impairment *n* 593, 595
impale *vb* 232, 860
impalement *n* 860
impalpability *n* 4, 283

impapable *adj* 4
impart *vb* 466
impartial *adj* 25, 27, 429, 756, 817, 831, 833
impartiality *n* 27, 429, 756, 817, 833
impassable *adj* 233
impasse *n* 233, 424
impassion *vb* 732
impassioned *adj* 729, 732
impassive *adj* 148, 403, 731, 733, 756, 810
impassiveness *n* 731
impassivity *n* 146, 148, 403, 733, 756, 760
impatience *n* 615, 729
impatient *adj* 615, 729, 730, 732, 802
impeach *vb* 826, 830
impeachment *n* 830
impeccability *n* 584, 839
impeccable *adj* 584, 837, 839
impecunious *adj* 713
impecuniousness *n* 713
impedance *n* 630
impede *vb* 630, 668
impediment *n* 628, 630
impedimenta *n* 694
impel *vb* 247, 255
impending *adj* 104, 261, 450, 806
impenetrability *n* 233, 287, 461
impenetrable *adj* 233, 287, 461
impenitence *n* 842
impenitent *adj* 842
imperative *adj* 536, 661, 664, *n* 536
imperceptibility *n* 373, 465
imperceptible *adj* 373, 465, 483
imperfect *adj* 32, 273, 585, 654, 767
imperfection *n* 273, 585, 654, 767, 851
imperial *adj* 177, *n* 765
imperil *vb* 599
imperious *adj* 781
imperishability *n* 95
imperishable *adj* 93, 95, 294
impermanence *n* 94, 121, 130
impermanent *adj* 94, 121, 130
impermeability *n* 143, 233, 287
impermeable *adj* 143, 233, 287
impersonal *adj* 756
impersonate *vb* 21, 128, 488, 498
impersonation *n* 21, 488, 498
impersonator *n* 21
impertinence *n* 781
impertinent *adj* 781, 792, 824
imperturbability *n* 731, 733
imperturbable *adj* 731, 733

imputation *n* 134, 830
impute *vb* 830
in *adj* 770
in/out of print *adj* 514
in abeyance *adj* 565, 608
in a big way *adv* 29
inability *n* 142, 625
in a body *adv* 66, 85
in absentia *adv* 163
inaccessibility *n* 172
inaccessible *adj* 172, 233, 424
in accord *adv* 19
inaccuracy *n* 407, 441, 479
inaccurate *adj* 441, 489, 818
inaction *n* 608
inactive *adj* 146, 235, 610
inactivity *n* 146, 610
in addition *adv* 35, 45
inadequacy *n* 50, 142, 144, 273, 574,
    579, 585
inadequate *adj* 50, 142, 273, 574, 585
inadmissibility *n* 546
inadmissible *adj* 52, 546
in advance *adv* 59, 98, 99, 113, 212
inadvertent *adj* 554
inadvisability *n* 581
inadvisable *adj* 581
in a flash *adv* 96
in agreement *adj* 636
inalienable *adj* 819
in all *adv* 47
in all directions *adv* 67
in all likelihood *adv* 3, 425
in all one's born days *adv* 1
inalterable *adj* 131
in a muddle *adv* 16
inane *adj* 397, 399, 443, 459
inanimate *adj* 321, 323
inanity *n* 397, 399, 443
in a nutshell *adv* 179, 505
inapposite *adj* 10
inappositeness *n* 10
inappropriate *adj* 10, 20, 512, 581,
    818, 820
inappropriateness *n* 10, 20, 512
in arrears *adj* 715, 717, 819
inarticulacy *n* 527, 529
inarticulate *adj* 527, 529
in a rush *adj* 615
in a sense *adv* 458
in a similar situation *adv* 17
in a temper *adj* 732
in a trice *adv* 245
inattention *n* 405, 449, 689, 792

inattentive *adj* 405, 407, 449, 689
inattentiveness *n* 407
inaudibility *n* 352, 356, 461
inaudible *adj* 352, 356, 461
inaugural *adj* 59, 61
inaugurate *vb* 59, 61, 672, 786
inauguration *n* 59, 61, 672, 786
inauspicious *adj* 116, 656, 749
in a word *adv* 505
in bad/poor taste *adj* 769
in between *adv* 63
in bits *adv* 41
in black and white *adv* 486
inborn *adj* 5
inbred *adj* 5, 12
inbreeding *n* 12
in brief *adv* 505
in Burke's Peerage *adj* 776
in cahoots *adv* 45
incalculable *adj* 89
incalculably *adv* 89
in camera *adv* 467
incandescence *n* 339, 383
incandescent *adj* 339, 374, 377
incantation *n* 876
incapable *adj* 625
incapacitated *adj* 142
incapacity *n* 142, 625
incarcerate *vb* 668
incarceration *n* 668
incarnate *vb* 3, 5, 282, 488
incarnation *n* 5, 282, 862, 868
incautious *adj* 753
incendiary *adj* 339, 341
incendiary bomb *n* 649
incense *n* 349, 881, *vb* 732, 802
incensed *adj* 802
incentive *n* 134
inception *n* 61
incessant *adj* 124
incessantly *adv* 95
incest *n* 12, 851
incestuous *adj* 12, 851
inch *vb* 246, 616
in charge *adj* 622
inchoate *adj* 217
in chorus *adv* 19
incident *n* 8, 101, 643
incidental *adj* 6, 8, 10, 85
incidentally *adv* 10
incidental music *n* 367
incineration *n* 339
incinerator *n* 339
incipient *adj* 61

indecency *n* 583, 769, 851
indecent *adj* 583, 769, 801, 838, 851
indecent assault *n* 851
indecent exposure *n* 205
indecipherability *n* 459, 461
indecipherable *adj* 461
indecision *n* 130, 280, 428, 541
indecisive *adj* 130, 280, 428, 541
in decline *adj* 593, *adv* 34
indecorous *adj* 769
indecorum *n* 769
in deep water *adv* 186
indefatigability *n* 540
indefatigable *adj* 294, 540
indefensible *adj* 830
indefinite *adj* 89, 217, 428, 504
indefinitely *adv* 89, 91
indefiniteness *n* 217, 428, 504
indelible *adj* 131, 448
indelicacy *n* 769
indelicate *adj* 769
in demand *adj* 558, 709, 825
indemnification *n* 704
indemnificatory *adj* 704, 814
indemnify *vb* 28, 687, 704, 814, 859
indemnity *n* 28, 687, 813, 814
indent *vb* 227, 229
indentation *n* 227, 229, 232
indented *adj* 227, 229
independence *n* 10, 44, 667
independent *adj* 41, 44, 73, 535, 667, 799, 822, *n* 667
in-depth *adj* 49, 186
indestructibility *n* 95
indestructible *adj* 95, 143
in detention *adj* 668
indeterminacy *n* 135
indeterminate *adj* 63, 217
index *n* 57, 76, 496, 516, *vb* 57, 76, 486
indexcard *n* 486
Indiaman *n* 243
Indian summer *n* 108
indiarubber *n* 293
indicate *vb* 249, 420, 484
indication *n* 420, 484
indicative *adj* 420, 484
indicator *n* 377, 484
indict *vb* 830, 856
indictment *n* 830, 856
indifference *n* 44, 335, 403, 538, 689, 733, 756, 833
indifferent *adj* 44, 146, 403, 538, 583, 610, 689, 733, 756, 833

indigence *n* 713
indigenous *adj* 164
indigent *adj* 713
indignant *adj* 802
indignation *n* 802
indignity *n* 802, 824
indigo *n* 391
indirect *adj* 195, 214, 251, 465
indirectness *n* 195
in disagreement *adj* 635
in disarray *adv* 56
indiscernible *adj* 373
indiscipline *n* 658, 753, 844
indiscreet *adj* 407, 445, 468, 753
indiscretion *n* 407, 445, 468, 753, 840
indiscriminate *adj* 419
in disorder *adv* 56
indispensable *adj* 536, 558
indisposed *adj* 589
indisposition *n* 589
in dispute *adj* 635
indissolubility *n* 79
indissoluble *adj* 79
indistinct *adj* 217, 352, 356, 360, 373, 376, 449, 529
indistinctness *n* 217, 352, 356, 360, 373, 376, 461, 529
indistinguishable *adj* 13
individual *adj* 22, 70, 79, 485, *n* 79, 322, 330
individualism *n* 44, 70, 79, 834
individualist *adj* 44, *n* 834
individualistic *adj* 70
individuality *n* 22, 70, 485
individuate *vb* 70
indivisibility *n* 79
indivisible *adj* 43, 79
in dock *adv* 142
indoctrinate *vb* 72, 475
indoctrination *n* 72, 475
indolence *n* 146, 610
indolent *adj* 146, 610
indomitability *n* 143
indomitable *adj* 143, 539
indoor *adj* 199
indoors *adv* 199
in dribs and drabs *adv* 48, 65, 87
in droves *adv* 86
induce *vb* 551
inducement *n* 132, 134, 551
induct *vb* 263, 475, 672, 786
induction *n* 263, 400, 475, 672, 786, 878
inductive *adj* 400

inflamed *adj* 737
inflammable *adj* 339, 341
inflammation *n* 170, 589, 737
inflatable *n* 286
inflate *vb* 33, 170, 225, 306, 482, 825
inflated *adj* 170, 306, 482, 510
inflatedness *n* 482
inflation *n* 33, 170, 723
inflationary *adj* 33, 723
inflationary spiral *n* 723
inflect *vb* 121, 500, 526
inflection *n* 121, 500, 526
inflexibility *n* 122, 222, 289, 542, 659
inflexible *adj* 122, 222, 289, 539, 542, 659, 810
in-flight *adj* 238
in flight *adv* 238
inflorescence *n* 327
influence *n* 132, 136, 139, 141, 257, 657, 876, *vb* 136, 138, 139, 140, 257, 729
influenced *adj* 729
influential *adj* 31, 132, 136, 138, 139, 141, 576, 657
influenza *n* 589
influx *n* 263
info *n* 466
in force *adv* 141
inform *vb* 5, 438, 466, 602, 830
informal *adj* 788
informality *n* 788
informant *n* 466
information *n* 420, 438, 466, 602
information retrieval *n* 75, 570
informative *adj* 466, 468, 471
informed *adj* 438, 466
informer *n* 466, 830
inform on *vb* 466
infraction *n* 272
infra dig *adj* 775
infrastructure *n* 189, 216, 298
infrequency *n* 87, 118, 183, 288
infrequent *adj* 87, 118, 183, 288
infrequently *adv* 87, 118
infringe *vb* 272, 662, 689, 818, 820, 853
infringement *n* 272, 662, 689, 853
in front *adv* 59, 212
in full view *adv* 372
infuriate *vb* 147, 802
infuriated *adj* 802
infuriating *adj* 597
infuse *vb* 38, 269
infusion *n* 38, 267, 303

in future *adv* 104
in general *adv* 27, 69
ingenious *adj* 457, 626
ingénue *n* 627
ingenuity *n* 457, 626
ingenuous *adj* 478, 627, 831
ingenuousness *n* 478, 627
ingest *vb* 166, 199, 267
ingestion *n* 199, 265, 267
inglorious *adj* 775
in good health *adj* 588
in good heart *adj* 742
in good taste *adj* 768
ingrained *adj* 5, 131, 199, 549
ingratiate oneself *vb* 782, 827
ingratiating *adj* 782, 791, 827
ingratiation *n* 782, 791
ingratitude *n* 812
ingredient *n* 35, 48, 53, 282
ingredients *n* 166
ingress *n* 263
in-group *n* 52, 634
ingrown *adj* 199
inhabit *vb* 158, 162, 165
inhabitant *n* 164
inhabited *adj* 164
inhalation *n* 316
inhale *vb* 199, 316, 347
in hand *adj* 565, 570, *adv* 37
inharmonious *adj* 366
inhere *vb* 5, 53
inherent *adj* 5, 53
inherit *vb* 690, 697, 699
inheritance *n* 100, 690, 697, 719
inherited *adj* 12, 133
inheritor *n* 100, 699
inherit the mantle of *vb* 100
inhibit *vb* 668
inhibited *adj* 668, 784
inhibition *n* 784
in hock *adj* 687
in-house *adj* 162, 199
inhuman *adj* 731, 806
inhumanity *n* 806, 810
inimical *adj* 794
inimitable *adj* 22, 70
iniquity *n* 838
in irons *adj* 668
initial *adj* 59, 61, *n* 495, *vb* 485, 495
initially *adv* 61
initials *n* 485
initiate *vb* 59, 61, 132, 263, 265, 475
initiation *n* 59, 61, 263, 265, 475
initiative *n* 59, 145, 607

initiatory *adj* 59, 61, 265
inject *vb* 269, 596, 849
injection *n* 199, 269, 596
in jeopardy *adj* 599
injunction *n* 71, 623, 661
injure *vb* 150, 337, 593, 595, 604, 806, 818
injured *adj* 337, 593, 595
injured party *n* 839
injurious *adj* 150, 604, 818
injury *n* 337, 593, 595, 604, 818, 836
injustice *n* 26, 430, 802, 818, 853
ink *n* 384, *vb* 490
in keeping *adv* 15, 19, 72
in kind *adv* 129
inkiness *n* 384
inkling *n* 456
inky *adj* 375, 384
inlaid *adj* 766
inland *adj* 311, *n* 311
inland revenue *n* 721
inland sea *n* 312
in-laws *n* 12
inlay *n* 201, 269, *vb* 201, 269, 766
in league *adj* 633, *adv* 40, 45
inlet *n* 263, 310
in lieu *adv* 28, 128
in limbo *adv* 161, 198
in line *adv* 15, 57, 72
in loco parentis *adv* 154
in love *adj* 795
inmate *n* 164, 199, 671
in mind *adv* 398
in mint condition *adv* 106
in moderation *adv* 148
in mothballs *adj* 565
in motion *adj* 609, *adv* 234
inn *n* 165
in name *adv* 4
in name only *adj* 497
innards *n* 53, 199
innate *adj* 5
in need *adj* 558, *adv* 558
inner *adj* 199
inner circle *n* 52
inner city *n* 157
inner man *n* 199
innermost *adj* 199
innings *n* 92
innocence *n* 627, 837, 839, 857
innocent *adj* 509, 627, 831, 837, 839, 850, 857, *n* 627, 839
innocent party *n* 839
innocuous *adj* 839

innocuousness *n* 148
innovate *vb* 106
innovation *n* 22, 106, 121
innovative *adj* 22, 59, 106, 121, 132
innovator *n* 22
innuendo *n* 465, 744, 828
innumerable *adj* 86, 89
inoculate *vb* 269, 590
inoculation *n* 269, 590, 596
inoffensive *adj* 780, 839
inoffensiveness *n* 780
in office *adj* 657
in one fell swoop *adv* 47, 96
in one piece *adj* 598
in one's absence *adv* 163
in ones and twos *adv* 87
in one's element *adv* 19
in one's lifetime *adv* 1
in one's own time *adv* 612
in one's place/stead *adv* 128
in one's right mind *adj* 847
in one's shoes *adv* 128
in operation *adj* 607, *adv* 141
inoperative *adj* 608
inopportune *adj* 20, 98, 116, 581
inopportunely *adv* 116
inopportuneness *n* 116
in orbit *adv* 238
in order *adv* 55, 57, 60
inordinate *adj* 482, 575
inorganic *adj* 321
in parallel *adv* 194
in parenthesis *adv* 10
in part *adv* 48
in particular *adv* 70
in partnership *adv* 45
in-patient *n* 164
in person *adv* 162
in phase *adv* 19, 103
in pieces *adv* 41
in place *adv* 19, 57, 72, 159, 160
in plain English *adv* 509
in point of fact *adv* 1
in poor health *adj* 589
in position *adv* 160
in possession of one's senses *adj* 847
in power *adj* 657, *adv* 141
in practice *adv* 3
in preparation *adj* 559, *adv* 50
in private *adv* 467
in profit *adv* 35
in proportion *adv* 9
in public *adv* 464
in pursuit *adj* 555

input *n* 570, *vb* 75
in quarantine *adj* 598
inquest *n* 323, 414, 417, 856
inquiring mind *n* 402
inquiry *n* 856
inquisition *n* 414
inquisitive *adj* 402, 414, 755
inquisitiveness *n* 402, 755
inquisitor *n* 860
inquisitorial *adj* 402
in rags *adj* 713
in readiness *adj* 559
in reality *adv* 3
in relation to *prep* 9
in reserve *adj* 565, 570
in return *adv* 129
in reverse *adv* 254
inroad *n* 263
in rotation *adv* 119
ins and outs *n* 70
insane *adj* 58, 445, 447
insanitary *adj* 591
insanity *n* 58, 445, 447
insatiability *n* 846
insatiable *adj* 755, 846
insatiable appetite *n* 846
inscribe *vb* 76, 263, 265
inscription *n* 499, 513
inscrutable *adj* 459, 461
in secret *adv* 467
insect *n* 326
insectivorous *adj* 326
insecure *adj* 144, 599
insecurity *n* 144, 599
inseminate *vb* 152
insemination *n* 152
insensibility *n* 335, 731
insensible *adj* 335, 731
insensitive *adj* 289, 297, 335, 419,
731, 756, 792, 842
insensitivity *n* 289, 297, 335, 419, 731,
756
insentience *n* 731
insentient *adj* 731
inseparable *adj* 5, 43, 85, 173, 793
in sequence *adv* 60
insert *n* 269, *vb* 35, 166, 269
inserted *adj* 269
insertion *n* 35, 199, 269
in service *adj* 666
inset *vb* 269
in seventh heaven *adj* 734
inshore *adj* 310
inshore waters *n* 310

in short *adv* 179
in short supply *adj* 574
inside *adj* 199, 668, *adv* 199, *n* 199
inside out *adv* 14, 126, 196
insider *n* 199
insides *n* 53, 166, 199
insidious *adj* 465, 604, 832
insidiousness *n* 465
insight *n* 370, 396, 401, 418, 444, 457
insightful *adj* 444
insignia *n* 484, 657
insignificance *n* 30, 459, 577
insignificant *adj* 30, 459, 577
insincere *adj* 479, 481, 771, 827, 832,
873
insincerity *n* 479, 481, 771, 827
insinuate *vb* 465
insinuation *n* 465, 828, 830
insipid *adj* 144, 148, 343, 382, 483,
508
insipidness *n* 144, 343, 382, 483, 508
insist *vb* 536, 659
insistence *n* 473, 507
insistent *adj* 473, 507, 681
insist on *vb* 422, 473, 507, 685
insist on one's rights *vb* 819
in situ *adv* 159
in snatches *adv* 48
insobriety *n* 848
insolence *n* 779, 781, 792
insolent *adj* 781, 792, 824
insoluble *adj* 424
insolvency *n* 652, 713, 717
insolvent *adj* 652, 713, 717, *n* 713
in some degree *adv* 24, 48
in someone's wake *adv* 85
in someone's wake/train *adv* 60
insouciance *n* 403
insouciant *adj* 403
inspect *vb* 370, 404, 414, 720
inspection *n* 370, 404, 414
inspector *n* 622
inspiration *n* 134, 433, 732, 868
inspire *vb* 132, 134, 732, 751
inspired *adj* 134, 507, 732, 868
inspiring *adj* 732
instability *n* 16, 94, 121, 130, 144,
544, 732
install *vb* 160, 672, 786
installation *n* 160, 614, 672, 878
installed *adj* 160
instalment *n* 48, 64, 716
instalment plan *n* 702
instant *adj* 96, 559

in the end *adv* 62, 93, 114
in the event *adv* 8
in the eyes of the law *adv* 852
in the family way *adv* 152
in the final analysis *adv* 62
in the first place *adv* 61
in the forefront *adv* 212
in the fullness of time *adv* 104
in the interim *adv* 90
in the long run *adv* 62, 93, 104
in the main *adv* 69
in the meantime *adv* 90
in the middle of nowhere *adv* 172
in the money *adj* 712
in the nick of time *adv* 114, 115
in the nude *adv* 205
in the offing *adv* 104
in the open *adv* 198
in theory *adv* 4
in the past *adv* 105
in the present situation *adv* 7
in the raw *adv* 205
in the rear *adv* 213
in the red *adj* 715, *adv* 36
in the region of *adv* 23
in the right ballpark *adv* 23
in the same boat *adv* 17, 45
in the same breath *adv* 103
in the same way *adv* 13
in the stocks *adj* 668
in the style/manner of *adv* 17
in this day and age *adv* 101
intimacy *n* 40, 173, 793
intimate *adj* 40, 173, 199, 793, *n* 793, 795, *vb* 623
intimation *n* 466, 623
in time *adv* 90
intimidate *vb* 552, 659, 750, 806
intimidating *adj* 552
intimidation *n* 552, 750, 806
into action *adv* 136
into force *adv* 136
intolerance *n* 181, 430, 659, 732
intolerant *adj* 181, 430, 659, 732, 806
intonation *n* 353, 365, 526
intone *vb* 368, 526
into operation *adv* 136
into pieces *adv* 46
into play *adv* 136
into smithereens *adv* 46
into the bargain *adv* 33, 35
in tow *adv* 85
in town *adv* 162
intoxicate *vb* 145, 604, 848

intoxicated *adj* 732, 848
intoxication *n* 732, 848
intractability *n* 289, 542, 662
intractable *adj* 289, 542, 662
intransigence *n* 542, 659
intransigent *adj* 539, 542
in transit *adv* 234, 239
intrepid *adj* 751
intrepidity *n* 751
intricacy *n* 224
intricate *adj* 56, 197, 224, 504, 766
intrigue *n* 469, 557, 626, 795, *vb* 469, 557, 626, 732
intrinsic *adj* 5, 53
intrinsically *adv* 5
in triplicate *adv* 82
introduce *vb* 35, 54, 59, 106, 207, 265, 269, 791, 793
introduction *n* 59, 61, 199, 265, 269, 791
introduction fee *n* 721
introductory *adj* 59, 61, 265
intromission *n* 199
introspect *vb* 398
introspection *n* 199, 398
introspective *adj* 199, 398
introversion *n* 199, 790
introverted *adj* 199, 790
intrude *vb* 54, 116, 272
intruder *n* 54, 263
in true *adv* 222
intrusion *n* 116, 263, 272
intrusive *adj* 116, 207, 263, 272
intuit *vb* 399, 401
intuition *n* 396, 397, 399, 401, 877
intuitive *adj* 396, 397, 399, 401
in tune *adj* 365, *adv* 19
in turn *adv* 11, 60, 64, 119
in twain *adv* 41
in two *adv* 41
inundate *vb* 147, 305, 314
inundation *n* 575
in unison *adv* 19, 79, 103
inured *adj* 549, 731
in use *adj* 564
inutility *n* 579
invade *vb* 263, 272, 639, 645
invader *n* 263, 639, 794
invalid *adj* 142, 144, 673, 820, *n* 144
invalidate *vb* 2, 4, 142, 413, 673, 820
invalidated *adj* 413
invalidation *n* 413, 673
invalidism *n* 144
invaluable *adj* 578

invariability *n* 122, 131
invariable *adj* 122, 131
invasion *n* 263, 272, 639, 645
invasive *adj* 263, 272
invective *n* 801
inveigh against *vb* 801
inveigle *vb* 827
invent *vb* 4, 22, 106, 149, 398, 433,
  457, 479, 830
invention *n* 149, 408, 433, 479
inventive *adj* 22, 132, 149, 457
inventiveness *n* 22, 457
inventor *n* 22, 132, 149
inventorize *vb* 76
inventory *n* 57, 76, 486
inverse *adj* 14, 196, *n* 215
inversely *adv* 196
inversion *n* 196
invert *vb* 196
invertebrate *n* 326
inverted *adj* 126, 196
invest *vb* 570, 639, 672, 701, 718
investigate *vb* 414, 433
investigation *n* 414
investigative *adj* 414, 433
investigator *n* 203
invest in *vb* 708
investiture *n* 672
investment *n* 570, 639, 672, 694, 701,
  718
investment surcharge *n* 721
investor *n* 701, 714
in view *adv* 104, 173
invigorate *vb* 141, 143, 145, 322
invigorating *adj* 145, 588, 620
invigoration *n* 620
inviolable *adj* 819
invisibility *n* 373, 465
invisible *adj* 373, 395, 465
invitation *n* 679, 681, 732, 791
invite *n* 681, *vb* 679, 681, 789, 791
invite tenders *vb* 679
inviting *adj* 261, 265
invocation *n* 532, 681, 874, 876
in vogue *adj* 770
invoice *n* 720, *vb* 720
invoke *vb* 532, 681, 874
involuntary *adj* 401, 536, 548, 554
involve *vb* 9, 197, 830
involved *adj* 56, 197, 224, 504, 628
involvement *n* 840
invulnerability *n* 143, 598
invulnerable *adj* 143, 598, 731
in want *adv* 558

inward-looking *adj* 199
inwardly *adv* 199
in words of one syllable *adj* 503, *adv*
  509
iota *n* 78
IOU *n* 683, 711
IQ *n* 396, 397
irascibility *n* 301, 803
irascible *adj* 803, 804
irate *adj* 802
ire *n* 802
iridescence *n* 374, 393
iridescent *adj* 393
irk *vb* 628, 762
irksome *adj* 737, 762
iron *n* 143, 191, 289, 292, 569
Iron Curtain *n* 52
ironic *adj* 744, 773
iron out *vb* 191, 222, 292
iron will *n* 539
irony *n* 744, 773, 826
irradiate *vb* 374, 604
irrational *adj* 397, 399, 401, 544
irrationality *n* 399, 401
irreconcilable *adj* 794
irrecoverable *adj* 691
irredeemable *adj* 749, 842
irreducible *adj* 39
irrefutable *adj* 412, 420
irregular *adj* 16, 65, 118, 120, 219,
  550, 818, *n* 648
irregularity *n* 16, 65, 118, 120, 219,
  550, 818
irregularly *adv* 120
irrelevance *n* 6, 10, 54, 459, 577
irrelevancy *n* 20
irrelevant *adj* 6, 10, 20, 54, 459, 577
irreligion *n* 869, 875
irreligious *adj* 869, 873, 880
irreproachability *n* 584, 839
irreproachable *adj* 584, 837
irresistible *adj* 257, 664
irresolute *adj* 44, 130, 144, 280, 428,
  541
irresolution *n* 44, 130, 428, 541
irresponsibility *n* 753
irresponsible *adj* 445, 544, 689, 753,
  853
irretrievable *adj* 691
irreverence *n* 824, 873
irreverent *adj* 824, 873
irreversible *adj* 105, 253
irrevocability *n* 749
irrevocable *adj* 105, 749

irrigate *vb* 152, 305, 328
irrigation *n* 152, 305
irrigator *n* 305
irritability *n* 730, 732, 803
irritable *adj* 730, 732, 803
irritant *adj* 301, *n* 597
irritate *vb* 301, 737, 741, 802
irritated *adj* 802, 803
irritating *adj* 737
irritation *n* 301, 739, 741, 802
irrupt *vb* 263
Islam *n* 868
island *n* 311
isle *n* 311
islet *n* 311
isochronous *adj* 103
isolate *vb* 41, 70, 79, 790, 860
isolated *adj* 79, 790
isolated instance *n* 79
isolation *n* 79, 790
isolationism *n* 41, 79
isolationist *adj* 41, 79, *n* 790
issue *n* 12, 48, 60, 100, 155, 264, 409,
 vb 133, 264, 711
issue a writ *vb* 661
isthmus *n* 42, 181, 311
italic *adj* 495, 513, *n* 495
itch *n* 338, 755, *vb* 755
itchiness *n* 281
itching *adj* 450, 755
itchy *adj* 281, 337
item *n* 48, 79
itemize *vb* 70
itinerant *adj* 236
itinerary *n* 236
ivory *n* 383
ivory tower *n* 79

J

jab *n* 561, 596, *vb* 561
jabber *vb* 459, 530
jack *n* 276, 332
jacket *n* 202, 210
jack of all trades *n* 49
jack of all trades and master of none
 n 625
jack o' lantern *n* 4
jackpot *n* 690
jack up *vb* 276
jacuzzi *n* 586
jade *n* 390, *vb* 575, 762
jaded *adj* 575, 762
jagged *adj* 220, 229, 291, 296

jaggedness *n* 291, 296
jail *n* 671, 861, *vb* 860
jail/gaolbird *n* 671
jailer *n* 668
jalousie *n* 378
jam *n* 123, 630, *vb* 235
jam-packed *adj* 49
jam session *n* 367
jangle *n* 359, 362, *vb* 359, 362, 366
jangling *adj* 366
jangly *adj* 362
janitor *n* 666, 668
January sales *n* 709
jar *n* 281, *vb* 20, 247, 281, 362, 366
jargon *n* 459, 461, 494
jarring *adj* 20, 362, 366, 512
jasmine *n* 389
jasper *n* 393
jaundice *n* 389
jaundiced *adj* 452, 804, 815
jaunt *n* 236, 761
javelin *n* 649
jaw *n* 530
jazz *n* 367
jazz-rock *n* 367
jazzy *adj* 367
jealous *adj* 739, 802, 815, 816, 834
jealousy *n* 815
jeer *n* 824, *vb* 682, 773
jeer at *vb* 824
jeers *n* 682
Jehovah *n* 862
jejune *adj* 508
jejuneness *n* 508
jelly *n* 182, 318, 649
jellyfish *n* 144
jemmy *n* 568
jeopardize *vb* 599
jeopardy *n* 599
jerk *n* 281, *vb* 247, 256, 281
jerkiness *n* 65, 120, 281
jerky *adj* 65, 120, 281
jeroboam *n* 167
jersey *n* 569
jest *n* 744, *vb* 744
jester *n* 744
Jesuitical *adj* 411
Jesus Christ *n* 862
jet *n* 244, 314, 384, 766, *vb* 238, 264
jet-black *adj* 384
jet engine *n* 568
jet set *n* 770
jetsetter *n* 770
jetstream *n* 316

jettison *vb* 286, 696
jewel *n* 766, 800
jeweller *n* 613
jewellery *n* 766
jib *n* 192, *vb* 538, 682
jig *n* 367, 524
jiggery-pokery *n* 480
jigsaw *n* 45, 761
jihad *n* 645
jilt *vb* 452
jingle *n* 359, 521, *vb* 359
jingling *adj* 359
jingoism *n* 331
jingoistic *adj* 331
jink *vb* 195
jinx *n* 656, 876
jitterbug *vb* 524
jitters *n* 281
jittery *adj* 281, 732, 750
jive *n* 524, 761, *vb* 524
job *n* 562, 607, 611
jobber *n* 613, 707
jobbing *n* 707
job half-done *n* 654
job losses *n* 673
job lot *n* 38
Job's comforter *n* 749
job-sharing *n* 45
Jock *n* 331
jocular *adj* 742, 744
jocularity *n* 742, 744
Joe Bloggs *n* 27, 69, 777
jog *n* 236, 616, *vb* 234, 236, 247, 616, 761
jogger *n* 236
jogging *n* 617, 761
jog the memory *vb* 448
John Doe *n* 777
joie de vivre *n* 145, 742
join *vb* 40, 43, 634, 797
joiner *n* 613
join forces *vb* 40, 45, 66
join in *vb* 633
join on *vb* 35
joint *adj* 19, 40, 45, 633, 634, 693, *n* 40, 849
joint account *n* 693
joint/concerted effort *n* 633
joint effort *n* 45
jointly owned *adj* 693
join together *vb* 633
joint ownership *n* 693
joint possession *n* 693
joist *n* 193, 569

joke *n* 744, *vb* 744
joker *n* 744
jokey *adj* 744
joking *adj* 744, *n* 744
jollity *n* 734, 742
jolly *adj* 734, 742, 761
jolly along *vb* 742
jolt *n* 247, 281, *vb* 247, 281, 451
jonquil *n* 389
joss stick *n* 349
jostle *vb* 173, 824
jot *n* 30, 78, *vb* 208, 513
jot down *vb* 486
jottings *n* 50, 486
journal *n* 97, 471, 486, 720
journalism *n* 471, 513
journalist *n* 471, 613
journey *n* 236, 271, *vb* 236, 271
journey's end *n* 236, 261
joust *n* 643
jovial *adj* 742, 761
joviality *n* 742
jowls *n* 192
joy *n* 734, 736
joyful *adj* 734
joylessness *n* 743
joyous *adj* 734
jubilant *adj* 746
jubilation *n* 746
jubilee *n* 92, 786
Judaism *n* 868
judder *n* 281, *vb* 281
judge *n* 429, 665, 854, *vb* 418, 429, 854, 856, 858
judged *adj* 840
judgment *n* 396, 418, 429, 856, 862, 867
judgmental *adj* 429
judicatory *adj* 429
judicature *n* 856
judicial *adj* 429, 854
judicial assembly *n* 855
judiciary *adj* 854
judicious *adj* 406, 418, 429
judiciousness *n* 406
judo *n* 643
jug *n* 167, 671
juggernaut *n* 150, 191, 242
juggler *n* 876
juice *n* 303
juiciness *n* 303, 317
juicy *adj* 303, 317
ju-jitsu *n* 643

K

keep oneself to oneself *vb* 790
keep one's eyes skinned/peeled *vb* 370
keep one's fingers crossed *vb* 748
keep one's hair/shirt on *vb* 733
keep one's head down *vb* 754
keep one's mouth shut *vb* 531
keep one's nose clean *vb* 71
keep one's temper *vb* 733
keep open house *vb* 789
keep order *vb* 854
keep out of harm's way *vb* 598
keepsake *n* 448
keep secret *vb* 467
keep smiling *vb* 742
keep sober *vb* 843
keep tabs on *vb* 406
keep the books *vb* 720
keep the faith *vb* 872
keep the peace *vb* 644
keep the wolf from the door *vb* 712
keep to oneself *vb* 834
keep to the straight and narrow *vb* 71, 837
keep under surveillance *vb* 406, 598
keep under wraps *vb* 467
keep up *vb* 103
keep up appearances *vb* 72
keep up with the Joneses *vb* 72, 770
keep well *vb* 588
keep well out of *vb* 754
keep within bounds *vb* 843
keg *n* 167
ken *n* 438
kennel *n* 165
kerb *n* 209
kernel *n* 5, 63, 199
kerosene *n* 319, 341
ketch *n* 243
kettle *n* 167
kettledrum *n* 369
key *adj* 200, *n* 232, 365
keyboard *n* 570
keyboard instrument *n* 369
keyed up *adj* 559, 729, 732
keyhole *n* 232
key moment *n* 115
khaki *adj* 386, 390, *n* 204
khan *n* 776
kibbutz *n* 328, 693
kibbutznik *n* 693
kick *n* 255, 336, 729, 734, *vb* 247, 255, 682
kick against *vb* 638
kickback *n* 248, 859

kick back *vb* 248
kick-off *n* 61
kick off *vb* 61
kick one's heels *vb* 608
kick over the traces *vb* 73, 127, 658
kick the bucket *vb* 323
kick up a fuss *vb* 682
kick upstairs *vb* 161, 673
kid *n* 111, *vb* 744, 773
kidnap *n* 703
kidnap *vb* 395, 703, 705
kidnapper *n* 703, 705
kidnapping *n* 703, 705
kidnap victim *n* 671, 706
kidney *n* 68
kid's stuff *n* 629
kill *vb* 90, 324, 860
killer *n* 147, 150, 324
killing *adj* 617, 744, *n* 147, 324
killingly funny *adj* 744
killjoy *n* 552, 745
kill oneself *vb* 324
kill the fatted calf *vb* 261, 725, 786
kill with kindness *vb* 800
kiln *n* 339
kilo *n* 23
kind *adj* 725, 791, 793, 805, 809, 837, *n* 68
kindergarten *n* 111, 477
kindhearted *adj* 805
kindheartedness *n* 805
kindle *n* 66, *vb* 132, 145, 339, 341
kindliness *n* 791
kindling *n* 341
kindly *adj* 660, 791, 805, 837
kindness *n* 660, 791, 793, 805, 837
kind offer *n* 725
kind person *n* 805, 807
kindred *adj* 12
kindred spirit *n* 17
kinetic *adj* 234
king *n* 665, 776
kingdom *n* 157
kingdom come *n* 866
kingdom of God *n* 866
kingdom of heaven *n* 866
kingfisher blue *adj* 391
kingly *adj* 776
King of Kings *n* 862
king-size *adj* 168
king's ransom *n* 712
kink *n* 224
kinky *adj* 224, 447

labour *n* 617, *vb* 617
laboured *adj* 512
labourer *n* 149, 611, 613
labour force *n* 613
labour of love *n* 724
labour of Sisyphus *n* 654
labour-saving *adj* 726
labours of Hercules *n* 628
labyrinth *n* 56, 224
labyrinthine *adj* 56, 224
lace *n* 232, 379, 766, *vb* 38
lacerate *vb* 41, 337
lack *n* 50, 163, 273, 558, 574, 691, *vb* 50, 273, 574, 588
lackadaisical *adj* 407
lack courage *vb* 752
lack courtesy *vb* 824
lack discipline *vb* 844
lackey *n* 666
lack foresight *vb* 454
lacking *adj* 50, 163, 273, 558, 574, 691
lacklustre *adj* 382
lack of appreciation *n* 812
lack of ceremony *n* 788
lack of consideration *n* 792
lack of curiosity *n* 403
lack of discrimination *n* 419
lack of emphasis *n* 508
lack of enthusiasm *n* 616
lack of entitlement *n* 820
lack of experience/practice *n* 625
lack of faith *n* 869
lack of fitness *n* 589
lack of foresight *n* 454
lack of formality *n* 788
lack of haste *n* 246, 616
lack of hygiene *n* 591
lack of intellect *n* 397
lack of interest *n* 756
lack of meaning *n* 459
lack of motive *n* 135
lack of preparation *n* 560
lack of refinement *n* 792
lack of rehearsal/training/practice *n* 560
lack of restraint *n* 844
lack of sanitation *n* 591
lack of self control *n* 844
lack of smell *n* 348
lack of success *n* 652
lack of thought *n* 399
lack of wonder *n* 760
lack self-control *vb* 844

laconic *adj* 179, 505, 531
laconicism *n* 505
laconism *n* 531
lacquer *n* 202, *vb* 202, 766
lacrosse *n* 761
lacuna *n* 50, 174, 232
lacy *adj* 174, 232, 379
lad *n* 332
ladder *n* 24, 42, 64, 274
laden *adj* 285
ladle *n* 227
lady *n* 333, 665
Lady *n* 778
lady-in-waiting *n* 666
ladylike *adj* 333, 791
lady of the house *n* 665
Ladyship *n* 778
lady's maid *n* 666
lag *vb* 60, 213, 246
laggard *n* 610
lagging *n* 202
lagoon *n* 310, 312
laical *adj* 880
laicize *vb* 880
laid *n* 569
laid back *adj* 618, 756
laid low *adj* 185
laid up *adj* 142, 565, 589
lair *n* 165, 469, 600
laird *n* 776
laissez-faire *n* 122, 658, 667
laissez-passer *n* 271
laity *n* 880
lake *n* 312
lake of fire and brimstone *n* 867
lama *n* 879
lamb *n* 326, 800, 839, *vb* 152
lambent *adj* 374
Lamb of God *n* 862
lame *adj* 144, *vb* 144
lame duck *n* 142, 144, 652
lamella *n* 175
lamellate *adj* 175
lament *n* 325, 747, *vb* 325, 747, 826
lamentable *adj* 747
lamentation *n* 747
lamented *adj* 323
lamenting *adj* 747
lamina *n* 175
laminate *vb* 175
laminated *adj* 175
lamp *n* 377
lamplight *n* 374
lampoon *n* 773, 828, *vb* 744, 773, 828

lance *n* 649, *vb* 296
lance corporal *n* 648
lancer *n* 648
land *n* 311, 694, *vb* 237, 238, 261, 275, 690, 699
landau *n* 242
landed *adj* 692, 694
landed gentry *n* 776
landfall *n* 261
landing *n* 238, 261, 275
landing strip *n* 238
landlady *n* 692
landlord *n* 692
landmark *n* 484
landowner *n* 692
landscape *n* 490, 763
landscape gardening *n* 329
land travel *n* 236
lane *n* 240
language *n* 494, 528
languid *adj* 144, 146, 246, 616
languish *vb* 144, 743
languor *n* 144, 146, 246, 762
lanky *adj* 183, 184
lanolin *n* 319
lantern *n* 377
Laodicean *adj* 27
lap *n* 127, 278, 356, *vb* 223, 251, 278, 314, 356
lapdog *n* 782
lapel *n* 230
lapidary *adj* 505
lapis lazuli *n* 391, 766
lap of luxury *n* 336
lapse *n* 405, 407, 441, 840, *vb* 838
lapsed *adj* 105, 435, 869
lapse from faith *n* 869
lap up *vb* 404
larboard *n* 214
lard *n* 319
larder *n* 570
large *adj* 23, 168
largely *adv* 29
largeness *n* 168
large quantity *n* 23
large-scale *adj* 168
largesse *n* 698, 725
largo *adv* 246
lark *n* 736
larva *n* 326
lascivious *adj* 851
lasciviousness *n* 851
laser *n* 374
lash *n* 247, *vb* 40, 147

lashings *n* 29, 573
lash out *vb* 147, 727
lass *n* 111, 333
lassitude *n* 144
last *adj* 62, 100, *vb* 1, 93, 122
last/family name *n* 497
last forever *vb* 89
last gasp *n* 62
last hour *n* 323
lasting *adj* 1, 93, 122
last judgment *n* 62
last lap *n* 62
last man in *n* 60
last-minute *adj* 114, 615
last minute *n* 114
last orders *n* 62
last post *n* 110
last resort *n* 536
last rites *n* 323, 325
last round *n* 62
last straw *n* 49, 653
last trump *n* 62
last will and testament *n* 323
last word *n* 106, 770
last words *n* 62, 323
latch *n* 42, 233
late *adj* 98, 105, 114, 323, 616, *adv* 114
latecomer *n* 100, 114
late developer *n* 114
late hour *n* 114
late in the day *adj* 114, *adv* 98
lately *adv* 106
latency *n* 465
lateness *n* 114
latent *adj* 373, 465, 469
later *adj* 60, *adv* 102
lateral *adj* 214
lateral thinking *n* 400
late riser *n* 616
latest *adj* 101, *n* 770
latest fashion *n* 770
latest thing *n* 106
lath *n* 569
lathe *n* 279
lather *n* 306, 339
Latin *n* 331
latitude *n* 23, 156, 180, 667
latitudes *n* 157
lattice *n* 174, 197, *vb* 174
latticed *adj* 174
laud *vb* 874
laudable *adj* 825
laudatory *adj* 825

laugh *vb* 744
laughable *adj* 443, 744, 772
laughableness *n* 772
laugh all the way to the bank *vb* 712
laugh at *vb* 824
laughing *adj* 742
laughing stock *n* 773
laugh in the face of *vb* 435
laugh like a drain *vb* 744
laugh off *vb* 399, 407
laugh out of court *vb* 435
laughter *n* 742, 744
launch *n* 61, 243, *vb* 61, 132, 237, 247, 255
launch into *vb* 562
launder *vb* 586
launderer *n* 586
launderette *n* 586
laundry *n* 586
laurels *n* 650
lava *n* 317
lavender *n* 349, 392
lavish *adj* 182, 510, 725, 727, *vb* 725
lavishness *n* 725, 727
law *n* 71, 661, 852
law-abiding *adj* 55, 72, 663, 831
law and order *n* 55, 854
lawbreaker *n* 838
lawbreaking *n* 853
lawcourt *n* 855
lawful *adj* 817, 819, 852
lawfulness *n* 817, 852
lawless *adj* 56, 658, 838, 853
lawlessness *n* 658, 662, 853
law-maker *n* 852
law-making *n* 852
lawn *n* 327, 569
law officer *n* 854
lawsuit *n* 635, 856
lawyer *n* 613, 623
lax *adj* 407, 658, 689, 788, 809
laxative *adj* 268, *n* 39, 596
laxity *n* 407, 658, 689
lay *adj* 880, *n* 521, *vb* 40
lay/put aside *vb* 565
layabout *n* 610, 838
lay at one's door *vb* 830
lay at the door of *vb* 134
lay bare *vb* 203, 464, 468
lay brethren *n* 880
lay claim to *vb* 819
lay down *vb* 422, 623, 661
lay down one's life *vb* 323
lay down the law *vb* 71, 661

layer *n* 175, 321, *vb* 175, 202, 207
layered *adj* 175
lay ghosts *vb* 876
lay in *vb* 570
lay into *vb* 147, 639
lay it on thick *vb* 482, 827
lay it on with a shovel/trowel *vb* 431, 510
lay low *vb* 185
layman *n* 880
lay-off *n* 161, 673
lay off *vb* 161, 673, 696
lay one's hands on *vb* 690
layout *n* 55, 57, 557
lay out *vb* 557, 718
layout artist *n* 557
lay people *n* 880
lay-preacher *n* 868, 880
lay-reader *n* 880
lay siege to *vb* 639
lay the foundations *vb* 559
lay to rest *vb* 325
lay up *vb* 570
lay waste *vb* 150
lazeabout *n* 610
laziness *n* 146, 610, 616
lazy *adj* 146, 610, 616
lazy-bones *n* 610
lea *n* 313
lead *n* 31, 285, 385, 569, 651, *vb* 31, 59, 212, 622
lead astray *vb* 441, 838
lead balloon *n* 285
lead captive *vb* 703
leaden *adj* 285, 385
leader *n* 31, 368, 519, 622, 665
leader of fashion *n* 770
leadership *n* 31, 622, 657
lead-in *n* 61
leading *adj* 31, 59, 140, 212, 576, 622, 657, 774
leading lady/man *n* 523
leading light *n* 774
leading seaman *n* 648
lead the fashion *vb* 770
lead up the garden path *vb* 480
leaf *n* 175, 327
leafiness *n* 390
leafless *adj* 203
leaflet *n* 516
leafy *adj* 327, 390
league *n* 40, 45, 633, 634, 684

legitimacy *n* 817, 852
legitimate *adj* 523, 817, 819, 852
legitimately *adv* 852
legless *adj* 848
Lego *n* 53, 761
leg-pulling *n* 773
legroom *n* 156
leg-up *n* 253, 276
leisure *n* 580, 608, 612, 616, 761
leisure activities *n* 612
leisure centre *n* 612
leisured *adj* 610, 612
leisured classes *n* 610
leisureliness *n* 246
leisurely *adj* 246, 616
lemon *n* 346, 389
lemon-yellow *adj* 389
lend *vb* 701, 714
lend a hand *vb* 631
lend an ear *vb* 351
lender *n* 571, 701, 714
lending *n* 701
length *n* 23, 178
lengthen *vb* 178
lengthening *n* 178
lengthily *adv* 178
lengthways *adv* 178
lengthy *adj* 178, 506
leniency *n* 660
lenient *adj* 429, 660, 677, 809, 813
lens *n* 491
Lent *n* 845, 881
leper *n* 54, 790
leprechaun *n* 865
leprosy *n* 589
lesbian *adj* 73, 333, *n* 73
lesbianism *n* 333
less *adv* 36
less and less *adv* 34
lessee *n* 692, 699
lessen *vb* 30, 34, 144, 148, 171
lesson *n* 475, 476, 602
less than one *n* 78
let *n* 701, *vb* 677, 697, 701
let alone *vb* 556, 667
let be *vb* 667
let bygones be bygones *vb* 449, 646, 813
let down *adj* 452
letdown *n* 452
let down *vb* 452
let fly *vb* 147
let fly at *vb* 639
let go *vb* 696

lethal *adj* 150, 323, 324, 604
lethargic *adj* 144, 146, 246, 731
lethargy *n* 144, 146, 246, 610, 731
let it all hang out *vb* 667
let off *adj* 813
let-off *n* 857
let off *vb* 606, 822, 857
let off steam *vb* 761
let off the lead *vb* 669
let oneself go *vb* 667
let oneself in for *vb* 562
let one's hair down *vb* 667, 746
let-out *n* 264, 422, 605
let out *vb* 669
let pass *vb* 813
let sleeping dogs lie *vb* 608
let slide *vb* 407
let slip *vb* 405, 468
let slip through one's fingers *vb* 691
letter *n* 495, 515, *vb* 485, 495
letterbox *n* 232
lettered *adj* 438, 476
lettering *n* 495
letter of credit *n* 711
letter of the law *n* 659
letterpress *n* 514
letters *n* 515
let the cat out of the bag *vb* 466
let the cat out the bag *vb* 468
let the grass grow under one's feet *vb* 407
let things slide *vb* 610
letting *n* 697, 701
letting off *n* 605
letup *n* 123
let up *vb* 246
leukaemia *n* 589
level *adj* 185, 191, 222, 292, *n* 24, 175, 191, 353, 502, *vb* 15, 150, 185, 191, 222, 249, 277, 292
level-headed *adj* 444, 446, 733
level-headedness *n* 444, 446, 733
levelling *n* 72, 277
levelness *n* 191, 292
level pegging *n* 25
level up/down *vb* 25
lever *n* 132, 193, 276, 568, *vb* 276
leverage *n* 31, 139
leviathan *n* 168
levitate *vb* 286
levitation *n* 274, 276
levity *n* 445, 742
levy *n* 699, 721, 819, *vb* 699, 721
lewd *adj* 851

light-fingered *adj* 705
light fitting *n* 377
light-footed *adj* 245
light-headed *adj* 445
light-headedness *n* 445
light-hearted *adj* 742
light-heartedness *n* 742
lighthouse *n* 377
lighting-up time *n* 110
light music *n* 367
lightness *n* 286, 306
light object *n* 286
light on *adj* 574
light red *adj* 387
light source *n* 377
lights out *n* 110, 375
light touch *n* 338
light up *vb* 374
light upon *vb* 135, 433
light verse *n* 521
lightweight *adj* 187, 286
light-year *n* 92
lignite *n* 321, 341
like *adj* 13, 17, *vb* 757, 795
likeable *adj* 736, 757
like a cat on hot bricks *adj* 281
like a dream *adv* 629
like a shot *adv* 537
like clockwork *adv* 629
like company *vb* 789
like falling off a log *adv* 629
likelihood *n* 140, 423, 425, 427, 434
likely *adj* 3, 140, 423, 425
like-minded *adj* 436, 636
liken *vb* 17, 194
likeness *n* 13, 17, 488
likewise *adv* 13, 17
liking *n* 757
lilac *n* 392
Lilliputian *adj* 30, 169
lilt *n* 353
lilting *adj* 365
lily-livered *adj* 752
lily-white *adj* 383
limb *n* 48
limb from limb *adv* 41
limbo *n* 2, 449, 867
lime *n* 390
lime-green *adj* 390
limerick *n* 521, 744
limestone *n* 311
limit *n* 62, 211, *vb* 211, 422, 630, 668

limitation *n* 422, 630, 685
limited *adj* 211, 668
limited patience *n* 803
limiting *adj* 630, 668, 685
limitless *adj* 89
limitlessness *n* 89
limn *vb* 490
limousine *n* 242
limp *adj* 144, 290, 508, *vb* 246
limpet *n* 43
limpid *adj* 379, 460, 503
limpidity *n* 379, 460, 503
limpness *n* 144, 290, 508
linchpin *n* 141, 576
linctus *n* 596
line *n* 60, 64, 154, 178, 181, 240, 249, 330, 493, 707, *vb* 201, 231
lineage *n* 12, 60, 155
lineal *adj* 155
linear *adj* 64, 222
linearity *n* 222
lined *adj* 230, 231
line drawing *n* 490
line engraving *n* 493
linen *n* 569
line of country *n* 7
line of least resistance *n* 629
line of work *n* 611
line one's pocket *vb* 712
liner *n* 201, 243
lines *n* 216, 521
line-up *n* 57
line up *vb* 64
linger *vb* 93, 114, 246, 616
lingerie *n* 204
lingering *adj* 359
lingo *n* 494
lingua franca *n* 494
linguistic *adj* 458, 494
linguistics *n* 494
liniment *n* 319
lining *n* 201
link *n* 9, 40, 42, 124, *vb* 9, 40
link-man *n* 42
linkup *n* 40, 42
linocut *n* 493
linoleum *n* 202
Linotype *n* 514
lionheart *n* 751
lionize *vb* 774, 786, 823
lion's share *n* 29, 48
lip *n* 209, 415, 781
lip gloss *n* 765
lip-reading *n* 352

lip-service *n* 481, 873
lipstick *n* 765
liquefaction *n* 125, 303
liquefied *adj* 303
liquefier *n* 303
liquefy *vb* 125, 183, 217, 303
liquid *adj* 217, 303, 305, *n* 303, 305
liquidate *vb* 150, 324, 487, 716, 717
liquidation *n* 150, 324, 487, 716, 717
liquidity *n* 217, 303, 711
liquidization *n* 303
liquidize *vb* 38, 303, 317
liquidizer *n* 38, 303
liquor *n* 303
lisp *n* 526, 529, *vb* 529
lissom *adj* 183
list *n* 26, 57, 76, 195, *vb* 70, 76, 195, 486, 603
listed building *n* 603
listen *vb* 351
listener *n* 351, 532
listen in on *vb* 351, 402
listing *n* 57, 76
listless *adj* 144, 246, 403, 610
listlessness *n* 144, 403, 610
list price *n* 721
lit *adj* 374, *n* 518
litany *n* 874, 881
literacy *n* 438
literal *adj* 458, 496, *n* 441, 514
literally *adv* 440
literary *adj* 502, 518
literate *adj* 438
literature *n* 518
lithe *adj* 183
lithography *n* 514
litigant *adj* 856, *n* 856
litigate *vb* 856
litigating *adj* 856
litigation *n* 635, 856
litigious *adj* 410, 635, 856
litmus test *n* 71, 416
litter *n* 37, 56, 66, 155, 241, *vb* 67, 152
litterateur *n* 518
little *adj* 30, 169, 577
little bird *n* 466
little by little *adv* 24, 246
little green men *n* 54
littleness *n* 30, 169
little people *n* 865
littoral *adj* 310, *n* 209, 310
liturgical *adj* 874, 881
liturgy *n* 874, 881

live *adj* 101, 136, 141, 322, *adv* 162, *vb 1*, 322
live alone *vb* 799
live and let live *vb* 667
live beyond one's means *vb* 727
live for the present *vb* 101
live from day to day *vb* 454, 560
live from hand to mouth *vb* 101, 454, 713
live-in *adj* 162
live in *vb* 162
live in hope *vb* 748
live like a lord *vb* 655
liveliness *n* 145, 322, 609, 742
lively *adj* 145, 245, 322, 507, 524, 609, 742
liven up *vb* 322
liverish *adj* 386
livery *n* 204, 484
livestock *n* 326
live the life of Riley *vb* 336
liveware *n* 75
livewire *n* 145
live within one's income *vb* 668
live within one's means/income *vb* 726
livid *adj* 382, 802
living *adj* 322, *n* 322
living apart *adj* 798, *n* 798
load *n* 166, 285, 570, 638, 737, *vb* 166, 285, 430, 559
loaded *adj* 219, 712
loaded dice *n* 26
loading *n* 559
load off one's mind *n* 740
loads *n* 29
load up *vb* 570
loaf *n* 188, 396, *vb* 246, 610
loafer *n* 610, 838
loam *n* 311
loamy *adj* 311
loan *n* 631, 701, 702, 714, *vb* 701
loan shark *n* 701
loath *adj* 538, 758
loathe *vb* 758, 796
loathing *n* 758, 796
loathsome *adj* 737, 758, 764, 796
loathsomeness *n* 737
lob *vb* 255, 276
lobby *n* 139, 681, *vb* 139, 414
lobbying *n* 139
lobbyist *n* 681
lobe *n* 192
lobster *n* 387

look out *vb* 754
look out! *vb* 602
look out for *vb* 370, 406
look out for oneself *vb* 834
look right through *vb* 792
look-see *n* 370
look to *vb* 821
look up and down *vb* 370
look up to *vb* 774, 823
loom *vb* 3, 29, 104, 372, 450, 599
loony *adj* 447, *n* 447
loop *n* 221, 223, 251, *vb* 221, 223, 224, 251, 278
loophole *n* 232, 264, 422, 605, 685, 853
loopy *adj* 224
loose *adj* 44, 67, 192, 300, 501, 504, 658, 788, 851, *vb* 669, 696
loose cover *n* 202
loose ends *n* 50, 407
looseleaf *adj* 516
loosely *adv* 180
loosen *vb* 44
looseness *n* 44, 192, 300, 407, 504
looseness of morals *n* 851
loosen up *vb* 667
loose off *vb* 255
loosing *n* 669
loot *n* 650, 706, *vb* 705
looter *n* 705
looting *n* 705
lop *vb* 179
lope *vb* 234
lopsided *adj* 26, 219
lopsidedness *n* 26, 219
loquacious *adj* 530
loquacity *n* 530
lord *n* 332, 665
Lord *n* 862
Lord/Lady Muck *n* 779
lord it *vb* 781
lord it over *vb* 657
lordly *adj* 774
Lord of Hosts *n* 862
Lord of Lords *n* 862
Lord of Misrule *n* 864
lord of the manor *n* 665
Lord's Day *n* 881
Lordship *n* 778
lords spiritual *n* 776
Lord's Supper *n* 881
lords temporal *n* 776
lore *n* 476
Lorelei *n* 865

lorry *n* 242
lorryload *n* 23
lose *vb* 34, 161, 652, 691
lose colour *vb* 382
lose consciousness *vb* 335
lose control *vb* 658
lose face *vb* 32, 775
lose faith in human nature *vb* 808
lose heart *vb* 743
lose hope *vb* 749
lose its novelty *vb* 762
lose no time *vb* 113, 615
lose one's bearings *vb* 252
lose one's heart *vb* 795
lose one's marbles *vb* 447
lose one's nerve *vb* 750, 752
lose one's rag *vb* 802
lose one's reputation *vb* 775
lose one's sight *vb* 371
lose one's temper *vb* 802
lose one's voice *vb* 527
loser *n* 32, 652
lose the thread *vb* 405
lose track of *vb* 405
lose weight *vb* 845
losing battle *n* 32
loss *n* 34, 36, 163, 323, 395, 572, 691
losses *n* 323
loss of memory *n* 449
lost *adj* 161, 163, 572, 691, 842, 869
lost for words *adj* 354
lost in thought *adj* 405
lost to view *adj* 395
lot *n* 7, 536, 700, *vb* 700
lotion *n* 302
lots *n* 29
lottery *n* 554
loud *adj* 351, 353, 355, 363, 381, 526, 769, 785
loudhailer *n* 355
loudly *adv* 355
loud-mouthed *adj* 355, 771
loudness *n* 351, 353, 355, 769
loud pedal *n* 355
loudspeaker *n* 355
loud voice *n* 526
lough *n* 312
lounge *vb* 610, 618
lounge suit *n* 787
lour *vb* 804
louse *n* 838
lousy *adj* 583
lout *n* 769, 792, 838
loutish *adj* 769

lovable *adj* 795
lovableness *n* 795
love *n* 2, 77, 795, 800, 800, *vb* 795, 800
love affair *n* 795
love child *n* 12, 155, 853
loved *adj* 795
loved one *n* 795
love-letter *n* 515, 800
loveliness *n* 736, 763
lovely *adj* 736, 763, 795
love-making *n* 795, 800
lover *n* 795
lovesick *adj* 795
lovey-dovey *adj* 800
loving *adj* 795, 800, 805, 862
loving words *n* 800
low *adj* 32, 185, 356, 743, 777, *n* 307, *vb* 364
lowbrow *adj* 367
low-density *adj* 87
lowdown *n* 466
lower *adj* 32, *vb* 185, 277, 360, 593, 824
lower-case *adj* 495
lower classes *n* 777
lowered *adj* 277
lowering *adj* 277, *n* 277
lower limit *n* 189
lower oneself *vb* 775, 780
lower one's sights *vb* 686
lower one's voice *vb* 526
lower orders *n* 777
lower world *n* 867
lowest *adj* 189
lowest common denominator *n* 27, 69
low esteem *n* 824
low-grade *adj* 583
low IQ *n* 397
low-key *adj* 148, 784
lowland *n* 185, 311, 313
lowliness *n* 780
lowly *adj* 30, 777, 780
low-lying *adj* 185
low-necked *adj* 205
lowness *n* 185, 356
low opinion *n* 824
low-paid *adj* 713
low point *n* 30, 185
low profile *n* 213
low relief *n* 492
low-risk *adj* 427
low sound *n* 356
low spirits *n* 743

low turnout *n* 87
loyal *adj* 663, 688, 793, 831, 870, 872
loyalty *n* 663, 688, 821, 831, 872
lozenge *n* 220, 596
LP *n* 369
Lsd *n* 711
LSD *n* 849
L-shaped *adj* 220
lubricant *n* 148, 302, 319
lubricate *vb* 292, 302, 319
lubricated *adj* 302, 319
lubrication *n* 302
lucid *adj* 446, 460, 503
lucidity *n* 446, 460, 503
Lucifer *n* 864
luck *n* 135, 554, 835
luck of the draw *n* 554
lucky *adj* 135, 554, 651
lucky break *n* 651
lucky charm *n* 876
lucrative *adj* 690
ludicrous *adj* 443, 772
ludicrousness *n* 426, 772
ludo *n* 761
lug *vb* 241
lugubrious *adj* 747, 804
lukewarm *adj* 27, 44, 339, 538, 541, 756
lukewarmness *n* 339
lull *n* 123, 235, 354, 644, 740, *vb* 148, 354, 740
lumbar *adj* 213
luminary *n* 774
luminescence *n* 374
luminescent *adj* 374
luminosity *n* 374
luminous *adj* 377
lump *n* 226, 228, 287
lumpiness *n* 182
lump in one's throat *n* 729
lumpishness *n* 512
lump together *vb* 40, 45, 419
lumpy *adj* 182, 226, 228, 512
lunacy *n* 445, 447
lunar *adj* 284
lunar month *n* 92
lunatic *adj* 445, 447, *n* 447
lunatic fringe *n* 73
lunch hour *n* 92, 618
lung *n* 316
lunge *vb* 245
lurch *vb* 275, 848
lure *n* 257, 601, *vb* 257
lurid *adj* 381, 785, 851

lurk *vb* 373, 395, 465, 469
luscious *adj* 736
lush *adj* 327, 573, *n* 848
lushness *n* 573
lust *n* 755, 795, 851
lust after *vb* 755, 816
lustful *adj* 795
lusting *adj* 755
lustre *n* 292, 374
lustrous *adj* 292, 374
lusty *adj* 355, 363
lute *n* 369
luxuriance *n* 573
luxuriant *adj* 573
luxuriate *vb* 336, 844
luxurious *adj* 336, 712, 734
luxury *n* 655, 712, 734, 844
lych-gate *n* 882
lying *adj* 479, 480, 481
lying-in-state *n* 325
lymph *n* 303
lynch *vb* 324, 826
lynch mob *n* 324
lynx-eyed *adj* 370
lyric *adj* 521
lyrical *adj* 732
lyricism *n* 732
lyrics *n* 367, 51

M

ma'am *n* 333, 778
macabre *adj* 750
mace *n* 649
Machiavellian *adj* 469
machinations *n* 469
machine *n* 568, *vb* 149
machine code *n* 75
machine code/language *n* 570
machine gun *n* 649
machinery *n* 53, 568
machismo *n* 332
macho *adj* 332, 751
mackerel sky *n* 307
macramé *n* 149, 766
macrobiotic *adj* 39
macrobiotics *n* 39
macrocosm *n* 29, 284
macrocosmic *adj* 284
mad *adj* 58, 443, 445, 447, 772
madam *n* 111, 333, 778
madame *n* 778
madcap *n* 753
madden *vb* 147, 447, 802

mademoiselle *n* 778
made of money *adj* 712
made-to-measure *adj* 19, 70, 204
made-to-order *adj* 70
made-up *adj* 479
madman *n* 447
madness *n* 58, 445, 447
madrigal *n* 367
maelstrom *n* 279
maestro *n* 368
mafia *n* 66
magazine *n* 471, 570
magenta *adj* 387, 392
magic *adj* 582, *n* 139, 876
magical *adj* 876
magician *n* 876
magic rite *n* 876
magic word *n* 876
magistrate *n* 665
magnanimity *n* 805, 833, 837
magnanimous *adj* 833
magnate *n* 141, 576
magnet *n* 256, 257
magnetic *adj* 139, 256, 257
magnetic tape *n* 570
magnetism *n* 139, 256, 257
magnetize *vb* 256, 257
magnificence *n* 763, 785
magnificent *adj* 582, 763, 785
magnify *vb* 170, 482, 741
magnifying glass *n* 370
magnitude *n* 23, 29, 168
magnolia *n* 383
magnum *n* 167
magnum opus *n* 29
maharajah *n* 665
mah jong *n* 761
mahogany *n* 386
maid *n* 613, 666
maiden *n* 333, 861
maiden aunt *n* 799
maidenhood *n* 799
maiden name *n* 497
maiden speech *n* 61
maiden voyage *n* 61
mail *n* 472, 515, *vb* 239, 515
mail order *n* 708
maim *vb* 144
main *adj* 29, 576, *n* 310
mainframe *n* 75
main ingredient *n* 5
mainland *adj* 311, *n* 311
main line *n* 240
mainline *vb* 849

mañana *n* 616
man and boy *adv* 1
man-at-arms *n* 648
mandarin *n* 141
mandate *n* 657, 661, 672, *vb* 661, 672
mandatory *adj* 71, 536, 623, 661, 664, 821
mandolin *n* 369
mangle *vb* 219
manhandle *vb* 338
man-hater *n* 808
manhole *n* 232
manhood *n* 112, 332
man hour *n* 90
mania *n* 447, 729, 755
maniac *n* 447
maniacal *adj* 447
manic *adj* 729
manic-depressive *adj* 447
manicure *n* 765
manicurist *n* 765
manifest *adj* 394, 464, *n* 720, *vb* 394, 464, 484
manifestation *n* 394, 464
manifold *adj* 86
manikin *n* 169
man in the street *n* 27, 69, 777
manipulate *vb* 139, 338
manipulation *n* 139, 338
manipulative *adj* 139
mankind *n* 330
manliness *n* 143, 332, 751
manly *adj* 143, 332, 751
man-made *adj* 149
manner *n* 7, 68, 240, 502, 621
mannered *adj* 502, 771
mannerism *n* 771
manners *n* 768
mannish *adj* 332
mannishness *n* 332
manoeuvre *n* 607
man of God *n* 863
man of honour *n* 831
man of many parts *n* 624
man of prayer *n* 863, 872, 874
man of property *n* 692
man of straw *n* 4, 142
man on the Clapham omnibus *n* 69, 777
manor *n* 165
man o' war *n* 243
manpower *n* 567, 613
manqué *adj* 652
man's best friend *n* 326

manse *n* 882
manservant *n* 666
man's estate *n* 322
mansion *n* 165
manslaughter *n* 324
mantissa *n* 74
mantle *n* 202, *vb* 387
mantrap *n* 601
manufacture *n* 149, *vb* 149
manufacturer *n* 149, 613
manure *n* 268, *vb* 152, 328, 329
manuscript *adj* 513, *n* 513, 516
many *adj* 80, 86
many a time *adv* 117
many happy returns *n* 786
map *n* 249, 488, 557, *vb* 488, 557
map-maker *n* 557
map out *vb* 208
mapreading *n* 159
maquette *n* 490, 492
mar *vb* 585, 764, 767, 775
maracas *n* 369
marathon *n* 93, 172, 236
marauding *adj* 705
marble *n* 289, 292, 393, 492, 569, *vb* 393
marbled *adj* 393
marbles *n* 761
march *n* 236, 253, 682, *vb* 234, 236, 682
marchioness *n* 776
mare *n* 326, 333
margin *n* 20, 156, 174, 209, 214, 667, 722
marginal *adj* 209, *n* 73
marginally *adv* 78
margrave *n* 665
marigold *n* 388
marijuana *n* 849
marimba *n* 369
marinade *n* 344, *vb* 344
marine *adj* 237, 243, 310, *n* 648
mariner *n* 237
marines *n* 648
marital *adj* 40, 797
maritime *adj* 237, 243, 310
mark *n* 484, 585, 587, 593, 595, 767, *vb* 5, 587, 593, 595, 767, 786
mark down *vb* 724
marked *adj* 464, 585, 587, 593, 595, 767
marked down *adj* 724
marker *n* 484
market *n* 464, 470, 708, 710, *vb* 709

meddlesome *adj* 402
media *n* 472
media coverage *n* 470
medial *adj* 63, 250
median *adj* 27, 63, *n* 27, 63, 207, 250
mediate *vb* 63, 138, 646, 647
mediation *n* 63, 138, 646, 647, 862
mediator *n* 63, 148, 647
mediatory *adj* 647
medical *adj* 596
medical assistance *n* 631
medicament *n* 596
medication *n* 596
medicinal *adj* 596
medicine *n* 596
medicine-man *n* 876
mediocre *adj* 27, 32, 583
mediocrity *n* 27, 583
meditate *vb* 398, 874
meditating *adj* 874
meditation *n* 398, 872, 874
meditative *adj* 398, 872
medium *n* 455, 567, 876, 877
medley *n* 16, 38
meek *adj* 642, 663, 733, 780, 784, 872
meekness *n* 642, 733, 780, 784
meet *n* 761, *vb* 66, 716, 718
meet an obligation *vb* 819
meet halfway *vb* 436, 686
meeting *n* 40, 66, 176, 259, 433, 789
meeting-house *n* 882
meeting point *n* 200, 207
meet one's needs *vb* 738
meet someone halfway *vb* 63
meet with approval *vb* 738, 825
megalomania *n* 783
megalomaniac *adj* 783
megaphone *n* 355
me generation *n* 70
melancholia *n* 447
melancholic *adj* 447
melancholy *adj* 735, 743, 804, *n* 735, 743, 804
melange *n* 38
melee *n* 56, 147, 643
mellifluous *adj* 365
mellifluousness *n* 365
mellow *adj* 290, 342, 736, *vb* 290
mellowness *n* 290
melodic *adj* 365, 367
melodious *adj* 365, 736
melodiousness *n* 365
melodrama *n* 482, 523, 732
melodramatic *adj* 482, 523, 732

melody *n* 365, 367, 736
melt *vb* 2, 4, 44, 94, 183, 217, 290, 303, 809
melt down *vb* 303
melting pot *n* 38, 125
melt into thin air *vb* 395
meltwater *n* 305
member *n* 48, 53, 634, 693
member of parliament *n* 657
membership *n* 43, 51
memento *n* 105, 448
memo *n* 448, 486
memoirs *n* 517, 518, 522
memorable *adj* 365, 448
memorandum *n* 448
memorial *n* 448, 484, 486
memorize *vb* 438, 448
memory *n* 75, 105, 448, 570
memsahib *n* 778
menace *n* 599, 796, 806, *vb* 599, 750, 806
menacing *adj* 599, 806
ménage *n* 164
menagerie *n* 326
mend *n* 594, *vb* 594, 817
mendable *adj* 594
mendacious *adj* 479, 481
mendaciousness *n* 479, 481
mended *adj* 594
mender *n* 594
mendicancy *n* 713
mendicant *adj* 681, *n* 681, 713
mending *n* 594
mend one's fences *vb* 636
mend one's ways *vb* 592
menhir *n* 190
menial *adj* 32, 666, *n* 613, 666
menopausal *adj* 112
menopause *n* 112, 153
menstrual *adj* 92
menstruation *n* 119
mensurate *vb* 177
mensuration *n* 177
mental *adj* 396
mental block *n* 449
mental defective *n* 397
mental deficiency *n* 397
mental illness *n* 447
mental image *n* 457
mentally deficient *adj* 397
mentally ill *adj* 447
mention *n* 650, *vb* 70, 404, 458
mentor *n* 444, 475, 623
Mephistopheles *n* 864

Mephistopholean *adj* 864
mercantile *adj* 707
mercenary *adj* 728, *n* 648
merchandise *n* 149, 707, *vb* 707
merchandising *n* 709
merchant *n* 571, 613, 707
merchantman *n* 243
merchant navy *n* 237
merciful *adj* 660, 805, 809, 813, 862
merciless *adj* 806, 810
mercilessness *n* 810
mercurial *adj* 130, 245, 405, 543, 544, 732
mercury *n* 130
Mercury *n* 862
mercy *n* 660, 805, 809, 813, 862
mercy killing *n* 323
mere *n* 312
merely *adv* 30, 39, 79
mere shadow *n* 489
meretricious *adj* 4, 394, 480, 769
meretriciousness *n* 480
merge *vb* 13, 38, 40, 45, 79, 633
merger *n* 38, 40, 45, 633, 708
meridian *n* 97, 103
meringue *n* 306
merit *n* 582, 837, *vb* 819
merited *adj* 819
meritorious *adj* 774, 819, 825
merits *n* 819
mermaid *n* 865
merriment *n* 734, 742
merry *adj* 734, 742, 848
merry-go-round *n* 279
merrymaking *n* 746
mésalliance *n* 20
mescalin *n* 849
mesh *n* 174, 197, 232, *vb* 174
mesmeric *adj* 139
mesmerism *n* 139
mesmerize *vb* 139, 257, 877
mess *n* 56, 587, 625, 764
message *n* 409, 466
messenger *n* 59, 241, 466, 470
Messiah *n* 862
mess up *vb* 56, 217, 587, 625
messy *adj* 56, 217, 587
metabolism *n* 121
metabolize *vb* 121
metal *n* 321, 569, *vb* 202
metalled *adj* 202
metallic *adj* 321, 359
metallurgical *adj* 321
metallurgy *n* 321

metalworking *n* 149
metamorphose *vb* 121, 125
metamorphosis *n* 121, 125
metaphor *n* 458
metaphorical *adj* 458
metaphysical *adj* 1
metaphysics *n* 1
metathesis *n* 196
meteor *n* 284
meteoric *adj* 245
meteorite *n* 284
meteorological *adj* 307
meteorologist *n* 307
mete out *vb* 700
meter *n* 177
meter maid *n* 854
method *n* 55, 71, 240, 567
methodical *adj* 55, 57, 246, 406
methodically *adv* 55
methodicalness *n* 246, 406
methods *n* 621
methuselah *n* 167
meticulous *adj* 404, 406, 440
meticulousness *n* 404, 406, 440
metre *n* 521
metric *adj* 177
metrical *adj* 521
metrics *n* 521
metronome *n* 97, 177, 280
metronymic *n* 497
metropolitan *adj* 165
mettle *n* 145, 539, 751
mew *vb* 364
mews *n* 165
mezzanine *n* 189
mezzo-relievo *n* 492
mezzosoprano *n* 368
mezzotint *n* 493
miaow *vb* 364
miasma *n* 304, 350, 591
Mick *n* 331
microbe *n* 169
microcomputer *n* 75, 169, 570
microcosm *n* 30, 47, 169
microelectronics *n* 169
microfiche *n* 486
microfilm *n* 491
microorganism *n* 169, 320
microphone *n* 355
microprocessor *n* 75, 169, 570
microscope *n* 370
microscopic *adj* 30, 320, 373
micturate *vb* 268
micturation *n* 268

mid *adj* 63
Midas *n* 712
midday *n* 109
midden *n* 56
middle *adj* 63, 250, *n* 63, 200
middle age *n* 27, 63, 112
middle-aged *adj* 27, 112
middlebrow *adj* 27, 69, 148, 367
middle-class *adj* 27, 777
middle class *n* 27, 777
middle course *n* 27, 250, 686
middle distance *n* 27, 63, 172
middle ground *n* 63, 686
middleman *n* 42, 63, 613, 647, 675, 707
middle name *n* 497
middle-of-the-road *adj* 27, 63, 148, 250
middle of the road *n* 27, 148, 250
middle way *n* 148, 250
middling *adj* 27, 585
midget *adj* 30, *n* 169
mid-life crisis *n* 27, 63, 112
midnight *n* 110
midnight blue *adj* 391
midnight sun *n* 284
midpoint *n* 27, 63, 207, 250
midriff *n* 63, 200, 207
midriff bulge *n* 168
midst *n* 63
midstream *n* 63
midsummer *n* 63, 108
midway *adj* 250, *adv* 63, *n* 27, 63
midweek *n* 63
midwifery *n* 152
midwinter *n* 63, 108
mien *n* 394
might *n* 29, 141, 143
mighty *adj* 29, 141, 143
migrant *n* 236
migrate *vb* 236
migratory *adj* 236
milch cow *n* 326
mild *adj* 148, 290, 339, 660, 733
mildew *n* 597
mildewed *adj* 597
mildness *n* 148, 290, 660, 733
mileage *n* 578
miles *n* 29
milestone *n* 8, 484
milieu *n* 8, 206
militancy *n* 43, 127, 645
militant *adj* 43, 127, 634, 645, *n* 127, 609

militarism *n* 645
militaristic *adj* 645
military *adj* 645
militate against *vb* 137
militiaman *n* 648
milk *n* 383, *vb* 270
milk and honey *n* 655
milkiness *n* 380, 383
milksop *n* 144
milk-white *adj* 383
milky *adj* 380, 383
mill *n* 300, 568, *vb* 66, 86, 229, 300
millboard *n* 569
millennium *n* 84, 92, 104, 866
milligram *n* 23
milling *adj* 66
million *n* 84
millionth *adj* 84
millpond *n* 292, 312
millrace *n* 314
millstone *n* 285
mime *n* 21, 484, 523, *vb* 484, 523
mimesis *n* 21
mimetic *adj* 21
mimic *n* 21, *vb* 21, 484, 488, 772
mimicry *n* 21, 772
mimosa *n* 389
mince *vb* 234
mind *n* 283, 396, 535, *vb* 85, 406
mind-blowing *adj* 849
mind-boggling *adj* 732, 759
minder *n* 85, 598
mindful *adj* 404, 406
mindfulness *n* 404, 406
mindless *adj* 397, 399
mindlessness *n* 397, 399
mind one's manners *vb* 791
mind one's P's and Q's *vb* 71, 406, 621, 791
mind one's step *vb* 406
mind-reader *n* 877
mind's eye *n* 370, 457
mine *n* 186, 570, 601, 614, 649, *vb* 270
minefield *n* 640
miner *n* 613
mineral *adj* 321, *n* 321, 569
mineralogical *adj* 321
mineralogy *n* 321
minginess *n* 728
mingle *vb* 38
mingy *adj* 574, 728
mini *adj* 169, 205, *n* 169
miniature *adj* 30, *n* 169, 490

miniaturized *adj* 169
minicab *n* 242
minicomputer *n* 75
minimal *adj* 30, 573
minimalist *adj* 490
minimally *adv* 30
minimization *n* 483
minimize *vb* 30, 432
minimum *n* 30, 32, 189, 573
mining *n* 275, 573
minion *n* 666
minister *n* 622, 657, 879, *vb* 881
ministerial *adj* 878
ministering *adj* 863
ministering spirit *n* 863
minister to *vb* 631, 666
ministration *n* 878
ministry *n* 878
minnow *n* 169
minor *adj* 30, 32, *n* 111
minority *n* 30, 48, 87
minster *n* 882
minstrel *n* 368, 521
mint *n* 712, *vb* 106, 149, 711
minuet *n* 367, 524
minus *adj* 2, 163, 273, *adv* 36
minuscule *n* 495
minute *adj* 30, 169, 373, *vb* 76, 486, 513
minuteness *n* 30, 169
minutes *n* 486, 513
minutiae *n* 70
minx *n* 111
miracle *n* 759, 868
miracle-worker *n* 759, 876
miracle-working *n* 876
miraculous *adj* 759
mirage *n* 4, 370, 394, 457
mire *n* 308
mirror *n* 248, 292, *vb* 13, 17, 81, 88, 248
mirror image *n* 11, 14
mirth *n* 742, 744
mirthful *adj* 742
MIRV *n* 649
misadventure *n* 656
misandry *n* 333
misanthrope *n* 808
misanthropic *adj* 808
misanthropize *vb* 808
misanthropy *n* 808
misapplication *n* 566
misapply *vb* 566

misapprehension *n* 463
misappropriate *vb* 566, 705
misappropriation *n* 705
misbehave *vb* 621, 662, 838
misbehaviour *n* 621, 662, 840
miscalculate *vb* 430, 441
miscalculation *n* 430, 441
miscall *vb* 498
miscalling *n* 498
miscarriage *n* 152, 323
miscarriage of justice *n* 853
miscarried *adj* 652
miscarry *vb* 153
miscellaneous *adj* 16, 38
miscellany *n* 16, 38, 45, 520
mischief *n* 662, 742, 806, 818, 836
mischief-maker *n* 662, 838
mischievous *adj* 662, 742
misconceive *vb* 430, 441
misconception *n* 430, 441, 463
misconduct *n* 621, 792, 840
misconstruction *n* 441, 463, 489, 501
misconstrue *vb* 219, 463
miscreant *n* 838
misdeed *n* 818
misdemeanour *n* 840, 853
misdemeanours *n* 621
miser *n* 728, 834
miserable *adj* 735, 743
miserliness *n* 728
miserly *adj* 574, 728, 834
misery *n* 735, 743
misfired *adj* 652
misfit *n* 20, 54, 73
misfortune *n* 554, 604, 656, 806, 836
misgiving *n* 435
misgivings *n* 428, 750
misgovern *vb* 658
misguided *adj* 430, 441
misguidedness *n* 441
mishandle *vb* 566, 625
mishandling *n* 566, 625
mishit *vb* 20
mishmash *n* 38
misinform *vb* 441
misinformation *n* 467
misinformed *adj* 441
misinterpret *vb* 441, 463
misinterpretation *n* 463, 489
misjudge *vb* 116, 430, 441
misjudged *adj* 116
misjudgment *n* 116, 430, 441
mislaid *adj* 161, 691
mislay *vb* 161, 691

mislead *vb* 411, 441, 480, 489
misleading *adj* 411, 441, 489
misled *adj* 441
mismanage *vb* 625
mismanagement *n* 625
mismatch *n* 20
misname *vb* 498
misnamed *adj* 498
misnaming *n* 498
misnomer *n* 498
misogynist *n* 332, 799, 808
misogyny *n* 808
misplace *vb* 20, 161
misplaced *adj* 161
misprint *n* 441
misread *vb* 463
misreading *n* 463, 489
misremember *vb* 449
misrepresent *vb* 219, 463, 489
misrepresentation *n* 219, 441, 463,
  479, 489
misrepresented *adj* 489
miss *vb* 50, 163, 273, 405, 407, 652,
  691
Miss *n* 778
misshapen *adj* 219, 764
missile *n* 255
missing *adj* 2, 50, 163, 273, 395, 585,
  691
missing link *n* 50, 65
missing person *n* 163
mission *n* 611, 645, 672, 675, 675,
  878, 882
missionary *adj* 125, *n* 807, 868, 872,
  879
missive *n* 515
miss one's cue *vb* 523
miss one's opportunity *vb* 116
miss out *vb* 50, 65
misspelling *n* 495
misspent *adj* 572
miss the boat *vb* 116
miss the point *vb* 6, 10, 411
miss the point of *vb* 731
mist *n* 307, 308, 376, 380, *vb* 4
mistake *n* 430, 441, 463, 501, 585, *vb*
  430, 463, 498
mistaken *adj* 430, 441
mistaken identity *n* 498
mister *n* 332, 778
mistime *vb* 20, 98, 116
mistimed *adj* 98, 116
mistiming *n* 98, 116
mistiness *n* 373, 376

mistral *n* 316
mistress *n* 475, 665, 778, 795
mistrust *n* 435, 815, *vb* 435, 815
mistrustful *adj* 435
mist up *vb* 376
misty *adj* 304, 307, 308, 373, 376, 380
misunderstand *vb* 441, 463
misunderstanding *n* 441, 463
misusage *n* 501
misuse *n* 566, 572, *vb* 566, 572
mite *n* 30, 111
mitigate *vb* 144, 148, 422, 740, 829
mitigating *adj* 422, 740, 829
mitigation *n* 148, 422, 740, 829
mitre *n* 657, 881, *vb* 40, 195
mix *vb* 16, 38, 45
mixed *adj* 16, 38
mixed bag *n* 16, 38, 419
mixer *n* 38
mixture *n* 38, 45, 596
mixture as before *n* 88
mix-up *n* 56
mix well *vb* 789
mnemonic *n* 448
moan *n* 356, 363, *vb* 356, 363, 682,
  739, 743, 747
moat *n* 210, 231, 315, 630, 640
mob *n* 66, 86, 777, *vb* 56
mobile *adj* 121, 130, 217, 234, *n* 492
mobile home *n* 165
mobility *n* 121, 130, 217, 234
mobilization *n* 645
mobilize *vb* 66, 640, 645
mobilized *adj* 645
Möbius strip *n* 64, 221
mob rule *n* 56, 147, 658, 853
mocha *n* 386
mock *adj* 21, 128, *vb* 21, 435, 744,
  773, 824, 828
mocker *n* 828, 873
mockery *n* 21, 435, 463, 489, 773, 824
mock-heroic *adj* 518
mocking *adj* 435, 773, 828
modal *adj* 7
modality *n* 7
mode *n* 7, 502, 770
model *n* 22, 31, 490, 492, 557, 584,
  761, 837, *vb* 22, 216, 492, 557
modelling *n* 492
model oneself on *vb* 21
model railway *n* 761
moderate *adj* 27, 148, 250, 843, *n*
  148, *vb* 144, 148, 422, 483
moderate drinker *n* 847

moderation *n* 27, 148, 250, 556, 843
modern *adj* 101, 106
modern dance *n* 524
modernism *n* 106, 871
modernity *n* 106
modernization *n* 106, 592
modernize *vb* 106, 592
modern times *n* 101
modest *adj* 30, 432, 483, 780, 784
modesty *n* 432, 483, 780, 784
modicum *n* 30
modification *n* 121, 422
modifier *n* 500
modify *vb* 121, 422, 500
modish *adj* 770
modular *adj* 53
modulate *vb* 121, 526
modulation *n* 121, 526
module *n* 53, 244
modus operandi *n* 7, 240
modus vivendi *n* 7, 686
moggy *n* 326
mogul *n* 141, 665
mohair *n* 569
Mohican *n* 765
moiety *n* 81
moiré *adj* 393
moist *adj* 303, 308
moisten *vb* 305, 308
moisture *n* 305, 308
moisturizer *n* 765
molasses *n* 345
mole *n* 139, 465, 466, 767
molecule *n* 169, 282
molest *vb* 737, 806
molestation *n* 737
mollification *n* 148, 646
mollify *vb* 646, 738
molten *adj* 303
moment *n* 90, 576
momentarily *adv* 94
momentary *adj* 94
moment of truth *n* 115
momentous *adj* 576, 732
momentum *n* 141, 234, 245, 247, 255
monad *n* 79
monarch *n* 665, 776
monarchical *adj* 657, 776
monastery *n* 882
monastic *adj* 799, 879
monetary *adj* 711
monetize *vb* 711
money *n* 567, 711, 712
moneybags *n* 712

money-belt *n* 167
money box *n* 711
moneyed *adj* 712
money for jam/old rope *n* 629
money-grubbing *adj* 728
moneylender *n* 701
money order *n* 711
money-saving *adj* 726
money-spinning *adj* 690
money to burn *n* 727
mongrel *adj* 38, *n* 38, 326
monies *n* 719
moniker *n* 497
monk *n* 790, 799, 850, 879
monkey *n* 838
monkey tricks *n* 772
mono *adj* 79, 353
monochromatic *adj* 382
monochrome *adj* 15, *n* 382
monocle *n* 370
monody *n* 534
monogamous *adj* 79
monogamy *n* 79, 797
monogram *n* 485, 495
monograph *n* 519
monolithic *adj* 15, 29
monologue *n* 79, 528, 534
monoplane *n* 244
monopolistic *adj* 52, 668, 692
monopolize *vb* 52, 692, 834
monopolize/hog the conversation *vb* 530
monopoly *n* 52, 79, 668, 692
Monopoly *n* 761
monorail *n* 240
monosyllabic *adj* 354, 505, 531
monotheism *n* 868
monotonous *adj* 13, 15, 88, 117, 124, 366, 762
monotony *n* 13, 15, 88, 117, 124, 366, 762
Monotype *n* 514
monsieur *n* 778
Monsignor *n* 778
monsoon *n* 307
monster *n* 168, 759, 838
monstrosity *n* 759
monstrous *adj* 759, 764, 772, 838
monstrousness *n* 806
montage *n* 525
month *n* 92
monthly *adj* 92
month of Sundays *n* 93
monument *n* 448, 484, 486

monumental *adj* 29, 168
moo *vb* 364
mooch *vb* 246
mood *n* 7, 206, 500, 544
moodiness *n* 804
moody *adj* 544, 803, 804
moon *n* 278, *vb* 405
moonless *adj* 375
moonlight *n* 374, *vb* 705
moonlight flit *n* 110, 262
moonlighting *n* 705
moonrise *n* 110
moonstone *n* 383, 766
moor *vb* 40, 160, 237, 261
mooring *n* 131
moorland *n* 313
moot *adj* 410, 428, *vb* 456
mop *n* 309, 586
mope *vb* 743, 804
moped *n* 242
moppet *n* 111
mopping up *n* 586
mop up *vb* 49, 309, 586
moral *adj* 821, 831, 837, 850, *n* 442
morale *n* 7, 751
moral fibre *n* 539, 831
moral imperative *n* 821
morality *n* 817, 821, 831, 837, 850
moralize *vb* 850
moral obligation *n* 821
morals *n* 837, 850
moral support *n* 631
moratorium *n* 114, 123
morbid curiosity *n* 402
mordancy *n* 296, 507
mordant *adj* 296, 507, 826
more and more *adv* 33
moreish *adj* 267, 342
more often than not *adv* 117
moreover *adv* 35, 45
mores *n* 549
morgue *n* 325
moribund *adj* 323
morn *n* 109
morning *adj* 109, *n* 61, 109
morning after the night before feeling
 n 848
morning dress *n* 787
moron *n* 397, 439, 445
moronic *adj* 397, 445
morose *adj* 743, 804
moroseness *n* 804
morphine *n* 849
morphological *adj* 500

morphology *n* 500
morris dance *n* 524
morrow *n* 104
Morse code *n* 472
morsel *n* 30, 48, 267
mortal *adj* 322, 323, 836, *n* 322, 330
mortality *n* 322, 323
mortar *n* 43, 569, 649
mortgage *n* 687, 701, 702, 714,
 715, *vb* 687, 702, 714, 715
mortgaged *adj* 687, 715
mortgagee *n* 701, 714
mortgagor *n* 687, 715
mortuary *adj* 325, *n* 325
mosaic *n* 16, 38, 45, 393
mosque *n* 882
moss-green *adj* 390
mossy *adj* 390
mostly *adv* 29
Most Reverend *n* 778
mote *n* 30, 169, 300
motel *n* 165
mothball *vb* 114, 123, 565, 570, 608
mothballed *adj* 565
motheaten *adj* 107
mother *n* 12, *vb* 800, 805
motherhood *n* 12, 152, 154
motherland *n* 165
motherliness *n* 333
motherly *adj* 154, 805
mother of pearl *n* 393, 766
Mother Superior *n* 879
mother-to-be *n* 154
mother tongue *n* 494
motif *n* 766
motile *adj* 234
motion *n* 234, 409, 681, *vb* 484
motionless *adj* 235, 610
motionlessness *n* 235
motion pictures *n* 525
motivate *vb* 134
motivated *adj* 134, 476
motivation *n* 132, 134, 755
motive *n* 132, 134
motiveless *adj* 135
mot juste *n* 19
motley *adj* 16, 38, *n* 393
motley crew *n* 16, 38
motor *n* 132, 141, 568
motorbike *n* 242
motor car *n* 242
motorcycle *n* 242
motorized *adj* 242
motorway *n* 240

mottle *vb* 393
mottled *adj* 38, 393
motto *n* 442, 499
mould *n* 15, 22, 68, 72, 216, 492, 597,
  vb 22, 72, 216, 492
mouldable *adj* 492
moulded *adj* 492
moulder *vb* 107
mouldering *adj* 107
mouldy *adj* 597
moult *vb* 203
moulting *n* 203
mound *n* 570
mount *vb* 40, 184, 193, 274
mountain *n* 23, 168, 184
mountaineer *n* 274
mountaineering *n* 274, 761
mountainous *adj* 184
mountebank *n* 21, 480
mounting *adj* 274, *n* 193, 209
mourn *vb* 325, 735, 747
mournful *adj* 735, 747, 804
mourning *adj* 747, *n* 204, 323, 325,
  735, 747
mouse *n* 784
mouser *n* 555
mousing *n* 555
mousse *n* 306
moustache *n* 765
mousy *adj* 382, 764
mouth *n* 232, 263, 310
mouthful *n* 496
mouthpiece *n* 528, 676
mouthwatering *adj* 342
movable *adj* 239, 694
movable feast *n* 120
movables *n* 694
move *n* 607, *vb* 130, 234, 239, 681,
  729, 732
moved *adj* 729, 732
move in the right circles *vb* 770
movement *n* 234, 271, 609, 634
move out *vb* 262
moves *n* 621
move slowly *vb* 246
move through *vb* 271
move to pity *vb* 809
move with the times *vb* 770
movie *n* 525
moving *adj* 234, 609, 732
moving force *n* 139
moving spirit *n* 141
mow *vb* 41, 328
Mr *n* 778

Mrs *n* 778
Mrs Grundy *n* 850
Mr X *n* 498
MS *n* 516
Ms *n* 778
much of a muchness *n* 17
muck *n* 268, 587
muck in *vb* 633
muck-raker *n* 828
muck-raking *n* 828
mucky *adj* 587
mucky pup *n* 587
mucous *adj* 318
mucus *n* 268, 303, 318
mud *n* 182, 290, 308, 317, 587
muddiness *n* 380
muddle *n* 56, 419, *vb* 56, 419
muddle-headed *adj* 56
muddle through *vb* 416, 454
muddy *adj* 308, 380, 587, *vb* 281, 376,
  380, 587
mudflat *n* 312
mud-slinger *n* 828
mud-slinging *n* 828
muffle *vb* 144, 148, 354, 360, 527
muffled *adj* 356, 360
muffledness *n* 360
mufti *n* 205, 788
mug *n* 167, 212, 480, *vb* 147, 639, 705
mugger *n* 639, 705
mugging *n* 147, 639, 705
muggy *adj* 308
mug up *vb* 476
mugwumpery *n* 27
mulatto *n* 38
mulberry *n* 392
mulch *vb* 329
mule *n* 241
mulish *adj* 542
mulishness *n* 542
mull *n* 569
mull over *vb* 398
multicoloured *adj* 381, 393
multifaceted *adj* 16
multifarious *adj* 80
multifariousness *n* 80
multilateralism *n* 80
multilateralist *adj* 80
multilingual *adj* 494
multimillionnaire *n* 712
multinational *n* 79
multiple *adj* 80, *n* 74, 80
multiple sclerosis *n* 589
multiplication *n* 75, 151, 152

mysticism *n* 283, 872, 877
mystification *n* 411
mystify *vb* 411, 439
mythical *adj* 865
mythological *adj* 107, 457
mythology *n* 10

N

nab *vb* 703
nabob *n* 776
nacreous *adj* 393
nada *n* 77
nadir *n* 30, 32, 185, 189
naff *adj* 769
nag *n* 326, *vb* 88, 739
nail *n* 42, 296, 568, *vb* 40, 232
nail-biting *adj* 732
nailbrush *n* 586
nail clippers *n* 765
nail file *n* 765
nail one's colours to the mast *vb* 43
nail polish *n* 765
nail scissors *n* 765
naive *adj* 434, 478, 509, 627, 839
naivety *n* 434, 478, 509, 627, 839
naked *adj* 203, 205
naked eye *n* 370
naked light *n* 377
nakedness *n* 203, 205
name *n* 485, 496, 497, *vb* 485, 497
named *adj* 485, 497
named after *adj* 497
nameless *adj* 498
namelessness *n* 498
namely *adv* 70, 462
name names *vb* 70
nameplate *n* 485
namesake *n* 497
naming *n* 485, 497
nanny *n* 333, 666, 668
nap *n* 299, 610, *vb* 610
narcissism *n* 783, 834
narcissist *n* 834
narcissistic *adj* 783, 834
Narcissus *n* 783
narcotic *adj* 849, *n* 335, 849
narcotism *n* 849
nark *n* 466
narrate *vb* 517
narration *n* 517
narrative *adj* 517, *n* 517
narrator *n* 517
narrow *adj* 30, 181, *vb* 171, 181, 183

narrow escape *n* 115, 605
narrowly *adv* 30
narrow-minded *adj* 181, 430, 850
narrow-mindedness *n* 181, 430
narrowness *n* 181
narrow space *n* 181
nasal *adj* 347, 529
nasalize *vb* 529
nascent *adj* 61
nastiness *n* 583, 737, 792
nasty *adj* 583, 737, 764, 792, 796, 806
nasty piece of work *n* 838
natation *n* 237
nation *n* 330, 331
national *adj* 331
National Insurance *n* 721
nationalism *n* 331
nationalistic *adj* 331
nationality *n* 331, 670
nationalization *n* 693, 703
nationalize *vb* 693, 697, 703
nationalized *adj* 693
nationhood *n* 331
native *adj* 164, *n* 164, 331
nativity *n* 322
natter *n* 533, *vb* 533
natty *adj* 763
natural *adj* 3, 39, 382, 509, 627
natural child *n* 12
natural death *n* 323
natural gas *n* 341
naturalism *n* 3
naturalistic *adj* 3, 488, 517
naturalize *vb* 54, 549
natural language *n* 494
naturalness *n* 509, 627
natural religion *n* 868
natural selection *n* 320
natural wastage *n* 673
nature reserve *n* 603
naturism *n* 205
naturist *n* 205
naught *n* 77
naughtiness *n* 662
naughty *adj* 662, 838
naughty child *n* 662
nausea *n* 266
nauseate *vb* 343, 737
nauseating *adj* 737
nautical *adj* 237, 243
naval *adj* 237
naval/submarine warfare *n* 645
nave *n* 882
navigate *vb* 237

neutral *adj* 27, 63, 250, 382, 385, 644, 756, 817, *n* 644, 647
neutrality *n* 27, 382, 644, 756, 833
neutralize *vb* 2, 137, 142
neutron bomb *n* 649
never *adv* 91
never-ending *adj* 89, 95, 124, 654
never forget *vb* 811
never have had it so good *vb* 655
never learn *vb* 445
never say die *vb* 540
nevertheless *adv* 28
never vary *vb* 762
new *adj* 106, 550, 565
new blood *n* 106
newborn *adj* 111
new boy *n* 61, 106
new broom *n* 106, 121, 592
new bug *n* 61, 106
newcomer *n* 106
new dawn *n* 127
new edition *n* 106
new face *n* 54
new Jerusalem *n* 866
new look *n* 106
newly *adv* 106
newlywed *adj* 797
newlyweds *n* 797
new-minted *adj* 106
newness *n* 106
new rich *n* 712
news *n* 101, 409, 466, 471
news blackout *n* 678
newsflash *n* 471
newshound *n* 402, 471
newsman *n* 471
newsmonger *n* 402
newspaper *n* 471
newspeak *n* 411, 461
newsprint *n* 514, 569
newsreader *n* 472
newsreel *n* 525
newsworthy *adj* 409, 471
newsy *adj* 466, 471, 533
new technology *n* 149
New Testament *n* 868
new to the game *adj* 106
new town *n* 67, 157
new wave *n* 106, 367
next *adj* 60, 100, *adv* 60
next of kin *n* 12
next world *n* 104, 323, 866
nexus *n* 40, 42
Niagara *n* 314

nibble *vb* 267
nice *adj* 418, 736
niceness *n* 736
nicety *n* 18, 418
niche *n* 57, 158, 160, 220
nick *n* 7, 229, 671, *vb* 229, 705
nickel *n* 383, 569
nickname *n* 497, 498, *vb* 497
nicotine *n* 849
niece *n* 12
niff *n* 350
niffy *adj* 350
niggard *n* 728, 834
niggardliness *n* 728
niggardly *adj* 728
nigger *n* 331, 384
nigger-brown *adj* 386
nigger in the woodpile *n* 465
nigh *adv* 173
night *n* 110, 375
night-blindness *n* 371
nightcap *n* 267
night club *n* 761
nightfall *n* 110, 375
night hawk *n* 110
nightly *adj* 110
nightmarish *adj* 865
night of the long knives *n* 324
night owl *n* 110
night school *n* 475
night-time *adj* 375, *n* 110
nihilism *n* 2
nihilistic *adj* 2
nil *adj* 77, *n* 2, 77
nimble *adj* 245, 338, 609
nimbleness *n* 609
nimbus *n* 223, 307, 374
nine *n* 84
nine days' wonder *n* 4, 94, 544, 651
nine tenths of the law *n* 692
nine to five *n* 119
ninety *n* 84
ninny *n* 445
ninth *adj* 84
nip *n* 344, *vb* 171
nip in the bud *vb* 113, 150
nipper *n* 111
nipple *n* 226
nirvana *n* 2, 866
nit-pick *vb* 18, 410
nit-picker *n* 739
nit-picking *adj* 411, *n* 18, 739
nitroglycerine *n* 649
nitty-gritty *n* 3

nix *n* 77
no *adj* 77
no apologies *n* 842
nob *n* 776
nobble *vb* 481, 705
nobility *n* 776, 776, 831, 833
noble *adj* 29, 774, 776, 831, 833, *n* 776
noble lord/lady *n* 776
nobleman *n* 776
noblewoman *n* 776
nobody *n* 777
no breeding *n* 769
no chance *n* 749
no charge *n* 724
no choice *n* 664
no comparison *n* 18
no compromise *n* 659
nocturnal *adj* 110, 375
nocturne *n* 367
nod *n* 484, 602, 791, *vb* 484, 791
noddle *n* 188
node *n* 40, 200
nod off *vb* 619
nodule *n* 226
no encouragement *n* 552
no frills *n* 509
no-go area *n* 52, 599
no heart *n* 731
no-hoper *n* 32, 652
no hurry *n* 616
noise *n* 353, 355, 363
noise abroad *vb* 470, 471
noiseless *adj* 354
noiselessness *n* 354
noisiness *n* 355
noisy *adj* 353, 355, 363
no laughing matter *n* 576
nomad *n* 94
nomadic *adj* 94, 234, 236
no-man's-land *n* 52, 63, 211, 599, 645
no matter what *adv* 427
nom de guerre *n* 498
nom de plume *n* 498
nomenclature *n* 497
nominal *adj* 4, 497, 500
nominate *vb* 672
nomination *n* 672
nominee *n* 643, 675
nomothetic *adj* 852
nonacceptance *n* 680, 826
nonadherence *n* 788
nonadhesion *n* 44
nonadhesive *adj* 44

nonage *n* 111
nonagenarian *n* 84
nonaggression *n* 644
nonaggression pact *n* 644, 684
nonagon *n* 84
nonagreement *n* 635
nonaligned *adj* 44, 644
nonalignment *n* 41, 44, 644
no name *n* 498
nonappearance *n* 163
nonary *adj* 84
nonattendance *n* 163
nonce word *n* 70, 496
nonchalance *n* 146, 403, 733
nonchalant *adj* 146, 403, 733
non-clerical *adj* 880
noncompletion *n* 654
noncompliance *n* 662, 680, 689
noncompliant *adj* 680, 689
non compos mentis *adj* 447
nonconformism *n* 73, 689, 871
nonconformist *adj* 73, 550, 635, 689, 871, *n* 73, 871
nonconformity *n* 73, 550, 689
noncontrition *n* 842
noncooperation *n* 556, 632
none *n* 77
nonentity *n* 2, 577, 777
nonet *n* 84
nonexistence *n* 2, 4, 163
nonexistent *adj* 2, 4, 163
nonfiction *n* 517, 518, 522
nonfriction *n* 302
nonfulfilment *n* 654, 689
non-heretical *adj* 870
noninterference *n* 658
nonintervention *n* 644, 658, 667
noninterventionist *adj* 644
noninvolvement *n* 556, 833
nonliability *n* 822
nonliable *adj* 822
nonmaterial world *n* 283
no-no *n* 424
nonobjective *adj* 490
nonobservance *n* 689, 788
nonobservant *adj* 689
no-nonsense *adj* 3, 145, 509
nonparticipation *n* 556
nonpayment *n* 717
nonperformance *n* 689
nonperson *n* 4, 163
nonphysical *adj* 283

nonplussed *adj* 461
nonporous *adj* 287
nonpractising *adj* 689, 869
nonrepresentational *adj* 490
nonresonance *n* 360
nonsense *n* 443, 459, 772
nonsensical *adj* 443, 459
non sequitur *n* 10, 65, 411
nonsmoker *n* 588
nonsmoking *n* 588
nonspecific *adj* 69
nonspecificness *n* 69
nonstandard *adj* 501
nonstarter *n* 32
nonstop *adj* 64, 124, *adv* 64, 95
non-toxic *adj* 598
non-U *adj* 769
nonuniform *adj* 16
nonuniformity *n* 16, 393
nonuse *n* 565
nonviolence *n* 644
nonviolent *adj* 644
no oil painting *n* 764
nook *n* 158, 181, 220, 227
nooky *n* 40
noon *n* 109
noose *n* 601, 861
no picnic *n* 628
no problem *n* 629
no proper drainage *n* 591
no quarter *n* 659
no regrets *n* 842
norm *n* 27
normal *adj* 27, 71, 446
normality *n* 446
normalization *n* 15
normalize *vb* 15, 71
normative *adj* 71
no room to swing a cat *n* 181
northern lights *n* 374
nose *n* 212, 228, 768, *vb* 347
nosedive *n* 238, *vb* 238, 275
nose job *n* 765
no sense of time *n* 616
nose to tail *adv* 64
nosh *n* 267
nosiness *n* 402
no spring chicken *n* 112
nostalgia *n* 105, 254, 448, 735
nostalgic *adj* 105, 254, 448, 735
nostril *n* 232, 316
nosy *adj* 402
nosy parker *n* 402
notable *adj* 576, *n* 576

not accept *vb* 680, 826
not act *vb* 608
not add up *vb* 459
not adhere *vb* 44
not a hair out of place *adj* 55
not allowed *adj* 678, 853
not all there *adj* 397, 447
not amused *adj* 826
not bad *adj* 582
not bat an eyelid *vb* 731, 733, 760
not be able to face *vb* 750
not be a patch on *vb* 32
not beat about the bush *vb* 505
not be entitled to *vb* 820
not before time *adv* 115
not be hurried *vb* 616
not be in the running *vb* 32
not believe one's eyes *vb* 759
not benefit *vb* 581
not be surprised *vb* 760
not born yesterday *adj* 626
not bothered *adj* 756
not breathe a word *vb* 467
not budge *vb* 539
not care *vb* 753, 756
not care for *vb* 756, 758
notch *n* 229, *vb* 229, 291
notched *adj* 229, 296
notch up *vb* 74, 486
not clash *vb* 580
not come up to *vb* 574
not come up to scratch *vb* 32, 50, 273
not come up to the mark *vb* 32
not complete *vb* 50, 654
not conform *vb* 73
not count *vb* 577
not countenance *vb* 659
not count the cost *vb* 725, 727
not cricket *adj* 818
not dare *vb* 752
not discriminate *vb* 419
not do *vb* 581
not drink *vb* 847
note *n* 364, *vb* 486, 513
not eating *adj* 845
not enforce *vb* 658
not enough *adj* 574, *n* 574
notepaper *n* 569
notes *n* 50, 486, 513
not excite oneself *vb* 733
not exist *vb* 2
not expect *vb* 451
not feel well *vb* 589
not finalized *adj* 654

nouveau riche *n* 712, 769
nouveaux riches *n* 106
nova *n* 284
novel *adj* 22, 106, 550, *n* 518, 522
novelette *n* 518
novelettish *adj* 508
novelist *n* 518
novelization *n* 518
novelize *vb* 518
novella *n* 518
novelty *n* 22, 106, 550
novena *n* 84
novice *n* 61, 106, 476, 880
novitiate *n* 476
now *adj* 101, *adv* 90, 101
nowadays *adv* 101
now and again *adv* 119
now and then *adv* 65, 92, 118, 174
no way *adv* 542
now or never *adv* 101
noxious *adj* 347, 350, 604
noxiousness *n* 604
nozzle *n* 232
nuance *n* 18, 24, 418
nuanced *adj* 418
nub *n* 5, 199
nubble *n* 226
nubbly *adj* 226
nubile *adj* 797
nuclear bomb *n* 649
nuclear family *n* 12
nuclear freeze *n* 644
nuclear power *n* 341
nuclear war *n* 645
nucleus *n* 5, 61, 63, 200
nude *adj* 205
nudge *n* 247, 484, *vb* 247
nudist *n* 205
nudity *n* 205
nugget *n* 287
nuisance *n* 597, 630, 737, 836
null *adj* 2, *n* 77
null and void *adj* 673
nullification *n* 2, 150, 673
nullify *vb* 2, 150, 673, 853
nullity *n* 77
numb *adj* 146, 335, *vb* 335, *adj* 731,
  vb 148, 731
number *n* 48, 74, 500, *vb* 74, 485
number among *vb* 51
numbercrunching *n* 75
numberless *adj* 86, 89
number one *n* 70
numbness *n* 335, 731

numeracy *n* 438
numeral *n* 74
numerate *adj* 438
numeration *n* 75
numerator *n* 74, 75
numerical *adj* 74
numerous *adj* 80, 86, 117
nun *n* 799, 850, 879
nuncio *n* 675
nunnery *n* 882
nuptial *adj* 797
nuptial mass *n* 881
nuptials *n* 797
nurse *n* 596, *vb* 596, 631, 805
nursemaid *n* 666, 668
nursery *n* 111, 132, 329, 477
nurseryman *n* 329, 613
nursery nurse *n* 666, 668
nursing *n* 631
nut *n* 447
nut-brown *adj* 386
nutcase *n* 447
nutcracker *n* 568
nutrition *n* 267
nutritious *adj* 267, 588
nuts *adj* 447
nutter *n* 447
nuzzle *vb* 338, 800
nylon *n* 569
nymph *n* 865
nymphet *n* 33, 111

O

oak *n* 289
oar *n* 255
oasis *n* 41, 305, 312
oasthouse *n* 339
oath *n* 496, 683, 801
oatmeal *adj* 386
obduracy *n* 542, 842
obdurate *adj* 542, 842
obedience *n* 537, 663, 688, 780
obedient *adj* 55, 537, 642, 663, 688,
  780, 821, 870
obediently *adv* 663
obeisance *n* 791
obelisk *n* 190, 486
obese *adj* 168, 575
obesity *n* 168, 575
obey *vb* 663, 688
obey orders *vb* 71
obfuscate *vb* 375, 461
obfuscation *n* 504

obfuscatory *adj* 461, 504
obituary *n* 262, 323, 325
object *n* 282, 500, *vb* 437, 538, 632, 635, 638, 682
objecter *n* 682
objectification *n* 6
objectify *vb* 3, 6, 282
objecting *adj* 856
objection *n* 437, 538, 632, 638, 682, 826
objectionable *adj* 758, 826
objective *adj* 3, 282, 400, 429, 817, 833, *n* 249, 553
objectivity *n* 3, 429, 833
object lesson *n* 442
object of one's desire *n* 755
object of worship *n* 862
objector *n* 856
object to *vb* 796, 826
obligation *n* 536, 558, 562, 664, 715, 817, 819, 821
obligatory *adj* 71, 536, 558, 661, 664, 821
oblige *vb* 536, 558, 664, 791, 805, 821
obliged *adj* 562, 715, 811, 821
obliging *adj* 631, 791, 805
oblique *adj* 195, 214
obliquely *adv* 195
obliqueness *n* 195
obliterate *vb* 2, 150, 395, 449, 487
obliteration *n* 2, 150, 395, 449, 487
oblivion *n* 2, 449
oblivious *adj* 405, 449, 731
obliviousness *n* 405, 731
oblong *n* 220
obloquy *n* 775
obnoxious *adj* 737, 758, 796
oboe *n* 369
obscene *adj* 583, 769, 801, 851
obscenity *n* 496, 583, 769, 801, 851
obscurantism *n* 411, 504
obscurantist *adj* 504
obscure *adj* 461, 465, 504, 577, 775, 777, *vb* 375, 376, 461
obscured *adj* 373, 376
obscurity *n* 32, 461, 465, 504
obsequies *n* 325
obsequious *adj* 663, 782, 823, 827
obsequiousness *n* 663, 782, 827
observable *adj* 372
observance *n* 688, 786, 821, 881
observant *adj* 370, 404, 688
observation *n* 370, 404, 528

observe *vb* 370, 404, 663, 688, 786, 881
observe neutrality *vb* 644
observer *n* 370
observe the formalities *vb* 787
obsess *vb* 398, 737
obsessed *adj* 404
obsession *n* 408, 447
obsessive *adj* 447, 729
obsessiveness *n* 729
obsidian *n* 321
obsolescence *n* 2, 107
obsolescent *adj* 107
obsolete *adj* 2, 105, 107
obsoleteness *n* 105, 107
obstacle *n* 628, 630
obstetric *adj* 152, 333
obstetrics *n* 152
obstinacy *n* 122, 430, 535, 538, 542, 632, 638
obstinate *adj* 122, 538, 542, 561, 628, 632, 638
obstreperous *adj* 662, 792
obstruct *vb* 233, 628, 630, 632
obstruction *n* 233, 630
obstructive *adj* 630
obstructiveness *n* 630
obtain *vb* 1, 69, 690, 699
obtainable *adj* 423
obtaining *n* 690
obtrusive *adj* 207
obtrusiveness *n* 575
obtuse *adj* 182, 297, 397, 731
obtuseness *n* 297, 397, 731
obviate *vb* 52, 99, 137
obvious *adj* 162, 372, 460, 464, 629
obviousness *n* 162, 372, 464
occasion *n* 8, 134, 786, *vb* 132, 134
occasional *adj* 118
occasionally *adv* 65, 87, 118
occasioned *adj* 134
occlude *vb* 233
occlusion *n* 233
occult *adj* 283, 876, 877
occultism *n* 283, 876, 877
occultist *n* 876
occult lore *n* 877
occupancy *n* 162, 692
occupant *n* 164, 692
occupation *n* 607, 611, 703
occupational *adj* 607, 611
occupied *adj* 164
occupier *n* 692
occupy *vb* 123, 162, 165, 692, 703

occupy oneself *vb* 607
occupy the middle ground *vb* 63
occur *vb* 101, 398
occurrence *n* 8, 101
ocean *n* 310
ocean-going *adj* 237, 243, 310
oceanic *adj* 310
oceanography *n* 310
ochre *n* 386, 389
octad *n* 84
octagon *n* 84, 220
octagonal *adj* 220
octave *n* 84
octavo *n* 84
octet *n* 84, 368
octogenarian *n* 84
octopus *n* 84
octoroon *n* 84
octuple *adj* 84
ocular *adj* 370
odd *adj* 20, 37, 73, 74, 447, 759
oddball *n* 73, 447
oddity *n* 73, 759
odd-job man *n* 613, 666
oddly enough *adv* 554
odd man out *n* 20, 73
oddness *n* 447
odd number *n* 26
odds and ends *n* 37
odds and sods *n* 37
ode *n* 521
odious *adj* 796
odium *n* 796
odoriferous *adj* 347
odorous *adj* 347, 349
odour *n* 347, 349
odourless *adj* 348
odourlessness *n* 348
odyssey *n* 236
oeuvre *n* 149
of a certain age *adj* 112
of a piece *adj* 15, 19
of assistance *adj* 631
of balance *adv* 26
of distinction *adj* 774
off *adj* 163, 343, 350, 709
off and on *adv* 65, 118, 120, 130, 174
off-beam *adj* 252
offbeat *adj* 22, 73
off-chance *n* 423
off-colour *adj* 589, 744
off-course *adj* 252
off course *adv* 58
offcut *n* 37

off-day *n* 116
offence *n* 802, 818, 838, 840, 853
offend *vb* 737, 802, 824
offender *n* 838
offensive *adj* 258, 350, 639, 737, 764, 781, 792, 824, 838, *n* 639, 645
offer *n* 679, *vb* 679, 698
offer a bribe *vb* 859
offered *adj* 679
offer for sale *vb* 679
offering *n* 698, 814
offer of marriage *n* 800
offer one's services *vb* 679
offer sacrifice *vb* 814
offer the hand of friendship *vb* 646
offertory *n* 698
off-guard *adj* 451
offhand *adj* 405, 781, 792, 824, *adv* 548
offhandedness *n* 405
office *n* 614, 821
officer *n* 613, 622
office worker *n* 613
official *adj* 657, *n* 622, 665
officialdom *n* 657
officiate *vb* 881
officious *adj* 402, 575
officiousness *n* 402, 575
off-key *adj* 366
off one's guard *adj* 407
off one's own bat *adv* 535
offprint *n* 514
off-putting *adj* 258, 737
offscourings *n* 37
offset *n* 514, *vb* 25, 28, 137
offshoot *n* 41, 48, 155, 634, 871
offshore *adj* 172, 310
off side *n* 214
offspring *n* 12, 60, 155
off the beaten track *adj* 790, *adv* 73, 172
off-the-cuff *adj* 454
off the cuff *adv* 96, 548, 560
off-the-peg *adj* 15, 204, 559
off the point *adj* 252, 506, *adv* 6, 10
off the premises *adv* 163
off the rails *adj* 441, *adv* 56, 58
off the top of one's head *adv* 548, 560
off white *n* 383
of good family *adj* 776
of good repute *adj* 774
of high birth *adj* 776
of late *adv* 106

of necessity *adv* 558, 664
of note *adj* 774
of one mind *adj* 636
of one's own accord *adv* 535
of royal blood *adj* 776
often *adv* 117
of the world *adj* 880
ogive *n* 221
ogle *vb* 370, 800
ogre *n* 865
oil *n* 302, 319, 490, 587, *vb* 292, 302, 319
oil and water *n* 14
oiled *adj* 302
oiliness *n* 292, 302, 319
oil the wheels *vb* 302, 629
oily *adj* 292, 302, 319, 587
ointment *n* 302, 319, 596
OK *adj* 582
okay *vb* 436
old *adj* 107, 112
old age *n* 107, 112
old-age pensioner *n* 112
old as the hills *adj* 107
old boy *n* 112
old-boy network *n* 139
old buffer *n* 112
old clothes *n* 204
old dear *n* 112
old dutch *n* 797
olden *adj* 107
older generation *n* 112
old-fashioned *adj* 98
old fogy *n* 112
old folks' home *n* 112
old gold *adj* 389
old hand *n* 107, 112, 624
Old Harry *n* 864
old hat *adj* 107, *n* 760
old lady *n* 797
old lag *n* 671
old maid *n* 333, 799, 850
old-maidish *adj* 850
old man *n* 797
old master *n* 490
oldness *n* 107
old news *n* 105
Old Nick *n* 864
old person *n* 112
old rose *adj* 387
old salt *n* 237
old school tie *n* 484, 818
old soak *n* 848
oldster *n* 112

Old Testament *n* 868
old-time dancing *n* 524
old-timer *n* 107, 112
old wives' tale *n* 479
old-world *adj* 107
oleaginous *adj* 319
olfactory *adj* 347
olive *n* 390
olive branch *n* 646
olive-green *adj* 390
ombudsman *n* 647
omega *n* 62
omen *n* 455, 484, 602
ominous *adj* 455, 602, 749, 806
ominousness *n* 455
omission *n* 50, 163, 407, 652, 689
omit *vb* 50, 52, 65, 407, 689
omnibus *adj* 47
omnipotence *n* 141
omnipotent *adj* 141, 862
omnipresence *n* 162
omnipresent *adj* 162, 862
omniscient *adj* 438, 862
omnivore *n* 326
omnivorous *adj* 267, 326, 846
on/under oath *adj* 683
on account of *prep* 134
on active service *adj* 645
on a large scale *adv* 29
on all sides *adv* 206
on and on *adv* 124, 506
on an even keel *adj* 446
on average *adv* 27
on bad terms *adj* 794
on balance *adv* 11, 27
on behalf of *prep* 138
on bended knee *adj* 681
on call *adv* 162
once *adv* 90
once and for all *adv* 62
once in a blue moon *adv* 118
once in a while *adv* 118
once more *adv* 88
once-over *n* 370
once upon a time *adv* 90, 105
oncoming *adj* 212, 259, 261
on consideration *adv* 398
on course *adv* 159, 249
on credit *adj* 715
on display *adv* 394, 464
one *adj* 79, *n* 79
one after another *adv* 64
one after the other *adv* 60
one-armed bandit *n* 554

one at a time *adv* 79
one by one *adv* 79
on edge *adj* 732
one fine day *adv* 90, 102
one-hander *n* 534
one hundred per cent *adj* 584, *adv* 47
one in a million *n* 837
one-liner *n* 744
one-man band *n* 79, 368, 534
one-man show *n* 79, 534
on end *adv* 190
oneness *n* 79
one of a series *n* 64
one-off *adj* 22, 70, *n* 70
one of these days *adv* 102
one of those days *n* 116
one over the limit *n* 848
one-parent family *n* 154
on equal terms *adv* 25
onerous *adj* 285, 737
one's born days *n* 322
one's generation *n* 101
one-sided *adj* 430, 818
one-sidedness *n* 430
one's own flesh and blood *n* 12
one's own time *n* 612
one-time *adj* 99, 105, 674
one too many *n* 848
one-to-one *adj* 25
one-track mind *n* 408
on everyone's lips *adv* 409
on foot *adv* 236
ongoing *adj* 1, 64, 90, 93, 101, 124, 253
on high *adv* 184
on holiday *adj* 612, *adv* 163
onion *n* 175
on leave *adv* 163
on-line *adj* 40
onlooker *n* 162, 370
only *adv* 30, 79
on-off *adj* 65
on offer *adj* 679
onomatopoeia *n* 21
onomatopoeic *adj* 21
on one's beam ends *adj* 713
on one's best behaviour *adj* 791
on one's mind *adv* 398
on one's own *adv* 79
on one's tail *adj* 555
on one's tod *adv* 79
on one's toes *adj* 730
on one's uppers *adj* 713
on pain of death *adv* 806

on record *adv* 486
on reflection *adv* 398
onrush *n* 147
on second thoughts *adv* 398
onset *n* 61, 261
onshore *adj* 311
on show *adv* 394, 464
on side *n* 214
on site *adv* 159
onslaught *n* 639
on someone's coat-tails *adv* 85
on-stream *adj* 136, 141
on supplementary benefit *adj* 574
on tap *adv* 162
on tape *adv* 486
on the agenda *adv* 104, 409
on the beat *adv* 236
on the blink *adv* 56
on the brain *adv* 398
on the breadline *adj* 713
on the cards *adv* 104
on the contrary *adv* 14
on the dot *adv* 96
on the face of it *adv* 198, 394
on the fiddle *adj* 705
on the go *adj* 609, *adv* 234
on the ground *adv* 162
on the high seas *adv* 237
on the horizon *adv* 104
on the house *adj* 724
on the increase *adv* 33
on the light/heavy side *adv* 26
on the loose *adj* 667
on the make *adj* 690
on the market *adj* 679
on the mend *adj* 588
on the move *adv* 234
on the nail *adv* 96
on the off chance *adv* 554
on the other hand *adv* 11, 14, 28
on the outside *adv* 6, 198
on the premises *adv* 162
on the quiet *adv* 467
on the rampage *adj* 732
on the right lines *adv* 249
on the right track *adv* 159, 249
on the road *adv* 234, 236
on the rocks *adj* 340, 717, 798, *adv* 39, 150
on the scrapheap *adj* 696, *adv* 150
on the shelf *adv* 37
on the sly *adv* 467
on the spot *adv* 101, 158, 162

on the spur of the moment *adv* 96, 548

on the stocks *adv* 50

on the throne *adj* 657

on the top rung of the ladder *adv* 188

on the trail *adv* 236

on the trot *adv* 64

on the up and up *adj* 655, *adv* 33, 274

on the wagon *adj* 847

on the wane *adv* 34

on the warpath *adj* 732

on the way *adv* 239

on the whole *adv* 27

on the wing *adv* 238

on the wrong track *adv* 58

on time *adv* 96

ontological *adj* 1

ontology *n* 1

on top of that *adv* 45

on top of the world *adj* 734, 742

onus *n* 821

on vacation *adv* 163

on view *adv* 394, 464

onward *adv* 253

onyx *n* 766

oodles *n* 29, 573

oomph *n* 145

ooze *n* 308, 317, *vb* 246, 264, 308, 314

oozy *adj* 264, 308

opacity *n* 376, 380

opal *n* 766

opalescence *n* 380

opalescent *adj* 380, 385, 393

opaque *adj* 376, 380, 459, 461, 504

opaqueness *n* 380, 459, 461, 504

open *adj* 232, 265, 464, 468, 478, 627, *n* 306, *vb* 232

open-air *adj* 306

open air *n* 198, 306

open-and-shut case *n* 629

open arms *n* 265

open country *n* 313

open door *n* 263

open-ended *adj* 89, 416

opener *n* 232

open-handed *adj* 698, 725, 859

open house *n* 69, 725

opening *n* 115, 232, 611

opening gambit *n* 61

opening night *n* 523

open letter *n* 69

openly *adv* 232, 464

open marriage *n* 797

open meeting *n* 69

open-mouthed *adj* 232, 759

openness *n* 232, 265, 478, 627

open one's heart *vb* 478

open one's mouth *vb* 528

open prison *n* 671

open sea *n* 310

open secret *n* 470

open sesame *n* 232, 876

open space *n* 232

open to the four winds *adv* 232

open up *vb* 468

openwork *n* 197, 232

opera *n* 367, 761

opera house *n* 761

operate *vb* 136, 596

operatic *adj* 367

operation *n* 136, 562, 645

operational *adj* 136, 607

operative *adj* 136, 141, *n* 613

operetta *n* 367

ophthalmic *adj* 370

opiate *adj* 849, *n* 148

opinion *n* 408, 429, 434

opinionated *adj* 430, 434, 542, 783

opium *n* 849

opium den *n* 849

oppo *n* 25

opponent *n* 632, 794, 826

opportune *adj* 19, 115, 580

opportuneness *n* 115

opportunism *n* 543, 580, 834

opportunist *adj* 580, *n* 834

opportunity *n* 115, 423, 580

oppose *vb* 14, 137, 215, 437, 632, 638, 794, 826

opposed *adj* 14, 215, 437, 474, 538, 656, 794, 826

opposed to *adj* 632

opposing *adj* 137, 632

opposite *adj* 14, 212, 215, *n* 14, 215, 632

oppositeness *n* 14

opposite number *n* 11, 25

opposite pole *n* 14

opposition *n* 14, 137, 215, 437, 632, 638, 656, 826

oppress *vb* 285, 657, 659, 670, 794, 806

oppressed *adj* 670

oppression *n* 659, 670

oppressive *adj* 285, 659, 737

oppressor *n* 659
opprobrium *n* 775
opt for *vb* 535, 545
optical *adj* 370
optical device *n* 370
optical illusion *n* 4, 370
optimal *adj* 29
optimism *n* 450, 742, 748
optimist *n* 748
optimistic *adj* 450, 742, 748
optimum *n* 29
option *n* 535, 545
optional *adj* 535, 545
opt out *vb* 608
opulence *n* 712
opulent *adj* 712
opus *n* 149, 367
oracle *n* 455, 877
oracular *adj* 455
oral *adj* 526, 528
oral history *n* 107
orange *adj* 388, *n* 388
orangery *n* 329
orangey *adj* 388
orate *vb* 528, 532
oration *n* 528, 532
orator *n* 528
oratorical *adj* 502, 528
oratorio *n* 367
oratory *n* 502
orb *n* 223, 225
orbit *n* 7, 223, 238, 240, 278, 279, *vb* 223, 238, 278, 279
orbital *adj* 278, *n* 278
orbital motion *n* 278
orbs *n* 370
orchard *n* 327, 329
orchestra *n* 368
orchestral *adj* 367
orchestrate *vb* 368, 557
orchestration *n* 367
ordain *vb* 71, 661, 672, 878, 881
ordained *adj* 879
ordeal *n* 628, 656
order *n* 55, 57, 68, 68, 622, 634, 650, 661, 881, *vb* 55, 57, 622, 661, 821, 878
ordered *adj* 57
order in council *n* 661
orderliness *n* 55, 406
orderly *adj* 55, 406
order of the day *n* 72, 547
ordinal *adj* 55, 74
ordinance *n* 623, 661, 852, 881

ordinariness *n* 27, 69
ordinary *adj* 27, 69, 577, 777
ordinary person *n* 777
ordination *n* 672, 878
ore *n* 321, 569
organ *n* 48, 369, 471
organic *adj* 5, 47, 298, 320
organism *n* 320, 322
organization *n* 55, 57, 298, 557, 621, 622, 634
organizational *adj* 57, 298, 622
organization man *n* 53
organize *vb* 40, 55, 132, 298, 557, 622
organized *adj* 55
organizer *n* 622
orgasm *n* 336, 732
orientate *vb* 159, 249
orientated *adj* 159
orientation *n* 159, 249
orienteering *n* 159, 761
orifice *n* 232, 263
origami *n* 492
origin *n* 61, 132
original *adj* 22, 70, 132, 457, *n* 22
originality *n* 22, 70, 457
originate *vb* 22, 61, 132, 149
originate in *vb* 133
origination *n* 149
originator *n* 22, 132, 149, 557
ormolu *n* 389
ornament *n* 510, *vb* 766
ornamental *adj* 766
ornamental art *n* 488
ornamentation *n* 510, 766
ornamented *adj* 766
ornate *adj* 510, 766
ornateness *n* 510
orographic *adj* 284
orography *n* 284
orotund *adj* 510
orphan *n* 37
orphanage *n* 323
orphaned *adj* 323
orthodox *adj* 71, 72, 549, 688, 870, 878
orthodoxy *n* 72, 549, 688, 870
orthography *n* 495
oscillate *vb* 65, 280
oscillating *adj* 280
oscillation *n* 234, 280
oscillator *n* 280
osmose *vb* 271
osmosis *n* 271
ossification *n* 289

overjoyed *adj* 734
overkill *n* 26, 482, 575
overlaid *adj* 175, 202
overland *adj* 311, *adv* 236
overlap *n* 20, 202, *vb* 64, 175, 176
overlapping *adj* 175
overlay *n* 175, 187, 202, *vb* 35, 175, 202
overload *n* 26, *vb* 285
overlook *vb* 184, 405, 407, 432, 660, 813
overlooked *adj* 432
overlord *n* 665
overmanned *adj* 86
overmuch *adj* 575
overnight *adj* 110, *adv* 96, 110
overnight bag *n* 167
over one's dead body *adv* 91, 542
over one's head *adv* 186
overoptimism *n* 431
overoptimistic *adj* 431
overpopulated *adj* 86
overpraise *vb* 431
overpraised *adj* 431
overpriced *adj* 431, 723
overproduction *n* 572
overrate *vb* 272, 431, 825
overrated *adj* 431, 452
overreach *vb* 272
override *vb* 139
overripe *adj* 317
overripeness *n* 317
overrule *vb* 673
overrun *vb* 49, 86, 272
overseas *adj* 172, *adv* 54, *n* 54
overseer *n* 622, 665
oversensitive *adj* 730
overshadow *vb* 31, 375, 774
overshoot *vb* 26, 272, 431
overshot *adj* 26
oversight *n* 405, 407, 441, 652
oversleep *vb* 114
overspend *n* 718, *vb* 718, 727
overspending *n* 572, 727
overspill *n* 67
overstate *vb* 482
overstated *adj* 431, 482
overstatement *n* 431, 482
overstep *vb* 272, 575
overstepping *n* 272
overstep the mark *vb* 820
overt *adj* 464
over the moon *adj* 734, 746
over the odds *adv* 35

over the top *adj* 272, 431, 482, 575, 772
overthrow *n* 121, 126, 127, 161, 277, 652, 673, *vb* 126, 127, 277, 657, 673
overthrown *adj* 652
overtime *n* 35, 90
overtone *n* 359
overture *n* 59, 367, 646, 679
overturn *n* 126, 277, *vb* 126, 127, 196
overuse *n* 566, *vb* 566
overvaluation *n* 431
overvalue *vb* 431
overvalued *adj* 431
overview *n* 47, 184, 370
overweight *adj* 26, 168, 285
overwhelm *vb* 49, 147, 759, 823
overwhelming *adj* 29, 147
overwork *vb* 566, 572
overwritten *adj* 482, 504
overwrought *adj* 729
ovine *adj* 326
ovoid *adj* 221
ovum *n* 152
owe *vb* 715
owed *adj* 715
owing *adj* 715, 819
owing to *prep* 132, 134
own *vb* 692
own-brand *adj* 70, 724
owner *n* 692
owner-occupier *n* 164, 692
ownership *n* 692
own up *vb* 468, 478, 841
own up to *vb* 473
ox *n* 326, 332
oxblood *adj* 387
oxbow *n* 221
Oxbridge *n* 477
Oxford blue *adj* 391
oxygen *n* 306
oxygenate *vb* 304, 306
oyster *adj* 385
ozone *n* 30

P

pace *n* 245, *vb* 236
pace out *vb* 177
pacification *n* 148, 646
pacificatory *adj* 646
pacifism *n* 644
pacifist *n* 644
pacify *vb* 55, 148, 646, 738

pack *n* 66, *vb* 49, 66, 166, 171, 201, 202, 287
package *n* 724, *vb* 66
package deal *n* 51
packaging *n* 167, 202
packed *adj* 66, 86, 173, 287
packet *n* 243, 712
packhorse *n* 241
pack up *vb* 652
pact *n* 636, 646, 683, 684
pad *n* 165, 356, *vb* 170, 182, 201, 290, 506
padding *n* 35, 124, 170, 182, 201, 290, 506
paddle *vb* 187, 237, 237
paddleboat *n* 243
paddle one's own canoe *vb* 44, 79
paddock *n* 158, 210
paddy *n* 802
Paddy *n* 331
padlock *n* 42
pad out *vb* 33, 35
padre *n* 778, 879
pagan *adj* 869, 875, *n* 869, 875
paganism *n* 869, 875
page *n* 514, 516, 666, 797
pageant *n* 464
pageantry *n* 785
pageboy *n* 765
paid *adj* 690
pail *n* 167
pain *n* 597, 617, 836
painful *adj* 337, 730, 735, 737, 836
pain in the arse/neck *n* 597
pain in the neck *n* 762
painkiller *n* 335, 740
painless *adj* 629
pains *n* 406, 617
painstaking *adj* 246, 404, 406, 616
paint *n* 202, 381, 766, *vb* 202, 381, 490, 517, 603, 766
painted *adj* 785
painter *n* 243, 490, 613
painterly *adj* 490
painting *n* 488, 490
paint-remover *n* 203
paint the town red *vb* 746, 761, 844
pair *n* 81, *vb* 40, 40, 81
pairing *n* 40
pair off *vb* 45
paisley *n* 766
Pakki *n* 331
pal *n* 793
palace revolution *n* 161

palaeography *n* 105
palaeology *n* 105
palatable *adj* 267, 342
palate *n* 342, 768
palatial *adj* 712, 734
pale *adj* 144, 381, 382, 383, *vb* 382, 383, 395
pale imitation *n* 489
paleness *n* 382, 383
palette *n* 381, 490
pale yellow *adj* 389
palindrome *n* 196
paling *n* 210
palisade *n* 210
pall *n* 202, 325, *vb* 343, 575, 762
palliate *vb* 829
palliative *n* 148
pallid *adj* 382, 483
pallidness *n* 483
pallor *n* 144, 382
pally *adj* 789, 793
palm *n* 650
palmist *n* 455, 877
palmistry *n* 455
palpability *n* 3, 282
palpable *adj* 3, 282, 338
palpitate *vb* 280, 281
palpitation *n* 280, 281
paltriness *n* 30
paltry *adj* 30, 577
pampas *n* 313
pamper *vb* 736, 800
pampered *adj* 336
pamphlet *n* 516
pan *n* 167, 227, *vb* 525, 828
Pan *n* 862
panacea *n* 69, 596
pandemonium *n* 56, 658
pander to *vb* 736, 782
panegyric *n* 825
panel *n* 657
panelling *n* 201
pang *n* 337
panic *n* 750, *vb* 750, 752
panicky *adj* 750
panicle *n* 327
panic-stricken *adj* 750
pannier *n* 167
panorama *n* 47, 180, 191, 232, 394
panoramic *adj* 47
pansy *n* 73
pant *n* 316, *vb* 316
pantechnicon *n* 242
pantheism *n* 868

pantheon *n* 882
panting *adj* 316, 729
pantomime *n* 523
pantry *n* 570
pap *n* 226, 317, 518
papa *n* 154
papacy *n* 878
papal *adj* 878, 879
papal bull *n* 661
paper *n* 519, 569
paperback *adj* 516
paperchase *n* 555
paper over the cracks *vb* 50
paper tiger *n* 4, 142
paperweight *n* 285
paperwork *n* 513
papery *adj* 295
papier mâché *n* 492, 569
papyrus *n* 513
par *n* 25, 27
parable *n* 458
parabola *n* 221
parachute *vb* 238
parachuting *n* 238, 761
parachutist *n* 238
Paraclete *n* 862
parade *n* 464, 785, *vb* 464, 785
paradigm *n* 22, 57
paradigmatic *adj* 57
paradise *n* 734, 866
paradox *n* 772
paradoxical *adj* 461, 772
paraffin *n* 319, 341
paragon *n* 31, 582, 584, 837
paragraph *n* 522
parallel *adj* 9, 17, 25, 85, 194, 218, *n*
    9, *17*, *157*, *178*
parallelism *n* 194, 218
parallelogram *n* 194, 220
paralyse *vb* 142, 630
paralysed *adj* 142, 146, 235, 335, 608,
    731
paralysis *n* 142, 335, 608, 731
paramount *adj* 31
paramour *n* 795
paranoia *n* 447
paranoiac *n* 447
paranoid *adj* 447
paranormal *adj* 877, *n* 283
parapet *n* 193
paraphase *n* 499
paraphernalia *n* 694
paraphrase *n* 462, *vb* 462, 499
parapsychology *n* 877

parascending *n* 761
parasite *n* 703
parasitical *adj* 703
parasol *n* 378
paratrooper *n* 238, 648
parboiled *adj* 654
parcel *n* 66, 700, *vb* 66
parcel out *vb* 700
parcel post *n* 472
parch *vb* 309
parched *adj* 309, 755
parchedness *n* 309
parchment *n* 513
pardon *n* 606, 660, 813, 822, 857, *vb*
    606, 660, 669, 809, 813, 822, 857
pardonable *adj* 813, 829, 839
pardoned *adj* 813
pare *vb* 36, 175
parent *n* 12, 154
parental *adj* 154
parenthesis *n* 35, 65, 252
parenthetical *adj* 65, 269
parenthood *n* 12, 154
parenting *n* 12, 154
par for the course *adj* 27
pariah *n* 54, 73, 790
parings *n* 175
pari passu *adv* 25
parish *n* 157, 878, 880
parishioner *n* 164, 880
parish priest *n* 879
parity *n* 25
park *n* 165, 313, 329, 761, *vb* 160
parky *adj* 340
parlance *n* 494, 499
parley *n* 533, *vb* 533, 685
parliament *n* 634, 657
parliamentarian *n* 657
parlour maid *n* 666
parochial *adj* 157, 165, 430
parochialism *n* 430
parodist *n* 21
parody *n* 21, 463, 489, 772, 773, *vb*
    21, 463, 489, 772
parole *n* 198, 669, 683, *vb* 669
paroxysm *n* 147, 281
paroxysmic *adj* 281
parrot *n* 21, *vb* 13, 21, 88
parrot-fashion *adv* 21
parry *n* 258, *vb* 123, 258, 415
parse *vb* 500
parsimonious *adj* 728
parson *n* 879
parsonage *n* 882

part *n* 48, 53, 78, 523, *vb* 41, 48, 232
part company *vb* 262
partial *adj* 48, 78, 140, 430, 818
partiality *n* 430, 757, 818
partially *adv* 30, 48, 50, 78
partial to *adj* 757
participant *adj* 162, *n* 162, 693
participate *vb* 162, 693
participate in *vb* 562
participating *adj* 693
participation *n* 162, 693
particle *n* 30, 78, 169, 282, 300
particoloured *adj* 393
particular *adj* 70, 545
particularity *n* 70, 485
particularize *vb* 70
particulars *n* 70
parting *n* 200, 207, 262
parting of the ways *n* 41, 260
parting shot *n* 262
partisan *adj* 140, 430, 818, 871
partisanship *n* 430, 818, 871
partition *n* 41, 52, 207, 700, *vb* 41, 48, 700
partly *adv* 48
partner *n* 85, 634, 693, 797, *vb* 85
partnership *n* 45, 633, 634, 693
part of speech *n* 500
part-payment *n* 48
parts *n* 157
parturition *n* 152
part with *vb* 696
partwork *n* 48
party *n* 66, 634, 761, 786, 789, 856, *vb* 789
party game *n* 761
party hack *n* 53, 72
party line *n* 72
party pooper *n* 745
party spirit *n* 871
party wall *n* 207
parvenu *n* 106, 769
pas de deux *n* 524
pass *n* 181, 651, 677, 800, *vb* 90, 94, 105, 268, 271, 651, 677, 697, 825, 852
passable *adj* 27, 582, 738
passage *n* 42, 48, 234, 240, 271
pass away *vb* 2
passbook *n* 677
passé *adj* 107
passenger *n* 236, 610
passenger ship *n* 243
passing *adj* 94, 234

passion *n* 147, 507, 729, 732, 795, 802
passionate *adj* 507, 729, 732, 795
passive *adj* 146, 500, 608, 642
passivity *n* 146, 608, 642
pass judgment on *vb* 429
pass mark *n* 573
pass muster *vb* 573, 825
pass on *vb* 470, 696, 697
pass oneself off as *vb* 481, 498
pass out *vb* 335, 786, 848
Passover *n* 881
pass over *vb* 52, 432, 546
pass over/away *vb* 323
passport *n* 271, 485, 661, 677
pass sentence *vb* 856
pass sentence on *vb* 858
pass the buck *vb* 608, 822
pass the hat round *vb* 681
pass the time of day *vb* 533
password *n* 232, 485
past *adj* 2, 105, *n* 102, 621
paste *n* 43, 317, 318, *vb* 43
pasteboard *n* 569
pastel *adj* 381, 483, *n* 490
pasteurization *n* 39, 590
pasteurize *vb* 39, 590
pasteurized *adj* 590
past hoping *adj* 749
pastiche *n* 21
pastime *n* 761
pastiness *n* 382
past it *adj* 107
pastor *n* 879
pastoral *adj* 328, 878, 879
pastoral care *n* 878
pastorship *n* 878
past time *n* 105
pasture *n* 313, 327
pasty *adj* 382
pat *n* 338, *vb* 338
patch *n* 158, 393, 587, 594, *vb* 393, 594
patchiness *n* 50, 585
patch up *vb* 50
patchwork *n* 16, 38, 45, 65, 149, 393
patchy *adj* 48, 50, 393, 585
pate *n* 188
patent *adj* 464, *n* 819, *vb* 22, 106
patent medicine *n* 596
pater *n* 154
paterfamilias *n* 154, 332
paternal *adj* 154
paternity *n* 154
path *n* 181, 240, 486

pathetic *adj* 735, 747, 809
pathfinder *n* 59
patience *n* 246, 540, 733, 761, 813
patient *adj* 246, 540, 733, 813
patois *n* 494
patriarch *n* 112, 154, 332, 879
patriarchal *adj* 12, 154
patriarchy *n* 12, 332
patrician *adj* 776, *n* 776
patrilineal *adj* 12
patriotic *adj* 331
patriotism *n* 331
patrol *n* 598, 640, *vb* 271, 598
patron *n* 193, 708, 807, 825
patronage *n* 139, 657, 708
patronize *vb* 631, 708, 779
patronizing *adj* 779
patron saint *n* 863
patronymic *n* 497
patsy *n* 480
patter *n* 356, 494, 528
pattern *n* 15, 22, 55, 57, 72, 216, 298,
   557, 584, 766, *vb* 22, 216, 298
patterned *adj* 766
pattern oneself after *vb* 21
paucity *n* 30, 87, 169
paunch *n* 225
paunchy *adj* 225
pauper *n* 713
pause *n* 65, 123, 235, 618, *vb* 65, 90,
   123, 235
pave *vb* 202
paved *adj* 202
pavement *n* 193
pave the way *vb* 559
paving *n* 202, 569
Pavlovian *adj* 401
Pavlovian reaction *n* 536
paw *vb* 338
pawn *n* 32, 577, 687, 702, *vb* 687, 702
pawnbroker *n* 701
pawnbroking *n* 701
pawned *adj* 687
pay *n* 690, 711, 716, 719, 859, *vb* 580,
   716, 718, 819, 821, 859
payable *adj* 715, 819
pay a dividend *vb* 690
pay-as-you-earn *n* 721
pay attention *vb* 404
pay back *vb* 641
pay by credit card *vb* 714, 715
pay damages *vb* 716
pay due attention to *vb* 688
payee *n* 699

payer *n* 716
pay for *vb* 631
pay homage *vb* 823
pay homage to *vb* 874
paying *adj* 690
paying guest *n* 164
paymaster *n* 711, 716
payment *n* 716, 718, 819, 859
payment in kind *n* 707
payoff *n* 62
pay off *vb* 651
pay one's last respects *vb* 325
pay one's respects *vb* 823
pay out *vb* 716
pay respect to *vb* 774
payroll *n* 613
pay the penalty *vb* 860
pay through the nose *vb* 723
pay tribute *vb* 811, 823, 825, 859
pay tribute to *vb* 786
pay up *vb* 716
PE *n* 617
pea *n* 225
peace *n* 55, 610, 636, 644
peaceable *adj* 55, 636, 644
peace and quiet *n* 354, 618
peaceful *adj* 55, 354, 610, 618, 636,
   644, 738,
peace-loving *adj* 644
peacemaker *n* 148, 644, 647
peacemaking *n* 646
peace offering *n* 646
peace of mind *n* 738
peace process *n* 644
peacetime *adj* 644, *n* 644
peace treaty *n* 684
peace treaty/agreement *n* 644
peach *n* 388, 763
peachy *adj* 387
peacock *n* 770, 783
peacock blue *adj* 391
pea-green *adj* 390
peak *n* 29, 31, 62, 184, 188, 584, *vb*
   31, 188
peal *n* 357, 359, *vb* 355, 357, 359
pearl *n* 766
pearl-grey *adj* 385
pearliness *n* 380, 383
pearly *adj* 380, 383, 385, 393
pear-shaped *adj* 221
peasant *n* 164, 328, 777
peashooter *n* 255
pea-souper *n* 307
peat *n* 341

peaty *adj* 386
pebble *n* 311
pebbly *adj* 311
peccadillo *n* 838, 840
peck at *vb* 267
pecking order *n* 55
peckish *adj* 755
peculiar *adj* 18, 70, 70
peculiarity *n* 70
pecuniary *adj* 711
pedagogic *adj* 475
pedagogue *n* 475
pedagogy *n* 475
pedal *n* 255
pedal car *n* 761
pedant *n* 438, 659
pedantic *adj* 406, 438, 440, 659, 688
pedantry *n* 438, 440, 659, 688
peddle *vb* 681, 709
pedestal *n* 189, 193
pedestrian *adj* 508, 522, 762, *n* 236
pedicure *n* 765
pedigree *adj* 39, *n* 59, 154, 776
pedlar *n* 681, 707
pee *n* 268, *vb* 268
peek *n* 370, *vb* 370
peel *n* 202, *vb* 175, 203
peeling *adj* 175
peelings *n* 175
peel off *vb* 205
peep *n* 370, *vb* 364, 370
peepers *n* 370
peephole *n* 232
peeping Tom *n* 402
peer *n* 25, 776, *vb* 370
peerage *n* 776
peeress *n* 776
peer group *n* 66, 101, 103
peerless *adj* 31, 584
peer of the realm *n* 776
peeve *vb* 737
peeved *adj* 802
peevish *adj* 739, 803
peg *n* 42
peg away *vb* 124, 540
peg out *vb* 323
pejorative *adj* 824, 828
pelagic *adj* 310
pellet *n* 255, 649
pell-mell *adv* 38, 56
pellucid *adj* 379
pellucidity *n* 379
pelt *n* 202, *vb* 96, 147, 245
pen *n* 158, 210, 328, *vb* 210, 513

penal *adj* 860
penalize *vb* 860
penalty *n* 685, 860
penance *n* 814, 841
penchant *n* 140, 537, 757
pencil *n* 374, *vb* 490
pendant *n* 35, 192, 377, 766
pendency *n* 192
pendent *adj* 192
pending *adj* 90
pendulous *adj* 192
pendulousness *n* 192
pendulum *n* 97, 119, 192, 280
penetrability *n* 232
penetrate *vb* 139, 232, 263, 271, 460
penetrating *adj* 444
penetration *n* 263, 271, 418, 444
penfriend *n* 515
peninsula *n* 311
peninsular *adj* 311
penis *n* 152
penitence *n* 814, 841
penitent *adj* 814, 841, *n* 841
penitential *adj* 814
penitentiary *adj* 814, *n* 671
penmanship *n* 513
pen name *n* 497, 498
pennant *n* 484
pennies from heaven *n* 835
penniless *adj* 713
pennilessness *n* 713
penny dreadful *n* 518
penny-pinching *adj* 728
penpal *n* 515
pension *n* 674, 716, 719, 859
pension off *vb* 696
pensive *adj* 398, 405
pensiveness *n* 398
pentad *n* 84
pentagon *n* 84
pentameter *n* 84
pentangle *n* 84, 220
Pentateuch *n* 84, 868
pentathlon *n* 84
Pentecost *n* 881
penthouse *n* 165, 184
penumbra *n* 376
penurious *adj* 713
penury *n* 713
people *n* 330, 331, *vb* 165
people's bureau *n* 672
pep *n* 145
pepper *n* 344, *vb* 232, 393
pepper-and-salt *adj* 385, 393

pepperiness *n* 344
peppery *adj* 342, 344
pep talk *n* 145, 532
per *prep* 138
perambulation *n* 234
per capita *adv* 700
perceive *vb* 370, 396
percentage *n* 35, 48, 78, 722
perceptibility *n* 372
perceptible *adj* 372
perception *n* 334, 370, 396, 729
perceptive *adj* 334, 370
perceptual *adj* 396
percolate *vb* 263, 271
percolation *n* 271
percussion *n* 369
perdition *n* 867
peregrination *n* 236
peremptory *adj* 473, 661
perennial *adj* 92, 93, 131, 327
perfect *adj* 584, 837, 839, 850, *vb* 49, 584, 653
perfectibility *n* 253
perfection *n* 31, 584, 653, 850
perfectionism *n* 406, 440
perfectionist *adj* 406, 440
perfidious *adj* 480, 481, 832
perfidy *n* 480, 543, 832
perforate *vb* 227, 232
perforated *adj* 227, 232
perforation *n* 227, 232
perform *vb* 136, 368, 488, 523, 607, 688, 786, 821
performance *n* 136, 367, 488, 523, 607, 688, 786, 821
performer *n* 368, 523, 607
performing arts *n* 488
perform ritual *vb* 881
perfume *n* 347, 349, *vb* 349
perfumed *adj* 347, 349
perfunctoriness *n* 50, 273
perfunctory *adj* 50, 187, 273
pergola *n* 165
perhaps *adv* 423
per head *adv* 700
peril *n* 599
perilous *adj* 599
perimeter *n* 198, 206, 209
period *n* 90, 92
periodic *adj* 65, 88, 92, 117, 119, 174
periodical *adj* 90, *n* 471
periodically *adv* 65, 92, 119
periodicity *n* 119
peripatetic *adj* 234, 236

peripheral *adj* 6, 10, 172, 198, 206, 209, 577
periphery *n* 6, 172, 198, 206, 208
perish *vb* 2, 323
perishability *n* 94
perishable *adj* 94
perishables *n* 707
perjure oneself *vb* 481, 830
perjury *n* 481, 830
perk *n* 35
perks *n* 690, 706
perk up *vb* 620, 742
perm *n* 765, *vb* 224
permanence *n* 93, 95, 122, 131
permanent *adj* 93, 122, 131
permanently *adv* 122
permanent overdraft *n* 727
permeability *n* 232
permeable *adj* 232
permeate *vb* 38, 139, 162, 232, 263, 271
permeation *n* 271
permissibility *n* 852
permissible *adj* 677, 825, 852
permission *n* 677, 822, 825
permissive *adj* 180, 658, 677
permissiveness *n* 180, 658
permissive society *n* 851
permit *n* 677, 819, *vb* 658, 677, 825
permitted *adj* 677, 852
permutation *n* 121
pernicious *adj* 150, 604
perorate *vb* 506, 532
peroration *n* 506, 528, 532
peroxide *n* 382
perpendicular *adj* 190, 222
perpendicularity *n* 190, 222
perpetrate *vb* 607
perpetration *n* 607
perpetrator *n* 607
perpetual *adj* 64, 89, 91, 95, 124
perpetually *adv* 89
perpetuate *vb* 95, 124
perpetuation *n* 124
perpetuity *n* 89, 91, 95
perplex *vb* 439, 461, 628, 628
perplexed *adj* 461
perplexity *n* 461
persecute *vb* 604, 659, 737, 794, 806, 810
persecution *n* 604, 737, 870
persecutor *n* 659, 860
perseverance *n* 43, 539, 540, 609, 872

persevere *vb* 43, 122, 124, 540, 542, 872

perseverence *n* 542

persevering *adj* 539, 540, 542

persist *vb* 37, 64, 93, 122, 124, 540, 542

persistence *n* 1, 93, 122, 540

persistent *adj* 43, 122, 540

person *n* 330, 500

personage *n* 330, 576

personal *adj* 70

personal/desk computer *n* 75

personal assistant *n* 613

personal column *n* 681

personality *n* 576

personalized *adj* 70

personally *adv* 70

personification *n* 5, 488

personify *vb* 5, 488

personnel *n* 613

perspective *n* 370

Perspex *n* 379, 569

perspicacious *adj* 370, 418, 444

perspicacity *n* 418, 444

perspicuity *n* 503

perspicuous *adj* 503

perspiration *n* 268, 305, 308

perspire *vb* 268, 308

persuadability *n* 551

persuadable *adj* 551

persuade *vb* 125, 139, 434, 507, 551, 623

persuader *n* 551

persuasion *n* 139, 434, 551, 623

persuasive *adj* 139, 434, 507, 551, 623

pert *adj* 781

pertain *vb* 9

pertinence *n* 9

pertinent *adj* 9

perturb *vb* 58

perturbation *n* 58, 281

perturbed *adj* 58, 281

peruse *vb* 370, 404

pervade *vb* 38, 162, 232

pervasive *adj* 139, 162

pervasiveness *n* 162

perverse *adj* 542, 838

perverseness *n* 542

perversion *n* 58, 219, 411, 463, 479, 489, 566, 871

perversity *n* 838

pervert *n* 851, *vb* 58, 219, 411, 463, 489, 566, 838

perverted *adj* 219, 447, 838, 871

pesky *adj* 597

pessimism *n* 432, 450, 743, 749

pessimist *n* 749

pessimistic *adj* 432, 450, 743, 749

pest *n* 597, 597, 737, 796, 836

pester *vb* 414, 737, 802

pestilential *adj* 597

pestle *n* 300

pet *adj* 795, *n* 326, 800, *vb* 736, 800

petal *n* 327

peter out *vb* 62, 123

pet hate *n* 758, 796

petite *adj* 169, 179, 185

petition *n* 414, 681, 874, *vb* 681, 856, 874

petitioner *n* 681, 874

pet name *n* 497, 498

petrification *n* 289, 321

petrified *adj* 750

petrify *vb* 289, 750

petrol/diesel engine *n* 568

petroleum *n* 319, 341

pettifogging *adj* 411

pettiness *n* 30, 577

petting *n* 800

petty *adj* 30, 430

petty cash *n* 711

petty office *n* 648

pew *n* 882

pewter *n* 385

phalanx *n* 43

phallus *n* 152

phantom *adj* 865, *n* 4, 370, 394, 457, 865

Pharisaic *adj* 872

Pharisee *n* 872

phase *n* 90, 92, *vb* 103

phenomenal *adj* 759

phenomenon *n* 394, 759

phial *n* 167

philander *vb* 795, 800

philanderer *n* 795

philanthropic *adj* 725, 805, 807

philanthropist *n* 805, 807

philanthropize *vb* 805

philanthropy *n* 805, 807, 833

philistine *adj* 439, *n* 439

philistinism *n* 439

philological *adj* 458, 494

philology *n* 494

philosophize *vb* 400

phlegm *n* 318, 733

phlegmatic *adj* 403, 616, 733

411

phobia n 447, 735, 750, 796
phobic adj 447
phone-in n 472
phoneme n 495
phonetic adj 494, 526
phonetics n 353, 494
phoney adj 4, 21, 479, 481, 771
phosphorescence n 374
phosphorescent adj 374
photo n 491
photocompose vb 514
photocomposition n 514
photocopy n 21, vb 21
photo finish n 25, 103
photogenic adj 491, 525
photograph n 488, 491, vb 486, 491
photographer n 613
photographic adj 491, 517
photographic memory n 448
photography n 488, 491
photogravure n 493
photojournalism n 491
photostat vb 491
phrase n 496, 499, vb 496, 499
phraseology n 494, 502
phrasing n 499
phylum n 68
physical adj 1, 3, 282, 334
physical condition n 7
physical education n 617
physicality n 334
physical pain n 337
physical pleasure n 336
physical training n 617
physical world n 3
physician n 596
physionomy n 212
piano adv 356, n 369
picaresque adj 518
pick n 545, 582, vb 545
pick and choose vb 545
picket n 682, vb 210, 630, 682
picketing n 630
pick holes vb 826
pick holes in vb 410
pickle n 603, 628, vb 570
pickled adj 603, 848
pick-me-up n 145, 594
pick out vb 70, 418, 766
pickpocket n 705, 838
pickpocketing n 705
pick pockets vb 705
pick someone up on vb 413
pick the short straw vb 554

pickup n 242
pick up vb 668
pick up the tab vb 716
picky adj 418
picnic n 629, 761, 789, vb 761
pictogram n 495, 513
pictorial adj 488, 490
picture n 490, 763, vb 488
picture house n 525
picture palace n 525
picturesque adj 490, 517, 763
picture writing n 495
piddle n 268, vb 268
pidgin n 494
piebald adj 38, 393
piece n 48, 53, 78, 149, 367, 519
pièce de résistance n 582
piecemeal adj 48, adv 48
piece of cake n 629
piece of luck n 115
pied adj 393
pied-à-terre n 165
pie in the sky n 4
pier n 193
pierce vb 232, 296
piercing adj 340, 355
pietism n 872
piety n 872
piffle n 459
pig n 326, 587, 846
pigeonhole n 57, 158, 232, vb 57, 485
pigeon post n 472
piggery n 328
piggybank n 711
pig-headed adj 542
pig-headedness n 542
pig in a poke n 428, 554
pig-in-the-middle n 42, 63
pig Latin n 494
piglet n 326
pigment n 381, vb 381
pigmentation n 381
pig's ear n 625
pigsty n 56, 587
pigtail n 765
pike n 649
pile n 66, 299, 570, 712, vb 66
pile on the agony vb 482
pile up vb 570
pilfer vb 705
pilfering n 705
pilgrim n 872
pill n 596
pillage n 705, vb 150, 705

pillager *n* 705
pillar *n* 131, 143, 190
pillarbox-red *adj* 387
pillar of society *n* 774, 837
pillar of the church *n* 870
pillbox *n* 167
pillory *n* 861, *vb* 773, 828
pillow *n* 193, 290, *vb* 193, 290
pillowcase *n* 202
pilot *n* 59, 237, 238, 559, 648, *vb* 237, 238
pilot officer *n* 648
pilot scheme *n* 416
pimp *n* 838
pimple *n* 226, 767
pimply *adj* 226
pin *n* 296, *vb* 40, 695
pince-nez *n* 370
pincers *n* 568
pinch *n* 23, 30, 115, *vb* 171, 181, 705, 728
pinched *adj* 171, 181
pin down *vb* 485
pine *vb* 735, 743
ping *n* 359, *vb* 359
pinguid *adj* 319
pinhead *n* 169, 181
pinhole *n* 232
pink *adj* 387, *vb* 229
pink elephants *n* 848
pinko *n* 148
pinnacle *n* 188
pinpoint *vb* 70, 158, 249
pinprick *n* 187, 577
pins and needles *n* 338
pinstripe *n* 766
pint-sized *adj* 169
pin-up *n* 763
pioneer *n* 59, 559, *vb* 59, 61
pioneering *adj* 59
pious *adj* 863, 872
pious hope *n* 426
pipeclay *n* 383
pipe down *vb* 526
pipe-dream *n* 4, 457, 748
pipeline *n* 42, 315
pipe of peace *n* 646
pipe up *vb* 528
piping *n* 209
piquancy *n* 342, 344
piquant *adj* 342, 344
pique *n* 739
piqued *adj* 739
piracy *n* 705

pirate *n* 648, 705, 838
piratical *adj* 705
pirogue *n* 243
pirouette *n* 223, 279, 524, *vb* 223, 279, 524
piss *n* 268, *vb* 268
pissed *adj* 848
pissed off *adj* 743
pistol *n* 649
pistol shot *n* 357
piston *n* 119
pit *n* 186, 227, 601, *vb* 227, 767
pitch *n* 158, 210, 255, 353, 365, 384, 526, 761, *vb* 160, 190, 195, 255
pitch-black *adj* 375, 384
pitcher *n* 167, 255
pitchfork *vb* 255
piteous *adj* 809
pitfall *n* 601
pith *n* 5, 166, 199, 458
pithiness *n* 505
pithy *adj* 442, 458, 505
pitiable *adj* 735, 747, 809
pitiful *adj* 809
pitiless *adj* 810
pitilessness *n* 810, 842
pittance *n* 30
pitted *adj* 227, 291, 767
pity *n* 805, 809, *vb* 809
pitying *adj* 809
pivot *n* 40, 42, 63, 132, 193, 200, 259, 279, *vb* 133, 279
pivotal *adj* 132, 200
pivot on *vb* 200
pixie *n* 865
pizzle *n* 152
placard *n* 470
placate *vb* 646
placatory *adj* 646
place *n* 158, *vb* 158, 160
placebo *n* 596
placed *adj* 160
place in the sun *n* 655
placement *n* 160
place name *n* 497
place of departed spirits *n* 867
place of work *n* 614
place of worship *n* 882
placid *adj* 733
placidity *n* 733
plagiarism *n* 21, 702
plagiarist *n* 21
plagiarize *vb* 21, 702
plague *n* 597, 737, 836, *vb* 628

413

plagued *adj* 656
plain *adj* 372, 460, 464, 473, 483, 503, 509, 762, 764, 843, *adv* 49, *n* 185, 311, 313
plain/honest truth *n* 478
plain clothes *n* 205
plain Jane *n* 764
plainness *n* 372, 483, 503, 509, 522
plain sailing *n* 629
plaint *n* 830
plaintiff *n* 681, 819, 830, 856
plaintive *adj* 747
plait *n* 197, 765, *vb* 197
plan *n* 298, 488, 547, 553, 557, 621, *vb* 298, 535, 547, 553, 557
plan ahead *vb* 453
planchette *n* 876
plane *adj* 191, *n* 191, 244, 568, *vb* 292, 301
planet *n* 278, 284
planetary *adj* 284
planet earth *n* 284
plangency *n* 359
plangent *adj* 355, 359
plank *n* 569
planned *adj* 547, 557, 621
planner *n* 557
planning *n* 754
plant *n* 320, 327, 614, *vb* 327
plantation *n* 327, 329
planter *n* 329
plant life *n* 327
plant out *vb* 329
plash *vb* 314
plasma *n* 303
plaster *n* 569, 596, *vb* 40, 43
plasterboard *n* 569
plastered *adj* 848
plasterer *n* 613
plastic *adj* 121, 130, 216, 290, 492, *n* 569
plastic arts *n* 492
plasticity *n* 130, 290
plastic surgeon *n* 765
plastic surgery *n* 765
plate *n* 167, 650, *vb* 175
plateau *n* 191, 313
plates of meat *n* 189
platform *n* 184, 193, 470
platinum *n* 383
platinum-blond *adj* 383
platitude *n* 442
platitudinous *adj* 442
platonic *adj* 850

Platonic love *n* 795
platoon *n* 648
platter *n* 167
plausibility *n* 3, 434
plausible *adj* 3, 394, 423, 425, 434, 551, 827, 829
play *n* 523, 667, 761, *vb* 368, 523
play-act *vb* 481
play-acting *n* 481
play ball *vb* 633
playboy *n* 770, 851
play by ear *vb* 368
play down *vb* 422, 432, 483, 577, 828
played out *adj* 62
player *n* 368, 761
play fair *vb* 831
play fast and loose *vb* 800
play for time *vb* 93, 114
play games *vb* 761
play havoc with *vb* 604
play hooky *vb* 163
playing field *n* 761
play it by ear *vb* 401, 416, 548
playmate *n* 793
play of light *n* 374
play one's cards well *vb* 624
play on words *n* 744
play safe *vb* 754
playschool *n* 111
play second fiddle *vb* 32, 577, 784
play the fool *vb* 772
play the game *vb* 817
plaything *n* 761
play to the gallery *vb* 523, 785
play truant *vb* 395, 605, 662
play up *vb* 482, 621, 662
play with fire *vb* 599, 753
plea *n* 551, 681, 829
pleach *vb* 197
pleached *adj* 197
plead *vb* 551, 681, 829
plead for *vb* 410
plead guilty *vb* 840, 841
pleadings *n* 856
plead with *vb* 809
pleasant *adj* 629, 734, 736, 761
pleasantness *n* 736
please *vb* 736, 738
pleased *adj* 734, 811
pleased as Punch *adj* 734
pleased with oneself *adj* 738
please oneself *vb* 667
pleasing *adj* 736
pleasurable *adj* 336, 734, 736

pleasurableness *n* 736
pleasure *n* 734, 761
pleasure-seeking *adj* 844, *n* 336
pleat *n* 230, *vb* 230
pleated *adj* 230
pleb *n* 777
plebeian *adj* 777, *n* 777
plebiscite *n* 545
pledge *n* 473, 683, 687, 702, 821, *vb* 473, 683, 687, 702
pledged *adj* 473, 683, 687
pledge oneself *vb* 821
plenipotentiary *n* 675
plenitude *n* 49
plenteous *adj* 573
plentiful *adj* 29, 152, 182, 573
plenty *adj* 86, *n* 573
pleonasm *n* 506
pleonastic *adj* 506
plethora *n* 29, 575
pliability *n* 293, 537
pliable *adj* 72, 216, 293, 541
pliancy *n* 290, 541
pliant *adj* 290, 642
plicate *adj* 230
pliers *n* 270, 568
plight *n* 7
plight one's troth *vb* 683, 797
Plimsoll line *n* 177
plinth *n* 185, 189, 193
plod *vb* 236, 246, 540, 617
plodder *n* 616
plodding *adj* 540, 616
plod on *vb* 124
plonk *n* 267, 360, *vb* 360
plop *n* 360, *vb* 360, 360
plot *n* 517, 557, 626, *vb* 469, 557, 626
plotter *n* 557, 626
plotting *adj* 557, *n* 469
plough *vb* 231, 328
plough a lonely furrow *vb* 79
pluck *n* 143, 145, 539, 751, *vb* 203, 256, 368
plucked *adj* 203
pluck up courage *vb* 751
plucky *adj* 143, 751
plug *n* 202, 233, 470, *vb* 233, 470
plug away *vb* 540
plug in *vb* 136, 141
plum *n* 392, 582
plumage *n* 202
plumb *adj* 190, *adv* 222, *n* 222, 285
plumber *n* 613
plumbline *n* 192

plumbness *n* 190
plumb the depths *vb* 186
plummet *vb* 186, 190, 275
plump *adj* 168, *vb* 545
plump for *vb* 535
plunder *n* 650, 705, 706, *vb* 705
plunge *n* 34, 186, 275, *vb* 34, 185, 186, 190, 269, 275
plunging *adj* 205
plural *adj* 80
pluralism *n* 80, 657
pluralist *adj* 80, 657, *n* 80
plurality *n* 80
plus *adv* 35, 45
plush *adj* 712
Pluto *n* 862
plutocrat *n* 712
ply *n* 175, *vb* 119, 237, 607
plywood *n* 569
p.m. *adv* 110
pneumatic *adj* 306
pneumonia *n* 589
poach *vb* 267, 272, 555, 705
poacher *n* 555, 705
poaching *n* 705
pocket *n* 232, *vb* 690, 699, 703
pocket money *n* 711, 719
pockmark *n* 227, *vb* 227
pockmarked *adj* 227
pod *n* 202, *vb* 203
podgy *adj* 168
poem *n* 521
poesy *n* 521
poet *n* 518, 521
poetaster *n* 521
poetic *adj* 518, 521
poetic justice *n* 817
poet laureate *n* 521
poetry *n* 518, 521
po-faced *adj* 745
pogrom *n* 324
point *n* 8, 9, 24, 228, 296, 409, 458, 564, *vb* 220, 249, 296, 484
point at issue *n* 410, 635
point-blank *adv* 249
point-blank range *n* 173
pointed *adj* 220, 296, 458, 507
pointedness *n* 296, 507
pointer *n* 484
point in the other direction *vb* 421
point in time *n* 90
pointless *adj* 445, 565, 579
pointlessness *n* 445, 579
point of departure *n* 262

point of honour *n* 831
point out *vb* 404
point the finger at *vb* 830
point to *vb* 484
poise *n* 25, 235, 511
poised *adj* 511
poison *n* 150, 267, 597, 604, 861, *vb*
604, 796, 806, 860
poisonous *adj* 589, 597, 604
poison pen letter *n* 515
poke/stick one's nose in *vb* 402
poke fun at *vb* 744, 773
poker *n* 222, 761
poker-faced *adj* 745
Polack *n* 331
polar *adj* 215
polarity *n* 14, 81, 215, 632
polarization *n* 41, 215
polarize *vb* 41
polder *n* 311
polemical *adj* 41, 410, 635
polemicist *n* 635
polemics *n* 410
poles apart *adj* 18
police *n* 598, 854, *vb* 55, 598, 622,
854
police force *n* 854
policeman *n* 854
police officer *n* 854
police state *n* 657
policewoman *n* 854
policy *n* 621
polio *n* 589
polish *n* 292, 301, 511, 586, 586, 592,
768, *vb* 292, 301, 511, 584, 586, 592
polished *adj* 292, 511, 586, 768
polish off *vb* 49, 267, 653, 846
polite *adj* 791, 823
politeness *n* 791
political *adj* 622
political party *n* 634
political prisoner *n* 671
politician *n* 622
politics *n* 622
polka *n* 367, 524, 761
polka dot *n* 766
poll *n* 75, 188, 414, 545, *vb* 414
pollen *n* 152, 300
pollinate *vb* 152
pollination *n* 152
poll tax *n* 721
pollute *vb* 572, 587, 591, 604
polluted *adj* 347, 350, 587, 591, 851
polluting *adj* 604

pollution *n* 347, 572, 587, 591, 604,
851
polo *n* 761
polonaise *n* 524
poltergeist *n* 865
poltroon *n* 752
poly *n* 477
polychromatic *adj* 393
polychrome *adj* 381
polycotton *n* 569
polyester *n* 569
polygamous *adj* 80
polygamy *n* 80, 797
polyglot *adj* 494, 528
polygon *n* 220
polygonal *adj* 220
polymath *n* 49, 80, 438
polyphonic *adj* 367
polysemous *adj* 80
polysemy *n* 80
polystyrene *n* 569
polysyllable *n* 496
polytechnic *n* 477
polytheism *n* 868
polytheist *adj* 80
polythene *n* 569
pomade *n* 319, 349
pomander *n* 349
Pommie *n* 331
pomp *n* 785
pomposity *n* 482, 510, 785
pompous *adj* 482, 510, 783, 785
ponce around *vb* 771
poncy *adj* 771
pond *n* 312
ponder *vb* 616
ponderous *adj* 285, 502, 508, 762
ponderousness *n* 285, 508
pong *n* 347, 350, *vb* 350
pongy *adj* 350
pontiff *n* 879
pontifical *adj* 878
pontificate *vb* 528, 532
pontoon *n* 761
pony *n* 326
ponytail *n* 765
pony-trekking *n* 761
pooch *n* 326
poofter *n* 73
pooh-pooh *vb* 407, 432
pool *n* 312
pool one's resources *vb* 45
pooped *adj* 619
poor *adj* 574, 713

poor-/low-quality *adj* 583
poor/low quality *n* 583
poor box *n* 698
poor health *n* 589
poor likeness *n* 489
poor lookout *n* 749
poorly *adj* 589
poorly fed *adj* 845
poor quality *n* 32
poor relation *n* 32
poor visibility *n* 373
poor whites *n* 777
pop *vb* 687, 702, 849
pope *n* 879
pop-eyed *adj* 228
popgun *n* 761
pop in *vb* 263
poplin *n* 569
pop music *n* 367
pop one's clogs *vb* 323
poppet *n* 800
poppy *n* 387
pop the question *vb* 800
populace *n* 330, 777
popular *adj* 69, 367, 757, 774, 825
popularity *n* 774
popularization *n* 460
popularize *vb* 69
populate *vb* 165
population *n* 164, 330
population drift *n* 67
population explosion *n* 152
pop up *vb* 394
porch *n* 209
porcine *adj* 326
pore *n* 232
pore over *vb* 370
porno *adj* 851
pornographic *adj* 851
pornography *n* 851
porosity *n* 232
porous *adj* 232
porridge *n* 317, 343, 668
porringer *n* 167
port *n* 214, 387, 553
portability *n* 286
portable *adj* 239, 286
portal *n* 232
portcullis *n* 630
portend *vb* 455
portent *n* 455
portentous *adj* 455
portentousness *n* 455
porter *n* 241, 666, 668

portfolio *n* 167
porthole *n* 232
portion *n* 23, 48, 78, 700
portliness *n* 168
portly *adj* 168
portmanteau word *n* 496
portrait *n* 488, 490
portray *vb* 488, 490
portrayal *n* 488, 490, 517
pose *n* 394, 771, *vb* 771
Poseidon *n* 862
poser *n* 414, 628, 771
poseur *n* 21, 771
posh *adj* 770, 776
posing *adj* 771
posit *vb* 456
position *n* 7, 8, 159, 160, 162, 434,
   611, 774, 776, *vb* 159, 160
positioned *adj* 159
positive *adj* 415, 434, 473, 633
positive discrimination *n* 25
positive thinking *n* 742
posse *n* 66
possess *vb* 40, 692, 876
possessed *adj* 447
possession *n* 692, 876
possessions *n* 694
possessive *adj* 692, 815, 834
possessiveness *n* 815
possessor *n* 692
possibilities *n* 423
possibility *n* 423
possible *adj* 423
possibly *adv* 423
post *n* 160, 472, 515, 611, *vb* 158,
   159, 160, 239, 241, 515, 720
postage *n* 721
postal *adj* 515
postal order *n* 711
postbag *n* 515
postcard *n* 515
post chaise *n* 242
postcode *n* 515
postdate *vb* 98, 100
posted *adj* 466
poster *n* 470, 490
posterior *adj* 60, 62, 100, *n* 60, 213
posterity *n* 60, 100, 155
post haste *adv* 245
posthumous *adj* 98, 100, 114, 323
postman *n* 241
post meridiem *adv* 110
post mortem *n* 60, 100, 323, 417
postpone *vb* 100, 114, 654

417

prearrange *vb* 547
prearranged *adj* 547
prearrangement *n* 547, 559
precarious *adj* 94, 144, 428, 599
precariousness *n* 94, 144, 599
precaution *n* 559, 598, 754
precautionary *adj* 559, 754
precede *vb* 59, 99
precedence *n* 31, 59, 99
precedent *n* 22, 59, 71, 549
preceding *adj* 59
precept *n* 71, 623, 821
precinct *n* 157
precincts *n* 206
precious *adj* 510, 723, *n* 800
precious metal *n* 321
preciousness *n* 510
precious stone *n* 766
precipice *n* 184, 190, 275
precipitate *adj* 615, *vb* 132, 615
precipitately *adv* 147
precipitation *n* 307, 308, 615
precipitous *adj* 184, 190, 245, 753
precipitousness *n* 190
precis *n* 36, 179, 520, *vb* 179, 520
precise *adj* 440, 503, 787, 817
preciseness *n* 503
precision *n* 406, 440
preclude *vb* 52, 59, 99
precocious *adj* 98, 113
precocity *n* 98, 113
precognition *n* 453, 455
preconceive *vb* 430, 547
preconceived *adj* 547
precondition *n* 536
precursor *n* 59, 99
predate *vb* 59, 99
predator *n* 703
predatory *adj* 703
predecease *vb* 99
predecessor *n* 59
predestination *n* 104, 547
predestine *vb* 547
predestined *adj* 104
predetermination *n* 547
predetermine *vb* 536, 547
predetermined *adj* 547
predicament *n* 628
predicate *n* 500
predict *vb* 104, 425, 450, 453, 455
predictability *n* 117, 119, 131, 425, 427
predictable *adj* 117, 119, 131, 425
prediction *n* 104, 453, 455, 877

predictive *adj* 455
predilection *n* 140, 545, 757, 795
predispose *vb* 140, 430
predisposed *adj* 140
predisposition *n* 140
predominate *vb* 29, 31, 69
preempt *vb* 59, 99, 113, 453
preemptive *adj* 99, 453
preen *vb* 765
preexist *vb* 99
preexistence *n* 99
preexisting *adj* 99
prefab *n* 165
preface *n* 59, 61, *vb* 59
prefatory *adj* 59, 61
prefect *n* 622, 665
prefer *vb* 545, 757
preference *n* 535, 545, 757, 795
preferential *adj* 545
preferential treatment *n* 818
preferment *n* 253
prefigure *vb* 455
prefix *n* 500
pregnancy *n* 152
pregnant *adj* 152, 458
prehistoric *adj* 105
prehistory *n* 99, 105
prejudice *n* 26, 140, 181, 430, 434, 758, 796, 818, 871, *vb* 26, 140, 430
prejudiced *adj* 26, 181, 430, 818
prelate *n* 879
preliminaries *n* 61, 559
preliminary *adj* 59, 61, 113, 414, 559, *n* 59
prelude *n* 59, 367
premarital *adj* 797
premature *adj* 98, 113
prematurely *adv* 98
prematurity *n* 98, 113
premeditate *vb* 453, 547
premeditated *adj* 453, 547
premeditation *n* 453, 547, 559
premier *n* 31, 622
premiere *n* 61, 523
premise *n* 400, 410, 456
premises *n* 158
premium *adj* 582, *n* 859
premium bond *n* 554
premonition *n* 99, 401, 602
preoccupation *n* 398, 404
preoccupied *adj* 398, 404
preoccupy *vb* 398, 404
preordain *vb* 536
preordained *adj* 536

preordination *n* 547
prep *n* 476, 559
preparation *n* 61, 149, 475, 547, 559
preparatory *adj* 61, 113, 559
prepare *vb* 267, 453, 475, 547, 559
prepare a brief *vb* 856
prepare a case *vb* 856
prepared *adj* 450, 453, 559
preparedness *n* 113, 453, 559
preparer *n* 559
prepare the ground *vb* 559
preposition *n* 500
prepositional *adj* 500
preposterous *adj* 443, 482, 772
prequel *n* 59
prerequisite *n* 85, 422, 536, 558
prerogative *n* 31, 657, 776, 819
presage *n* 455, 602, *vb* 59, 99, 455
presbyopia *n* 370
presbyopic *adj* 370
presbytery *n* 882
preschool *adj* 111
prescience *n* 453, 455
prescient *adj* 453, 455
prescribe *vb* 71, 623, 661, 819
prescription *n* 71, 623, 661
prescriptive *adj* 71, 623
presence *n* 1, 162, 865
presence of God *n* 866
present *adj* 1, 90, 101, 162, *n* 101, 698, *vb* 464, 523, 698, 720, 791, 793, 859
present arms *vb* 791
presentation *n* 464, 621, 698, 791
present-day *adj* 101
present day *n* 101
presenter *n* 212, 472
present event *n* 101
presentiment *n* 99, 401, 453
presently *adv* 1
present no difficulties *vb* 629
present oneself *vb* 162
present time *n* 101
present with a fait accompli *vb* 99
preservation *n* 598, 603, 640, 862
preservative *adj* 603, *n* 603
preserve *vb* 95, 124, 570, 598, 603, 640
preserved *adj* 603
Preserver *n* 862
preserving *adj* 603, *n* 603
president *n* 665
press *n* 66, 86, 471, 568, *vb* 173, 247
press-gang *vb* 703

press officer/secretary *n* 647
press on *vb* 253
press release *n* 466
pressure *n* 23, 136, 141, 285, 338, 551, 615, 617, 656, 664
pressure group *n* 139, 681
pressurize *vb* 139, 285, 664
pressurized *adj* 615
prestige *n* 29, 657, 774, 825
prestigious *adj* 29, 31, 657, 774
presume *vb* 456, 748, 781, 820
presume upon *vb* 812
presumption *n* 431, 748, 781, 820
presumptuous *adj* 781, 820
presuppose *vb* 400, 430
pretence *n* 469, 481, 551
pretend *vb* 457, 479, 481, 551, 771
pretended *adj* 481
pretender *n* 820
pretension *n* 769, 771
pretentious *adj* 510, 769, 771, 783, 785
pretentiousness *n* 510, 771
pretext *n* 134, 551, 829
prettify *vb* 765
prettiness *n* 763
pretty *adj* 763
pretty as a picture *adj* 763
prevail *vb* 1, 29, 31, 69, 141, 651
prevailing *adj* 139
prevail on *vb* 139
prevalent *adj* 1, 69, 117
prevaricate *vb* 461
prevent *vb* 52, 99, 137, 556
preventative *adj* 630
preventive *adj* 99, 598, 630
preventive measure *n* 598
preventive medicine *n* 590
preview *n* 59, 523
previous *adj* 59, 98, 99, 105, 113
previous engagement *n* 581
previously *adv* 59, 99, 102, 105
prey *n* 555
price *n* 582, 721, *vb* 721
price control *n* 668, 721
price-fixing *n* 668
price freeze *n* 721
price label/tag/ticket *n* 721
priceless *adj* 582, 723
price reduction *n* 724
prices and incomes policy *n* 668
pricey *adj* 723
prick *n* 152, 296, *vb* 232, 296, 551
prickle *n* 291, 296, *vb* 291

prickliness *n* 296, 301, 730
prickly *adj* 291, 296, 730, 803
prickly heat *n* 338
prick out *vb* 79, 329
prick up *vb* 190, 228
prick up one's ears *vb* 351, 404
pride *n* 66, 779
pride of place *n* 31, 59
pride oneself on *vb* 779
priest *n* 879
priesthood *n* 878
priestly *adj* 878
prig *n* 850
priggish *adj* 850
prim *adj* 745, 771, 850
primacy *n* 31, 878
prima donna *n* 31, 368, 779
prima facie *adj* 198, *adv* 6, 394
primal *adj* 61
primary *adj* 3, 61, 132, 576
primary/secondary/complementary
  colour *n* 381
primary school *n* 477
primate *n* 879
prime *adj* 74, 582, *n* 112, 655, *vb* 559
prime constituent *n* 5
primed *adj* 466, 559
prime minister *n* 31
prime mover *n* 132, 862
primeval *adj* 61
priming *n* 559
primness *n* 745, 850
primogeniture *n* 59, 99
primordial *adj* 61, 107
primordial soup *n* 61
primp *vb* 765
primrose *n* 389
primrose-yellow *adj* 389
primum mobile *n* 284
prince *n* 665, 776
princely *adj* 774, 776
Prince of Darkness *n* 864
Prince of Peace *n* 862
princess *n* 665, 776
principal *adj* 31, 576, *n* 665
principalities *n* 863
principally *adv* 31
principle *n* 71, 434, 831
principled *adj* 831, 837
principles *n* 837
prink *vb* 204
print *n* 491, 514, *vb* 491, 513, 514
printable *adj* 677
printed *adj* 514

printer *n* 514, 570, 613
printer's error *n* 514
printing *n* 514
print off *vb* 514
printout *n* 75, 514, 570
print run *n* 514
prior *adj* 59, 99, *n* 879, 879
priority *n* 59, 99, 576, 657
prior notice *n* 99
prior warning *n* 113
priory *n* 882
prism *n* 130, 220, 381, 393
prison *n* 671, 790, 861
prisoner *n* 671
prisoner at the bar *n* 856
prisoner in the dock *n* 671
prisoner of war *n* 671
prisoner-of-war camp *n* 671
prison officer *n* 668
prison sentence *n* 860
pristine *adj* 39, 47, 106, 565, 584
privacy *n* 467
private *adj* 199, 467, *n* 648
private devotion *n* 874
private eye *n* 203
privately *adv* 467
private parts *n* 152
privation *n* 691, 713
privatization *n* 704
privatize *vb* 704
privilege *n* 26, 31, 776, 819, 822
privileged *adj* 822
privileged class *n* 776
prize *n* 650, 698, 703, 706, 719, 859,
  vb 774, 795
prizewinner *n* 31, 651
prizewinning *adj* 651
PR man *n* 470
pro- *adj* 676
probability *n* 425
probable *adj* 425
probably *adv* 425
probationary *adj* 416
probationer *n* 61, 476
probe *n* 414, *vb* 186, 414, 433
probing *adj* 186, 433
probity *n* 478, 817, 831, 837, 839
problem *n* 409, 414, 628, 735
problematic *adj* 628
problematical *adj* 414
proboscis *n* 228
procedural *adj* 71, 787
procedure *n* 71, 240, 621, 787
proceed *vb* 124, 234, 253, 271

prolongation n 93, 124, 178
prolonged adj 178
promenade n 240
prominence n 31, 212, 228, 372, 464, 576, 774
prominent adj 31, 212, 228, 372, 464, 576, 774
promiscuity n 851
promiscuous adj 756
promiscuousness n 756
promise n 104, 423, 425, 473, 562, 683, 748, 821, vb 473, 562, 683
promised adj 683
promised land n 748
promising adj 104, 425, 655, 748
promissory adj 683
promissory note n 683, 711
promontory n 228, 311
promote vb 132, 138, 253, 470, 576, 592, 631
promoter n 470, 631
promotion n 253, 276, 470, 592
prompt adj 96, 113, 245, 537, n 523, vb 61, 448, 551
promptly adv 245
promptness n 96, 113, 245, 537
promulgate vb 468
promulgation n 468
prone adj 140, 191
proneness n 140, 191
prong n 296
pronoun n 500
pronounce vb 429, 473, 526, 856
pronounced adj 464
pronounce man and wife vb 797
pronouncement n 473
pronto adv 96, 245
pronunciation n 526
proof adj 638, n 412, 417, 420, 514
proof of identity n 485
proofread vb 592
proofreader n 514, 592, 613
proofreading n 592
prop n 131, 193, vb 193
propaganda n 139, 475
propaganda war n 645
propagate vb 67, 149, 152, 329
propagation n 67, 152, 322
propel vb 141, 247, 255, 664
propellant n 255
propellent adj 255
propeller n 255, 279
propensity n 140, 537, 757
proper adj 511, 817, 819, 837

propertied adj 692, 694, 712
property n 5, 694
prophecy n 455, 868
prophesy vb 453, 455
prophet n 455, 868, 877
prophetic adj 453, 455, 868
prophylactic adj 598, 754, n 754
prophylaxis n 598, 754
propinquity n 173
propitiate vb 646, 738, 814
propitiation n 814, 862
propitiatory adj 646, 814
propitious adj 115
proportion n 9, 24, 48, 78, 218, 511
proportional adj 9, 24, 218
proportionally adv 9
proportionately adv 700
proportions n 156, 168
proposal n 409, 557, 679, 681, 795, 800
propose vb 456, 553, 557, 623, 679, 681, 800
propose conditions vb 685
proposed adj 557
proposer n 557
proposition n 456, 679, 800, vb 800
proprietary adj 694
proprietor n 692
proprietorial adj 692
proprietorship n 692
propriety n 511, 768, 817, 850
props n 523
propulsion n 141, 234, 247, 255
propulsive adj 255
prop up vb 131, 276
pro rata adv 700
prosaic adj 502, 508, 522, 762
prosaicness n 522
pros and cons n 410
proscenium n 523
proscribe vb 678
proscription n 678
prose n 518, 522
prosecute vb 607, 830, 856
prosecution n 555, 830, 856
prosecutor n 830, 856
proselyte n 125
proselytize vb 125, 872
proselytizing adj 125
prose poem n 522
prosiness n 508, 522
prosodic adj 521
prosody n 521
prospect n 104, 425, 450

prospecting n 433
prospective adj 104, 425, 450
prospectus n 76, 516
prosper vb 33, 336, 651, 655, 712, 835
prosperity n 655, 712, 835
prosperous adj 651, 655, 712, 835
prostitute vb 566
prostitution n 566, 851
prostrate adj 142, 144, 185, 191, 823, vb 142
prostrate oneself vb 874
prostration n 142, 144, 619
prosy adj 506, 508, 522
protean adj 121, 130, 217
protect vb 378, 598, 603, 640
protected adj 378
protection n 598, 603, 640
protectionism n 668
protectionist adj 52, 668
protective adj 598, 603, 640
protective clothing n 640
protector n 598, 640, 807
protectorate n 157, 672
protein n 320
protest n 73, 437, 638, 682, 826, vb 73, 437, 538, 632, 638, 682, 826
protestant adj 682
protester n 682, 739
protesting adj 682
protest meeting n 682
protocol n 549, 787, 791
protoplasm n 320
prototypal adj 22
prototype n 22, 216
protract vb 93, 124, 178, 506
protracted adj 93, 178, 506
protraction n 93, 178
protractor n 177
protrude vb 228
protuberance n 228
protuberant adj 228
proud adj 779
proud person n 779
provable adj 417
prove vb 412, 417, 829
prove accurate vb 440
prove guilty vb 858
prove innocent vb 857
proven adj 417
provender n 267
prove one's point vb 412
proverb n 442, 499
proverbial adj 442
prove wrong vb 413

provide vb 559, 571
provided adj 571
provide for vb 453
providence n 835
Providence n 862
provident adj 453
providential adj 115, 862
provider n 571
provide the means vb 567
province n 157
provincial adj 157, 430, 777
provincialism n 430
proving n 416
provision n 453, 559, 570, 571, 685, vb 559, 571
provisional adj 8, 50, 94, 101, 121, 416, 422, 685
provisionally adv 8, 94, 101
provisioning n 559, 571
provisions n 267, 559, 567, 571
proviso n 422, 685
provocation n 132, 637, 732
provocative adj 410, 635, 637, 732
provoke vb 61, 132, 637, 732, 794, 802
provost n 665
prow n 212
prowess n 751
proximity n 104, 173, 176
proxy n 128, 672, 675, 676
prude n 850
prudence n 398, 406, 726, 754
prudent adj 406, 453, 726, 754
prudery n 850
prudish adj 784, 850
prudishness n 784, 850
prune adj 36, vb 41, 179, 183
prurience n 402, 851
prurient adj 402, 851
Prussian blue n 391
pry vb 402
prying n 402
psalm n 367, 874
Psalms n 868
psalter n 881
pseudo adj 21
pseudonym n 469, 497, 498
pseudonymous adj 498
psyche n 283, 396
psychedelic adj 38, 381
psychiatrist n 396
psychic adj 283, 396, 401, 455, 877, n 877
psychical adj 877

psychics *n* 877
psychic science *n* 877
psychoanalyst *n* 396
psychokinesis *n* 877
psychological *adj* 396
psychological moment *n* 115
psychological warfare *n* 645
psychologist *n* 396
psychopath *n* 447
psychopathic *adj* 324
psychopathy *n* 447
psychosis *n* 447
psychosomatic *adj* 396
psychotherapist *n* 396
psychotic *adj* 447
PT *n* 617
pub *n* 165
pub bore *n* 762
pub-crawl *n* 848
puberty *n* 111
pubescence *n* 111
pubescent *adj* 111
public *adj* 198, 330, 464, 468, 470, 693, *n* 330, 470
public address *n* 532
public-address system *n* 355
publication *n* 464, 468, 470, 514, 516
public baths *n* 586
public enemy *n* 794, 838
public health *n* 590
public house *n* 165
publicist *n* 470
publicity *n* 470
publicize *vb* 464, 470
public ownership *n* 693
public place *n* 470
public property *n* 470, 693
public relations *n* 470
public relations officer *n* 647
public speaking *n* 528
public-spirited *adj* 807
public spiritedness *n* 807
public weal *n* 835
publish *vb* 468, 470, 471, 514
published *adj* 470
puce *adj* 392
puck *n* 865
pucker *n* 230, *vb* 171, 219, 230
puckered *adj* 230, 231
pudding *n* 267
puddle *n* 187, 312
pudenda *n* 152
puerile *adj* 111, 445

puff *n* 316, 431, 470, *vb* 306, 316, 825, 827
puffiness *n* 170
puff up *vb* 170
puffy *adj* 226
pugnacious *adj* 643
puke *vb* 266
pulchritude *n* 763
pull *n* 139, 256, 257, 617, *vb* 234, 256, 257
pull a face *vb* 219, 764
pull a long face *vb* 743
pull at *vb* 256
pulley *n* 568
pulling *n* 256
pull off *vb* 651
pull oneself together *vb* 742
pull one's finger out *vb* 61, 617
pull one's punches *vb* 660
pull one's socks up *vb* 592
pull out *vb* 123, 262
pull out all the stops *vb* 49, 145, 617, 785
pull rank *vb* 141
pull someone's leg *vb* 744, 773
pull together *vb* 19, 633
pullulate *vb* 86
pull up *vb* 123, 235
pulp *n* 182, 290, 317, 569
pulp *vb* 150, 290, 317
pulp fiction *n* 518
pulpiness *n* 182, 317
pulpit *n* 470, 882
pulpy *adj* 182, 290, 317
pulsar *n* 284
pulsate *vb* 280
pulsating *adj* 280
pulse *n* 88, 119, 280, 358
pulverization *n* 46, 300
pulverize *vb* 46, 147, 300
pulverized *adj* 300
pumice *n* 301, 586
pummel *vb* 247
pump *n* 270, *vb* 270
pumping iron *n* 143
pun *n* 461, 496, 744, *vb* 744
punch *n* 38, 145, 232, 247, 507, 568, *vb* 147, 232, 247
punch-drunk *adj* 335, 731
punched cards *n* 570
punch-up *n* 56, 147, 643
punchy *adj* 145, 507
punctilious *adj* 404, 440, 688, 787
punctiliousness *n* 404, 440, 688

put in store *vb* 570
put in the hands of a receiver *vb* 717
put in the picture *vb* 466
put in the shade *vb* 31
put into effect *vb* 607, 852
put into effect/practice *vb* 136
put into practice *vb* 564
put into service *vb* 564
put into words *vb* 496, 499
put into writing *vb* 513
put money up *vb* 701
put off *vb* 100, 114, 405, 552, 654, 758
put off one's stride/stroke *vb* 58
put on *adj* 481, *vb* 523, 771
put-on *n* 771
put on a back burner *vb* 565
put on a brave face *vb* 742
put on airs *vb* 771, 783
put on a pedestal *vb* 276, 576, 774, 823, 875
put on a show *vb* 785
put on a war footing *vb* 645
put one off *vb* 737
put one over on *vb* 480, 626
put oneself first *vb* 834
put oneself last *vb* 833
put oneself out *vb* 617
put oneself to a lot of bother *vb* 617
put one's feet up *vb* 618
put one's finger on *vb* 70
put one's foot down *vb* 539, 542, 659
put one's foot in it *vb* 116, 441
put one's hand in one's pocket *vb* 698
put one's money into *vb* 708
put one's oar in *vb* 65
put one's shirt on *vb* 427
put on ice *vb* 123, 608, 654
put on ice/in cold storage *vb* 114
put on the black cap *vb* 858
put on the market *vb* 679, 709
put on the slate *vb* 714
put out *adj* 743, *vb* 581, 628, 737
put out at interest *vb* 701
put out feelers *vb* 414
put out of action *vb* 142
put out of one's mind *vb* 399
put pen to paper *vb* 513
putrefaction *n* 350
putrid *adj* 350
put right *vb* 594, 596, 817
put someone's nose out of joint *vb* 31
put the cart before the horse *vb* 196
put the clock back *vb* 98, 105

put the fear of God into *vb* 750
put the finishing touches to *vb* 49, 653
put the mockers/kibosh on *vb* 150
put the wind up *vb* 750
put to death *vb* 860
put to rights *vb* 55
put to sea *vb* 237
put to shame *vb* 775, 824
put to trouble *vb* 737
put to trouble/inconvenience *vb* 628
put to use *vb* 564
put two and two together *vb* 400
putty *n* 290
put under *vb* 335
put under a curse *vb* 876
put under an obligation *vb* 821
put under the microscope *vb* 46
put up *vb* 276, 571, 723
put up a fight *vb* 638
put up at *vb* 165
put up for auction *vb* 679
put up for sale *vb* 709
put-up job *n* 547, 830
put up with *vb* 660, 733
puzzle *n* 467, 628, *vb* 461, 628
puzzled *adj* 461
puzzlement *n* 461
puzzle out *vb* 462
puzzling *adj* 414, 461, 628
PVC *n* 569
pygmy *n* 169
pyramid *n* 168, 220
pyramidal *adj* 220
pyre *n* 325
Pyrrhic victory *n* 65

Q

quack *n* 480, *vb* 364
quack remedy *n* 596
quad *n* 83
quadrangle *n* 83, 158
quadrant *n* 177
quadraphonic *adj* 83, 353
quadrate *adj* 83, *vb* 83
quadrennial *adj* 83
quadricentennial *n* 84
quadriga *n* 83
quadrilateral *adj* 83
quadruped *n* 83, 326
quadruple *adj* 83, *vb* 83
quadruplet *n* 83
quadruplicate *n* 83, *vb* 83

quaff *vb* 267
quagmire *n* 308
quail *vb* 750, 752
quake *vb* 280, 281, 750
quaking *adj* 281
qualification *n* 422
qualifier *n* 61
qualify *vb* 422, 500, 573
qualifying *adj* 422, 685
quality *adj* 582, *n* 31, 471, 582
quality of life *n* 322
qualm *n* 538
qualms *n* 435, 750
quantification *n* 177
quantify *vb* 23, 177
quantitative *adj* 23
quantity *n* 23
quantum *n* 23
quantum jump *n* 274
quantum leap *n* 33
quarantine *n* 41, 52, 590, 598, 668, 790, *vb* 41, 52, 790
quarrel *n* 410, 437, 635, 802, *vb* 410, 437, 635
quarrelling *adj* 635
quarrelsome *adj* 410, 635
quarrelsomeness *n* 410
quarry *n* 555, 570, 614, *vb* 270
quarter *n* 78, 83, 92, 157, 660, 809, *vb* 83, 158
quarterly *adj* 83, 92, *n* 83
quartermaster *n* 571
quarters *n* 158, 165
quartet *n* 83, 368
quarto *n* 83
quartz *n* 321
quasar *n* 284
quash *vb* 150, 487, 673
quashed *adj* 673
quaternary *adj* 83
quaternity *n* 83
quatrain *n* 83, 521
quaver *n* 358, *vb* 144, 358
queen *n* 665, 776
queenly *adj* 776
Queen's English *n* 494
queer *adj* 73, 447, *n* 73
queerness *n* 447
queer street *n* 713
quell *vb* 2, 148, 150, 354, 630
querulous *adj* 739, 803
query *n* 414, 428, *vb* 428
quest *n* 414, 555, 562, *vb* 555
question *n* 409, 414, *vb* 402, 414

questionable *adj* 410, 428, 435, 775, 832
questioning *adj* 402, 414
question mark *n* 428
questionnaire *n* 414
queue *n* 64, 178
quibble *vb* 410, 411, 739
quibbling *n* 411
quick *adj* 245, 322, *n* 199
quick-change *adj* 130
quicken *vb* 245, 729, 732
quick-fire *adj* 245, 533
quickness *n* 245
quicksand *n* 308, 601
quicksilver *adj* 732, *n* 130
quickstep *n* 524, 761
quick-tempered *adj* 732
quick-witted *adj* 396
quid pro quo *n* 28, 129
quiescent *adj* 465
quiet *adj* 55, 354, 356, 618, *n* 55, 235, 610
quieten *vb* 354
quietly *adv* 663
quietness *n* 531
quiet time *n* 874
quilt *vb* 201
quilting *n* 201
quin *n* 84
quincentenary *n* 84
quincunx *n* 84
quinquagenarian *n* 84
quintessence *n* 5
quintessential *adj* 5
quintet *n* 84, 368
quintuple *adj* 84
quintuplet *n* 84
quip *n* 744, *vb* 744
quirk *n* 70
quirky *adj* 70, 485, 502
quit *vb* 262, 563, 674, 752
quits *n* 25
quitter *n* 752
quitting *n* 752
quiver *n* 280, 281, 729, *vb* 280, 281, 750
quivering *adj* 281
quixotic *adj* 457, 833
quiz *n* 414, 472, *vb* 402
quizzical *adj* 414
quizzing *n* 402
quorate *adj* 573
quorum *n* 573
quota *n* 700

quotation *n* 721
quote *vb* 70, 721
quotidian *adj* 92
quotient *n* 7

R

rabbet *vb* 40
rabbi *n* 868, 879
rabbit *n* 752, *vb* 445, 506
rabbit on *vb* 459, 530
rabbitter *n* 555
rabbitting *n* 555
rabble *n* 777
rabid *adj* 147
rabies *n* 589
race *n* 68, 236, 245, 615, 643, *vb* 234, 236, 245, 314, 615, 643
racehorse *n* 245
raceme *n* 327
racer *n* 245
racial *adj* 331
raciness *n* 502, 507
racism *n* 331, 430
racist *adj* 331, 430
rack *n* 861, *vb* 860
racket *n* 355, 358, 366, 480, 832
racketeer *n* 707, 838, *vb* 707
rack one's brains *vb* 398
raconteur *n* 517
racy *adj* 145, 494, 507, 732
raddle *vb* 387
radial *adj* 260
radiance *n* 374, 763
radiant *adj* 374, 742, 763
radiate *vb* 48, 67, 260, 374
radiating *adj* 67
radiation *n* 67, 260, 374
radiator *n* 339
radical *adj* 49, 73, 121, 127, 550, *n* 73, 121, 127, 662
radicalism *n* 127
radio *n* 472, 761
radioactive *adj* 604
radioactivity *n* 604
radiographic *adj* 491
radiography *n* 491
radiophonic *adj* 353
radius *n* 156
raffle *n* 554
raft *n* 66
rafter *n* 193, 569
rag *n* 471, 569, *vb* 773
ragbag *n* 16, 38

rage *n* 147, 732, 770, 802, *vb* 147, 316, 732, 802
ragged *adj* 50, 229
ragging *n* 773
raging *adj* 147, 732
ragout *n* 38
rags *n* 204
rag trade *n* 204
raid *n* 639, 645, 705, *vb* 639, 645, 705
raider *n* 639, 705
railing *n* 210
railroad *n* 240, *vb* 615
railway *n* 240
railway lines *n* 194
raiment *n* 204
rain *n* 307, *vb* 307
rainbow *adj* 38, *n* 16, 381, 393
rainfall *n* 307
rainless *adj* 309
rainproof *adj* 309
rains *n* 307
rainwater *n* 305
rainy *adj* 307
rainy season *n* 307
raise *vb* 184, 190, 276, 298, 328, 492, 721
raise Cain *vb* 355
raised *adj* 226, 228, 276, 492
raised eyebrows *n* 682
raised voices *n* 363, 682
raise objections *vb* 682
raise one's eyebrows *vb* 682
raise one's glass to *vb* 786
raise one's hat *vb* 791
raise one's voice *vb* 526
raise one's voice against *vb* 682
raise someone's hopes *vb* 748
raise spirits *vb* 876
raise the money *vb* 567
raise the roof *vb* 355
raising *n* 276
raising agent *n* 276, 286, 306
rajah *n* 776
rake *n* 183, 195, 838, 851, *vb* 328
rake it in *vb* 712
rake-off *n* 33, 722
rakish *adj* 336, 770
rally *n* 66, *vb* 66, 751
rallying point *n* 200
ram *n* 247, 326, 332, *vb* 247
Ramadan *n* 845
ramble *n* 236, *vb* 236, 445, 447, 506, 530, 761
rambler *n* 236

rambling *adj* 56, 252, 506
ramekin *n* 167
ram home *vb* 507
ramification *n* 67, 260
ramify *vb* 48, 67, 220, 260
ramp *n* 195, 274
rampage *vb* 56, 147
rampant *adj* 147, 190, *n* 143
rampart *n* 640
ramrod *n* 190, 222
ramshackle *adj* 144
ranch *n* 328, *vb* 328
rancid *adj* 343, 350
rancidness *n* 343, 350
rancorous *adj* 794, 796, 802
rancour *n* 794, 802, 806
random *adj* 10, 56, 120, 135, 416, 419, 554
randomize *vb* 56, 58
randomness *n* 10, 120, 135, 419
randy *adj* 851
range *n* 156, 172, 180, 339, 707, 854, *vb* 57, 64, 68, 156
ranger *n* 668
rangy *adj* 184
rank *adj* 49, 327, 343, 347, 350, *n* 7, 24, 55, 64, 68, 776, *vb* 24, 57, 64, 68, 774
rank and file *n* 32
ranking *adj* 774
rankle *vb* 802, 806
rankness *n* 343, 350
ransack *vb* 150
ransom *n* 706
rant *vb* 147, 363, 443, 459, 771, 802
rap *n* 247, 357, 860, *vb* 247
rapacious *adj* 703, 728, 755
rapacity *n* 755
rape *n* 147, 639, 703, 851, *vb* 147, 639, 703, 851
rapid *adj* 245
rapid-fire *adj* 96
rapidity *n* 245
rapids *n* 314
rapier *n* 649
rapist *n* 639, 703
rap over the knuckles *vb* 826, 860
rapport *n* 9, 42, 173, 636
rapt *adj* 404, 759
raptness *n* 404
rapture *n* 734, 795, 866
rapturous *adj* 734
rara avis *n* 70

rare *adj* 30, 73, 118, 267, 288, 574, 759
rarefaction *n* 288
rarefied *adj* 4
rarefy *vb* 4, 87, 183, 288
rarely *adv* 87, 118
rarity *n* 73, 87, 118, 183, 288, 759
rascal *n* 662, 838
rash *adj* 615, 753
rashness *n* 753
rasp *n* 301, 362, *vb* 301, 361, 362
raspberry *n* 484, 826
rasping *adj* 301, 362
rat *n* 838, *vb* 466
rat-at-tat *n* 357
ratchet *n* 229
rate *n* 24, 245, *vb* 24, 582, 721
rateable value *n* 721
rate of knots *n* 245
rates *n* 721
ratification *n* 131, 436, 684
ratify *vb* 131, 420, 436, 684
rating assessment *n* 721
ratio *n* 9, 24
ratiocination *n* 400
ration *n* 23, 700, *vb* 23, 700
rational *adj* 148, 396, 400, 410, 446
rationale *n* 132, 134
rationalism *n* 869
rationalist *n* 869
rationalistic *adj* 869
rationality *n* 148, 396, 400, 446
rationalization *n* 400, 411
rationalize *vb* 55, 400
rationing *n* 700
ration oneself *vb* 843
rations *n* 267, 571
ratter *n* 555
rattle *n* 358, 761, *vb* 358, 750
rattle on *vb* 459
ratty *adj* 802, 803
raucous *adj* 362, 366
raucousness *n* 362, 366
ravage *vb* 150
ravaged *adj* 595
ravages *n* 150
rave *vb* 443, 447, 459
rave about *vb* 734, 825
ravel *vb* 197
ravelled *adj* 197
raven-haired *adj* 384
ravenous *adj* 755, 846
ravine *n* 181, 227
raving *adj* 447

ravishing *adj* 736, 763
raw *adj* 39, 50, 106, 217, 334, 337, 340, 439, 560
raw-boned *adj* 183
raw deal *n* 818, 836
raw material *n* 104, 132, 217
raw materials *n* 569
rawness *n* 50, 106, 334, 439, 654
raw recruit *n* 106
raw sienna *n* 386
ray *n* 30, 374
ray of sunshine *n* 740
rayon *n* 569
raze *vb* 150, 185, 191, 277
razor *n* 296, 765
razor-sharp *adj* 296
re *prep* 9
reach *n* 141, 156, 172, 178, *vb* 172, 261
reach a compromise *vb* 684
reach an understanding *vb* 19
react *vb* 126, 137, 248, 334, 415, 729
reacting *adj* 126
reaction *n* 126, 133, 137, 248, 334, 415
reactionary *adj* 126, 137, *n* 122
reactive *adj* 248
reactor *n* 141
read *vb* 462
readability *n* 460
readable *adj* 460, 629
read between the lines *vb* 462
reader *n* 516
readership *n* 470
readily *adv* 537, 629
readiness *n* 162, 453, 537, 559, 609, 653
reading *n* 462
reading list *n* 516
read into *vb* 463
read the future *vb* 455
ready *adj* 162, 450, 453, 535, 537, 559
ready for anything *adj* 751
ready-made *adj* 149, 559
ready money *n* 711
ready reckoner *n* 75
ready to eat *adj* 559
ready-to-wear *adj* 204
real *adj* 1, 3, 22, 74, 282, 694
real estate *n* 694
realism *n* 3, 440, 444
realist *adj* 3
realistic *adj* 3, 444, 488, 490, 517
realities *n* 3

reality *n* 1, 3
realizable *adj* 423
realization *n* 1, 394, 433, 464, 653, 690
realize *vb* 3, 6, 334, 396, 433, 653, 690, 721
really *adv* 1, 3
realm *n* 7, 157
real McCoy *n* 22
real thing *n* 22
realty *n* 694
real world *n* 3
reams *n* 29
reap *vb* 328, 690
reappear *vb* 88
reappearance *n* 88
rear *adj* 60, 62, 100, 213, *n* 60, 213, *vb* 152, 190, 276, 328
rear admiral *n* 648
rearguard *n* 60, 213
rearmost *adj* 213
reason *n* 132, 134, 396, 400, *vb* 396, 400
reasonable *adj* 148, 400, 423, 425, 446, 724
reasonableness *n* 148, 446, 724
reasoned *adj* 396
reason falsely *vb* 411
reasoning *n* 856
rebarbative *adj* 758
rebate *n* 36, 704, 722, *vb* 704, 722
rebel *n* 73, 127, 635, 662, 871, *vb* 73, 127, 637, 662
rebellion *n* 127, 635, 637, 662, 853
rebellious *adj* 73, 127, 635, 637, 662
rebirth *n* 88, 151
reborn *adj* 125
rebound *n* 248, *vb* 126, 248, 293
rebuff *n* 248, 258, 546, 680, 792, 824, *vb* 248, 258, 546, 680, 790, 824
rebuild *vb* 151
rebuke *n* 602, 826, *vb* 602, 826, 860
rebut *vb* 413, 415, 421, 474
rebuttal *n* 413, 415, 421, 474
recalcitrance *n* 437, 538, 632, 638, 662, 680
recalcitrant *adj* 137, 538, 632, 638, 662, 680
recall *n* 448, 673, *vb* 105, 448, 673
recant *vb* 435, 543, 841
recantation *n* 435, 543
recapitulate *vb* 88
recapitulation *n* 88
recapture *vb* 448

recede *vb* 34, 126, 254
receding *adj* 254
receipt *n* 703, 719, 720
receipts *n* 690, 699, 719
receive *vb* 51, 261, 265, 699, 703, 791
received idea *n* 72
Received Pronunciation *n* 494
received wisdom *n* 549
receiver *n* 699
receive with open arms *vb* 811
receiving *n* 699
recently *adv* 106
recentness *n* 106
receptacle *n* 167
reception *n* 261, 265, 699, 789, 791, 797
reception committee *n* 786
receptive *adj* 265, 537, 699
receptiveness *n* 537
receptivity *n* 265
recess *n* 158, 220, 227, 612, *vb* 227, 493
recessed *adj* 227, 493
recession *n* 34, 126, 171, 254
recessive *adj* 254
recharge one's batteries *vb* 620
recherché *adj* 504, 545
recidivism *n* 126
recipe *n* 557
recipient *n* 515, 699
reciprocal *adj* 9, 11, 81, 129
reciprocate *vb* 11, 119, 129, 280
reciprocating *adj* 280
reciprocation *n* 280
reciprocity *n* 9, 11, 129
recital *n* 367, 517
recite *vb* 528
recite an incantation *vb* 876
recite a spell *vb* 876
reckless *adj* 407, 445, 615, 727, 753
recklessness *n* 407, 445, 615, 732, 753
reckon *vb* 74, 177, 716
reckoning *n* 716
reckon on *vb* 553
reclaim *vb* 328
recline *vb* 191
reclining *adj* 191
recluse *n* 790
recognition *n* 370, 811, 825, 859
recognizable *adj* 460, 485
recognizance *n* 687
recognize *vb* 370, 460, 811, 825, 859
recoil *n* 126, 137, 248, 293, *vb* 126, 248, 293, 538

recoil at *vb* 796
recollect *vb* 105, 448
recollection *n* 105, 448
recommence *vb* 61
recommend *vb* 420, 623, 825
recommendation *n* 420, 623
recommended retail price *n* 721
recompense *n* 704, 716, 859, *vb* 704, 716, 859
reconcile *vb* 9, 646, 738, 814
reconciled *adj* 19, 636, 813
reconciliation *n* 19, 636, 646, 813, 814
reconciliatory *adj* 814
recondite *adj* 461, 504
recondition *vb* 594
reconditioned *adj* 594
reconditioning *n* 594
reconnaissance *n* 370
reconsider *vb* 398
reconstruct *vb* 121, 127
reconstruction *n* 121
record *n* 76, 369, 486, 621, *vb* 76, 97, 486
record-breaker *n* 31
record-breaking *adj* 651
recorded delivery *n* 472
recorder *n* 486
recording *n* 472
recording session *n* 367
record low *n* 32
record-player *n* 353, 369
record sleeve *n* 202
recount *vb* 517
recoup *vb* 690, 704
recouping *n* 690
recover *vb* 126, 594, 620, 704
recovered *adj* 620
recovery *n* 126, 588, 592, 594, 620, 704
recreation *n* 612, 620, 761
recreational *adj* 475, 761
recreation ground *n* 761
recreation period *n* 618
recrimination *n* 641
recriminatory *adj* 641
recrudescence *n* 126
recruit *n* 476, *vb* 611
rectangle *n* 194, 220
rectangular *adj* 220
rectified *adj* 594
rectify *vb* 594, 817
rectilinear *adj* 222
rectitude *n* 817, 831, 837
recto *n* 212, 516

refrain *n* 88, 119, 365, *vb* 123, 556, 608, 660, 843
refresh *vb* 620
refreshed *adj* 620
refreshing *adj* 620, 736
refreshment *n* 594, 620
refresh one's memory *vb* 448
refrigerate *vb* 340, 570, 603
refrigeration *n* 340, 603
refrigerator *n* 340, 570
refuge *n* 165, 469, 600
refugee *n* 54, 161, 600, 790
refund *n* 28, 704, 716, *vb* 28, 704, 716
refurbish *vb* 106, 121, 594
refurbished *adj* 594
refurbisher *n* 594
refurbishment *n* 594
refusal *n* 437, 474, 546, 556, 678, 680, 826
refusal to obey *n* 662
refusal to recant *n* 842
refuse *n* 37, 696, *vb* 437, 474, 546, 556, 678, 680, 796
refuse/withhold payment *vb* 717
refuse food *vb* 845
refuse permission *vb* 678
refuse to budge *vb* 638
refuse to recant *vb* 842
refutation *n* 413, 421, 474
refute *vb* 4, 413, 421, 474
refuted *adj* 413
regain *vb* 704
regal *adj* 774, 776
regalia *n* 204, 657, 787
regard *n* 404, 406, 688, 774, 823, *vb* 9, 688, 774
regard highly *vb* 823
regards *n* 823
regency *n* 672
regeneration *n* 151
regenerative *adj* 151
regent *n* 665
reggae *n* 367
regiment *n* 66, 648, *vb* 15
regimentation *n* 15
region *n* 156, 157, 206
regional *adj* 157, 494
regionalism *n* 494
register *n* 57, 76, 365, 486, 502, *vb* 76, 265, 334, 404, 486
registered post *n* 472
registrar *n* 486
registration *n* 265
regress *vb* 88, 98, 105, 126, 254

regression *n* 105, 126, 234, 254
regressive *adj* 105, 126
regret *n* 452, 735, 739, 747, 809, 841, *vb* 325, 747, 826, 841
regretful *adj* 452, 841
regular *adj* 15, 49, 88, 117, 119, 124, 131, 218, 549
regularity *n* 15, 55, 88, 117, 119, 124, 131, 218, 549
regularize *vb* 15, 71
regularly *adv* 117, 119
regulate *vb* 71, 622
regulation *n* 71, 622, 623, 852, 852
regulatory *adj* 71
rehabilitate *vb* 15, 72, 704
rehabilitated *adj* 813
rehabilitation *n* 72, 704, 813
rehabilitation centre *n* 671
rehash *n* 88, *vb* 88
rehearsal *n* 88, 416, 523, 547, 559
rehearse *vb* 88, 416, 523, 547, 559
rehearsed *adj* 559
rehoboam *n* 167
reign *vb* 657
reigning *adj* 657
reign of terror *n* 750
reimburse *vb* 28, 704, 716, 859
reimbursement *n* 28, 704, 716, 859
rein *n* 42, 148, 668
reincarnation *n* 151
reinforce *vb* 33, 35, 143, 193, 289, 640
reinforced *adj* 289
reinforcement *n* 35, 143, 193
reinstate *vb* 126, 704
reinstated *adj* 813
reinstatement *n* 126, 704
reinvigorate *vb* 620
reissue *n* 88, 151, 516, *vb* 88, 151
reiterate *vb* 88, 473, 507
reiteration *n* 88, 507
reiterative *adj* 88, 507
reject *n* 54, 546, *vb* 52, 258, 435, 437, 474, 546, 556, 565, 635, 680, 796, 826
rejected *adj* 546
rejection *n* 52, 258, 437, 474, 546, 556, 565, 680, 826
rejects *n* 724
rejoice *vb* 734, 746
rejoicing *adj* 746, *n* 746
rejoin *vb* 641
rejoinder *n* 129, 415, 641
rejuvenate *vb* 106
rejuvenated *adj* 151

relapse *n* 88, 105, 126, 254, *vb* 88,
126, 254
relate *vb* 9, 517
related *adj* 9
relatedness *n* 9
relation *n* 9, 42
relationship *n* 9, 795
relative *adj* 8, 9, 24
relatively *adv* 9
relativeness *n* 9
relatives *n* 12
relax *vb* 290, 612, 618, 669, 761, 788,
809
relaxation *n* 148, 612, 618, 658, 669,
761
relaxed *adj* 618, 658, 738, 788
relaxing *adj* 618
relay *n* 472, *vb* 470
release *n* 323, 669, 696, 813, 822, 857,
vb 44, 132, 525, 669, 696, 822,
857
released *adj* 813, 857
relegate *vb* 161, 266
relegation *n* 161, 266
relent *vb* 290, 660, 809, 813
relentless *adj* 95, 117, 124, 810
relentlessly *adv* 95
relentlessness *n* 539, 806, 810
relevance *n* 9, 200
relevant *adj* 9
reliability *n* 119, 131, 425, 427, 714,
774, 831
reliable *adj* 119, 131, 420, 427, 434,
478, 774, 831
reliance *n* 434, 748
relic *n* 37, 105, 107, 448, 486
relict *n* 37, 798
relief *n* 16, 128, 148, 208, 228, 492,
596, 620, 631, 673, 740, 809
relieve *vb* 148, 596, 631, 673, 740, 805
relieve oneself *vb* 268, 740
relieving *adj* 740
religion *n* 634, 868, 877
religiosity *n* 872
religious *adj* 688, 862, 868, 874, 877
religious education *n* 868
religious knowledge *n* 868
religious teacher *n* 868
religious teaching *n* 868
relinquish *vb* 563, 674, 696
relinquished *adj* 563
relinquishment *n* 563, 674, 696
relish *n* 145, 342, 344, 734, 757, *vb*
336, 342, 734, 757

relive *vb* 448
relocate *vb* 161
relocation *n* 161, 239
reluctance *n* 246, 437, 538, 638, 680,
784
reluctant *adj* 246, 437, 538, 556, 556,
638, 680, 784
rely *vb* 434, 748
rely on *vb* 427, 450
remain *vb* 1, 37, 93, 122
remainder *n* 37, 74, 516, *vb* 709
remaining *adj* 37
remains *n* 37, 324, 486
remake *n* 88, 151, 525, *vb* 88, 151
remand *n* 668
remand centre/home *n* 671
remand in custody *vb* 668
remark *n* 528
remarkable *adj* 29, 759
remarry *vb* 797
remedial *adj* 137, 594, 596, 740
remedied *adj* 594
remedy *n* 137, 594, 596, 740, *vb* 137,
594, 596, 740, 817
remember *vb* 105, 448, 786
remembered *adj* 448
remembrance *n* 105, 448, 786
remind *vb* 448
reminder *n* 448
reminisce *vb* 448
reminiscence *n* 448
reminiscent *adj* 448
remiss *adj* 407
remission *n* 606, 813, 857
remit *vb* 698, 716, 813
remittance *n* 716
remnant *n* 37
remodel *vb* 121, 127
remonstrate *vb* 437, 682
remonstration *n* 437, 682
remorse *n* 735, 809, 840, 841
remorseful *adj* 841
remorseless *adj* 117, 810
remorselessness *n* 810
remote *adj* 172, 790
remote/outside/slim chance *n* 426
remoteness *n* 172
removal *n* 36, 161, 239, 266, 270
removal from office *n* 673
remove *adj* 36, *n* 24, *vb* 161, 270
remove from office *vb* 673
remove from the scene *vb* 395
remunerate *vb* 716, 859

remuneration *n* 690, 711, 716, 719, 859
remunerative *adj* 690, 859
renaissance *n* 88, 151
Renaissance man *n* 49, 80, 438
rend *vb* 41, 174, 232
render *vb* 202, 303, 462, 698
render a service *vb* 805
render assistance *vb* 631
rendering *n* 488, 490
render null and void *vb* 673
rendezvous *n* 66, *vb* 66
rendition *n* 462
renegade *n* 44, 73
renege *vb* 689
renew *vb* 88, 106, 151
renewal *n* 88, 151, 620
renounce *vb* 435, 474, 563, 696, 674
renovate *vb* 106, 594
renovated *adj* 594
renovation *n* 106, 594
renovator *n* 594
renown *n* 29, 774
renowned *adj* 29, 774
rent *adj* 41, *n* 41, 719, 721, *vb* 697, 702
rental *n* 697, 702, 721
rented *adj* 164
renunciation *n* 435, 474, 563, 674, 696
reorganization *n* 121
reorganize *vb* 121
rep *n* 709
repair *vb* 7, 594, *vb* 594
repaired *adj* 594
repairer *n* 594
repairman *n* 613
reparable *adj* 594
reparation *n* 28, 646, 704, 814, 859
reparatory *adj* 28
repartee *n* 129, 415, 533, 641, 744
repatriate *vb* 266
repatriation *n* 266
repay *vb* 28, 641, 704, 716, 811, 814
repayment *n* 28, 704, 716, 814
repeal *n* 474, 487, 673, *vb* 474, 487, 673
repeat *adj* 81, *n* 88, 151, 472, *vb* 13, 21, 81, 88, 151
repeated *adj* 117, 119
repeatedly *adv* 88, 117, 124
repeated sound *n* 358
repeater *n* 97
repeat performance *n* 88
repel *vb* 258, 343, 638, 680, 737, 758

repellent *adj* 258, 737, 796
repent *vb* 841
repentance *n* 814, 841
repent and believe *vb* 872
repentant *adj* 814, 841
repercussion *n* 64, 126, 137, 248
repercussive *adj* 126, 248
répétiteur *n* 559
repetition *n* 81, 88, 117, 119, 151
repetitious *adj* 88, 762
repetitive *adj* 15, 88, 506, 762
repetitiveness *n* 88, 506
rephrase *vb* 499
rephrasing *n* 499
replace *vb* 128, 676
replacement *n* 128
replay *n* 88, *vb* 88
replenish *vb* 49
replete *adj* 49
repleteness *n* 49
replica *n* 13, 21
replicate *vb* 13
reply *n* 248, 415, 515, *vb* 248, 415, 515
reply-paid *adj* 724
report *n* 355, 357, 466, 471, 486, 517, *vb* 471, 486, 517
reportage *n* 517, 522
reporter *n* 466, 471
repose *n* 610, 618, *vb* 191
repository *n* 160, 570
repossess *vb* 704
repossession *n* 704
repoussé *492*
reprehend *vb* 826
reprehensible *adj* 818, 826
represent *vb* 22, 484, 488, 517, 676
representation *n* 488, 490, 672
representational *adj* 484, 488, 490
representative *adj* 68, 69, 488, 814, *n* 657, 675, 676, 814
repress *vb* 630, 668
repression *n* 668
repressive *adj* 668
reprieve *n* 114, 605, 606, 673, 813, 857, *vb* 605, 606, 673, 809, 813, 857
reprieved *adj* 857
reprimand *n* 602, 826, 860, *vb* 602, 826, 860
reprint *n* 88, 151, 514, 516, *vb* 88, 151
reprisal *n* 641
reprisals *n* 129, 137
reprise *n* 88, *vb* 88

reproach *n* 826, 840, *vb* 826
reproachable *adj* 840
reproachful *adj* 826
reprobate *n* 838, 873
reproduce *vb* 17, 21, 88, 151, 491
reproduction *n* 21, 81, 88, 151, 152, 488
reproductive *adj* 151
reproof *n* 826, 860
reprove *vb* 602, 826, 830
reproving *adj* 826
reptile *n* 326
reptilian *adj* 326
republic *n* 157, 331
republican *adj* 657
republicanism *n* 657
repudiate *vb* 413, 437, 474, 546, 673, 717
repudiation *n* 413, 437, 474, 546, 673
repugnance *n* 538, 758, 796
repugnant *adj* 758, 796, 838
repulse *vb* 680
repulsion *n* 258, 758, 796
repulsive *adj* 258, 758, 764
repulsiveness *n* 764
reputable *adj* 774, 823, 831
reputation *n* 714, 774, 779
repute *n* 774, 823
request *n* 414, 681, 874, *vb* 414, 681
requiem *n* 325, 367, 747
requiem mass *n* 881
require *vb* 132, 273, 536, 558, 574, 661, 664, 685, 755, 821
required *adj* 536, 558
requirement *n* 536, 558, 661, 755
require no effort *vb* 629
requisite *adj* 536, *n* 558
requisition *n* 681, 703, *vb* 564, 681, 703
requisitioning *n* 703
requital *n* 814
requite *vb* 811, 814
requittal *n* 129
rerun *n* 88, *vb* 88
rescind *vb* 673
rescission *n* 673
rescue *n* 605, 606, 669, *vb* 605, 606, 669
rescuer *n* 606
research *n* 416, 433, *vb* 416
resemblance *n* 17
resemble *vb* 17
resent *vb* 796, 802, 815
resentful *adj* 739, 794, 802, 815

resentment *n* 739, 802, 815, 816
reservation *n* 422, 538, 685, 790
reserve *adj* 35, *n* 35, 41, 128, 172, 483, 531, 784, 790, *vb* 113, 545
reserved *adj* 172, 483, 531, 668, 733, 784
reserves *n* 570, 571, 694, 711
reservist *n* 648
reservoir *n* 167, 312, 570
reside *vb* 162, 165
reside in *vb* 53, 158
residence *n* 158, 162, 165, 694
resident *adj* 162, *n* 164, 675, 692
residential *adj* 162, 165
residual *adj* 37
residue *n* 37
resign *vb* 123, 563, 674
resignation *n* 642, 674, 733, 749, 780
resigned *adj* 642, 733, 749, 780
resign oneself *vb* 733, 749, 780
resilience *n* 143, 289, 293, 294
resilient *adj* 143, 289, 293
resin *n* 318
resinous *adj* 318
resist *vb* 437, 542, 630, 632, 638, 640
resistance *n* 137, 258, 289, 294, 301, 630, 632, 638
resistance fighter *n* 648
resistant *adj* 137, 258, 289, 294, 638
resistor *n* 638
resist temptation *vb* 837
resolute *adj* 43, 143, 539
resoluteness *n* 289
resolution *n* 43, 62, 143, 409, 535, 539, 553, 751
resolve *n* 539, 553, *vb* 539, 553
resolved *adj* 539
resonance *n* 353, 359
resonant *adj* 248, 355, 359, 510
resonate *vb* 359
resort to *vb* 564
resound *vb* 353, 355
resource *vb* 567
resourceful *adj* 626
resourcefulness *n* 626
resources *n* 567
respect *n* 688, 754, 791, 823, 874, *vb* 688, 774, 823, 874
respectability *n* 768, 774
respectable *adj* 29, 768, 776, 831
respected *adj* 823
respectful *adj* 754, 791, 823
respective *adj* 9
respectively *adv* 9, 70

respects *n* 823
respiration *n* 316
respite *n* 123, 606, 740
resplendence *n* 763
resplendent *adj* 763
respond *vb* 126, 137, 248, 334, 415, 729
response *n* 126, 137, 248, 334, 415
responsibility *n* 134, 819, 821, 840, 854
responsible *adj* 134, 688, 821, 840
responsive *adj* 126, 248, 334, 415, 730
responsiveness *n* 730
rest *n* 123, 235, 608, 610, 612, 618, 738, 761, *vb* 235, 610, 618
rest assured *vb* 748
restate *vb* 88, 499
restatement *n* 499
restaurant *n* 165
rest day *n* 92
restful *adj* 618
restfulness *n* 618
resting *adj* 565, 608, 612
resting-place *n* 160
restitute *vb* 704
restitution *n* 28, 126, 704, 716, 814
restitutory *adj* 704
restiveness *n* 739
restless *adj* 130, 234, 236, 281, 732, 739
restlessness *n* 130, 281, 732, 739
rest on one's oars *vb* 235
restorable *adj* 594
restoration *n* 106, 126, 594, 620, 704
restorative *adj* 137, 594, 620, 740
restore *vb* 126, 137, 594, 620, 704
restored *adj* 594, 813
restore order *vb* 55
restorer *n* 594
restoring *adj* 620
restrain *vb* 630, 668
restrained *adj* 148, 483, 509, 511, 668, 784, 843
restraining *adj* 668
restrain oneself *vb* 843
restraint *n* 34, 148, 246, 483, 509, 511, 630, 668, 784, 843
restrict *vb* 181, 211, 422, 630, 668, 678
restricted *adj* 181
restrictedness *n* 181
restriction *n* 211, 422, 630, 668, 685
restrictive *adj* 52, 422, 630, 668, 678
restrictive practice *n* 668

restrictive practices *n* 52
rest with *vb* 821
result *n* 133, 651, *vb* 60, 133
resultant *adj* 133
resulting *adj* 60
results *n* 433
résumé *n* 179, 505, 520
resume *vb* 61, 88
resumption *n* 88
resurgence *n* 151
resurgent *adj* 151
resurrect *vb* 105, 151
resurrection *n* 105, 866
resuscitate *vb* 105, 151, 322
resuscitation *n* 105, 151, 322
retail *adj* 707, *vb* 709
retailer *n* 613, 707, 709
retail price index *n* 721
retain *vb* 448, 695
retainer *n* 32, 721
retaliate *vb* 11, 129, 137, 415, 641
retaliation *n* 126, 129, 137, 415, 638, 641
retaliatory *adj* 11, 137, 415, 641
retard *vb* 98, 246, 630, 668
retardation *n* 114, 246, 397, 630, 668
retarded *adj* 114, 397
retch *vb* 266
retention *n* 448, 695
retentive *adj* 695
reticence *n* 432, 467, 483, 531, 784, 790
reticent *adj* 467, 483, 531, 556, 784, 790
reticulate *vb* 174
reticulation *n* 174, 197
retire *vb* 123, 254, 262, 563, 612, 674, 790
retired *adj* 612, 674
retire defeated *vb* 32
retirement *n* 254, 563, 612, 674, 790
retiring *adj* 432, 674, 784, 790
retort *n* 129, 137, 248, 415, 641, *vb* 126, 129, 137, 248, 415, 641
retrace one's steps *vb* 88, 126, 213, 254
retract *vb* 256, 435, 543, 673
retractable *adj* 256
retractile *adj* 254
retraction *n* 126, 254, 435, 474, 673
retractive *adj* 256
retreat *n* 126, 165, 234, 254, 262, 469, 600, 605, 790, *vb* 126, 163, 262, 605
retreating *adj* 254

retrench vb 34, 726
retrenchment n 34, 36, 126, 668, 726
retrial n 856
retribution n 641, 814, 817, 860
retributive adj 641
retrieval n 126, 704
retrieve vb 126, 606, 704
retroaction n 254
retroactive adj 105, 126, 254
retrograde adj 126, 254
retrogress vb 593
retrogression n 126, 593
retrogressive adj 126, 254, 593
retrospection n 254, 448
retrospective adj 105, 126, 254, 448, n 105
retroussé adj 179, 221
retroversion n 196
return n 88, 126, 672, 690, 704, 859, vb 88, 126, 254, 672, 704
return a favour vb 811
return a verdict vb 856
return from the dead vb 865
return in kind vb 11
returns n 719
reunion n 40, 789
reuse vb 564
revalue vb 723
revamp vb 121
reveal vb 203, 420, 464, 466, 468, 484
revealed adj 468, 868
revealed religion n 868
revealing adj 205, 379, 458, 468, 484
reveille n 109
revel vb 336, 746
revelation n 203, 433, 451, 464, 468, 868
Revelation n 868
revelatory adj 455
revel in vb 734
revelling n 746
revelry n 746
revels n 746
revenge n 641
revengeful adj 641
revengefulness n 641
revenue n 690, 719
reverberant adj 359
reverberate vb 248, 353, 355, 358, 359
reverberation n 126, 248, 353, 355, 358, 359
reverberative adj 126, 248
revere vb 774, 795, 823, 874
revered adj 874

reverence n 754, 823, 872, 874
Reverence n 778
Reverend n 778
Reverend Father n 778
Reverend Mother n 778
reverent adj 872, 874
reverential adj 823, 874
reversal n 126, 196, 543, 673
reversal of judgment n 856
reverse adj 14, 213, n 14, 213, 215, vb 14, 196, 213, 254, 673
reversed charges n 724
reversible adj 126
reversion n 88, 105, 126, 254
revert vb 88, 105, 126, 254, 697
reverted adj 126
review n 414, 429, 519, vb 398, 429, 519
revile vb 801, 828
revise n 514, vb 106, 121, 476, 592
revised adj 592
reviser n 592
revision n 106, 121, 476, 592
revitalization n 151
revitalize vb 322
revival n 88, 105, 151, 523, 620
revivalist adj 125, n 872
revive vb 88, 105, 151, 322, 620
reviving adj 620
revocation n 474, 487, 673
revoke vb 474, 487, 673
revoking n 673
revolt n 73, 127, 637, 662, 853, vb 127, 637, 662
revolting adj 737, 796
revolution n 106, 119, 121, 127, 196, 223, 278, 279
revolutionary adj 121, 127, n 121, 127, 662
revolutionize vb 121, 127
revolve vb 119, 196, 223, 278, 279
revolver n 649
revolving adj 279
revue n 523
revulsion n 796
reward n 650, 690, 698, 811, 817, 819, 859, vb 774, 811, 859
reward for service n 859
rewarding adj 859
rewardingly adv 859
reword vb 462, 499
rewording n 499
rewrite vb 592
rhapsodic adj 521

rhetoric *n* 502, 510, 528, 785
rhetorical *adj* 502, 510, 528
rheum *n* 303
rheumatism *n* 589
rheumy *adj* 303
rhizome *n* 327
rhomboid *adj* 220
rhombus *n* 220
rhubarb *n* 358
rhyme *n* 88, 521, *vb* 521
rhymester *n* 521
rhyming slang *n* 494
rhythm *n* 88, 117, 119, 218, 511, 521
rhythmic *adj* 15, 117, 119, 511, 524
rhythmical *adj* 88, 280, 521
rib *vb* 231, 773
ribald *adj* 801
ribaldry *n* 851
ribbed *adj* 231, 299
ribbing *n* 231, 773
ribbon *n* 181, 650, 766
ribbon development *n* 67
rich *adj* 149, 152, 342, 381, 510, 712
riches *n* 655, 712
richness *n* 152, 342
rich person *n* 712
rickety *adj* 144
rickshaw *n* 242
ricochet *n* 248, *vb* 248
riddle *n* 232, 414, 467, *vb* 232
riddled *adj* 232
ride *n* 236
rider *n* 35
ride roughshod over *vb* 824
ride to hounds *vb* 761
ridge *n* 226, 228, 230, *vb* 291
ridged *adj* 230, 231, 291
ridicule *n* 435, 773, 824, 828, *vb* 744,
  773, 824, 828
ridiculous *adj* 443, 744, 772
ridiculousness *n* 443, 772
rife *adj* 471
riffraff *n* 32, 777, 838
rifle *n* 255, 649, *vb* 231
rifleman *n* 648
rifling *n* 231
rift *n* 174, 635
rig *vb* 481, 547
rigged *adj* 481
right *adj* 214, 440, 817, 819, 831, 852,
  adv 817, *n* 214, 657, 817, 819, 829,
  852
right amount *n* 573
right-angled *adj* 220

righteous *adj* 817, 837, 863
righteousness *n* 837
rightful *adj* 817, 819
rightfulness *n* 817
right hand *n* 214
right-hand man *n* 631, 666, 676
Right Honourable *n* 778
rightly *adv* 817
right-minded *adj* 870
right moment *n* 19, 115
rightness *n* 440
right of reply *n* 415
right of way *n* 99, 240, 271
Right Reverend *n* 778
right royal *adj* 725
rights *n* 694
right side *n* 212
rigid *adj* 122, 222, 235, 289, 659
rigidity *n* 122, 222, 289
rigorous *adj* 406, 418, 440, 659
rigorousness *n* 659
rigour *n* 406, 440, 659
rig-out *n* 204
rile *vb* 802
riled *adj* 802, 803
rill *n* 314
rim *n* 208, 209, *vb* 209
rime *n* 340, 383, *vb* 383
rind *n* 202
ring *n* 210, 223, 359, 587, 766, *vb*
  206, 251, 278, 359
ring a bell *vb* 448
ring down the curtain *vb* 62, 123
ringing *adj* 355, 359
ringlet *n* 224
ringlets *n* 765
ring off *vb* 123
ring out *vb* 353, 355, 357
ring road *n* 240, 251, 278
ringside seat *n* 173
ring the changes *vb* 121
ring true *vb* 440
rink *n* 210
rinse *n* 765, *vb* 305, 586
riot *n* 56, 147, 573, 853, *vb* 56, 147
rioter *n* 662
rioting *n* 658
riotous *adj* 56, 147, 658, 662, 853
rip *n* 595, *vb* 595
riparian *adj* 209, 311
ripen *vb* 653
ripeness *n* 107, 653
ripe old age *n* 112
rip-off *n* 480, 705, 723

rip off *vb* 480, 705, 705, 723
rip-off merchant *n* 705
riposte *n* 129, 137, 248, 415, 641, *vb* 137, 415, 641
ripple *n* 224, 231, *vb* 291
ripple effect *n* 133
rippling *adj* 224
rise *n* 33, 184, 274, *vb* 33, 184, 226, 228, 274, 286, 723
rise up *vb* 127
risibility *n* 772
risible *adj* 772
rising *adj* 274, 425, 655, 723
rising/spiralling prices *n* 723
rising damp *n* 308
rising generation *n* 106
rising tide *n* 33
risk *n* 554, 599, *vb* 554, 599
risk one's neck *vb* 753
risky *adj* 428, 554, 599
risqué *adj* 744, 851
rite *n* 874, 881
rite of passage *n* 265
ritual *adj* 787, 881, *n* 549, 786, 787, 881
ritual object *n* 881
rival *adj* 643, *n* 632, 643, 815, *vb* 632, 643
rivalry *n* 632, 815
river *n* 314
riverbank *n* 311
riverbed *n* 315
riverine *adj* 311
riverside *adj* 209
riveted *adj* 404
rivulet *n* 314
road *n* 240
road block *n* 233, 630
roadblock *n* 668
roadhouse *n* 165
roadside *adj* 209, *n* 209
roadsweeper *n* 586
roam *vb* 234, 236
roan *n* 386
roar *n* 355, 363, 526, *vb* 355, 363, 364, 526, 802
roaring/runaway success *n* 651
roar with laughter *vb* 744
roast *vb* 267, 339
roasting *n* 826
rob *vb* 705
robber *n* 705
robbery *n* 705
robbery with violence *n* 639, 705

robe *n* 202, *vb* 204
robot *n* 568, 731
rob Peter to pay Paul *vb* 25
robust *adj* 143, 588
rock *n* 289, 311, 321, 367, *vb* 280
rock-bottom *adj* 724
rock bottom *n* 30, 32, 185, 189
rock-climbing *n* 761
rocker *n* 280
rockery *n* 329
rocket *n* 244, 255, 649, 826, *vb* 33, 274, 723
rocket motor *n* 568
rock-hard *adj* 289
rock'n roll *n* 524, 761
rock-solid *adj* 427
rock the boat *vb* 73
rocky *adj* 144, 289, 311
rod *n* 861
rodent *n* 326
rod of iron *n* 659
rogation *n* 874
rogue *n* 480, 705, 838
roguery *n* 832, 838
role *n* 523
roll *n* 66, 76, 224, 279, 358, 486, *vb* 90, 191, 221, 224, 225, 234, 279, 292, 314, 358, 525
roll call *n* 75, 497
roller *n* 225, 292, 310
roller coaster *n* 221
rollers *n* 765
roller skates *n* 761
rolling *adj* 221
rolling in it *adj* 712
rolling stone *n* 236
roll in the aisles *vb* 744
roll into one *vb* 419
roll out the red carpet *vb* 786
roll up *vb* 261
roly-poly *adj* 168
roman *adj* 495, 513
romance *n* 457, 479, 518, 795
romantic *adj* 367, 457, 518, 729, 730, 732, 795
romanticism *n* 732
romanticize *vb* 457
rondo *n* 367
roof *n* 188, 202, *vb* 202
roofing felt *n* 569
rooftop *n* 184
rook *vb* 705
room *n* 156
roommate *n* 693, 793

rush off *vb* 262
russet *adj* 386, 387, 388
rust *n* 388, 593, 595, 597, 767, *vb* 107, 593, 595, 767
rustic *adj* 165, 328, *n* 164
rusticate *vb* 266
rustication *n* 266
rustiness *n* 550, 625
rustle *n* 356, *vb* 356, 361, 705
rustler *n* 705
rustling *n* 705
rusty *adj* 107, 362, 550, 593, 595, 625, 767
rut *n* 15, 231, 549, *vb* 231
ruthless *adj* 539, 731, 806, 810
ruthlessness *n* 539, 731, 806, 810
rutted *adj* 231, 29

S

Sabbath *n* 84, 881
sabbatical *adj* 612, *n* 84, 612
sable *n* 384
sabotage *n* 58, 150, *vb* 58, 150, 579
saboteur *n* 150
sabre *n* 649
sabre-rattling *n* 645, 750
saccharin *n* 345
saccharine *adj* 345, 827
saccharinity *n* 345
sacerdotal *adj* 878
sack *vb* 161, 266, 673, 705
sackcloth *n* 291
sackcloth and ashes *n* 747, 841
sackful *n* 23
sacking *n* 161, 569, 673
sacrament *n* 881
sacred *adj* 862, 868, 872, 874
sacredness *n* 872
sacred relics *n* 881
sacred writings *n* 868
sacrifice *n* 698, 814, *vb* 698
sacrificial *adj* 698, 814
sacrilege *n* 801, 873
sacrilegious *adj* 801, 873
sad *adj* 735, 743
sadden *vb* 743
saddle *vb* 285
saddlebag *n* 167
saddle with *vb* 821
sadism *n* 806
sadness *n* 735, 739
safari *n* 236
safari park *n* 326

safe *adj* 598, *n* 570, 711
safe and sound *adj* 598
safe bet *n* 425, 427
safe-blower/-breaker/-cracker *n* 705
safe-blowing/-breaking/-cracking *n* 705
safe conduct *n* 271, 598, 677
safeguard *vb* 598, 640
safe house *n* 600
safekeeping *n* 570, 598, 603, 640
safety *n* 598
safety curtain *n* 378
safety first *n* 754
safety net *n* 28, 598
safety precaution *n* 640
saffron *n* 389
sag *n* 192, *vb* 144, 192, 290
sagacious *adj* 444
sagacity *n* 444
sage *n* 444
sage-green *adj* 390
sagging *adj* 275
saggy *adj* 192
Sahara *n* 309
sahib *n* 778
sail *n* 237, *vb* 237, 761
sailcloth *n* 569
sailing *n* 237, 761
sailing ship *n* 243
sailor *n* 237, 648
sail through *vb* 629
sail too near the wind *vb* 599
saint *n* 807, 837, 863
sainted *adj* 323
saintliness *n* 837, 863, 872
saintly *adj* 837, 863, 872
saint's day *n* 92
salacious *adj* 402, 851
salaciousness *n* 402, 851
salad days *n* 111, 655
salaried *adj* 690
salaried classes *n* 777
salary *n* 690, 711, 716, 719
sale *n* 697, 709
saleable *adj* 696, 709
sale goods *n* 724
sale of work *n* 709
sale price *n* 724
salesman *n* 551, 681, 709
salesmanship *n* 551
sales representative *n* 709
sales talk/pitch *n* 709
sales tax *n* 721
saleswoman *n* 709

salient *adj* 228, *n* 228
saliva *n* 268, 303, 305
salivate *vb* 268
sallow *adj* 382, 389
sallowness *n* 382, 389
sally *n* 264, 639, *vb* 639
sally forth *vb* 264
salmon-pink *adj* 387
saloon *n* 242
salt *n* 603, *vb* 570
SALT *n* 646
salted *adj* 603
saltiness *n* 342, 344
saltire *n* 197
salt of the earth *n* 837
salt tax *n* 721
salt water *n* 305
salty *adj* 342, 344
salubrious *adj* 588
salubrity *n* 588
salutation *n* 532, 791, 823
salute *n* 786, 791, 823, *vb* 532, 786, 791, 823
salvage *n* 606, *vb* 606
salvation *n* 606, 669, 862
salve *n* 148, 302, 319
salver *n* 167
salvo *n* 255, 357, 639
samba *n* 761
same *adj* 13, 15, 17, 25, 762
same age *n* 103
sameness *n* 13, 15, 17, 17, 25, 762
same old story *n* 13, 88
same time *n* 103
samey *adj* 13
sampan *n* 243
sample *n* 59, *vb* 267, 342, 416
Samson *n* 143
sanctified *adj* 862, 863
sanctify *vb* 872, 878
sanctimonious *adj* 771, 872
sanctimoniousness *n* 872
sanction *n* 436, 664, 677, 825, 852, *vb* 436, 672, 677, 825
sanctioned *adj* 852
sanctity *n* 837, 863, 872
sanctuary *n* 165, 598, 600, 882
sand *n* 300, 569, *vb* 300
sandalwood *n* 349
sandbag *n* 285
sandbank *n* 311, 601
sand dune *n* 309
sander *n* 301
sandpaper *n* 291, 292, 301

sandstone *n* 311
sandwich *n* 175, *vb* 207
sandwich course *n* 475
sandy *adj* 300, 309, 311, 389
sane *adj* 148, 446
saneness *n* 446
sangfroid *n* 731, 733
sanguine *adj* 387, 450, 742, 748
sanitary *adj* 586, 590
sanitary engineer *n* 590
sanitary inspector *n* 590
sanitation *n* 39, 586, 590
sanitize *vb* 586, 590
sanitized *adj* 39
sanity *n* 148, 444, 446
sanspareil *n* 584
sansserif *n* 514
sap *n* 5, 303, 445, *vb* 142, 144
sapience *n* 444
sapient *adj* 444
sapling *n* 327
sapphire *n* 391, 766
sappiness *n* 317
sappy *adj* 303, 317
sarcasm *n* 744, 773, 826
sarcastic *adj* 744, 773, 828
sarcophagus *n* 325
sardines *n* 761
sardonic *adj* 744
Sassenach *n* 331
Satan *n* 864
satanic *adj* 806, 864
Satanism *n* 864
Satanist *n* 864
satchel *n* 167
sate *vb* 49, 575
sated *adj* 49, 575
satellite *n* 85, 244, 278, 284
satiate *vb* 575
satiated *adj* 575
satiety *n* 49, 575
satin *n* 292, 569
satiny *adj* 292, 299
satire *n* 21, 744, 828
satirical *adj* 744, 773
satirist *n* 21, 744, 828
satirize *vb* 21, 744, 773, 828
satisfaction *n* 336, 646, 734, 738, 742, 814, 825
satisfactory *adj* 573, 582, 738, 825
satisfied *adj* 734, 738, 742, 825
satisfy *vb* 49, 573, 736, 738, 814
satisfying *adj* 734, 738

saturate *vb* 49, 305, 575

saturated *adj* 305, 575

saturation *n* 287, 305, 381, 575

saturation point *n* 49, 211

saturnine *adj* 804

satyr *n* 865

sauce *n* 781

saucer *n* 223, 227

saucy *adj* 732, 792, 824

sauna *n* 586

saunter *n* 246, 616, *vb* 234, 236, 246, 616

savage *adj* 147, 604, 806, *n* 147, 330, 838

savagery *n* 147, 806

savannah *n* 313

save *adv* 52, *vb* 570, 603, 605, 606, 669, 690, 711, 726

save one's breath *vb* 531

save up *vb* 570

saving *n* 603, 606

saving grace *n* 582, 837

savings *n* 570, 690, 711, 726

savings bank *n* 711

saviour *n* 606

Saviour *n* 862

savoir faire *n* 768

savour *n* 342, *vb* 336, 342

savouriness *n* 344

savour of *vb* 17, 342

savoury *adj* 342, 344

savvy *n* 396, 438

saw *n* 229, 442, 568, *vb* 362

sawdust *n* 343

saw-toothed *adj* 229

saxophone *n* 369

say *vb* 528

say 'I do' *vb* 797

say a prayer *vb* 874

say goodbye to *vb* 691

say grace *vb* 811

saying *n* 442, 499

say in no uncertain terms *vb* 507

say nothing *vb* 527

say one's piece *vb* 528

say one's prayers *vb* 872, 874

say one thing and mean another *vb* 543

say thank-you *vb* 811

say what one thinks *vb* 627

S-bend *n* 221

scab *n* 73, 202, 291

scabbard *n* 202

scabby *adj* 291

scaffold *n* 861

scald *n* 339, *vb* 339

scale *n* 9, 24, 64, 175, 201, 291, *vb* 24, 184, 274

scales *n* 177, 285

scaliness *n* 291

scallop *n* 221, 229, *vb* 221, 229

scalloped *adj* 209, 229

scallywag *n* 838

scalp *vb* 203

scalpel *n* 296

scaly *adj* 175, 291

scamp *n* 838, *vb* 50, 407

scamper *vb* 245

scan *vb* 370, 521

scandal *n* 471, 604, 775, 828

scandalize *vb* 737

scandalmonger *n* 402, 471, 828

scandalous *adj* 471, 838

scansion *n* 521

scant *adj* 30, 87, 574

scantiness *n* 50, 87, 169, 179

scantness *n* 30, 118

scanty *adj* 50, 169, 179

scapegoat *n* 128, 814

scar *n* 595

scarce *adj* 30, 87, 118, 179, 574

scarcely *adv* 30

scarcity *n* 30, 87, 118, 163, 179, 273, 574

scare *n* 750, *vb* 750, 806

scarecrow *n* 183, 764

scared *adj* 750

scaredy *n* 752

scarlet *adj* 387

scarlet fever *n* 589

scarper *vb* 245, 262

scarred *adj* 595

scary *adj* 750

scatter *vb* 41, 46, 56, 58, 67, 87, 288, 395

scatterbrain *n* 405

scatterbrained *adj* 56, 397, 445

scattered *adj* 67, 87, 288

scatty *adj* 405, 445

scenario *n* 516, 517, 525

scene *n* 159, 732

scenery *n* 523

scenic *adj* 490, 517, 763

scent *n* 347, 349, *vb* 349

scented *adj* 347

scentless *adj* 348

sceptic *n* 869

sceptical *adj* 435

scepticism *n* 435, 869
sceptre *n* 657
schadenfreude *n* 734
schedule *n* 57, 76, 97, 547, 557, *vb* 57, 76, 97, 547, 557
schema *n* 57
schematic *adj* 57, 557
scheme *n* 557, 626, *vb* 557, 626
schemer *n* 626
scheming *adj* 557, 626
scherzo *n* 367
schism *n* 41, 73, 635, 871
schismatic *adj* 871
schismatism *n* 871
schist *n* 311
schizoid *adj* 447
schizophrenia *n* 447
schizophrenic *n* 447
schmaltz *n* 508
schmaltzy *adj* 508
scholar *n* 438, 476, 868
scholarliness *n* 438, 444, 476
scholarly *adj* 438, 444, 476
scholarship *n* 631, 690, 719
scholastic *adj* 475
school *n* 66, 477, *vb* 475
schooling *n* 438, 475
schoolroom *n* 477
schooner *n* 167, 243
science fiction *n* 518
science of law *n* 852
sci-fi *n* 518
scimitar *n* 649
scion *n* 155
scissors *n* 296
sclerosis *n* 289
scoff *vb* 773, 824, 846
scoffer *n* 828, 873
scoffing *adj* 773, *n* 773, 873
scold *n* 803, *vb* 826
scoop *n* 106, 227, 270, 471
scoot *vb* 245
scooter *n* 242
scope *n* 156, 180
scorch *n* 339, *vb* 339, 386
scorched-earth policy *n* 150
scorcher *n* 307
scorching *adj* 307, 339
score *n* 75, 84, 367, *vb* 41, 231, 368, 486
score out *vb* 487
scorn *n* 435, 773, 796, 824, *vb* 435, 637, 680, 773, 824
scornful *adj* 435, 773, 824

scoundrel *n* 838
scour *vb* 301, 586
scourge *n* 597, 659, 836, 861
scouring *n* 586
Scouse *n* 494
scout *n* 59, 666, 668
scowl *n* 802, 804, *vb* 219, 484, 792, 802, 804
scrabble *vb* 338
Scrabble *n* 761
scraggy *adj* 183
scram *vb* 262
scramble *n* 615, *vb* 463, 615
scrambled egg *n* 657
scrap *n* 30, 48, 78, 572, 643, *vb* 150, 546, 565, 643
scrapbook *n* 486
scrape *n* 187, 301, 362, 628, 772, *vb* 187, 301, 362, 728, 823
scraper *n* 301
scrapings *n* 37
scrappiness *n* 50
scrapping *n* 565
scrappy *adj* 48, 50
scraps *n* 37
scratch *adj* 625, *n* 187, 338, 362, 585, 595, *vb* 41, 123, 301, 362, 595
scratched *adj* 585, 595
scratchiness *n* 291
scratch the surface *vb* 187
scratchy *adj* 291, 362
scrawl *n* 217, 489, 513, *vb* 513
scrawny *adj* 183
scream *n* 355, 357, 363, *vb* 355, 357, 364
scree *n* 311
screech *n* 355, 357, 362, 363, *vb* 355, 362, 363, 364
screed *n* 202
screen *n* 202, 207, 378, 600, *vb* 373, 378, 414, 525, 640
screened *adj* 378
screen idol *n* 525
screenplay *n* 516, 525
screw *n* 224, 279, 568, 668, *vb* 40, 219
screwdriver *n* 568
screwing *n* 40
screw up one's courage *vb* 751
screwy *adj* 447
scribble *n* 217, 513, *vb* 513
scribe *n* 486, 872
scrimp *vb* 728
script *n* 513, 525, *vb* 525

scriptural *adj* 868, 870
scroll *n* 224, 513
scrollwork *n* 766
scrooge *n* 728
scrounge *vb* 681
scrounger *n* 610, 681
scrub *n* 327, *vb* 487, 586
scrubbing *n* 586
scrubbing brush *n* 586
scrubby *adj* 327
scrub out *vb* 673
scruffiness *n* 56
scruffy *adj* 56, 775
scrum *n* 66
scrumptious *adj* 267, 342
scruple *n* 538, *vb* 538
scruples *n* 435, 831
scrupulous *adj* 404, 406, 688, 831
scrupulousness *n* 404, 688
scrutinize *vb* 370, 404, 414
scrutiny *n* 370, 404, 414
scuff *vb* 301
scuffle *n* 643, *vb* 643
scull *n* 243, *vb* 237
sculling *n* 237, 761
sculpt *vb* 216, 492
sculpted *adj* 492
sculpture *n* 492, *vb* 492
sculptured *adj* 492
scum *n* 32, 37, 777
scupper *vb* 150
scurf *n* 37
scurrility *n* 801
scurrilous *adj* 801
scurry *n* 615, *vb* 615
scuttle *vb* 150, 245, 277
scythe *vb* 41
sea *n* 86, 310
seaboard *n* 209, 310
sea change *n* 121
sea dog *n* 237
seafarer *n* 237
seafaring *adj* 237, *n* 237
sea-girt *adj* 311
seagoing *adj* 243, 310
sea-green *adj* 390
seal *n* 40, 43, 233, 485, 515, *vb* 40, 233, 485, 515, 584
sea legs *n* 237
sea level *n* 185
sea loch *n* 310, 312
seal of approval *n* 420, 825
seal off *vb* 210
seam *n* 40, 42, 175, 570

seaman *n* 237, 648
seamanship *n* 237
seamless *adj* 47, 64, 124
séance *n* 876, 877
seaplane *n* 244
sear *vb* 731
search *n* 414, 555, *vb* 555
searcher *n* 555
searching *adj* 414, 555, *n* 186
searchlight *n* 377
search party *n* 555
search warrant *n* 856
seascape *n* 490, 763
seaside *n* 311
season *n* 90, 92, 108, *vb* 38, 344, 559
seasonable *adj* 115
seasonal *adj* 90, 92, 108, 119
seasonally *adv* 119
seasoned *adj* 549, 559
seasoning *n* 35, 344, 559
seat *n* 158, 165, 165
seat of justice *n* 855
sea water *n* 305
seaworthy *adj* 237
secateurs *n* 296
secede *vb* 563, 871
secession *n* 41, 437, 563, 871
secessionist *adj* 41
seclude *vb* 41
secluded *adj* 378, 790
seclusion *n* 41, 790
second *adj* 81, *n* 676, *vb* 81, 436, 473
secondary *adj* 32, 133
secondary picketing *n* 682
secondary school *n* 477
second best *n* 32, 128
second chance *n* 809
second childhood *n* 112
second-class *adj* 32
second cousin *n* 12
second fiddle *n* 577
second-hand *adj* 21, 564
second helping *n* 49, 88
second-in-command *n* 676
second lieutenant *n* 648
second marriage *n* 797
second nature *n* 549
second-rate *adj* 32, 583
seconds *n* 32, 546, 724
second self *n* 13
second sight *n* 401, 453, 877
second-strike *adj* 641
second strike *n* 641
second string *n* 32

second thoughts *n* 100, 398, 543
secrecy *n* 465, 467
secret *adj* 465, 467, 469, *n* 467
secret agent *n* 465
secretary *n* 486, 613, 666
secretary of state *n* 622
secrete *vb* 264, 268, 469
secretion *n* 264, 268, 303
secretive *adj* 467
secretiveness *n* 467
secretly *adv* 467
sect *n* 41, 634, 871
sectarian *adj* 41, 634, 871
sectarianism *n* 871
section *n* 48, 78, *vb* 48
sectional *adj* 48, 634
sector *n* 48
secular *adj* 869, 880
secularism *n* 869
secularize *vb* 880
secure *adj* 598, *vb* 40, 687, 690, 695
secured *adj* 687
secure oneself *vb* 28
securities *n* 694
security *n* 28, 598, 687, 819
security forces *n* 598, 640
sedate *vb* 335, *adj* 733, 745
sedateness *n* 733, 745
sedative *n* 148, 335, 740
sedentary *adj* 235
sediment *n* 37, 182
sedimentary *adj* 37
sedition *n* 127, 662, 832
seditious *adj* 127
seduce *vb* 257, 795, 838, 851
seduction *n* 139
seductive *adj* 257, 551, 551, 736, 795
seductiveness *n* 257
sedulous *adj* 404, 540
sedulousness *n* 540
see *n* 878, *vb* 334, 370
see both sides of the question *vb* 27
see coming *vb* 450
seed *n* 61, 132, 152, 327
seed bed *n* 132
see double *vb* 848
seedsman *n* 329
seedtime *n* 108
see eye to eye *vb* 19, 436, 633, 636
see fair play *vb* 817
see how the wind blows *vb* 754
seeing *n* 370
seeing distance *n* 372

seeing double *adj* 848
seek *vb* 555, 561
seek/take advice *vb* 623
seeker *n* 555
seek refuge *vb* 600
seek to know *vb* 402
seem *vb* 394
seeming *adj* 394, 481
seemly *adj* 768
see nothing remarkable *vb* 760
see one's solicitor *vb* 623
seep *vb* 264, 308, 314
seepage *n* 264, 308, 605
seer *n* 455, 876, 877
see reason *vb* 446
see red *vb* 147, 802
seesaw *adj* 11, *n* 11, 121, 280, *vb* 11, 280, 541
seethe *n* 281, *vb* 66, 86, 281, 802
see the error of one's ways *vb* 872
see the funny side of *vb* 744
see the light *vb* 433, 841, 872
see the light of day *vb* 61, 322
seething *adj* 66, 281
see things *vb* 447
see-through *adj* 379
see through *vb* 653
segment *n* 48, 78, *vb* 48
segmented *adj* 48
segregate *vb* 41, 52, 790
segregation *n* 41, 52, 430, 790
segregationist *adj* 41
seize *vb* 703
seize one's opportunity *vb* 115
seize power *vb* 657
seize up *vb* 123, 652
seizure *n* 281, 589, 703
seldom *adv* 87, 118
select *adj* 545, 582, *vb* 418, 545, 611
selection *n* 520, 545
selective *adj* 18, 418, 545
selectiveness *n* 545
selectivity *n* 418
self *n* 70, 283, 396
self-abasement *n* 780
self-abasing *adj* 780
self-absorbed *adj* 834
self-absorption *n* 199, 834
self-accusation *n* 841
self-accusing *adj* 841
self-centred *adj* 70, 834
self-coloured *adj* 15
self-condemnation *n* 841
self-congratulation *n* 783

senior citizen *n* 112
seniority *n* 31, 107, 112, 657
señor *n* 778
señora *n* 778
señorita *n* 778
sensation *n* 299, 334, 338, 729, 759
sensational *adj* 471, 482, 732, 759
sensationalism *n* 471, 482, 732, 785
sense *n* 334, 396, 458, *vb* 334, 338, 396, 399, 401, 729
senseless *adj* 399, 443, 445, 459, 565
senselessness *n* 399, 443, 445, 459
sense of *n* 729
sense of duty *n* 821
sense of humour *n* 744
sense of obligation *n* 811
senses *n* 396
sensibility *n* 334, 730
sensible *adj* 148, 282, 334, 396, 400, 729, 730
sensitive *adj* 334, 729, 730, 803
sensitiveness *n* 730
sensitivity *n* 334, 418, 729, 730, 803
sensitize *vb* 334
sensory *adj* 334
sensual *adj* 336, 729, 844, 851
sensuality *n* 334, 336, 844, 851
sensuous *adj* 334, 729, 844
Sensurround *n* 525
sentence *vb* 856, 858, 860
sentenced *adj* 858
sentence to death *vb* 858
sententious *adj* 505, 510
sententiousness *n* 510
sentient *adj* 334, 729
sentiment *n* 434, 729, 795
sentimental *adj* 508, 729, 795, 800
sentimentality *n* 508, 729
sentry *n* 640, 668
separate *adj* 41, 44, *vb* 41, 207, 262, 270, 798, 871
separated *adj* 798
separateness *n* 10, 44
separates *n* 204
separate the sheep from the goats *vb* 18, 418
separation *n* 41, 262, 270, 790, 794, 798, 867, 871
separatism *n* 41, 44, 79, 871
separatist *adj* 41, 44, 79, *n* 871
sepia *n* 386
sept *n* 330
septet *n* 84
septic tank *n* 570

septuagenarian *n* 84
septuple *adj* 84
sepulchral *adj* 325
sepulchre *n* 325
sequel *n* 35, 60, 133
sequence *n* 60, 64
sequential *adj* 60
sequester *vb* 41
sequestrate *vb* 661
sequestration *n* 661, 672
sequin *n* 766
seraph *n* 863
sere *adj* 309
serenade *n* 367
serene *adj* 733, 738
serenity *n* 733, 738
serf *n* 328, 666, 777
serge *n* 569
sergeant *n* 648
sergeant major *n* 648
serial *adj* 24, 55, 60, 64
series *n* 24, 55, 60, 64, 516
serif *n* 514
serious *adj* 285, 507, 576, 745
seriousness *n* 285, 576, 745
sermon *n* 532
sermonize *vb* 528, 532
serpent *n* 864
serpentine *adj* 224
serrate *vb* 229, 291
serrated *adj* 229, 291, 296
serratedness *n* 296
serration *n* 229
serried *adj* 173, 287
serried ranks *n* 43
serum *n* 303
servant *n* 32, 613, 666
servant of God *n* 879
serve *vb* 40, 138, 571, 578, 666, 835
serve one right *vb* 819
serve up *vb* 267
service *n* 580, 611, 670, 805, 835, 874, 881
serviceability *n* 138, 578
serviceable *adj* 138, 578
services *n* 138, 648
servile *adj* 780, 782, 823, 827
servility *n* 780, 782
serving *adj* 666, *n* 700
servitude *n* 32, 664, 670
sesquipedalian *adj* 496
session *n* 855
sestina *n* 84, 521

set *adj* 211, 249, 539, *n* 516, 523, 524, 643, *vb* 43, 189, 287, 596
set about *vb* 61
set against *adj* 796, *vb* 28
set a good example *vb* 837
set an example *vb* 621
set apart *vb* 822
set aside *vb* 673
setback *n* 452, 630, 836
set by the ears *vb* 796
set down *vb* 486
set down in black and white *vb* 513, 683
set foot in *n* 261, *vb* 263
set free *adj* 857, *vb* 669, 857
set in motion *vb* 61
set in one's ways *adj* 542, 549
set off *vb* 766
set one's cap at *vb* 795
set one's face against *vb* 680
set one's heart on *vb* 539, 748, 755
set one's teeth on edge *vb* 346, 362
set out *vb* 61, 262, 557
set phrase *n* 499
set sail *vb* 237, 262
sett *n* 165
set the ball rolling *vb* 61
set the seal on *vb* 49
setting *n* 8, 159, 206, 367
setting out *n* 262
settle *vb* 122, 160, 165, 235, 275, 427, 429, 697, 703, 716
settled *adj* 684
settle down *vb* 131
settlement *n* 160, 429, 636, 684, 697, 703, 716
settle on *vb* 545
settle one's differences *vb* 633, 646
settler *n* 164, 263
set-to *n* 635
set to *vb* 617
set to music *vb* 368
set trends *vb* 770
set-up *n* 8
set up *vb* 132
set upon *vb* 639
seven *n* 84
seven seas *n* 310
seventh *adj* 84
seventh heaven *n* 866
seventy *n* 84
seven wonders of the world *n* 759
sever *vb* 41
several *adj* 80

severance *n* 41
severe *adj* 659, 806, 810
severity *n* 659, 806
sew *vb* 40, 149
sewage *n* 37
sewer *n* 315, 587
sewn up *adj* 653
sexagenarian *n* 84
sex appeal *n* 763, 795
sexism *n* 430
sexist *adj* 430
sextant *n* 177
sextet *n* 84, 368
sexton *n* 880
sextuple *adj* 84
sextuplet *n* 84
sexual *adj* 40
sexual assault *n* 851
sexual intercourse *n* 40
sexual union *n* 40
sexy *adj* 795
shabby *adj* 583, 775, 832
shack *n* 165
shackle *n* 42, *vb* 40
shade *n* 376, 378, 381, *vb* 378, 381, 490
shaded *adj* 378
shade of meaning *n* 418
shades *n* 323
shadow *n* 4, 37, 85, 375, 376, *vb* 60, 85, 173, 555
shadowy *adj* 4, 283, 375, 376
shady *adj* 378, 626, 775, 832
shaft *n* 186, 227, 232, 279, 374
shagginess *n* 291
shaggy *adj* 291
shaggy-dog story *n* 744
shake *n* 280, *vb* 38, 144, 281, 750, 750
shake hands *vb* 646, 684, 791
shaken *adj* 281
shakeup *n* 127
shake up *vb* 16, 127
shakiness *n* 144
shaky *adj* 144, 281
shale *n* 311
shallow *adj* 23, 187, 445
shallowness *n* 187, 445
shallows *n* 187
sham *adj* 21, 481, 771, *n* 21, 481, 771, 827, *vb* 21, 771
shaman *n* 876
shamble *vb* 246, 616
shambles *n* 56, 150, 625

shambolic *adj* 56
shame *n* 775, 818, 832, 841
shamefaced *adj* 840
shameful *adj* 583, 775, 824
shameless *adj* 781, 785, 851
shamelessness *n* 769, 781, 851
shampoo *n* 586, 765
shampoo and set *n* 765
shanghai *vb* 705
Shank's pony *n* 236
shanty town *n* 165
shape *n* 7, 208, 216, 298, *vb* 216, 298, 492
shaped *adj* 216
shapeless *adj* 217
shapelessness *n* 217
shapeliness *n* 763
shapely *adj* 221, 763
shard *n* 48
share *n* 23, 48, 700, *vb* 693, 700
shareholder *n* 693
share-out *n* 700
share out *vb* 698
sharing *n* 700
shark *n* 705
sharp *adj* 295, 296, 342, 346, 366, 626, 803
sharpen *vb* 296, 741
sharpener *n* 296
sharpening *n* 741
sharp-eyed *adj* 370
sharpness *n* 295, 296, 342, 344, 346, 737
sharp practice *n* 480
shatter *vb* 46, 147, 150
shattered *adj* 46, 619
shattering *adj* 619
shatterproof *adj* 289
shave *n* 765, *vb* 175
shaver *n* 765
shavings *n* 175, 183
she *n* 333
sheaf *n* 66
shear *vb* 41
shears *n* 296
sheath *n* 167, 202
sheathe *vb* 202, 256, 269
shed *vb* 203, 696
shedding *n* 203
sheen *n* 292, 374
sheep *n* 21, 72, 326, 880
sheepfold *n* 328
sheepish *adj* 784, 840
sheep's eyes *n* 370

sheer *adj* 49, 183, 190, 379
sheer drop *n* 190
sheerness *n* 183, 190
sheet *n* 175, 202
sheet music *n* 367
sheikh *n* 665, 776
shekels *n* 711
shelf *n* 191, 193, 228
shell *n* 37, 198, 202, 255, 289, 649, *vb* 203, 639
shell out *vb* 698, 716
shell pink *adj* 387
shelter *n* 378, 598, 600, *vb* 265, 378, 598, 640
sheltered *adj* 378
shelve *vb* 114, 123, 195, 565, 608, 654
Sheol *n* 867
shepherd *n* 328, 613, *vb* 66
sheriff *n* 665, 854
shibboleth *n* 485
shield *n* 202, 378, 600, 650, *vb* 378, 598
shift *n* 121, 234, 239, 252, *vb* 121, 130, 234, 239
shiftiness *n* 467, 543
shifting *adj* 234
shifting sand *n* 94
shiftless *adj* 454
shift the blame *vb* 822
shifty *adj* 130, 467, 480, 481, 543, 775, 832
shillelagh *n* 649
shilly-shally *vb* 428, 541
shimmer *n* 374, *vb* 130, 374
shimmery *adj* 374
shine *n* 292, 374, 586, *vb* 70, 292, 307, 374, 586, 624, 774
shingle *vb* 175
shingled *adj* 175
shininess *n* 292
Shintoism *n* 868
shin up *vb* 274
shiny *adj* 292, 374, 586
ship *n* 243, *vb* 166, 239, 241
shipment *n* 166, 239
shipper *n* 241
shipping *n* 237
ship that passes in the night *n* 94
shire *n* 157
shirk *vb* 407, 538, 556, 610
shirker *n* 556, 752
shirting *n* 569
shirtsleeves *n* 788
shirty *adj* 802, 803

show-off n 771, 783
show off vb 464, 771, 783, 785
show of piety n 872
show one's gratitude vb 859
show one's mettle vb 751
show partiality vb 818
showpiece n 464, 584, 763
show promise vb 423, 748
show respect vb 791, 823
showroom n 464
show the door vb 258, 546
show the ropes vb 265, 475, 631
show the white flag vb 642
show up n 261, vb 101, 162, 372, 394, 413
show willing vb 537
showy adj 510, 785
shrapnel n 649
shred n 48, 78, 169, vb 41, 150
shrew n 803
shrewd adj 429, 444, 626
shrewdness n 418, 444, 626
shriek n 355, 357, 362, 363, vb 355, 362, 363
shrift n 814
shrill adj 355, 362, 526
shrillness n 355, 362
shrimp n 169
shrine n 325, 882
shrink n 396, vb 30, 34, 183, 395, 750, 752, 784
shrinkage n 34, 171, 395
shrink from vb 758
shrinking violet n 784
shrivel vb 171, 309
shrivelled adj 171, 309
shroud n 202, 325, vb 202, 378
Shrove Tuesday n 881
shrub n 327
shrubbery n 329
shrubby adj 327
shrug n 484, vb 484
shrug off vb 822
shrunk adj 171
shudder n 281, vb 281, 750
shudder at vb 758
shuffle n 128, vb 16, 56, 58, 128, 129, 234, 246, 524
shun vb 556
shun company vb 790
shunt vb 161
shun the limelight vb 784
shut adj 233, vb 233
shutdown n 123, 610

shut-eye n 610
shut in vb 199
shut oneself up vb 790
shut one's eyes to vb 813
shut out vb 678
shutter n 202, 233, 378
shuttered adj 233, 378
shuttle n 244, 280, vb 236
shuttle diplomacy n 647
shuttle service n 119
shut up vb 527, 531
shut up shop vb 62, 123
shy adj 556, 750, 784, 790
Shylock n 701
shyness n 750, 784, 790
shyster n 480
SI adj 177
Siberian adj 340
sibilant adj 361, 529
sibling adj 12, n 12
sick adj 447, 589
sick as a parrot adj 452
sicken vb 343, 589, 737
sick joke n 744
sickle n 221
sickliness n 144, 345
sickly adj 144, 343, 345, 589
sickness n 266, 589
sick of adj 762
side adj 214, n 214
sideboards n 765
sideburns n 765
side by side adv 40, 43, 176, 194, 214
side effect n 133
sidekick n 631
sidelight n 377
sidelines n 198, 214
sidelong adj 195, 214
sidereal adj 284
side-splitting adj 744
sidestep n 214, 252, 556, vb 195, 214, 252, 556
sidestreet n 240
sidetrack vb 214
sideways adj 195, adv 214
side with vb 634
siding n 214, 240
sidle vb 195, 214
siege n 639
siesta n 610
sieve n 232, vb 39
sift vb 39, 55, 418, 545
sigh n 316, 356, vb 316, 356, 361, 747

sight *n* 370, 370, 394, 764, *vb* 433
sight for sore eyes *n* 370, 763
sighting *n* 433
sightless *adj* 371
sightlessness *n* 371
sight-read *vb* 368
sightseeing *n* 236
sightseer *n* 236
sign *n* 420, 455, 484, 495, 868, *vb* 485, 495
signal *n* 484, *vb* 484
signalling *n* 472
signature *n* 367, 485, 497, 683
signed *adj* 436
signet ring *n* 766
significance *n* 458, 576
significant *adj* 458, 484, 576
signify *vb* 458, 484, 488
sign language *n* 352, 484, 494
sign off *vb* 62, 262
sign on *vb* 76, 263
sign on/up *vb* 634
sign on the dotted line *vb* 683
signora *n* 778
signore *n* 778
signorina *n* 778
sign over *vb* 697
signpost *n* 249, 484, *vb* 249, 484
sign someone's death warrant *vb* 858
sign the pledge *vb* 847
silence *n* 354, 527, 531, *vb* 354, 527, 668
silencer *n* 354, 360
silent *adj* 354, 527, 531, *n* 525
silent majority *n* 27, 72
silhouette *n* 208, 216, 375, *vb* 208
silk *n* 569
silkiness *n* 292
silky *adj* 292, 299
sill *n* 193, 209
silliness *n* 443, 445
silly *adj* 443, 445, 772
silo *n* 167, 570
silt *n* 182, 317
silver *n* 569; *vb* 383
silver/big screen *n* 525
silver-grey *adj* 385
silverness *n* 383
silversmith *n* 613
silversmithing *n* 149
silvery *adj* 365, 383, 385
similar *adj* 9, 13, 17, 194, 218
similarity *n* 9, 13, 17, 194

similarly *adv* 13, 17
simile *n* 17, 458
similitude *n* 17
simmer *vb* 267, 306
simper *n* 744, *vb* 744
simple *adj* 39, 460, 483, 503, 509, 511, 627, 629, 839
simpleton *n* 445, 627
simplicity *n* 460, 483, 503, 509, 511, 627, 629
simplification *n* 460, 629
simplify *vb* 39, 460, 629
simply *adv* 30, 39, 79, 509
simulacrum *n* 4
simulate *vb* 21, 481
simulated *adj* 17, 481
simulation *n* 17, 21, 481
simulcast *n* 472
simultaneity *n* 96, 101, 103
simultaneous *adj* 85, 96, 101, 103
simultaneously *adv* 103
sin *n* 689, 818, 838, 838, 840, *vb* 689
since Adam was a boy *adv* 107
sincere *adj* 478, 627, 831
sincerity *n* 478, 627
since the year dot *adv* 107
sinecure *n* 629
sine die *adv* 89, 91
sine qua non *n* 85, 558
sinew *n* 294
sinewy *adj* 183, 294
sinful *adj* 818, 869, 873
sinfulness *n* 840, 851, 869
sing *vb* 368
singable *adj* 365
singe *vb* 384
singer *n* 368
sing hymns *vb* 874
single *adj* 39, 79, 79, 799, *n* 369
single-celled *adj* 320
single entry *n* 720
single-handed *adj* 79
single-minded *adj* 404, 535, 539
single-mindedness *n* 539
single out *vb* 70, 79, 418, 545
single parent *n* 79, 154, 798
single person *n* 79, 799
single state *n* 799
singly *adv* 79
sing psalms *vb* 874
singsong *adj* 366, 526
sing the praises of *vb* 786, 825, 875
singular *adj* 18, 70
singularity *n* 70, 73

sinister *adj* 836
sinistral *adj* 214
sink *vb* 32, 150, 186, 275
sinker *n* 285
sinking *adj* 275
sink without trace *vb* 395
sinless *adj* 839, 850
sinlessness *n* 850
sinner *n* 838, 873
sinning *adj* 689
sinuosity *n* 221
sinuous *adj* 221, 224
sinuousness *n* 224
sip *n* 30, 267, *vb* 267, 342
siphon *n* 270
siphon off *vb* 270
sir *n* 332, 778
Sir *n* 778
sire *n* 154, *vb* 12, 152, 154
siren *n* 97, 257, 355, 484, 602
sirocco *n* 316
sissy *adj* 752, *n* 144, 752
sister *n* 12, 778, 879
sisterhood *n* 333, 634
sisterly *adj* 12, 333, 793
Sisyphean *adj* 654
sit *vb* 7
sitcom *n* 472, 744
site *n* 158, 614, *vb* 158, 159
sit-in *n* 123, 682
sit in judgment *vb* 854
sit on the fence *vb* 27, 44
sit tight *vb* 235
sitting *n* 877
sitting duck *n* 142, 629
situate *vb* 7, 158, 159, 249
situated *adj* 159
situation *n* 7, 8, 158, 159, 162, 249, 611
situational *adj* 7, 8
situation comedy *n* 744
sit up and take notice *vb* 404
six *n* 84
sixer *n* 84
six feet under *adj* 325
six of one and half a dozen of the other *n* 17, 25
sixth *adj* 84
sixth-form college *n* 477
sixth sense *n* 401
sixty *n* 84
sizable *adj* 29, 168
size *n* 29, 156, 168, 318, *vb* 15, 24, 57
size up *vb* 429

sizzle *vb* 361
skate *vb* 292, 761
skateboard *n* 761
skate on thin ice *vb* 599
skate over *vb* 50, 407
skating *n* 761
skedaddle *vb* 245, 262
skein *n* 66, 197
skeletal *adj* 183, 298
skeleton *n* 37, 208, 216, 298
sketch *n* 50, 208, 488, 490, 520, 557, *vb* 208, 216, 488, 490, 517, 557
sketchiness *n* 50
sketchy *adj* 50, 520
skew *n* 219, *vb* 26, 219, 430
skewbald *adj* 38, 393
skewed *adj* 219
skewer *n* 232, *vb* 232
skew-whiff *adj* 26, 219
ski *vb* 761
skiff *n* 243
skiing *n* 761
ski-jumping *n* 761
skilful *adj* 438, 624
skill *n* 149, 438, 476, 567, 624
skilled *adj* 624
skilled person *n* 624
skim *vb* 173, 187, 338
skimp *vb* 50, 654, 728
skimped *adj* 615
skimpiness *n* 169, 179
skimpy *adj* 169, 179, 205
skin *n* 202, 569, *vb* 203
skin-deep *adj* 187, 198
skinflick *n* 525
skinflint *n* 728
skinful *n* 49
skin graft *n* 765
skinhead *n* 111
skinned *adj* 203
skinniness *n* 183
skinny *adj* 183
skint *adj* 713
skintight *adj* 43, 181
skip *n* 274, *vb* 50, 65, 163, 274, 407, 524, 654, 746
skirl *n* 362, *vb* 362
skirmish *n* 639, *vb* 639
skirt *n* 192, 333, *vb* 173, 176, 209, 214, 251
skit *n* 523, 828
skive *vb* 610
skivvy *n* 613, 666
skulduggery *n* 480, 832

457

skulk *n* 66, *vb* 469, 752
skull and crossbones *n* 484
skunk *n* 350
sky *n* 184
sky-blue *adj* 391
skydiving *n* 238, 761
sky-high *adj* 184, 276
skyjack *vb* 705
skyjacker *n* 705
skyjacking *n* 705
skylight *n* 232
skyline *n* 172, 191, 211
skyscraper *n* 168, 184
slab *n* 48
slack *adj* 44, 144, 192, 246, 290, 407, *vb* 538
slacken *vb* 34, 44, 144, 246, 290
slacker *n* 610
slackness *n* 44, 144, 246, 290, 407
slag *n* 851
slam *vb* 826
slander *n* 604, 775, 828, 830, *vb* 604, 828, 830
slanderer *n* 828
slanderous *adj* 604, 828
slang *n* 494
slanging match *n* 410, 533, 635
slangy *adj* 494
slant *n* 195, *vb* 195, 430
slap *n* 247, 860, *vb* 247, 860
slapdash *adj* 625
slap-happy *adj* 753
slap in the face *n* 680
slap on *vb* 35
slapstick *adj* 523, *n* 744
slap-up *adj* 725
slap-up meal *n* 267
slash *adj* 36, *n* 231, *vb* 34, 41, 231, 722, 724
slate *n* 385, 569, *vb* 202, 828
slater *n* 613
slaty *adj* 311, 385, 391
slaughter *n* 147, 150, 324, 860, *vb* 150, 324, 860
slave *n* 613, 666
slave labour *n* 670
slaver *n* 703
slavery *n* 664, 670
slave trade *n* 703
slave trader *n* 707
slavish *adj* 642, 663
slavishness *n* 642, 663
slay *vb* 324
sleek *adj* 292

sleekness *n* 292
sleep *n* 610, *vb* 146, 610
sleep around *vb* 851
sleepiness *n* 619
sleeping around *n* 851
sleeping partner *n* 610
sleep it off *vb* 847
sleep on it *vb* 114, 616
sleep together *vb* 795
sleep with *vb* 40, 795
sleepy *adj* 146, 610, 619
sleet *n* 307, 340, *vb* 307, 340
sleight of hand *n* 480, 626
slender *adj* 183
slenderness *n* 183
sleuth *n* 203
slew *n* 66, *vb* 252
slice *n* 175, 700
slice of life *n* 3
slice of the cake *n* 23, 48
slick *vb* 292
slide *n* 34, 275, 491, 593, 765, *vb* 34, 44, 292, 314
slide rule *n* 75
sliding scale *n* 24
slight *adj* 30, 78, 144, 187, *n* 775, 824, *vb* 432, 824, 828
slighting *adj* 824, 828
slightly *adv* 30, 78
slightness *n* 144, 187
slim *adj* 183, 763, *vb* 171, 845
slim down *adj* 36, *vb* 183
slime *n* 308, 317, 318, 587
slimmer *n* 168
slimming *n* 845
slimness *n* 183
slimy *adj* 318, 587, 827
sling *n* 255
slink *vb* 465, 469
slink away *vb* 752
slinky *adj* 181, 763
slip *n* 652, 840, *vb* 44, 292
slip of the tongue/pen *n* 501
slip on *vb* 204
slip one's mind *vb* 449
slip out of *vb* 205
slipperiness *n* 44, 292, 302, 543
slippery *adj* 44, 292, 302, 319, 543, 599
slipping away *adj* 323
slipshod *adj* 56, 407
slipstream *n* 316
slip up *vb* 441
slit *n* 231, *vb* 41

slitheriness *n* 292
slithery *adj* 292
sliver *n* 48, 183
Sloane Ranger *n* 776
slobber *vb* 268
slog *n* 617, *vb* 236, 540
slogan *n* 442, 470, 496
slog away *vb* 617
slogger *n* 609
sloop *n* 243
slope *n* 184, 195, 274, *vb* 195
slope off *vb* 262
sloppiness *n* 407, 441, 504
sloppy *adj* 56, 317, 407, 501, 504
slops *n* 317, 343
slosh *vb* 247, 308, 314
sloshed *adj* 848
slot *n* 57, 158, 231, 232
sloth *n* 146, 246, 610
slothful *adj* 146, 610, 616
slough *n* 37, *vb* 203
slovenliness *n* 407
slovenly *adj* 407
slow *adj* 114, 246, 616, 762, *vb* 668
slowcoach *n* 246, 616
slow creature *n* 246
slow down *n* 246, *vb* 246, 618
slow handclap *n* 484, 682
slow-handclap *vb* 682
slowing *n* 668
slowly *adv* 246
slow motion *n* 246
slow-moving *adj* 610
slowness *n* 114, 178, 246, 397, 616, 762
slow off the mark *adj* 246
slow on the uptake *adj* 397
slow starter *n* 114
slow-witted *adj* 397
sludge *n* 308, 317
sludgy *adj* 308, 317
slug *n* 649, *vb* 247
sluggish *adj* 146, 246, 314, 610, 616
sluggishness *n* 146, 246
sluice *n* 315, *vb* 305, 586
slum *n* 165, 587
slumber *vb* 146, 610
slum dweller *n* 713
slump *n* 34, 171, 254, 275, 593, 724, *vb* 32, 34, 275, 593, 724
slur *n* 529, 775, 775, 818, 828, 830, *vb* 529, 828, 830
slurred *adj* 529
slush *n* 317

slushy *adj* 308
slut *n* 587, 851
sly *adj* 480, 481, 626, 832
slyboots *n* 626
slyness *n* 626
smack *n* 243, 247, 849, 860, *vb* 247, 860
smack of *vb* 17, 342
smack one's lips *vb* 342
small *adj* 23, 30, 78, 169, 185, 495
small ad *n* 681
small arms *n* 649
small beer *n* 30, 577
small change *n* 711
smallest part *n* 30
small fry *n* 30, 169
smallholder *n* 164, 328
smallholding *n* 328
small hours *n* 92, 110, 114
smallness *n* 30, 169, 185
small piece *n* 48
smallpox *n* 589
small print *n* 685
small quantity *n* 23, 30
small-scale *adj* 169
small screen *n* 472
small talk *n* 533
smarmy *adj* 782, 827
smart *adj* 55, 204, 245, 511, 626, 763, 770, *vb* 337
smart aleck *n* 781
smarten *vb* 765
smarten up *vb* 55, 204, 511, 766
smarting *adj* 337, 802
smartish *adv* 245
smartness *n* 511
smart set *n* 770
smash *n* 247, *vb* 46, 147, 247
smash-and-grab raid *n* 705
smash hit *n* 523
smash-up *n* 150
smash up *vb* 150
smattering *n* 288
smear *n* 587, 767, 775, 828, 830, *vb* 202, 302, 319, 376, 587, 767, 775, 828
smear campaign *n* 150, 828
smeared *adj* 587
smell *n* 347, *vb* 334, 347, 350
smelly *adj* 347, 350
smelt *vb* 303
smile *n* 744, 791, *vb* 484, 744, 791
smiling *adj* 789
smirk *n* 744, 773, *vb* 744, 773

smith *n* 613
smocking *n* 766
smog *n* 307, 350
smoke *n* 304, *vb* 304, 380, 603, 849
smoked *adj* 603
smoked glass *n* 380
smokeless zone *n* 348
smokescreen *n* 373, 380, 469
smokiness *n* 376
smoking *n* 849
smoky *adj* 304, 350, 376, 380, 385
smooch *vb* 800
smooth *adj* 44, 292, 297, 299, 314,
   511, 827, *vb* 222, 292, 301, 629
smoothie *n* 782
smoothly *adv* 629
smoothness *n* 44, 124, 292, 297, 302,
   511
smooth over *vb* 302
smooth-running *adj* 292, 302
smother *vb* 150, 202, 324
smudge *n* 587, 595, 767, *vb* 217, 384,
   587, 595, 767
smudged *adj* 587, 595, 767
smug *adj* 738, 783
smuggle *vb* 705
smuggled *adj* 853
smuggler *n* 705
smuggling *n* 705
smugness *n* 738, 783
smut *n* 851
smutty *adj* 851
snack *n* 267
snack bar *n* 165
snaffle *vb* 705
snag *n* 123, 452, 585
snail *n* 246
snail's pace *n* 246, 616
snake *vb* 224
snake in the grass *n* 465, 626
snakes and ladders *n* 761
snaky *adj* 224
snap *adj* 560, *n* 491, 761, 804, *vb* 295,
   491, 794, 802, 803, 804
snap decision *n* 548
snap-happy *adj* 491
snap one's fingers at *vb* 637, 781
snap out of it *vb* 742
snappy *adj* 245, 803
snapshot *n* 491
snare *n* 257, 555, 601
snarl *n* 56, 197, 802, 804, *vb* 197, 364,
   794, 802, 804
snarl-up *n* 630

snatch *n* 703, *vb* 703
snazzy *adj* 770
sneak *n* 466
sneer *n* 824, 826
sneer at *vb* 824, 828
sneeze *n* 316
snick *n* 229, *vb* 229
snicker *vb* 364
snide *adj* 828
sniff *n* 316, *vb* 316, 347, 849
sniff out *vb* 555
snigger *n* 744, 773, *vb* 744, 773
snip *n* 724, *vb* 229
sniper *n* 255, 648
snippet *n* 48
snob *n* 769, 779
snobbery *n* 779
snobbish *adj* 52, 771, 779
snog *vb* 800
snooker *n* 761, *vb* 630
snoop *vb* 402
snooper *n* 402
snooze *n* 610
snopake *vb* 487
Snopake *n* 487
snort *n* 267, 804, *vb* 316, 364, 781,
   849
snotty *adj* 781
snout *n* 228
snow *n* 307, 340, 383, 849, *vb* 307,
   340
snow-blindness *n* 371
snowfall *n* 307
snowiness *n* 383
snowstorm *n* 307
snow under *vb* 86
snow-white *adj* 383
snowy *adj* 307, 383
snub *adj* 297, *n* 258, 680, 792, 824, *vb*
   258, 680, 790, 792, 824
snuff it *vb* 323
snuffle *vb* 316
snuffly *adj* 316
snuff out *vb* 2, 375
snug *adj* 19, 738
snuggle *vb* 800
snugness *n* 738
soak *vb* 305
soaked *adj* 305
so-and-so *n* 498
soap *n* 319, 586, *vb* 319
soapbox *n* 470
soapiness *n* 319
soap opera *n* 472

soapy *adj* 319
soar *vb* 29, 184, 274, 286, 723
soaring *adj* 184, 723
sob *n* 747, *vb* 363, 747, 747
sobbing *n* 747
sober *adj* 148, 446, 733, 745, 843, 847
sober as a judge *adj* 847
sobered *adj* 847
sobered up *adj* 847
soberness *n* 847
sober person *n* 847
sobersides *n* 745
sober up *vb* 847
sobriety *n* 148, 446, 733, 745, 847
sobriquet *n* 497, 498
so-called *adj* 456, 479, 497, 498
soccer *n* 761
sociability *n* 789, 793
sociable *adj* 789, 793
sociableness *n* 789
social *adj* 330, 634, 789, *n* 789
social climber *n* 769
social conscience *n* 807
social gathering *n* 789
social group *n* 66
socialism *n* 657
socialist *adj* 657
socialize *vb* 85
social security *n* 631
social services *n* 807
social work *n* 807
society *n* 85, 330, 634, 770
sociological *adj* 330
socket *n* 227
sod *n* 327
sodden *adj* 308
soft *adj* 144, 290, 292, 356, 381, 658, 660, 730
softback *adj* 516
soften *vb* 144, 290, 360, 740, 813, 829
soften up *vb* 559
soft-hearted *adj* 660, 809
soft-heartedness *n* 809
softie *n* 730
soft in the head *adj* 445
softly softly *adv* 148, 246
softness *n* 144, 290, 292, 352, 356, 660
soft option *n* 629
soft pedal *n* 360
soft-pedal *vb* 432
soft porn *n* 851
soft sell *n* 139, 470
soft soap *n* 827

soft-soap *vb* 827
soft-spoken *adj* 356
soft spot *n* 140, 144, 730, 757
soft touch *n* 480, 730
soft voice *n* 526
software *n* 75, 570
sogginess *n* 317
soggy *adj* 290, 308, 317
soigné *adj* 204, 511
soil *n* 311, *vb* 268, 587
soirée *n* 110, 789
sojourn *vb* 165
solace *n* 809
solar *adj* 284
solar energy *n* 141, 341
solarium *n* 765
solar panel *n* 339
solar system *n* 284
solar year *n* 92
solder *n* 43, *vb* 40, 43
soldier *n* 648
soldier of fortune *n* 648
sold out *adj* 709
sole *vb* 594
solecism *n* 496, 498, 501
solely *adv* 79
solemn *adj* 507, 576, 745, 787, 872, 874, 881
solemnity *n* 507, 576, 745, 787
solemnization *n* 786
solemnize *vb* 786
solicit *vb* 681
solicitation *n* 681
solicitor *n* 613, 681
solicitous *adj* 404, 406
solicitude *n* 404, 406
solid *adj* 3, 40, 43, 122, 131, 182, 216, 282, 285, 287, 633, 636, *n* 287
solidarity *n* 19, 40, 43, 633, 636, 793
solidification *n* 125, 287
solidify *vb* 43, 125, 182, 287, 289
solidity *n* 3, 43, 122, 131, 182, 282, 287
solid object *n* 282
soliloquize *vb* 534
soliloquy *n* 79, 534
solipsism *n* 70
solipsistic *adj* 70
solitaire *n* 761
solitariness *n* 79
solitary *adj* 41, 79, 790, *n* 799, 808
solitary confinement *n* 860
solitude *n* 79, 790
solo *adj* 79, 79, 367, *n* 524, 534

461

solo effort *n* 79
soloist *n* 79, 368
Solomon *n* 444
soluble *adj* 46, 303, 696
solution *n* 303, 305
solve *vb* 462
solvent *n* 203, 303
solvent abuse *n* 849
sombre *adj* 375, 384, 804
somebody *n* 774
somersault *n* 196, *vb* 196
something for everyone *n* 51, 69
something on one's mind *n* 735
sometime *adj* 99, 105, 674
some time *adv* 102
sometimes *adv* 90, 92
somewhat *adv* 24, 30
somnolence *n* 619
somnolent *adj* 610, 619
son *n* 12
sonata *n* 367
song *n* 364, 365, 367, 874
song and dance *n* 281, 732
songbook *n* 367
song of praise *n* 874
songster *n* 368
songwriter *n* 368
sonic *adj* 353
sonic boom *n* 357
sonnet *n* 521
Son of God *n* 862
Son of Man *n* 862
sonority *n* 353, 355
sonorous *adj* 353, 355, 359
sonorousness *n* 359
soon *adv* 90
sooner or later *adv* 102
soot *n* 384
soothe *vb* 148, 596, 736, 740
soothing *adj* 148, 596, 736, 740
soothsayer *n* 455, 876
sootiness *n* 384
sooty *adj* 384
sophistical *adj* 411
sophisticate *n* 768
sophisticated *adj* 511, 768
sophistication *n* 511, 768
sophistry *n* 411
sopping *adj* 305
soppy *adj* 730, 800
soprano *n* 368
sorcerer *n* 876
sorcerous *adj* 876
sorcery *n* 139, 875, 876

sordid *adj* 583
sore *adj* 334, 337, 737, 802
soreness *n* 334, 737
sore point *n* 635, 730
sore throat *n* 589
sorrel *n* 386
sorrow *n* 735, 747, *vb* 735, 747
sorrowful *adj* 735
sorrowing *adj* 735
sorry *adj* 809, 814, 841
sort *n* 68, *vb* 24, 55, 57, 68, 418
sorted *adj* 57
sortie *n* 264, 639, *vb* 639
SOS *n* 602
so-so *adj* 27
so to speak *adv* 17, 458
sotto voce *adv* 356
sou *n* 30
soufflé *n* 306
sough *vb* 316, 356, 361
sought after *adj* 709
soul *n* 5, 283, 322, 330, 367
soulmate *n* 17, 795
soul-searching *n* 398
sound *adj* 143, 446, 582, 584, 588,
   870, *n* 310, 353, *vb* 177, 186, 353,
   368
sound effect *n* 353
sounding *adj* 353, *n* 177
sounding board *n* 248, 416
soundless *adj* 354
soundlessness *n* 354
soundness *n* 143, 588, 870
sound off *vb* 528, 530
soundproof *adj* 354
soundproofing *n* 201
sound system *n* 353, 369
soundtrack *n* 353, 525
sound wave *n* 353
soup *n* 182, 317
souped-up *adj* 141
soupiness *n* 182
soup-strainer *n* 765
soupy *adj* 182, 317
sour *adj* 343, 344, 346, 804, 815, *vb*
   346, 741, 796
source *n* 22, 132, 466, 570
soured *adj* 452
sourish *adj* 346
sourness *n* 344, 346, 804
souse *vb* 269, 305
southpaw *n* 214
souvenir *n* 105, 448
sovereign *adj* 31, 657, 862, *n* 665, 776

sovereignty *n* 31, 657
sow *n* 326, *vb* 328, 329
sow one's wild oats *vb* 844
sow the seeds of *vb* 61
sozzled *adj* 848
space *n* 156, 174, 232, 284
space-age *adj* 54
spaced out *adj* 118, 174
space flight *n* 238
space heater *n* 339
spaceman/woman *n* 238
space out *vb* 174
spaceship *n* 244, 278
spaceship earth *n* 284
space-time *n* 90, 156
space travel *n* 238
space traveller *n* 238
spacious *adj* 29, 156, 180
spadework *n* 61
spaghetti western *n* 525
span *n* 42, 81, 90, 92, 156, 172, 178, 180, *vb* 40, 156, 271
spangle *vb* 393
spank *vb* 247, 860
spanner *n* 568
spanner in the works *n* 54, 630
spar *n* 192, *vb* 643
spare *adj* 35, 37, 183, 565, 570, 575, *n* 575, *vb* 696, 809
spare no effort *vb* 617
spare no expense *vb* 725
spare part *n* 53
spare the rod *vb* 660
spare time *n* 580, 612, 761
spare tyre *n* 168
sparing *adj* 726, 728, 843
spark *n* 339
sparkle *n* 374, 507, *vb* 281, 306, 374
sparkling *adj* 304, 507, 742
sparkly *adj* 374
spark off *vb* 61
sparring match *n* 643
sparse *adj* 30, 67, 87, 118, 183, 187, 288
sparseness *n* 30, 87, 118, 183, 288
spartan *adj* 843
spasm *n* 147, 281
spasmodic *adj* 65, 120, 130, 281
spasmodically *adv* 120, 130
spasmodicness *n* 120
spate *n* 29, 66, 314
spatial *adj* 156
spatio-temporal *adj* 156
spatter *vb* 67, 308

spawn *n* 155, *vb* 152
spay *adj* 36, *vb* 153
speak *vb* 353, 526, 528
speak badly *vb* 529
speaker *n* 528
speak for *vb* 676
speak for itself *vb* 460
speaking clock *n* 97
speak one's mind *vb* 478, 627
speak out *vb* 528
speak plainly *vb* 509
speak up *vb* 478, 526, 528
speak well of *vb* 825
speak with a plum in one's mouth *vb* 529
spear *n* 649, *vb* 232
spearhead *n* 212, *vb* 31, 59, 212
spear side *n* 12, 332
special *adj* 70
special case *n* 70, 73
special dispensation *n* 667
special effects *n* 525
specialist *n* 624
speciality *n* 70
special offer *n* 722
special price/rate *n* 722
special purchase *n* 709
special treatment *n* 822
species *n* 68
specific *adj* 70
specifically *adv* 70
specification *n* 422
specifications *n* 70
specificity *n* 70
specify *vb* 70, 79, 422
specimen *n* 464
specious *adj* 4, 394, 411, 480
speciousness *n* 411, 480
speck *n* 169, 300, 393, 767, *vb* 767
speckle *n* 393, *vb* 393
speckled *adj* 393
specs *n* 370
spectacle *n* 370, 394, 523, 785
spectacles *n* 370
spectacular *adj* 785
spectate *vb* 162
spectator *n* 162, 370
spectre *n* 4, 865
spectrum *n* 64, 381, 393
speculate *vb* 398, 400, 416, 456, 554, 701
speculation *n* 398, 400, 416, 456, 554, 707

speculative *adj* 398, 400, 416, 456, 554
speculator *n* 554, 707
speech *n* 494, 522, 526, 528, 532
speech defect *n* 529
speechify *vb* 528, 532
speech impediment *n* 529
speechless *adj* 354, 527, 531, 759
speechlessness *n* 354, 527, 531
speech sound *n* 353, 495
speed *n* 245, 580, 849, *vb* 245
speediness *n* 96
speed limit *n* 668
speed merchant *n* 245
speedometer *n* 177
speed up *vb* 615
speedwriting *n* 513
speedy *adj* 96, 245
speleologist *n* 275
speleology *n* 275
spell *n* 90, 92, 801, 876, *vb* 455, 495
spellbind *vb* 256, 876
spellbinder *n* 876
spellbinding *adj* 876
spellbound *adj* 235, 759, 876
spell danger *vb* 806
spelling *n* 495
spell it out *vb* 509
spell out *vb* 70, 507
spelt out *adj* 503
spend *vb* 90, 716, 718
spend a penny *vb* 268
spending *n* 718
spending spree *n* 718
spend money as if it were going out of fashion *vb* 727
spend money like water *vb* 727
spendthrift *adj* 727, 844, *n* 727
spent *adj* 144
sperm *n* 152
spew *vb* 266
sphere *n* 7, 157, 223, 225, 284
spherical *adj* 223, 225
spice *n* 344, 349, 603, *vb* 38, 344, 349
spiciness *n* 342, 344
spicy *adj* 342, 344, 349, 732
spidery *adj* 513
spiel *n* 528, 551, 709
spigot *n* 233
spike *n* 296, *vb* 38, 579
spiky *adj* 296
spill *n* 275, 341, 377, *vb* 275, 314
spill the beans *vb* 468

spin *n* 223, 236, *vb* 149, 197, 223, 279, 479, 524
spin a coin *vb* 554
spin a yarn *vb* 4
spindle *n* 279
spindly *adj* 183
spindrift *n* 94, 306
spin-dry *vb* 309
spin-dryer *n* 309
spine *n* 193, 296, 516
spineless *adj* 142, 144, 541, 752
spinelessness *n* 541, 752
spinet *n* 369
spinney *n* 327
spinning *adj* 279
spin-off *n* 37, 60, 133
spin out *vb* 93, 124, 178, 506, 616
spinster *n* 79, 333, 799
spinsterhood *n* 799
spiny *adj* 296
spiral *adj* 224, *n* 33, 224, 274, 278, 279, *vb* 33, 223, 274, 278, 279
spiralling *adj* 33, 723
spire *n* 184, 188
spirit *n* 145, 283, 322, 539, 751, 865, 865
Spirit *n* 862
spirit away *vb* 395
spirit communication *n* 876, 877
spirited *adj* 145, 322, 751
spiritism *n* 876
spirit manifestation *n* 877
spirit message *n* 877
spirit raiser *n* 876
spirits *n* 7, 267, 323
spiritual *adj* 283, 862, 868, 872, 878, *n* 367
spiritual guidance *n* 878
spiritualism *n* 283, 876, 877
spiritualist *adj* 283, *n* 876, 877
spirituality *n* 283, 872
spiritualize *vb* 283
spit *n* 228, 311, *vb* 268, 361, 364
spite *n* 604, 641, 796, 806, 816, *vb* 806
spiteful *adj* 604, 641, 796, 806
spitefully *adv* 806
spitfire *n* 147
spit out *vb* 266
spitting distance *n* 173
spitting image *n* 13
spittle *n* 268, 305
spit upon *vb* 796
spiv *n* 480

splash *n* 30, *vb* 308, 314, 361, 393
splashdown *n* 238
splash down *vb* 238
splash out *vb* 718
splashy *adj* 308, 361
splay *vb* 170, 180, 260
splayed *adj* 170, 260
spleen *n* 802, 804
splendid *adj* 582, 763, 785
splendiferous *adj* 785
splendour *n* 763, 785
splice *n* 40, *vb* 40
splint *n* 193, 596
splinter *n* 48, 183, *vb* 41, 46, 295
splinter group *n* 41, 634
split *adj* 81, 635, *n* 41, 635, 871, *vb*
  41, 41, 46, 48, 81, 174, 232, 295, 635
split down the middle *vb* 63, 686
split hairs *vb* 18, 410, 411, 739
split infinitive *n* 501
split one's sides *vb* 744
split personality *n* 447
split the difference *vb* 27, 686
split up *vb* 798
sploshy *adj* 361
splotch *n* 393
splurge *n* 727, *vb* 727, 785
spoil *vb* 585, 593, 595, 625, 767, 800
spoils *n* 650, 703, 706
spoilsport *n* 745
spoken *adj* 528
spokeshave *n* 568
spokesman *n* 466, 647, 676
spokesperson *n* 212, 528, 647, 676
spokeswoman *n* 647, 676
sponge *n* 309, 487, 586, 702, *vb* 309,
  586, 681, 702
sponger *n* 681
sponginess *n* 144, 290, 317
spongy *adj* 144, 290, 317
sponsor *n* 193, 631, *vb* 193, 631, 698
sponsorship *n* 193, 631, 698
spontaneity *n* 96, 399, 401, 454, 537,
  548
spontaneous *adj* 96, 399, 401, 535,
  537, 548
spoof *n* 21, 744, 773
spook *n* 865
spooky *adj* 865
spool *n* 491
spoon *n* 227, 568
spoon-bending *n* 877
spoonerism *n* 196, 496
spoonfeed *vb* 800

spoonful *n* 30
spoor *n* 37, 485
sporadic *adj* 65, 67, 120, 130, 174
sporadicness *n* 65, 120
sport *n* 20, 612, 617, 761, *vb* 204
sporting *adj* 643, 761, 766, 817
sporting chance *n* 425
sportsman *n* 761, 831
sportswoman *n* 761
sporty *adj* 761
spot *n* 158, 169, 393, 767, *vb* 370,
  404, 433
spotless *adj* 584, 586, 831, 839, 850
spotlessness *n* 586, 850
spotlight *n* 377, *vb* 464
spotlit *adj* 374
spot on *adj* 440
spotted *adj* 393, 767
spouse *n* 797
spout *n* 232, 264, *vb* 264, 314, 528,
  530
sprain *n* 337, 595, *vb* 337, 595
sprained *adj* 595
sprat *n* 169
sprawl *n* 170, *vb* 67, 170, 180, 191
sprawling *adj* 67
spray *n* 66, 304, 306, 308, *vb* 308
spread *n* 33, 67, 156, 170, *vb* 33, 67,
  69, 156, 170, 202, 319, 471
spreadeagle *vb* 180, 260
spreadeagled *adj* 170, 260
spread one's wings *vb* 16, 180
spread the word *vb* 470
spree *n* 727
sprightly *adj* 112
spring *n* 108, 224, 248, 274, 293, 314,
  vb 245, 248, 274, 293, 451
springboard *n* 262, 276
spring-clean *vb* 586
springiness *n* 290
springlike *adj* 108
springtime *n* 108, 111
spring up *vb* 61, 101, 133
springy *adj* 248, 290, 293
sprinkle *vb* 38, 67, 87, 288, 300, 305,
  308, 393
sprinkler *n* 305
sprinkling *n* 30, 38, 87, 288
sprint *n* 236, 245, 615, *vb* 236, 245,
  615
sprinter *n* 236, 245
sprite *n* 865
sprocket *n* 229
sprout *vb* 33, 152, 327

stalker *n* 555
stall *n* 165, 710, *vb* 114, 123, 610, 652
stallion *n* 326, 332
stalls *n* 523
stalwart *adj* 143, 540
stalwartness *n* 540
stamina *n* 43, 93, 143, 294, 540
stammer *n* 529, *vb* 529
stamp *n* 5, 15, 68, 216, 485, 515, *vb* 5, 68, 191, 216, 485, 493, 515, 825
stamp/fix on one's memory *vb* 448
stamp duty *n* 721
stampede *n* 245, 750, *vb* 147, 245
stamping ground *n* 158, 165
stamp out *vb* 150
stance *n* 408
stand *n* 189, 193, 638, 710, *vb* 7, 190, 679, 716, 718
stand above the law *vb* 853
stand alone *vb* 79
standard *adj* 15, 22, 27, 69, 71, 72, 500, *n* 71, 484, 584, 657
Standard English *n* 494
standardization *n* 15
standardize *vb* 15, 71, 72
standard lamp *n* 377
standards *n* 831
standard time *n* 90, 97
stand by *vb* 193, 450, 559, 608
stand down *vb* 123, 674
stand erect *vb* 779
stand firm *vb* 43, 539
stand firm/fast *vb* 131
stand for *vb* 458, 484, 488
stand-in *n* 128, 676
stand in fear of *vb* 750
stand in for *vb* 128, 676
standing *adj* 190, 823, *n* 7, 24
standing by *adj* 559
standing on one's head *adv* 629
standing order *n* 71
standing-stone *n* 190
stand in need of *adj* 558
stand no nonsense *vb* 659
standoffish *adj* 172, 790
standoffishness *n* 172, 790
stand on ceremony *vb* 787
stand one's ground *vb* 539, 638, 659
stand on its head *vb* 196
stand on one's own two feet *vb* 44, 79
stand out *vb* 70, 162, 228, 372
standpipe *n* 305
standpoint *n* 159, 434

standstill *n* 123, 235
stand still *vb* 90, 122, 235
stand surety *vb* 687
stand to reason *vb* 400
stand up to *vb* 637, 638
stanza *n* 521
staple *vb* 40
star *n* 31, 284, 525, 650, 657, 774, *vb* 774
starboard *n* 214
starch *n* 182, *vb* 289
starchy *adj* 182
stare *n* 370, *vb* 370, 759
stargazing *n* 284
stark *adj* 483, 509, *adv* 49
starkers *adj* 205
starkness *n* 509
starless *adj* 375
starlet *n* 525
starlight *n* 374
Star of David *n* 220
starry *adj* 284
stars *n* 104
Stars and Stripes *n* 484
star-studded *adj* 525
start *n* 61, 248, 281, *vb* 61, 96
starter *n* 59, 267
starting-point *n* 61, 189, 262
startle *vb* 451, 732
startled *adj* 451
starvation *n* 574, 755, 845
starvation diet *n* 574
starve *vb* 755, 845
starving *adj* 713, 755, 845
stash *vb* 469
stash away *vb* 570
stasis *n* 25, 122, 123, 235, 608
state *n* 7, 157, 331, *vb* 473, 496, 499
statehood *n* 331
stateliness *n* 511
stately *adj* 511, 524, 779, 787
stately home *n* 165
statement *n* 420, 466, 473, 720
state of affairs *n* 8
state of mind *n* 7
state of play *n* 8
state of war *n* 794
state-owned *adj* 693
statesman *n* 622, 657
statesmanlike *adj* 622
static *adj* 25, 122, 235, 608
station *n* 160, 472, 553, 614, 776, 821 *vb* 158, 159, 160
stationary *adj* 122, 235

stationery *n* 513
station wagon *n* 242
statistical *adj* 75
statistician *n* 75
statistics *n* 75, 466
stative *adj* 7
statuary *n* 492
statue *n* 486, 488, 492, 875
statuette *n* 492
stature *n* 184
status *n* 7, 24, 774
status quo *n* 8, 25, 122
statute *n* 71, 852
statute book *n* 71, 852
statutory *adj* 71, 623, 661, 852
staunch *adj* 143, 233, 539, 540, 793
staunchness *n* 233, 539, 540
stave in *vb* 227
stay *n* 193, *vb* 122, 193
stay-at-home *adj* 235, 790, *n* 199, 790
stay at home *vb* 790
stay away *vb* 163
staying power *n* 43, 93, 143, 540
stay neutral *vb* 608
stay of execution *n* 606
stay put *vb* 122, 131, 235
stay the course *vb* 43, 294, 540
steadfast *adj* 122, 540
steadfastness *n* 540
steadiness *n* 119, 122, 124, 131, 616, 733
steady *adj* 119, 122, 124, 131, 616, *n* 795
steal *vb* 465, 469, 690, 705
steal a march on *vb* 99
stealing *n* 705
steal someone's thunder *vb* 31
stealth *n* 467, 626
steal the limelight *vb* 523
stealthiness *n* 465
stealthy *adj* 465, 467
steam *n* 304, 305, 308, *vb* 237, 304
steam engine *n* 568
steamer *n* 243
steam radio *n* 472
steamroller *n* 150, 191
steamy *adj* 304
steel *n* 143, 289, 296, 569, *vb* 143
steel oneself *vb* 731
steelworker *n* 613
steely *adj* 143, 289, 385, 391, 539
steep *adj* 184, 190, 723, *vb* 269, 305
steeple *n* 184, 188, 882
steeplechase *n* 555

steeplechaser *n* 274
steeplechasing *n* 761
steeplejack *n* 274
steepness *n* 184, 190
steer *vb* 237, 249, 622
steer a middle course *vb* 63, 686
steer clear of *vb* 406, 556
steering *adj* 623
steering committee *n* 623
stellar *adj* 284
stem *n* 327, *vb* 123, 638
stench *n* 347, 350
stenography *n* 513
stentorian *adj* 355
step *n* 24, 253, 607
stepbrother *n* 12
step by step *adv* 24, 55
step forward *vb* 212
step into someone's shoes *vb* 60
step into the shoes of *vb* 100
step on it *vb* 245
step out of line *vb* 73, 781
step-parent *n* 12
steppe *n* 311, 313
stepped *adj* 229
stepping-stone *n* 8, 42
steps *n* 240, 274
stepsister *n* 12
step up *vb* 33
stereo *n* 353
stereophonic *adj* 353
stereotype *n* 15, 72, *vb* 15, 22, 72
stereotyped *adj* 15
stereotypical *adj* 22, 68
sterile *adj* 39, 153, 586, 590
sterility *n* 153
sterilization *n* 39, 153, 586, 590
sterilize *vb* 39, 153, 586, 590
sterilized *adj* 590
sterling *adj* 831, 837, *n* 711
stern *adj* 659, 745, 745, 826, *n* 213
sternness *n* 745
stethoscope *n* 351
stew *n* 317, *vb* 267, 317
steward *n* 571, 622, 666
stewardess *n* 666
stick *n* 861, *vb* 40, 43, 124, 235, 695
stick at *vb* 538
sticker *n* 485
stickiness *n* 43, 318
sticking point *n* 211
stick in one's throat *vb* 527
stick-in-the-mud *n* 122
stick it out *vb* 540

stool *n* 268
stool pigeon *n* 466
stoop *n* 277, *vb* 185, 277, 775, 780
stooping *adj* 185
stop *n* 123, 235, *vb* 62, 123, 233, 235, 618, 717
stop a cheque *vb* 717
stop at nothing *vb* 810
stopcock *n* 233
stopgap *adj* 101, *n* 25, 124, 128
stop-go *adj* 65, 120
stop in one's tracks *vb* 123, 235
stop off/over *vb* 65
stopover *n* 65, 236
stoppage *n* 123, 233, 235, 717
stopper *n* 202, 233
stop press *n* 471
stop short *vb* 123, 235
stopwatch *n* 97
stop working *vb* 652
storage *n* 565, 570
store *n* 167, 565, 570, 710, *vb* 570
store away *vb* 570
stored *adj* 570
storehouse *n* 160
storekeeper *n* 571
storeroom *n* 570
stores *n* 571
store up *vb* 690
storey *n* 64, 175
storm *n* 66, 147, 307, 316, *vb* 56, 147, 316, 639
storm in a teacup *n* 482, 577
storming *n* 639, 639
storm of protest *n* 682
stormy *adj* 147, 281, 307, 316, 410
story *n* 471, 517
storyline *n* 517
story so far *n* 8
story-teller *n* 517
stout *adj* 168
stout-hearted *adj* 751
stove *n* 339
stow away *vb* 469
strabismus *n* 370
straddle *vb* 40, 63, 156, 271
strafe *vb* 639
straggle *vb* 67, 192, 213
straggler *n* 60
straggling *adj* 67
straggly *adj* 87, 288
straight *adj* 39, 222, 250, 367, 523, 817, 831, *adv* 39, 222, 249
straighten *vb* 222

straight-faced *adj* 745
straightforward *adj* 297, 460, 478, 503, 509, 627, 629, 817, 831
straightforwardness *n* 297, 460, 478, 503, 509, 580, 627, 629
straight from the horse's mouth *adj* 420
straight line *n* 222
straight man *n* 773
straightness *n* 222
strain *n* 23, 68, 154, 365, 502, 595, 617, 739, *vb* 561, 595, 617
strained *adj* 595
strainer *n* 232
strait *n* 181, 310
straitened *adj* 181, 713
straitjacket *n* 171, 668
straitlaced *adj* 668, 745, 850
strand *n* 183, 311
strange *adj* 54, 550, 759
strangeness *n* 550
stranger *n* 54
strangle *vb* 150, 324, 860
stranglehold *n* 43, 695
strangling *n* 860
strangulate *vb* 233
strangulation *n* 233, 860
strap *n* 861, *vb* 860
strapping *adj* 29, 143, 588
stratagem *n* 480
strategic *adj* 557, 621, 645
strategist *n* 557
strategy *n* 557, 621, 645
stratify *vb* 175
stratum *n* 175, 321
stratus *n* 307
strawberry blond *adj* 387
strawberry mark *n* 767
strawboard *n* 569
stray *adj* 67, 252, *n* 161, *vb* 67, 234, 252, 838
streak *n* 181, 183, 374, *vb* 245, 393
streaker *n* 205
streaks *n* 765
streaky *adj* 183, 393
stream *n* 29, 314, *vb* 86, 192, 303, 314
streaming *adj* 305
streamline *vb* 181, 183, 592
streamlined *adj* 292
stream of consciousness *n* 522
street *n* 240
streetcar *n* 242
street party *n* 746, 761
street violence *n* 853

street-walking *n* 851
strength *n* 23, 141, 143, 294, 507
strengthen *vb* 141, 143, 294, 741, 751
strengthening *n* 741
strength of character *n* 143
strenuous *adj* 617
stress *n* 23, 136, 473, 507, 521, *vb*
  143, 473, 507, 576
stretch *n* 92, 156, 178, 293, 668, *vb*
  156, ·172, 178, 180, 191, 222, 293
stretcher *n* 241
stretchiness *n* 170
stretch one's legs *vb* 620
stretchy *adj* 170, 293
strew *vb* 67, 288
striate *vb* 393
striated *adj* 231
stricken *adj* 656
strict *adj* 659, 870
strictness *n* 659, 870
stride *n* 234, 253, *vb* 234
stridency *n* 355, 362
strident *adj* 355, 362, 526
strife *n* 635, 643
strike *n* 123, 235, 433, 610, 639, 682,
  vb 123, 147, 247, 327
strike a balance *vb* 25
strike a balance between *vb* 27
strike a bargain *vb* 684
strike camp *vb* 262
strike it rich *vb* 712
strike off *vb* 266, 673
strike one *vb* 398
strike out *vb* 487
strike up an acquaintance *vb* 793
strike while the iron is hot *vb* 115
striking *adj* 464
string *n* 60, 64, 66, 175, 178, 299
string along *vb* 85
stringed instrument *n* 369
string-pulling *n* 139
strings *n* 685
string up *vb* 324
stringy *adj* 183, 294
strip *n* 175, 181, *vb* 203, 205
stripe *n* 5, 68, 181, 657, *vb* 393
striped *adj* 393
strip lighting *n* 377
stripling *n* 111, 332
stripped *adj* 203, 691
stripper *n* 203, 205
stripping *n* 203
striptease *n* 205
strive *vb* 561, 617, 643

strobe light *n* 377
stroke *n* 247, 338, 589, 800, *vb* 338,
  736, 800
stroll *n* 236, 246, 616, *vb* 234, 236,
  246, 616
strong *adj* 141, 143, 294
strong-arm tactics *n* 664
strong emotion *n* 732
stronghold *n* 600
strongly *adv* 143
strongly worded *adj* 507
strong man *n* 143
strongpoint *n* 640
strongroom *n* 167, 711
strong-willed *adj* 539
stroppy *adj* 804
struck dumb *adj* 759
struck off *adj* 52
structural *adj* 5, 193, 216, 298
structure *n* 57, 216, 298, 299, *vb* 298
struggle *n* 632, 656, *vb* 561, 643
strum *vb* 358
strumming *n* 358
strung out *adj* 67, 87, 288
strut *n* 193, *vb* 234, 771, 779, 783
strutting *adj* 779
stub *n* 485, 719
stubbiness *n* 179, 297
stubble *n* 37
stubborn *adj* 122, 540, 542, 628,
  842
stubbornness *n* 122, 542, 842
stubby *adj* 179, 297
stuck *adj* 235
stuck-up *adj* 771, 779, 783
stud *n* 223, 332, 851
studded *adj* 393, 766
student *n* 438, 476
stud farm *n* 328
studied *adj* 771
studio *n* 165, 490, 525, 614
studious *adj* 398, 404, 476
studiousness *n* 404
study *n* 414, 476, 519, 559, 614, *vb*
  438, 476, 559
study of religion *n* 868
study spiritualism *vb* 877
stuff *n* 5, 282, 569, 694, 707, *vb* 49,
  66, 166, 170, 182, 201, 603, 846
stuffed *adj* 49, 575
stuffiness *n* 745
stuffing *n* 166, 170, 182, 201, 269
stuff oneself *vb* 846
stuffy *adj* 350, 745

stumble vb 275
stumble across vb 433
stumble upon vb 135
stumbling block n 628
stump n 37, vb 236
stumped adj 461
stump up vb 716
stun vb 451
stunned adj 451
stunner n 451, 763
stunning adj 763
stunt n 785, vb 171, 219
stunted adj 169, 171, 179, 185, 219
stupefaction n 759
stupefied adj 335, 759
stupefy vb 731
stupefying adj 759
stupendous adj 759
stupid adj 182, 397, 399, 439, 445, 731
stupidity n 182, 397, 399, 439, 445, 731
stupid person n 397
stupor n 335, 610, 731
stutter n 529, vb 529
sty n 165, 328
Stygian adj 384
style n 216, 494, 497, 502, 511, 621, 770, vb 216, 497
styling n 765
stylish adj 511, 763, 770
stylishness n 511, 770
stylist n 765
stylistic adj 502
stylized adj 502
stymie vb 630
suave adj 292
suavity n 292
subaltern n 666
subconscious adj 396, 401
subdivide vb 48
subdivision n 48
subdue vb 139, 148, 354, 360, 668, 670
subdued adj 148, 356, 360, 381
subeditor n 514
subfertile adj 153
subfusc n 204
subject adj 32, 670, 685, n 409, 416, 500, vb 670
subjecthood n 670
subjection n 32, 670
subjective adj 4, 70, 401
subjectivity n 4, 70, 283

subject to adj 821
subjugate vb 670
subjugation n 32, 670
subjunctive adj 500
sublet n 701, vb 701
subletting n 701
sublieutenant n 648
sublimate n 270
sublime adj 276, 507, 862
subliminal adj 396, 401
sublimity n 276
sub-machine gun n 649
submarine n 310
submariner n 237, 275, 648
submerge vb 186, 275, 373, 487
submerged adj 373, 465
submerged rock n 601
submersion n 186
submission n 436, 551, 642, 663, 679
submissive adj 436, 537, 551, 642, 663, 733, 780, 821, 823
submissiveness n 642, 733, 780
submit vb 32, 436, 551, 623, 642, 663, 679, 733, 780, 821, 823
subnormal adj 397
subordinate adj 32, 670, n 32, vb 670
subordination n 32, 670
subplot n 517
subpoena n 661, 856, vb 661
subscribe vb 634, 698, 716
subscriber n 698
subscribe to vb 43
subscription n 698, 716
subsequent adj 60, 100, 133
subsequently adv 60, 100
subservience n 642, 663, 780, 782
subservient adj 642, 663, 780, 782
subside vb 34, 235, 275
subsidence n 275
subsidiary adj 32, 670, n 634
subsidize vb 631, 698, 701, 746
subsidy n 631, 698, 716
subsist vb 1, 122
subsistence n 122, 573, 631
subsistence level n 713
substance n 1, 3, 5, 282, 458, 520, 576, 712
substandard adj 32, 273, 501
substantial adj 1, 3, 29, 287, 576
substantially adv 29
substantiate vb 3, 412, 417, 440, 819
substantiation n 417
substitutable adj 128, 129

substitute *adj* 128, *n* 128, 676, 814, *vb* 121, 128, 129
substitute for *vb* 676
substitution *n* 121, 128, 129, 196
substratum *n* 189
subsume *vb* 51
subterfuge *n* 469
subterranean *adj* 185, 186, 465
subtle *adj* 381, 418, 483
subtlety *n* 418, 483
subtract *adj* 36, *vb* 34, 75
subtraction *n* 34, 36, 75
subtractive *adj* 34
suburb *n* 157
suburban *adj* 157, 777
suburbanite *n* 164
suburbia *n* 67
subvention *n* 716
subversion *n* 58, 127, 139, 662
subversive *adj* 127, 139, 662, *n* 662
subvert *vb* 58, 127, 139
subway *n* 240, 242
succeed *vb* 60, 64, 100, 651, 835
succeeding *adj* 60
succeed to *vb* 697, 699
success *n* 651, 655, 835
successful *adj* 561, 651, 655, 835
successful candidate *n* 651
succession *n* 60, 64, 100, 155
successive *adj* 60, 64, 100
successively *adv* 64
successor *n* 37, 100, 155
succinct *adj* 179, 505, 520
succinctness *n* 179, 505
succour *n* 631, *vb* 631
succubus *n* 864
succulence *n* 317
succulent *adj* 317
succumb *vb* 150, 551
suck *vb* 270
sucker *n* 480
suckling *n* 111
suck up to *vb* 782, 827
suction *n* 270
sudden *adj* 96, 245, 451, 548
sudden decrease *n* 34
sudden increase *n* 33
suddenly *adv* 96
suddenness *n* 96, 245, 451
sudden sound *n* 357
suds *n* 306
sue *vb* 635, 830, 856
sue for peace *vb* 646

suet *n* 319
suffer *vb* 677, 733
sufferance *n* 660
suffer defeat *vb* 652
suffer from *vb* 589
suffering *n* 337, 735
suffer punishment *vb* 860
suffer purgatory *vb* 814
suffer with *vb* 729
suffice *vb* 573
sufficiency *n* 573
sufficient *adj* 573
suffix *n* 500
suffocate *vb* 150, 324
suffuse *vb* 38
sugar *n* 345, 603, *vb* 345
sugar-coat *vb* 345
sugared *adj* 345
sugariness *n* 345
sugary *adj* 345, 827
suggest *vb* 17, 420, 456, 458, 465, 557, 623, 679, 681
suggestibility *n* 541
suggestible *adj* 541
suggestion *n* 139, 409, 456, 458, 483, 557, 623, 679, 681
suggestive *adj* 139, 420, 458, 465, 484, 517
suicidal *adj* 150, 324, 743, 753
suicide *n* 323, 324
sui generis *adj* 22, 70
suing *adj* 856
suit *n* 795, 800, 830, 856, *vb* 19, 580
suitability *n* 19, 265, 578, 580, 817
suitable *adj* 19, 265, 578, 580, 797, 817
suitcase *n* 167
suite *n* 64, 367
suiting *n* 569
suitor *n* 795, 856
sulk *vb* 743, 804
sulkiness *n* 804
sulky *adj* 739, 804
sullen *adj* 538, 804
sullenly *adv* 804
sullenness *n* 538, 542, 804
sullied *adj* 851
sully *vb* 767, 775, 828
sulphur *n* 350
sulphur-yellow *adj* 389
sultan *n* 665, 776
sultry *adj* 339
sum *n* 47, 74
summarize *adj* 36, *vb* 179, 505, 520

suppress *vb* 150, 467, 487, 659, 668, 678
suppressed *adj* 678
suppression *n* 467, 487, 659, 668, 678
suppressive *adj* 668
suppurating *adj* 303
suppuration *n* 303
supremacy *n* 31, 657
supreme *adj* 31, 582, 584, 862, *n* 188
Supreme Being *n* 862
supreme deity *n* 862
surburban *adj* 165
surcharge *n* 721
sure *adj* 427, 434, 598
sureness *n* 131
sure thing *n* 427
surety *n* 598, 687
surf *n* 310, *vb* 237
surface *adj* 187, 198, *n* 6, 187, 198, 202, 299, *vb* 202, 286, 394
surfaced *adj* 202
surface wound *n* 187
surfeit *n* 575
surfing *n* 237, 761
surge *vb* 147, 274, 314
surgeon *n* 596
surgery *n* 596
surgical *adj* 596
surgical collar *n* 193
surly *adj* 792, 804
surmise *n* 456, *vb* 456
surname *n* 497
surpass *vb* 31, 272
surplice *n* 881
surplus *adj* 37, 565, 575, *n* 20, 37, 575
surprise *n* 451, 560
surprised *adj* 451
surprising *adj* 451
surrender *n* 563, 642, *vb* 563, 642
surreptitious *adj* 469
surrogate *adj* 128, *n* 128
surrogate mother *n* 12, 154
surround *n* 208, *vb* 198, 206, 210, 223
surrounding *adj* 8, *n* 206
surroundings *n* 8, 206
surtax *n* 721
surveillance *n* 370, 404
survey *n* 47, 370, 414, 519, *vb* 414, 519
surveying *n* 177
survival *n* 1, 122, 322
survival instinct *n* 93
survive *vb* 1, 37, 93, 122, 294, 322

surviving *adj* 1, 37, 93, 122, 322, 323
survivor *n* 37, 798
susceptibility *n* 140, 551, 730
susceptible *adj* 140, 334, 551, 730
suspect *adj* 435, 830, *n* 830, *vb* 428, 435, 815
suspected *adj* 840
suspend *vb* 65, 114, 123, 192, 565, 673, 853, 860
suspended *adj* 114, 192, 565, 608
suspended sentence *n* 857
suspender *n* 192
suspense *n* 450
suspension *n* 114, 123, 192, 235, 303, 565, 608, 673
suspicion *n* 435, 483, 754, 815
suspicious *adj* 435, 754, 815, 832
sustain *vb* 122, 124, 193, 631
sustained *adj* 117
sustaining *adj* 193
sustenance *n* 267
suture *n* 40, 42
svelte *adj* 183
swaddling clothes *n* 202
swag *n* 221, 706, *vb* 221
swagger *vb* 234
swallow *vb* 434, 733
swallow one's pride *vb* 642
swallow one's words *vb* 529
swallowtail *n* 81
swallow up *vb* 150
swamp *n* 308, *vb* 49, 86, 150, 305
swampy *adj* 308
swank *n* 779, *vb* 771, 785
swanking *n* 771
swan-necked *adj* 221
swansong *n* 62
swap *n* 28, 128, 129, 196, 707, *vb* 11, 121, 128, 129, 707
sward *n* 327
swarm *n* 66, 86, *vb* 29, 66, 86, 573
swarming *adj* 29
swarthiness *n* 384
swarthy *adj* 384, 386
swash *vb* 314, 361
swastika *n* 197
swath *n* 486
swathe *vb* 202, 230
sway *n* 31, 139, 141, 657, *vb* 29, 139, 280
swear *vb* 473, 683, 792, 801, 873
swear by *vb* 434
swearing *adj* 873
swear like a trooper *vb* 801

swear off *vb* 843
swearword *n* 496, 801
sweat *n* 268, 305, 308, 339, 617, *vb* 268, 308, 617
sweatshop *n* 670
sweaty *adj* 308
sweep *n* 156, 170, 172, 180, 191, 221, *vb* 156, 191, 221, 586
sweeper *n* 60, 213
sweeping *adj* 47, 127, 147, 180
sweep under the carpet *vb* 467
sweet *adj* 342, 345, 365, 763, *n* 267
sweet-and-sour *adj* 344
sweeten *vb* 290, 345, 349
sweetener *n* 345
sweet f *n* 77
sweetheart *n* 795, 800
sweetmeat *n* 345
sweetness *n* 342, 345, 348, 365
sweetness and light *n* 636
sweet nothings *n* 800
sweet smell *n* 349
sweet-smelling *adj* 347, 348, 349
sweet-talk *vb* 827
sweet tooth *n* 342
swell *n* 281, 770, *vb* 33, 35, 170, 225, 226, 355
swelling *n* 225, 226
sweltering *adj* 307, 339
swerve *n* 221, 252, *vb* 221
swift *adj* 245
swiftly *adv* 245
swiftness *n* 245
swig *n* 267, *vb* 848
swim *vb* 237, 761
swimming *n* 237, 761
swim with the tide *vb* 72
swindle *n* 480, 705, *vb* 480, 705, 832
swindler *n* 480, 705
swine *n* 326, 838
swing *n* 119, 192, 280, 367, *vb* 119, 192, 280
swinger *n* 770
swinging *adj* 770
swing of the pendulum *n* 126, 248
swings and roundabouts *n* 11
swipe *vb* 705
swirl *n* 224, 279, 314, *vb* 279, 314
swish *adj* 770, *n* 356, *vb* 356, 361
switch *n* 121, 125, 128, *vb* 121, 128, 129
switchback *n* 221
switchboard *n* 42
switch off *vb* 375, 731

switch on *vb* 136, 141, 732
swivel *vb* 279
swiz *n* 480
swollen *adj* 170, 225, 226
swollen-headed *adj* 779, 783
swollenness *n* 170, 226
swoon *vb* 335, *n* 335
swoop *n* 275, *vb* 245, 275
sword *n* 649
sword of Damocles *n* 599
swordsman *n* 648
sworn *adj* 473
swot *n* 476, *vb* 476
sycophancy *n* 782, 791
sycophant *n* 782, 827
sycophantic *adj* 782, 791, 827
syllabary *n* 495
syllabic *adj* 495
syllabify *vb* 495
syllable *n* 495
syllabus *n* 475
sylvan *adj* 327
symbiosis *n* 40, 85
symbiotic *adj* 40, 45, 85
symbol *n* 484, 495
symbolic *adj* 458, 484, 488
symbolism *n* 458
symbolization *n* 488
symbolize *vb* 458, 484, 488
symbol of authority *n* 657
symmetrical *adj* 17, 25, 218, 511, 636
symmetry *n* 17, 25, 218, 511, 636
sympathetic *adj* 436, 633, 660, 729, 805, 809
sympathetic to *adj* 757
sympathize *vb* 729, 809
sympathize with *vb* 436
sympathy *n* 42, 633, 660, 729, 757, 793, 795, 805, 809
symphonic *adj* 367
symphony *n* 367
symposium *n* 533
symptom *n* 85, 420, 484
symptomatic *adj* 420, 484, 602
synagogue *n* 882
sync *n* 103
synchronic *adj* 103
synchronism *n* 103
synchronization *n* 19, 103
synchronize *vb* 19, 25, 103
synchronous *adj* 103
syncretic *adj* 38
syndicate *n* 40, 66, 634
synergic *adj* 633

synergy *n* 633
synod *n* 878
synonym *n* 496
synonymous *adj* 17, 458
synonymy *n* 17
synopsis *n* 47, 520
syntactic *adj* 500
syntax *n* 500
synthesis *n* 40, 45
synthesize *vb* 45, 149
synthesizer *n* 369
synthetic *adj* 17, 21, 149
syringe *n* 270
syrup *n* 318, 345
syrupy *adj* 318, 345
system *n* 55, 57, 68, 71, 621
systematic *adj* 55, 57
systematically *adv* 55
systematize *vb* 15, 55
systems analyst *n* 7

T

tab *n* 657
tabby *n* 326
tabernacle *n* 882
table *n* 57, 76, *vb* 76, 486
tableland *n* 191, 313
table of contents *n* 76
tablet *n* 596
table-turning *n* 876
tabloid *n* 471
taboo *adj* 678, *n* 678
tabular *adj* 57
tabula rasa *n* 127, 487
tabulate *vb* 57
tacheograph *n* 177
tacit *adj* 465
taciturn *adj* 354, 527, 531, 790
taciturnity *n* 354, 531, 790
tack *n* 240, 249
tackiness *n* 43, 182, 318
tackle *vb* 61, 562
tack on *vb* 35
tacky *adj* 43, 182, 318, 583, 695
tact *n* 768, 791
tactful *adj* 768, 791
tactfulness *n* 768
tactical *adj* 621, 645
tactics *n* 621, 645
tactile *adj* 338
tactless *adj* 625, 769, 792
tactlessness *n* 625, 769
taffeta *n* 569

Taffy *n* 331
tag *n* 485, *vb* 485, 497
tag along *vb* 85
tail *n* 60, 85, 213, *vb* 60, 85, 173, 555
tailback *n* 64, 630
tail end *n* 37
tail-end Charlie *n* 60
tail light *n* 377
tail off *vb* 62
tailor *n* 204, 613
tailored *adj* 204
tailpiece *n* 60
tails *n* 213
tailwind *n* 316
taint *vb* 775
taintedness *n* 851
take *vb* 491, 500, 690, 703, 733
take a back seat *vb* 32, 784, 833
take a beating/hammering *vb* 32
take a break *vb* 612, 618
take a breather *vb* 235, 620
take a dim view of *vb* 826
take a dislike to *vb* 758
take advantage of *vb* 115, 564, 851
take after *vb* 12, 17
take a holiday *vb* 618
take a job *vb* 611
take amiss *vb* 802
take an average *vb* 27
take apart *vb* 48
take as read *vb* 760
take a trip *vb* 849
takeaway *n* 165
take away *vb* 860
take away one's good name *vb* 775
take by storm *vb* 703
take care *vb* 754
take comfort *vb* 740
take command *vb* 657
take communion *vb* 881
take courage *vb* 751
take credit *vb* 714
take down *vb* 513
take down a peg *vb* 775
take early retirement *vb* 674
take effect *vb* 136
take exception *vb* 682, 802
take flight *vb* 605
take forever *vb* 93
take for granted *vb* 760, 812
take fright *vb* 750
take heart *vb* 740, 742, 751
take holy orders *vb* 799, 878, 879
take in *vb* 166, 265, 460, 699

talk to a brick wall *vb* 534
talk to oneself *vb* 534
talk up *vb* 431, 482
tall *adj* 184
tall, dark, and handsome *adj* 763
tallness *n* 184
tall order *n* 628
tallow *n* 302, 319
tall story *n* 479, 482
tally *n* 75, *vb* 9, 11, 17, 19, 25, 72, 194
Talmud *n* 868
tambourine *n* 369
tame *adj* 148, 326, 642, *vb* 148
tampon *n* 233
tan *adj* 386, 388, *vb* 386, 860
tandem *n* 81, 242
tang *n* 342, 344
tangency *n* 176
tangent *n* 195, 214, 252
tangential *adj* 6, 10, 214
tangerine *n* 388
tangibility *n* 3, 282
tangible *adj* 3, 282, 338
tanginess *n* 342
tangle *n* 56, 197
tangled *adj* 56, 197
tango *n* 524
tangy *adj* 342, 344
tank *n* 167
tankard *n* 167
tanker *n* 242, 243
tanned *adj* 386
tanning *n* 765
tantalizing *adj* 732
tantamount *adj* 458
tantrum *n* 732, 802
Taoism *n* 868
tap *n* 233, 247, 305, 338, 357, *vb* 247, 270
tap dance *n* 524
tape *n* 369
tape measure *n* 177
taper *n* 341, 377, *vb* 171, 181, 183, 296
tape reader *n* 570
tape-record *vb* 486
tape-recorder *n* 369
tape recording *n* 486
tapestry *n* 149, 569, 766
tar *n* 318
tar and feather *vb* 860
tardily *adv* 98, 114
tardiness *n* 114, 246

tardy *adj* 98, 114, 246, 616
tare *n* 36
target *n* 249, 553
tariff *n* 668, 721
tarmac *n* 202, 569, *vb* 202
tarn *n* 312
tarnish *n* 587, 595, 767, 775, *vb* 384, 587, 595, 767, 775, 828
tarnished *adj* 587, 595, 767
tarot *n* 455
tarpaulin *n* 202
tarry *adj* 318, *vb* 98, 114, 122, 235
tart *adj* 344, 346, 803
tartan *n* 393, 484
Tartar *n* 803
tarted up *adj* 204, 785
tartness *n* 344, 346
tart up *vb* 765
Tarzan *n* 143
task *n* 562, 607, 611, 672, 821
tassel *n* 192, 766
taste *n* 342, 418, 511, *vb* 267, 334, 342, 729
tastebuds *n* 342
tasteful *adj* 511, 768
tastefulness *n* 768
tasteless *adj* 144, 343, 512, 737, 769
tastelessness *n* 144, 343, 483, 512, 737, 769
taste of *vb* 342
tastiness *n* 342, 344
tasty *adj* 267, 342, 344, 736
tat *n* 32
tatting *n* 766
tattoo *n* 358, *vb* 232, 485
tatty *adj* 32
taunt *n* 824, 826, *vb* 824
taupe *n* 385
taut *adj* 170
tautness *n* 222
tautological *adj* 88
tautologous *adj* 458, 506
tautology *n* 88, 506
tavern *n* 165
tawny *adj* 386, 389
tax *n* 699, 721, *vb* 619, 699, 721
taxable *adj* 721
taxation *n* 721
tax collector *n* 699
tax credit *n* 721
tax-deductible *adj* 722
tax demand *n* 661
tax dodger *n* 717
tax evader *n* 705

thankless task *n* 812
thank one's lucky stars *vb* 740
thanks *n* 811, 859
thanksgiving *n* 746, 811, 874
thanks to *prep* 138
thank-you *n* 811
thank-you letter *n* 811
thatch *n* 202, 569, *vb* 202
that is *adv* 462
that is to say *adv* 458
thaumaturgist *n* 876
thaumaturgy *n* 876
thaw *n* 303, *vb* 44, 217, 303, 809
theatre *n* 157, 470, 523, 761, 761, 785
theatre-in-the-round *n* 523
theatreland *n* 523
theatre of war *n* 645
theatrical *adj* 523, 785
theatricality *n* 523, 785
theatricals *n* 523
the blue *n* 310
the blues *n* 743
the boot *n* 266, 673
the brightest and best *n* 31
the bum's rush *n* 266
the church *n* 878
the creeps *n* 750
thé dansant *n* 524
the dead *n* 323
the deep *n* 186, 310
the doldrums *n* 743
the done thing *n* 688
the elect *n* 863
the Eternal *n* 862
the Evil One *n* 864
the faithful *n* 870
the fleshpots *n* 844
theft *n* 690, 705
the gallows *n* 324
the giggles *n* 744
the gods *n* 862
the Good Book *n* 868
the great unwashed *n* 777
the happy couple *n* 797
the hard way *adv* 617, 628
the heave *n* 673
the hereafter *n* 866
the here and now *n* 3
theism *n* 868
the just *n* 863, 872
the Law and the Prophets *n* 868
the little man *n* 577
the long and short of it *n* 520
the lot *n* 47

the lowest of the low *n* 32
them *n* 657
the masses *n* 777
theme *n* 367, 409
then *adv* 60, 102
the needful *n* 711
the never-never *n* 702, 708
theodolite *n* 177
theologian *n* 868
theological *adj* 868
theology *n* 868
theophany *n* 862, 868
theorem *n* 400
theoretical *adj* 396, 400, 408, 456
theorize *vb* 396, 398, 400, 456
theory *n* 134, 408, 456
the people *n* 777
the pick of the bunch *n* 31
the poor *n* 713
the push *n* 266
the rank and file *n* 777
therapeutic *adj* 588, 594, 596
therapist *n* 596
therapy *n* 596
thereabouts *adv* 173
the ready *n* 711
thereafter *adv* 100
therefore *adv* 60, 134
thereupon *adv* 100, 100
the righteous *n* 863, 872
thermal *n* 316
thermometer *n* 177
the rope *n* 324
the sack *n* 266, 673
the saints *n* 863, 872
thesaurus *n* 76, 496, 570
these days *adv* 101
thesis *n* 400, 409, 410, 519
thespian *n* 523
the stake *n* 324
the thing to do *n* 787
the underprivileged *n* 777
the way the cookie crumbles *n* 554
the whole kit and caboodle *n* 47
the whole shooting match *n* 47
the willies *n* 750
the works *n* 47
the worse for drink *adj* 848
they *n* 657
thick *adj* 182, 287, 317, 397, 494, 529,
 n 63
thick and fast *adv* 86
thick as thieves *adj* 85
thicken *vb* 182, 287, 317

tight-/close-fisted *adj* 728
tighten *vb* 171, 181
tighten one's belt *vb* 34, 656, 668
tighten up on *vb* 55, 659
tight fit *n* 181
tight-fitting *adj* 43
tight-lipped *adj* 467, 531
tightness *n* 181
tight squeeze *n* 181
tile *n* 569, *vb* 175, 202
tiler *n* 613
till *n* 711, *vb* 328
till all hours *adv* 114
till doomsday *adv* 95
till the cows come home *adv* 91
tilt *n* 26, *vb* 195, 196
tilt at windmills *vb* 579
timber *n* 569
timbre *n* 353, 526
time *n* 90, 668, *vb* 97
time after time *adv* 88
time and time again *adv* 117
time-consuming *adj* 93
time-honoured *adj* 107, 549, 823
time immemorial *n* 90, 105
timekeeping *adj* 97, *n* 97
time lag *n* 65, 90, 114
timeless *adj* 91, 95, 862
timelessness *n* 91, 95
time limit *n* 211
timeliness *n* 19, 113, 115
timely *adj* 19, 113, 115
time off *n* 612
time out of mind *n* 90
timepiece *n* 97
timeserver *n* 72, 782
timeserving *adj* 543, 580, 782, *n* 543,
 580, 782
time-sharing *n* 693
timesheet *n* 97
time signal *n* 97
timetable *n* 57, 76, 97, 475, 547, *vb*
 57, 76, 97, 547
time to come *n* 104
time to kill *n* 762
time to spare *n* 616
time up *n* 62
timewarp *n* 65, 90
time was *adv* 105
time zone *n* 90, 97, 103
timid *adj* 750, 752, 784
timidity *n* 750, 752, 784
timing *n* 97
timorous *adj* 750

timorousness *n* 750
timpani *n* 369
tin *n* 167, 569
tincture *n* 381
tinder *n* 341
tine *n* 296
tin-eared *adj* 352
ting *vb* 359
tinge *n* 30, 38, 381, *vb* 38, 381
tingle *n* 338
tingling *n* 729
tinker *vb* 187
tinkle *n* 356, 359, *vb* 356, 359
tinkly *adj* 359
tinned *adj* 603
tinny *adj* 362
tin-opener *n* 232, 568
tinsel *n* 4, 785
tint *n* 381, *vb* 381, 490
tinted *adj* 381
tiny *adj* 30, 78, 169
tip *n* 56, 188, 209, 587, 623, 698, 811,
 859, *vb* 188, 195, 196, 698, 811
tip-off *n* 466
tip off *vb* 466, 602
tipper *n* 698
tipple *n* 267, *vb* 267, 848
tippler *n* 848
tipsiness *n* 848
tipsy *adj* 848
tip the scales *vb* 26, 285
tip the wink *vb* 602
tip-tilted *adj* 221
tirade *n* 506, 532
tire *vb* 619, 619
tired *adj* 610, 619
tiredness *n* 619
tireless *adj* 540, 609
tirelessness *n* 540, 609
tiresome *adj* 737, 762
tiring *adj* 619
tissue *n* 299
tissue paper *n* 569
titbit *n* 267, 342
titchy *adj* 169
tit for tat *n* 11, 129, 641
tithe *n* 84, 721
titian *adj* 387
titillate *vb* 336
titillating *adj* 336, 732
titivate *vb* 204, 765
title *n* 497, 516, 650, 778, 819, *vb* 497
titled *adj* 497, 776
title deed *n* 819

titled person *n* 776

tits *n* 226

titter *n* 744, 773, *vb* 744, 773

tittle-tattle *n* 471, 530, 533, *vb* 533

titular *adj* 497

tizz *n* 281

tizzy *n* 802

TNT *n* 649

toady *n* 782, 827, *vb* 782

to all appearances *adv* 4, 198, 394

to all intents and purposes *adv* 173

to and fro *adv* 119, 280, *n* 119

toast *n* 532, 786, 791, *vb* 309, 339, 386, 786, 791, 823

tobacco *n* 849

to begin with *adv* 61

to blame *adj* 840

toboggan *vb* 761

tobogganning *n* 761

to boot *adv* 35

to clear *adj* 724

to crown/cap it all *adv* 31

tocsin *n* 602

to cut a long story short *adv* 179

to date *adv* 101

today *adv* 101

toddler *n* 111

to-do *n* 56, 482, 609, 732

toe *n* 189

toehold *n* 43

toe the line *vb* 71, 663

toff *n* 770, 776

toffee-nosed *adj* 779

together *adv* 85

togetherness *n* 85, 789, 793

togs *n* 204

to hand *adv* 162

toil *n* 617, *vb* 617

toilette *n* 204

toilet-trained *adj* 268

toilet water *n* 349

token *adj* 4, 484, *n* 484, 687

tolerable *adj* 582

tolerance *n* 180, 658, 660, 733

tolerant *adj* 180, 658, 660, 677, 733, 788, 805

tolerate *vb* 658, 660, 677, 733, 813

toleration *n* 788

to let *adj* 679

toll *n* 699, 721

toll-free *adj* 724

tollgate *n* 630

tom *n* 326, 332

tomb *n* 325

tombola *n* 554, 761

tomboy *n* 111

Tom, Dick, and Harry *n* 47, 69, 777

tome *n* 516

tomfool *adj* 772

tomfoolery *n* 772

tomorrow *n* 104

Tom Thumb *n* 169

tonality *n* 365

tone *n* 353, 381, 502, 526

tone-deaf *adj* 352, 366

tone-deafness *n* 352, 366

tone down *vb* 144, 148, 354, 360, 483

toneless *adj* 366

tonelessness *n* 366

tone of voice *n* 621

tongue *n* 228, 342, 494, 526, 528

tongue-in-cheek *adj* 744, 771

tongue-tied *adj* 354, 527, 531

tongue twister *n* 496

tonic *adj* 145, *n* 145, 594, 620

to no avail *adj* 749

ton of bricks *n* 285

tons *n* 29

tonsillitis *n* 589

too big for one's boots *adj* 783

too few *adj* 574, *n* 574

tool *n* 32, 568, *vb* 766

tooled *adj* 766

too little *adj* 574, *n* 574

tools *n* 567

too many *adj* 575, *n* 575

too much *adj* 575, *n* 575

too much of a good thing *n* 575

to one's face *adv* 162

to one side *adv* 195

to one's name *adj* 692

tooth *n* 229, 296, *vb* 229

tooth and nail *adv* 147, 617

toothbrush *n* 586

toothbrush moustache *n* 765

toothed *adj* 296

toothless *adj* 142

toothpaste *n* 586

tootsie *n* 189

top *n* 31, 188, 233, *adj* 188, *vb* 188, 202, 274

topaz *n* 321, 766

top brass *n* 31

topcoat *n* 175, 187

top-drawer *adj* 776

topdress *vb* 329

top-flight *adj* 31

top-heaviness *n* 26

top-heavy *adj* 26, 285
topiary *n* 329
topic *n* 409
topical *adj* 101, 106, 409, 471
topicality *n* 101, 106
to play with *adv* 37
top-level *adj* 31
topmost *adj* 188
top-notch *adj* 31, 582
top of the heap *n* 31
topographical *adj* 159
topography *n* 159
toponym *n* 497
top people *n* 31
topping *n* 202
topple *vb* 191, 196, 277
toppling *n* 277
top-priority *adj* 615
top rung of the ladder *n* 31
top-secret *adj* 467
topside *n* 212
topsoil *n* 311
topsy-turvy *adj* 196, *adv* 14, 56, 196
top-up *n* 49
top up *vb* 35, 49
Torah *n* 868
torch *n* 377
to right and to left *adv* 206
torment *n* 735, *vb* 337, 735, 737, 806
torn *adj* 41, 595
tornado *n* 279, 307, 316
toroid *adj* 223
torpedo *n* 255, 649, *vb* 150, 277
torpid *adj* 142, 146, 610, 731
torpor *n* 142, 146, 610, 731
torque *n* 23
torrent *n* 29, 147, 314
torrid *adj* 339
torsion *n* 224
torso *n* 48, 492
tortoise *n* 246
tortoiseshell *n* 393
tortuous *adj* 219, 224
tortuousness *n* 219, 224
torture *n* 806, 860, *vb* 806, 860
torture chamber *n* 861
torturer *n* 860
torus *n* 223
to scale *adv* 9
to shreds *adv* 41
to smithereens *adv* 41
to some extent *adv* 24
to spare *adv* 37
toss *n* 255, *vb* 247, 255

toss and turn *vb* 281
toss aside *vb* 637
toss for it *vb* 554
toss-up *n* 428, 554
tot *n* 111
total *adj* 47, 49, *n* 47, 74, *vb* 74
total abstainer *n* 843, 847
totalitarianism *n* 657
totality *n* 47, 49
totally *adv* 47
total recall *n* 448
to tatters *adv* 41
tote *n* 554, *vb* 241
tote bag *n* 241
totem *n* 875
to the bitter end *adv* 124, 540
to the core *adv* 49
to the ends of the earth *adv* 172
to the four corners of the earth *adv* 67
to the four winds *adv* 67
to the good *adv* 35
to the hilt *adv* 49
to the letter *adv* 440
to the life *adv* 21
to the nth degree *adv* 89
to the second *adv* 96
to the top of one's bent *adv* 49
to the tune of *adv* 23
to the utmost *adv* 29
totter *vb* 144, 275
touch *n* 299, 334, 338, 381, 624, *vb* 9, 173, 334, 338, 681, 702, 729
touchable *adj* 338
touch and go *adj* 428
touchdown *n* 238, 261, 275
touch down *vb* 238, 261, 275
touched *adj* 447, 729
touchiness *n* 730, 803
touch one's cap *vb* 791
touchpaper *n* 341
touchstone *n* 416
touch up *vb* 187
touchy *adj* 730, 803
tough *adj* 93, 143, 147, 289, 294, 542, 628, 731, 806, *n* 838
toughen *vb* 289, 294, 731
toughness *n* 93, 143, 289, 294, 542
tough time *n* 656
toupee *n* 765
tour *n* 278, *vb* 236
tourism *n* 236
tourist *n* 236
tournament *n* 643

tourniquet *n* 171, 233, 630
tousle *vb* 56, 291
tousled *adj* 56, 291
tout *n* 470, 681, 707, 709, *vb* 681,
  707, 709
tovarisch *n* 778
tow *n* 256, 299, *vb* 256
towel *n* 309, *vb* 309
towelling *n* 569
tower *n* 184, 882, *vb* 29, 184
tower block *n* 165, 184
towering *adj* 184
tower of strength *n* 143, 193, 631
to wit *adv* 462
town *n* 157
town crier *n* 470
townee *n* 164
townhouse *n* 165
town planner *n* 613
towpath *n* 240
towrope *n* 256
toxic *adj* 324, 589, 597, 604
toxin *n* 150, 597, 604
toxophily *n* 255
toy *adj* 30, 169, *n* 761, *vb* 800
toy soldier *n* 761
trace *n* 30, 37, 38, 483, 486, *vb* 208,
  513
tracer *n* 649
tracery *n* 197, 766
tracing paper *n* 569
track *n* 37, 231, 240, 485, 486, *vb* 85,
  158, 249, 525, 555
track down *vb* 433
tracker *n* 555
tracking device *n* 249
tracking shot *n* 525
tract *n* 156, 516
tractability *n* 290, 537
tractable *adj* 290, 537, 642, 663,
  821
traction *n* 256
tractor *n* 256
trad *n* 367
trade *n* 129, 149, 611, 697, 707, 708,
  vb 129, 611, 697, 707
trade fair *n* 710
trade-in *n* 707
trade in *vb* 707
trademark *n* 70, 485, *vb* 22
trader *n* 613, 707, 709
tradesman *n* 613, 707
trade union *n* 40
trade wind *n* 316

trading *adj* 707, *n* 609, 707
tradition *n* 107, 122, 549, 871
traditional *adj* 107, 549, 870
traditionalism *n* 72
traditionalist *adj* 72, *n* 72, 870
traffic *n* 234, 271, 707, *vb* 707
traffic island *n* 250, 600
traffic jam *n* 630
trafficker *n* 707
trafficking *n* 707
traffic light *n* 377
traffic warden *n* 854
tragedy *n* 523, 836
tragic *adj* 523, 836
trail *n* 37, 60, 240, 486, *vb* 59, 60,
  192, 213, 470, 555
trail-blazer *n* 59, 559
trailer *n* 59, 470, 525
trailing *adj* 192
train *n* 60, 64, 192, 213, 242, *vb* 475,
  476, 559
trained *adj* 624
trainer *n* 475, 559
training *n* 475, 476, 624
train set *n* 761
traipse *vb* 236
trait *n* 70
traitor *n* 480, 794, 838
traitorous *adj* 662, 794
trajectory *n* 221, 240
tram *n* 242
tramlines *n* 194
tramp *n* 236, 243, 681, 777, 851,
  vb 234, 236
trample *vb* 191
trance *n* 335, 610, 876
tranquil *adj* 618, 733, 738
tranquillity *n* 618, 733, 738
tranquillize *vb* 335
tranquillizer *n* 148, 335
transact *vb* 707
transaction *n* 101, 707
transatlantic *adj* 243
transcend *vb* 272
transcendence *n* 283
transcendent *adj* 283, 862
transcendental *adj* 877
transcribe *vb* 129, 462, 513
transcript *n* 513
transcription *n* 129, 462
transept *n* 882
transfer *n* 129, 161, 234, 239, *vb* 121,
  129, 161, 234, 239, 696, 697
transferable *adj* 239, 696, 697

transferal *n* 239
transference *n* 121
transfer of property *n* 697
transfiguration *n* 121, 862
transfigure *vb* 121
transfix *vb* 232
transfixed *adj* 235, 759
transform *vb* 121, 125, 877
transformation *n* 121, 125
transformer *n* 121
transfuse *vb* 269
transfusion *n* 239, 269
transgress *vb* 272, 662, 689, 818, 838, 853
transgression *n* 272, 662, 689, 838, 840, 853
transience *n* 94, 179, 395
transient *adj* 94, 179, 395
transistor *n* 472
transit *n* 234, 271, *vb* 271
transition *n* 121
transitional *adj* 121, 234
transitoriness *n* 395
transitory *adj* 94
translate *vb* 460, 462
translation *n* 460, 462, 866
transliterate *vb* 495
transliteration *n* 129, 495
translucence *n* 286, 379
translucency *n* 183
translucent *adj* 183, 286, 379
transmissible *adj* 239
transmission *n* 239, 466, 472
transmit *vb* 239, 466
transmitter *n* 472
transmogrification *n* 121
transmogrify *vb* 121
transmute *vb* 121
transparency *n* 183, 286, 379, 491, 503
transparent *adj* 183, 286, 379, 460, 503
transpire *vb* 101
transplant *vb* 329
transplantation *n* 239
transport *n* 234, 239, 242, *vb* 166, 234, 239, 241, 860
transportation *n* 239, 860
transporter *n* 241
transpose *vb* 121, 129, 161, 196, 368
transposition *n* 121, 129, 161, 196
transsexual *adj* 38, *n* 38, 73
transship *vb* 239
transshipment *n* 239

transverse *adj* 195
transvestite *n* 73
trap *n* 232, 242, 555, 601, *vb* 451, 601
trapdoor *n* 202, 232
trapezium *n* 194
trapper *n* 555
trappings *n* 35, 694
Trappist *n* 879
trash *n* 32, 518
trashy *adj* 32, 583
trattoria *n* 165
trauma *n* 337
traumatized *adj* 337
travel *vb* 234, 236
travel/ticket agent *n* 709
traveller *n* 236
traveller's cheque *n* 711
travelling *adj* 236
travelogue *n* 517
traverse *vb* 271
travesty *n* 21, 463, 489, 772, *vb* 21, 463, 489
trawl *n* 256, *vb* 256, 555
trawler *n* 243, 555
treacherous *adj* 465, 480, 481, 599, 662, 806, 832
treacherousness *n* 465
treachery *n* 480, 543, 832
treacle *n* 318, 345
treacly *adj* 318, 345
tread *n* 234, *vb* 191
treadmill *n* 64, 119, 762
tread on someone's heels *vb* 173
tread on someone's toes *vb* 824
tread on the heels of *vb* 60
tread the boards *vb* 523
tread warily *vb* 406, 754
tread water *vb* 122, 237
treason *n* 480, 481, 662, 832
treasure *n* 570, 800, *vb* 774, 795, 875
treasure hunt *n* 555
treasurer *n* 699, 711
treasure trove *n* 706, 835
treasury *n* 167, 711
treasury note *n* 683, 711
treat *n* 736, *vb* 121, 125, 149, 519, 596, 631, 685, 718
treatise *n* 519
treatment *n* 125, 490, 596, 631
treaty *n* 633, 636, 646
treble *n* 82, 368, *vb* 33, 82
trebly *adv* 82
tree *n* 327
trek *n* 172, 236, *vb* 236

trellis *n* 174, 197
tremble *vb* 144, 280, 281, 358, 750
trembling *adj* 281, *n* 729
tremendous *adj* 759
tremolo *n* 358
tremor *n* 234, 280, 281, 729, 750
tremulous *adj* 281
tremulousness *n* 281
trench *n* 210, 227, 231, 315, 600
trench/jungle/desert/guerrilla warfare
   n 645
trenchancy *n* 296, 507
trenchant *adj* 296, 505, 507, 826
trencherman *n* 267
trenches *n* 640
trend *n* 64, 140, 249, 770
trendiness *n* 106
trendsetter *n* 59, 770
trendy *adj* 106, 770, *n* 106
trepidation *n* 750
trespass *n* 272, 662, 818, 838, 840,
   853, *vb* 54, 263, 272, 662, 818, 820
trespasser *n* 54
trestle *n* 193
triad *n* 82
trial *n* 416, 559, 656, 836
trial and error *n* 416
trial balance *n* 720
trial run *n* 61, 559
triangle *n* 82, 220, 369
triangular *adj* 82, 220
triangulation *n* 177
tribal *adj* 12, 330
tribalism *n* 12, 330
tribe *n* 66, 68, 330
tribunal *n* 855, 878
tributary *adj* 670, *n* 48, 314
tribute *n* 699, 716, 721, 786, 811, 825,
   859
trick *n* 480, 626, *vb* 626
trick cyclist *n* 396
trickery *n* 480, 481
trickle *n* 30, 87, *vb* 246, 308, 314
trick photography *n* 370
trickster *n* 480, 626
tricky *adj* 480, 628
tricolour *n* 484
tricycle *n* 82, 242, 761
trident *n* 82
tried and tested *adj* 417
trifle *n* 30, 577, *vb* 800
trifling *adj* 30
trigger *n* 134, *vb* 132
trigger-happy *adj* 753

trigger off *vb* 61
trigonometry *n* 75, 177
trike *n* 242
trilateral *adj* 82
trill *n* 358, *vb* 358, 368, 526
trillion *n* 84
trilogy *n* 82
trim *adj* 36, 55, 763, *n* 7, 209, 765, *vb*
   209, 766
trimester *n* 82, 92
trimmed *adj* 766
trimming *n* 766
trimmings *n* 35
trinity *n* 82
Trinity *n* 862
trio *n* 82, 368
trip *n* 236, 761, *vb* 275
tripartite *adj* 82
triple *adj* 82, *vb* 82
triplet *n* 82, 521
triplex *adj* 82
triplicate *adj* 82, *vb* 82
tripod *n* 82, 193
tripper *n* 236
trip the light fantastic *vb* 524
triptych *n* 82
tripwire *n* 640
trishaw *n* 242
trite *adj* 88, 442, 459, 508, 762
triteness *n* 459
triumph *n* 651, 746, *vb* 31, 651, 746
triumphal *adj* 746
triumphant *adj* 31, 651, 746
triumvirate *n* 82
triune *n* 82
trivet *n* 193
trivial *adj* 30, 187, 459
triviality *n* 187, 577
troglodyte *n* 330
troika *n* 82
troll *n* 865
trolley *n* 241
trolleybus *n* 242
trollop *n* 851
trombone *n* 369
trompe l'oeil *n* 4
troop *n* 648, *vb* 86
trophy *n* 650, 859
tropical *adj* 339
trot *n* 616, *vb* 616
troth *n* 683
trot out *vb* 528
trots *n* 268
troubadour *n* 368, 521

490

trouble *n* 56, 406, 617, 628, 656, 735, 737, 836, *vb* 628, 735, 737, 836
trouble and strife *n* 797
troubled *adj* 281, 656, 735
troublemaker *n* 662, 838
troublesome *adj* 628, 737
trouble spot *n* 599
trough *n* 32, 231
trounce *vb* 31, 651
troupe *n* 66, 523
trouper *n* 523
trousseau *n* 570
trowel *n* 227
troy *adj* 177
truancy *n* 163, 605, 662
truant *adj* 605, *n* 556, 605
truce *n* 123, 235, 606, 644, 646
truck *n* 242
truculent *adj* 806
trudge *vb* 236, 246
true *adj* 3, 222, 365, 793, 817, 870
true believer *n* 870
true love *n* 795
true-to-life *adj* 3, 440, 488, 517
true up *vb* 19
truism *n* 442
truly *adv* 1
trump card *n* 31
trumped-up *adj* 481
trumpet *n* 355, 369, *vb* 470
trump up *vb* 830
truncate *vb* 179
truncated *adj* 179
truncheon *n* 247, 649
trundle *vb* 234
trunk *n* 48, 167, 225, 327, 570
trunk road *n* 240
truss *n* 66, 193, *vb* 66
trust *n* 434, 450, 714, 748, *vb* 434, 748
trustee *n* 675, 699
trusteeship *n* 672
trust in *vb* 427
trusting *adj* 434, 748
trustworthiness *n* 427, 774
trustworthy *adj* 427, 434, 478, 774, 793, 831, 868
trusty *adj* 434, 831
trusty soul *n* 831
truth *n* 440, 478, 868
truthful *adj* 478, 831
truthfulness *n* 478, 831
try *n* 561, *vb* 342, 561, 617, 762, 856
trying *adj* 737

try on *vb* 204
try-out *n* 416
try out *vb* 414, 416
tryst *n* 66
tsar *n* 665, 776
tsunami *n* 314
tub *n* 167, 243
tuba *n* 369
tubby *adj* 168
tube *n* 225, 232, 240
tuber *n* 327
tuberculosis *n* 589
tub-thumping *adj* 528
tubular *adj* 223, 225
tubular bells *n* 359
tuck *n* 230, 267, *vb* 230
tuck into *vb* 267
tug *n* 243, 256, 617, *vb* 234, 247, 256
tugboat *n* 256
tug of war *n* 256
tug one's forelock *vb* 663, 782
tuition *n* 475
tulle *n* 183
tumble *n* 34, 275, *vb* 34, 185, 275, 314
tumbledown *adj* 593
tumble-dry *vb* 309
tumble-dryer *n* 309
tumbler *n* 167
tumble to *vb* 433, 460
tumbril *n* 242
tumescence *n* 170, 226
tumescent *adj* 170, 226
tumid *adj* 170, 226
tumour *n* 226, 589
tumult *n* 56, 281
tumultuous *adj* 56, 147
tun *n* 167
tundra *n* 153, 311, 313
tune *n* 365, 367, 367, *vb* 103, 559
tuned *adj* 559
tuneful *adj* 365, 367
tunefulness *n* 365
tuning *n* 559
tunnel *n* 42, 227, 232
tunnel vision *n* 371
turbid *adj* 380
turbidity *n* 380
turbine *n* 141, 255, 279, 568
turbulence *n* 56, 147, 281, 732
turbulent *adj* 56, 147, 281, 732
turd *n* 268
tureen *n* 167
turf *n* 327, 390

turf accountant *n* 554
turf out *vb* 266
turgid *adj* 170, 508, 510, 762
turgidity *n* 170, 508, 510
Turkish bath *n* 586
turmeric *n* 389
turmoil *n* 56, 147, 281, 658
turn *n* 127, 221, 279, 523, *vb* 133, 216, 221, 278, 279, 346
turn a blind eye to *vb* 407, 658
turn a deaf ear *vb* 352, 680
turn a deaf ear to *vb* 810
turn and turn about *adv* 11
turncoat *n* 125
turn down *vb* 546, 680
turned on *adj* 732
turned-up *adj* 221
turning point *n* 8, 115
turnip *n* 97
turn loose *vb* 669
turn of events *n* 101
turn of phrase *n* 499
turn-on *n* 336
turn on *vb* 200, 336, 732, 795, 803, 849
turn one's back on *vb* 262, 680
turn one's head *vb* 783
turn one's nose up at *vb* 758
turn one's stomach *vb* 343
turn on one's heel *vb* 254
turn out *vb* 60, 149, 266
turnover *n* 690, 711
turn over *vb* 690
turn over a new leaf *vb* 121, 550, 592, 841
turntable *n* 279
turn tail *vb* 213, 254, 752
turn the other cheek *vb* 780
turn the tables *vb* 196
turn the tables on *vb* 14
turn to good account *vb* 115
turn turtle *vb* 196
turn-up *n* 230
turn up *vb* 101, 162, 261, 394
turquoise *adj* 390, 391, *n* 391, 766
tusk *n* 296
tussle *vb* 643
tutee *n* 476
tutelage *n* 111, 476
tutor *n* 475, 623, 668, *vb* 475
tutorial *n* 475
TV dinner *n* 267
twaddle *n* 443, 459
twang *n* 359, 526, 529, *vb* 359

twangy *adj* 529
twat *n* 152
tweak *vb* 256
twee *adj* 510
tweed *n* 291, 569
Tweedledum and Tweedledee *n* 13
tweedy *adj* 291, 299
tweeness *n* 510
tweeny *n* 613, 666
tweet *vb* 364
tweezers *n* 270, 568
twelfth *adj* 84
twelve *n* 84
twelvemonth *n* 92
twenty and over *n* 84
twenty-four hours a day *adv* 97
twerp *n* 445
twice *adv* 81
twiddle one's thumbs *vb* 608
twiddling one's thumbs *adj* 762
twig *n* 327, *vb* 433, 460
twilight *adj* 110, *n* 110, 374, 376
twilight of the gods *n* 62
twilit *adj* 376
twill *n* 569
twin *adj* 81, *n* 12, 13, 17, 25, *vb* 13, 81
twinge *n* 337
twinkle *n* 374, *vb* 130, 281, 374
twinkly *adj* 374
twins *n* 81
twirl *n* 279, *vb* 279
twist *n* 224, 524, 761, *vb* 197, 217, 219, 224, 463, 524
twisted *adj* 219, 224, 447
twistedness *n* 219
twister *n* 838
twist round one's little finger *vb* 551
twit *n* 445, *vb* 773
twitch *n* 281, *vb* 281
twitchiness *n* 281
twitchy *adj* 281
twitter *vb* 364
two *n* 81
two a penny *adj* 117
two-faced *adj* 81, 479, 481, 543, 832
twofold *adj* 81, *adv* 81
two-hander *n* 81
two of a kind *n* 17
two-seater *n* 81
twosome *n* 81
two-time *vb* 832
two-way *adj* 81, 126, 129
two-wheeler *n* 81

tycoon *n* 141, 576
tyke *n* 326
type *n* 68, 514, *vb* 513
typecast *adj* 15, *vb* 15
typeface *n* 514
typescript *n* 513
typeset *adj* 514, *vb* 514
typesetter *n* 514
typesetting *n* 514
typewriting *n* 513
typhoid *n* 589
typhoon *n* 307, 316
typical *adj* 68, 69, 70, 72, 485, 488
typically *adv* 69
typification *n* 488
typify *vb* 22, 68, 488
typo *n* 514
typographic *adj* 514
typography *n* 514
tyrannical *adj* 622, 659
tyrannize *vb* 657, 659, 806
tyranny *n* 622, 657, 659
tyrant *n* 665
Tyrian purple *n* 392
tyro *n* 61, 106, 47

U

U *adj* 776
ubiquitous *adj* 69, 162
ubiquitousness *n* 162
udder *n* 226
ugliness *n* 512, 737, 764
ugly *adj* 512, 737, 764
ugly customer *n* 838
ugly duckling *n* 764
ukelele *n* 369
ulcer *n* 589
ultimate *adj* 62
ultimately *adv* 114
ultimatum *n* 62, 211, 681
ultramarine *n* 391
umbrage *n* 802
umbrella *n* 202, 378
umpirage *n* 429
umpire *n* 429, 647, *vb* 429, 647
umpteen *adj* 86
unabashed *adj* 842
unable *adj* 142
unable to pay *adj* 717
unabridged *adj* 47, 178
unaccented *adj* 522
unacceptable *adj* 501, 574
unaccompanied *adj* 367

unaccountability *n* 135
unaccountable *adj* 135, 822
unaccustomed *adj* 550
unaccustomedness *n* 550
unacknowledged *adj* 812
unadaptable *adj* 579
unadorned *adj* 483, 503, 509
unadornedness *n* 503
unadulterated *adj* 39, 47, 584
unaffected *adj* 509, 627, 667, 822
unaffectedness *n* 509, 627
unafraid *adj* 751
unaided *adj* 144
unalloyed *adj* 39
unambiguous *adj* 427, 458, 460, 503
unambiguousness *n* 460, 503
unambitious *adj* 756
unanimity *n* 19, 436, 633, 636
unanimous *adj* 19, 436, 633, 636
unannounced *adj* 451
unanswerable *adj* 412
unappealing *adj* 737
unappetizing *adj* 343
unappreciative *adj* 812
unapproachability *n* 790
unapproachable *adj* 172, 790
unarmed *adj* 144
unashamed *adj* 842
unasked *adj* 535, 756
unassailable *adj* 131
unassertive *adj* 784
unassuming *adj* 483, 509, 780, 784
unassuming nature *n* 784
unattached *adj* 41, 667, 799
unattainable *adj* 424
unattractive *adj* 737, 756
unauthorized *adj* 820, 853, 871
unavailability *n* 579
unavailable *adj* 163, 424, 565, 579
unavoidability *n* 536
unavoidable *adj* 427, 536, 556, 664
unaware *adj* 405, 439, 449, 731
unawareness *n* 405, 439, 449, 731
unbalance *vb* 26, 58, 447
unbalanced *adj* 10, 20, 26, 58, 447, 818
unbeatable *adj* 584
unbeaten *adj* 651
unbecoming *adj* 20, 764
unbelief *n* 435, 869
unbelievable *adj* 426, 435, 759
unbeliever *n* 869, 873
unbelieving *adj* 435, 869
unbend *vb* 222, 809, 813

unearned income *n* 690
unearth *vb* 325, 433, 464
unearthliness *n* 283
unearthly *adj* 283
unease *n* 130
uneasiness *n* 739, 750
uneasy *adj* 130, 739, 750
uneconomical *adj* 844
unedited *adj* 47
uneducated *adj* 439
unemotional *adj* 731
unemphatic *adj* 508
unemployable *adj* 579
unemployed *adj* 565, 608
unemployment *n* 565, 608
unenlightened *adj* 439
unenterprising *adj* 610
unenthusiastic *adj* 403, 538, 541, 616
unentitled *adj* 820
unenvious *adj* 738
unequal *adj* 20, 26, 219
unequivocal *adj* 427, 458, 473
unethical *adj* 832
uneven *adj* 16, 26, 48, 50, 65, 120,
    219, 291, 585, 818
unevenness *n* 16, 26, 50, 65, 120, 291,
    585
uneventful *adj* 762
unexceptional *adj* 72
unexciting *adj* 762
unexpected *adj* 135, 451
unexpectedly *adv* 135, 451
unexpectedness *n* 451
unextreme *adj* 250
unfailing *adj* 540
unfair *adj* 26, 430, 818, 820
unfairness *n* 430, 818
unfaithful *adj* 689, 794, 832, 851, 869
unfaithfulness *n* 689, 815, 851
unfamiliar *adj* 439, 550
unfamiliarity *n* 439, 550
unfashionableness *n* 98
unfasten *vb* 232
unfathomable *adj* 89, 461
unfavourable *adj* 538, 630, 656, 749,
    826
unfavourable verdict *n* 856, 858
unfeeling *adj* 335, 731, 810
unfetter *vb* 629
unfettered *adj* 667
unfinished *adj* 48, 50, 217, 291, 654
unfit *adj* 142, 589
unfit for human habitation *adj* 591
unfitness *n* 142

unfitting *adj* 20
unfittingness *n* 820
unflagging *adj* 143, 294, 540, 609
unflappable *adj* 733
unflinching *adj* 751
unfold *vb* 133, 203, 221, 222, 464
unforeseeable *adj* 428
unforeseen *adj* 451
unforgettable *adj* 448
unforgivable *adj* 818, 838
unforgiving *adj* 810
unformed *adj* 217
unforthcoming *adj* 467, 531, 556, 790
unfortunate *adj* 652, 656, 836
unfounded *adj* 441, 481
unfriendliness *n* 790, 792
unfriendly *adj* 632, 656, 790, 792,
    794, 806
unfrock *vb* 673, 860
unfrocking *n* 673
unfunny *adj* 745, 762
unfurl *vb* 221, 464
ungainliness *n* 512
ungainly *adj* 512, 764
ungentlemanly *adj* 792
ungodliness *n* 869
ungodly *adj* 869, 873
ungracious *adj* 792, 806
ungrammatical *adj* 501
ungrammaticality *n* 501
ungrateful *adj* 812
ungratefulness *n* 812
ungrateful wretch *n* 812
unguent *n* 319
unhand *vb* 696
unhappiness *n* 735, 739, 743
unhappy *adj* 581, 735, 743
unharmed *adj* 598
unharness *vb* 629
unhealthy *adj* 589
unheard-of *adj* 22, 775
unhelpful *adj* 538, 579, 630
unhindered *adj* 667
unhinge *vb* 58, 447
unhinged *adj* 58, 447
unholiness *n* 869
unholy *adj* 869, 873, 880
unholy alliance *n* 45
unhurried *adj* 246, 616
unhurriedness *n* 246
unhygienic *adj* 591, 604
unidentified *adj* 498
unification *n* 45
unified *adj* 79

unsavoury *adj* 343
unscathed *adj* 598
unscented *adj* 348
unscrupulous *adj* 832, 838
unseasonable *adj* 98
unseasoned *adj* 560
unseat *vb* 58, 161, 673
unseeing *adj* 371
unseemly *adj* 818, 820
unseen *adj* 373, 465
unselective *adj* 419
unselfish *adj* 725, 805, 833
unselfishness *n* 833
unserviceable *adj* 579
unsettled *adj* 94, 715, 819
unshackled *adj* 667
unshakable *adj* 43, 131, 427, 539, 542
unshapeliness *n* 512
unshapely *adj* 512
unshaven *adj* 291
unsheathe *vb* 464
unsightliness *n* 512, 764
unsightly *adj* 512, 764
unskilful *adj* 439, 625
unskilfulness *n* 439, 625
unsociability *n* 790, 804, 808
unsociable *adj* 790, 804, 808
unsoiled *adj* 839
unsophisticated *adj* 509, 627, 769, 839
unsophistication *n* 509, 627
unsound *adj* 411, 585, 871
unsoundness *n* 441, 585
unsparing *adj* 833, 859
unspiritual *adj* 869
unspoken *adj* 354, 465
unsportsmanlike *adj* 818
unstable *adj* 16, 94, 121, 130, 144,
   217, 541
unsteadiness *n* 120, 144, 281
unsteady *adj* 120
unstick *vb* 44
unstinting *adj* 49, 725
unstudied *adj* 627
unstuffy *adj* 788
unsubtle *adj* 419
unsuccessful *adj* 652
unsuccessful candidate/competitor *n*
   652
unsuitability *n* 20, 546, 579, 581
unsuitable *adj* 20, 546, 579, 581, 818
unsung *adj* 432, 465
unsure *adj* 428, 435
unsureness *n* 435
unsurprised *adj* 760

unsuspecting *adj* 454
unsweetened *adj* 346, 346
unswerving *adj* 222
unsympathetic *adj* 810
untainted *adj* 839, 850
untaintedness *n* 850
unthanked *adj* 812
unthinkable *adj* 424
unthinking *adj* 399, 548, 753
untidiness *n* 56, 407
untidy *adj* 56, 407, *vb* 56
untie *vb* 205
until now *adv* 101
untimeliness *n* 20, 98, 116
untimely *adj* 20, 98, 116, 581
untold *adj* 86, 89
untouchable *n* 777, 790
untoward *adj* 116
untraced *adj* 691
untrained *adj* 560
untreated *adj* 39
untried *adj* 106
untrue *adj* 441, 479, 481
untrustworthiness *n* 428, 543, 775
untrustworthy *adj* 428, 435, 543, 775
untruth *n* 479
untuneful *adj* 366
unusable *adj* 565, 579
unused *adj* 550, 565
unusual *adj* 18, 73, 118, 550
unutilized *adj* 565
unvarnished *adj* 509
unvarying *adj* 13, 15
unveil *vb* 203, 464, 468
unveiling *n* 203
unwanted *adj* 54, 546, 756
unwarranted *adj* 272, 820
unwavering *adj* 43, 122, 131, 540
unwed *adj* 799
unwelcome *adj* 756
unwelcome guest *n* 789
unwelcoming *adj* 790
unwholesome *adj* 343, 589, 604
unwholesomeness *n* 343, 604
unwieldiness *n* 512
unwieldy *adj* 285, 581, 628
unwilling *adj* 246, 437, 538, 556, 638
unwillingly *adv* 538
unwillingness *n* 246, 437, 538, 638
unwise *adj* 445
unwitting *adj* 439
unwonted *adj* 550
unwontedness *n* 550
unworkable *adj* 424

utensil *n* 568
uterus *n* 152
utilitarian *adj* 580
utilitarianism *n* 580, 807
utility *n* 138, 578
utilization *n* 564
utilize *vb* 564
utilized *adj* 564
utopia *n* 748
utopian *n* 807
utter *adj* 49, *vb* 353, 526, 528
utterance *n* 353, 526, 528
utterly *adv* 49
U-turn *n* 121, 126, 196, 221, 254, 54

V

vacancy *n* 163, 611
vacant *adj* 2, 163
vacation *n* 163, 612, 618
vaccinate *vb* 269, 590
vaccination *n* 269, 590, 596
vaccine *n* 596
vacillate *vb* 44, 121, 130, 280, 428, 541
vacillating *adj* 44, 130, 280, 541
vacillation *n* 44, 121, 130, 280, 428, 541
vacuity *n* 397
vacuous *adj* 163, 397, 399
vacuum *n* 2, 163, *vb* 270, 586
vacuum cleaner *n* 586
vagabond *adj* 236, *n* 236, 777, 838
vagary *n* 457
vagina *n* 152
vagrant *adj* 236, *n* 236, 777
vague *adj* 4, 217, 373, 376, 405, 428, 504
vagueness *n* 217, 373, 376, 405, 428, 504
vain *adj* 579, 652, 749, 783, 834
vainglorious *adj* 779
vainglory *n* 779
vain hope *n* 4
valediction *n* 262
valedictory *adj* 262
valentine *n* 795, 800
Valentine *n* 515
valet *n* 613, 666
valetudinarianism *n* 144
Valhalla *n* 323
valiant *adj* 751
valid *adj* 3, 817
validate *vb* 3, 131, 412, 417, 440

validation *n* 131, 412, 417
validity *n* 3
valley *n* 185, 227, 313
valour *n* 751
valuable *adj* 578, 582, 835
valuables *n* 694
valuate *vb* 177
valuation *n* 177
value *n* 576, 578, 582, *vb* 576, 721, 768, 774, 795, 823
value-added tax *n* 721
valued *adj* 823
value for money *n* 724
valve *n* 233
vamoose *vb* 262
vamp *vb* 548
vampire *n* 865
van *n* 242
vandal *n* 150, 838
vandalism *n* 150
vandalize *vb* 150
vanguard *n* 59, 212
vanish *vb* 2, 94, 373, 395
vanished *adj* 395
vanishing *adj* 395
vanity *n* 783, 834
vantage point *n* 31, 184
vapidness *n* 508
vaporization *n* 304
vaporize *vb* 304
vaporizer *n* 304
vaporous *adj* 304
vapour *n* 305, 308, 347
variability *n* 16, 120, 130
variable *adj* 16, 120, 130, *n* 74, 120
variation *n* 121
varied *adj* 16
variegate *vb* 16, 393
variegated *adj* 16, 38, 381, 393
variegation *n* 16, 393
variety *n* 16, 68, 80, 393, 523
various *adj* 16, 80
variously *adv* 18
varnish *n* 202, 292, *vb* 202, 603, 766, 829
varsity *n* 477
vary *vb* 16, 120, 121, 130
vase *n* 167
vasectomy *n* 153
vast *adj* 29, 86, 89, 168
vastly *adv* 29, 89
vastness *n* 89, 168
vat *n* 167
Vatican *n* 882

vaudeville *n* 523
vault *n* 186, 221, 274, 325, 570, 711, *vb* 221, 274
vaunt *vb* 771
VC *n* 751
VDU *n* 570
Vedas *n* 868
veer *n* 252, *vb* 121, 252
vegan *n* 843
veganism *n* 843
vegetable *n* 327
vegetal *adj* 327
vegetarian *adj* 267, *n* 843
vegetarianism *n* 843
vegetate *vb* 1, 90, 146
vegetation *n* 327
vehemence *n* 147, 473, 507, 732
vehement *adj* 147, 507
vehicle *n* 242, 523
vehicular *adj* 242
veil *n* 202, 373, 378, 469, *vb* 373, 378, 469
veiled *adj* 202, 465
vein *n* 175, 181, 321, 502, 570, *vb* 393
veined *adj* 393
veld *n* 313
vellum *n* 513
velocity *n* 245
velour *n* 569
velvet *n* 290, 292, 569
velvety *adj* 290, 292
venal *adj* 728
venality *n* 728
vend *vb* 709
vendetta *n* 635, 641, 794
vendor *n* 709
veneer *n* 175, 187, 202, 212, 394, *vb* 175, 187, 202
venerable *adj* 107, 549, 823
venerate *vb* 874
veneration *n* 823, 874
venerator *n* 874
venereal *adj* 40
venereal disease *n* 589
vengeance *n* 641
vengeful *adj* 641, 810
venial *adj* 813
venomous *adj* 806, 826, 828
vent *n* 232, 264
ventilate *vb* 306, 316, 348, 468
ventilation *n* 306, 348
venture *n* 611, *vb* 554, 751
venturesome *adj* 561, 562
venue *n* 159

Venus *n* 763, 862
veracious *adj* 478
veracity *n* 478
verb *n* 500
verbal *adj* 496, 500, 528
verbal diarrhoea *n* 530
verbalize *vb* 496, 526, 528
verbatim *adj* 496, *adv* 21, 440
verbiage *n* 459
verbose *adj* 459, 496, 504, 506, 530, 762
verbosity *n* 504, 506, 530
verdant *adj* 327, 390
verdict *n* 429, 856
verdict of not guilty *n* 857
verdigris *n* 390
verdure *n* 327, 390
verge *n* 173, 209, 209, *vb* 140, 173, 209
verger *n* 880
verifiable *adj* 412, 417
verification *n* 416, 417, 420
verified *adj* 417
verify *vb* 417, 420
verisimilitude *n* 3, 440
vermilion *n* 387
vermin *n* 326, 597
vernacular *adj* 69, 164, *n* 494
vernal *adj* 108
vernal equinox *n* 108
versatile *adj* 16, 69, 80, 125, 130, 578
versatility *n* 16, 125, 130
verse *n* 521
versed *adj* 438
verse form *n* 521
verses *n* 521
versification *n* 521
versifier *n* 521
versify *vb* 521
version *n* 121, 462
verso *n* 14, 213, 516
vertebral *adj* 213
vertebrate *n* 326
vertex *n* 188
vertical *adj* 184, 190, 222, 276, *n* 190, 222
verticality *n* 184, 190, 222
vertically *adv* 190
vertiginous *adj* 184, 190
verve *n* 145, 322, 507
very much *adv* 29
Very Reverend *n* 778
vespers *n* 110, 881
vessel *n* 167, 243

warehouse *n* 167, 570, 710, *vb* 570
warehousing *n* 570
wares *n* 707
warfare *n* 643, 645
wariness *n* 435, 754
warm *adj* 339, 387, 729, *vb* 339
warm-hearted *adj* 793, 805
warm-heartedness *n* 809
warming *adj* 742
warmonger *n* 645
warmongering *adj* 645, *n* 645
warmth *n* 339, 729, 793
warm to *vb* 729
warm up *vb* 559
warn *vb* 466, 602, 623
warning *adj* 602, *n* 455, 466, 599, 602, 623
warning light *n* 377, 602
warning shot *n* 602
warning sign *n* 484
war of attrition *n* 645
war of independence *n* 645
war of nerves *n* 645
war of words *n* 410, 643
warp *n* 299, *vb* 195, 217, 219, 430
warped *adj* 447
warrant *n* 819, *vb* 687, 819, 829
warranted *adj* 819
warranty *n* 420, 598, 683, 687
war rations *n* 845
warren *n* 56, 165, 224
warring *adj* 635, 643, 645
warrior *n* 648
warship *n* 243
wart *n* 767
war widow *n* 798
wary *adj* 406, 435, 750, 754
wash *n* 305, 312, 314, 381, 486, *vb* 39, 305, 314, 381, 490, 586
wash and brush-up *n* 765
washed out *adj* 144, 382
washed up *adj* 62, 150, 717
washerwoman *n* 586
washing *n* 586
washing machine *n* 586
washing powder *n* 586
wash one's hands of *vb* 62, 680, 822
washout *n* 452, 652
waspish *adj* 803
wastage *n* 691
waste *n* 149, 566, 572, 579, 696, 844, *vb* 90, 566, 572, 727
wasted *adj* 572, 691
wasted effort *n* 652

wasteful *adj* 572, 727, 844
wastefulness *n* 572, 727, 844
waste ground *n* 232
wasteland *n* 153, 309
waste nothing *vb* 726
waste of time *n* 579
waste one's breath *vb* 534
waste product *n* 572
wastrel *n* 727, 838
watch *n* 92, 370, 640, *vb* 162, 370, 404
watcher *n* 370
watchful *adj* 370, 404, 754, 815
watchfulness *n* 404, 754, 815
watchmaker *n* 613
watchman *n* 598, 668
watch oneself *vb* 843
watch one's step *vb* 754
watch out *vb* 406
watch over *vb* 598
watchtower *n* 184
watchword *n* 442, 485, 496
water *n* 268, 303, 305, 379, *vb* 305
waterborne *adj* 237
waterclock *n* 97
watercolour *adj* 483, *n* 381, 490
watercourse *n* 314
water down *vb* 144, 183, 305, 483
watered down *adj* 305
watered silk *n* 393
waterfall *n* 275, 314
watergate *n* 315
water glass *n* 603
waterhole *n* 312
wateriness *n* 44, 144, 303, 305
water line *n* 177
waterlog *vb* 305
waterlogged *adj* 305, 308
water pistol *n* 761
waterproof *adj* 309
water rate *n* 721
waters *n* 310
watershed *n* 176, 200, 207
waterskiing *n* 761
water sport *n* 237
waterspout *n* 314, 315
watertight *adj* 233, 309
water torture *n* 861
water tower *n* 570
water travel *n* 237
waterway *n* 314, 315
watery *adj* 44, 144, 183, 303, 305, 317, 343
wattle *n* 192

weightiness *n* 285
weighting *n* 28
weightless *adj* 286, 306
weightlessness *n* 286, 306
weightlifter *n* 143
weightlifting *n* 143
weight watcher *n* 168
weighty *adj* 285, 507, 576
weigh up *vb* 177, 429, 616
weir *n* 314, 315, 630
weird *adj* 73, 447, 750, 759, 865, 876
weirdness *n* 447
weirdo *n* 73, 447
welcome *adj* 115, 734, 736, 755, *n* 261, 791, *vb* 261, 265, 436, 755, 786, 791, 793, 823, 825
welcoming *adj* 261, 265, 699, 786, 789
weld *n* 40, *vb* 43
welder *n* 613
welfare *n* 655, 835
welfare state *n* 807
well *adj* 588, *n* 186, 227, 305, 312
well-adjusted *adj* 19
well-argued *adj* 410
well-armed *adj* 143
well-behaved *adj* 55, 663, 791
wellbeing *n* 336, 588, 655, 734, 835
well-born *adj* 776
well-bred *adj* 768, 791
well crafted *adj* 502
well-deserved *adj* 819
well-disposed *adj* 633
well-dressed *adj* 204, 770
well-equipped *adj* 571
well-formed *adj* 500, 763
well-groomed *adj* 511
well-heeled *adj* 712
well-intentioned *adj* 805, 837
well-kept *adj* 763
well-known *adj* 576
well-lit *adj* 377
well-meaning *adj* 793, 805
well-meant *adj* 805
well-off *adj* 655, 712
well-preserved *adj* 603
well-proportioned *adj* 511
well-put *adj* 511
well-read *adj* 438
well-stacked *adj* 226
well thought of *adj* 774, 823, 825
well-timed *adj* 115
well-to-do *adj* 655, 712
well turned *adj* 502
well turned-out *adj* 204

well up *vb* 303, 314
well up on *adj* 438
well-wisher *n* 805
welsh *vb* 717
welt *n* 209
welter *n* 56
weltschmerz *n* 743
wench *n* 333
werewolf *n* 865
West End *n* 523
western *n* 525
wet *adj* 144, 305, 308, 784, *n* 144, 305, 308, *vb* 305
wet behind the ears *adj* 111
wet blanket *n* 148, 552, 745
wether *n* 326
wetlands *n* 308
wet-look *adj* 374
wetness *n* 305, 308
wet nurse *n* 666
wet one's whistle *vb* 848
whack *n* 48, 700, *vb* 247, 860
whacked *adj* 619
whacking *adj* 29
whale *n* 168
whaler *n* 243, 555
what is acceptable *n* 573
what is right *n* 817
what one expected *n* 760
what's-its-name *n* 498
wheedle *vb* 551, 827
wheedling *n* 827
wheel *n* 223, 278, 568, 861, *vb* 223, 234, 254, 278
wheel and deal *vb* 707
wheeled *adj* 242
wheeler-dealer *n* 707
wheeler-dealing *n* 685
wheels *n* 242
wheeze *n* 316, 408, 480, *vb* 316, 361
wheeziness *n* 527
wheezy *adj* 316, 361, 527
whelp *vb* 152
when it comes to the crunch *adv* 3
when the chips are down *adv* 3, 62
when you get down to it *adv* 189
whereabouts *n* 158, 162
wherewithal *n* 567, 711
wherry *n* 243
whet *vb* 296
whetstone *n* 296
whey *n* 303
whicker *vb* 364
whiff *n* 316, 347

wreck *n* 37, 150, *vb* 150, 604
wreckage *n* 150
wrecker *n* 150
wrench *n* 270, 568, *vb* 247, 337
wrest *vb* 703
wrestling *n* 643
wretch *n* 838
wretched *adj* 577, 583, 597, 656, 735
wretchedness *n* 735
wriggle *vb* 224
wring *vb* 309
wringer *n* 309
wringing *adj* 305
wringing out *n* 270
wring out *vb* 270
wrinkle *n* 230, 231, 408, 626, *vb* 171, 230, 231
wrinkled *adj* 231
wristwatch *n* 97
writ *n* 661, 856
write *vb* 513, 515, 518
write off *vb* 62, 150, 749
writer *n* 518, 613
write-up *n* 519
write up *vb* 519
writhe *vb* 224, 281, 337
writing *n* 513, 522
writing on the wall *n* 602
written *adj* 513
written matter *n* 513
wrong *adj* 441, 604, 818, 838, 840, 853, *adv* 836, *n* 566, 604, 802, 818, 836, 838, 853, *vb* 566, 604, 818
wrong belief *n* 871
wrongdoer *n* 838
wrongdoing *n* 838
wrongful *adj* 818
wrongfulness *n* 818
wrong-headed *adj* 430, 441
wrongheadedness *n* 430
wrong moment *n* 98, 116
wrong name *n* 498
wrongness *n* 441, 818
wrong side *n* 14
wrong time *n* 98
wrong turning *n* 252
wrong verdict *n* 853
wynd *n* 24

X

X-ray *n* 374, 491, *vb* 491
xylophone *n* 36

Y

yacht *n* 243
yachting *n* 237, 761
yahoo *n* 792
Yahweh *n* 862
yak *vb* 530
yank *vb* 256
Yank *n* 331
yap *vb* 364, 530
yard *n* 210, 614
yardstick *n* 177, 416
yarn *n* 197, 299, 479, 482
yawl *n* 243
yawn *vb* 174, 232
yawning *adj* 186, 227, 232
year *n* 92
yearbook *n* 76
yearly *adj* 92
yearn *vb* 735, 755, 795
yearning *n* 735, 755
yeast *n* 121, 276, 286, 306
yeasty *adj* 306
yell *n* 355, 357, 363, 526, *vb* 355, 363, 746
yellow *adj* 389, 752, *n* 389
yellow-bellied *adj* 752
yellow card *n* 602
yellow metal *n* 389
yellowness *n* 389
yellow press *n* 471
yellow streak *n* 752
yellowy *adj* 389
yelp *n* 363, *vb* 357, 363, 364
yen *n* 755
yeoman *n* 328, 777
yes-man *n* 72, 782, 827
yesterday's man *n* 105
yesteryear *n* 105
yeti *n* 865
Yid *n* 331
yield *n* 149, 328, 690, 690, *vb* 32, 290, 551, 642, 690, 696
yielding *adj* 290, *n* 642
yin and yang *n* 14
yob *n* 111, 147, 769, 792
yobbish *adj* 769
yobbo *n* 838
yodel *vb* 363
yogi *n* 877
yoke *n* 32, 40, 42, 670, *vb* 40
yokel *n* 164, 627, 777
Yom Kippur *n* 845

Z

MORE ABOUT PENGUINS, PELICANS
AND PUFFINS

For further information about books available from Penguins please write to Dept EP, Penguin Books Ltd, Harmondsworth, Middlesex UB7 0DA.

In the U.S.A.: For a complete list of books available from Penguins in the United States write to Dept DG, Penguin Books, 299 Murray Hill Parkway, East Rutherford, New Jersey 07073.

In Canada: For a complete list of books available from Penguins in Canada write to Penguin Books Canada Ltd, 2801 John Street, Markham, Ontario L3R 1B4.

In Australia: For a complete list of books available from Penguins in Australia write to the Marketing Department, Penguin Books Australia Ltd, P.O. Box 257, Ringwood, Victoria 3134.

In New Zealand: For a complete list of books available from Penguins in New Zealand write to the Marketing Department, Penguin Books (N.Z.) Ltd, Private Bag, Takapuna, Auckland 9.

In India: For a complete list of books available from Penguins in India write to Penguin Overseas Ltd, 706 Eros Apartments, 56 Nehru Place, New Delhi 110019.

A CHOICE OF PENGUINS

☐ **Monsignor Quixote** Graham Greene £1.95

'Greene's best, most absorbing, adept and effortless novel', as the *Spectator* described it, circulates around the shrines and fleshpots of Spain, with an endearing, modern-day Don Quixote and his unlikely travelling companion, a deposed communist mayor. 'A deliciously funny novel' – *The Times*

☐ **The Philosopher's Pupil** Iris Murdoch £2.95

'We are back, of course, with great delight, in the land of Iris Murdoch, which is like no other but Prospero's . . .' – *Sunday Telegraph*. And, as expected, her new masterpiece is 'marvellous . . . compulsive reading, hugely funny' – *Spectator*

☐ **The Orlando Trilogy** Isabel Colegate £3.95

Orlando King's rise to success, amid the gaiety and splintering ideals of the thirties and forties, is charted in this compelling family saga by the award-winning author of *The Shooting Party*. 'Tender, intelligent . . . highly recommended' – *Guardian*

☐ **White Mischief** James Fox £1.95

Who did kill the 22nd Earl of Erroll in Nairobi? The bestselling reconstruction of 'one of the most fascinating and intriguing cases of this century . . . Eccentric settlers and shady aristos, neurotic wives and lounge-lizards. The cast and setting are unique' – William Boyd. 'Marvellously entertaining' – Auberon Waugh

☐ **The Penguin Collected Stories of Isaac Bashevis Singer** £4.95

Forty-seven unforgettable tales of Jewish faith, magic and exile. 'Never was the Nobel Prize more deserved . . . He belongs with the giants' – *Sunday Times*

☐ **Holy Pictures** Clare Boylan £1.95

The beautifully drawn comedy of a young girl's awakening to adolescence in the Dublin of 1925. 'Sharp as a serpent's tooth . . . it is a very long time since a first novel of such fun and wit and style has come so confidently out of Ireland' – William Trevor

A CHOICE OF PENGUINS

☐ *Castaway* **Lucy Irvine**   £2.50

'Writer seeks "wife" for a year on tropical island.' This is the extra-ordinary, candid, sometimes shocking account of what happened when Lucy Irvine answered the advertisement and discovered for herself the realities of such a 'marriage' – and all our desert island dreams. 'Fascinating' – *Daily Mail*

☐ *Nineteen Eighty-Four* **George Orwell**   £2.25

The story of Winston Smith's rebellion against the Party, of Big Brother, Newspeak, Doublethink and the Thought Police is Orwell's world-famous masterpiece, and a political satire so brilliant that it has become an irreplaceable part of our modern vocabulary and imagination.

☐ *The Penguin Essays of George Orwell*   £4.95

All the famous pieces – on 'The Decline of the English Murder', 'Shooting an Elephant', politics, English life and P. G. Wodehouse – feature in this edition of forty-one essays, criticism and sketches.

☐ *The Penguin Classic Crime Omnibus*   £4.95

Julian Symons's original anthology includes twenty-five masters – Doyle, Poe, Highsmith, Graham Greene and P. D. James among them – represented by some of their less familiar but most surprising and ingenious crime stories.

☐ *An Ice-Cream War* **William Boyd**   £1.95

At the end of the First World War, a ridiculous and little-reported campaign is still being waged in East Africa. Boyd's bestselling novel, a brilliant depiction of the men and women swept into love and battle, has been acclaimed by John Carey as 'a towering achievement'.

☐ *People Who Knock on the Door*
   Patricia Highsmith   £2.95

Fanaticism, family tensions and life in American suburbia are un-erringly dissected by the author of the *Ripley* books. 'Relentless, compulsive, mutedly ominous' – *Observer*

KING PENGUIN

☐ **The Stories of William Trevor** £5.95

'Trevor packs into each separate five or six thousand words more richness, more laughter, more ache, more multifarious human-ness than many good writers manage to get into a whole novel' – *Punch*. 'Classics of the genre' – Auberon Waugh

☐ **A Confederacy of Dunces** John Kennedy Toole £3.25

In this Pulitzer Prize-winning novel, in the bulky figure of Ignatius J. Reilly an immortal comic character has been born. 'I succumbed, stunned and seduced . . . it is a masterwork of comedy' – *The New York Times*

☐ **War Music** Christopher Logue £2.50

An account of Books 16 to 19 of Homer's *Iliad*. 'Stunning . . . an explosive re-living of the splendours . . . with its sweating, bloody battles' – *Spectator*. 'A small triumph of skill and beauty . . . the perfect introduction to Homer' – Lawrence Durrell

☐ **The Samurai** Shasaku Endo £2.95

In 1613 the unlikely contingent of a Catholic priest and a small group of Japanese Samurai set sail for Mexico, Spain and Rome. A double-sided mirroring of East and West, by the author of *Silence* – 'one of the finest living novelists' – Graham Greene

☐ **The Book of Laughter and Forgetting**
Milan Kundera £2.95

'No question about it. The most important novel published in Britain this year . . . A whirling dance of a book . . . a masterpiece full of angels, terror, ostriches and love' – Salman Rushdie in the *Sunday Times*

☐ **A Midnight Clear** William Wharton £2.50

Six men – the crack bridge-players and poets of a US Army Intelligence squad – spend a nerve-shredding Christmas in a château in the Ardennes Forest during the Second World War. 'The most original war book I've read since *Catch 22*' – *Guardian*

PENGUINS ON HEALTH, SPORT AND PHYSICAL FITNESS

☐ **The F-Plan Audrey Eyton** £1.95

The book that started the diet revolution of the decade, *The F-Plan* is, quite simply, a phenomenon! Here Britain's top diet expert, Audrey Eyton, provides the recipes, menus and remarkable health revelations – everything you need to know to make that slim, fit future realistically possible.

☐ **The F-Plan Calorie Counter and Fibre Chart Audrey Eyton** £1.95

An indispensable companion to the F-Plan diet. High-fibre fresh, canned and packaged foods are listed, there's a separate chart for drinks, *plus* a wonderful new selection of effortless F-Plan meals.

☐ **The Arthritis Book Ephraim P. Engleman and Milton Silverman** £2.50

Written for patients and their families, this is a clear, expert and up-to-date handbook on arthritis, containing information on the latest drugs and treatments, and advice on how to cope.

☐ **Vogue Natural Health and Beauty Bronwen Meredith** £7.50

Health foods, yoga, spas, recipes, natural remedies and beauty preparations are all included in this superb, fully illustrated guide and companion to the bestselling *Vogue Body and Beauty Book*.

☐ **Alternative Medicine Andrew Stanway** £3.25

From Acupuncture and Alexander Technique to Macrobiotics, Radionics and Yoga, Dr Stanway provides an expert and objective guide to thirty-two therapies, for everyone interested in alternatives to conventional medicine.

☐ **The Runner's Handbook Bob Glover and Jack Shepherd** £2.95

Supplementary exercises, injuries, women on the run, running shoes and clothing, training for competitions and lots more information is included in this internationally famous manual.

PENGUIN COOKERY BOOKS

☐ *Mediterranean Cookbook* **Arabella Boxer** £2.50

A gastronomic grand tour of the region: 'The best book on Mediterranean cookery I have read since Elizabeth David' – *Sunday Express*

☐ *Josceline Dimbleby's Book of Puddings, Desserts and Savouries* £1.75

By the *Sunday Telegraph*'s popular cookery columnist, a book 'full of the most delicious and novel ideas for every type of pudding, from the tasty, filling family variety to exotic pastry concoctions' – *Lady*

☐ *Penguin Cordon Bleu Cookery* £2.50

Find the highest quality of European cooking with a French accent in this classic Penguin cookery book, prepared by Rosemary Hume and Muriel Downes, co-principals of the English Cordon Bleu School.

☐ *A Concise Encyclopedia of Gastronomy* **André Simon** £7.50

Expertly edited, with wit and wisdom, this is the most comprehensive survey ever published, and a treasure-house of good food.

☐ *An Invitation to Indian Cooking* **Madhur Jaffrey** £2.95

A witty, practical and irresistible handbook on Indian cooking by the presenter of the highly successful BBC television series.

☐ *The Chocolate Book* **Helge Rubinstein** £2.95

Part cookery book, part social history, this sumptuous book offers an unbeatable selection of recipes – chocolate cakes, ice-creams, pies, truffles, drinks and savoury dishes galore.

A CHOICE OF
PELICANS AND PEREGRINES

☐ **A Radical Reader** Christopher Hampton £9.95

With extracts from the writings of Wycliff, Shakespeare, Bacon, Milton, Swift, Blake, Byron, Dickens and Marx, among many others, this major new anthology spans five hundred years of radical protest from the Peasants' Revolt to the First World War.

☐ **Computer Power and Human Reason**
  Joseph Weizenbaum £2.95

Internationally acclaimed by scientists and humanists alike: 'This is the best book I have read on the impact of computers on society, and on technology and on man's image of himself' – *Psychology Today*

☐ **Astrology** H. J. Eysenck and D. K. B. Nias £2.50

Is astrology science or superstition? Two well-known analytical psychologists discuss the latest research and findings in a book that – for adherents of either side – will be an adventure.

☐ **The Germans** Gordon A. Craig £2.95

'This elegant and enticing work . . . dwells not on the familiar facts of German history but on some often neglected fundamental facets of German life and culture' – *The New York Times Book Review*

☐ **Mind in Science** Richard L. Gregory £7.95

Integrating and discussing ancient myth and philosophy, the rise of Western science, the developments of psychology and technology, and recent scientific discoveries, Gregory illuminates the nature of Mind. 'Few recent books can rival . . . its scope or its engaging enthusiasm' – *The Times Literary Supplement*

☐ **Who Cares about English Usage?** David Crystal £1.95

Including cartoons and quizzes to stimulate the mind, this is a highly entertaining guide to English usage by David Crystal, deviser of the popular Radio 4 programme, *Speak Out.*

A CHOICE OF
PELICANS AND PEREGRINES

☐ **Know Your Own Mind**
James Green and David Lewis £1.95

How do you *know* if you have a talent for solving problems, or creative work, or learning languages . . . ? This book contains nine assessments to help you build your own profile, discover your potential – and act on it.

☐ **The Mathematical Experience**
Philip J. Davis and Reuben Hersh £6.95

Not since *Gödel, Escher, Bach* has such an entertaining book been written on the relationship of mathematics to the arts and sciences. 'It deserves to be read by everyone . . . an instant classic' – *New Scientist*

☐ **The Tangled Wing** **Melvin Konner** £4.95

How far are our emotions and actions affected by our biology? This new study has been acclaimed by *The Times Higher Education Supplement* as 'a pleasure to read . . . an outstanding work of scholarship'.

☐ **The World Turned Upside Down** **Christopher Hill** £4.50

A portrait of radical groups and ideas during the English Revolution. 'Christopher Hill has that supreme gift of being able to show us the seventeenth-century world from the inside' – Arthur Marwick in *New Society*

☐ **Exploring the Earth and the Cosmos**
Isaac Asimov £3.95

From dinosaurs to black holes and space probes, this exhilarating book (and superb reference-source) guides us through the facts, figures, people and discoveries that have shaped our changing view of the earth and the cosmos.

☐ **Hen's Teeth and Horse's Toes**
Stephen Jay Gould £3.95

Essays on natural history by the author of *Ever Since Darwin*. 'He has the rare gift of communicating excitement . . . he challenges one furiously to think' – *Nature*

A CHOICE OF
PELICANS AND PEREGRINES

☐ *Three Who Made a Revolution* **Bertram D. Wolfe** £4.95

The classic historical biography of Lenin, Trotsky and Stalin. 'The best book in its field in any language' – Edmund Wilson

☐ *Montaillou* **Emmanuel Le Roy Ladurie** £5.95

The world-famous portrait of life in a medieval French village. 'A Chaucerian gallery of vivid medieval persons' – Hugh Trevor-Roper. 'A classic adventure in eavesdropping across time' – *The Times*

☐ *The Pelican History of the World* **J. M. Roberts** £5.95

'A stupendous achievement . . . This is the unrivalled World History for our day' – A J P Taylor

---

These books should be available at all good bookshops or news-agents, but if you live in the UK or the Republic of Ireland and have difficulty in getting to a bookshop, they can be ordered by post. Please indicate the titles required and fill in the form below.

NAME _____ BLOCK CAPITALS

ADDRESS _____

_____

_____

Enclose a cheque or postal order payable to The Penguin Bookshop to cover the total price of books ordered, plus 50p for postage. Readers in the Republic of Ireland should send £IR equivalent to the sterling prices, plus 67p for postage. Send to: The Penguin Bookshop, 54/56 Bridlesmith Gate, Nottingham, NG1 2GP.

You can also order by phoning (0602) 599295, and quoting your Barclaycard or Access number.

Every effort is made to ensure the accuracy of the price and availability of books at the time of going to press, but it is sometimes necessary to increase prices and in these circumstances retail prices may be shown on the covers of books which may differ from the prices shown in this list or elsewhere. This list is not an offer to supply any book.

This order service is only available to residents in the UK and the Republic of Ireland.